# NEW TESTAMENT

## CONTEMPORARY ENGLISH VERSION

# NEW TESTAMENT

# CONTEMPORARY ENGLISH VERSION

AMERICAN BIBLE SOCIETY
NEW YORK

# NEW TESTAMENT

## Contemporary English Version

### Quotation Rights for the Contemporary English Version

Cover Photo: © Corel
Text: Copyright © 1995, American Bible Society
Maps: Copyright © 1976, 1978. 1979, United Bible Societies

ISBN 1 – 58516 – 244 – 2

Printed in the United States of America
Eng. N.T. CEV250 – 106335
ABS – 9/02 – 20,000 – 160,000 — MW6

# THE CONTEMPORARY ENGLISH VERSION

*Translation it is that opens the window, to let in the light; that breaks the shell, that we may eat the kernel; that puts aside the curtain, that we may look into the most holy place; that removes the cover of the well, that we may come by the water* ("The Translators to the Reader," King James Version, 1611).

The most important document in the history of the English language is the *King James Version* of the Bible. To measure its spiritual impact on the English speaking world would be more impossible than counting the grains of sand along the ocean shores. Historically, many Bible translators have attempted in some measure to *retain the form* of the *King James Version*. But the translators of the *Contemporary English Version* of the Bible have diligently sought to *capture the spirit* of the *King James Version* by following certain principles set forth by its translators in the document "The Translators to the Reader," which was printed in the earliest editions.

### This is the Word of God, which we translate

Accuracy, beauty, clarity, and dignity—all of these can and must be achieved in the translation of the Bible. After all, as the translators of the *King James Version* stated, "This is the Word of God, which we translate."

Every attempt has been made to produce a text that is faithful to the *meaning* of the original. In order to assure the *accuracy* of the *Contemporary English Version,* the Old Testament was translated directly from the Hebrew and Aramaic texts published by the United Bible Societies (*Biblia Hebraica Stuttgartensia,* fourth edition corrected). And the New Testament was translated directly from the Greek text published by the United Bible Societies (third edition corrected and compared with the fourth revised edition).

The drafts in their earliest stages were sent for review and comment to a number of biblical scholars, theologians, and educators representing a wide variety of church traditions. In addition, drafts were sent for review and comment to all English-speaking Bible Societies and to more than forty United Bible Societies translation consultants around the world. Final approval of the text was given by the American Bible Society Board of Trustees on the recommendation of its Translations Subcommittee.

### We desire that the Scripture . . . may be understood

That the Scripture may be understood even by ordinary people was a primary goal of the translators of the *King James Version*. And they raised the question, "What can be more available thereto than to deliver God's book unto God's people in a tongue which they understand?" Martin Luther also did his translation for the common people, and he established the following guidelines:

> We do not have to inquire of the literal Latin, how we are to speak German . . . Rather we must inquire about this of the mother in the home, the children on the street, the common man in the marketplace. *We must be guided by their language, the way they speak, and do our translating accordingly.*

Today more people *hear* the Bible read aloud than read it for themselves! And statistics released by the National Center for Education indicate that "almost half of U.S. adults have very limited reading and writing skills." If this is the case, a contemporary translation must be a text that an inexperienced reader can *read aloud* without stumbling, that someone unfamiliar with traditional biblical terminology can *hear without misunderstanding,* and that everyone can *listen to with enjoyment* because the style is lucid and lyrical.

In order to attain these goals of clarity, beauty, and dignity, the translators of the *Contemporary English Version* carefully studied every word, phrase, clause, and paragraph of the original. Then, with equal care, they struggled to discover the best way to translate the text, so that it would be suitable both for *private* and *public* reading, and for *memorizing.* The result is an English text that is enjoyable and easily understood by the vast majority of English speakers, regardless of their religious or educational background.

In the *hearing* of a translation, even the inclusion of a simple word like "and" can make a significant difference. Matthew 2.9 of the *Contemporary English Version* reads as follows: "The wise men listened to what the king said and then left. *And* the star they had seen in the east went on ahead of them until it stopped over the place where the child was."

"And" at the beginning of the second sentence assists both the person who reads the text aloud and those who must depend upon hearing it read. Like all other punctuation marks, the period after "left" is silent, and so the text without "And" could possibly be *heard* as, "The wise men listened to what the king said and then left the star they had seen in the east." However, as the text now stands, the oral reader must pause briefly for a breath before "And," which will signal the hearer that a new sentence has begun.

As another example, try reading the following two sentences aloud: "You yourselves admit, then, that you agree with what your ancestors did" and "for it was better with me then than now." Both suffer from potential tongue twisters ("admit, then, that" and "then than"). But the first is doubly difficult because it consists of a lengthy series of unaccented syllables that do not allow the reader to take a breath. In the *Contemporary English Version* every attempt has been made to avoid these and other kinds of constructions that could possibly prove problematic for oral reading.

According to the rules of English grammar, the pronoun *he* must refer back to *God* in the following sentence: "The other, however, rebuked him saying, 'Don't you fear *God?* You received the same sentence *he* did.' " But the reference is actually to Jesus, who is mentioned earlier in the passage. Traditional translations assume that the reader can study the printed text and finally figure out the meaning, but the *Contemporary English Version* is concerned equally with the reader and the *hearer.* And in many situations, the hearer may have only *one* chance to understand what is read aloud.

In poetry, the *appearance of the text on the page* is important, since in oral reading there is a tendency to stress the last word on a line and to pause momentarily before going to the next line, especially if the second line is indented. Compare the three following examples, where the lines of the same text have been broken improperly (left column) and properly (right column):

| | |
|---|---|
| He brought me out into a broad place. | He brought me out into a broad place. |
| With the loyal you show yourself loyal. | With the loyal you show yourself loyal. |
| The Lord my God lights up my darkness. | The Lord my God lights up my darkness. |

No fault is to be found with the translation itself. Yet there is a significant difference in the *appearance* of the text on the page, because the lines on the right have been *measured*, in order to prevent unfortunate runovers. In this form, the text not only looks better on the page, but it is easier to read and memorize, and it avoids such disastrous combinations as "He brought me out into a broad" or "With the loyal you show yourself" or "The Lord my God lights up." Moreover, both formats require exactly the same amount of lines.

The first translation in the history of the English Bible to develop a text with measured poetry lines is the *Contemporary English Version,* in which the translators have consciously created a text that will not suffer from unfortunate line breaks when published in double columns. *Accuracy* is the main concern of translators, but it must be realized that in the translation of biblical poetry, what the reader *sees* is what will be *said,* and what others will *hear.* This means that lines improperly broken can easily lead to a misunderstanding of the text, especially for those who must depend upon *hearing* the Scriptures read.

Hebrew poetry has its own systems of sound, rhyme, and rhythm, as well as a *form* that involves much repetition. It is impossible in English to retain the sounds, rhymes, and rhythms of the Hebrew text, but traditional translations have attempted to reproduce the frequent repetition, in which a second line will repeat or expand, either negatively or positively, the thoughts of the previous line. However, this repetition is often ineffective for those English speakers who are unaccustomed to the poetic style of the biblical authors. And so, the translators of the *Contemporary English Version* have followed the example of Martin Luther in the translation of poetry:

> Whoever would speak German *must not use Hebrew style.* Rather he must see to it—once he understands the Hebrew author—that he concentrates on the *sense* of the text, asking himself, "Pray tell, what do the Germans say in such a situation?" Once he has the German words to serve his purpose, let him drop the Hebrew words and *express the meaning freely* in the best German he knows.

The qualities that many critics value most in modern poetry are effortless *economy* and *exactness* of language. It is hoped that readers will discover similar features in the poetry of the *Contemporary English Version,* which strives for beauty and dignity, as much as for accuracy and clarity. In this translation, the poetry often requires fewer lines than do traditional translations, but the *integrity, intent,* and *impact* of the original are consistently maintained. Note, for example, the rendering of Job 38.14, 15:

> Early dawn outlines the hills
> like stitches on clothing
>     or sketches on clay.
> But its light is too much
> for those who are evil,
>     and their power is broken.

Whenever the contents of two or more verses have been joined together and rearranged in the poetic sections of the *Contemporary English Version,* this is signaled by an asterisk (*) before the first verse number in the series.

In everyday speech, "gender generic" or "inclusive" language is used, because it sounds most natural to people today. This means that where the biblical languages require masculine nouns or pronouns when both men and women are intended, this intention must be reflected in translation, though the English *form* may be very different from that of the original. The Greek text of Matthew 16.24 is literally, "If anyone wants to follow me, *he* must deny *himself* and take up *his* cross and follow me." The *Contemporary English Version* shifts to a form which is still accurate, and at the same time more effective in English: "If any of *you* want to be my followers, *you* must forget about *yourself. You* must take up *your* cross and follow me."

### Variety of translations is profitable

The translators of the *King James Version* said, ". . . variety of translations is profitable for the finding out of the sense of the Scriptures" and "We affirm and avow that the very meanest translation of the Bible in English, set forth by men of our profession . . . contains the Word of God, nay is the Word of God." They even stated, "No cause therefore why the Word translated should be denied to be the Word, or forbidden to be current, notwithstanding that some imperfections and blemishes may be noted in the setting forth of it."

Each English translation is, in its own right, the Word of God, yet each translation serves to meet the needs of a different audience. In this regard, the *Contemporary English Version* should be considered a *companion*—the *mission* arm—of traditional translations, because it takes seriously the words of the apostle Paul that "faith comes by *hearing.*"

### It has pleased God in his divine providence

Translating the Bible may be compared to living the life of faith. God has not given us all the answers for our pilgrim journey, but we have been provided with all that we need to know in order to be saved. As the translators of the *King James Version* observed:

> . . . it has pleased God in His divine providence here and there to scatter those words and sentences of that difficulty and doubtfulness, not in doctrinal points that concern salvation (for in such it has been vouched that the Scriptures are plain), but in matters of less moment, that fearfulness would better beseem us than confidence . . .

For as it is a fault of incredulity, to doubt of those things that are evident; so to determine of such things that the Spirit of God has left (even in the mind of the judicious) questionable, can be no less than presumption.

Bible translators do not have the privilege and luxury of working from the original manuscripts of either the Old or New Testament. Indeed, there are numerous difficult passages where decisions must be made concerning what word or words actually belong in the text, and what these words may, in fact, mean. At such places, the best a translator can do is to give what seems to be one possible meaning for the difficult text and to indicate this by a note, which was also what the King James translators did: "... so diversity of signification and sense in the margin, where the text is not clear, must needs be good; yea, is necessary, as we are persuaded." Fortunately, these "words and sentences of that difficulty and doubtfulness" do not in any way leave unclear the central message of the Bible or any of its major doctrines.

## Having and using as great helps as were needful

The translators of the *Contemporary English Version* have not created new or novel interpretations of the text. Rather, it was their goal to express mainstream interpretations of the text in current, everyday English. To do so required *listening* carefully to each word of the biblical text, to the way in which English is spoken today, to the remarks of their reviewers, and especially to the Spirit of God. Once again the comments of the translators of the *King James Version* are appropriate:

Neither did we think much to consult the translators or commentators ... but neither did we disdain to revise that which we had done, and to bring to the anvil that which we had hammered; but having and using as great helps as were needful, and fearing no reproach for slowness, nor coveting praise for expedition, we have at the length, through the good hand of the Lord upon us, brought forth the work to that pass that you see.

Accordingly, the translators of the *Contemporary English Version* are indebted to all translators and biblical scholars who have gone before them and have made it possible to understand something of the languages, cultures, and history of biblical times. And, together with the apostle Paul, they confess: *We don't have the right to claim that we have done anything on our own. God gives us what it takes to do all that we do.* (2 Corinthians 3.5)

*Offer praise to God our Savior because of our Lord Jesus Christ!*
(Jude 24, 25)

# CONTENTS

# ABOUT THE
# NEW TESTAMENT

The New Testament is a collection of 27 books and letters written in Greek. They are arranged in four groups:

*(1) Gospels and Acts.* This group contains the four Gospels, which are Matthew, Mark, Luke, and John. The term "gospel" means "good news," and these four Gospels tell the good news about Jesus Christ. The group also contains the book of Acts, which tells how the good news spread in the years after Jesus died and was raised from death.

*(2) Letters of Paul.* This group is made up of Romans, 1 and 2 Corinthians, Galatians, Ephesians, Philippians, Colossians, 1 and 2 Thessalonians, 1 and 2 Timothy, Titus, and Philemon. These letters have traditionally been called "epistles," and each one is named for the group or person that it was written to.

*(3) Other Letters.* This group contains letters written by people other than Paul. It contains Hebrews, James, 1 and 2 Peter, 1, 2, and 3 John, and Jude. The Letter to the Hebrews doesn't give its author's name, but each of the other letters is named for the person who wrote it.

*(4) Revelation.* This book is quite different from the other New Testament books, because it is a book of visions and prophecies.

# MATTHEW

## ABOUT THIS BOOK

The Sermon on the Mount (5.1—7.28), the Lord's Prayer (6.9-13), and the Golden Rule (7.12: "Treat others as you want them to treat you") are all in this book. It is perhaps the best known and the most quoted of all the books that have ever been written about Jesus. That is one reason why Matthew was placed first among the four books about Jesus called Gospels.

One of the most important ideas found here is that God expects his people to obey him, and this is what is meant by the Greek word that appears in many translations as righteousness. It is used seven times by Matthew, but only once by Luke, and not at all by Mark. So it is an important clue to much of what Matthew wants his readers to understand about the teaching of Jesus.

Jesus first uses this word at his own baptism, when he tells John the Baptist, "We must do all that God wants us to do" (3.15). Then, during his Sermon on the Mount, he speaks five more times of what God's people must do to obey him (5.6, 10, 20; 6.1, 33). And finally, he reminds the chief priests and leaders of the people, "John the Baptist showed you how to do right" (21.32).

Matthew wanted to provide for the people of his time a record of Jesus' message and ministry. It is clear that the Old Testament Scriptures were very important to these people. And Matthew never fails to show when these texts point to the coming of Jesus as the Messiah sent from God. Matthew wrote this book to make sure Christians knew that their faith in Jesus as the Messiah was well anchored in the Old Testament Scriptures, and to help them grow in faith.

Matthew ends his story with the words of Jesus to his followers, which tell what they are to do after he leaves them:

> I have been given all authority in heaven and on earth! Go to the people of all nations and make them my disciples. Baptize them in the name of the Father, the Son, and the Holy Spirit, and teach them to do everything I have told you. I will be with you always, even until the end of the world.
>
> (28.18b-20)

## A QUICK LOOK AT THIS BOOK

1

## The Ancestors of Jesus
*(Luke 3.23-38)*

**1** Jesus Christ came from the family of King David and also from the family of Abraham. And this is a list of his ancestors. 2-6a From Abraham to King David, his ancestors were:

Abraham, Isaac, Jacob, Judah and his brothers (Judah's sons were Perez and Zerah, and their mother was Tamar), Hezron;

Ram, Amminadab, Nahshon, Salmon, Boaz (his mother was Rahab), Obed (his mother was Ruth), Jesse, and King David.

6b-11 From David to the time of the exile in Babylonia, the ancestors of Jesus were:

David, Solomon (his mother had been Uriah's wife), Rehoboam, Abijah, Asa, Jehoshaphat, Jehoram;

Uzziah, Jotham, Ahaz, Hezekiah, Manasseh, Amon, Josiah, and Jehoiachin and his brothers.

12-16 From the exile to the birth of Jesus, his ancestors were:

Jehoiachin, Shealtiel, Zerubbabel, Abiud, Eliakim, Azor, Zadok, Achim;

Eliud, Eleazar, Matthan, Jacob, and Joseph, the husband of Mary, the mother of Jesus, who is called the Messiah.

17 There were fourteen generations from Abraham to David. There were also fourteen from David to the exile in Babylonia and fourteen more to the birth of the Messiah.

## The Birth of Jesus
*(Luke 2.1-7)*

18 This is how Jesus Christ was born. A young woman named Mary was engaged to Joseph from King David's family. But before they were married, she learned that she was going to have a baby by God's Holy Spirit. 19 Joseph was a good man*a* and did not want to embarrass Mary in front of everyone. So he decided to quietly call off the wedding.

20 While Joseph was thinking about this, an angel from the Lord came to him in a dream. The angel said, "Joseph, the baby that Mary will have is from the Holy Spirit. Go ahead and marry her. 21 Then after her baby is born, name him Jesus,*b* because he will save his people from their sins."

22 So the Lord's promise came true, just as the prophet had said, 23 "A virgin will have a baby boy, and he will be called Immanuel," which means "God is with us."

24 After Joseph woke up, he and Mary were soon married, just as the Lord's angel had told him to do. 25 But they did not sleep together before her baby was born. Then Joseph named him Jesus.

## The Wise Men

**2** When Jesus was born in the village of Bethlehem in Judea, Herod was king. During this time some wise men*c* from the east came to Jerusalem 2 and said, "Where is the child born to be king of the Jews? We saw his star in the east*d* and have come to worship him."

3 When King Herod heard about this, he was worried, and so was everyone else in Jerusalem. 4 Herod brought together the chief priests and the teachers of the Law of Moses and asked them, "Where will the Messiah be born?"

5 They told him, "He will be born in Bethlehem, just as the prophet wrote,

6 'Bethlehem in the land
    of Judea,
you are very important
    among the towns of Judea.
From your town
    will come a leader,
who will be like a shepherd
    for my people Israel.' "

7 Herod secretly called in the wise men and asked them when they had first seen the star. 8 He told them, "Go to Bethlehem and search carefully for the child. As soon as you find him, let me know. I want to go and worship him too."

*a* **1.19** *good man*: Or "kind man," or "man who always did the right thing." *b* **1.21** *name him Jesus*: In Hebrew the name "Jesus" means "the Lord saves." *c* **2.1** *wise men*: People famous for studying the stars. *d* **2.2** *his star in the east*: Or "his star rise."

⁹The wise men listened to what the king said and then left. And the star they had seen in the east went on ahead of them until it stopped over the place where the child was. ¹⁰They were thrilled and excited to see the star.

¹¹When the men went into the house and saw the child with Mary, his mother, they knelt down and worshiped him  They took out their gifts of gold, frankincense, and myrrhᵉ and gave them to him. ¹²Later they were warned in a dream not to return to Herod, and they went back home by another road.

## The Escape to Egypt

¹³After the wise men had gone, an angel from the Lord appeared to Joseph in a dream and said, "Get up! Hurry and take the child and his mother to Egypt! Stay there until I tell you to return, because Herod is looking for the child and wants to kill him."

¹⁴That night, Joseph got up and took his wife and the child to Egypt, ¹⁵where they stayed until Herod died. So the Lord's promise came true, just as the prophet had said, "I called my son out of Egypt."

## The Killing of the Children

¹⁶When Herod found out that the wise men from the east had tricked him, he was very angry. He gave orders for his men to kill all the boys who lived in or near Bethlehem and were two years old and younger. This was based on what he had learned from the wise men.

¹⁷So the Lord's promise came true, just as the prophet Jeremiah had said,

¹⁸ "In Ramah a voice was heard
crying and weeping loudly.
Rachel was mourning
for her children,
and she refused
to be comforted,
because they were dead."

## The Return from Egypt

¹⁹After King Herod died, an angel from the Lord appeared in a dream to Joseph while he was still in Egypt. ²⁰The angel said, "Get up and take the child and his mother back to Israel. The people who wanted to kill him are now dead."

²¹Joseph got up and left with them for Israel. ²²But when he heard that Herod's son Archelaus was now ruler of Judea, he was afraid to go there. Then in a dream he was told to go to Galilee, ²³and they went to live there in the town of Nazareth. So the Lord's promise came true, just as the prophet had said, "He will be called a Nazarene."ᶠ

## The Preaching of John the Baptist
### (Mark 1.1-8; Luke 3.1-18; John 1.19-28)

**3** Years later, John the Baptist started preaching in the desert of Judea. ²He said, "Turn back to God! The kingdom of heavenᵍ will soon be here."ʰ ³John was the one the prophet Isaiah was talking about, when he said,

"In the desert someone
is shouting,
'Get the road ready
for the Lord!
Make a straight path
for him.' "

⁴John wore clothes made of camel's hair. He had a leather strap around his waist and ate grasshoppers and wild honey. ⁵From Jerusalem and all Judea and from the Jordan River Valley crowds of people went to John. ⁶They told how sorry they were for their sins, and he baptized them in the river.

⁷Many Pharisees and Sadducees also came to be baptized. But John said to them:

You bunch of snakes! Who warned you to run from the coming judgment? ⁸Do something to show

ᵉ2.11 frankincense, and myrrh: Frankincense was a valuable powder that was burned to make a sweet smell. Myrrh was a valuable sweet-smelling powder often used in perfume. ᶠ2.23 He will be called a Nazarene: The prophet who said this is not known. ᵍ3.2 kingdom of heaven: In the Gospel of Matthew "kingdom of heaven" is used with the same meaning as "God's kingdom" in Mark and Luke. ʰ3.2 will soon be here: Or "is already here."

that you have really given up your sins. ⁹ And don't start telling yourselves that you belong to Abraham's family. I tell you that God can turn these stones into children for Abraham. ¹⁰ An ax is ready to cut the trees down at their roots. Any tree that doesn't produce good fruit will be chopped down and thrown into a fire.

¹¹ I baptize you with water so that you will give up your sins.ⁱ But someone more powerful is going to come, and I am not good enough even to carry his sandals.ʲ He will baptize you with the Holy Spirit and with fire. ¹² His threshing fork is in his hand, and he is ready to separate the wheat from the husks.ᵏ He will store the wheat in a barn and burn the husks in a fire that never goes out.

### The Baptism of Jesus
(Mark 1.9-11; Luke 3.21, 22)

¹³ Jesus left Galilee and went to the Jordan River to be baptized by John. ¹⁴ But John kept objecting and said, "I ought to be baptized by you. Why have you come to me?"

¹⁵ Jesus answered, "For now this is how it should be, because we must do all that God wants us to do." Then John agreed.

¹⁶ So Jesus was baptized. And as soon as he came out of the water, the sky opened, and he saw the Spirit of God coming down on him like a dove. ¹⁷ Then a voice from heaven said, "This is my own dear Son, and I am pleased with him."

### Jesus and the Devil
(Mark 1.12, 13; Luke 4.1-13)

**4** The Holy Spirit led Jesus into the desert, so that the devil could test him. ² After Jesus had gone without eatingˡ for forty days and nights, he was very hungry. ³ Then the devil came to him and said, "If you are God's Son, tell these stones to turn into bread."

⁴ Jesus answered, "The Scriptures say:

'No one can live only on food.
People need every word
that God has spoken.' "

⁵ Next, the devil took Jesus to the holy city and had him stand on the highest part of the temple. ⁶ The devil said, "If you are God's Son, jump off. The Scriptures say:

'God will give his angels
orders about you.
They will catch you
in their arms,
and you won't hurt
your feet on the stones.' "

⁷ Jesus answered, "The Scriptures also say, 'Don't try to test the Lord your God!' "

⁸ Finally, the devil took Jesus up on a very high mountain and showed him all the kingdoms on earth and their power. ⁹ The devil said to him, "I will give all this to you, if you will bow down and worship me."

¹⁰ Jesus answered, "Go away Satan! The Scriptures say:

'Worship the Lord your God
and serve only him.' "

¹¹ Then the devil left Jesus, and angels came to help him.

### Jesus Begins His Work
(Mark 1.14, 15; Luke 4.14, 15)

¹² When Jesus heard that John had been put in prison, he went to Galilee. ¹³ But instead of staying in Nazareth, Jesus moved to Capernaum. This town

---

ⁱ**3.11** *so that you will give up your sins*: Or "because you have given up your sins." ʲ**3.11** *carry his sandals*: This was one of the duties of a slave. ᵏ**3.12** *His threshing fork is in his hand, and he is ready to separate the wheat from the husks*: After Jewish farmers had trampled out the grain, they used a large fork to pitch the grain and the husks into the air. Wind would blow away the light husks, and the grain would fall back to the ground, where it could be gathered up. ˡ**4.2** *went without eating*: The Jewish people sometimes went without eating (also called "fasting") to show their love for God or to show sorrow for their sins.

was beside Lake Galilee in the territory of Zebulun and Naphtali.*m* ¹⁴So God's promise came true, just as the prophet Isaiah had said,

¹⁵ "Listen, lands of Zebulun
      and Naphtali,
   lands along the road
   to the sea and east
      of the Jordan¹
   Listen Galilee,
      land of the Gentiles!
¹⁶ Although your people
      live in darkness,
   they will see
      a bright light.
   Although they live
      in the shadow of death,
   a light will shine
      on them."

¹⁷Then Jesus started preaching, "Turn back to God! The kingdom of heaven will soon be here."*n*

## Jesus Chooses
## Four Fishermen
### (Mark 1.16-20; Luke 5.1-11)

¹⁸While Jesus was walking along the shore of Lake Galilee, he saw two brothers. One was Simon, also known as Peter, and the other was Andrew. They were fishermen, and they were casting their net into the lake. ¹⁹Jesus said to them, "Come with me! I will teach you how to bring in people instead of fish." ²⁰Right then the two brothers dropped their nets and went with him.
²¹Jesus walked on until he saw James and John, the sons of Zebedee. They were in a boat with their father, mending their nets. Jesus asked them to come with him too. ²²Right away they left the boat and their father and went with Jesus.

## Jesus Teaches, Preaches, and Heals
### (Luke 6.17-19)

²³Jesus went all over Galilee, teaching in the Jewish meeting places and preaching the good news about God's kingdom. He also healed every kind of disease and sickness. ²⁴News about him spread all over Syria, and people with every kind of sickness or disease were brought to him. Some of them had a lot of demons in them, others were thought to be crazy,*o* and still others could not walk. But Jesus healed them all.
²⁵Large crowds followed Jesus from Galilee and the region around the ten cities known as Decapolis.*p* They also came from Jerusalem, Judea, and from across the Jordan River.

## The Sermon on the Mount

**5** When Jesus saw the crowds, he went up on the side of a mountain and sat down.*q*

## Blessings
### (Luke 6.20-23)

Jesus' disciples gathered around him, ²and he taught them:

³ God blesses those people
      who depend only on him.
   They belong to the kingdom
      of heaven!*r*
⁴ God blesses those people
      who grieve.
   They will find comfort!
⁵ God blesses those people
      who are humble.
   The earth will belong
      to them!
⁶ God blesses those people
      who want to obey him*s*
      more than to eat or drink.
   They will be given
      what they want!

---

*m***4.13** *Zebulun and Naphtali*: In Old Testament times these tribes were in northern Palestine, and in New Testament times many Gentiles lived where these tribes had once been. *n***4.17** *The kingdom of heaven will soon be here*: See the two notes at 3.2. *o***4.24** *thought to be crazy*: In ancient times people with epilepsy were thought to be crazy. *p***4.25** *the ten cities known as Decapolis*: A group of ten cities east of Samaria and Galilee, where the people followed the Greek way of life. *q***5.1** *sat down*: Teachers in the ancient world, including Jewish teachers, usually sat down when they taught. *r***5.3** *They belong to the kingdom of heaven*: Or "The kingdom of heaven belongs to them." *s***5.6** *who want to obey him*: Or "who want to do right" or "who want everyone to be treated right."

7 God blesses those people
who are merciful.
They will be treated
with mercy!
8 God blesses those people
whose hearts are pure.
They will see him!
9 God blesses those people
who make peace.
They will be called
his children!
10 God blesses those people
who are treated badly
for doing right.
They belong to the kingdom
of heaven. *t*

11 God will bless you when people insult you, mistreat you, and tell all kinds of evil lies about you because of me. 12 Be happy and excited! You will have a great reward in heaven. People did these same things to the prophets who lived long ago.

### Salt and Light
*(Mark 9.50; Luke 14.34, 35)*

13 You are like salt for everyone on earth. But if salt no longer tastes like salt, how can it make food salty? All it is good for is to be thrown out and walked on.
14 You are like light for the whole world. A city built on top of a hill cannot be hidden, 15 and no one would light a lamp and put it under a clay pot. A lamp is placed on a lampstand, where it can give light to everyone in the house. 16 Make your light shine, so that others will see the good that you do and will praise your Father in heaven.

### The Law of Moses

17 Don't suppose that I came to do away with the Law and the Prophets. *u* I did not come to do away with them, but to give them their full meaning. 18 Heaven and earth may disappear. But I promise you that not even a period or comma

will ever disappear from the Law. Everything written in it must happen.
19 If you reject even the least important command in the Law and teach others to do the same, you will be the least important person in the kingdom of heaven. But if you obey and teach others its commands, you will have an important place in the kingdom. 20 You must obey God's commands better than the Pharisees and the teachers of the Law obey them. If you don't, I promise you that you will never get into the kingdom of heaven.

### Anger

21 You know that our ancestors were told, "Do not murder" and "A murderer must be brought to trial." 22 But I promise you that if you are angry with someone, *v* you will have to stand trial. If you call someone a fool, you will be taken to court. And if you say that someone is worthless, you will be in danger of the fires of hell.
23 So if you are about to place your gift on the altar and remember that someone is angry with you, 24 leave your gift there in front of the altar. Make peace with that person, then come back and offer your gift to God.
25 Before you are dragged into court, make friends with the person who has accused you of doing wrong. If you don't, you will be handed over to the judge and then to the officer who will put you in jail. 26 I promise you that you will not get out until you have paid the last cent you owe.

### Marriage

27 You know the commandment which says, "Be faithful in marriage." 28 But I tell you that if you

look at another woman and want her, you are already unfaithful in your thoughts. ²⁹If your right eye causes you to sin, poke it out and throw it away. It is better to lose one part of your body, than for your whole body to end up in hell. ³⁰If your right hand causes you to sin, chop it off and throw it away! It is better to lose one part of your body, than for your whole body to be thrown into hell.

## Divorce
### (Matthew 19.9; Mark 10.11, 12; Luke 16.18)

³¹You have been taught that a man who divorces his wife must write out divorce papers for her.ʷ ³²But I tell you not to divorce your wife unless she has committed some terrible sexual sin.ˣ If you divorce her, you will cause her to be unfaithful, just as any man who marries her is guilty of taking another man's wife.

## Promises

³³You know that our ancestors were told, "Don't use the Lord's name to make a promise unless you are going to keep it." ³⁴But I tell you not to swear by anything when you make a promise! Heaven is God's throne, so don't swear by heaven. ³⁵The earth is God's footstool, so don't swear by the earth. Jerusalem is the city of the great king, so don't swear by it. ³⁶Don't swear by your own head. You cannot make one hair white or black. ³⁷When you make a promise, say only "Yes" or "No." Anything else comes from the devil.

## Revenge
### (Luke 6.29, 30)

³⁸You know that you have been taught, "An eye for an eye and a tooth for a tooth." ³⁹But I tell you not to try to get even with a person who has done something to you. When someone slaps your right cheek,ʸ turn and let that person slap your other cheek. ⁴⁰If someone sues you for your shirt, give up your coat as well. ⁴¹If a soldier forces you to carry his pack one mile, carry it two miles.ᶻ ⁴²When people ask you for something, give it to them. When they want to borrow money, lend it to them.

## Love
### (Luke 6.27, 28, 32-36)

⁴³You have heard people say, "Love your neighbors and hate your enemies." ⁴⁴But I tell you to love your enemies and pray for anyone who mistreats you. ⁴⁵Then you will be acting like your Father in heaven. He makes the sun rise on both good and bad people. And he sends rain for the ones who do right and for the ones who do wrong. ⁴⁶If you love only those people who love you, will God reward you for that? Even tax collectorsᵃ love their friends. ⁴⁷If you greet only your friends, what's so great about that? Don't even unbelievers do that? ⁴⁸But you must always act like your Father in heaven.

## Giving

**6** When you do good deeds, don't try to show off. If you do, you won't get a reward from your Father in heaven. ²When you give to the poor, don't

---

ʷ**5.31** *write out divorce papers for her*: Jewish men could divorce their wives, but the women could not divorce their husbands. The purpose of writing these papers was to make it harder for a man to divorce his wife. Before this law was made, all a man had to do was to send his wife away and say that she was no longer his wife. ˣ**5.32** *some terrible sexual sin*: This probably refers to the laws about the wrong kinds of marriages that are forbidden in Leviticus 18.6-18 or to some serious sexual sin. ʸ**5.39** *right cheek*: A slap on the right cheek was a bad insult. ᶻ**5.41** *two miles*: A Roman soldier had the right to force a person to carry his pack as far as one mile. ᵃ**5.46** *tax collectors*: These were usually Jewish people who paid the Romans for the right to collect taxes. They were hated by other Jews who thought of them as traitors to their country and to their religion.

blow a loud horn. That's what show-offs do in the meeting places and on the street corners, because they are always looking for praise. I can assure you that they already have their reward.

3 When you give to the poor, don't let anyone know about it.[b] 4 Then your gift will be given in secret. Your Father knows what is done in secret, and he will reward you.

## Prayer
### (Luke 11.2-4)

5 When you pray, don't be like those show-offs who love to stand up and pray in the meeting places and on the street corners. They do this just to look good. I can assure you that they already have their reward.

6 When you pray, go into a room alone and close the door. Pray to your Father in private. He knows what is done in private, and he will reward you.

7 When you pray, don't talk on and on as people do who don't know God. They think God likes to hear long prayers. 8 Don't be like them. Your Father knows what you need before you ask.

9 You should pray like this:

Our Father in heaven,
help us to honor
  your name.
10 Come and set up
  your kingdom,
so that everyone on earth
  will obey you,
as you are obeyed
  in heaven.
11 Give us our food for today.[c]
12 Forgive us for doing wrong,
  as we forgive others.
13 Keep us from being tempted
  and protect us from evil.[d]

14 If you forgive others for the wrongs they do to you, your Father in heaven will forgive you. 15 But if you don't forgive others, your Father will not forgive your sins.

## Worshiping God by Going without Eating

16 When you go without eating,[e] don't try to look gloomy as those show-offs do when they go without eating. I can assure you that they already have their reward. 17 Instead, comb your hair and wash your face. 18 Then others won't know that you are going without eating. But your Father sees what is done in private, and he will reward you.

## Treasures in Heaven
### (Luke 12.33, 34)

19 Don't store up treasures on earth! Moths and rust can destroy them, and thieves can break in and steal them. 20 Instead, store up your treasures in heaven, where moths and rust cannot destroy them, and thieves cannot break in and steal them. 21 Your heart will always be where your treasure is.

## Light
### (Luke 11.34-36)

22 Your eyes are like a window for your body. When they are good, you have all the light you need. 23 But when your eyes are bad, everything is dark. If the light inside you is dark, you surely are in the dark.

## Money
### (Luke 16.13)

24 You cannot be the slave of two masters! You will like one more than the other or be more loyal to one than the other. You cannot serve both God and money.

b 6.3 *don't let anyone know about it*: The Greek text has, "Don't let your left hand know what your right hand is doing." c 6.11 *our food for today*: Or "the food that we need" or "our food for the coming day." d 6.13 *evil*: Or "the evil one," that is, the devil. Some manuscripts add, "The kingdom, the power, and the glory are yours forever. Amen." e 6.16 *without eating*: See the note at 4.2.

## Worry
*(Luke 12.22-31)*

25 I tell you not to worry about your life. Don't worry about having something to eat, drink, or wear. Isn't life more than food or clothing? 26 Look at the birds in the sky! They don't plant or harvest. They don't even store grain in barns. Yet your Father in heaven takes care of them. Aren't you worth more than birds? 27 Can worry make you live longer?*f* 28 Why worry about clothes? Look how the wild flowers grow. They don't work hard to make their clothes. 29 But I tell you that Solomon with all his wealth*g* wasn't as well clothed as one of them. 30 God gives such beauty to everything that grows in the fields, even though it is here today and thrown into a fire tomorrow. He will surely do even more for you! Why do you have such little faith? 31 Don't worry and ask yourselves, "Will we have anything to eat? Will we have anything to drink? Will we have any clothes to wear?" 32 Only people who don't know God are always worrying about such things. Your Father in heaven knows that you need all of these. 33 But more than anything else, put God's work first and do what he wants. Then the other things will be yours as well. 34 Don't worry about tomorrow. It will take care of itself. You have enough to worry about today.

## Judging Others
*(Luke 6.37, 38, 41, 42)*

7 Don't condemn others, and God won't condemn you. 2 God will be as hard on you as you are on others! He will treat you exactly as you treat them.

3 You can see the speck in your friend's eye, but you don't notice the log in your own eye. 4 How can you say, "My friend, let me take the speck out of your eye," when you don't see the log in your own eye?

5 You're nothing but show-offs! First, take the log out of your own eye. Then you can see how to take the speck out of your friend's eye.

6 Don't give to dogs what belongs to God. They will only turn and attack you. Don't throw pearls down in front of pigs. They will trample all over them.

## Ask, Search, Knock
*(Luke 11.9-13)*

7 Ask, and you will receive. Search, and you will find. Knock, and the door will be opened for you. 8 Everyone who asks will receive. Everyone who searches will find. And the door will be opened for everyone who knocks. 9 Would any of you give your hungry child a stone, if the child asked for some bread? 10 Would you give your child a snake if the child asked for a fish? 11 As bad as you are, you still know how to give good gifts to your children. But your heavenly Father is even more ready to give good things to people who ask.

12 Treat others as you want them to treat you. This is what the Law and the Prophets*h* are all about.

## The Narrow Gate
*(Luke 13.24)*

13 Go in through the narrow gate. The gate to destruction is wide, and the road that leads there is easy to follow. A lot of people go through that gate. 14 But the gate to life is very narrow. The road that leads there is so hard to follow that only a few people find it.

## A Tree and Its Fruit
*(Luke 6.43-45)*

15 Watch out for false prophets! They dress up like sheep, but inside they are wolves who have come to attack you. 16 You can tell what they are by what they do. No one picks

*f*6.27 *live longer*: Or "grow taller." *g*6.29 *Solomon with all his wealth*: The Jewish people thought that Solomon was the richest person who had ever lived. *h*7.12 *the Law and the Prophets*: See the note at 5.17.

grapes or figs from thornbushes.
[17] A good tree produces good fruit,
and a bad tree produces bad fruit.
[18] A good tree cannot produce bad
fruit, and a bad tree cannot produce
good fruit. [19] Every tree that produces bad fruit will be chopped
down and burned. [20] You can tell
who the false prophets are by their
deeds.

### A Warning
(Luke 13.26, 27)

[21] Not everyone who calls me their
Lord will get into the kingdom of
heaven. Only the ones who obey my
Father in heaven will get in. [22] On
the day of judgment many will call
me their Lord. They will say, "We
preached in your name, and in your
name we forced out demons and
worked many miracles." [23] But I will
tell them, "I will have nothing to do
with you! Get out of my sight, you
evil people!"

### Two Builders
(Luke 6.47-49)

[24] Anyone who hears and obeys
these teachings of mine is like a
wise person who built a house
on solid rock. [25] Rain poured
down, rivers flooded, and winds
beat against that house. But it did
not fall, because it was built on solid
rock.
[26] Anyone who hears my teachings and doesn't obey them is like
a foolish person who built a house
on sand. [27] The rain poured
down, the rivers flooded, and
the winds blew and beat against
that house. Finally, it fell with a
crash.
[28] When Jesus finished speaking, the
crowds were surprised at his teaching.
[29] He taught them like someone with
authority, and not like their teachers
of the Law of Moses.

### Jesus Heals a Man
(Mark 1.40-45; Luke 5.12-16)

**8** As Jesus came down the mountain,
he was followed by large crowds.
[2] Suddenly a man with leprosy[i] came
and knelt in front of Jesus. He said,
"Lord, you have the power to make me
well, if only you wanted to."
[3] Jesus put his hand on the man and
said, "I want to! Now you are well."
At once the man's leprosy disappeared.
[4] Jesus told him, "Don't tell anyone
about this, but go and show the priest
that you are well. Then take a gift to
the temple just as Moses commanded,
and everyone will know that you have
been healed."[j]

### Jesus Heals an Army Officer's Servant
(Luke 7.1-10; John 4.43-54)

[5] When Jesus was going into the town
of Capernaum, an army officer came
up to him and said, [6] "Lord, my servant
is at home in such terrible pain that he
can't even move."
[7] "I will go and heal him," Jesus
replied.
[8] But the officer said, "Lord, I'm not
good enough for you to come into my
house. Just give the order, and my
servant will get well. [9] I have officers
who give orders to me, and I have soldiers who take orders from me. I can
say to one of them, 'Go!' and he goes.
I can say to another, 'Come!' and he
comes. I can say to my servant, 'Do
this!' and he will do it."
[10] When Jesus heard this, he was so
surprised that he turned and said to the
crowd following him, "I tell you that
in all of Israel I've never found anyone
with this much faith! [11] Many people
will come from everywhere to enjoy the
feast in the kingdom of heaven with
Abraham, Isaac, and Jacob. [12] But the
ones who should have been in the kingdom will be thrown out into the dark.
They will cry and grit their teeth in
pain."

[i]8.2 *leprosy*: In biblical times the word "leprosy" was used for many different kinds of
skin diseases. [j]8.4 *everyone will know that you have been healed*: People with leprosy
had to be examined by a priest and told that they were well (that is "clean") before they
could once again live a normal life in the Jewish community. The gift that Moses
commanded was the sacrifice of some lambs together with flour mixed with olive oil.

13 Then Jesus said to the officer, "You may go home now. Your faith has made it happen."

Right then his servant was healed.

## Jesus Heals Many People
(Mark 1.29-34; Luke 4.38-41)

14 Jesus went to the home of Peter, where he found that Peter's mother-in-law was sick in bed with fever. 15 He took her by the hand, and the fever left her. Then she got up and served Jesus a meal.

16 That evening many people with demons in them were brought to Jesus. And with only a word he forced out the evil spirits and healed everyone who was sick. 17 So God's promise came true, just as the prophet Isaiah had said,

"He healed our diseases
and made us well."

## Some Who Wanted To Go with Jesus
(Luke 9.57-62)

18 When Jesus saw the crowd,k he went across Lake Galilee. 19 A teacher of the Law of Moses came up to him and said, "Teacher, I'll go anywhere with you!"

20 Jesus replied, "Foxes have dens, and birds have nests. But the Son of Man doesn't have a place to call his own."

21 Another disciple said to Jesus, "Lord, let me wait till I bury my father."

22 Jesus answered, "Come with me, and let the dead bury their dead."l

## A Storm
(Mark 4.35-41; Luke 8.22-25)

23 After Jesus left in a boat with his disciples, 24 a terrible storm suddenly struck the lake, and waves started splashing into their boat.

Jesus was sound asleep, 25 so the disciples went over to him and woke him up. They said, "Lord, save us! We're going to drown!"

26 But Jesus replied, "Why are you so afraid? You surely don't have much faith." Then he got up and ordered the wind and the waves to calm down. And everything was calm.

27 The men in the boat were amazed and said, "Who is this? Even the wind and the waves obey him."

## Two Men with Demons in Them
(Mark 5.1-20; Luke 8.26-39)

28 After Jesus had crossed the lake, he came to shore near the town of Gadaram and started down the road. Two men with demons in them came to him from the tombs.n They were so fierce that no one could travel that way. 29 Suddenly they shouted, "Jesus, Son of God, what do you want with us? Have you come to punish us before our time?"

30 Not far from there a large herd of pigs was feeding. 31 So the demons begged Jesus, "If you force us out, please send us into those pigs!" 32 Jesus told them to go, and they went out of the men and into the pigs. All at once the pigs rushed down the steep bank into the lake and drowned.

33 The people taking care of the pigs ran to the town and told everything, especially what had happened to the two men. 34 Everyone in town came out to meet Jesus. When they saw him, they begged him to leave their part of the country.

## Jesus Heals a Crippled Man
(Mark 2.1-12; Luke 5.17-26)

9 Jesus got into a boat and crossed back over to the town where he lived.o 2 Some people soon brought to him a crippled man lying on a mat. When Jesus saw how much faith they had, he said to the crippled man, "My

k8.18 saw the crowd: Some manuscripts have "large crowd." Others have "large crowds." l8.22 let the dead bury their dead: For the Jewish people a proper burial of their dead was a very important duty. But Jesus teaches that following him is even more important. m8.28 Gadara: Some manuscripts have "Gergesa." Others have "Gerasa." n8.28 tombs: It was thought that demons and evil spirits lived in tombs and in caves that were used for burying the dead. o9.1 where he lived: Capernaum (see 4.13).

friend, don't worry! Your sins are
forgiven."
3 Some teachers of the Law of Moses
said to themselves, "Jesus must think
he is God!"
4 But Jesus knew what was in their
minds, and he said, "Why are you
thinking such evil things? 5 Is it easier
for me to tell this crippled man that his
sins are forgiven or to tell him to get
up and walk? 6 But I will show you that
the Son of Man has the right to forgive
sins here on earth." So Jesus said to
the man, "Get up! Pick up your mat and
go on home." 7 The man got up and
went home. 8 When the crowds saw
this, they were afraid[p] and praised God
for giving such authority to people.

### *Jesus Chooses Matthew*

*(Mark 2.13-17; Luke 5.27-32)*

9 As Jesus was leaving, he saw a tax
collector[q] named Matthew sitting at the
place for paying taxes. Jesus said to
him, "Come with me." Matthew got up
and went with him.
10 Later, Jesus and his disciples were
having dinner at Matthew's house.[r]
Many tax collectors and other sinners
were also there. 11 Some Pharisees
asked Jesus' disciples, "Why does your
teacher eat with tax collectors and
other sinners?"
12 Jesus heard them and answered,
"Healthy people don't need a doctor,
but sick people do. 13 Go and learn what
the Scriptures mean when they say, 'Instead of offering sacrifices to me, I want
you to be merciful to others.' I didn't
come to invite good people to be my
followers. I came to invite sinners."

### *People Ask about Going without Eating*

*(Mark 2.18-22; Luke 5.33-39)*

14 One day some followers of John
the Baptist came and asked Jesus,
"Why do we and the Pharisees often
go without eating,[s] while your disciples
never do?"
15 Jesus answered:

The friends of a bridegroom don't go without eating while he is still with them. But the time will come when he will be taken from them. Then they will go without eating.

16 No one uses a new piece of cloth
to patch old clothes. The patch
would shrink and tear a bigger hole.
17 No one pours new wine into old
wineskins. The wine would swell
and burst the old skins.[t] Then the
wine would be lost, and the skins
would be ruined. New wine must be
put into new wineskins. Both the
skins and the wine will then be safe.

### *A Dying Girl and a Sick Woman*

*(Mark 5.21-43; Luke 8.40-56)*

18 While Jesus was still speaking, an
official came and knelt in front of him.
The man said, "My daughter has just
now died! Please come and place your
hand on her. Then she will live again."
19 Jesus and his disciples got up and
went with the man.
20 A woman who had been bleeding
for twelve years came up behind Jesus
and barely touched his clothes. 21 She
had said to herself, "If I can just touch
his clothes, I will get well."
22 Jesus turned. He saw the woman
and said, "Don't worry! You are now
well because of your faith." At that moment she was healed.
23 When Jesus went into the home of
the official and saw the musicians and
the crowd of mourners,[u] 24 he said,
"Get out of here! The little girl isn't
dead. She is just asleep." Everyone
started laughing at Jesus. 25 But after
the crowd had been sent out of the
house, Jesus went to the girl's bedside.
He took her by the hand and helped
her up.
26 News about this spread all over
that part of the country.

[p]**9.8** *afraid*: Some manuscripts have "amazed." [q]**9.9** *tax collector*: See the note at 5.46.
[r]**9.10** *Matthew's house*: Or "Jesus' house." [s]**9.14** *without eating*: See the note at 4.2.
[t]**9.17** *swell and burst the old skins*: While the juice from grapes was becoming wine, it would swell and stretch the skins in which it had been stored. If the skins were old and stiff, they would burst. [u]**9.23** *the crowd of mourners*: The Jewish people often hired mourners for funerals.

## Jesus Heals Two Blind Men

27 As Jesus was walking along, two blind men began following him and shouting, "Son of David,v have pity on us!" 28 After Jesus had gone indoors, the two blind men came up to him. He asked them, "Do you believe I can make you well?"

"Yes, Lord," they answered.

29 Jesus touched their eyes and said, "Because of your faith, you will be healed." 30 They were able to see, and Jesus strictly warned them not to tell anyone about him. 31 But they left and talked about him to everyone in that part of the country.

## Jesus Heals a Man Who Could Not Talk

32 As Jesus and his disciples were on their way, some people brought to him a man who could not talk because a demon was in him. 33 After Jesus had forced the demon out, the man started talking. The crowds were so amazed that they began saying, "Nothing like this has ever happened in Israel!" 34 But the Pharisees said, "The leader of the demons gives him the power to force out demons."

## Jesus Has Pity on People

35 Jesus went to every town and village. He taught in their meeting places and preached the good news about God's kingdom. Jesus also healed every kind of disease and sickness. 36 When he saw the crowds, he felt sorry for them. They were confused and helpless, like sheep without a shepherd. 37 He said to his disciples, "A large crop is in the fields, but there are only a few workers. 38 Ask the Lord in charge of the harvest to send out workers to bring it in."

## Jesus Chooses His Twelve Apostles
### (Mark 3.13-19; Luke 6.12-16)

10 Jesus called together his twelve disciples. He gave them the power to force out evil spirits and to heal every kind of disease and sickness. 2 The first of the twelve apostles was Simon, better known as Peter. His brother Andrew was an apostle, and so were James and John, the two sons of Zebedee. 3 Philip, Bartholomew, Thomas, Matthew the tax collector,w James the son of Alphaeus, and Thaddaeus were also apostles. 4 The others were Simon, known as the Eager One,x and Judas Iscariot,y who later betrayed Jesus.

## Instructions for the Twelve Apostles
### (Mark 6.7-13; Luke 9.1-6)

5 Jesus sent out the twelve apostles with these instructions:

Stay away from the Gentiles and don't go to any Samaritan town. 6 Go only to the people of Israel, because they are like a flock of lost sheep. 7 As you go, announce that the kingdom of heaven will soon be here.z 8 Heal the sick, raise the dead to life, heal people who have leprosy,a and force out demons. You received without paying, now give without being paid. 9 Don't take along any gold, silver, or copper coins. 10 And don't carryb a traveling bag or an extra shirt or sandals or a walking stick.

Workers deserve their food. 11 So when you go to a town or a village, find someone worthy enough to have you as their guest and stay with them until you leave. 12 When you go to a home, give it your blessing of peace. 13 If the home is deserving, let your blessing remain with

---

v 9.27 *Son of David*: The Jewish people expected the Messiah to be from the family of King David, and for this reason the Messiah was often called the "Son of David." w 10.3 *tax collector*: See the note at 5.46. x 10.4 *known as the Eager One*: The Greek text has "Cananaean," which probably comes from a Hebrew word meaning "zealous" (see Luke 6.15). "Zealot" was the name later given to the members of a Jewish group that resisted and fought against the Romans. y 10.4 *Iscariot*: This may mean "a man from Kerioth" (a place in Judea). But more probably it means "a man who was a liar" or "a man who was a betrayer." z 10.7 *will soon be here*: Or "is already here." a 10.8 *leprosy*: See the note at 8.2. b 10.9, 10 *Don't take along . . . don't carry*: Or "Don't accept . . . don't accept."

them. But if the home isn't deserving, take back your blessing of peace. [14] If someone won't welcome you or listen to your message, leave their home or town. And shake the dust from your feet at them.[c] [15] I promise you that the day of judgment will be easier for the towns of Sodom and Gomorrah[d] than for that town.

## Warning about Trouble
### (Mark 13.9-13; Luke 21.12-17)

[16] I am sending you like lambs into a pack of wolves. So be as wise as snakes and as innocent as doves. [17] Watch out for people who will take you to court and have you beaten in their meeting places. [18] Because of me, you will be dragged before rulers and kings to tell them and the Gentiles about your faith. [19] But when someone arrests you, don't worry about what you will say or how you will say it. At that time you will be given the words to say. [20] But you will not really be the one speaking. The Spirit from your Father will tell you what to say.

[21] Brothers and sisters will betray one another and have each other put to death. Parents will betray their own children, and children will turn against their parents and have them killed. [22] Everyone will hate you because of me. But if you remain faithful until the end, you will be saved. [23] When people mistreat you in one town, hurry to another one. I promise you that before you have gone to all the towns of Israel, the Son of Man will come.

[24] Disciples are not better than their teacher, and slaves are not better than their master. [25] It is enough for disciples to be like their teacher and for slaves to be like their master. If people call the head of the family Satan, what will they say about the rest of the family?

## The One To Fear
### (Luke 12.2-7)

[26] Don't be afraid of anyone! Everything that is hidden will be found out, and every secret will be known. [27] Whatever I say to you in the dark, you must tell in the light. And you must announce from the housetops whatever I have whispered to you. [28] Don't be afraid of people. They can kill you, but they cannot harm your soul. Instead, you should fear God who can destroy both your body and your soul in hell. [29] Aren't two sparrows sold for only a penny? But your Father knows when any one of them falls to the ground. [30] Even the hairs on your head are counted. [31] So don't be afraid! You are worth much more than many sparrows.

## Telling Others about Christ
### (Luke 12.8, 9)

[32] If you tell others that you belong to me, I will tell my Father in heaven that you are my followers. [33] But if you reject me, I will tell my Father in heaven that you don't belong to me.

## Not Peace, but Trouble
### (Luke 12.51-53; 14.26, 27)

[34] Don't think that I came to bring peace to the earth! I came to bring trouble, not peace. [35] I came to turn sons against their fathers, daughters against their mothers, and daughters-in-law against their mothers-in-law. [36] Your worst enemies will be in your own family.

[37] If you love your father or mother or even your sons and daughters more than me, you are not fit to be my disciples. [38] And unless you are willing to take up your cross and come with me, you are not fit to be my disciples. [39] If you try to save your life, you will lose it. But if you give it up for me, you will surely find it.

---

[c] 10.14 *shake the dust from your feet at them*: This was a way of showing rejection (see Acts 13.51).    [d] 10.15 *Sodom and Gomorrah*: During the time of Abraham the Lord destroyed these towns because the people there were so evil.

### Rewards
(Mark 9.41)

**40** Anyone who welcomes you welcomes me. And anyone who welcomes me also welcomes the one who sent me. **41** Anyone who welcomes a prophet, just because that person is a prophet, will be given the same reward as a prophet. Anyone who welcomes a good person, just because that person is good, will be given the same reward as a good person. **42** And anyone who gives one of my most humble followers a cup of cool water, just because that person is my follower, will surely be rewarded.

### John the Baptist
(Luke 7.18-35)

**11** After Jesus had finished instructing his twelve disciples, he left and began teaching and preaching in the towns.*e*

**2** John was in prison when he heard what Christ was doing. So John sent some of his followers **3** to ask Jesus, "Are you the one we should be looking for? Or must we wait for someone else?"

**4** Jesus answered, "Go and tell John what you have heard and seen. **5** The blind are now able to see, and the lame can walk. People with leprosy*f* are being healed, and the deaf can hear. The dead are raised to life, and the poor are hearing the good news. **6** God will bless everyone who doesn't reject me because of what I do."

**7** As John's followers were going away, Jesus spoke to the crowds about John:

What sort of person did you go out into the desert to see? Was he like tall grass blown about by the wind? **8** What kind of man did you go out to see? Was he someone dressed in fine clothes? People who dress like that live in the king's palace. **9** What did you really go out to see? Was he a prophet? He certainly was. I tell

you that he was more than a prophet. **10** In the Scriptures God says about him, "I am sending my messenger ahead of you to get things ready for you." **11** I tell you that no one ever born on this earth is greater than John the Baptist. But whoever is least in the kingdom of heaven is greater than John.

**12** From the time of John the Baptist until now, violent people have been trying to take over the kingdom of heaven by force. **13** All the Books of the Prophets and the Law of Moses*g* told what was going to happen up to the time of John. **14** And if you believe them, John is Elijah, the prophet you are waiting for. **15** If you have ears, pay attention!

**16** You people are like children sitting in the market and shouting to each other,

**17** "We played the flute,
  but you would not dance!
We sang a funeral song,
  but you would not mourn!"

**18** John the Baptist did not go around eating and drinking, and you said, "That man has a demon in him!" **19** But the Son of Man goes around eating and drinking, and you say, "That man eats and drinks too much! He is even a friend of tax collectors*h* and sinners." Yet Wisdom is shown to be right by what it does.

### The Unbelieving Towns
(Luke 10.13-15)

**20** In the towns where Jesus had worked most of his miracles, the people refused to turn to God. So Jesus was upset with them and said:

**21** You people of Chorazin are in for trouble! You people of Bethsaida are in for trouble too! If the miracles that took place in your towns had happened in Tyre and Sidon, the people there would have turned to

*e* **11.1** *the towns*: The Greek text has "their towns," which may refer to the towns of Galilee or to the towns where Jesus' disciples had lived.   *f* **11.5** *leprosy*: See the note at 8.2.
*g* **11.13** *the Books of the Prophets and the Law of Moses*: The Jewish Scriptures, that is, the Old Testament.   *h* **11.19** *tax collectors*: See the note at 5.46.

God long ago. They would have dressed in sackcloth and put ashes on their heads.ⁱ ²² I tell you that on the day of judgment the people of Tyre and Sidon will get off easier than you will.

²³ People of Capernaum, do you think you will be honored in heaven? You will go down to hell! If the miracles that took place in your town had happened in Sodom, that town would still be standing. ²⁴ So I tell you that on the day of judgment the people of Sodom will get off easier than you.

## Come to Me and Rest
(Luke 10.21, 22)

²⁵ At that moment Jesus said:

My Father, Lord of heaven and earth, I am grateful that you hid all this from wise and educated people and showed it to ordinary people. ²⁶ Yes, Father, that is what pleased you.

²⁷ My Father has given me everything, and he is the only one who knows the Son. The only one who truly knows the Father is the Son. But the Son wants to tell others about the Father, so that they can know him too.

²⁸ If you are tired from carrying heavy burdens, come to me and I will give you rest. ²⁹ Take the yokeʲ I give you. Put it on your shoulders and learn from me. I am gentle and humble, and you will find rest. ³⁰ This yoke is easy to bear, and this burden is light.

## A Question about the Sabbath
(Mark 2.23-28; Luke 6.1-5)

**12** One Sabbath, Jesus and his disciples were walking through some wheat fields.ᵏ His disciples were hungry and began picking and eating grains of wheat. ² Some Pharisees noticed this and said to Jesus, "Why are your disciples picking grain on the Sabbath? They are not supposed to do that!"

³ Jesus answered:

You surely must have read what David did when he and his followers were hungry. ⁴ He went into the house of God, and then they ate the sacred loaves of bread that only priests are supposed to eat. ⁵ Haven't you read in the Law of Moses that the priests are allowed to work in the temple on the Sabbath? But no one says that they are guilty of breaking the law of the Sabbath. ⁶ I tell you that there is something here greater than the temple. ⁷ Don't you know what the Scriptures mean when they say, "Instead of offering sacrifices to me, I want you to be merciful to others?" If you knew what this means, you would not condemn these innocent disciples of mine. ⁸ So the Son of Man is Lord over the Sabbath.

## A Man with a Crippled Hand
(Mark 3.1-6; Luke 6.6-11)

⁹ Jesus left and went into one of the Jewish meeting places, ¹⁰ where there was a man whose hand was crippled. Some Pharisees wanted to accuse Jesus of doing something wrong, and they asked him, "Is it right to heal someone on the Sabbath?"

¹¹ Jesus answered, "If you had a sheep that fell into a ditch on the Sabbath, wouldn't you lift it out? ¹² People are worth much more than sheep, and so it is right to do good on the Sabbath." ¹³ Then Jesus told the man, "Hold out your hand." The man did, and it became as healthy as the other one.

¹⁴ The Pharisees left and started making plans to kill Jesus.

## God's Chosen Servant

¹⁵ When Jesus found out what was happening, he left there and large

ⁱ11.21 *sackcloth . . . ashes on their heads*: This was one way that people showed how sorry they were for their sins. ʲ11.29 *yoke*: Yokes were put on the necks of animals, so that they could pull a plow or wagon. A yoke was a symbol of obedience and hard work. ᵏ12.1 *walking through some wheat fields*: It was the custom to let hungry travelers pick grains of wheat.

crowds followed him. He healed all of their sick, [16] but warned them not to tell anyone about him. [17] So God's promise came true, just as Isaiah the prophet had said,

[18] "Here is my chosen servant!
I love him,
and he pleases me.
I will give him my Spirit,
and he will bring justice
to the nations.
[19] He won't shout or yell
or call out in the streets.
[20] He won't break off a bent reed
or put out a dying flame,
but he will make sure
that justice is done.
[21] All nations will place
their hope in him."

### Jesus and the Ruler of the Demons
(Mark 3.20-30; Luke 11.14-23; 12.10)

[22] Some people brought to Jesus a man who was blind and could not talk because he had a demon in him. Jesus healed the man, and then he was able to talk and see. [23] The crowds were so amazed that they asked, "Could Jesus be the Son of David?"[l]

[24] When the Pharisees heard this, they said, "He forces out demons by the power of Beelzebul, the ruler of the demons!"

[25] Jesus knew what they were thinking, and he said to them:
Any kingdom where people fight each other will end up ruined. And a town or family that fights will soon destroy itself. [26] So if Satan fights against himself, how can his kingdom last? [27] If I use the power of Beelzebul to force out demons, whose power do your own followers use to force them out? Your followers are the ones who will judge you. [28] But when I force out demons by the power of God's Spirit, it proves that God's kingdom has already come to you. [29] How can anyone break into a strong man's house and

steal his things, unless he first ties up the strong man? Then he can take everything. [30] If you are not on my side, you are against me. If you don't gather in the harvest with me, you scatter it. [31-32] I tell you that any sinful thing you do or say can be forgiven. Even if you speak against the Son of Man, you can be forgiven. But if you speak against the Holy Spirit, you can never be forgiven, either in this life or in the life to come.

### A Tree and Its Fruit
(Luke 6.43-45)

[33] A good tree produces only good fruit, and a bad tree produces bad fruit. You can tell what a tree is like by the fruit it produces. [34] You are a bunch of evil snakes, so how can you say anything good? Your words show what is in your hearts. [35] Good people bring good things out of their hearts, but evil people bring evil things out of their hearts. [36] I promise you that on the day of judgment, everyone will have to account for every careless word they have spoken. [37] On that day they will be told that they are either innocent or guilty because of the things they have said.

### A Sign from Heaven
(Mark 8.11, 12; Luke 11.29-32)

[38] Some Pharisees and teachers of the Law of Moses said, "Teacher, we want you to show us a sign from heaven." [39] But Jesus replied:
You want a sign because you are evil and won't believe! But the only sign you will get is the sign of the prophet Jonah. [40] He was in the stomach of a big fish for three days and nights, just as the Son of Man will be deep in the earth for three days and nights. [41] On the day of judgment the people of Nineveh[m] will stand there with you and

condemn you. They turned to God when Jonah preached, and yet here is something far greater than Jonah. [42] The Queen of the South[n] will also stand there with you and condemn you. She traveled a long way to hear Solomon's wisdom, and yet here is something much greater than Solomon.

### Return of an Evil Spirit
(Luke 11.24-26)

[43] When an evil spirit leaves a person, it travels through the desert, looking for a place to rest. But when the demon doesn't find a place, [44] it says, "I will go back to the home I left." When it gets there and finds the place empty, clean, and fixed up, [45] it goes off and finds seven other evil spirits even worse than itself. They all come and make their home there, and the person ends up in worse shape than before. That's how it will be with you evil people of today.

### Jesus' Mother and Brothers
(Mark 3.31-35; Luke 8.19-21)

[46] While Jesus was still speaking to the crowds, his mother and brothers came and stood outside because they wanted to talk with him. [47] Someone told Jesus, "Your mother and brothers are standing outside and want to talk with you."[o]
[48] Jesus answered, "Who is my mother and who are my brothers?" [49] Then he pointed to his disciples and said, "These are my mother and my brothers! [50] Anyone who obeys my Father in heaven is my brother or sister or mother."

### A Story about a Farmer
(Mark 4.1-9; Luke 8.4-8)

**13** That same day Jesus left the house and went out beside Lake Galilee, where he sat down to teach.[p] [2] Such large crowds gathered around

him that he had to sit in a boat, while the people stood on the shore. [3] Then he taught them many things by using stories. He said:

A farmer went out to scatter seed in a field. [4] While the farmer was scattering the seed, some of it fell along the road and was eaten by birds. [5] Other seeds fell on thin, rocky ground and quickly started growing because the soil wasn't very deep. [6] But when the sun came up, the plants were scorched and dried up, because they did not have enough roots. [7] Some other seeds fell where thornbushes grew up and choked the plants. [8] But a few seeds did fall on good ground where the plants produced a hundred or sixty or thirty times as much as was scattered. [9] If you have ears, pay attention!

### Why Jesus Used Stories
(Mark 4.10-12; Luke 8.9, 10)

[10] Jesus' disciples came to him and asked, "Why do you use nothing but stories when you speak to the people?" [11] Jesus answered:
I have explained the secrets about the kingdom of heaven to you, but not to others. [12] Everyone who has something will be given more. But people who don't have anything will lose even what little they have. [13] I use stories when I speak to them because when they look, they cannot see, and when they listen, they cannot hear or understand. [14] So God's promise came true, just as the prophet Isaiah had said,

"These people will listen
and listen,
    but never understand.
They will look and look,
    but never see.
[15] All of them have
    stubborn minds!
Their ears are stopped up,
    and their eyes are covered.
They cannot see or hear
    or understand.

n 12.42 Queen of the South: Sheba, probably a country in southern Arabia.  o 12.47 with you: Some manuscripts do not have verse 47.  p 13.1 sat down to teach: Teachers in the ancient world, including Jewish teachers, usually sat down when they taught.

If they could,
they would turn to me,
    and I would heal them."

16 But God has blessed you, because your eyes can see and your
ears can hear! 17 Many prophets and
good people were eager to see what
you see and to hear what you hear.
But I tell you that they did not see
or hear.

### Jesus Explains the Story about the Farmer
#### (Mark 4.13-20; Luke 8.11-15)

18 Now listen to the meaning of the
story about the farmer:
19 The seeds that fell along the
road are the people who hear the
message about the kingdom, but
don't understand it. Then the evil
one comes and snatches the message from their hearts. 20 The seeds
that fell on rocky ground are the
people who gladly hear the message
and accept it right away. 21 But they
don't have deep roots, and they
don't last very long. As soon as life
gets hard or the message gets them
in trouble, they give up.
22 The seeds that fell among the
thornbushes are also people who
hear the message. But they start
worrying about the needs of this life
and are fooled by the desire to get
rich. So the message gets choked
out, and they never produce anything. 23 The seeds that fell on good
ground are the people who hear and
understand the message. They produce as much as a hundred or sixty
or thirty times what was planted.

### Weeds among the Wheat

24 Jesus then told them this story:
The kingdom of heaven is like
what happened when a farmer scattered good seed in a field. 25 But
while everyone was sleeping, an enemy came and scattered weed seeds
in the field and then left.
26 When the plants came up and
began to ripen, the farmer's servants

could see the weeds. 27 The servants
came and asked, "Sir, didn't you
scatter good seed in your field?
Where did these weeds come from?"
28 "An enemy did this," he replied.
His servants then asked, "Do you
want us to go out and pull up the
weeds?"
29 "No!" he answered. "You might
also pull up the wheat. 30 Leave the
weeds alone until harvest time.
Then I'll tell my workers to gather
the weeds and tie them up and burn
them. But I'll have them store the
wheat in my barn."

### Stories about a Mustard Seed and Yeast
#### (Mark 4.30-32; Luke 13.18-21)

31 Jesus told them another story:
The kingdom of heaven is like
what happens when a farmer plants
a mustard seed in a field. 32 Although it is the smallest of all seeds,
it grows larger than any garden
plant and becomes a tree. Birds
even come and nest on its branches.
33 Jesus also said:
The kingdom of heaven is like
what happens when a woman mixes
a little yeast into three big batches
of flour. Finally, all the dough rises.

### The Reason for Teaching with Stories
#### (Mark 4.33, 34)

34 Jesus used stories when he spoke
to the people. In fact, he did not tell
them anything without using stories.
35 So God's promise came true, just as
the prophet q had said,

"I will use stories
    to speak my message
and to explain things
    that have been hidden
since the creation
    of the world."

### Jesus Explains the Story about the Weeds

36 After Jesus left the crowd and went
inside,r his disciples came to him and

q 13.35 the prophet: Some manuscripts have "the prophet Isaiah."    r 13.36 went inside: Or
"went home."

said, "Explain to us the story about the weeds in the wheat field."

37 Jesus answered:

The one who scattered the good seed is the Son of Man. 38 The field is the world, and the good seeds are the people who belong to the kingdom. The weed seeds are those who belong to the evil one, 39 and the one who scattered them is the devil. The harvest is the end of time, and angels are the ones who bring in the harvest.

40 Weeds are gathered and burned. That's how it will be at the end of time. 41 The Son of Man will send out his angels, and they will gather from his kingdom everyone who does wrong or causes others to sin. 42 Then he will throw them into a flaming furnace, where people will cry and grit their teeth in pain. 43 But everyone who has done right will shine like the sun in their Father's kingdom. If you have ears, pay attention!

### A Hidden Treasure

44 The kingdom of heaven is like what happens when someone finds treasure hidden in a field and buries it again. A person like that is happy and goes and sells everything in order to buy that field.

### A Valuable Pearl

45 The kingdom of heaven is like what happens when a shop owner is looking for fine pearls. 46 After finding a very valuable one, the owner goes and sells everything in order to buy that pearl.

### A Fish Net

47 The kingdom of heaven is like what happens when a net is thrown into a lake and catches all kinds of fish. 48 When the net is full, it is dragged to the shore, and the fishermen sit down to separate the fish. They keep the good ones, but throw the bad ones away. 49 That's how it

will be at the end of time. Angels will come and separate the evil people from the ones who have done right. 50 Then those evil people will be thrown into a flaming furnace, where they will cry and grit their teeth in pain.

### New and Old Treasures

51 Jesus asked his disciples if they understood all these things. They said, "Yes, we do."

52 So he told them, "Every student of the Scriptures who becomes a disciple in the kingdom of heaven is like someone who brings out new and old treasures from the storeroom."

### The People of Nazareth Turn against Jesus
#### (Mark 6.1-6; Luke 4.16-30)

53 When Jesus had finished telling these stories, he left 54 and went to his hometown. He taught in their meeting place, and the people were so amazed that they asked, "Where does he get all this wisdom and the power to work these miracles? 55 Isn't he the son of the carpenter? Isn't Mary his mother, and aren't James, Joseph, Simon, and Judas his brothers? 56 Don't his sisters still live here in our town? How can he do all this?" 57 So the people were very unhappy because of what he was doing.

But Jesus said, "Prophets are honored by everyone, except the people of their hometown and their own family." 58 And because the people did not have any faith, Jesus did not work many miracles there.

### The Death of John the Baptist
#### (Mark 6.14-29; Luke 9.7-9)

**14** About this time Herod the ruler[s] heard the news about Jesus 2 and told his officials, "This is John the Baptist! He has come back from death, and that's why he has the power to work these miracles."

3-4 Herod had earlier arrested John

---

[s] 14.1 Herod the ruler: Herod Antipas, the son of Herod the Great (see 2.1).

and had him chained and put in prison. He did this because John had told him, "It isn't right for you to take Herodias, the wife of your brother Philip." [5] Herod wanted to kill John. But the people thought John was a prophet, and Herod was afraid of what they might do.

[6] When Herod's birthday came, the daughter of Herodias danced for the guests. She pleased Herod [7] so much that he swore to give her whatever she wanted. [8] But the girl's mother told her to say, "Here on a platter I want the head of John the Baptist!"

[9] The king was sorry for what he had said. But he did not want to break the promise he had made in front of his guests. So he ordered a guard [10] to go to the prison and cut off John's head. [11] It was taken on a platter to the girl, and she gave it to her mother. [12] John's followers took his body and buried it. Then they told Jesus what had happened.

### Jesus Feeds Five Thousand
*(Mark 6.30-44; Luke 9.10-17; John 6.1-14)*

[13] After Jesus heard about John, he crossed Lake Galilee[t] to go to some place where he could be alone. But the crowds found out and followed him on foot from the towns. [14] When Jesus got out of the boat, he saw the large crowd. He felt sorry for them and healed everyone who was sick.

[15] That evening the disciples came to Jesus and said, "This place is like a desert, and it is already late. Let the crowds leave, so they can go to the villages and buy some food."

[16] Jesus replied, "They don't have to leave. Why don't you give them something to eat?"

[17] But they said, "We have only five small loaves of bread[u] and two fish."

[18] Jesus asked his disciples to bring the food to him, [19] and he told the crowd to sit down on the grass. Jesus took the five loaves and the two fish. He looked up toward heaven and blessed the food. Then he broke the bread and handed

it to his disciples, and they gave it to the people.

[20] After everyone had eaten all they wanted, Jesus' disciples picked up twelve large baskets of leftovers.

[21] There were about five thousand men who ate, not counting the women and children.

### Jesus Walks on the Water
*(Mark 6.45-52; John 6.15-21)*

[22] Right away, Jesus made his disciples get into a boat and start back across the lake.[v] But he stayed until he had sent the crowds away. [23] Then he went up on a mountain where he could be alone and pray. Later that evening, he was still there.

[24] By this time the boat was a long way from the shore. It was going against the wind and was being tossed around by the waves. [25] A little while before morning, Jesus came walking on the water toward his disciples. [26] When they saw him, they thought he was a ghost. They were terrified and started screaming.

[27] At once, Jesus said to them, "Don't worry! I am Jesus. Don't be afraid."

[28] Peter replied, "Lord, if it is really you, tell me to come to you on the water."

[29] "Come on!" Jesus said. Peter then got out of the boat and started walking on the water toward him.

[30] But when Peter saw how strong the wind was, he was afraid and started sinking. "Save me, Lord!" he shouted.

[31] Right away, Jesus reached out his hand. He helped Peter up and said, "You surely don't have much faith. Why do you doubt?"

[32] When Jesus and Peter got into the boat, the wind died down. [33] The men in the boat worshiped Jesus and said, "You really are the Son of God!"

### Jesus Heals Sick People in Gennesaret
*(Mark 6.53-56)*

[34] Jesus and his disciples crossed the lake and came to shore near the town

---

[t] **14.13** *crossed Lake Galilee*: To the east side. have been flat and round or in the shape of a bun. [u] **14.17** *small loaves of bread*: These would [v] **14.22** *back across the lake*: To the west side.

of Gennesaret. [35] The people found out that he was there, and they sent word to everyone who lived in that part of the country. So they brought all the sick people to Jesus. [36] They begged him just to let them touch his clothes, and everyone who did was healed.

## The Teaching of the Ancestors
### (Mark 7.1-13)

**15** About this time some Pharisees and teachers of the Law of Moses came from Jerusalem. They asked Jesus, [2] "Why don't your disciples obey what our ancestors taught us to do? They don't even wash their hands[w] before they eat."

[3] Jesus answered:

Why do you disobey God and follow your own teaching? [4] Didn't God command you to respect your father and mother? Didn't he tell you to put to death all who curse their parents? [5] But you let people get by without helping their parents when they should. You let them say that what they have has been offered to God.[x] [6] Is this any way to show respect to your parents? You ignore God's commands in order to follow your own teaching. [7] And you are nothing but show-offs! Isaiah the prophet was right when he wrote that God had said,

[8] "All of you praise me
    with your words,
but you never really
    think about me.
[9] It is useless for you
    to worship me,
when you teach rules
    made up by humans."

## What Really Makes People Unclean
### (Mark 7.14-23)

[10] Jesus called the crowd together and said, "Pay attention and try to understand what I mean. [11] The food that you put into your mouth doesn't make you unclean and unfit to worship God. The bad words that come out of your mouth are what make you unclean."

[12] Then his disciples came over to him and asked, "Do you know that you insulted the Pharisees by what you said?"

[13] Jesus answered, "Every plant that my Father in heaven did not plant will be pulled up by the roots. [14] Stay away from those Pharisees! They are like blind people leading other blind people, and all of them will fall into a ditch."

[15] Peter replied, "What did you mean when you talked about the things that make people unclean?"

[16] Jesus then said:

Don't any of you know what I am talking about by now? [17] Don't you know that the food you put into your mouth goes into your stomach and then out of your body? [18] But the words that come out of your mouth come from your heart. And they are what make you unfit to worship God. [19] Out of your heart come evil thoughts, murder, unfaithfulness in marriage, vulgar deeds, stealing, telling lies, and insulting others. [20] These are what make you unclean. Eating without washing your hands will not make you unfit to worship God.

## A Woman's Faith
### (Mark 7.24-30)

[21] Jesus left and went to the territory near the cities of Tyre and Sidon. [22] Suddenly a Canaanite woman[y] from there came out shouting, "Lord and Son of David,[z] have pity on me! My daughter is full of demons." [23] Jesus did not say a word. But the woman kept following along and shouting, so his disciples came up and asked him to send her away.

[24] Jesus said, "I was sent only to the people of Israel! They are like a flock of lost sheep."

---

[w] 15.2 *wash their hands*: The Jewish people had strict laws about washing their hands before eating, especially if they had been out in public.   [x] 15.5 *has been offered to God*: According to Jewish custom, when people said something was offered to God, it belonged to him and could not be used for anyone else, not even for their own parents.
[y] 15.22 *Canaanite woman*: This woman was not Jewish.   [z] 15.22 *Son of David*: See the note at 9.27.

25 The woman came closer. Then she knelt down and begged, "Please help me, Lord!"

26 Jesus replied, "It isn't right to take food away from children and feed it to dogs."ᵃ

27 "Lord, that's true," the woman said, "but even dogs get the crumbs that fall from their owner's table."

28 Jesus answered, "Dear woman, you really do have a lot of faith, and you will be given what you want." At that moment her daughter was healed.

### Jesus Heals Many People

29 From there, Jesus went along Lake Galilee. Then he climbed a hill and sat down. 30 Large crowds came and brought many people who were crippled or blind or lame or unable to talk. They placed them, and many others, in front of Jesus, and he healed them all. 31 Everyone was amazed at what they saw and heard. People who had never spoken could now speak. The lame were healed, the crippled could walk, and the blind were able to see. Everyone was praising the God of Israel.

### Jesus Feeds Four Thousand
*(Mark 8.1-10)*

32 Jesus called his disciples together and told them, "I feel sorry for these people. They have been with me for three days, and they don't have anything to eat. I don't want to send them away hungry. They might faint on their way home."

33 His disciples said, "This place is like a desert. Where can we find enough food to feed such a crowd?"

34 Jesus asked them how much food they had. They replied, "Seven small loaves of breadᵇ and a few little fish."

35 After Jesus had told the people to sit down, 36 he took the seven loaves of bread and the fish and gave thanks. He then broke them and handed them to his disciples, who passed them around to the crowds.

37 Everyone ate all they wanted, and the leftovers filled seven large baskets.

38 There were four thousand men who ate, not counting the women and children.

39 After Jesus had sent the crowds away, he got into a boat and sailed across the lake. He came to shore near the town of Magadon.ᶜ

### A Demand for a Sign from Heaven
*(Mark 8.11-13; Luke 12.54-56)*

**16** The Pharisees and Sadducees came to Jesus and tried to test him by asking for a sign from heaven. 2 He told them:

If the sky is red in the evening, you say the weather will be good. 3 But if the sky is red and gloomy in the morning, you say it is going to rain. You can tell what the weather will be like by looking at the sky. But you don't understand what is happening now.ᵈ 4 You want a sign because you are evil and won't believe! But the only sign you will be given is what happened to Jonah.ᵉ

Then Jesus left.

### The Yeast of the Pharisees and Sadducees
*(Mark 8.14-21)*

5 The disciples had forgotten to bring any bread when they crossed the lake.ᶠ 6 Jesus then warned them, "Watch out! Guard against the yeast of the Pharisees and Sadducees."

7 The disciples talked this over and said to each other, "He must be saying this because we didn't bring along any bread."

8 Jesus knew what they were thinking and said:

You surely don't have much faith! Why are you talking about not having any bread? 9 Don't you understand? Have you forgotten about the five thousand people and all those

---

ᵃ 15.26 *feed it to dogs*: The Jewish people sometimes referred to Gentiles as dogs.
ᵇ 15.34 *small loaves of bread*: See the note at 14.17.    ᶜ 15.39 *Magadan*: The location is unknown.    ᵈ 16.2, 3 *If the sky is red ... what is happening now*: The words of Jesus in verses 2 and 3 are not in some manuscripts.    ᵉ 16.4 *what happened to Jonah*: Jonah was in the stomach of a big fish for three days and nights (see 12.40).    ᶠ 16.5 *crossed the lake*: To the east side.

baskets of leftovers from just five loaves of bread? [10] And what about the four thousand people and all those baskets of leftovers from only seven loaves of bread? [11] Don't you know by now that I am not talking to you about bread? Watch out for the yeast of the Pharisees and Sadducees! [12] Finally, the disciples understood that Jesus wasn't talking about the yeast used to make bread, but about the teaching of the Pharisees and Sadducees.

### Who Is Jesus?
(Mark 8.27-30; Luke 9.18-21)

[13] When Jesus and his disciples were near the town of Caesarea Philippi, he asked them, "What do people say about the Son of Man?" [14] The disciples answered, "Some people say you are John the Baptist or maybe Elijah[g] or Jeremiah or some other prophet." [15] Then Jesus asked them, "But who do you say I am?" [16] Simon Peter spoke up, "You are the Messiah, the Son of the living God." [17] Jesus told him:

Simon, son of Jonah, you are blessed! You didn't discover this on your own. It was shown to you by my Father in heaven. [18] So I will call you Peter, which means "a rock." On this rock I will build my church, and death itself will not have any power over it. [19] I will give you the keys to the kingdom of heaven, and God in heaven will allow whatever you allow on earth. But he will not allow anything that you don't allow. [20] Jesus told his disciples not to tell anyone that he was the Messiah.

### Jesus Speaks about His Suffering and Death
(Mark 8.31—9.1; Luke 9.22-27)

[21] From then on, Jesus began telling his disciples what would happen to him. He said, "I must go to Jerusalem. There the nation's leaders, the chief priests, and the teachers of the Law of Moses will make me suffer terribly. I will be killed, but three days later I will rise to life."

[22] Peter took Jesus aside and told him to stop talking like that. He said, "God would never let this happen to you, Lord!"

[23] Jesus turned to Peter and said, "Satan, get away from me! You're in my way because you think like everyone else and not like God."

[24] Then Jesus said to his disciples:

If any of you want to be my followers, you must forget about yourself. You must take up your cross and follow me. [25] If you want to save your life,[h] you will destroy it. But if you give up your life for me, you will find it. [26] What will you gain, if you own the whole world but destroy yourself? What would you give to get back your soul?

[27] The Son of Man will soon come in the glory of his Father and with his angels to reward all people for what they have done. [28] I promise you that some of those standing here will not die before they see the Son of Man coming with his kingdom.

### The True Glory of Jesus
(Mark 9.2-13; Luke 9.28-36)

**17** Six days later Jesus took Peter and the brothers James and John with him. They went up on a very high mountain where they could be alone. [2] There in front of the disciples, Jesus was completely changed. His face was shining like the sun, and his clothes became white as light.

[3] All at once Moses and Elijah were there talking with Jesus. [4] So Peter said to him, "Lord, it is good for us to be here! Let us make three shelters, one for you, one for Moses, and one for Elijah."

[5] While Peter was still speaking, the shadow of a bright cloud passed over

---

g **16.14** *Elijah*: Many of the Jewish people expected the prophet Elijah to come and prepare the way for the Messiah.   h **16.25** *life*: In verses 25 and 26 the same Greek word is translated "life," "yourself," and "soul."

them. From the cloud a voice said, "This is my own dear Son, and I am pleased with him. Listen to what he says!" ⁶ When the disciples heard the voice, they were so afraid that they fell flat on the ground. ⁷ But Jesus came over and touched them. He said, "Get up and don't be afraid!" ⁸ When they opened their eyes, they saw only Jesus.

⁹ On their way down from the mountain, Jesus warned his disciples not to tell anyone what they had seen until after the Son of Man had been raised from death.

¹⁰ The disciples asked Jesus, "Don't the teachers of the Law of Moses say that Elijah must come before the Messiah does?"

¹¹ Jesus told them, "Elijah certainly will come and get everything ready. ¹² In fact, he has already come. But the people did not recognize him and treated him just as they wanted to. They will soon make the Son of Man suffer in the same way." ¹³ Then the disciples understood that Jesus was talking to them about John the Baptist.

### Jesus Heals a Boy
(Mark 9.14-29; Luke 9.37-43a)

¹⁴ Jesus and his disciples returned to the crowd. A man knelt in front of him ¹⁵ and said, "Lord, have pity on my son! He has a bad case of epilepsy and often falls into a fire or into water. ¹⁶ I brought him to your disciples, but none of them could heal him."

¹⁷ Jesus said, "You people are too stubborn to have any faith! How much longer must I be with you? Why do I have to put up with you? Bring the boy here." ¹⁸ Then Jesus spoke sternly to the demon. It went out of the boy, and right then he was healed.

¹⁹ Later the disciples went to Jesus in private and asked him, "Why couldn't we force out the demon?"

²⁰⁻²¹ Jesus replied:

It is because you don't have enough faith! But I can promise you this. If you had faith no larger than

a mustard seed, you could tell this mountain to move from here to there. And it would. Everything would be possible for you. ⁱ

### Jesus Again Speaks about His Death
(Mark 9.30-32; Luke 9.43b-45)

²² While Jesus and his disciples were going from place to place in Galilee, he told them, "The Son of Man will be handed over to people ²³ who will kill him. But three days later he will rise to life." All of this made the disciples very sad.

### Paying the Temple Tax

²⁴ When Jesus and the others arrived in Capernaum, the collectors for the temple tax came to Peter and asked, "Does your teacher pay the temple tax?"

²⁵ "Yes, he does," Peter answered.

After they had returned home, Jesus went up to Peter and asked him, "Simon, what do you think? Do the kings of this earth collect taxes and fees from their own people or from foreigners?" ʲ

²⁶ Peter answered, "From foreigners."

Jesus replied, "Then their own people ᵏ don't have to pay. ²⁷ But we don't want to cause trouble. So go cast a line into the lake and pull out the first fish you hook. Open its mouth, and you will find a coin. Use it to pay your taxes and mine."

### Who Is the Greatest?
(Mark 9.33-37; Luke 9.46-48)

**18** About this time the disciples came to Jesus and asked him who would be the greatest in the kingdom of heaven. ² Jesus called a child over and had the child stand near him. ³ Then he said:

I promise you this. If you don't change and become like a child, you will never get into the kingdom of heaven. ⁴ But if you are as humble

ⁱ **17.20,21** *for you:* Some manuscripts add, "But the only way to force out that kind of demon is by praying and going without eating." ʲ **17.25** *from their own people or from foreigners:* Or "from their children or from others." ᵏ **17.26** *From foreigners ... their own people:* Or "From other people ... their children."

as this child, you are the greatest in the kingdom of heaven. [5] And when you welcome one of these children because of me, you welcome me.

## Temptations To Sin
### (Mark 9.42-48; Luke 17.1, 2)

[6] It will be terrible for people who cause even one of my little followers to sin. Those people would be better off thrown into the deepest part of the ocean with a heavy stone tied around their necks! [7] The world is in for trouble because of the way it causes people to sin. There will always be something to cause people to sin, but anyone who does this will be in for trouble.

[8] If your hand or foot causes you to sin, chop it off and throw it away! You would be better off to go into life crippled or lame than to have two hands or two feet and be thrown into the fire that never goes out. [9] If your eye causes you to sin, poke it out and get rid of it. You would be better off to go into life with only one eye than to have two eyes and be thrown into the fires of hell.

## The Lost Sheep
### (Luke 15.3-7)

[10-11] Don't be cruel to any of these little ones! I promise you that their angels are always with my Father in heaven.[l] [12] Let me ask you this. What would you do if you had a hundred sheep and one of them wandered off? Wouldn't you leave the ninety-nine on the hillside and go look for the one that had wandered away? [13] I am sure that finding it would make you happier than having the ninety-nine that never wandered off. [14] That's how it is with your Father in heaven. He doesn't want any of these little ones to be lost.

## When Someone Sins
### (Luke 17.3)

[15] If one of my followers[m] sins against you, go and point out what was wrong. But do it in private, just between the two of you. If that person listens, you have won back a follower. [16] But if that one refuses to listen, take along one or two others. The Scriptures teach that every complaint must be proven true by two or more witnesses. [17] If the follower refuses to listen to them, report the matter to the church. Anyone who refuses to listen to the church must be treated like an unbeliever or a tax collector.[n]

## Allowing and Not Allowing

[18] I promise you that God in heaven will allow whatever you allow on earth, but he will not allow anything you don't allow. [19] I promise that when any two of you on earth agree about something you are praying for, my Father in heaven will do it for you. [20] Whenever two or three of you come together in my name,[o] I am there with you.

## An Official Who Refused To Forgive

[21] Peter came up to the Lord and asked, "How many times should I forgive someone[p] who does something wrong to me? Is seven times enough?" [22] Jesus answered:

Not just seven times, but seventy-seven times! [q] [23] This story will show you what the kingdom of heaven is like:

One day a king decided to call in his officials and ask them to give an account of what they owed him. [24] As he was doing this, one official was brought in who owed him fifty million silver coins. [25] But he didn't have any money to pay what he

---

[l]**18.10,11** *in heaven*: Some manuscripts add, "The Son of Man came to save people who are lost." [m]**18.15** *followers*: The Greek text has "brother," which is used here and elsewhere in this chapter to refer to a follower of Christ. [n]**18.17** *tax collector*: See the note at 5.46. [o]**18.20** *in my name*: Or "as my followers." [p]**18.21** *someone*: Or "a follower." See the note at 18.15. [q]**18.22** *seventy-seven times*: Or "seventy times seven." The large number means that one follower should never stop forgiving another.

owed. The king ordered him to be sold, along with his wife and children and all he owned, in order to pay the debt.
²⁶ The official got down on his knees and began begging, "Have pity on me, and I will pay you every cent I owe!" ²⁷ The king felt sorry for him and let him go free. He even told the official that he did not have to pay back the money.
²⁸ As the official was leaving, he happened to meet another official, who owed him a hundred silver coins. So he grabbed the man by the throat. He started choking him and said, "Pay me what you owe!"
²⁹ The man got down on his knees and began begging, "Have pity on me, and I will pay you back." ³⁰ But the first official refused to have pity. Instead, he went and had the other official put in jail until he could pay what he owed.
³¹ When some other officials found out what had happened, they felt sorry for the man who had been put in jail. Then they told the king what had happened. ³² The king called the first official back in and said, "You're an evil man! When you begged for mercy, I said you did not have to pay back a cent. ³³ Don't you think you should show pity to someone else, as I did to you?" ³⁴ The king was so angry that he ordered the official to be tortured until he could pay back everything he owed. ³⁵ That is how my Father in heaven will treat you, if you don't forgive each of my followers with all your heart.

## Teaching about Divorce
### (Mark 10.1-12)

**19** When Jesus finished teaching, he left Galilee and went to the part of Judea that is east of the Jordan River. ² Large crowds followed him, and he healed their sick people.

³ Some Pharisees wanted to test Jesus. They came up to him and asked, "Is it right for a man to divorce his wife for just any reason?"
⁴ Jesus answered, "Don't you know that in the beginning the Creator made a man and a woman? ⁵ That's why a man leaves his father and mother and gets married. He becomes like one person with his wife. ⁶ Then they are no longer two people, but one. And no one should separate a couple that God has joined together."
⁷ The Pharisees asked Jesus, "Why did Moses say that a man could write out divorce papers and send his wife away?"
⁸ Jesus replied, "You are so heartless! That's why Moses allowed you to divorce your wife. But from the beginning God did not intend it to be that way. ⁹ I say that if your wife has not committed some terrible sexual sin,ʳ you must not divorce her to marry someone else. If you do, you are unfaithful."
¹⁰ The disciples said, "If that's how it is between a man and a woman, it's better not to get married."
¹¹ Jesus told them, "Only those people who have been given the gift of staying single can accept this teaching. ¹² Some people are unable to marry because of birth defects or because of what someone has done to their bodies. Others stay single in order to serve God better. Anyone who can accept this teaching should do so."

## Jesus Blesses Little Children
### (Mark 10.13-16; Luke 18.15-17)

¹³ Some people brought their children to Jesus, so that he could place his hands on them and pray for them. His disciples told the people to stop bothering him. ¹⁴ But Jesus said, "Let the children come to me, and don't try to stop them! People who are like these children belong to God's kingdom."ˢ ¹⁵ After Jesus had placed his hands on the children, he left.

ʳ19.9 *some terrible sexual sin*: See the note at 5.32. ˢ19.14 *People who are like these children belong to God's kingdom*: Or "God's kingdom belongs to people who are like these children."

## A Rich Young Man
### (Mark 10.17-31; Luke 18.18-30)

**16** A man came to Jesus and asked, "Teacher, what good thing must I do to have eternal life?"

**17** Jesus said to him, "Why do you ask me about what is good? Only God is good. If you want to have eternal life, you must obey his commandments."

**18** "Which ones?" the man asked.

Jesus answered, "Do not murder. Be faithful in marriage. Do not steal. Do not tell lies about others. **19** Respect your father and mother. And love others as much as you love yourself." **20** The young man said, "I have obeyed all of these. What else must I do?"

**21** Jesus replied, "If you want to be perfect, go sell everything you own! Give the money to the poor, and you will have riches in heaven. Then come and be my follower." **22** When the young man heard this, he was sad, because he was very rich.

**23** Jesus said to his disciples, "It's terribly hard for rich people to get into the kingdom of heaven! **24** In fact, it's easier for a camel to go through the eye of a needle than for a rich person to get into God's kingdom."

**25** When the disciples heard this, they were greatly surprised and asked, "How can anyone ever be saved?"

**26** Jesus looked straight at them and said, "There are some things that people cannot do, but God can do anything."

**27** Peter replied, "Remember, we have left everything to be your followers! What will we get?"

**28** Jesus answered:

Yes, all of you have become my followers. And so in the future world, when the Son of Man sits on his glorious throne, I promise that you will sit on twelve thrones to judge the twelve tribes of Israel. **29** All who have given up home or brothers and sisters or father and mother or children or land for me will be given a hundred times as much. They will also have eternal life. **30** But many who are now first will be last, and many who are last will be first.

## Workers in a Vineyard

**20** As Jesus was telling what the kingdom of heaven would be like, he said:

Early one morning a man went out to hire some workers for his vineyard. **2** After he had agreed to pay them the usual amount for a day's work, he sent them off to his vineyard.

**3** About nine that morning, the man saw some other people standing in the market with nothing to do. **4** He said he would pay them what was fair, if they would work in his vineyard. **5** So they went.

At noon and again about three in the afternoon he returned to the market. And each time he made the same agreement with others who were loafing around with nothing to do.

**6** Finally, about five in the afternoon the man went back and found some others standing there. He asked them, "Why have you been standing here all day long doing nothing?"

**7** "Because no one has hired us," they answered. Then he told them to go work in his vineyard.

**8** That evening the owner of the vineyard told the man in charge of the workers to call them in and give them their money. He also told the man to begin with the ones who were hired last. **9** When the workers arrived, the ones who had been hired at five in the afternoon were given a full day's pay.

**10** The workers who had been hired first thought they would be given more than the others. But when they were given the same, **11** they began complaining to the owner of the vineyard. **12** They said, "The ones who were hired last worked for only one hour. But you paid them the same that you did us. And we worked in the hot sun all day long!"

**13** The owner answered one of them, "Friend, I didn't cheat you. I paid you exactly what we agreed on. **14** Take your money now and go! What business is it of yours if I want

to pay them the same that I paid you? 15 Don't I have the right to do what I want with my own money? Why should you be jealous, if I want to be generous?"
16 Jesus then said, "So it is. Everyone who is now first will be last, and everyone who is last will be first."

### Jesus Again Tells about His Death
(Mark 10.32-34; Luke 18.31-34)

17 As Jesus was on his way to Jerusalem, he took his twelve disciples aside and told them in private:
18 We are now on our way to Jerusalem, where the Son of Man will be handed over to the chief priests and the teachers of the Law of Moses. They will sentence him to death, 19 and then they will hand him over to foreigners t who will make fun of him. They will beat him and nail him to a cross. But on the third day he will rise from death.

### A Mother's Request
(Mark 10.35-45)

20 The mother of James and John u came to Jesus with her two sons. She knelt down and started begging him to do something for her. 21 Jesus asked her what she wanted, and she said, "When you come into your kingdom, please let one of my sons sit at your right side and the other at your left." v
22 Jesus answered, "Not one of you knows what you are asking. Are you able to drink from the cup w that I must soon drink from?"
James and John said, "Yes, we are!"
23 Jesus replied, "You certainly will drink from my cup! But it isn't for me to say who will sit at my right side and at my left. That is for my Father to say."
24 When the ten other disciples heard this, they were angry with the two

brothers. 25 But Jesus called the disciples together and said:
You know that foreign rulers like to order their people around. And their great leaders have full power over everyone they rule. 26 But don't act like them. If you want to be great, you must be the servant of all the others. 27 And if you want to be first, you must be the slave of the rest. 28 The Son of Man did not come to be a slave master, but a slave who will give his life to rescue x many people.

### Jesus Heals Two Blind Men
(Mark 10.46-52; Luke 18.35-43)

29 Jesus was followed by a large crowd as he and his disciples were leaving Jericho. 30 Two blind men were sitting beside the road. And when they heard that Jesus was coming their way, they shouted, "Lord and Son of David, y have pity on us!"
31 The crowd told them to be quiet, but they shouted even louder, "Lord and Son of David, have pity on us!"
32 When Jesus heard them, he stopped and asked, "What do you want me to do for you?"
33 They answered, "Lord, we want to see!"
34 Jesus felt sorry for them and touched their eyes. Right away they could see, and they became his followers.

### Jesus Enters Jerusalem
(Mark 11.1-11; Luke 19.28-38; John 12.12-19)

21 When Jesus and his disciples came near Jerusalem, he went to Bethphage on the Mount of Olives and sent two of them on ahead. 2 He told them, "Go into the next village, where you will at once find a donkey and her colt. Untie the two donkeys and bring them to me. 3 If anyone asks why you

---

t 20.19 foreigners: The Romans, who ruled Judea at this time.  u 20.20 mother of James and John: The Greek text has "mother of the sons of Zebedee" (see 26.37).  v 20.21 right side . . . left: The most powerful people in a kingdom sat at the right and left side of the king.  w 20.22 drink from the cup: In the Scriptures a cup is sometimes used as a symbol of suffering. To "drink from the cup" is to suffer.  x 20.28 rescue: The Greek word often, though not always, means the payment of a price to free a slave or a prisoner.  y 20.30 Son of David: See the note at 9.27.

are doing that, just say, 'The Lord[z] needs them.' Right away he will let you have the donkeys."

[4] So God's promise came true, just as the prophet had said,

[5] "Announce to the people
   of Jerusalem:
'Your king is coming to you!
He is humble
   and rides on a donkey.
He comes on the colt
   of a donkey.' "

[6] The disciples left and did what Jesus had told them to do. [7] They brought the donkey and its colt and laid some clothes on their backs. Then Jesus got on. [8] Many people spread clothes in the road, while others put down branches[a] which they had cut from trees. [9] Some people walked ahead of Jesus and others followed behind. They were all shouting,

"Hooray[b] for the Son of David![c]
God bless the one who comes
   in the name of the Lord.
Hooray for God
   in heaven above!"

[10] When Jesus came to Jerusalem, everyone in the city was excited and asked, "Who can this be?" [11] The crowd answered, "This is Jesus, the prophet from Nazareth in Galilee."

## Jesus in the Temple
(Mark 11.15-19; Luke 19.45-48; John 2.13-22)

[12] Jesus went into the temple and chased out everyone who was selling or buying. He turned over the tables of the moneychangers and the benches of the ones who were selling doves. [13] He told them, "The Scriptures say, 'My house should be called a place of worship.' But you have turned it into a place where robbers hide."

[14] Blind and lame people came to Jesus in the temple, and he healed

them. [15] But the chief priests and the teachers of the Law of Moses were angry when they saw his miracles and heard the children shouting praises to the Son of David.[c] [16] The men said to Jesus, "Don't you hear what those children are saying?"

"Yes, I do!" Jesus answered. "Don't you know that the Scriptures say, 'Children and infants will sing praises'?" [17] Then Jesus left the city and went out to the village of Bethany, where he spent the night.

## Jesus Puts a Curse on a Fig Tree
(Mark 11.12-14, 20-24)

[18] When Jesus got up the next morning, he was hungry. He started out for the city, [19] and along the way he saw a fig tree. But when he came to it, he found only leaves and no figs. So he told the tree, "You will never again grow any fruit!" Right then the fig tree dried up.

[20] The disciples were shocked when they saw how quickly the tree had dried up. [21] But Jesus said to them, "If you have faith and don't doubt, I promise that you can do what I did to this tree. And you will be able to do even more. You can tell this mountain to get up and jump into the sea, and it will. [22] If you have faith when you pray, you will be given whatever you ask for."

## A Question about Jesus' Authority
(Mark 11.27-33; Luke 20.1-8)

[23] Jesus had gone into the temple and was teaching when the chief priests and the leaders of the people came up to him. They asked, "What right do you have to do these things? Who gave you this authority?"

[24] Jesus answered, "I have just one question to ask you. If you answer it, I will tell you where I got the right to do these things. [25] Who gave John the right to baptize? Was it God in heaven or merely some human being?"

[z]21.3 *The Lord*: Or "The master of the donkeys." [a]21.8 *spread clothes . . . put down branches*: This was one way that the Jewish people welcomed a famous person. [b]21.9 *Hooray*: This translates a word that can mean "please save us." But it is most often used as a shout of praise to God. [c]21.9 *Son of David*: See the note at 9.27. [c]21.15 *Son of David*: See the note at 9.27.

They thought it over and said to each other, "We can't say that God gave John this right. Jesus will ask us why we didn't believe John. [26] On the other hand, these people think that John was a prophet, and we are afraid of what they might do to us. That's why we can't say that it was merely some human who gave John the right to baptize." [27] So they told Jesus, "We don't know."

Jesus said, "Then I won't tell you who gave me the right to do what I do."

## A Story about Two Sons

[28] Jesus said:

I will tell you a story about a man who had two sons. Then you can tell me what you think. The father went to the older son and said, "Go work in the vineyard today!" [29] His son told him that he would not do it, but later he changed his mind and went. [30] The man then told his younger son to go work in the vineyard. The boy said he would, but he didn't go. [31] Which one of the sons obeyed his father?

"The older one," the chief priests and leaders answered.

Then Jesus told them:

You can be sure that tax collectors[d] and prostitutes will get into the kingdom of God before you ever will! [32] When John the Baptist showed you how to do right, you would not believe him. But these evil people did believe. And even when you saw what they did, you still would not change your minds and believe.

## Renters of a Vineyard
### (Mark 12.1-12; Luke 20.9-19)

[33] Jesus told the chief priests and leaders to listen to this story:

A land owner once planted a vineyard. He built a wall around it and dug a pit to crush the grapes in. He also built a lookout tower. Then he rented out his vineyard and left the country.

[34] When it was harvest time, the owner sent some servants to get his share of the grapes. [35] But the renters grabbed those servants. They beat up one, killed one, and stoned one of them to death. [36] He then sent more servants than he did the first time. But the renters treated them in the same way.

[37] Finally, the owner sent his own son to the renters, because he thought they would respect him. [38] But when they saw the man's son, they said, "Someday he will own the vineyard. Let's kill him! Then we can have it all for ourselves." [39] So they grabbed him, threw him out of the vineyard, and killed him.

[40] Jesus asked, "When the owner of that vineyard comes, what do you suppose he will do to those renters?"

[41] The chief priests and leaders answered, "He will kill them in some horrible way. Then he will rent out his vineyard to people who will give him his share of grapes at harvest time."

[42] Jesus replied, "You surely know that the Scriptures say,

'The stone that the builders
    tossed aside
is now the most important
    stone of all.
This is something
the Lord has done,
    and it is amazing to us.'

[43] I tell you that God's kingdom will be taken from you and given to people who will do what he demands. [44] Anyone who stumbles over this stone will be crushed, and anyone it falls on will be smashed to pieces."[e]

[45] When the chief priests and the Pharisees heard these stories, they knew that Jesus was talking about them. [46] So they looked for a way to arrest Jesus. But they were afraid to, because the people thought he was a prophet.

[d]**21.31** *tax collectors*: See the note at 5.46.    [e]**21.44** *pieces*: Verse 44 is not in some manuscripts.

### The Great Banquet
*(Luke 14.15-24)*

**22** Once again Jesus used stories to teach the people:

² The kingdom of heaven is like what happened when a king gave a wedding banquet for his son. ³ The king sent some servants to tell the invited guests to come to the banquet, but the guests refused. ⁴ He sent other servants to say to the guests, "The banquet is ready! My cattle and prize calves have all been prepared. Everything is ready. Come to the banquet!"

⁵ But the guests did not pay any attention. Some of them left for their farms, and some went to their places of business. ⁶ Others grabbed the servants, then beat them up and killed them.

⁷ This made the king so furious that he sent an army to kill those murderers and burn down their city. ⁸ Then he said to the servants, "It is time for the wedding banquet, and the invited guests don't deserve to come. ⁹ Go out to the street corners and tell everyone you meet to come to the banquet." ¹⁰ They went out on the streets and brought in everyone they could find, good and bad alike. And the banquet room was filled with guests.

¹¹ When the king went in to meet the guests, he found that one of them wasn't wearing the right kind of clothes for the wedding. ¹² The king asked, "Friend, why didn't you wear proper clothes for the wedding?" But the guest had no excuse. ¹³ So the king gave orders for that person to be tied hand and foot and to be thrown outside into the dark. That's where people will cry and grit their teeth in pain. ¹⁴ Many are invited, but only a few are chosen.

### Paying Taxes
*(Mark 12.13-17; Luke 20.20-26)*

¹⁵ The Pharisees got together and planned how they could trick Jesus into saying something wrong. ¹⁶ They sent some of their followers and some of Herod's followers[f] to say to him, "Teacher, we know that you are honest. You teach the truth about what God wants people to do. And you treat everyone with the same respect, no matter who they are. ¹⁷ Tell us what you think! Should we pay taxes to the Emperor or not?"

¹⁸ Jesus knew their evil thoughts and said, "Why are you trying to test me? You show-offs! ¹⁹ Let me see one of the coins used for paying taxes." They brought him a silver coin, ²⁰ and he asked, "Whose picture and name are on it?"

²¹ "The Emperor's," they answered.

Then Jesus told them, "Give the Emperor what belongs to him and give God what belongs to God." ²² His answer surprised them so much that they walked away.

### Life in the Future World
*(Mark 12.18-27; Luke 20.27-40)*

²³ The Sadducees did not believe that people would rise to life after death. So that same day some of the Sadducees came to Jesus and said:

²⁴ Teacher, Moses wrote that if a married man dies and has no children, his brother should marry the widow. Their first son would then be thought of as the son of the dead brother.

²⁵ Once there were seven brothers who lived here. The first one married, but died without having any children. So his wife was left to his brother. ²⁶ The same thing happened to the second and third brothers and finally to all seven of them. ²⁷ At last the woman died. ²⁸ When God raises people from death, whose wife will this woman be? She had been married to all seven brothers.

²⁹ Jesus answered:

You are completely wrong! You don't know what the Scriptures teach. And you don't know anything about the power of God. ³⁰ When

---

f**22.16** *Herod's followers*: People who were political followers of the family of Herod the Great (see 2.1) and his son Herod Antipas (see 14.1), and who wanted Herod to be king in Jerusalem.

God raises people to life, they won't marry. They will be like the angels in heaven. ³¹ And as for people being raised to life, God was speaking to you when he said, ³² "I am the God worshiped by Abraham, Isaac, and Jacob." ᵍ He isn't the God of the dead, but of the living.

³³ The crowds were surprised to hear what Jesus was teaching.

### The Most Important Commandment
*(Mark 12.28-34; Luke 10.25-28)*

³⁴ After Jesus had made the Sadducees look foolish, the Pharisees heard about it and got together. ³⁵ One of them was an expert in the Jewish Law. So he tried to test Jesus by asking, ³⁶ "Teacher, what is the most important commandment in the Law?"

³⁷ Jesus answered:

Love the Lord your God with all your heart, soul, and mind. ³⁸ This is the first and most important commandment. ³⁹ The second most important commandment is like this one. And it is, "Love others as much as you love yourself." ⁴⁰ All the Law of Moses and the Books of the Prophets ʰ are based on these two commandments.

### About David's Son
*(Mark 12.35-37; Luke 20.41-44)*

⁴¹ While the Pharisees were still there, Jesus asked them, ⁴² "What do you think about the Messiah? Whose family will he come from?"

They answered, "He will be a son of King David." ⁱ

⁴³ Jesus replied, "How then could the Spirit have David call the Messiah his Lord? David said,

⁴⁴ 'The Lord said to my Lord: Sit at my right side ʲ

until I make your enemies into a footstool for you.'

⁴⁵ If David called the Messiah his Lord, how can the Messiah be a son of King David?" ⁴⁶ No one was able to give Jesus an answer, and from that day on, no one dared ask him any more questions.

### Jesus Condemns the Pharisees and the Teachers of the Law of Moses
*(Mark 12.38-40; Luke 11.37-52; 20.45-47)*

**23** Jesus said to the crowds and to his disciples:

² The Pharisees and the teachers of the Law are experts in the Law of Moses. ³ So obey everything they teach you, but don't do as they do. After all, they say one thing and do something else.

⁴ They pile heavy burdens on people's shoulders and won't lift a finger to help. ⁵ Everything they do is just to show off in front of others. They even make a big show of wearing Scripture verses on their foreheads and arms, and they wear big tassels ᵏ for everyone to see. ⁶ They love the best seats at banquets and the front seats in the meeting places. ⁷ And when they are in the market, they like to have people greet them as their teachers.

⁸ But none of you should be called a teacher. You have only one teacher, and all of you are like brothers and sisters. ⁹ Don't call anyone on earth your father. All of you have the same Father in heaven. ¹⁰ None of you should be called the leader. The Messiah is your only leader. ¹¹ Whoever is the greatest should be the servant of the others. ¹² If you put yourself above others, you will be put down. But if you humble yourself, you will be honored.

ᵍ22.32 *I am the God worshiped by Abraham, Isaac, and Jacob*: Jesus argues that if God is worshiped by these three, they must still be alive, because he is the God of the living. ʰ22.40 *the Law of Moses and the Books of the Prophets*: The Jewish Scriptures, that is, the Old Testament. ⁱ22.42 *son of King David*: See the note at 9.27. ʲ22.44 *right side*: The place of power and honor. ᵏ23.5 *wearing Scripture verses on their foreheads and arms ... tassels*: As a sign of their love for the Lord and his teachings, the Jewish people had started wearing Scripture verses in small leather boxes. But the Pharisees tried to show off by making the boxes bigger than necessary. The Jewish people were also taught to wear tassels on the four corners of their robes to show their love for God.

¹³⁻¹⁴ You Pharisees and teachers of the Law of Moses are in for trouble! You're nothing but show-offs. You lock people out of the kingdom of heaven. You won't go in yourselves, and you keep others from going in. *l*

¹⁵ You Pharisees and teachers of the Law of Moses are in for trouble! You're nothing but show-offs. You travel over land and sea to win one follower. And when you have done so, you make that person twice as fit for hell as you are.

¹⁶ You are in for trouble! You are supposed to lead others, but you are blind. You teach that it doesn't matter if a person swears by the temple. But you say that it does matter if someone swears by the gold in the temple. ¹⁷ You blind fools! Which is greater, the gold or the temple that makes the gold sacred?

¹⁸ You also teach that it doesn't matter if a person swears by the altar. But you say that it does matter if someone swears by the gift on the altar. ¹⁹ Are you blind? Which is more important, the gift or the altar that makes the gift sacred? ²⁰ Anyone who swears by the altar also swears by everything on it. ²¹ And anyone who swears by the temple also swears by God, who lives there. ²² To swear by heaven is the same as swearing by God's throne and by the one who sits on that throne.

²³ You Pharisees and teachers are show-offs, and you're in for trouble! You give God a tenth of the spices from your garden, such as mint, dill, and cumin. Yet you neglect the more important matters of the Law, such as justice, mercy, and faithfulness. These are the important things you should have done, though you should not have left the others un-

done either. ²⁴ You blind leaders! You strain out a small fly but swallow a camel.

²⁵ You Pharisees and teachers are show-offs, and you're in for trouble! You wash the outside of your cups and dishes, while inside there is nothing but greed and selfishness. ²⁶ You blind Pharisee! First clean the inside of a cup, and then the outside will also be clean.

²⁷ You Pharisees and teachers are in for trouble! You're nothing but show-offs. You're like tombs that have been whitewashed. *m* On the outside they are beautiful, but inside they are full of bones and filth. ²⁸ That's what you are like. Outside you look good, but inside you are evil and only pretend to be good.

²⁹ You Pharisees and teachers are nothing but show-offs, and you're in for trouble! You build monuments for the prophets and decorate the tombs of good people. ³⁰ And you claim that you would not have taken part with your ancestors in killing the prophets. ³¹ But you prove that you really are the relatives of the ones who killed the prophets. ³² So keep on doing everything they did. ³³ You are nothing but snakes and the children of snakes! How can you escape going to hell?

³⁴ I will send prophets and wise people and experts in the Law of Moses to you. But you will kill them or nail them to a cross or beat them in your meeting places or chase them from town to town. ³⁵ That's why you will be held guilty for the murder of every good person, beginning with the good man Abel. This also includes Barachiah's son Zechariah, *n* the man you murdered between the temple and the altar. ³⁶ I can promise that you people living

---

*l***23.13,14** *from going in*: Some manuscripts add, "You Pharisees and teachers are in for trouble! And you're nothing but show-offs! You cheat widows out of their homes and then pray long prayers just to show off. So you will be punished most of all."

*m***23.27** *whitewashed*: Tombs were whitewashed to keep anyone from accidentally touching them. A person who touched a dead body or a tomb was considered unclean and could not worship with the rest of the Jewish people.   *n***23.35** *Zechariah*: Genesis is the first book in the Jewish Scriptures, and it tells that Abel was the first person to be murdered. Second Chronicles is the last book in the Jewish Scriptures, and the last murder that it tells about is that of Zechariah.

today will be punished for all these things!

## Jesus Loves Jerusalem
### (Luke 13.34, 35)

37 Jerusalem, Jerusalem! Your people have killed the prophets and have stoned the messengers who were sent to you. I have often wanted to gather your people, as a hen gathers her chicks under her wings. But you wouldn't let me. 38 And now your temple will be deserted. 39 You won't see me again until you say,

"Blessed is the one who comes in the name of the Lord."

## The Temple Will Be Destroyed
### (Mark 13.1, 2; Luke 21.5, 6)

24 After Jesus left the temple, his disciples came over and said, "Look at all these buildings!" 2 Jesus replied, "Do you see these buildings? They will certainly be torn down! Not one stone will be left in place."

## Warning about Trouble
### (Mark 13.3-13; Luke 21.7-19)

3 Later, as Jesus was sitting on the Mount of Olives, his disciples came to him in private and asked, "When will this happen? What will be the sign of your coming and of the end of the world?" 4 Jesus answered:

Don't let anyone fool you. 5 Many will come and claim to be me. They will say that they are the Messiah, and they will fool many people. 6 You will soon hear about wars and threats of wars, but don't be afraid. These things will have to happen first, but that isn't the end. 7 Nations and kingdoms will go to war against each other. People will starve to death, and in some places there will be earthquakes. 8 But this is just the beginning of troubles.

9 You will be arrested, punished, and even killed. Because of me, you will be hated by people of all nations. 10 Many will give up and will betray and hate each other. 11 Many false prophets will come and fool a lot of people. 12 Evil will spread and cause many people to stop loving others. 13 But if you keep on being faithful right to the end, you will be saved. 14 When the good news about the kingdom has been preached all over the world and told to all nations, the end will come.

## The Horrible Thing
### (Mark 13.14-23; Luke 21.20-24)

15 Someday you will see that "Horrible Thing" in the holy place, just as the prophet Daniel said. Everyone who reads this must try to understand! 16 If you are living in Judea at that time, run to the mountains. 17 If you are on the roof o of your house, don't go inside to get anything. 18 If you are out in the field, don't go back for your coat. 19 It will be a terrible time for women who are expecting babies or nursing young children. 20 And pray that you won't have to escape in winter or on a Sabbath. p 21 This will be the worst time of suffering since the beginning of the world, and nothing this terrible will ever happen again. 22 If God doesn't make the time shorter, no one will be left alive. But because of God's chosen ones, he will make the time shorter.

23 Someone may say, "Here is the Messiah!" or "There he is!" But don't believe it. 24 False messiahs and false prophets will come and work great miracles and signs. They will even try to fool God's chosen

---

o24.17 *roof*: In Palestine the houses usually had a flat roof. Stairs on the outside led up to the roof, which was made of beams and boards covered with packed earth. p24.20 *in winter or on a Sabbath*: In Palestine the winters are cold and rainy and make travel difficult. The Jewish people were not allowed to travel much more than half a mile on the Sabbath. For these reasons it was hard for them to escape from their enemies in the winter or on a Sabbath.

ones. 25 But I have warned you ahead of time. 26 If you are told that the Messiah is out in the desert, don't go there! And if you are told that he is in some secret place, don't believe it! 27 The coming of the Son of Man will be like lightning that can be seen from east to west. 28 Where there is a corpse, there will always be buzzards. q

## When the Son of Man Appears
### (Mark 13.24-27; Luke 21.25-28)

29 Right after those days of suffering,

"The sun will become dark,
and the moon
  will no longer shine.
The stars will fall,
and the powers in the sky r
  will be shaken."

30 Then a sign will appear in the sky. And there will be the Son of Man. s All nations on earth will weep when they see the Son of Man coming on the clouds of heaven with power and great glory. 31 At the sound of a loud trumpet, he will send his angels to bring his chosen ones together from all over the earth.

## A Lesson from a Fig Tree
### (Mark 13.28-31; Luke 21.29-33)

32 Learn a lesson from a fig tree. When its branches sprout and start putting out leaves, you know that summer is near. 33 So when you see all these things happening, you will know that the time has almost come. t 34 I can promise you that some of the people of this generation will still be alive when all this happens. 35 The sky and the earth

won't last forever, but my words will.

## No One Knows the Day or Time
### (Mark 13.32-37; Luke 17.26-30, 34-36)

36 No one knows the day or hour. The angels in heaven don't know, and the Son himself doesn't know. u Only the Father knows. 37 When the Son of Man appears, things will be just as they were when Noah lived. 38 People were eating, drinking, and getting married right up to the day that the flood came and Noah went into the big boat. 39 They didn't know anything was happening until the flood came and swept them all away. That is how it will be when the Son of Man appears. 40 Two men will be in the same field, but only one will be taken. The other will be left. 41 Two women will be together grinding grain, but only one will be taken. The other will be left. 42 So be on your guard! You don't know when your Lord will come. 43 Homeowners never know when a thief is coming, and they are always on guard to keep one from breaking in. 44 Always be ready! You don't know when the Son of Man will come.

## Faithful and Unfaithful Servants
### (Luke 12.35-48)

45 Who are faithful and wise servants? Who are the ones the master will put in charge of giving the other servants their food supplies at the proper time? 46 Servants are fortunate if their master comes and finds them doing their job. 47 You may be sure that a servant who is always faithful will be put in charge of everything the master owns. 48 But

q 24.28 Where there is a corpse, there will always be buzzards: This saying may mean that when anything important happens, people soon know about it. Or the saying may mean that whenever something bad happens, curious people gather around and stare. But the word translated "buzzard" also means "eagle" and may refer to the Roman army, which had an eagle as its symbol. r 24.29 the powers in the sky: In ancient times people thought that the stars were spiritual powers. s 24.30 And there will be the Son of Man: Or "And it will be the Son of Man." t 24.33 the time has almost come: Or "he (that is, the Son of Man) will soon be here." u 24.36 and the Son himself doesn't know: These words are not in some manuscripts.

suppose one of the servants thinks that the master won't return until late. [49] Suppose that evil servant starts beating the other servants and eats and drinks with people who are drunk. [50] If that happens, the master will surely come on a day and at a time when the servant least expects him. [51] That servant will then be punished and thrown out with the ones who only pretended to serve their master. There they will cry and grit their teeth in pain.

## A Story about Ten Girls

**25** The kingdom of heaven is like what happened one night when ten girls took their oil lamps and went to a wedding to meet the groom. [v] [2] Five of the girls were foolish and five were wise. [3] The foolish ones took their lamps, but no extra oil. [4] The ones who were wise took along extra oil for their lamps. [5] The groom was late arriving, and the girls became drowsy and fell asleep. [6] Then in the middle of the night someone shouted, "Here's the groom! Come to meet him!"

[7] When the girls got up and started getting their lamps ready, [8] the foolish ones said to the others, "Let us have some of your oil! Our lamps are going out."

[9] The girls who were wise answered, "There's not enough oil for all of us! Go and buy some for yourselves."

[10] While the foolish girls were on their way to get some oil, the groom arrived. The girls who were ready went into the wedding, and the doors were closed. [11] Later the other girls returned and shouted, "Sir, sir! Open the door for us!"

[12] But the groom replied, "I don't even know you!"

[13] So, my disciples, always be ready! You don't know the day or the time when all this will happen.

## A Story about Three Servants
### (Luke 19.11-27)

[14] The kingdom is also like what happened when a man went away and put his three servants in charge of all he owned. [15] The man knew what each servant could do. So he handed five thousand coins to the first servant, two thousand to the second, and one thousand to the third. Then he left the country.

[16] As soon as the man had gone, the servant with the five thousand coins used them to earn five thousand more. [17] The servant who had two thousand coins did the same with his money and earned two thousand more. [18] But the servant with one thousand coins dug a hole and hid his master's money in the ground.

[19] Some time later the master of those servants returned. He called them in and asked what they had done with his money. [20] The servant who had been given five thousand coins brought them in with the five thousand that he had earned. He said, "Sir, you gave me five thousand coins, and I have earned five thousand more."

[21] "Wonderful!" his master replied. "You are a good and faithful servant. I left you in charge of only a little, but now I will put you in charge of much more. Come and share in my happiness!"

[22] Next, the servant who had been given two thousand coins came in and said, "Sir, you gave me two thousand coins, and I have earned two thousand more."

[23] "Wonderful!" his master replied. "You are a good and faithful servant. I left you in charge of only a little, but now I will put you in charge of much more. Come and share in my happiness!"

[24] The servant who had been given one thousand coins then came in and said, "Sir, I know that you are hard to get along with. You harvest

---

[v]25.1 *to meet the groom*: Some manuscripts add "and the bride." It was the custom for the groom to go to the home of the bride's parents to get his bride. Young girls and other guests would then go with them to the home of the groom's parents, where the wedding feast would take place.

what you don't plant and gather crops where you haven't scattered seed. ²⁵ I was frightened and went out and hid your money in the ground. Here is every single coin!"

²⁶ The master of the servant told him, "You are lazy and good-for-nothing! You know that I harvest what I don't plant and gather crops where I haven't scattered seed. ²⁷ You could have at least put my money in the bank, so that I could have earned interest on it."

²⁸ Then the master said, "Now your money will be taken away and given to the servant with ten thousand coins! ²⁹ Everyone who has something will be given more, and they will have more than enough. But everything will be taken from those who don't have anything. ³⁰ You are a worthless servant, and you will be thrown out into the dark where people will cry and grit their teeth in pain."

## The Final Judgment

³¹ When the Son of Man comes in his glory with all of his angels, he will sit on his royal throne. ³² The people of all nations will be brought before him, and he will separate them, as shepherds separate their sheep from their goats. ³³ He will place the sheep on his right and the goats on his left. ³⁴ Then the king will say to those on his right, "My father has blessed you! Come and receive the kingdom that was prepared for you before the world was created. ³⁵ When I was hungry, you gave me something to eat, and when I was thirsty, you gave me something to drink. When I was a stranger, you welcomed me, ³⁶ and when I was naked, you gave me clothes to wear. When I was sick, you took care of me, and when I was in jail, you visited me."

³⁷ Then the ones who pleased the Lord will ask, "When did we give you something to eat or drink? ³⁸ When did we welcome you as a

stranger or give you clothes to wear ³⁹ or visit you while you were sick or in jail?"

⁴⁰ The king will answer, "Whenever you did it for any of my people, no matter how unimportant they seemed, you did it for me."

⁴¹ Then the king will say to those on his left, "Get away from me! You are under God's curse. Go into the everlasting fire prepared for the devil and his angels! ⁴² I was hungry, but you did not give me anything to eat, and I was thirsty, but you did not give me anything to drink. ⁴³ I was a stranger, but you did not welcome me, and I was naked, but you did not give me any clothes to wear. I was sick and in jail, but you did not take care of me."

⁴⁴ Then the people will ask, "Lord, when did we fail to help you when you were hungry or thirsty or a stranger or naked or sick or in jail?"

⁴⁵ The king will say to them, "Whenever you failed to help any of my people, no matter how unimportant they seemed, you failed to do it for me."

⁴⁶ Then Jesus said, "Those people will be punished forever. But the ones who pleased God will have eternal life."

## The Plot To Kill Jesus
(Mark 14.1, 2; Luke 22.1, 2; John 11.45-53)

**26** When Jesus had finished teaching, he told his disciples, ² "You know that two days from now will be Passover. That is when the Son of Man will be handed over to his enemies and nailed to a cross."

³ At that time the chief priests and the nation's leaders were meeting at the home of Caiaphas the high priest. ⁴ They planned how they could sneak around and have Jesus arrested and put to death. ⁵ But they said, "We must not do it during Passover, because the people will riot."

## At Bethany
(Mark 14.3-9; John 12.1-8)

⁶ Jesus was in the town of Bethany, eating at the home of Simon, who had

leprosy.[w] [7] A woman came in with a bottle of expensive perfume and poured it on Jesus' head. [8] But when his disciples saw this, they became angry and complained, "Why such a waste? [9] We could have sold this perfume for a lot of money and given it to the poor."

[10] Jesus knew what they were thinking, and he said:

Why are you bothering this woman? She has done a beautiful thing for me. [11] You will always have the poor with you, but you won't always have me. [12] She has poured perfume on my body to prepare it for burial.[x] [13] You may be sure that wherever the good news is told all over the world, people will remember what she has done. And they will tell others.

## Judas and the Chief Priests
### (Mark 14.10, 11; Luke 22.3-6)

[14] Judas Iscariot[y] was one of the twelve disciples. He went to the chief priests [15] and asked, "How much will you give me if I help you arrest Jesus?" They paid Judas thirty silver coins, [16] and from then on he started looking for a good chance to betray Jesus.

## Jesus Eats the Passover Meal with His Disciples
### (Mark 14.12-21; Luke 22.7-13; John 13.21-30)

[17] On the first day of the Festival of Thin Bread, Jesus' disciples came to him and asked, "Where do you want us to prepare the Passover meal?"

[18] Jesus told them to go to a certain man in the city and tell him, "Our teacher says, 'My time has come! I want to eat the Passover meal with my disciples in your home.'" [19] They did as Jesus told them and prepared the meal.

[20-21] When Jesus was eating with his twelve disciples that evening, he said, "One of you will surely hand me over to my enemies."

[22] The disciples were very sad, and each one said to Jesus, "Lord, you can't mean me!"

[23] He answered, "One of you men who has eaten with me from this dish will betray me. [24] The Son of Man will die, as the Scriptures say. But it's going to be terrible for the one who betrays me! That man would be better off if he had never been born."

[25] Judas said, "Teacher, you surely don't mean me!"

"That's what you say!" Jesus replied. But later, Judas did betray him.

## The Lord's Supper
### (Mark 14.22-26; Luke 22.14-23; 1 Corinthians 11.23-25)

[26] During the meal Jesus took some bread in his hands. He blessed the bread and broke it. Then he gave it to his disciples and said, "Take this and eat it. This is my body."

[27] Jesus picked up a cup of wine and gave thanks to God. He then gave it to his disciples and said, "Take this and drink it. [28] This is my blood, and with it God makes his agreement with you. It will be poured out, so that many people will have their sins forgiven. [29] From now on I am not going to drink any wine, until I drink new wine with you in my Father's kingdom." [30] Then they sang a hymn and went out to the Mount of Olives.

## Peter's Promise
### (Mark 14.27-31; Luke 22.31-34; John 13.36-38)

[31] Jesus said to his disciples, "During this very night, all of you will reject me, as the Scriptures say,

'I will strike down
  the shepherd,
and the sheep
  will be scattered.'

[32] But after I am raised to life, I will go to Galilee ahead of you."

[33] Peter spoke up, "Even if all the others reject you, I never will!"

---

[w]26.6 *leprosy*: See the note at 8.2.  [x]26.12 *poured perfume on my body to prepare it for burial*: The Jewish people taught that giving someone a proper burial was even more important than helping the poor.  [y]26.14 *Iscariot*: See the note at 10.4.

³⁴ Jesus replied, "I promise you that before a rooster crows tonight, you will say three times that you don't know me." ³⁵ But Peter said, "Even if I have to die with you, I will never say I don't know you."

All the others said the same thing.

## Jesus Prays
(Mark 14.32-42; Luke 22.39-46)

³⁶ Jesus went with his disciples to a place called Gethsemane. When they got there, he told them, "Sit here while I go over there and pray."

³⁷ Jesus took along Peter and the two brothers, James and John.ᶻ He was very sad and troubled, ³⁸ and he said to them, "I am so sad that I feel as if I am dying. Stay here and keep awake with me."

³⁹ Jesus walked on a little way. Then he knelt with his face to the ground and prayed, "My Father, if it is possible, don't make me suffer by having me drink from this cup.ᵃ But do what you want, and not what I want."

⁴⁰ He came back and found his disciples sleeping. So he said to Peter, "Can't any of you stay awake with me for just one hour? ⁴¹ Stay awake and pray that you won't be tested. You want to do what is right, but you are weak."

⁴² Again Jesus went to pray and said, "My Father, if there is no other way, and I must suffer, I will still do what you want."

⁴³ Jesus came back and found them sleeping again. They simply could not keep their eyes open. ⁴⁴ He left them and prayed the same prayer once more.

⁴⁵ Finally, Jesus returned to his disciples and said, "Are you still sleeping and resting?ᵇ The time has come for the Son of Man to be handed over to sinners. ⁴⁶ Get up! Let's go. The one who will betray me is already here."

## Jesus Is Arrested
(Mark 14.43-50; Luke 22.47-53; John 18.3-12)

⁴⁷ Jesus was still speaking, when Judas the betrayer came up. He was one of the twelve disciples, and a large mob armed with swords and clubs was with him. They had been sent by the chief priests and the nation's leaders. ⁴⁸ Judas had told them ahead of time, "Arrest the man I greet with a kiss."ᶜ

⁴⁹ Judas walked right up to Jesus and said, "Hello, teacher." Then Judas kissed him.

⁵⁰ Jesus replied, "My friend, why are you here?"ᵈ

The men grabbed Jesus and arrested him. ⁵¹ One of Jesus' followers pulled out a sword. He struck the servant of the high priest and cut off his ear.

⁵² But Jesus told him, "Put your sword away. Anyone who lives by fighting will die by fighting. ⁵³ Don't you know that I could ask my Father, and right away he would send me more than twelve armies of angels? ⁵⁴ But then, how could the words of the Scriptures come true, which say that this must happen?"

⁵⁵ Jesus said to the mob, "Why do you come with swords and clubs to arrest me like a criminal? Day after day I sat and taught in the temple, and you didn't arrest me. ⁵⁶ But all this happened, so that what the prophets wrote would come true."

All of Jesus' disciples left him and ran away.

## Jesus Is Questioned by the Council
(Mark 14.53-65; Luke 22.54, 55, 63-71; John 18.13, 14, 19-24)

⁵⁷ After Jesus had been arrested, he was led off to the house of Caiaphas the high priest. The nation's leaders and the teachers of the Law of Moses were meeting there. ⁵⁸ But Peter followed along at a distance and came to the courtyard of the high priest's pal-

ace. He went in and sat down with the guards to see what was going to happen. [59] The chief priests and the whole council wanted to put Jesus to death. So they tried to find some people who would tell lies about him in court.[e] [60] But they could not find any, even though many did come and tell lies. At last, two men came forward [61] and said, "This man claimed that he would tear down God's temple and build it again in three days."

[62] The high priest stood up and asked Jesus, "Why don't you say something in your own defense? Don't you hear the charges they are making against you?" [63] But Jesus did not answer. So the high priest said, "With the living God looking on, you must tell the truth. Tell us, are you the Messiah, the Son of God?"[f]

[64] "That is what you say!" Jesus answered. "But I tell all of you,

'Soon you will see
    the Son of Man
sitting at the right side[g]
    of God All-Powerful
and coming on the clouds
    of heaven.' "

[65] The high priest then tore his robe and said, "This man claims to be God! We don't need any more witnesses! You have heard what he said. [66] What do you think?"

They answered, "He is guilty and deserves to die!" [67] Then they spit in his face and hit him with their fists. Others slapped him [68] and said, "You think you are the Messiah! So tell us who hit you!"

### Peter Says He Doesn't Know Jesus
(Mark 14.66-72; Luke 22.56-62;
John 18.15-18, 25-27)

[69] While Peter was sitting out in the courtyard, a servant girl came up to him and said, "You were with Jesus from Galilee." [70] But in front of everyone Peter said,

"That isn't so! I don't know what you are talking about!"

[71] When Peter had gone out to the gate, another servant girl saw him and said to some people there, "This man was with Jesus from Nazareth." [72] Again Peter denied it, and this time he swore, "I don't even know that man!"

[73] A little while later some people standing there walked over to Peter and said, "We know that you are one of them. We can tell it because you talk like someone from Galilee."

[74] Peter began to curse and swear, "I don't know that man!"

Right then a rooster crowed, [75] and Peter remembered that Jesus had said, "Before a rooster crows, you will say three times that you don't know me." Then Peter went out and cried hard.

### Jesus Is Taken to Pilate
(Mark 15.1; Luke 23.1, 2; John 18.28-32)

**27** Early the next morning all the chief priests and the nation's leaders met and decided that Jesus should be put to death. [2] They tied him up and led him away to Pilate the governor.

### The Death of Judas
(Acts 1.18, 19)

[3] Judas had betrayed Jesus, but when he learned that Jesus had been sentenced to death, he was sorry for what he had done. He returned the thirty silver coins to the chief priests and leaders [4] and said, "I have sinned by betraying a man who has never done anything wrong."

"So what? That's your problem," they replied. [5] Judas threw the money into the temple and then went out and hanged himself.

[6] The chief priests picked up the money and said, "This money was paid to have a man killed. We can't put it in the temple treasury." [7] Then they had

---

[e]26.59 *some people who would tell lies about him in court*: The Law of Moses taught that two witnesses were necessary before a person could be put to death (see verse 60).
[f]26.63 *Son of God*: One of the titles used for the kings of Israel. [g]26.64 *right side*: See the note at 22.44.

a meeting and decided to buy a field that belonged to someone who made clay pots. They wanted to use it as a graveyard for foreigners. [8] That's why people still call that place "Field of Blood." [9] So the words of the prophet Jeremiah came true,

"They took
the thirty silver coins,
the price of a person
among the people of Israel.
[10] They paid it
for a potter's field, [h]
as the Lord
had commanded me."

### Pilate Questions Jesus
#### (Mark 15.2-5; Luke 23.3-5; John 18.33-38)

[11] Jesus was brought before Pilate the governor, who asked him, "Are you the king of the Jews?"

"Those are your words!" Jesus answered. [12] And when the chief priests and leaders brought their charges against him, he did not say a thing. [13] Pilate asked him, "Don't you hear what crimes they say you have done?" [14] But Jesus did not say anything, and the governor was greatly amazed.

### The Death Sentence
#### (Mark 15.6-15; Luke 23.13-26; John 18.39—19.16)

[15] During Passover the governor always freed a prisoner chosen by the people. [16] At that time a well-known terrorist named Jesus Barabbas [i] was in jail. [17] So when the crowd came together, Pilate asked them, "Which prisoner do you want me to set free? Do you want Jesus Barabbas or Jesus who is called the Messiah?" [18] Pilate knew that the leaders had brought Jesus to him because they were jealous. [19] While Pilate was judging the case,

his wife sent him a message. It said, "Don't have anything to do with that innocent man. I have had nightmares because of him."

[20] But the chief priests and the leaders convinced the crowds to ask for Barabbas to be set free and for Jesus to be killed. [21] Pilate asked the crowd again, "Which of these two men do you want me to set free?"

"Barabbas!" they replied.

[22] Pilate asked them, "What am I to do with Jesus, who is called the Messiah?"

They all yelled, "Nail him to a cross!"
[23] Pilate answered, "But what crime has he done?"

"Nail him to a cross!" they yelled even louder.

[24] Pilate saw that there was nothing he could do and that the people were starting to riot. So he took some water and washed his hands [j] in front of them and said, "I won't have anything to do with killing this man. You are the ones doing it!"

[25] Everyone answered, "We and our descendants will take the blame for his death!"

[26] Pilate set Barabbas free. Then he ordered his soldiers to beat Jesus with a whip and nail him to a cross.

### Soldiers Make Fun of Jesus
#### (Mark 15.16-21; John 19.2, 3)

[27] The governor's soldiers led Jesus into the fortress [k] and brought together the rest of the troops. [28] They stripped off Jesus' clothes and put a scarlet robe [l] on him. [29] They made a crown out of thorn branches and placed it on his head, and they put a stick in his right hand. The soldiers knelt down and pretended to worship him. They made fun of him and shouted, "Hey, you king of the Jews!" [30] Then they spit on him.

[h] 27.10 *a potter's field*: Perhaps a field owned by someone who made clay pots. But it may have been a field where potters came to get clay or to make pots or to throw away their broken pieces of pottery.   [i] 27.16 *Jesus Barabbas*: Here and in verse 17 many manuscripts have "Barabbas."   [j] 27.24 *washed his hands*: To show that he was innocent.
[k] 27.27 *fortress*: The place where the Roman governor stayed. It was probably at Herod's palace west of Jerusalem, though it may have been Fortress Antonia north of the temple, where the Roman troops were stationed.   [l] 27.28 *scarlet robe*: This was probably a Roman soldier's robe.

They took the stick from him and beat him on the head with it.

## Jesus Is Nailed to a Cross
### (Mark 15.22-32; Luke 23.27-43; John 19.17-27)

**31** When the soldiers had finished making fun of Jesus, they took off the robe. They put his own clothes back on him and led him off to be nailed to a cross. **32** On the way they met a man from Cyrene named Simon, and they forced him to carry Jesus' cross.

**33** They came to a place named Golgotha, which means "Place of a Skull." *m* **34** There they gave Jesus some wine mixed with a drug to ease the pain. But when Jesus tasted what it was, he refused to drink it.

**35** The soldiers nailed Jesus to a cross and gambled to see who would get his clothes. **36** Then they sat down to guard him. **37** Above his head they put a sign that told why he was nailed there. It read, "This is Jesus, the King of the Jews." **38** The soldiers also nailed two criminals on crosses, one to the right of Jesus and the other to his left.

**39** People who passed by said terrible things about Jesus. They shook their heads and **40** shouted, "So you're the one who claimed you could tear down the temple and build it again in three days! If you are God's Son, save yourself and come down from the cross!"

**41** The chief priests, the leaders, and the teachers of the Law of Moses also made fun of Jesus. They said, **42** "He saved others, but he can't save himself. If he is the king of Israel, he should come down from the cross! Then we will believe him. **43** He trusted God, so let God save him, if he wants to. He even said he was God's Son." **44** The two criminals also said cruel things to Jesus.

## The Death of Jesus
### (Mark 15.33-41; Luke 23.44-49; John 19.28-30)

**45** At noon the sky turned dark and stayed that way until three o'clock. **46** Then about that time Jesus shouted, "Eli, Eli, lema sabachthani?" *n* which means, "My God, my God, why have you deserted me?"

**47** Some of the people standing there heard Jesus and said, "He's calling for Elijah." *o* **48** One of them at once ran and grabbed a sponge. He soaked it in wine, then put it on a stick and held it up to Jesus.

**49** Others said, "Wait! Let's see if Elijah will come *p* and save him." **50** Once again Jesus shouted, and then he died.

**51** At once the curtain in the temple *q* was torn in two from top to bottom. The earth shook, and rocks split apart. **52** Graves opened, and many of God's people were raised to life. **53** They left their graves, and after Jesus had risen to life, they went into the holy city, where they were seen by many people.

**54** The officer and the soldiers guarding Jesus felt the earthquake and saw everything else that happened. They were frightened and said, "This man really was God's Son!"

**55** Many women had come with Jesus from Galilee to be of help to him, and they were there, looking on at a distance. **56** Mary Magdalene, Mary the mother of James and Joseph, and the mother of James and John *r* were some of these women.

## Jesus Is Buried
### (Mark 15.42-47; Luke 23.50-56; John 19.38-42)

**57** That evening a rich disciple named Joseph from the town of Arimathea **58** went and asked for Jesus' body. Pilate gave orders for it to be given to Joseph, **59** who took the body and

---

*m* **27.33** *Place of a Skull*: The place was probably given this name because it was near a large rock in the shape of a human skull. *n* **27.46** *Eli . . . sabachthani*: These words are in Aramaic, a language spoken in Palestine during the time of Jesus. *o* **27.47** *Elijah*: In Aramaic the name "Elijah" sounds like "Eli," which means "my God." *p* **27.49** *Elijah will come*: See the note at 16.14. *q* **27.51** *curtain in the temple*: There were two curtains in the temple. One was at the entrance, and the other separated the holy place from the most holy place that the Jewish people thought of as God's home on earth. The second curtain is probably the one that is meant. *r* **27.56** *of James and John*: The Greek text has "of Zebedee's sons" (see 26.37).

wrapped it in a clean linen cloth. [60] Then Joseph put the body in his own tomb that had been cut into solid rock[s] and had never been used. He rolled a big stone against the entrance to the tomb and went away.

[61] All this time Mary Magdalene and the other Mary were sitting across from the tomb.

[62] On the next day, which was a Sabbath, the chief priests and the Pharisees went together to Pilate. [63] They said, "Sir, we remember what that liar said while he was still alive. He claimed that in three days he would come back from death. [64] So please order the tomb to be carefully guarded for three days. If you don't, his disciples may come and steal his body. They will tell the people that he has been raised to life, and this last lie will be worse than the first one."[t]

[65] Pilate said to them, "All right, take some of your soldiers and guard the tomb as well as you know how." [66] So they sealed it tight and placed soldiers there to guard it.

## Jesus Is Alive
### (Mark 16.1-8; Luke 24.1-12; John 20.1-10)

**28** The Sabbath was over, and it was almost daybreak on Sunday when Mary Magdalene and the other Mary went to see the tomb. [2] Suddenly a strong earthquake struck, and the Lord's angel came down from heaven. He rolled away the stone and sat on it. [3] The angel looked as bright as lightning, and his clothes were white as snow. [4] The guards shook from fear and fell down, as though they were dead.

[5] The angel said to the women, "Don't be afraid! I know you are looking for Jesus, who was nailed to a cross. [6] He isn't here! God has raised him to life, just as Jesus said he would. Come, see the place where his body was lying. [7] Now hurry! Tell his disciples that he has been raised to life and is on his way to Galilee. Go there, and you will see

him. That is what I came to tell you."

[8] The women were frightened and yet very happy, as they hurried from the tomb and ran to tell his disciples. [9] Suddenly Jesus met them and greeted them. They went near him, held on to his feet, and worshiped him. [10] Then Jesus said, "Don't be afraid! Tell my followers to go to Galilee. They will see me there."

## Report of the Guard

[11] While the women were on their way, some soldiers who had been guarding the tomb went into the city. They told the chief priests everything that had happened. [12] So the chief priests met with the leaders and decided to bribe the soldiers with a lot of money. [13] They said to the soldiers, "Tell everyone that Jesus' disciples came during the night and stole his body while you were asleep. [14] If the governor[u] hears about this, we will talk to him. You won't have anything to worry about." [15] The soldiers took the money and did what they were told. The people of Judea still tell each other this story.

## What Jesus' Followers Must Do
### (Mark 16.14-18; Luke 24.36-49; John 20.19-23; Acts 1.6-8)

[16] Jesus' eleven disciples went to a mountain in Galilee, where Jesus had told them to meet him. [17] They saw him and worshiped him, but some of them doubted. [18] Jesus came to them and said:

I have been given all authority in heaven and on earth! [19] Go to the people of all nations and make them my disciples. Baptize them in the name of the Father, the Son, and the Holy Spirit, [20] and teach them to do everything I have told you. I will be with you always, even until the end of the world.

[s]**27.60** *tomb . . . solid rock*: Some of the Jewish people buried their dead in rooms carved into solid rock. A heavy stone was rolled against the entrance. [t]**27.64** *the first one*: Probably the belief that Jesus is the Messiah. [u]**28.14** *governor*: Pontius Pilate.

# MARK

## ABOUT THIS BOOK

This is the shortest of the four New Testament books that tell about the life and teachings of Jesus, but it is also the most action-packed. From the very beginning of his ministry, Jesus worked mighty wonders. After choosing four followers (1.16-20), he immediately performed many miracles of healing. Among those healed were a man with an evil spirit in him (1.21-28), Simon's mother-in-law (1.30, 31), crowds of sick people (1.32-34), and a man with leprosy (1.40-45). Over and over Mark tells how Jesus healed people, but always in such a way as to show that he did these miracles by the power of God.

The religious leaders refused to accept Jesus. This led to conflicts (2.2—3.6) that finally made them start looking for a way to kill him (11.18). But the demons saw the power of Jesus, and they knew that he was the Son of God, although Jesus would not let them tell anyone.

This book is full of miracles that amazed the crowds and Jesus' followers. But, according to Mark, the most powerful miracle of Jesus is his suffering and death. The first person to understand this miracle was the Roman soldier who saw Jesus die on the cross and said, "This man really was the Son of God!" (15.39).

This Gospel is widely thought to be the first one written. The many explanations of Aramaic words and Jewish customs in Mark suggest that Mark wrote to Gentile or non-Jewish Christians. He wants to tell about Jesus and to encourage readers to believe in the power of Jesus to rescue them from sickness, demons, and death. He also wants to remind them that the new life of faith is not an easy life, and that they must follow Jesus by serving others and being ready to suffer as he did.

The first followers of Jesus to discover the empty tomb were three women, and the angel told them:

> Don't be alarmed! You are looking for Jesus from Nazareth, who was nailed to a cross. God has raised him to life, and he isn't here. (16.6)

## A QUICK LOOK AT THIS BOOK

The Message of John the Baptist (1.1-8)
The Baptism and Temptation of Jesus (1.9-13)
Jesus in Galilee (1.14—9.50)
Jesus Goes from Galilee to Jerusalem (10.1-52)
Jesus' Last Week: His Trial and Death (11.1—15.47)
Jesus Is Alive (16.1-8)
Jesus Appears to His Followers (16.9-20)

## The Preaching
## of John the Baptist
### (Matthew 3.1-12; Luke 3.1-18; John 1.19-28)

1 This is the good news about Jesus Christ, the Son of God.[a] 2 It began just as God had said in the book written by Isaiah the prophet,

"I am sending my messenger
to get the way ready
for you.
3 In the desert
someone is shouting,
'Get the road ready
for the Lord!
Make a straight path
for him.'"

4 So John the Baptist showed up in the desert and told everyone, "Turn back to God and be baptized! Then your sins will be forgiven."
5 From all Judea and Jerusalem crowds of people went to John. They told how sorry they were for their sins, and he baptized them in the Jordan River.
6 John wore clothes made of camel's hair. He had a leather strap around his waist and ate grasshoppers and wild honey.
7 John also told the people, "Someone more powerful is going to come. And I am not good enough even to stoop down and untie his sandals.[b] 8 I baptize you with water, but he will baptize you with the Holy Spirit!"

## The Baptism of Jesus
### (Matthew 3.13-17; Luke 3.21, 22)

9 About that time Jesus came from Nazareth in Galilee, and John baptized him in the Jordan River. 10 As soon as Jesus came out of the water, he saw the sky open and the Holy Spirit coming down to him like a dove. 11 A voice from heaven said, "You are my own dear Son, and I am pleased with you."

## Jesus and Satan
### (Matthew 4.1-11; Luke 4.1-13)

12 Right away God's Spirit made Jesus go into the desert. 13 He stayed there for forty days while Satan tested him. Jesus was with the wild animals, but angels took care of him.

## Jesus Begins His Work
### (Matthew 4.12-17; Luke 4.14, 15)

14 After John was arrested, Jesus went to Galilee and told the good news that comes from God.[c] 15 He said, "The time has come! God's kingdom will soon be here.[d] Turn back to God and believe the good news!"

## Jesus Chooses Four Fishermen
### (Matthew 4.18-22; Luke 5.1-11)

16 As Jesus was walking along the shore of Lake Galilee, he saw Simon and his brother Andrew. They were fishermen and were casting their nets into the lake. 17 Jesus said to them, "Come with me! I will teach you how to bring in people instead of fish." 18 Right then the two brothers dropped their nets and went with him.
19 Jesus walked on and soon saw James and John, the sons of Zebedee. They were in a boat, mending their nets. 20 At once Jesus asked them to come with him. They left their father in the boat with the hired workers and went with him.

## A Man with an Evil Spirit
### (Luke 4.31-37)

21 Jesus and his disciples went to the town of Capernaum. Then on the next Sabbath he went into the Jewish meeting place and started teaching. 22 Everyone was amazed at his teaching. He taught with authority, and not like the teachers of the Law of Moses. 23 Suddenly a man with an evil spirit[e] in him entered the meeting place and

---

[a] 1.1 the Son of God: These words are not in some manuscripts.  [b] 1.7 untie his sandals: This was the duty of a slave.  [c] 1.14 that comes from God: Or "that is about God."
[d] 1.15 will soon be here: Or "is already here."  [e] 1.23 evil spirit: A Jewish person who had an evil spirit was considered "unclean" and was not allowed to eat or worship with other Jewish people.

yelled, [24] "Jesus from Nazareth, what do you want with us? Have you come to destroy us? I know who you are! You are God's Holy One."

[25] Jesus told the evil spirit, "Be quiet and come out of the man!" [26] The spirit shook him. Then it gave a loud shout and left.

[27] Everyone was completely surprised and kept saying to each other, "What is this? It must be some new kind of powerful teaching! Even the evil spirits obey him." [28] News about Jesus quickly spread all over Galilee.

## Jesus Heals Many People
### (Matthew 8.14-17; Luke 4.38-41)

[29] As soon as Jesus left the meeting place with James and John, they went home with Simon and Andrew. [30] When they got there, Jesus was told that Simon's mother-in-law was sick in bed with fever. [31] Jesus went to her. He took hold of her hand and helped her up. The fever left her, and she served them a meal.

[32] That evening after sunset,[f] all who were sick or had demons in them were brought to Jesus. [33] In fact, the whole town gathered around the door of the house. [34] Jesus healed all kinds of terrible diseases and forced out a lot of demons. But the demons knew who he was, and he did not let them speak.

[35] Very early the next morning, Jesus got up and went to a place where he could be alone and pray. [36] Simon and the others started looking for him. [37] And when they found him, they said, "Everyone is looking for you!"

[38] Jesus replied, "We must go to the nearby towns, so that I can tell the good news to those people. This is why I have come." [39] Then Jesus went to Jewish meeting places everywhere in Galilee, where he preached and forced out demons.

## Jesus Heals a Man
### (Matthew 8.1-4; Luke 5.12-16)

[40] A man with leprosy[g] came to Jesus and knelt down.[h] He begged, "You have the power to make me well, if only you wanted to."

[41] Jesus felt sorry for[i] the man. So he put his hand on him and said, "I want to! Now you are well." [42] At once the man's leprosy disappeared, and he was well.

[43] After Jesus strictly warned the man, he sent him on his way. [44] He said, "Don't tell anyone about this. Just go and show the priest that you are well. Then take a gift to the temple as Moses commanded, and everyone will know that you have been healed."[j]

[45] The man talked about it so much and told so many people, that Jesus could no longer go openly into a town. He had to stay away from the towns, but people still came to him from everywhere.

## Jesus Heals a Crippled Man
### (Matthew 9.1-8; Luke 5.17-26)

2 Jesus went back to Capernaum, and a few days later people heard that he was at home.[k] [2] Then so many of them came to the house that there wasn't even standing room left in front of the door.

Jesus was still teaching [3] when four people came up, carrying a crippled man on a mat. [4] But because of the crowd, they could not get him to Jesus. So they made a hole in the roof[l] above him and let the man down in front of everyone.

[5] When Jesus saw how much faith

---

[f] **1.32** *after sunset*: The Sabbath was over, and a new day began at sunset. [g] **1.40** *leprosy*: In biblical times the word "leprosy" was used for many different kinds of skin diseases. [h] **1.40** *and knelt down*: These words are not in some manuscripts. [i] **1.41** *felt sorry for*: Some manuscripts have "was angry with." [j] **1.44** *everyone will know that you have been healed*: People with leprosy had to be examined by a priest and told that they were well (that is, "clean") before they could once again live a normal life in the Jewish community. The gift that Moses commanded was the sacrifice of some lambs together with flour mixed with olive oil. [k] **2.1** *at home*: Or "in the house" (perhaps Simon Peter's home). [l] **2.4** *roof*: In Palestine the houses usually had a flat roof. Stairs on the outside led up to the roof that was made of beams and boards covered with packed earth.

they had, he said to the crippled man, "My friend, your sins are forgiven."

6 Some of the teachers of the Law of Moses were sitting there. They started wondering, 7 "Why would he say such a thing? He must think he is God! Only God can forgive sins."

8 Right away, Jesus knew what they were thinking, and he said, "Why are you thinking such things? 9 Is it easier for me to tell this crippled man that his sins are forgiven or to tell him to get up and pick up his mat and go on home? 10 I will show you that the Son of Man has the right to forgive sins here on earth." So Jesus said to the man, 11 "Get up! Pick up your mat and go on home."

12 The man got right up. He picked up his mat and went out while everyone watched in amazement. They praised God and said, "We have never seen anything like this!"

### Jesus Chooses Levi
#### (Matthew 9.9-13; Luke 5.27-32)

13 Once again, Jesus went to the shore of Lake Galilee. A large crowd gathered around him, and he taught them. 14 As he walked along, he saw Levi, the son of Alphaeus. Levi was sitting at the place for paying taxes, and Jesus said to him, "Come with me!" So he got up and went with Jesus.

15 Later, Jesus and his disciples were having dinner at Levi's house.m Many tax collectorsn and other sinners had become followers of Jesus, and they were also guests at the dinner.

16 Some of the teachers of the Law of Moses were Pharisees, and they saw that Jesus was eating with sinners and tax collectors. So they asked his disciples, "Why does he eat with tax collectors and sinners?"

17 Jesus heard them and answered, "Healthy people don't need a doctor,

but sick people do. I didn't come to invite good people to be my followers. I came to invite sinners."

### People Ask about Going without Eating
#### (Matthew 9.14-17; Luke 5.33-39)

18 The followers of John the Baptist and the Pharisees often went without eating.o Some people came and asked Jesus, "Why do the followers of John and those of the Pharisees often go without eating, while your disciples never do?"

19 Jesus answered:

The friends of a bridegroom don't go without eating while he is still with them. 20 But the time will come when he will be taken from them. Then they will go without eating.

21 No one patches old clothes by sewing on a piece of new cloth. The new piece would shrink and tear a bigger hole.

22 No one pours new wine into old wineskins. The wine would swell and burst the old skins.p Then the wine would be lost, and the skins would be ruined. New wine must be put into new wineskins.

### A Question about the Sabbath
#### (Matthew 12.1-8; Luke 6.1-5)

23 One Sabbath Jesus and his disciples were walking through some wheat fields. His disciples were picking grains of wheat as they went along.q 24 Some Pharisees asked Jesus, "Why are your disciples picking grain on the Sabbath? They are not supposed to do that!"

25 Jesus answered, "Haven't you read what David did when he and his followers were hungry and in need? 26 It was during the time of Abiathar the high priest. David went into the house of

---

m2.15 Levi's house: Or "Jesus' house." n2.15 tax collectors: These were usually Jewish people who paid the Romans for the right to collect taxes. They were hated by other Jews who thought of them as traitors to their country and to their religion. o2.18 without eating: The Jewish people sometimes went without eating (also called "fasting") to show their love for God or to show sorrow for their sins. p2.22 swell and burst the old skins: While the juice from grapes was becoming wine, it would swell and stretch the skins in which it had been stored. If the skins were old and stiff, they would burst. q2.23 went along: It was the custom to let hungry travelers pick grains of wheat.

God and ate the sacred loaves of bread
that only priests are allowed to eat. He
also gave some to his followers."
   27 Jesus finished by saying, "People
were not made for the good of the Sabbath. The Sabbath was made for the
good of people. 28 So the Son of Man
is Lord over the Sabbath."

## A Man with a Crippled Hand
### (Matthew 12.9-14; Luke 6.6-11)

**3** The next time that Jesus went into
the meeting place, a man with a
crippled hand was there. 2 The Pharisees r wanted to accuse Jesus of doing
something wrong, and they kept watching to see if Jesus would heal him on
the Sabbath.
   3 Jesus told the man to stand up
where everyone could see him. 4 Then
he asked, "On the Sabbath should we
do good deeds or evil deeds? Should
we save someone's life or destroy it?"
But no one said a word.
   5 Jesus was angry as he looked
around at the people. Yet he felt sorry
for them because they were so stubborn. Then he told the man, "Stretch
out your hand." He did, and his bad
hand was healed.
   6 The Pharisees left. And right away
they started making plans with Herod's
followers s to kill Jesus.

## Large Crowds Come to Jesus

   7 Jesus led his disciples down to the
shore of the lake. Large crowds followed him from Galilee, Judea, 8 and
Jerusalem. People came from Idumea,
as well as other places east of the Jordan River. They also came from the region around the cities of Tyre and Sidon. All of these crowds came because
they had heard what Jesus was doing.
9 He even had to tell his disciples to get
a boat ready to keep him from being
crushed by the crowds.
   10 After Jesus had healed many people, the other sick people begged him
to let them touch him. 11 And whenever
any evil spirits saw Jesus, they would
fall to the ground and shout, "You are
the Son of God!" 12 But Jesus warned
the spirits not to tell who he was.

## Jesus Chooses His Twelve Apostles
### (Matthew 10.1-4; Luke 6.12-16)

   13 Jesus decided to ask some of his
disciples to go up on a mountain with
him, and they went. 14 Then he chose
twelve of them to be his apostles, t so
that they could be with him. He also
wanted to send them out to preach
15 and to force out demons. 16 Simon
was one of the twelve, and Jesus named
him Peter. 17 There were also James
and John, the two sons of Zebedee.
Jesus called them Boanerges, which
means "Thunderbolts." 18 Andrew,
Philip, Bartholomew, Matthew,
Thomas, James son of Alphaeus, and
Thaddaeus were also apostles. The
others were Simon, known as the Eager
One, u 19 and Judas Iscariot, v who later
betrayed Jesus.

## Jesus and the Ruler of Demons
### (Matthew 12.22-32; Luke 11.14-23; 12.10)

   20 Jesus went back home, w and once
again such a large crowd gathered that
there was no chance even to eat.
21 When Jesus' family heard what he
was doing, they thought he was crazy
and went to get him under control.
   22 Some teachers of the Law of Moses
came from Jerusalem and said, "This
man is under the power of Beelzebul, the ruler of demons! He is even
forcing out demons with the help of
Beelzebul."

r 3.2 *Pharisees*: The Greek text has "they" (but see verse 6).   s 3.6 *Herod's followers*: People
who were political followers of the family of Herod the Great and his son Herod Antipas.
t 3.14 *to be his apostles*: These words are not in some manuscripts.   u 3.18 *known as the
Eager One*: The Greek text has "Cananaean," which probably comes from a Hebrew word
meaning "zealous" (see Luke 6.15). "Zealot" was the name later given to the members of
a Jewish group which resisted and fought against the Romans.   v 3.19 *Iscariot*: This may
mean "a man from Kerioth" (a place in Judea). But more probably it means "a man who
was a liar" or "a man who was a betrayer."   w 3.20 *went back home*: Or "entered a house"
(perhaps the home of Simon Peter).

²³ Jesus told the people to gather around him. Then he spoke to them in riddles and said:

How can Satan force himself out? ²⁴ A nation whose people fight each other won't last very long. ²⁵ And a family that fights won't last long either. ²⁶ So if Satan fights against himself, that will be the end of him.

²⁷ How can anyone break into the house of a strong man and steal his things, unless he first ties up the strong man? Then he can take everything.

²⁸ I promise you that any of the sinful things you say or do can be forgiven, no matter how terrible those things are. ²⁹ But if you speak against the Holy Spirit, you can never be forgiven. That sin will be held against you forever.

³⁰ Jesus said this because the people were saying that he had an evil spirit in him.

### Jesus' Mother and Brothers
*(Matthew 12.46-50; Luke 8.19-21)*

³¹ Jesus' mother and brothers came and stood outside. Then they sent someone with a message for him to come out to them. ³² The crowd that was sitting around Jesus told him, "Your mother and your brothers and sistersˣ are outside and want to see you."

³³ Jesus asked, "Who is my mother and who are my brothers?" ³⁴ Then he looked at the people sitting around him and said, "Here are my mother and my brothers. ³⁵ Anyone who obeys God is my brother or sister or mother."

### A Story about a Farmer
*(Matthew 13.1-9; Luke 8.4-8)*

**4** The next time Jesus taught beside Lake Galilee, a big crowd gathered. It was so large that he had to sit in a boat out on the lake, while the people stood on the shore. ² He used stories to teach them many things, and this is part of what he taught:

³ Now listen! A farmer went out to scatter seed in a field. ⁴ While the farmer was scattering the seed, some of it fell along the road and was eaten by birds. ⁵ Other seeds fell on thin, rocky ground and quickly started growing because the soil wasn't very deep. ⁶ But when the sun came up, the plants were scorched and dried up, because they did not have enough roots. ⁷ Some other seeds fell where thornbushes grew up and choked out the plants. So they did not produce any grain. ⁸ But a few seeds did fall on good ground where the plants grew and produced thirty or sixty or even a hundred times as much as was scattered.

⁹ Then Jesus said, "If you have ears, pay attention."

### Why Jesus Used Stories
*(Matthew 13.10-17; Luke 8.9, 10)*

¹⁰ When Jesus was alone with the twelve apostles and some others, they asked him about these stories. ¹¹ He answered:

I have explained the secret about God's kingdom to you, but for others I can use only stories. ¹² The reason is,

"These people will look
and look, but never see.
They will listen and listen,
but never understand.
If they did,
they would turn to God,
and he would forgive them."

### Jesus Explains the Story about the Farmer
*(Matthew 13.18-23; Luke 8.11-15)*

¹³ Jesus told them:

If you don't understand this story, you won't understand any others. ¹⁴ What the farmer is spreading is really the message about the kingdom. ¹⁵ The seeds that fell along the road are the people who hear the message. But Satan soon comes and snatches it away from them. ¹⁶ The seeds that fell on rocky ground are the people who gladly hear the mes-

ˣ**3.32** *and sisters*: These words are not in some manuscripts.

sage and accept it right away. 17 But they don't have any roots, and they don't last very long. As soon as life gets hard or the message gets them in trouble, they give up.

18 The seeds that fell among the thornbushes are also people who hear the message. 19 But they start worrying about the needs of this life. They are fooled by the desire to get rich and to have all kinds of other things. So the message gets choked out, and they never produce anything. 20 The seeds that fell on good ground are the people who hear and welcome the message. They produce thirty or sixty or even a hundred times as much as was planted.

## Light
### (Luke 8.16-18)

21 Jesus also said:
You don't light a lamp and put it under a clay pot or under a bed. Don't you put a lamp on a lampstand? 22 There is nothing hidden that will not be made public. There is no secret that will not be well known. 23 If you have ears, pay attention!

24 Listen carefully to what you hear! The way you treat others will be the way you will be treated—and even worse. 25 Everyone who has something will be given more. But people who don't have anything will lose what little they have.

## Another Story about Seeds

26 Again Jesus said:
God's kingdom is like what happens when a farmer scatters seed in a field. 27 The farmer sleeps at night and is up and around during the day. Yet the seeds keep sprouting and growing, and he doesn't understand how. 28 It is the ground that makes the seeds sprout and grow into plants that produce grain. 29 Then when harvest season comes and the grain is ripe, the farmer cuts it with a sickle.y

## A Mustard Seed
### (Matthew 13.31, 32; Luke 13.18, 19)

30 Finally, Jesus said:
What is God's kingdom like? What story can I use to explain it? 31 It is like what happens when a mustard seed is planted in the ground. It is the smallest seed in all the world. 32 But once it is planted, it grows larger than any garden plant. It even puts out branches that are big enough for birds to nest in its shade.

## The Reason for Teaching with Stories
### (Matthew 13.34, 35)

33 Jesus used many other stories when he spoke to the people, and he taught them as much as they could understand. 34 He did not tell them anything without using stories. But when he was alone with his disciples, he explained everything to them.

## A Storm
### (Matthew 8.23-27; Luke 8.22-25)

35 That evening, Jesus said to his disciples, "Let's cross to the east side." 36 So they left the crowd, and his disciples started across the lake with him in the boat. Some other boats followed along. 37 Suddenly a windstorm struck the lake. Waves started splashing into the boat, and it was about to sink.

38 Jesus was in the back of the boat with his head on a pillow, and he was asleep. His disciples woke him and said, "Teacher, don't you care that we're about to drown?"

39 Jesus got up and ordered the wind and the waves to be quiet. The wind stopped, and everything was calm. 40 Jesus asked his disciples, "Why were you afraid? Don't you have any faith?"

41 Now they were more afraid than ever and said to each other, "Who is this? Even the wind and the waves obey him!"

y4.29 sickle: A knife with a long curved blade, used to cut grain and other crops.

## A Man with Evil Spirits
### (Matthew 8.28-34; Luke 8.26-39)

5 Jesus and his disciples crossed Lake Galilee and came to shore near the town of Gerasa.z 2 When he was getting out of the boat, a man with an evil spirit quickly ran to him 3 from the graveyarda where he had been living. No one was able to tie the man up anymore, not even with a chain. 4 He had often been put in chains and leg irons, but he broke the chains and smashed the leg irons. No one could control him. 5 Night and day he was in the graveyard or on the hills, yelling and cutting himself with stones.

6 When the man saw Jesus in the distance, he ran up to him and knelt down. 7 He shouted, "Jesus, Son of God in heaven, what do you want with me? Promise me in God's name that you won't torture me!" 8 The man said this because Jesus had already told the evil spirit to come out of him.

9 Jesus asked, "What is your name?"

The man answered, "My name is Lots, because I have 'lots' of evil spirits." 10 He then begged Jesus not to send them away.

11 Over on the hillside a large herd of pigs was feeding. 12 So the evil spirits begged Jesus, "Send us into those pigs! Let us go into them." 13 Jesus let them go, and they went out of the man and into the pigs. The whole herd of about two thousand pigs rushed down the steep bank into the lake and drowned.

14 The men taking care of the pigs ran to the town and the farms to spread the news. Then the people came out to see what had happened. 15 When they came to Jesus, they saw the man who had once been full of demons. He was sitting there with his clothes on and in his right mind, and they were terrified.

16 Everyone who had seen what had happened told about the man and the pigs. 17 Then the people started begging Jesus to leave their part of the country.

18 When Jesus was getting into the boat, the man begged to go with him. 19 But Jesus would not let him. Instead, he said, "Go home to your family and tell them how much the Lord has done for you and how good he has been to you."

20 The man went away into the region near the ten cities known as Decapolisb and began telling everyone how much Jesus had done for him. Everyone who heard what had happened was amazed.

## A Dying Girl and a Sick Woman
### (Matthew 9.18-26; Luke 8.40-56)

21 Once again Jesus got into the boat and crossed Lake Galilee.c Then as he stood on the shore, a large crowd gathered around him. 22 The person in charge of the Jewish meeting place was also there. His name was Jairus, and when he saw Jesus, he went over to him. He knelt at Jesus' feet 23 and started begging him for help. He said, "My daughter is about to die! Please come and touch her, so she will get well and live." 24 Jesus went with Jairus. Many people followed along and kept crowding around.

25 In the crowd was a woman who had been bleeding for twelve years. 26 She had gone to many doctors, and they had not done anything except cause her a lot of pain. She had paid them all the money she had. But instead of getting better, she only got worse. 27 The woman had heard about Jesus, so she came up behind him in the crowd and barely touched his clothes. 28 She had said to herself, "If I can just touch his clothes, I will get well." 29 As soon as she touched them, her bleeding stopped, and she knew she was well.

30 At that moment Jesus felt power go out from him. He turned to the crowd and asked, "Who touched my clothes?"

31 His disciples said to him, "Look at all these people crowding around you! How can you ask who touched you?" 32 But Jesus turned to see who had touched him.

33 The woman knew what had happened to her. She came shaking with

z5.1 *Gerasa*: Some manuscripts have "Gadara," and others have "Gergesa."
a5.3 *graveyard*: It was thought that demons and evil spirits lived in graveyards.   b5.20 *the ten cities known as Decapolis*: A group of ten cities east of Samaria and Galilee, where the people followed the Greek way of life.   c5.21 *crossed Lake Galilee*: To the west side.

fear and knelt down in front of Jesus. Then she told him the whole story.

34 Jesus said to the woman, "You are now well because of your faith. May God give you peace! You are healed, and you will no longer be in pain."

35 While Jesus was still speaking, some men came from Jairus' home and said, "Your daughter has died! Why bother the teacher anymore?"

36 Jesus heard[d] what they said, and he said to Jairus, "Don't worry. Just have faith!"

37 Jesus did not let anyone go with him except Peter and the two brothers, James and John. 38 They went home with Jairus and saw the people crying and making a lot of noise.[e] 39 Then Jesus went inside and said to them, "Why are you crying and carrying on like this? The child isn't dead. She is just asleep." 40 But the people laughed at him.

After Jesus had sent them all out of the house, he took the girl's father and mother and his three disciples and went to where she was. 41-42 He took the twelve-year-old girl by the hand and said, "Talitha, koum!"[f] which means, "Little girl, get up!" The girl got right up and started walking around. Everyone was greatly surprised. 43 But Jesus ordered them not to tell anyone what had happened. Then he said, "Give her something to eat."

### The People of Nazareth Turn against Jesus
*(Matthew 13.53-58; Luke 4.16-30)*

6 Jesus left and returned to his hometown[g] with his disciples. 2 The next Sabbath he taught in the Jewish meeting place. Many of the people who heard him were amazed and asked, "How can he do all this? Where did he get such wisdom and the power to work these miracles? 3 Isn't he the carpenter,[h] the son of Mary? Aren't James, Joseph, Judas, and Simon his brothers? Don't his sisters still live here in our town?" The people were very unhappy because of what he was doing.

4 But Jesus said, "Prophets are honored by everyone, except the people of their hometown and their relatives and their own family." 5 Jesus could not work any miracles there, except to heal a few sick people by placing his hands on them. 6 He was surprised that the people did not have any faith.

### Instructions for the Twelve Apostles
*(Matthew 10.5-15; Luke 9.1-6)*

Jesus taught in all the neighboring villages. 7 Then he called together his twelve apostles and sent them out two by two with power over evil spirits. 8 He told them, "You may take along a walking stick. But don't carry food or a traveling bag or any money. 9 It's all right to wear sandals, but don't take along a change of clothes. 10 When you are welcomed into a home, stay there until you leave that town. 11 If any place won't welcome you or listen to your message, leave and shake the dust from your feet[i] as a warning to them."

12 The apostles left and started telling everyone to turn to God. 13 They forced out many demons and healed a lot of sick people by putting olive oil[j] on them.

### The Death of John the Baptist
*(Matthew 14.1-12; Luke 9.7-9)*

14 Jesus became so well-known that Herod the ruler[k] heard about him. Some people thought he was John the Baptist, who had come back to life with the power to work miracles. 15 Others thought he was Elijah[l] or some other

d5.36 *heard*: Or "ignored." e5.38 *crying and making a lot of noise*: The Jewish people often hired mourners for funerals. f5.41,42 *Talitha, koum*: These words are in Aramaic, a language spoken in Palestine during the time of Jesus. g6.1 *hometown*: Nazareth. h6.3 *carpenter*: The Greek word may also mean someone who builds or works with stone or brick. i6.11 *shake the dust from your feet*: This was a way of showing rejection. j6.13 *olive oil*: The Jewish people used olive oil as a way of healing people. Sometimes olive oil is a symbol for healing by means of a miracle (see James 5.14). k6.14 *Herod the ruler*: Herod Antipas, the son of Herod the Great. l6.15 *Elijah*: Many of the Jewish people expected the prophet Elijah to come and prepare the way for the Messiah.

prophet who had lived long ago. [16] But when Herod heard about Jesus, he said, "This must be John! I had his head cut off, and now he has come back to life."

[17-18] Herod had earlier married Herodias, the wife of his brother Philip. But John had told him, "It isn't right for you to take your brother's wife!" So, in order to please Herodias, Herod arrested John and put him in prison.

[19] Herodias had a grudge against John and wanted to kill him. But she could not do it [20] because Herod was afraid of John and protected him. He knew that John was a good and holy man. Even though Herod was confused by what John said,[m] he was glad to listen to him. And he often did.

[21] Finally, Herodias got her chance when Herod gave a great birthday celebration for himself and invited his officials, his army officers, and the leaders of Galilee. [22] The daughter of Herodias[n] came in and danced for Herod and his guests. She pleased them so much that Herod said, "Ask for anything, and it's yours! [23] I swear that I will give you as much as half of my kingdom, if you want it."

[24] The girl left and asked her mother, "What do you think I should ask for?"

Her mother answered, "The head of John the Baptist!"

[25] The girl hurried back and told Herod, "Right now on a platter I want the head of John the Baptist!"

[26] The king was very sorry for what he had said. But he did not want to break the promise he had made in front of his guests. [27] At once he ordered a guard to cut off John's head there in prison. [28] The guard put the head on a platter and took it to the girl. Then she gave it to her mother.

[29] When John's followers learned that he had been killed, they took his body and put it in a tomb.

## Jesus Feeds Five Thousand
(Matthew 14.13-21; Luke 9.10-17; John 6.1-14)

[30] After the apostles returned to Jesus,[o] they told him everything they had done and taught. [31] But so many people were coming and going that Jesus and the apostles did not even have a chance to eat. Then Jesus said, "Let's go to a place[p] where we can be alone and get some rest." [32] They left in a boat for a place where they could be alone. [33] But many people saw them leave and figured out where they were going. So people from every town ran on ahead and got there first.

[34] When Jesus got out of the boat, he saw the large crowd that was like sheep without a shepherd. He felt sorry for the people and started teaching them many things.

[35] That evening the disciples came to Jesus and said, "This place is like a desert, and it is already late. [36] Let the crowds leave, so they can go to the farms and villages near here and buy something to eat."

[37] Jesus replied, "You give them something to eat."

But they asked him, "Don't you know that it would take almost a year's wages[q] to buy all of these people something to eat?"

[38] Then Jesus said, "How much bread do you have? Go and see!"

They found out and answered, "We have five small loaves of bread[r] and two fish." [39] Jesus told his disciples to have the people sit down on the green grass. [40] They sat down in groups of a hundred and groups of fifty.

[41] Jesus took the five loaves and the two fish. He looked up toward heaven and blessed the food. Then he broke the bread and handed it to his disciples to give to the people. He also divided the two fish, so that everyone could have some.

[42] After everyone had eaten all they wanted, [43] Jesus' disciples picked up

---

[m]6.20 *was confused by what John said*: Some manuscripts have "did many things because of what John said."   [n]6.22 *Herodias*: Some manuscripts have "Herod."   [o]6.30 *the apostles returned to Jesus*: From the mission on which he had sent them (see 6.7, 12, 13).   [p]6.31 *a place*: This was probably northeast of Lake Galilee (see verse 45).   [q]6.37 *almost a year's wages*: The Greek text has "two hundred silver coins." Each coin was the average day's wage for a worker.   [r]6.38 *small loaves of bread*: These would have been flat and round or in the shape of a bun.

twelve large baskets of leftover bread and fish. ⁴⁴ There were five thousand men who ate the food.

## Jesus Walks on the Water
### (Matthew 14.22-33; John 6.15-21)

⁴⁵ Right away, Jesus made his disciples get into the boat and start back across to Bethsaida. But he stayed until he had sent the crowds away. ⁴⁶ Then he told them goodby and went up on the side of a mountain to pray.

⁴⁷ Later that evening he was still there by himself, and the boat was somewhere in the middle of the lake. ⁴⁸ He could see that the disciples were struggling hard, because they were rowing against the wind. Not long before morning, Jesus came toward them. He was walking on the water and was about to pass the boat.

⁴⁹ When the disciples saw Jesus walking on the water, they thought he was a ghost, and they started screaming. ⁵⁰ All of them saw him and were terrified. But at that same time he said, "Don't worry! I am Jesus. Don't be afraid." ⁵¹ He then got into the boat with them, and the wind died down. The disciples were completely confused. ⁵² Their minds were closed, and they could not understand the true meaning of the loaves of bread.

## Jesus Heals Sick People in Gennesaret
### (Matthew 14.34-36)

⁵³ Jesus and his disciples crossed the lake and brought the boat to shore near the town of Gennesaret. ⁵⁴ As soon as they got out of the boat, the people recognized Jesus. ⁵⁵ So they ran all over that part of the country to bring their sick people to him on mats. They brought them each time they heard where he was. ⁵⁶ In every village or farm or marketplace where Jesus went, the people brought their sick to

him. They begged him to let them just touch his clothes, and everyone who did was healed.

## The Teaching of the Ancestors
### (Matthew 15.1-9)

7 Some Pharisees and several teachers of the Law of Moses from Jerusalem came and gathered around Jesus. ² They noticed that some of his disciples ate without first washing their hands.ˢ

³ The Pharisees and many others obey the teachings of their ancestors. They always wash their hands in the proper wayᵗ before eating. ⁴ None of them will eat anything they buy in the market until it is washed. They also follow a lot of other teachings, such as washing cups, pitchers, and bowls.ᵘ

⁵ The Pharisees and teachers asked Jesus, "Why don't your disciples obey what our ancestors taught us to do? Why do they eat without washing their hands?"

⁶ Jesus replied:

You are nothing but show-offs! The prophet Isaiah was right when he wrote that God had said,

"All of you praise me
    with your words,
but you never really
    think about me.
⁷ It is useless for you
    to worship me,
when you teach rules
    made up by humans."

⁸ You disobey God's commands in order to obey what humans have taught. ⁹ You are good at rejecting God's commands so that you can follow your own teachings! ¹⁰ Didn't Moses command you to respect your father and mother? Didn't he tell you to put to death all who curse their parents? ¹¹ But you let people get by without helping their parents when they should. You let them say that what they own has been offered

---

ˢ7.2 *without first washing their hands*: The Jewish people had strict laws about washing their hands before eating, especially if they had been out in public.   ᵗ7.3 *in the proper way*: The Greek text has "with the fist," but the exact meaning is not clear. It could mean "to the wrist" or "to the elbow."   ᵘ7.4 *bowls*: Some manuscripts add "and sleeping mats."

to God.ᵛ ¹²You won't let those people help their parents. ¹³And you ignore God's commands in order to follow your own teaching. You do a lot of other things that are just as bad.

## What Really Makes People Unclean
### (Matthew 15.10-20)

¹⁴Jesus called the crowd together again and said, "Pay attention and try to understand what I mean. ¹⁵⁻¹⁶The food that you put into your mouth doesn't make you unclean and unfit to worship God. The bad words that come out of your mouth are what make you unclean."ʷ

¹⁷After Jesus and his disciples had left the crowd and had gone into the house, they asked him what these sayings meant. ¹⁸He answered, "Don't you know what I am talking about by now? You surely know that the food you put into your mouth cannot make you unclean. ¹⁹It doesn't go into your heart, but into your stomach, and then out of your body." By saying this, Jesus meant that all foods were fit to eat.

²⁰Then Jesus said:

What comes from your heart is what makes you unclean. ²¹Out of your heart come evil thoughts, vulgar deeds, stealing, murder, ²²unfaithfulness in marriage, greed, meanness, deceit, indecency, envy, insults, pride, and foolishness. ²³All of these come from your heart, and they are what make you unfit to worship God.

## A Woman's Faith
### (Matthew 15.21-28)

²⁴Jesus left and went to the region near the city of Tyre, where he stayed in someone's home. He did not want people to know he was there, but they found out anyway. ²⁵A woman whose daughter had an evil spirit in her heard where Jesus was. And right away she came and knelt down at his feet. ²⁶The woman was Greek and had been born in the part of Syria known as Phoenicia. She begged Jesus to force the demon out of her daughter. ²⁷But Jesus said, "The children must first be fed! It isn't right to take away their food and feed it to dogs."ˣ

²⁸The woman replied, "Lord, even dogs eat the crumbs that children drop from the table."

²⁹Jesus answered, "That's true! You may go now. The demon has left your daughter." ³⁰When the woman got back home, she found her child lying on the bed. The demon had gone.

## Jesus Heals a Man Who Was Deaf and Could Hardly Talk

³¹Jesus left the region around Tyre and went by way of Sidon toward Lake Galilee. He went through the land near the ten cities known as Decapolis.ʸ ³²Some people brought to him a man who was deaf and could hardly talk. They begged Jesus just to touch him.

³³After Jesus had taken him aside from the crowd, he stuck his fingers in the man's ears. Then he spit and put it on the man's tongue. ³⁴Jesus looked up toward heaven, and with a groan he said, "Effatha!"ᶻ which means "Open up!" ³⁵At once the man could hear, and he had no more trouble talking clearly.

³⁶Jesus told the people not to say anything about what he had done. But the more he told them, the more they talked about it. ³⁷They were completely amazed and said, "Everything he does is good! He even heals people who cannot hear or talk."

## Jesus Feeds Four Thousand
### (Matthew 15.32-39)

**8** One day another large crowd gathered around Jesus. They had not brought along anything to eat. So Jesus

---

ᵛ**7.11** *has been offered to God*: According to Jewish custom, when anything was offered to God, it could not be used for anyone else, not even for a person's parents. ʷ**7.15,16** *unclean*: Some manuscripts add, "If you have ears, pay attention." ˣ**7.27** *feed it to dogs*: The Jewish people often referred to Gentiles as dogs. ʸ**7.31** *the ten cities known as Decapolis*: See the note at 5.20. ᶻ**7.34** *Effatha*: This word is in Aramaic, a language spoken in Palestine during the time of Jesus.

called his disciples together and said, ² "I feel sorry for these people. They have been with me for three days, and they don't have anything to eat. ³ Some of them live a long way from here. If I send them away hungry, they might faint on their way home."

⁴ The disciples said, "This place is like a desert. Where can we find enough food to feed such a crowd?"

⁵ Jesus asked them how much food they had. They replied, "Seven small loaves of bread."ᵃ

⁶ After Jesus told the crowd to sit down, he took the seven loaves and blessed them. He then broke the loaves and handed them to his disciples, who passed them out to the crowd. ⁷ They also had a few little fish, and after Jesus had blessed these, he told the disciples to pass them around.

⁸⁻⁹ The crowd of about four thousand people ate all they wanted, and the leftovers filled seven large baskets.

As soon as Jesus had sent the people away, ¹⁰ he got into the boat with the disciples and crossed to the territory near Dalmanutha.ᵇ

### A Sign from Heaven
#### (Matthew 16.1-4)

¹¹ The Pharisees came out and started an argument with Jesus. They wanted to test him by asking for a sign from heaven. ¹² Jesus groaned and said, "Why are you always looking for a sign? I can promise you that you will not be given one!" ¹³ Then he left them. He again got into a boat and crossed over to the other side of the lake.

### The Yeast of the Pharisees and of Herod
#### (Matthew 16.5-12)

¹⁴ The disciples had forgotten to bring any bread, and they had only one loaf with them in the boat. ¹⁵ Jesus warned them, "Watch out! Guard against the yeast of the Pharisees and of Herod."ᶜ ¹⁶ The disciples talked this over and said to each other, "He must be saying

this because we don't have any bread."

¹⁷ Jesus knew what they were thinking and asked, "Why are you talking about not having any bread? Don't you understand? Are your minds still closed? ¹⁸ Are your eyes blind and your ears deaf? Don't you remember ¹⁹ how many baskets of leftovers you picked up when I fed those five thousand people with only five small loaves of bread?"

"Yes," the disciples answered. "There were twelve baskets."

²⁰ Jesus then asked, "And how many baskets of leftovers did you pick up when I broke seven small loaves of bread for those four thousand people?"

"Seven," they answered.

²¹ "Don't you know what I am talking about by now?" Jesus asked.

### Jesus Heals a Blind Man at Bethsaida

²² As Jesus and his disciples were going into Bethsaida, some people brought a blind man to him and begged him to touch the man. ²³ Jesus took him by the hand and led him out of the village, where he spit into the man's eyes. He placed his hands on the blind man and asked him if he could see anything. ²⁴ The man looked up and said, "I see people, but they look like trees walking around."

²⁵ Once again Jesus placed his hands on the man's eyes, and this time the man stared. His eyes were healed, and he saw everything clearly. ²⁶ Jesus said to him, "You may return home now, but don't go into the village."

### Who Is Jesus?
#### (Matthew 16.13-20; Luke 9.18-21)

²⁷ Jesus and his disciples went to the villages near the town of Caesarea Philippi. As they were walking along, he asked them, "What do people say about me?"

²⁸ The disciples answered, "Some say you are John the Baptist or maybe Elijah.ᵈ Others say you are one of the prophets."

**29** Then Jesus asked them, "But who do you say I am?"

"You are the Messiah!" Peter replied. **30** Jesus warned the disciples not to tell anyone about him.

### Jesus Speaks about His Suffering and Death
*(Matthew 16.21-28; Luke 9.22-27)*

**31** Jesus began telling his disciples what would happen to him. He said, "The nation's leaders, the chief priests, and the teachers of the Law of Moses will make the Son of Man suffer terribly. He will be rejected and killed, but three days later he will rise to life." **32** Then Jesus explained clearly what he meant.

Peter took Jesus aside and told him to stop talking like that. **33** But when Jesus turned and saw the disciples, he corrected Peter. He said to him, "Satan, get away from me! You are thinking like everyone else and not like God." **34** Jesus then told the crowd and the disciples to come closer, and he said:

If any of you want to be my followers, you must forget about yourself. You must take up your cross and follow me. **35** If you want to save your life,*e* you will destroy it. But if you give up your life for me and for the good news, you will save it. **36** What will you gain, if you own the whole world but destroy yourself? **37** What could you give to get back your soul?

**38** Don't be ashamed of me and my message among these unfaithful and sinful people! If you are, the Son of Man will be ashamed of you when he comes in the glory of his Father with the holy angels.

**9** I can assure you that some of the people standing here will not die before they see God's kingdom come with power.

### The True Glory of Jesus
*(Matthew 17.1-13; Luke 9.28-36)*

**2** Six days later Jesus took Peter, James, and John with him. They went up on a high mountain, where they could be alone. There in front of the disciples, Jesus was completely changed. **3** And his clothes became much whiter than any bleach on earth could make them. **4** Then Moses and Elijah were there talking with Jesus.

**5** Peter said to Jesus, "Teacher, it is good for us to be here! Let us make three shelters, one for you, one for Moses, and one for Elijah." **6** But Peter and the others were terribly frightened, and he did not know what he was talking about.

**7** The shadow of a cloud passed over and covered them. From the cloud a voice said, "This is my Son, and I love him. Listen to what he says!" **8** At once the disciples looked around, but they saw only Jesus.

**9** As Jesus and his disciples were coming down the mountain, he told them not to say a word about what they had seen, until the Son of Man had been raised from death. **10** So they kept it to themselves. But they wondered what he meant by the words "raised from death."

**11** The disciples asked Jesus, "Don't the teachers of the Law of Moses say that Elijah must come before the Messiah does?"

**12** Jesus answered:

Elijah certainly will come*f* to get everything ready. But don't the Scriptures also say that the Son of Man must suffer terribly and be rejected? **13** I can assure you that Elijah has already come. And people treated him just as they wanted to, as the Scriptures say they would.

### Jesus Heals a Boy
*(Matthew 17.14-20; Luke 9.37-43a)*

**14** When Jesus and his three disciples came back down, they saw a large crowd around the other disciples. The teachers of the Law of Moses were arguing with them. **15** The crowd was really surprised to see Jesus, and everyone hurried over to greet him.

---

*e***8.35** *life:* In verses 35-37 the same Greek word is translated "life," "yourself," and "soul."
*f***9.12** *Elijah certainly will come:* See the note at 6.15.

¹⁶ Jesus asked, "What are you arguing about?"

¹⁷ Someone from the crowd answered, "Teacher, I brought my son to you. A demon keeps him from talking. ¹⁸ Whenever the demon attacks my son, it throws him to the ground and makes him foam at the mouth and grit his teeth in pain. Then he becomes stiff. I asked your disciples to force out the demon, but they couldn't do it."

¹⁹ Jesus said, "You people don't have any faith! How much longer must I be with you? Why do I have to put up with you? Bring the boy to me."

²⁰ They brought the boy, and as soon as the demon saw Jesus, it made the boy shake all over. He fell down and began rolling on the ground and foaming at the mouth.

²¹ Jesus asked the boy's father, "How long has he been like this?"

The man answered, "Ever since he was a child. ²² The demon has often tried to kill him by throwing him into a fire or into water. Please have pity and help us if you can!"

²³ Jesus replied, "Why do you say 'if you can'? Anything is possible for someone who has faith!"

²⁴ Right away the boy's father shouted, "I do have faith! Please help me to have even more."

²⁵ When Jesus saw that a crowd was gathering fast, he spoke sternly to the evil spirit that had kept the boy from speaking or hearing. He said, "I order you to come out of the boy! Don't ever bother him again."

²⁶ The spirit screamed and made the boy shake all over. Then it went out of him. The boy looked dead, and almost everyone said he was. ²⁷ But Jesus took hold of his hand and helped him stand up.

²⁸ After Jesus and the disciples had gone back home and were alone, they asked him, "Why couldn't we force out that demon?"

²⁹ Jesus answered, "Only prayer can force out that kind of demon."

## Jesus Again Speaks about His Death
(Matthew 17.22, 23; Luke 9.43b-45)

³⁰ Jesus left with his disciples and started through Galilee. He did not want anyone to know about it, ³¹ because he was teaching the disciples that the Son of Man would be handed over to people who would kill him. But three days later he would rise to life. ³² The disciples did not understand what Jesus meant, and they were afraid to ask.

## Who Is the Greatest?
(Matthew 18.1-5; Luke 9.46-48)

³³ Jesus and his disciples went to his home in Capernaum. After they were inside the house, Jesus asked them, "What were you arguing about along the way?" ³⁴ They had been arguing about which one of them was the greatest, and so they did not answer.

³⁵ After Jesus sat down and told the twelve disciples to gather around him, he said, "If you want the place of honor, you must become a slave and serve others!"

³⁶ Then Jesus had a child stand near him. He put his arm around the child and said, ³⁷ "When you welcome even a child because of me, you welcome me. And when you welcome me, you welcome the one who sent me."

## For or against Jesus
(Luke 9.49, 50)

³⁸ John said, "Teacher, we saw a man using your name to force demons out of people. But he wasn't one of us, and we told him to stop."

³⁹ Jesus said to his disciples:

Don't stop him! No one who works miracles in my name will soon turn and say something bad about me. ⁴⁰ Anyone who isn't against us is for us. ⁴¹ And anyone who gives you a cup of water in my name, just because you belong to me, will surely be rewarded.

## Temptations To Sin
(Matthew 18.6-9; Luke 17.1, 2)

⁴² It will be terrible for people who cause even one of my little followers to sin. Those people would be better off thrown into the ocean with a heavy stone tied around their necks. ⁴³⁻⁴⁴ So if your hand causes you to sin, cut it off! You would be better

off to go into life crippled than to have two hands and be thrown into the fires of hell that never go out. g 45-46 If your foot causes you to sin, chop it off. You would be better off to go into life lame than to have two feet and be thrown into hell. h 47 If your eye causes you to sin, get rid of it. You would be better off to go into God's kingdom with only one eye than to have two eyes and be thrown into hell. 48 The worms there never die, and the fire never stops burning.

49 Everyone must be salted with fire. i

50 Salt is good. But if it no longer tastes like salt, how can it be made salty again? Have salt among you and live at peace with each other. j

## Teaching about Divorce
### (Matthew 19.1-12; Luke 16.18)

**10** After Jesus left, he went to Judea and then on to the other side of the Jordan River. Once again large crowds came to him, and as usual, he taught them.

2 Some Pharisees wanted to test Jesus. So they came up to him and asked if it was right for a man to divorce his wife. 3 Jesus asked them, "What does the Law of Moses say about that?"

4 They answered, "Moses allows a man to write out divorce papers and send his wife away."

5 Jesus replied, "Moses gave you this law because you are so heartless. 6 But in the beginning God made a man and a woman. 7 That's why a man leaves his father and mother and gets married. 8 He becomes like one person with his wife. Then they are no longer two people, but one. 9 And no one should sepa-

rate a couple that God has joined together."

10 When Jesus and his disciples were back in the house, they asked him about what he had said. 11 He told them, "A man who divorces his wife and marries someone else is unfaithful to his wife. 12 A woman who divorces her husband k and marries again is also unfaithful."

## Jesus Blesses Little Children
### (Matthew 19.13-15; Luke 18.15-17)

13 Some people brought their children to Jesus so that he could bless them by placing his hands on them. But his disciples told the people to stop bothering him.

14 When Jesus saw this, he became angry and said, "Let the children come to me! Don't try to stop them. People who are like these little children belong to the kingdom of God. l 15 I promise you that you cannot get into God's kingdom, unless you accept it the way a child does." 16 Then Jesus took the children in his arms and blessed them by placing his hands on them.

## A Rich Man
### (Matthew 19.16-30; Luke 18.18-30)

17 As Jesus was walking down a road, a man ran up to him. He knelt down, and asked, "Good teacher, what can I do to have eternal life?"

18 Jesus replied, "Why do you call me good? Only God is good. 19 You know the commandments. 'Do not murder. Be faithful in marriage. Do not steal. Do not tell lies about others. Do not cheat. Respect your father and mother.' "

20 The man answered, "Teacher, I

---

g 9.43,44 *never go out:* Some manuscripts add, "The worms there never die, and the fire never stops burning." h 9.45,46 *thrown into hell:* Some manuscripts add, "The worms there never die, and the fire never stops burning." i 9.49 *salted with fire:* Some manuscripts add "and every sacrifice will be seasoned with salt." The verse may mean that Christ's followers must suffer because of their faith. j 9.50 *Have salt among you and live at peace with each other:* This may mean that when Christ's followers have to suffer because of their faith, they must still try to live at peace with each other. k 10.12 *A woman who divorces her husband:* Roman law let a woman divorce her husband, but Jewish law did not let a woman do this. l 10.14 *People who are like these little children belong to the kingdom of God:* Or "The kingdom of God belongs to people who are like these little children."

have obeyed all these commandments since I was a young man."

²¹ Jesus looked closely at the man. He liked him and said, "There's one thing you still need to do. Go sell everything you own. Give the money to the poor, and you will have riches in heaven. Then come with me."

²² When the man heard Jesus say this, he went away gloomy and sad because he was very rich.

²³ Jesus looked around and said to his disciples, "It's hard for rich people to get into God's kingdom!" ²⁴ The disciples were shocked to hear this. So Jesus told them again, "It's terribly hard$^m$ to get into God's kingdom! ²⁵ In fact, it's easier for a camel to go through the eye of a needle than for a rich person to get into God's kingdom."

²⁶ Jesus' disciples were even more amazed. They asked each other, "How can anyone ever be saved?"

²⁷ Jesus looked at them and said, "There are some things that people cannot do, but God can do anything."

²⁸ Peter replied, "Remember, we left everything to be your followers!"

²⁹ Jesus told him:

You can be sure that anyone who gives up home or brothers or sisters or mother or father or children or land for me and for the good news ³⁰ will be rewarded. In this world they will be given a hundred times as many houses and brothers and sisters and mothers and children and pieces of land, though they will also be mistreated. And in the world to come, they will have eternal life. ³¹ But many who are now first will be last, and many who are now last will be first.

### Jesus Again Tells about His Death
(Matthew 20.17-19; Luke 18.31-34)

³² The disciples were confused as Jesus led them toward Jerusalem, and his other followers were afraid. Once

again, Jesus took the twelve disciples aside and told them what was going to happen to him. He said:

³³ We are now on our way to Jerusalem where the Son of Man will be handed over to the chief priests and the teachers of the Law of Moses. They will sentence him to death and hand him over to foreigners, $^n$ ³⁴ who will make fun of him and spit on him. They will beat him and kill him. But three days later he will rise to life.

### The Request of James and John
(Matthew 20.20-28)

³⁵ James and John, the sons of Zebedee, came up to Jesus and asked, "Teacher, will you do us a favor?"

³⁶ Jesus asked them what they wanted, ³⁷ and they answered, "When you come into your glory, please let one of us sit at your right side and the other at your left." $^o$

³⁸ Jesus told them, "You don't really know what you're asking! Are you able to drink from the cup$^p$ that I must soon drink from or be baptized as I must be baptized?" $^q$

³⁹ "Yes, we are!" James and John answered.

Then Jesus replied, "You certainly will drink from the cup from which I must drink. And you will be baptized just as I must! ⁴⁰ But it isn't for me to say who will sit at my right side and at my left. That is for God to decide."

⁴¹ When the ten other disciples heard this, they were angry with James and John. ⁴² But Jesus called the disciples together and said:

You know that those foreigners who call themselves kings like to order their people around. And their great leaders have full power over the people they rule. ⁴³ But don't act like them. If you want to be great, you must be the servant of all the others. ⁴⁴ And if you want to be first,

---

$^m$**10.24** *hard*: Some manuscripts add "for people who trust in their wealth." Others add "for the rich." $^n$**10.33** *foreigners*: The Romans who ruled Judea at this time. $^o$**10.37** *right side . . . left*: The most powerful people in a kingdom sat at the right and left side of the king. $^p$**10.38** *drink from the cup*: In the Scriptures a "cup" is sometimes used as a symbol of suffering. To "drink from the cup" would be to suffer. $^q$**10.38** *as I must be baptized*: Baptism is used with the same meaning that "cup" has in this verse.

you must be everyone's slave. [45] The Son of Man did not come to be a slave master, but a slave who will give his life to rescue[r] many people.

## Jesus Heals Blind Bartimaeus
### (Matthew 20.29-34; Luke 18.35-43)

[46] Jesus and his disciples went to Jericho. And as they were leaving, they were followed by a large crowd. A blind beggar by the name of Bartimaeus son of Timaeus was sitting beside the road. [47] When he heard that it was Jesus from Nazareth, he shouted, "Jesus, Son of David,[s] have pity on me!" [48] Many people told the man to stop, but he shouted even louder, "Son of David, have pity on me!"

[49] Jesus stopped and said, "Call him over!"

They called out to the blind man and said, "Don't be afraid! Come on! He is calling for you." [50] The man threw off his coat as he jumped up and ran to Jesus.

[51] Jesus asked, "What do you want me to do for you?"

The blind man answered, "Master,[t] I want to see!"

[52] Jesus told him, "You may go. Your eyes are healed because of your faith."

Right away the man could see, and he went down the road with Jesus.

## Jesus Enters Jerusalem
### (Matthew 21.1-11; Luke 19.28-40; John 12.12-19)

**11** Jesus and his disciples reached Bethphage and Bethany near the Mount of Olives. When they were getting close to Jerusalem, Jesus sent two of them on ahead. [2] He told them, "Go into the next village. As soon as you enter it, you will find a young donkey that has never been ridden. Untie the donkey and bring it here. [3] If anyone asks why you are doing that, say, 'The Lord[u] needs it and will soon bring it back.'"

[4] The disciples left and found the donkey tied near a door that faced the street. While they were untying it, [5] some of the people standing there asked, "Why are you untying the donkey?" [6] They told them what Jesus had said, and the people let them take it.

[7] The disciples led the donkey to Jesus. They put some of their clothes on its back, and Jesus got on. [8] Many people spread clothes on the road, while others went to cut branches from the fields.[v]

[9] In front of Jesus and behind him, people went along shouting,

"Hooray![w]
God bless the one who comes
  in the name of the Lord!
[10] God bless the coming kingdom
  of our ancestor David.
Hooray for God
  in heaven above!"

[11] After Jesus had gone to Jerusalem, he went into the temple and looked around at everything. But since it was already late in the day, he went back to Bethany with the twelve disciples.

## Jesus Puts a Curse on a Fig Tree
### (Matthew 21.18, 19)

[12] When Jesus and his disciples left Bethany the next morning, he was hungry. [13] From a distance Jesus saw a fig tree covered with leaves, and he went to see if there were any figs on the tree. But there were not any, because it wasn't the season for figs. [14] So Jesus said to the tree, "Never again will anyone eat fruit from this tree!" The disciples heard him say this.

---

[r] **10.45** *rescue*: The Greek word often, though not always, means the payment of a price to free a slave or a prisoner.   [s] **10.47** *Son of David*: The Jewish people expected the Messiah to be from the family of King David, and for this reason the Messiah was often called the "Son of David."   [t] **10.51** *Master*: A Hebrew word that may also mean "Teacher."   [u] **11.3** *The Lord*: Or "The master of the donkey."   [v] **11.8** *spread . . . branches from the fields*: This was one way that the Jewish people welcomed a famous person.   [w] **11.9** *Hooray*: This translates a word that can mean "please save us." But it is most often used as a shout of praise to God.

## Jesus in the Temple
*(Matthew 21.12-17; Luke 19.45-48; John 2.13-22)*

15 After Jesus and his disciples reached Jerusalem, he went into the temple and began chasing out everyone who was selling and buying. He turned over the tables of the moneychangers and the benches of those who were selling doves. 16 Jesus would not let anyone carry things through the temple. 17 Then he taught the people and said, "The Scriptures say, 'My house should be called a place of worship for all nations.' But you have made it a place where robbers hide!"

18 The chief priests and the teachers of the Law of Moses heard what Jesus said, and they started looking for a way to kill him. They were afraid of him, because the crowds were completely amazed at his teaching.

19 That evening, Jesus and the disciples went outside the city.

## A Lesson from the Fig Tree
*(Matthew 21.20-22)*

20 As the disciples walked past the fig tree the next morning, they noticed that it was completely dried up, roots and all. 21 Peter remembered what Jesus had said to the tree. Then Peter said, "Teacher, look! The tree you put a curse on has dried up."

22 Jesus told his disciples:

Have faith in God! 23 If you have faith in God and don't doubt, you can tell this mountain to get up and jump into the sea, and it will. 24 Everything you ask for in prayer will be yours, if you only have faith.

25-26 Whenever you stand up to pray, you must forgive what others have done to you. Then your Father in heaven will forgive your sins.ˣ

## A Question about Jesus' Authority
*(Matthew 21.23-27; Luke 20.1-8)*

27 Jesus and his disciples returned to Jerusalem. And as he was walking through the temple, the chief priests, the nation's leaders, and the teachers of the Law of Moses came over to him. 28 They asked, "What right do you have to do these things? Who gave you this authority?"

29 Jesus answered, "I have just one question to ask you. If you answer it, I will tell you where I got the right to do these things. 30 Who gave John the right to baptize? Was it God in heaven or merely some human being?"

31 They thought it over and said to each other, "We can't say that God gave John this right. Jesus will ask us why we didn't believe John. 32 On the other hand, these people think that John was a prophet. So we can't say that it was merely some human who gave John the right to baptize."

They were afraid of the crowd 33 and told Jesus, "We don't know."

Jesus replied, "Then I won't tell you who gave me the right to do what I do."

## Renters of a Vineyard
*(Matthew 21.33-46; Luke 20.9-19)*

12 Jesus then told them this story: A farmer once planted a vineyard. He built a wall around it and dug a pit to crush the grapes in. He also built a lookout tower. Then he rented out his vineyard and left the country.

2 When it was harvest time, he sent a servant to get his share of the grapes. 3 The renters grabbed the servant. They beat him up and sent him away without a thing.

4 The owner sent another servant, but the renters beat him on the head and insulted him terribly. 5 Then the man sent another servant, and they killed him. He kept sending servant after servant. They beat some of them and killed others.

6 The owner had a son he loved very much. Finally, he sent his son to the renters because he thought they would respect him. 7 But they said to themselves, "Someday he will own this vineyard. Let's kill him! That way we can have it all for ourselves." 8 So they grabbed the

ˣ 11.25,26 *your sins*: Some manuscripts add, "But if you do not forgive others, God will not forgive you."

owner's son and killed him. Then they threw his body out of the vineyard.

⁹ Jesus asked, "What do you think the owner of the vineyard will do? He will come and kill those renters and let someone else have his vineyard. ¹⁰ You surely know that the Scriptures say,

'The stone that the builders
   tossed aside
is now the most important
   stone of all.
¹¹ This is something
   the Lord has done,
      and it is amazing to us.' "

¹² The leaders knew that Jesus was really talking about them, and they wanted to arrest him. But because they were afraid of the crowd, they let him alone and left.

### Paying Taxes
*(Matthew 22.15-22; Luke 20.20-26)*

¹³ The Pharisees got together with Herod's followers.ʸ Then they sent some men to trick Jesus into saying something wrong. ¹⁴ They went to him and said, "Teacher, we know that you are honest. You treat everyone with the same respect, no matter who they are. And you teach the truth about what God wants people to do. Tell us, should we pay taxes to the Emperor or not?"

¹⁵ Jesus knew what they were up to, and he said, "Why are you trying to test me? Show me a coin!"

¹⁶ They brought him a silver coin, and he asked, "Whose picture and name are on it?"

"The Emperor's," they answered.

¹⁷ Then Jesus told them, "Give the Emperor what belongs to him and give God what belongs to God." The men were amazed at Jesus.

### Life in the Future World
*(Matthew 22.23-33; Luke 20.27-40)*

¹⁸ The Sadducees did not believe that people would rise to life after death. So some of them came to Jesus and said:

¹⁹ Teacher, Moses wrote that if a married man dies and has no children, his brother should marry the widow. Their first son would then be thought of as the son of the dead brother. ²⁰ There were once seven brothers. The first one married, but died without having any children. ²¹ The second brother married his brother's widow, and he also died without having children. The same thing happened to the third brother, ²² and finally to all seven brothers. At last the woman died. ²³ When God raises people from death, whose wife will this woman be? After all, she had been married to all seven brothers.

²⁴ Jesus answered:

You are completely wrong! You don't know what the Scriptures teach. And you don't know anything about the power of God. ²⁵ When God raises people to life, they won't marry. They will be like the angels in heaven. ²⁶ You surely know about people being raised to life. You know that in the story about Moses and the burning bush, God said, "I am the God worshiped by Abraham, Isaac, and Jacob."ᶻ ²⁷ He isn't the God of the dead, but of the living. You Sadducees are all wrong.

### The Most Important Commandment
*(Matthew 22.34-40; Luke 10.25-28)*

²⁸ One of the teachers of the Law of Moses came up while Jesus and the Sadducees were arguing. When he heard Jesus give a good answer, he asked him, "What is the most important commandment?"

²⁹ Jesus answered, "The most important one says: 'People of Israel, you have only one Lord and God. ³⁰ You must love him with all your heart, soul, mind, and strength.' ³¹ The second most important commandment says: 'Love others as much as you love yourself.'

No other commandment is more important than these."

[32] The man replied, "Teacher, you are certainly right to say there is only one God. [33] It is also true that we must love God with all our heart, mind, and strength, and that we must love others as much as we love ourselves. These commandments are more important than all the sacrifices and offerings that we could possibly make."

[34] When Jesus saw that the man had given a sensible answer, he told him, "You are not far from God's kingdom." After this, no one dared ask Jesus any more questions.

### About David's Son
#### (Matthew 22.41-46; Luke 20.41-44)

[35] As Jesus was teaching in the temple, he said, "How can the teachers of the Law of Moses say that the Messiah will come from the family of King David? [36] The Holy Spirit had David say,

'The Lord said to my Lord:
Sit at my right side[a]
until I make your enemies
into a footstool for you.'

[37] If David called the Messiah his Lord, how can the Messiah be his son?"[b]

The large crowd enjoyed listening to Jesus teach.

### Jesus Condemns the Pharisees and the Teachers of the Law of Moses
#### (Matthew 23.1-36; Luke 20.45-47)

[38] As Jesus was teaching, he said:
Guard against the teachers of the Law of Moses! They love to walk around in long robes and be greeted in the market. [39] They like the front seats in the meeting places and the best seats at banquets. [40] But they cheat widows out of their homes and pray long prayers just to show off. They will be punished most of all.

### A Widow's Offering
#### (Luke 21.1-4)

[41] Jesus was sitting in the temple near the offering box and watching people put in their gifts. He noticed that many rich people were giving a lot of money. [42] Finally, a poor widow came up and put in two coins that were worth only a few pennies. [43] Jesus told his disciples to gather around him. Then he said:

I tell you that this poor widow has put in more than all the others. [44] Everyone else gave what they didn't need. But she is very poor and gave everything she had. Now she doesn't have a cent to live on.

### The Temple Will Be Destroyed
#### (Matthew 24.1, 2; Luke 21.5, 6)

**13** As Jesus was leaving the temple, one of his disciples said to him, "Teacher, look at these beautiful stones and wonderful buildings!"

[2] Jesus replied, "Do you see these huge buildings? They will certainly be torn down! Not one stone will be left in place."

### Warning about Trouble
#### (Matthew 24.3-14; Luke 21.7-19)

[3] Later, as Jesus was sitting on the Mount of Olives across from the temple, Peter, James, John, and Andrew came to him in private. [4] They asked, "When will these things happen? What will be the sign that they are about to take place?"

[5] Jesus answered:
Watch out and don't let anyone fool you! [6] Many will come and claim to be me. They will use my name and fool many people.

[7] When you hear about wars and threats of wars, don't be afraid. These things will have to happen first, but that isn't the end. [8] Nations and kingdoms will go to war against each other. There will be earthquakes in many places, and people will starve to death. But this is just the beginning of troubles.

[9] Be on your guard! You will be taken to courts and beaten with whips in their meeting places. And because of me, you will have to stand before rulers and kings to tell

about your faith. [10] But before the end comes, the good news must be preached to all nations.

[11] When you are arrested, don't worry about what you will say. You will be given the right words when the time comes. But you will not really be the ones speaking. Your words will come from the Holy Spirit.

[12] Brothers and sisters will betray each other and have each other put to death. Parents will betray their own children, and children will turn against their parents and have them killed. [13] Everyone will hate you because of me. But if you keep on being faithful right to the end, you will be saved.

### The Horrible Thing
(Matthew 24.15-21; Luke 21.20-24)

[14] Someday you will see that "Horrible Thing" where it should not be. [c] Everyone who reads this must try to understand! If you are living in Judea at that time, run to the mountains. [15] If you are on the roof [d] of your house, don't go inside to get anything. [16] If you are out in the field, don't go back for your coat. [17] It will be an awful time for women who are expecting babies or nursing young children. [18] Pray that it won't happen in winter. [e] [19] This will be the worst time of suffering since God created the world, and nothing this terrible will ever happen again. [20] If the Lord doesn't make the time shorter, no one will be left alive. But because of his chosen and special ones, he will make the time shorter.

[21] If someone should say, "Here is the Messiah!" or "There he is!" don't believe it. [22] False messiahs and false prophets will come and work miracles and signs. They will even try to fool God's chosen ones. [23] But be on your guard! That's why I am telling you these things now.

### When the Son of Man Appears
(Matthew 24.29-31; Luke 21.25-28)

[24] In those days, right after that time of suffering,

"The sun will become dark,
and the moon
    will no longer shine.
[25] The stars will fall,
and the powers in the sky [f]
    will be shaken."

[26] Then the Son of Man will be seen coming in the clouds with great power and glory. [27] He will send his angels to gather his chosen ones from all over the earth.

### A Lesson from a Fig Tree
(Matthew 24.32-35; Luke 21.29-33)

[28] Learn a lesson from a fig tree. When its branches sprout and start putting out leaves, you know summer is near. [29] So when you see all these things happening, you will know that the time has almost come. [g] [30] You can be sure that some of the people of this generation will still be alive when all this happens. [31] The sky and the earth will not last forever, but my words will.

### No One Knows the Day or Time
(Matthew 24.36-44)

[32] No one knows the day or the time. The angels in heaven don't know, and the Son himself doesn't know. Only the Father knows. [33] So watch out and be ready! You don't know when the time will come. [34] It is like what happens when a man goes away for a while and places his servants in charge of everything. He tells each of them what to do, and he orders the guard to keep alert. [35] So be alert! You don't know when the master of the house will come back. It could be in the evening or

---

[c] **13.14** *where it should not be*: Probably the holy place in the temple.   [d] **13.15** *roof*: See the note at 2.4.   [e] **13.18** *in winter*: In Palestine the winters are cold and rainy and make travel difficult.   [f] **13.25** *the powers in the sky*: In ancient times people thought that the stars were spiritual powers.   [g] **13.29** *the time has almost come*: Or "he (that is, the Son of Man) will soon be here."

at midnight or before dawn or in the morning. ³⁶But if he comes suddenly, don't let him find you asleep. ³⁷I tell everyone just what I have told you. Be alert!

## A Plot To Kill Jesus
(Matthew 26.1 5; Luke 22.1, 2, John 11.45-53)

**14** It was now two days before Passover and the Festival of Thin Bread. The chief priests and the teachers of the Law of Moses were planning how they could sneak around and have Jesus arrested and put to death. ²They were saying, "We must not do it during the festival, because the people will riot."

## At Bethany
(Matthew 26.6-13; John 12.1-8)

³Jesus was eating in Bethany at the home of Simon, who once had leprosy,ʰ when a woman came in with a very expensive bottle of sweet-smelling perfume.ⁱ After breaking it open, she poured the perfume on Jesus' head. ⁴This made some of the guests angry, and they complained, "Why such a waste? ⁵We could have sold this perfume for more than three hundred silver coins and given the money to the poor!" So they started saying cruel things to the woman.

⁶But Jesus said:

Leave her alone! Why are you bothering her? She has done a beautiful thing for me. ⁷You will always have the poor with you. And whenever you want to, you can give to them. But you won't always have me here with you. ⁸She has done all she could by pouring perfume on my body to prepare it for burial. ⁹You may be sure that wherever the good news is told all over the world, people will remember what she has done. And they will tell others.

## Judas and the Chief Priests
(Matthew 26.14-16; Luke 22.3-6)

¹⁰Judas Iscariotʲ was one of the twelve disciples. He went to the chief priests and offered to help them arrest Jesus. ¹¹They were glad to hear this, and they promised to pay him. So Judas started looking for a good chance to betray Jesus.

## Jesus Eats with His Disciples
(Matthew 26.17-25; Luke 22.7-14, 21-23; John 13.21-30)

¹²It was the first day of the Festival of Thin Bread, and the Passover lambs were being killed. Jesus' disciples asked him, "Where do you want us to prepare the Passover meal?"

¹³Jesus said to two of the disciples, "Go into the city, where you will meet a man carrying a jar of water.ᵏ Follow him, ¹⁴and when he goes into a house, say to the owner, 'Our teacher wants to know if you have a room where he can eat the Passover meal with his disciples.' ¹⁵The owner will take you upstairs and show you a large room furnished and ready for you to use. Prepare the meal there."

¹⁶The two disciples went into the city and found everything just as Jesus had told them. So they prepared the Passover meal.

¹⁷⁻¹⁸While Jesus and the twelve disciples were eating together that evening, he said, "The one who will betray me is now eating with me."

¹⁹This made the disciples sad, and one after another they said to Jesus, "You surely don't mean me!"

²⁰He answered, "It is one of you twelve men who is eating from this dish with me. ²¹The Son of Man will die, just as the Scriptures say. But it is going to be terrible for the one who betrays me. That man would be better off if he had never been born."

ʰ14.3 leprosy: In biblical times the word "leprosy" was used for many different skin diseases. ⁱ14.3 sweet-smelling perfume: The Greek text has "perfume made of pure spikenard," a plant used to make perfume. ʲ14.10 Iscariot: See the note at 3.19. ᵏ14.13 a man carrying a jar of water: A male slave carrying water could mean that the family was rich.

## The Lord's Supper

(Matthew 26.26-30; Luke 22.14-23;
1 Corinthians 11.23-25)

22 During the meal Jesus took some bread in his hands. He blessed the bread and broke it. Then he gave it to his disciples and said, "Take this. It is my body."

23 Jesus picked up a cup of wine and gave thanks to God. He gave it to his disciples, and they all drank some. 24 Then he said, "This is my blood, which is poured out for many people, and with it God makes his agreement. 25 From now on I will not drink any wine, until I drink new wine in God's kingdom." 26 Then they sang a hymn and went out to the Mount of Olives.

## Peter's Promise

(Matthew 26.31-35; Luke 22.31-34; John 13.36-38)

27 Jesus said to his disciples, "All of you will reject me, as the Scriptures say,

'I will strike down
   the shepherd,
and the sheep
   will be scattered.'

28 But after I am raised to life, I will go ahead of you to Galilee."

29 Peter spoke up, "Even if all the others reject you, I never will!"

30 Jesus replied, "This very night before a rooster crows twice, you will say three times that you don't know me."

31 But Peter was so sure of himself that he said, "Even if I have to die with you, I will never say that I don't know you!"

All the others said the same thing.

## Jesus Prays

(Matthew 26.36-46; Luke 22.39-46)

32 Jesus went with his disciples to a place called Gethsemane, and he told them, "Sit here while I pray."

33 Jesus took along Peter, James, and John. He was sad and troubled and

34 told them, "I am so sad that I feel as if I am dying. Stay here and keep awake with me."

35-36 Jesus walked on a little way. Then he knelt down on the ground and prayed, "Father, l if it is possible, don't let this happen to me! Father, you can do anything. Don't make me suffer by having me drink from this cup. m But do what you want, and not what I want."

37 When Jesus came back and found the disciples sleeping, he said to Simon Peter, "Are you asleep? Can't you stay awake for just one hour? 38 Stay awake and pray that you won't be tested. You want to do what is right, but you are weak."

39 Jesus went back and prayed the same prayer. 40 But when he returned to the disciples, he found them sleeping again. They simply could not keep their eyes open, and they did not know what to say.

41 When Jesus returned to the disciples the third time, he said, "Are you still sleeping and resting? n Enough of that! The time has come for the Son of Man to be handed over to sinners. 42 Get up! Let's go. The one who will betray me is already here."

## Jesus Is Arrested

(Matthew 26.47-56; Luke 22.47-53; John 18.3-12)

43 Jesus was still speaking, when Judas the betrayer came up. He was one of the twelve disciples, and a mob of men armed with swords and clubs were with him. They had been sent by the chief priests, the nation's leaders, and the teachers of the Law of Moses. 44 Judas had told them ahead of time, "Arrest the man I greet with a kiss. o Tie him up tight and lead him away."

45 Judas walked right up to Jesus and said, "Teacher!" Then Judas kissed him, 46 and the men grabbed Jesus and arrested him.

47 Someone standing there pulled out a sword. He struck the servant of the high priest and cut off his ear.

l 14.35,36 Father: The Greek text has "Abba," which is an Aramaic word meaning "father." m 14.35,36 by having me drink from this cup: See the note at 10.38. n 14.41 Are you still sleeping and resting?: Or "You may as well keep on sleeping and resting." o 14.44 greet with a kiss: It was the custom for people to greet each other with a kiss on the cheek.

48 Jesus said to the mob, "Why do you come with swords and clubs to arrest me like a criminal? 49 Day after day I was with you and taught in the temple, and you didn't arrest me. But what the Scriptures say must come true."

50 All of Jesus' disciples ran off and left him. 51 One of them was a young man who was wearing only a linen cloth. And when the men grabbed him, 52 he left the cloth behind and ran away naked.

### Jesus Is Questioned by the Council

*(Matthew 26.57-68; Luke 22.54, 55, 63-71; John 18.13, 14, 19-24)*

53 Jesus was led off to the high priest. Then the chief priests, the nation's leaders, and the teachers of the Law of Moses all met together. 54 Peter had followed at a distance. And when he reached the courtyard of the high priest's house, he sat down with the guards to warm himself beside a fire.

55 The chief priests and the whole council tried to find someone to accuse Jesus of a crime, so they could put him to death. But they could not find anyone to accuse him. 56 Many people did tell lies against Jesus, but they did not agree on what they said. 57 Finally, some men stood up and lied about him. They said, 58 "We heard him say he would tear down this temple that we built. He also claimed that in three days he would build another one without any help." 59 But even then they did not agree on what they said.

60 The high priest stood up in the council and asked Jesus, "Why don't you say something in your own defense? Don't you hear the charges they are making against you?" 61 But Jesus kept quiet and did not say a word. The high priest asked him another question, "Are you the Messiah, the Son of the glorious God?"p

62 "Yes, I am!" Jesus answered.

"Soon you will see
the Son of Man

sitting at the right sideq
of God All-Powerful,
and coming with the clouds
of heaven."

63 At once the high priest ripped his robe apart and shouted, "Why do we need more witnesses? 64 You heard him claim to be God! What is your decision?" They all agreed that he should be put to death.

65 Some of the people started spitting on Jesus. They blindfolded him, hit him with their fists, and said, "Tell us who hit you!" Then the guards took charge of Jesus and beat him.

### Peter Says He Doesn't Know Jesus

*(Matthew 26.69-75; Luke 22.56-62; John 18.15-18, 25-27)*

66 While Peter was still in the courtyard, a servant girl of the high priest came up 67 and saw Peter warming himself by the fire. She stared at him and said, "You were with Jesus from Nazareth!"

68 Peter replied, "That isn't true! I don't know what you're talking about. I don't have any idea what you mean." He went out to the gate, and a rooster crowed.r

69 The servant girl saw Peter again and said to the people standing there, "This man is one of them!"

70 "No, I'm not!" Peter replied.

A little while later some of the people said to Peter, "You certainly are one of them. You're a Galilean!"

71 This time Peter began to curse and swear, "I don't even know the man you're talking about!"

72 Right away the rooster crowed a second time. Then Peter remembered that Jesus had told him, "Before a rooster crows twice, you will say three times that you don't know me." So Peter started crying.

p 14.61 *Son of the glorious God*: "Son of God" was one of the titles used for the kings of Israel.  q 14.62 *right side*: See the note at 12.36.  r 14.68 *a rooster crowed*: These words are not in some manuscripts.

### Pilate Questions Jesus
*(Matthew 27.1, 2, 11-14; Luke 23.1-5; John 18.28-38)*

**15** Early the next morning the chief priests, the nation's leaders, and the teachers of the Law of Moses met together with the whole Jewish council. They tied up Jesus and led him off to Pilate.

2 He asked Jesus, "Are you the king of the Jews?"

"Those are your words," Jesus answered.

3 The chief priests brought many charges against Jesus. 4 Then Pilate questioned him again, "Don't you have anything to say? Don't you hear what crimes they say you have done?" 5 But Jesus did not answer, and Pilate was amazed.

### The Death Sentence
*(Matthew 27.15-26; Luke 23.13-25; John 18.39—19.16)*

6 During Passover, Pilate always freed one prisoner chosen by the people. 7 And at that time there was a prisoner named Barabbas. He and some others had been arrested for murder during a riot. 8 The crowd now came and asked Pilate to set a prisoner free, just as he usually did.

9 Pilate asked them, "Do you want me to free the king of the Jews?" 10 Pilate knew that the chief priests had brought Jesus to him because they were jealous. 11 But the chief priests told the crowd to ask Pilate to free Barabbas.

12 Then Pilate asked the crowd, "What do you want me to do with this man you say is *s* the king of the Jews?"

13 They yelled, "Nail him to a cross!"

14 Pilate asked, "But what crime has he done?"

"Nail him to a cross!" they yelled even louder.

15 Pilate wanted to please the crowd. So he set Barabbas free. Then he ordered his soldiers to beat Jesus with a whip and nail him to a cross.

### Soldiers Make Fun of Jesus
*(Matthew 27.27-30; John 19.2, 3)*

16 The soldiers led Jesus inside the courtyard of the fortress *t* and called together the rest of the troops. 17 They put a purple robe *u* on him, and on his head they placed a crown that they had made out of thorn branches. 18 They made fun of Jesus and shouted, "Hey, you king of the Jews!" 19 Then they beat him on the head with a stick. They spit on him and knelt down and pretended to worship him.

20 When the soldiers had finished making fun of Jesus, they took off the purple robe. They put his own clothes back on him and led him off to be nailed to a cross. 21 Simon from Cyrene happened to be coming in from a farm, and they forced him to carry Jesus' cross. Simon was the father of Alexander and Rufus.

### Jesus Is Nailed to a Cross
*(Matthew 27.31-44; Luke 23.27-43; John 19.17-27)*

22 The soldiers took Jesus to Golgotha, which means "Place of a Skull." *v* 23 There they gave him some wine mixed with a drug to ease the pain, but he refused to drink it.

24 They nailed Jesus to a cross and gambled to see who would get his clothes. 25 It was about nine o'clock in the morning when they nailed him to the cross. 26 On it was a sign that told why he was nailed there. It read, "This is the King of the Jews." 27-28 The soldiers also nailed two criminals on crosses, one to the right of Jesus and the other to his left. *w*

29 People who passed by said terrible things about Jesus. They shook their heads and shouted, "Ha! So you're the one who claimed you could tear down

---

*s* **15.12** *this man you say is:* These words are not in some manuscripts.   *t* **15.16** *fortress:* The place where the Roman governor stayed. It was probably at Herod's palace west of Jerusalem, though it may have been Fortress Antonia, north of the temple, where the Roman troops were stationed.   *u* **15.17** *purple robe:* This was probably a Roman soldier's robe.   *v* **15.22** *Place of a Skull:* The place was probably given this name because it was near a large rock in the shape of a human skull.   *w* **15.27-28** *left:* Some manuscripts add, "So the Scriptures came true which say, 'He was accused of being a criminal.'"

the temple and build it again in three days. [30] Save yourself and come down from the cross!"

[31] The chief priests and the teachers of the Law of Moses also made fun of Jesus. They said to each other, "He saved others, but he can't save himself. [32] If he is the Messiah, the king of Israel, let him come down from the cross! Then we will see and believe." The two criminals also said cruel things to Jesus.

### The Death of Jesus

*(Matthew 27.45-56; Luke 23.44-49; John 19.28-30)*

[33] About noon the sky turned dark and stayed that way until around three o'clock. [34] Then about that time Jesus shouted, "Eloi, Eloi, lema sabachthani?"[x] which means, "My God, my God, why have you deserted me?"

[35] Some of the people standing there heard Jesus and said, "He is calling for Elijah."[y] [36] One of them ran and grabbed a sponge. After he had soaked it in wine, he put it on a stick and held it up to Jesus. He said, "Let's wait and see if Elijah will come[z] and take him down!" [37] Jesus shouted and then died.

[38] At once the curtain in the temple[a] tore in two from top to bottom.

[39] A Roman army officer was standing in front of Jesus. When the officer saw how Jesus died, he said, "This man really was the Son of God!"

[40-41] Some women were looking on from a distance. They had come with Jesus to Jerusalem. But even before this they had been his followers and had helped him while he was in Galilee. Mary Magdalene and Mary the mother of the younger James and of Joseph were two of these women. Salome was also one of them.

### Jesus Is Buried

*(Matthew 27.57-61; Luke 23.50-56; John 19.38-42)*

[42] It was now the evening before the Sabbath, and the Jewish people were getting ready for that sacred day. [43] A man named Joseph from Arimathea was brave enough to ask Pilate for the body of Jesus. Joseph was a highly respected member of the Jewish council, and he was also waiting for God's kingdom to come.

[44] Pilate was surprised to hear that Jesus was already dead, and he called in the army officer to find out if Jesus had been dead very long. [45] After the officer told him, Pilate let Joseph have Jesus' body.

[46] Joseph bought a linen cloth and took the body down from the cross. He had it wrapped in the cloth, and he put it in a tomb that had been cut into solid rock. Then he rolled a big stone against the entrance to the tomb.

[47] Mary Magdalene and Mary the mother of Joseph were watching and saw where the body was placed.

### Jesus Is Alive

*(Matthew 28.1-8; Luke 24.1-12; John 20.1-10)*

**16** After the Sabbath, Mary Magdalene, Salome, and Mary the mother of James bought some spices to put on Jesus' body. [2] Very early on Sunday morning, just as the sun was coming up, they went to the tomb. [3] On their way, they were asking one another, "Who will roll the stone away from the entrance for us?" [4] But when they looked, they saw that the stone had already been rolled away. And it was a huge stone!

[5] The women went into the tomb, and on the right side they saw a young man in a white robe sitting there. They were alarmed.

[6] The man said, "Don't be alarmed! You are looking for Jesus from Nazareth, who was nailed to a cross. God has raised him to life, and he isn't here. You can see the place where they put his body. [7] Now go and tell his disciples, and especially Peter, that he will go

---

[x] 15.34 *Eloi . . . sabachthani:* These words are in Aramaic, a language spoken in Palestine during the time of Jesus. [y] 15.35 *Elijah:* The name "Elijah" sounds something like "Eloi," which means "my God." [z] 15.36 *see if Elijah will come:* See the note at 6.15. [a] 15.38 *curtain in the temple:* There were two curtains in the temple. One was at the entrance, and the other separated the holy place from the most holy place that the Jewish people thought of as God's home on earth. The second curtain is probably the one which is meant.

ahead of you to Galilee. You will see him there, just as he told you."

⁸ When the women ran from the tomb, they were confused and shaking all over. They were too afraid to tell anyone what had happened.

## ONE OLD ENDING
## TO MARK'S GOSPEL ᵇ

### Jesus Appears to Mary Magdalene
*(Matthew 28.9, 10; John 20.11-18)*

⁹ Very early on the first day of the week, after Jesus had risen to life, he appeared to Mary Magdalene. Earlier he had forced seven demons out of her. ¹⁰ She left and told his friends, who were crying and mourning. ¹¹ Even though they heard that Jesus was alive and that Mary had seen him, they would not believe it.

### Jesus Appears to Two Disciples
*(Luke 24.13-35)*

¹² Later, Jesus appeared in another form to two disciples, as they were on their way out of the city. ¹³ But when these disciples told what had happened, the others would not believe.

### What Jesus' Followers Must Do
*(Matthew 28.16-20; Luke 24.36-49; John 20.19-23; Acts 1.6-8)*

¹⁴ Afterwards, Jesus appeared to his eleven disciples as they were eating. He scolded them because they were too stubborn to believe the ones who had seen him after he had been raised to life. ¹⁵ Then he told them:

Go and preach the good news to everyone in the world. ¹⁶ Anyone who believes me and is baptized will be saved. But anyone who refuses to believe me will be condemned. ¹⁷ Everyone who believes me will be able to do wonderful things. By using my name they will force out demons, and they will speak new languages. ¹⁸ They will handle snakes and will drink poison and not be hurt. They will also heal sick people by placing their hands on them.

### Jesus Returns to Heaven
*(Luke 24.50-53; Acts 1.9-11)*

¹⁹ After the Lord Jesus had said these things to the disciples, he was taken back up to heaven where he sat down at the right side ᶜ of God. ²⁰ Then the disciples left and preached everywhere. The Lord was with them, and the miracles they worked proved that their message was true.

## ANOTHER OLD ENDING
## TO MARK'S GOSPEL ᵈ

⁹⁻¹⁰ The women quickly told Peter and his friends what had happened. Later, Jesus sent the disciples to the east and to the west with his sacred and everlasting message of how people can be saved forever.

ᵇ 16.9 *One Old Ending to Mark's Gospel*: Verses 9-20 are not in some manuscripts.
ᶜ 16.19 *right side*: See the note at 12.36.   ᵈ 16.9,10 *Another Old Ending to Mark's Gospel*: Some manuscripts and early translations have both this shorter ending and the longer one (verses 9-20).

# LUKE

## ABOUT THIS BOOK

God's love is for everyone! Jesus came into the world to be the Savior of all people! These are two of the main thoughts in this book. Several of the best known stories that Jesus used for teaching about God's love are found only in Luke's Gospel: The Good Samaritan (10.25-37), A Lost Sheep (15.1-7), and A Lost Son (15.11-32). Only Luke tells how Jesus visited in the home of a hated tax collector (19.1-10) and promised life in paradise to a dying criminal (23.39-43).

Luke mentions God's Spirit more than any of the other New Testament writers. For example, the power of the Spirit was with John the Baptist from the time he was born (1.15). And the angel promised Mary, "The Holy Spirit will come down to you . . . So your child will be called the holy Son of God" (1.35). Jesus followed the Spirit (4.1, 14, 8; 10.21) and taught that the Spirit is God's greatest gift (11.13).

Luke shows how important prayer was to Jesus. Jesus prayed often: after being baptized (3.21), before choosing the disciples (6.12), before asking his disciples who they thought he was (9.18), and before giving up his liffe on the cross (23.34, 46). From Luke we learn of three stories that Jesus told to teach about prayer (11.5-9; 18.1-8, 9-14).

An important part of Luke's story is the way in which he shows the concern of Jesus for the poor: the good news is preached to them (4.18; 7.22), they receive God's blessings (6.20), they are invited to the great feast (14.13, 21), the poor man Lazarus is taken to heaven by angels (16.20, 22), and Jesus commands his disciples to sell what they have and give the money to the poor (12.33).

To make sure that readers would understand that Jesus was raised physically from death, Luke reports that the risen Jesus ate a piece of fish (24.42, 43). There could be no mistake about the risen Jesus: he was not a ghost. His being raised from death was real and not someone's imagination. Luke also wrote another book—the Acts of the Apostles—to show what happened to Jesus' followers after he was raised from death and taken up to heaven. No other Gospel has a second volume that continues the story.

Luke closes this first book that he wrote by telling that Jesus returned to heaven. But right before Jesus leaves, he tells his disciples:

> The Scriptures say that the Messiah must suffer, then three days later he will rise from death. They also say that all people of every nation must be told in my name to turn to God, in order to be forgiven. So beginning in Jerusalem, you must tell everything that has happened. (24.46-48)

## A QUICK LOOK AT THIS BOOK

73

---

**1** Many people have tried to tell the story of what God has done among us. ² They wrote what we had been told by the ones who were there in the beginning and saw what happened. ³ So I made a careful study*a* of everything and then decided to write and tell you exactly what took place. Honorable Theophilus, ⁴ I have done this to let you know the truth about what you have heard.

### An Angel Tells about the Birth of John

⁵ When Herod was king of Judea, there was a priest by the name of Zechariah from the priestly group of Abijah. His wife Elizabeth was from the family of Aaron.*b* ⁶ Both of them were good people and pleased the Lord God by obeying all that he had commanded. ⁷ But they did not have children. Elizabeth could not have any, and both Zechariah and Elizabeth were already old.

⁸ One day Zechariah's group of priests were on duty, and he was serving God as a priest. ⁹ According to the custom of the priests, he had been chosen to go into the Lord's temple that day and to burn incense,*c* ¹⁰ while the people stood outside praying.

¹¹ All at once an angel from the Lord appeared to Zechariah at the right side of the altar. ¹² Zechariah was confused and afraid when he saw the angel. ¹³ But the angel told him:

Don't be afraid, Zechariah! God has heard your prayers. Your wife Elizabeth will have a son, and you must name him John. ¹⁴ His birth will make you very happy, and many people will be glad. ¹⁵ Your son will be a great servant of the Lord. He must never drink wine or beer, and the power of the Holy Spirit will be with him from the time he is born.

¹⁶ John will lead many people in Israel to turn back to the Lord their God. ¹⁷ He will go ahead of the Lord with the same power and spirit that Elijah*d* had. And because of John, parents will be more thoughtful of their children. And people who now disobey God will begin to think as they ought to. That is how John will get people ready for the Lord.

¹⁸ Zechariah said to the angel, "How will I know this is going to happen? My wife and I are both very old."

¹⁹ The angel answered, "I am Gabriel, God's servant, and I was sent to tell you this good news. ²⁰ You have not believed what I have said. So you will not be able to say a thing until all this happens. But everything will take place when it is supposed to."

²¹ The crowd was waiting for Zechariah and kept wondering why he was staying so long in the temple. ²² When he did come out, he could not speak, and they knew he had seen a vision. He motioned to them with his hands, but did not say a thing.

²³ When Zechariah's time of service in the temple was over, he went home. ²⁴ Soon after that, his wife was expecting a baby, and for five months she did not leave the house. She said to herself, ²⁵ "What the Lord has done for me will keep people from looking down on me."*e*

---

*a* **1.3** *a careful study*: Or "a study from the beginning." *b* **1.5** *Aaron*: The brother of Moses and the first priest. *c* **1.9** *burn incense*: This was done twice a day, once in the morning and again in the late afternoon. *d* **1.17** *Elijah*: The prophet Elijah was known for his power to work miracles. *e* **1.25** *keep people from looking down on me*: When a married woman could not have children, it was thought that the Lord was punishing her.

## An Angel Tells about the Birth of Jesus

26 One month later God sent the angel Gabriel to the town of Nazareth in Galilee 27 with a message for a virgin named Mary. She was engaged to Joseph from the family of King David. 28 The angel greeted Mary and said, "You are truly blessed! The Lord is with you."

29 Mary was confused by the angel's words and wondered what they meant. 30 Then the angel told Mary, "Don't be afraid! God is pleased with you, 31 and you will have a son. His name will be Jesus. 32 He will be great and will be called the Son of God Most High. The Lord God will make him king, as his ancestor David was. 33 He will rule the people of Israel forever, and his kingdom will never end."

34 Mary asked the angel, "How can this happen? I am not married!"

35 The angel answered, "The Holy Spirit will come down to you, and God's power will come over you. So your child will be called the holy Son of God. 36 Your relative Elizabeth is also going to have a son, even though she is old. No one thought she could ever have a baby, but in three months she will have a son. 37 Nothing is impossible for God!"

38 Mary said, "I am the Lord's servant! Let it happen as you have said." And the angel left her.

## Mary Visits Elizabeth

39 A short time later Mary hurried to a town in the hill country of Judea. 40 She went into Zechariah's home, where she greeted Elizabeth. 41 When Elizabeth heard Mary's greeting, her baby moved within her.

The Holy Spirit came upon Elizabeth. 42 Then in a loud voice she said to Mary:
God has blessed you more than any other woman! He has also blessed the child you will have. 43 Why should the mother of my Lord come to me? 44 As soon as I heard your greeting, my baby became happy and moved within me.

45 The Lord has blessed you because you believed that he will keep his promise.

## Mary's Song of Praise

46 Mary said:

With all my heart
47    I praise the Lord,
and I am glad
    because of God my Savior.
48 God cares for me,
    his humble servant.
From now on,
all people will say
    God has blessed me.
49 God All-Powerful has done
great things for me,
    and his name is holy.
50 He always shows mercy
to everyone
    who worships him.
51 The Lord has used
    his powerful arm
to scatter those
    who are proud.
52 God drags strong rulers
    from their thrones
and puts humble people
    in places of power.
53 God gives the hungry
    good things to eat,
and sends the rich away
    with nothing.
54 God helps his servant Israel
and is always merciful
    to his people.
55 The Lord made this promise
    to our ancestors,
to Abraham and his family
    forever!

56 Mary stayed with Elizabeth about three months. Then she went back home.

## The Birth of John the Baptist

57 When Elizabeth's son was born, 58 her neighbors and relatives heard how kind the Lord had been to her, and they too were glad.

59 Eight days later they did for the child what the Law of Moses commands.f They were going to name him

---

f 1.59 what the Law of Moses commands: This refers to circumcision. It is the cutting off of skin from the private part of Jewish boys eight days after birth to show that they belong to the Lord.

Zechariah, after his father. ⁶⁰ But Elizabeth said, "No! His name is John."

⁶¹ The people argued, "No one in your family has ever been named John." ⁶² So they motioned to Zechariah to find out what he wanted to name his son.

⁶³ Zechariah asked for a writing tablet. Then he wrote, "His name is John." Everyone was amazed. ⁶⁴ Right away, Zechariah started speaking and praising God.

⁶⁵ All the neighbors were frightened because of what had happened, and everywhere in the hill country people kept talking about these things. ⁶⁶ Everyone who heard about this wondered what this child would grow up to be. They knew that the Lord was with him.

### Zechariah Praises the Lord

⁶⁷ The Holy Spirit came upon Zechariah, and he began to speak:

⁶⁸ Praise the Lord,
    the God of Israel!
He has come
    to save his people.
⁶⁹ Our God has given us
    a mighty Savior ᵍ
from the family
    of David his servant.
⁷⁰ Long ago the Lord promised
    by the words
    of his holy prophets
⁷¹ to save us from our enemies
    and from everyone
    who hates us.
⁷² God said he would be kind
    to our people and keep
    his sacred promise.
⁷³ He told our ancestor Abraham
⁷⁴ that he would rescue us
    from our enemies.
Then we could serve him
    without fear,

⁷⁵ by being holy and good
    as long as we live.

⁷⁶ You, my son, will be called
    a prophet of God
    in heaven above.
You will go ahead of the Lord
    to get everything ready
    for him.
⁷⁷ You will tell his people
    that they can be saved
    when their sins
    are forgiven.
⁷⁸ God's love and kindness
    will shine upon us
like the sun that rises
    in the sky. ʰ
⁷⁹ On us who live
    in the dark shadow
    of death
this light will shine
    to guide us
    into a life of peace.

⁸⁰ As John grew up, God's Spirit gave him great power. John lived in the desert until the time he was sent to the people of Israel.

### The Birth of Jesus
#### (Matthew 1.18-25)

**2** About that time Emperor Augustus gave orders for the names of all the people to be listed in record books. ⁱ ² These first records were made when Quirinius was governor of Syria. ʲ ³ Everyone had to go to their own hometown to be listed. ⁴ So Joseph had to leave Nazareth in Galilee and go to Bethlehem in Judea. Long ago Bethlehem had been King David's hometown, and Joseph went there because he was from David's family. ⁵ Mary was engaged to Joseph and traveled with him to Bethlehem. She was soon going to have a baby, ⁶ and while they were there, ⁷ she gave birth to her first-born ᵏ son. She dressed him

---

ᵍ **1.69** *a mighty Savior*: The Greek text has "a horn of salvation." In the Scriptures animal horns are often a symbol of great strength.   ʰ **1.78** *like the sun that rises in the sky*: Or "like the Messiah coming from heaven."   ⁱ **2.1** *names . . . listed in record books*: This was done so that everyone could be made to pay taxes to the Emperor.   ʲ **2.2** *Quirinius was governor of Syria*: It is known that Quirinius made a record of the people in A.D. 6 or 7. But the exact date of the record taking that Luke mentions is not known.   ᵏ **2.7** *first-born*: The Jewish people said that the first-born son in each of their families belonged to the Lord.

in baby clothes<sup>l</sup> and laid him on a bed of hay, because there was no room for them in the inn.

## The Shepherds

8 That night in the fields near Bethlehem some shepherds were guarding their sheep. 9 All at once an angel came down to them from the Lord, and the brightness of the Lord's glory flashed around them. The shepherds were frightened. 10 But the angel said, "Don't be afraid! I have good news for you, which will make everyone happy. 11 This very day in King David's hometown a Savior was born for you. He is Christ the Lord. 12 You will know who he is, because you will find him dressed in baby clothes and lying on a bed of hay."

13 Suddenly many other angels came down from heaven and joined in praising God. They said:

14 "Praise God in heaven!
   Peace on earth to everyone
      who pleases God."

15 After the angels had left and gone back to heaven, the shepherds said to each other, "Let's go to Bethlehem and see what the Lord has told us about." 16 They hurried off and found Mary and Joseph, and they saw the baby lying on a bed of hay. 17 When the shepherds saw Jesus, they told his parents what the angel had said about him. 18 Everyone listened and was surprised. 19 But Mary kept thinking about all this and wondering what it meant.

20 As the shepherds returned to their sheep, they were praising God and saying wonderful things about him. Everything they had seen and heard was just as the angel had said.

21 Eight days later Jesus' parents did for him what the Law of Moses commands.<sup>m</sup> And they named him Jesus,

just as the angel had told Mary when he promised she would have a baby.

## Simeon Praises the Lord

22 The time came for Mary and Joseph to do what the Law of Moses says a mother is supposed to do after her baby is born.<sup>n</sup>

They took Jesus to the temple in Jerusalem and presented him to the Lord, 23 just as the Law of the Lord says, "Each first-born<sup>o</sup> baby boy belongs to the Lord." 24 The Law of the Lord also says that parents have to offer a sacrifice, giving at least a pair of doves or two young pigeons. So that is what Mary and Joseph did.

25 At this time a man named Simeon was living in Jerusalem. Simeon was a good man. He loved God and was waiting for God to save the people of Israel. God's Spirit came to him 26 and told him that he would not die until he had seen Christ the Lord.

27 When Mary and Joseph brought Jesus to the temple to do what the Law of Moses says should be done for a new baby, the Spirit told Simeon to go into the temple. 28 Simeon took the baby Jesus in his arms and praised God,

29 "Lord, I am your servant,
   and now I can die in peace,
   because you have kept
      your promise to me.
30 With my own eyes I have seen
   what you have done
      to save your people,
31 and foreign nations
      will also see this.
32 Your mighty power is a light
   for all nations,
   and it will bring honor
      to your people Israel."

33 Jesus' parents were surprised at what Simeon had said. 34 Then he blessed them and told Mary, "This child of yours will cause many people in Israel to fall and others to stand. The

child will be like a warning sign. Many people will reject him, [35] and you, Mary, will suffer as though you had been stabbed by a dagger. But all this will show what people are really thinking."

## Anna Speaks about the Child Jesus

[36] The prophet Anna was also there in the temple. She was the daughter of Phanuel from the tribe of Asher, and she was very old. In her youth she had been married for seven years, but her husband died. [37] And now she was eighty-four years old.[p] Night and day she served God in the temple by praying and often going without eating.[q] [38] At that time Anna came in and praised God. She spoke about the child Jesus to everyone who hoped for Jerusalem to be set free.

## The Return to Nazareth

[39] After Joseph and Mary had done everything that the Law of the Lord commands, they returned home to Nazareth in Galilee. [40] The child Jesus grew. He became strong and wise, and God blessed him.

## The Boy Jesus in the Temple

[41] Every year Jesus' parents went to Jerusalem for Passover. [42] And when Jesus was twelve years old, they all went there as usual for the celebration. [43] After Passover his parents left, but they did not know that Jesus had stayed on in the city. [44] They thought he was traveling with some other people, and they went a whole day before they started looking for him. [45] When they could not find him with their relatives and friends, they went back to Jerusalem and started looking for him there. [46] Three days later they found Jesus

sitting in the temple, listening to the teachers and asking them questions. [47] Everyone who heard him was surprised at how much he knew and at the answers he gave.

[48] When his parents found him, they were amazed. His mother said, "Son, why have you done this to us? Your father and I have been very worried, and we have been searching for you!"

[49] Jesus answered, "Why did you have to look for me? Didn't you know that I would be in my Father's house?"[r] [50] But they did not understand what he meant.

[51] Jesus went back to Nazareth with his parents and obeyed them. His mother kept on thinking about all that had happened.

[52] Jesus became wise, and he grew strong. God was pleased with him and so were the people.

## The Preaching of John the Baptist

*(Matthew 3.1-12; Mark 1.1-8; John 1.19-28)*

**3** For fifteen years[s] Emperor Tiberius had ruled that part of the world. Pontius Pilate was governor of Judea, and Herod[t] was the ruler of Galilee. Herod's brother, Philip, was the ruler in the countries of Iturea and Trachonitis, and Lysanias was the ruler of Abilene. [2] Annas and Caiaphas were the Jewish high priests.[u]

At that time God spoke to Zechariah's son John, who was living in the desert. [3] So John went along the Jordan Valley, telling the people, "Turn back to God and be baptized! Then your sins will be forgiven." [4] Isaiah the prophet wrote about John when he said,

"In the desert
someone is shouting,
'Get the road ready
for the Lord!
Make a straight path
for him.

5 Fill up every valley
    and level every mountain
    and hill.
   Straighten the crooked paths
   and smooth out
    the rough roads.
6 Then everyone will see
   the saving power of God.' "

7 Crowds of people came out to be baptized, but John said to them, "You bunch of snakes! Who warned you to run from the coming judgment? 8 Do something to show that you really have given up your sins. Don't start saying that you belong to Abraham's family. God can turn these stones into children for Abraham.v 9 An ax is ready to cut the trees down at their roots. Any tree that doesn't produce good fruit will be cut down and thrown into a fire."

10 The crowds asked John, "What should we do?"

11 John told them, "If you have two coats, give one to someone who doesn't have any. If you have food, share it with someone else."

12 When tax collectorsw came to be baptized, they asked John, "Teacher, what should we do?"

13 John told them, "Don't make people pay more than they owe."

14 Some soldiers asked him, "And what about us? What do we have to do?"

John told them, "Don't force people to pay money to make you leave them alone. Be satisfied with your pay."

15 Everyone became excited and wondered, "Could John be the Messiah?"

16 John said, "I am just baptizing with water. But someone more powerful is going to come, and I am not good enough even to untie his sandals.x He will baptize you with the Holy Spirit and with fire. 17 His threshing forky is in his hand, and he is ready to separate the wheat from the husks. He will store the wheat in his barn and burn the husks with a fire that never goes out."

18 In many different ways John preached the good news to the people. 19 But to Herod the ruler, he said, "It was wrong for you to take Herodias, your brother's wife." John also said that Herod had done many other bad things. 20 Finally, Herod put John in jail, and this was the worst thing he had done.

## The Baptism of Jesus
(Matthew 3.13-17; Mark 1.9-11)

21 While everyone else was being baptized, Jesus himself was baptized. Then as he prayed, the sky opened up, 22 and the Holy Spirit came down upon him in the form of a dove. A voice from heaven said, "You are my own dear Son, and I am pleased with you."

## The Ancestors of Jesus
(Matthew 1.1-17)

23 When Jesus began to preach, he was about thirty years old. Everyone thought he was the son of Joseph. But his family went back through Heli, 24 Matthat, Levi, Melchi, Jannai, Joseph, 25 Mattathias, Amos, Nahum, Esli, Naggai, 26 Maath, Mattathias, Semein, Josech, Joda;

27 Joanan, Rhesa, Zerubbabel, Shealtiel, Neri, 28 Melchi, Addi, Cosam, Elmadam, Er, 29 Joshua, Eliezer, Jorim, Matthat, Levi;

30 Simeon, Judah, Joseph, Jonam, Eliakim, 31 Melea, Menna, Mattatha, Nathan, David, 32 Jesse, Obed, Boaz, Salmon, Nahshon;

33 Amminadab, Admin, Arni, Hezron, Perez, Judah, 34 Jacob, Isaac, Abraham, Terah, Nahor, 35 Serug, Reu, Peleg, Eber, Shelah;

36 Cainan, Arphaxad, Shem, Noah, Lamech, 37 Methuselah, Enoch, Jared, Mahalaleel, Kenan, 38 Enosh, and Seth.

v3.8 children for Abraham: The Jewish people thought they were God's chosen people because of God's promises to their ancestor Abraham. w3.12 tax collectors: These were usually Jewish people who paid the Romans for the right to collect taxes. They were hated by other Jews who thought of them as traitors to their country and to their religion. x3.16 untie his sandals: This was the duty of a slave. y3.17 threshing fork: After Jewish farmers had trampled out the grain, they used a large fork to pitch the grain and the husks into the air. Wind would blow away the light husks, and the grain would fall back to the ground, where it could be gathered up.

The family of Jesus went all the way back to Adam and then to God.

## Jesus and the Devil
### (Matthew 4.1-11; Mark 1.12, 13)

4 When Jesus returned from the Jordan River, the power of the Holy Spirit was with him, and the Spirit led him into the desert. [2] For forty days Jesus was tested by the devil, and during that time he went without eating.[z] When it was all over, he was hungry.

[3] The devil said to Jesus, "If you are God's Son, tell this stone to turn into bread."

[4] Jesus answered, "The Scriptures say, 'No one can live only on food.' "

[5] Then the devil led Jesus up to a high place and quickly showed him all the nations on earth. [6] The devil said, "I will give all this power and glory to you. It has been given to me, and I can give it to anyone I want to. [7] Just worship me, and you can have it all."

[8] Jesus answered, "The Scriptures say:

'Worship the Lord your God
    and serve only him!' "

[9] Finally, the devil took Jesus to Jerusalem and had him stand on top of the temple. The devil said, "If you are God's Son, jump off. [10-11] The Scriptures say:

'God will tell his angels
    to take care of you.
They will catch you
    in their arms,
and you will not hurt
    your feet on the stones.' "

[12] Jesus answered, "The Scriptures also say, 'Don't try to test the Lord your God!' "

[13] After the devil had finished testing Jesus in every way possible, he left him for a while.

## Jesus Begins His Work
### (Matthew 4.12-17; Mark 1.14, 15)

[14] Jesus returned to Galilee with the power of the Spirit. News about him spread everywhere. [15] He taught in the Jewish meeting places, and everyone praised him.

## The People of Nazareth Turn against Jesus
### (Matthew 13.53-58; Mark 6.1-6)

[16] Jesus went back to Nazareth, where he had been brought up, and as usual he went to the meeting place on the Sabbath. When he stood up to read from the Scriptures, [17] he was given the book of Isaiah the prophet. He opened it and read,

[18] "The Lord's Spirit
    has come to me,
because he has chosen me
to tell the good news
    to the poor.
The Lord has sent me
to announce freedom
    for prisoners,
to give sight to the blind,
to free everyone
    who suffers,
[19] and to say, 'This is the year
    the Lord has chosen.' "

[20] Jesus closed the book, then handed it back to the man in charge and sat down. Everyone in the meeting place looked straight at Jesus. [21] Then Jesus said to them, "What you have just heard me read has come true today."

[22] All the people started talking about Jesus and were amazed at the wonderful things he said. They kept on asking, "Isn't he Joseph's son?"

[23] Jesus answered:
You will certainly want to tell me this saying, "Doctor, first make yourself well." You will tell me to do the same things here in my own hometown that you heard I did in Capernaum. [24] But you can be sure that no prophets are liked by the people of their own hometown. [25] Once during the time of Elijah there was no rain for three and a half years, and people everywhere were starving. There were many widows in Israel, [26] but Elijah was sent only to a widow in the town of

z**4.2** went without eating: See the note at 2.37.

Zarephath near the city of Sidon.
²⁷ During the time of the prophet Elisha, many men in Israel had lep-
rosy.ᵃ But no one was healed, except Naaman who lived in Syria.

²⁸ When the people in the meeting
place heard Jesus say this, they became
so angry ²⁹ that they got up and threw
him out of town. They dragged him to
the edge of the cliff on which the town
was built, because they wanted to
throw him down from there. ³⁰ But
Jesus slipped through the crowd and
got away.

### A Man with an Evil Spirit
*(Mark 1.21-28)*

³¹ Jesus went to the town of Capernaum in Galilee and taught the people
on the Sabbath. ³² His teaching amazed
them because he spoke with power.
³³ There in the Jewish meeting place
was a man with an evil spirit. He yelled
out, ³⁴ "Hey, Jesus of Nazareth, what
do you want with us? Are you here to
get rid of us? I know who you are! You
are God's Holy One."
³⁵ Jesus ordered the evil spirit to be
quiet and come out. The demon threw
the man to the ground in front of everyone and left without harming him.
³⁶ They all were amazed and kept
saying to each other, "What kind of
teaching is this? He has power to order
evil spirits out of people!" ³⁷ News
about Jesus spread all over that part
of the country.

### Jesus Heals Many People
*(Matthew 8.14-17; Mark 1.29-34)*

³⁸ Jesus left the meeting place and
went to Simon's home. When Jesus got
there, he was told that Simon's mother-
in-law was sick with a high fever. ³⁹ So
Jesus went over to her and ordered the
fever to go away. Right then she was
able to get up and serve them a
meal.
⁴⁰ After the sun had set, people with
all kinds of diseases were brought to
Jesus. He put his hands on each one
of them and healed them. ⁴¹ Demons
went out of many people and shouted,
"You are the Son of God!" But Jesus
ordered the demons not to speak
because they knew he was the
Messiah.

⁴² The next morning Jesus went out
to a place where he could be alone, and
crowds came looking for him. When
they found him, they tried to stop him
from leaving. ⁴³ But Jesus said, "People
in other towns must hear the good news
about God's kingdom. That's why I
was sent." ⁴⁴ So he kept on preaching
in the Jewish meeting places in
Judea.ᵇ

### Jesus Chooses His First Disciples
*(Matthew 4.18-22; Mark 1.16-20)*

5 Jesus was standing on the shore of
Lake Gennesaret,ᶜ teaching the
people as they crowded around him to
hear God's message. ² Near the shore
he saw two boats left there by some
fishermen who had gone to wash their
nets. ³ Jesus got into the boat that belonged to Simon and asked him to row
it out a little way from the shore. Then
Jesus sat downᵈ in the boat to teach
the crowd.
⁴ When Jesus had finished speaking,
he told Simon, "Row the boat out into
the deep water and let your nets down
to catch some fish."
⁵ "Master," Simon answered, "we
have worked hard all night long and
have not caught a thing. But if you tell
me to, I will let the nets down." ⁶ They
did it and caught so many fish that their
nets began ripping apart. ⁷ Then they
signaled for their partners in the other
boat to come and help them. The men
came, and together they filled the two
boats so full that they both began to
sink.
⁸ When Simon Peter saw this happen,
he knelt down in front of Jesus and
said, "Lord, don't come near me! I am
a sinner." ⁹ Peter and everyone with
him were completely surprised at all

ᵃ4.27 *leprosy*: In biblical times the word "leprosy" was used for many different kinds of
skin diseases.   ᵇ4.44 *Judea*: Some manuscripts have "Galilee."   ᶜ5.1 *Lake Gennesaret*:
Another name for Lake Galilee.   ᵈ5.3 *sat down*: Teachers in the ancient world, including
Jewish teachers, usually sat down when they taught.

the fish they had caught. [10] His partners James and John, the sons of Zebedee, were surprised too.

Jesus told Simon, "Don't be afraid! From now on you will bring in people instead of fish." [11] The men pulled their boats up on the shore. Then they left everything and went with Jesus.

### Jesus Heals a Man
*(Matthew 8.1-4; Mark 1.40-45)*

[12] Jesus came to a town where there was a man who had leprosy.[e] When the man saw Jesus, he knelt down to the ground in front of Jesus and begged, "Lord, you have the power to make me well, if only you wanted to."

[13] Jesus put his hand on him and said, "I want to! Now you are well." At once the man's leprosy disappeared. [14] Jesus told him, "Don't tell anyone about this, but go and show yourself to the priest. Offer a gift to the priest, just as Moses commanded, and everyone will know that you have been healed."[f]

[15] News about Jesus kept spreading. Large crowds came to listen to him teach and to be healed of their diseases. [16] But Jesus would often go to some place where he could be alone and pray.

### Jesus Heals a Crippled Man
*(Matthew 9.1-8; Mark 2.1-12)*

[17] One day some Pharisees and experts in the Law of Moses sat listening to Jesus teach. They had come from every village in Galilee and Judea and from Jerusalem.

God had given Jesus the power to heal the sick, [18] and some people came carrying a crippled man on a mat. They tried to take him inside the house and put him in front of Jesus. [19] But because of the crowd, they could not get him to Jesus. So they went up on the roof,[g] where they removed some tiles and let the mat down in the middle of the room.

[20] When Jesus saw how much faith they had, he said to the crippled man, "My friend, your sins are forgiven."

[21] The Pharisees and the experts began arguing, "Jesus must think he is God! Only God can forgive sins."

[22] Jesus knew what they were thinking, and he said, "Why are you thinking that? [23] Is it easier for me to tell this crippled man that his sins are forgiven or to tell him to get up and walk? [24] But now you will see that the Son of Man has the right to forgive sins here on earth." Jesus then said to the man, "Get up! Pick up your mat and walk home."

[25] At once the man stood up in front of everyone. He picked up his mat and went home, giving thanks to God. [26] Everyone was amazed and praised God. What they saw surprised them, and they said, "We have seen a great miracle today!"

### Jesus Chooses Levi
*(Matthew 9.9-13; Mark 2.13-17)*

[27] Later, Jesus went out and saw a tax collector[h] named Levi sitting at the place for paying taxes. Jesus said to him, "Come with me." [28] Levi left everything and went with Jesus.

[29] In his home Levi gave a big dinner for Jesus. Many tax collectors and other guests were also there.

[30] The Pharisees and some of their teachers of the Law of Moses grumbled to Jesus' disciples, "Why do you eat and drink with those tax collectors and other sinners?"

[31] Jesus answered, "Healthy people don't need a doctor, but sick people do. [32] I didn't come to invite good people to turn to God. I came to invite sinners."

---

[e]**5.12** *leprosy:* See the note at 4.27. [f]**5.14** *everyone will know that you have been healed:* People with leprosy had to be examined by a priest and told that they were well (that is, "clean") before they could once again live a normal life in the Jewish community. The gift that Moses commanded was the sacrifice of some lambs together with flour mixed with olive oil. [g]**5.19** *roof:* In Palestine the houses usually had a flat roof. Stairs on the outside led up to the roof, which was made of beams and boards covered with packed earth. Luke says that the roof was made of (clay) tiles, which were also used for making roofs in New Testament times. [h]**5.27** *tax collector:* See the note at 3.12.

## People Ask about Going without Eating
*(Matthew 9.14-17; Mark 2.18-22)*

**33** Some people said to Jesus, "John's followers often pray and go without eating,[i] and so do the followers of the Pharisees. But your disciples never go without eating or drinking."

**34** Jesus told them, "The friends of a bridegroom don't go without eating while he is still with them. **35** But the time will come when he will be taken from them. Then they will go without eating."

**36** Jesus then told them these sayings:
No one uses a new piece of cloth to patch old clothes. The patch would shrink and make the hole even bigger.

**37** No one pours new wine into old wineskins. The new wine would swell and burst the old skins.[j] Then the wine would be lost, and the skins would be ruined. **38** New wine must be put only into new wineskins.

**39** No one wants new wine after drinking old wine. They say, "The old wine is better."

## A Question about the Sabbath
*(Matthew 12.1-8; Mark 2.23-28)*

**6** One Sabbath when Jesus and his disciples were walking through some wheat fields,[k] the disciples picked some wheat. They rubbed the husks off with their hands and started eating the grain.

**2** Some Pharisees said, "Why are you picking grain on the Sabbath? You're not supposed to do that!"

**3** Jesus answered, "You surely have read what David did when he and his followers were hungry. **4** He went into the house of God and took the sacred loaves of bread that only priests were supposed to eat. He not only ate some himself, but even gave some to his followers."

**5** Jesus finished by saying, "The Son of Man is Lord over the Sabbath."

## A Man with a Crippled Hand
*(Matthew 12.9-14; Mark 3.1-6)*

**6** On another Sabbath[l] Jesus was teaching in a Jewish meeting place, and a man with a crippled right hand was there. **7** Some Pharisees and teachers of the Law of Moses kept watching Jesus to see if he would heal the man. They did this because they wanted to accuse Jesus of doing something wrong.

**8** Jesus knew what they were thinking. So he told the man to stand up where everyone could see him. And the man stood up. **9** Then Jesus asked, "On the Sabbath should we do good deeds or evil deeds? Should we save someone's life or destroy it?"

**10** After he had looked around at everyone, he told the man, "Stretch out your hand." He did, and his bad hand became completely well.

**11** The teachers and the Pharisees were furious and started saying to each other, "What can we do about Jesus?"

## Jesus Chooses His Twelve Apostles
*(Matthew 10.1-4; Mark 3.13-19)*

**12** About that time Jesus went off to a mountain to pray, and he spent the whole night there. **13** The next morning he called his disciples together and chose twelve of them to be his apostles. **14** One was Simon, and Jesus named him Peter. Another was Andrew, Peter's brother. There were also James, John, Philip, Bartholomew, **15** Matthew, Thomas, and James the son of Alphaeus. The rest of the apostles were Simon, known as the Eager One,[m] **16** Jude, who was the son of James, and

---

[i]**5.33** *without eating:* See the note at 2.37.   [j]**5.37** *swell and burst the old skins:* While the juice from grapes was becoming wine, it would swell and stretch the skins in which it had been stored. If the skins were old and stiff, they would burst.   [k]**6.1** *walking through some wheat fields:* It was the custom to let hungry travelers pick grains of wheat.   [l]**6.6** *On another Sabbath:* Some manuscripts have a reading which may mean "the Sabbath after the next."   [m]**6.15** *known as the Eager One:* The word "eager" translates the Greek word "zealot," which was a name later given to the members of a Jewish group that resisted and fought against the Romans.

Judas Iscariot,[n] who later betrayed Jesus.

## Jesus Teaches, Preaches, and Heals
### (Matthew 4.23-25)

[17] Jesus and his apostles went down from the mountain and came to some flat, level ground. Many other disciples were there to meet him. Large crowds of people from all over Judea, Jerusalem, and the coastal cities of Tyre and Sidon were there too. [18] These people had come to listen to Jesus and to be healed of their diseases. All who were troubled by evil spirits were also healed. [19] Everyone was trying to touch Jesus, because power was going out from him and healing them all.

## Blessings and Troubles
### (Matthew 5.1-12)

[20] Jesus looked at his disciples and said:
God will bless you people
who are poor.
His kingdom belongs to you!
[21] God will bless
you hungry people.
You will have plenty
to eat!
God will bless you people
who are crying.
You will laugh!

[22] God will bless you when others hate you and won't have anything to do with you. God will bless you when people insult you and say cruel things about you, all because you are a follower of the Son of Man. [23] Long ago your own people did these same things to the prophets. So when this happens to you, be happy and jump for joy! You will have a great reward in heaven.

[24] But you rich people
are in for trouble.
You have already had
an easy life!
[25] You well-fed people
are in for trouble.
You will go hungry!
You people
who are laughing now
are in for trouble.
You are going to cry
and weep!
[26] You are in for trouble when everyone says good things about you. That is what your own people said about those prophets who told lies.

## Love for Enemies
### (Matthew 5.38-48; 7.12a)

[27] This is what I say to all who will listen to me:
Love your enemies, and be good to everyone who hates you. [28] Ask God to bless anyone who curses you, and pray for everyone who is cruel to you. [29] If someone slaps you on one cheek, don't stop that person from slapping you on the other cheek. If someone wants to take your coat, don't try to keep back your shirt. [30] Give to everyone who asks and don't ask people to return what they have taken from you. [31] Treat others just as you want to be treated.

[32] If you love only someone who loves you, will God praise you for that? Even sinners love people who love them. [33] If you are kind only to someone who is kind to you, will God be pleased with you for that? Even sinners are kind to people who are kind to them. [34] If you lend money only to someone you think will pay you back, will God be pleased with you for that? Even sinners lend to sinners because they think they will get it all back.

[35] But love your enemies and be good to them. Lend without expecting to be paid back.[o] Then you will get a great reward, and you will be the true children of God in heaven. He is good even to people who are unthankful and cruel. [36] Have pity

---

[n]**6.16** *Iscariot*: This may mean "a man from Kerioth" (a place in Judea). But more probably it means "a man who was a liar" or "a man who was a betrayer." [o]**6.35** *without expecting to be paid back*: Some manuscripts have "without giving up on anyone."

on others, just as your Father has pity on you.

## Judging Others
*(Matthew 7.1-5)*

³⁷ Jesus said:

Don't judge others, and God won't judge you. Don't be hard on others, and God won't be hard on you. Forgive others, and God will forgive you. ³⁸ If you give to others, you will be given a full amount in return. It will be packed down, shaken together, and spilling over into your lap. The way you treat others is the way you will be treated.

³⁹ Jesus also used some sayings as he spoke to the people. He said:

Can one blind person lead another blind person? Won't they both fall into a ditch? ⁴⁰ Are students better than their teacher? But when they are fully trained, they will be like their teacher.

⁴¹ You can see the speck in your friend's eye. But you don't notice the log in your own eye. ⁴² How can you say, "My friend, let me take the speck out of your eye," when you don't see the log in your own eye? You show-offs! First, get the log out of your own eye. Then you can see how to take the speck out of your friend's eye.

## A Tree and Its Fruit
*(Matthew 7.17-20; 12.34b, 35)*

⁴³ A good tree cannot produce bad fruit, and a bad tree cannot produce good fruit. ⁴⁴ You can tell what a tree is like by the fruit it produces. You cannot pick figs or grapes from thornbushes. ⁴⁵ Good people do good things because of the good in their hearts. Bad people do bad things because of the evil in their hearts. Your words show what is in your heart.

## Two Builders
*(Matthew 7.24-27)*

⁴⁶ Why do you keep on saying that I am your Lord, when you refuse to do what I say? ⁴⁷ Anyone who comes and listens to me and obeys me ⁴⁸ is like someone who dug down deep and built a house on solid rock. When the flood came and the river rushed against the house, it was built so well that it didn't even shake. ⁴⁹ But anyone who hears what I say and doesn't obey me is like someone whose house wasn't built on solid rock. As soon as the river rushed against that house, it was smashed to pieces!

## Jesus Heals an Army Officer's Servant
*(Matthew 8.5-13; John 4.43-54)*

**7** After Jesus had finished teaching the people, he went to Capernaum. ² In that town an army officer's servant was sick and about to die. The officer liked this servant very much. ³ And when he heard about Jesus, he sent some Jewish leaders to ask him to come and heal the servant.

⁴ The leaders went to Jesus and begged him to do something. They said, "This man deserves your help! ⁵ He loves our nation and even built us a meeting place." ⁶ So Jesus went with them.

When Jesus wasn't far from the house, the officer sent some friends to tell him, "Lord, don't go to any trouble for me! I am not good enough for you to come into my house. ⁷ And I am certainly not worthy to come to you. Just say the word, and my servant will get well. ⁸ I have officers who give orders to me, and I have soldiers who take orders from me. I can say to one of them, 'Go!' and he goes. I can say to another, 'Come!' and he comes. I can say to my servant, 'Do this!' and he will do it."

⁹ When Jesus heard this, he was so surprised that he turned and said to the crowd following him, "In all of Israel I've never found anyone with this much faith!"

¹⁰ The officer's friends returned and found the servant well.

## A Widow's Son

¹¹ Soon Jesus and his disciples were on their way to the town of Nain, and a big crowd was going along with them. ¹² As they came near the gate of the

town, they saw people carrying out the
body of a widow's only son. Many people from the town were walking along
with her.
13 When the Lord saw the woman, he
felt sorry for her and said, "Don't cry!"
14 Jesus went over and touched the
stretcher on which the people were carrying the dead boy. They stopped, and
Jesus said, "Young man, get up!" 15 The
boy sat up and began to speak. Jesus
then gave him back to his mother.
16 Everyone was frightened and
praised God. They said, "A great
prophet is here with us! God has come
to his people."
17 News about Jesus spread all over
Judea and everywhere else in that part
of the country.

### *John the Baptist*

*(Matthew 11.1-19)*

18-19 John's followers told John everything that was being said about Jesus.
So he sent two of them to ask the Lord,
"Are you the one we should be looking
for? Or must we wait for someone
else?"
20 When these messengers came to
Jesus, they said, "John the Baptist sent
us to ask, 'Are you the one we should
be looking for? Or are we supposed to
wait for someone else?' "
21 At that time Jesus was healing
many people who were sick or in pain
or were troubled by evil spirits, and he
was giving sight to a lot of blind people.
22 Jesus said to the messengers sent by
John, "Go and tell John what you have
seen and heard. Blind people are now
able to see, and the lame can walk. People who have leprosy[p] are being
healed, and the deaf can now hear. The
dead are raised to life, and the poor are
hearing the good news. 23 God will
bless everyone who doesn't reject me
because of what I do."
24 After John's messengers had gone,
Jesus began speaking to the crowds
about John:

What kind of person did you go
out to the desert to see? Was he like
tall grass blown about by the wind?
25 What kind of man did you really
go out to see? Was he someone
dressed in fine clothes? People who
wear expensive clothes and live in
luxury are in the king's palace.
26 What then did you go out to see?
Was he a prophet? He certainly was!
I tell you that he was more than a
prophet. 27 In the Scriptures, God
calls John his messenger and says,
"I am sending my messenger ahead
of you to get things ready for you."
28 No one ever born on this earth is
greater than John. But whoever is
least important in God's kingdom
is greater than John.

29 Everyone had been listening to
John. Even the tax collectors[q] had
obeyed God and had done what was
right by letting John baptize them.
30 But the Pharisees and the experts in
the Law of Moses refused to obey God
and be baptized by John.
31 Jesus went on to say:

What are you people like? What
kind of people are you? 32 You are
like children sitting in the market
and shouting to each other,

"We played the flute,
but you would not dance!
We sang a funeral song,
but you would not cry!"

33 John the Baptist did not go around
eating and drinking, and you said,
"John has a demon in him!" 34 But
because the Son of Man goes around
eating and drinking, you say, "Jesus
eats and drinks too much! He is even
a friend of tax collectors and sinners." 35 Yet Wisdom is shown to be
right by what its followers do.

### *Simon the Pharisee*

36 A Pharisee invited Jesus to have
dinner with him. So Jesus went to the
Pharisee's home and got ready to eat.[r]

[p] **7.22** *leprosy*: See the note at 4.27. [q] **7.29** *tax collectors*: See the note at 3.12. [r] **7.36** *got ready to eat*: On special occasions the Jewish people often followed the Greek and Roman custom of lying down on their left side and leaning on their left elbow, while eating with their right hand. This is how the woman could come up behind Jesus and wash his feet (see verse 38).

37 When a sinful woman in that town found out that Jesus was there, she bought an expensive bottle of perfume. 38 Then she came and stood behind Jesus. She cried and started washing his feet with her tears and drying them with her hair. The woman kissed his feet and poured the perfume on them.

39 The Pharisee who had invited Jesus saw this and said to himself, "If this man really were a prophet, he would know what kind of woman is touching him! He would know that she is a sinner."

40 Jesus said to the Pharisee, "Simon, I have something to say to you."

"Teacher, what is it?" Simon replied.

41 Jesus told him, "Two people were in debt to a moneylender. One of them owed him five hundred silver coins, and the other owed him fifty. 42 Since neither of them could pay him back, the moneylender said that they didn't have to pay him anything. Which one of them will like him more?"

43 Simon answered, "I suppose it would be the one who had owed more and didn't have to pay it back."

"You are right," Jesus said.

44 He turned toward the woman and said to Simon, "Have you noticed this woman? When I came into your home, you didn't give me any water so I could wash my feet. But she has washed my feet with her tears and dried them with her hair. 45 You didn't greet me with a kiss, but from the time I came in, she has not stopped kissing my feet. 46 You didn't even pour olive oil on my head,s but she has poured expensive perfume on my feet. 47 So I tell you that all her sins are forgiven, and that is why she has shown great love. But anyone who has been forgiven for only a little will show only a little love."

48 Then Jesus said to the woman, "Your sins are forgiven."

49 Some other guests started saying to one another, "Who is this who dares to forgive sins?"

50 But Jesus told the woman, "Because of your faith, you are now saved.t May God give you peace!"

## Women Who Helped Jesus

8 Soon after this, Jesus was going through towns and villages, telling the good news about God's kingdom. His twelve apostles were with him, 2 and so were some women who had been healed of evil spirits and all sorts of diseases. One of the women was Mary Magdalene,u who once had seven demons in her. 3 Joanna, Susanna, and many others had also used what they owned to help Jesusv and his disciples. Joanna's husband Chuza was one of Herod's officials.w

## A Story about a Farmer
### (Matthew 13.1-9; Mark 4.1-9)

4 When a large crowd from several towns had gathered around Jesus, he told them this story:

5 A farmer went out to scatter seed in a field. While the farmer was doing it, some of the seeds fell along the road and were stepped on or eaten by birds. 6 Other seeds fell on rocky ground and started growing. But the plants did not have enough water and soon dried up. 7 Some other seeds fell where thornbushes grew up and choked the plants. 8 The rest of the seeds fell on good ground where they grew and produced a hundred times as many seeds.

When Jesus had finished speaking, he said, "If you have ears, pay attention!"

s 7.44, 46 washed my feet ... greet me with a kiss ... pour olive oil on my head: Guests in a home were usually offered water so they could wash their feet, because most people either went barefoot or wore sandals and would come in the house with very dusty feet. Guests were also greeted with a kiss on the cheek, and special ones often had sweet-smelling olive oil poured on their head. t 7.50 saved: Or "healed." The Greek word may have either meaning. u 8.2 Magdalene: Meaning "from Magdala," a small town on the western shore of Lake Galilee. There is no hint that she is the sinful woman in 7.36-50. v 8.3 used what they owned to help Jesus: Women often helped Jewish teachers by giving them money. w 8.3 Herod's officials: Herod Antipas, the son of Herod the Great.

## Why Jesus Used Stories
*(Matthew 13.10-17; Mark 4.10-12)*

⁹ Jesus' disciples asked him what the story meant. ¹⁰ So he answered:

I have explained the secrets about God's kingdom to you, but for others I can only use stories. These people look, but they don't see, and they hear, but they don't understand.

## Jesus Explains the Story about a Farmer
*(Matthew 13.18-23; Mark 4.13-20)*

¹¹ This is what the story means: The seed is God's message, ¹² and the seeds that fell along the road are the people who hear the message. But the devil comes and snatches the message out of their hearts, so that they will not believe and be saved. ¹³ The seeds that fell on rocky ground are the people who gladly hear the message and accept it. But they don't have deep roots, and they believe only for a little while. As soon as life gets hard, they give up. ¹⁴ The seeds that fell among the thornbushes are also people who hear the message. But they are so eager for riches and pleasures that they never produce anything. ¹⁵ Those seeds that fell on good ground are the people who listen to the message and keep it in good and honest hearts. They last and produce a harvest.

## Light
*(Mark 4.21-25)*

¹⁶ No one lights a lamp and puts it under a bowl or under a bed. A lamp is always put on a lampstand, so that people who come into a house will see the light. ¹⁷ There is nothing hidden that will not be found. There is no secret that will not be well known. ¹⁸ Pay attention to how you listen! Everyone who has something will be given more, but people who have nothing will lose what little they think they have.

## Jesus' Mother and Brothers
*(Matthew 12.46-50; Mark 3.31-35)*

¹⁹ Jesus' mother and brothers went to see him, but because of the crowd they could not get near him. ²⁰ Someone told Jesus, "Your mother and brothers are standing outside and want to see you." ²¹ Jesus answered, "My mother and my brothers are those people who hear and obey God's message."

## A Storm
*(Matthew 8.23-27; Mark 4.35-41)*

²² One day, Jesus and his disciples got into a boat, and he said, "Let's cross the lake."ˣ They started out, ²³ and while they were sailing across, he went to sleep.

Suddenly a windstorm struck the lake, and the boat started sinking. They were in danger. ²⁴ So they went to Jesus and woke him up, "Master, Master! We are about to drown!"

Jesus got up and ordered the wind and waves to stop. They obeyed, and everything was calm. ²⁵ Then Jesus asked the disciples, "Don't you have any faith?"

But they were frightened and amazed. They said to each other, "Who is this? He can give orders to the wind and the waves, and they obey him!"

## A Man with Demons in Him
*(Matthew 8.28-34; Mark 5.1-20)*

²⁶ Jesus and his disciples sailed across Lake Galilee and came to shore near the town of Gerasa.ʸ ²⁷ As Jesus was getting out of the boat, he was met by a man from that town. The man had demons in him. He had gone naked for a long time and no longer lived in a house, but in the graveyard.ᶻ ²⁸ The man saw Jesus and screamed. He knelt down in front of him and shouted, "Jesus, Son of God in heaven, what do you want with me? I beg you not to torture me!" ²⁹ He said this because Jesus had already told the evil spirit to go out of him.

ˣ**8.22** *cross the lake*: To the eastern shore of Lake Galilee, where most of the people were not Jewish. ʸ**8.26** *Gerasa*: Some manuscripts have "Gergesa." ᶻ**8.27** *graveyard*: It was thought that demons and evil spirits lived in graveyards.

The man had often been attacked by the demon. And even though he had been bound with chains and leg irons and kept under guard, he smashed whatever bound him. Then the demon would force him out into lonely places. <sup>30</sup> Jesus asked the man, "What is your name?"

He answered, "My name is Lots." He said this because there were 'lots' of demons in him. <sup>31</sup> They begged Jesus not to send them to the deep pit,<sup>a</sup> where they would be punished.

<sup>32</sup> A large herd of pigs was feeding there on the hillside. So the demons begged Jesus to let them go into the pigs, and Jesus let them go. <sup>33</sup> Then the demons left the man and went into the pigs. The whole herd rushed down the steep bank into the lake and drowned.

<sup>34</sup> When the men taking care of the pigs saw this, they ran to spread the news in the town and on the farms. <sup>35</sup> The people went out to see what had happened, and when they came to Jesus, they also found the man. The demons had gone out of him, and he was sitting there at the feet of Jesus. He had clothes on and was in his right mind. But the people were terrified. <sup>36</sup> Then all who had seen the man healed told about it. <sup>37</sup> Everyone from around Gerasa<sup>b</sup> begged Jesus to leave, because they were so frightened.

When Jesus got into the boat to start back, <sup>38</sup> the man who had been healed begged to go with him. But Jesus sent him off and said, <sup>39</sup> "Go back home and tell everyone how much God has done for you." The man then went all over town, telling everything that Jesus had done for him.

### A Dying Girl and a Sick Woman
(Matthew 9.18-26; Mark 5.21-43)

<sup>40</sup> Everyone had been waiting for Jesus, and when he came back, a crowd was there to welcome him. <sup>41</sup> Just then the man in charge of the Jewish meeting place came and knelt down in front of Jesus. His name was Jairus, and he begged Jesus to come to his home <sup>42</sup> because his twelve-year-old child was dying. She was his only daughter.

While Jesus was on his way, people were crowding all around him. <sup>43</sup> In the crowd was a woman who had been bleeding for twelve years. She had spent everything she had on doctors,<sup>c</sup> but none of them could make her well.

<sup>44</sup> As soon as she came up behind Jesus and barely touched his clothes, her bleeding stopped.

<sup>45</sup> "Who touched me?" Jesus asked. While everyone was denying it, Peter said, "Master, people are crowding all around and pushing you from every side."<sup>d</sup>

<sup>46</sup> But Jesus answered, "Someone touched me, because I felt power going out from me." <sup>47</sup> The woman knew that she could not hide, so she came trembling and knelt down in front of Jesus. She told everyone why she had touched him and that she had been healed right away.

<sup>48</sup> Jesus said to the woman, "You are now well because of your faith. May God give you peace!"

<sup>49</sup> While Jesus was speaking, someone came from Jairus' home and said, "Your daughter has died! Why bother the teacher anymore?"

<sup>50</sup> When Jesus heard this, he told Jairus, "Don't worry! Have faith, and your daughter will get well."

<sup>51</sup> Jesus went into the house, but he did not let anyone else go with him, except Peter, John, James, and the girl's father and mother. <sup>52</sup> Everyone was crying and weeping for the girl. But Jesus said, "The child isn't dead. She is just asleep." <sup>53</sup> The people laughed at him because they knew she was dead.

<sup>54</sup> Jesus took hold of the girl's hand and said, "Child, get up!" <sup>55</sup> She came back to life and got right up. Jesus told them to give her something to eat. <sup>56</sup> Her parents were surprised, but Jesus ordered them not to tell anyone what had happened.

<sup>a</sup>8.31 deep pit: The place where evil spirits are kept and punished. <sup>b</sup>8.37 Gerasa: See the note at 8.26. <sup>c</sup>8.43 She had spent everything she had on doctors: Some manuscripts do not have these words. <sup>d</sup>8.45 from every side: Some manuscripts add "and you ask, 'Who touched me?' "

LUKE 9   90

## Instructions for the Twelve Apostles
*(Matthew 10.5-15; Mark 6.7-13)*

**9** Jesus called together his twelve apostles and gave them complete power over all demons and diseases. ²Then he sent them to tell about God's kingdom and to heal the sick. ³He told them, "Don't take anything with you! Don't take a walking stick or a traveling bag or food or money or even a change of clothes. ⁴When you are welcomed into a home, stay there until you leave that town. ⁵If people won't welcome you, leave the town and shake the dust from your feet*e* as a warning to them."

⁶The apostles left and went from village to village, telling the good news and healing people everywhere.

## Herod Is Worried
*(Matthew 14.1-12; Mark 6.14-29)*

⁷Herod*f* the ruler heard about all that was happening, and he was worried. Some people were saying that John the Baptist had come back to life. ⁸Others were saying that Elijah had come*g* or that one of the prophets from long ago had come back to life. ⁹But Herod said, "I had John's head cut off! Who is this I hear so much about?" Herod was eager to meet Jesus.

## Jesus Feeds Five Thousand
*(Matthew 14.13-21; Mark 6.30-44; John 6.1-14)*

¹⁰The apostles came back and told Jesus everything they had done. He then took them with him to the village of Bethsaida, where they could be alone. ¹¹But a lot of people found out about this and followed him. Jesus welcomed them. He spoke to them about God's kingdom and healed everyone who was sick.

¹²Late in the afternoon the twelve apostles came to Jesus and said, "Send the crowd to the villages and farms around here. They need to find a place to stay and something to eat. There is nothing in this place. It is like a desert!"

¹³Jesus answered, "You give them something to eat."

But they replied, "We have only five small loaves of bread*h* and two fish. If we are going to feed all these people, we will have to go and buy food." ¹⁴There were about five thousand men in the crowd.

Jesus said to his disciples, "Have the people sit in groups of fifty." ¹⁵They did this, and all the people sat down. ¹⁶Jesus took the five loaves and the two fish. He looked up toward heaven and blessed the food. Then he broke the bread and fish and handed them to his disciples to give to the people.

¹⁷Everyone ate all they wanted. What was left over filled twelve baskets.

## Who Is Jesus?
*(Matthew 16.13-19; Mark 8.27-29)*

¹⁸When Jesus was alone praying, his disciples came to him, and he asked them, "What do people say about me?"

¹⁹They answered, "Some say that you are John the Baptist or Elijah*i* or a prophet from long ago who has come back to life."

²⁰Jesus then asked them, "But who do you say I am?"

Peter answered, "You are the Messiah sent from God."

²¹Jesus strictly warned his disciples not to tell anyone about this.

## Jesus Speaks about His Suffering and Death
*(Matthew 16.20-28; Mark 8.30—9.1)*

²²Jesus told his disciples, "The nation's leaders, the chief priests, and the teachers of the Law of Moses will make the Son of Man suffer terribly. They will reject him and kill him, but three days later he will rise to life."

²³Then Jesus said to all the people:

*e9.5 shake the dust from your feet*: This was a way of showing rejection. *f9.7 Herod*: Herod Antipas, the son of Herod the Great. *g9.8 Elijah had come*: Many of the Jewish people expected the prophet Elijah to come and prepare the way for the Messiah. *h9.13 small loaves of bread*: These would have been flat and round or in the shape of a bun. *i9.19 Elijah*: See the note at 9.8.

If any of you want to be my followers, you must forget about yourself. You must take up your cross each day and follow me. 24 If you want to save your life,j you will destroy it. But if you give up your life for me, you will save it. 25 What will you gain, if you own the whole world but destroy yourself or waste your life? 26 If you are ashamed of me and my message, the Son of Man will be ashamed of you when he comes in his glory and in the glory of his Father and the holy angels. 27 You can be sure that some of the people standing here will not die before they see God's kingdom.

### The True Glory of Jesus
*(Matthew 17.1-8; Mark 9.2-8)*

28 About eight days later Jesus took Peter, John, and James with him and went up on a mountain to pray. 29 While he was praying, his face changed, and his clothes became shining white. 30 Suddenly Moses and Elijah were there speaking with him. 31 They appeared in heavenly glory and talked about all that Jesus' deathk in Jerusalem would mean.
32 Peter and the other two disciples had been sound asleep. All at once they woke up and saw how glorious Jesus was. They also saw the two men who were with him.
33 Moses and Elijah were about to leave, when Peter said to Jesus, "Master, it is good for us to be here! Let us make three shelters, one for you, one for Moses, and one for Elijah." But Peter did not know what he was talking about.
34 While Peter was still speaking, a shadow from a cloud passed over them, and they were frightened as the cloud covered them. 35 From the cloud a voice spoke, "This is my chosen Son. Listen to what he says!"
36 After the voice had spoken, Peter, John, and James saw only Jesus. For some time they kept quiet and did not say anything about what they had seen.

### Jesus Heals a Boy
*(Matthew 17.14-18; Mark 9.14-27)*

37 The next day Jesus and his three disciples came down from the mountain and were met by a large crowd. 38 Just then someone in the crowd shouted, "Teacher, please do something for my son! He is my only child! 39 A demon often attacks him and makes him scream. It shakes him until he foams at the mouth, and it won't leave him until it has completely worn the boy out. 40 I begged your disciples to force out the demon, but they couldn't do it."
41 Jesus said to them, "You people are stubborn and don't have any faith! How much longer must I be with you? Why do I have to put up with you?"
Then Jesus said to the man, "Bring your son to me." 42 While the boy was being brought, the demon attacked him and made him shake all over. Jesus ordered the demon to stop. Then he healed the boy and gave him back to his father. 43 Everyone was amazed at God's great power.

### Jesus Again Speaks about His Death
*(Matthew 17.22, 23; Mark 9.30-32)*

While everyone was still amazed at what Jesus was doing, he said to his disciples, 44 "Pay close attention to what I am telling you! The Son of Man will be handed over to his enemies." 45 But the disciples did not know what he meant. The meaning was hidden from them. They could not understand it, and they were afraid to ask.

### Who Is the Greatest?
*(Matthew 18.1-5; Mark 9.33-37)*

46 Jesus' disciples were arguing about which one of them was the greatest. 47 Jesus knew what they were thinking, and he had a child stand there beside him. 48 Then he said to his disciples, "When you welcome even a child because of me, you welcome me. And

j9.24 *life*: In verses 24, 25 a Greek word which often means "soul" is translated "life" and "yourself." k9.31 *Jesus' death*: In Greek this is "his departure," which probably includes his rising to life and his return to heaven.

when you welcome me, you welcome the one who sent me. Whichever one of you is the most humble is the greatest."

## For or against Jesus
*(Mark 9.38-40)*

⁴⁹ John said, "Master, we saw a man using your name to force demons out of people. But we told him to stop, because he isn't one of us."
⁵⁰ "Don't stop him!" Jesus said. "Anyone who isn't against you is for you."

## A Samaritan Village Refuses To Receive Jesus

⁵¹ Not long before it was time for Jesus to be taken up to heaven, he made up his mind to go to Jerusalem. ⁵² He sent some messengers on ahead to a Samaritan village to get things ready for him. ⁵³ But he was on his way to Jerusalem, so the people there refused to welcome him. ⁵⁴ When the disciples James and John saw what was happening, they asked, "Lord, do you want us to call down fire from heaven to destroy these people?"*l*
⁵⁵ But Jesus turned and corrected them for what they had said.*m* ⁵⁶ Then they all went on to another village.

## Three People Who Wanted To Be Followers
*(Matthew 8.19-22)*

⁵⁷ Along the way someone said to Jesus, "I'll go anywhere with you!"
⁵⁸ Jesus said, "Foxes have dens, and birds have nests, but the Son of Man doesn't have a place to call his own."
⁵⁹ Jesus told someone else to come with him. But the man said, "Lord, let me wait until I bury my father."*n*

⁶⁰ Jesus answered, "Let the dead take care of the dead, while you go and tell about God's kingdom."
⁶¹ Then someone said to Jesus, "I want to go with you, Lord, but first let me go back and take care of things at home."
⁶² Jesus answered, "Anyone who starts plowing and keeps looking back isn't worth a thing to God's kingdom!"

## The Work of the Seventy-Two Followers

**10** Later the Lord chose seventy-two*o* other followers and sent them out two by two to every town and village where he was about to go. ² He said to them:

A large crop is in the fields, but there are only a few workers. Ask the Lord in charge of the harvest to send out workers to bring it in. ³ Now go, but remember, I am sending you like lambs into a pack of wolves. ⁴ Don't take along a money-bag or a traveling bag or sandals. And don't waste time greeting people on the road.*p* ⁵ As soon as you enter a home, say, "God bless this home with peace." ⁶ If the people living there are peace-loving, your prayer for peace will bless them. But if they are not peace-loving, your prayer will return to you. ⁷ Stay with the same family, eating and drinking whatever they give you, because workers are worth what they earn. Don't move around from house to house.

⁸ If the people of a town welcome you, eat whatever they offer. ⁹ Heal their sick and say, "God's kingdom will soon be here!"*q*
¹⁰ But if the people of a town refuse to welcome you, go out into the

---

*l***9.54** *to destroy these people*: Some manuscripts add "as Elijah did." *m***9.55** *what they had said*: Some manuscripts add, "and said, 'Don't you know what spirit you belong to? The Son of Man did not come to destroy people's lives, but to save them.'" *n***9.59** *bury my father*: The Jewish people taught that giving someone a proper burial was even more important than helping the poor. *o***10.1** *seventy-two*: Some manuscripts have "seventy." According to the book of Genesis, there were seventy nations on earth. But the ancient Greek translation of the Old Testament has "seventy-two" in place of "seventy." Jesus probably chose this number of followers to show that his message was for everyone in the world. *p***10.4** *waste time greeting people on the road*: In those days a polite greeting could take a long time. *q***10.9** *will soon be here*: Or "is already here."

street and say, 11 "We are shaking the dust from our feet r as a warning to you. And you can be sure that God's kingdom will soon be here!" s 12 I tell you that on the day of judgment the people of Sodom will get off easier than the people of that town!

## The Unbelieving Towns
### (Matthew 11.20-24)

13 You people of Chorazin are in for trouble! You people of Bethsaida are also in for trouble! If the miracles that took place in your towns had happened in Tyre and Sidon, the people there would have turned to God long ago. They would have dressed in sackcloth and put ashes on their heads. t 14 On the day of judgment the people of Tyre and Sidon will get off easier than you will. 15 People of Capernaum, do you think you will be honored in heaven? Well, you will go down to hell!

16 My followers, whoever listens to you is listening to me. Anyone who says "No" to you is saying "No" to me. And anyone who says "No" to me is really saying "No" to the one who sent me.

## The Return of the Seventy-Two

17 When the seventy-two u followers returned, they were excited and said, "Lord, even the demons obeyed when we spoke in your name!" 18 Jesus told them:

I saw Satan fall from heaven like a flash of lightning. 19 I have given you the power to trample on snakes and scorpions and to defeat the power of your enemy Satan. Nothing can harm you. 20 But don't be happy because evil spirits obey you. Be happy that your names are written in heaven!

## Jesus Thanks His Father
### (Matthew 11.25-27; 13.16, 17)

21 At that same time, Jesus felt the joy that comes from the Holy Spirit, v and he said:

My Father, Lord of heaven and earth, I am grateful that you hid all this from wise and educated people and showed it to ordinary people. Yes, Father, that is what pleased you.

22 My Father has given me everything, and he is the only one who knows the Son. The only one who really knows the Father is the Son. But the Son wants to tell others about the Father, so that they can know him too.

23 Jesus then turned to his disciples and said to them in private, "You are really blessed to see what you see! 24 Many prophets and kings were eager to see what you see and to hear what you hear. But I tell you that they did not see or hear."

## The Good Samaritan

25 An expert in the Law of Moses stood up and asked Jesus a question to see what he would say. "Teacher," he asked, "what must I do to have eternal life?"

26 Jesus answered, "What is written in the Scriptures? How do you understand them?"

27 The man replied, "The Scriptures say, 'Love the Lord your God with all your heart, soul, strength, and mind.' They also say, 'Love your neighbors as much as you love yourself.' "

28 Jesus said, "You have given the right answer. If you do this, you will have eternal life."

29 But the man wanted to show that he knew what he was talking about. So he asked Jesus, "Who are my neighbors?"

30 Jesus replied:

As a man was going down from

r 10.11 shaking the dust from our feet: This was a way of showing rejection. s 10.11 will soon be here: Or "is already here." t 10.13 dressed in sackcloth . . . ashes on their heads: This was one way that people showed how sorry they were for their sins. u 10.17 seventy-two: See the note at 10.1. v 10.21 the Holy Spirit: Some manuscripts have "his spirit."

Jerusalem to Jericho, robbers attacked him and grabbed everything he had. They beat him up and ran off, leaving him half dead.

31 A priest happened to be going down the same road. But when he saw the man, he walked by on the other side. 32 Later a temple helperʷ came to the same place. But when he saw the man who had been beaten up, he also went by on the other side.

33 A man from Samaria then came traveling along that road. When he saw the man, he felt sorry for him 34 and went over to him. He treated his wounds with olive oil and wineˣ and bandaged them. Then he put him on his own donkey and took him to an inn, where he took care of him. 35 The next morning he gave the innkeeper two silver coins and said, "Please take care of the man. If you spend more than this on him, I will pay you when I return."

36 Then Jesus asked, "Which one of these three people was a real neighbor to the man who was beaten up by robbers?"

37 The teacher answered, "The one who showed pity."

Jesus said, "Go and do the same!"

### Martha and Mary

38 The Lord and his disciples were traveling along and came to a village. When they got there, a woman named Martha welcomed him into her home. 39 She had a sister named Mary, who sat down in front of the Lord and was listening to what he said. 40 Martha was worried about all that had to be done. Finally, she went to Jesus and said, "Lord, doesn't it bother you that my sister has left me to do all the work by myself? Tell her to come and help me!"

41 The Lord answered, "Martha, Martha! You are worried and upset about so many things, 42 but only one thing

is necessary. Mary has chosen what is best, and it will not be taken away from her."

### Prayer
*(Matthew 6.9-13; 7.7-11)*

11 When Jesus had finished praying, one of his disciples said to him, "Lord, teach us to pray, just as John taught his followers to pray."

2 So Jesus told them, "Pray in this way:

'Father, help us
   to honor your name.
Come and set up
   your kingdom.
3 Give us each day
   the food we need.ʸ
4 Forgive our sins,
   as we forgive everyone
   who has done wrong to us.
And keep us
   from being tempted.' "

5 Then Jesus went on to say:

Suppose one of you goes to a friend in the middle of the night and says, "Let me borrow three loaves of bread. 6 A friend of mine has dropped in, and I don't have a thing for him to eat." 7 And suppose your friend answers, "Don't bother me! The door is bolted, and my children and I are in bed. I cannot get up to give you something."

8 He may not get up and give you the bread, just because you are his friend. But he will get up and give you as much as you need, simply because you are not ashamed to keep on asking.

9 So I tell you to ask and you will receive, search and you will find, knock and the door will be opened for you. 10 Everyone who asks will receive, everyone who searches will find, and the door will be opened for everyone who knocks. 11 Which one of you fathers would give your hungry child a snake if the child asked

---

ʷ 10.32 *temple helper*: A man from the tribe of Levi, whose job it was to work around the temple.   ˣ 10.34 *olive oil and wine*: In New Testament times these were used as medicine. Sometimes olive oil is a symbol for healing by means of a miracle (see James 5.14).
ʸ 11.3 *the food we need*: Or "food for today" or "food for the coming day."

for a fish? 12 Which one of you would give your child a scorpion if the child asked for an egg? 13 As bad as you are, you still know how to give good gifts to your children. But your heavenly Father is even more ready to give the Holy Spirit to anyone who asks.

## Jesus and the Ruler of Demons
### (Matthew 12.22-30; Mark 3.20-27)

14 Jesus forced a demon out of a man who could not talk. And after the demon had gone out, the man started speaking, and the crowds were amazed. 15 But some people said, "He forces out demons by the power of Beelzebul, the ruler of the demons!"

16 Others wanted to put Jesus to the test. So they asked him to show them a sign from God. 17 Jesus knew what they were thinking, and he said:

A kingdom where people fight each other will end up in ruin. And a family that fights will break up. 18 If Satan fights against himself, how can his kingdom last? Yet you say that I force out demons by the power of Beelzebul. 19 If I use his power to force out demons, whose power do your own followers use to force them out? They are the ones who will judge you. 20 But if I use God's power to force out demons, it proves that God's kingdom has already come to you.

21 When a strong man arms himself and guards his home, everything he owns is safe. 22 But if a stronger man comes and defeats him, he will carry off the weapons in which the strong man trusted. Then he will divide with others what he has taken. 23 If you are not on my side, you are against me. If you don't gather in the crop with me, you scatter it.

## Return of an Evil Spirit
### (Matthew 12.43-45)

24 When an evil spirit leaves a person, it travels through the desert, looking for a place to rest. But when it doesn't find a place, it says, "I will go back to the home I left." 25 When it gets there and finds the place clean and fixed up, 26 it goes off and finds seven other evil spirits even worse than itself. They all come and make their home there, and that person ends up in worse shape than before.

## Being Really Blessed

27 While Jesus was still talking, a woman in the crowd spoke up, "The woman who gave birth to you and nursed you is blessed!"

28 Jesus replied, "That's true, but the people who are really blessed are the ones who hear and obey God's message!" z

## A Sign from God
### (Matthew 12.38-42; Mark 8.12)

29 As crowds were gathering around Jesus, he said:

You people of today are evil! You keep looking for a sign from God. But what happened to Jonah a is the only sign you will be given. 30 Just as Jonah was a sign to the people of Nineveh, the Son of Man will be a sign to the people of today. 31 When the judgment comes, the Queen of the South b will stand there with you and condemn you. She traveled a long way to hear Solomon's wisdom, and yet here is something far greater than Solomon. 32 The people of Nineveh will also stand there with you and condemn you. They turned to God when Jonah preached, and yet here is something far greater than Jonah.

---

z 11.28 "That's true, but the people who are really blessed ... message": Or " 'That's not true, the people who are blessed ... message.' "   a 11.29 what happened to Jonah: Jonah was in the stomach of a big fish for three days and nights (see Matthew 12.40). b 11.31 Queen of the South: Sheba, probably a country in southern Arabia.

### Light
*(Matthew 5.15; 6.22, 23)*

33 No one lights a lamp and then hides it or puts it under a clay pot. A lamp is put on a lampstand, so that everyone who comes into the house can see the light. 34 Your eyes are the lamp for your body. When your eyes are good, you have all the light you need. But when your eyes are bad, everything is dark. 35 So be sure that your light isn't darkness. 36 If you have light, and nothing is dark, then light will be everywhere, as when a lamp shines brightly on you.

### Jesus Condemns the Pharisees and Teachers of the Law of Moses
*(Matthew 23.1-36; Mark 12.38-40; Luke 20.45-47)*

37 When Jesus finished speaking, a Pharisee invited him home for a meal. Jesus went and sat down to eat.c 38 The Pharisee was surprised that he did not wash his handsd before eating. 39 So the Lord said to him:

You Pharisees clean the outside of cups and dishes, but on the inside you are greedy and evil. 40 You fools! Didn't God make both the outside and the inside?e 41 If you would only give what you have to the poor, everything you do would please God.

42 You Pharisees are in for trouble! You give God a tenth of the spices from your gardens, such as mint and rue. But you cheat people, and you don't love God. You should be fair and kind to others and still give a tenth to God.

43 You Pharisees are in for trouble! You love the front seats in the meeting places, and you like to be greeted with honor in the market.

44 But you are in for trouble! You are like unmarked gravesf that people walk on without even knowing it.

45 A teacher of the Law of Moses spoke up, "Teacher, you said cruel things about us."

46 Jesus replied:

You teachers are also in for trouble! You load people down with heavy burdens, but you won't lift a finger to help them carry the loads. 47 Yes, you are really in for trouble. You build monuments to honor the prophets your own people murdered long ago. 48 You must think that was the right thing for your people to do, or else you would not have built monuments for the prophets they murdered.

49 Because of your evil deeds, the Wisdom of God said, "I will send prophets and apostles to you. But you will murder some and mistreat others." 50 You people living today will be punished for all the prophets who have been murdered since the beginning of the world. 51 This includes every prophet from the time of Abel to the time of Zechariah,g who was murdered between the altar and the temple. You people will certainly be punished for all of this.

52 You teachers of the Law of Moses are really in for trouble! You carry the keys to the door of knowledge about God. But you never go in, and you keep others from going in.

53 Jesus was about to leave, but the teachers and the Pharisees wanted to get even with him. They tried to make him say what he thought about other things, 54 so that they could catch him saying something wrong.

---

c 11.37 *sat down to eat*: See the note at 7.36. d 11.38 *did not wash his hands*: The Jewish people had strict laws about washing their hands before eating, especially if they had been out in public. e 11.40 *Didn't God make both the outside and the inside?*: Or "Doesn't the person who washes the outside always wash the inside too?" f 11.44 *unmarked graves*: Tombs were whitewashed to keep anyone from accidentally touching them. A person who touched a dead body or a tomb was considered unclean and could not worship with other Jewish people. g 11.51 *from the time of Abel ... Zechariah*: Genesis is the first book in the Jewish Scriptures, and it tells that Abel was the first person to be murdered. Second Chronicles is the last book in the Jewish Scriptures, and the last murder that it tells about is that of Zechariah.

## Warnings

**12** As thousands of people crowded around Jesus and were stepping on each other, he told his disciples:

Be sure to guard against the dishonest teaching[h] of the Pharisees! It is their way of fooling people. ²Everything that is hidden will be found out, and every secret will be known. ³Whatever you say in the dark will be heard when it is day. Whatever you whisper in a closed room will be shouted from the housetops.

## The One To Fear
*(Matthew 10.28-31)*

⁴My friends, don't be afraid of people. They can kill you, but after that, there is nothing else they can do. ⁵God is the one you must fear. Not only can he take your life, but he can throw you into hell. God is certainly the one you should fear!

⁶Five sparrows are sold for just two pennies, but God doesn't forget a one of them. ⁷Even the hairs on your head are counted. So don't be afraid! You are worth much more than many sparrows.

## Telling Others about Christ
*(Matthew 10.32, 33; 12.32; 10.19, 20)*

⁸If you tell others that you belong to me, the Son of Man will tell God's angels that you are my followers. ⁹But if you reject me, you will be rejected in front of them. ¹⁰If you speak against the Son of Man, you can be forgiven, but if you speak against the Holy Spirit, you cannot be forgiven.

¹¹When you are brought to trial in the Jewish meeting places or before rulers or officials, don't worry about how you will defend yourselves or what you will say. ¹²At that time the Holy Spirit will tell you what to say.

## A Rich Fool

¹³A man in a crowd said to Jesus, "Teacher, tell my brother to give me my share of what our father left us when he died."

¹⁴Jesus answered, "Who gave me the right to settle arguments between you and your brother?"

¹⁵Then he said to the crowd, "Don't be greedy! Owning a lot of things won't make your life safe."

¹⁶So Jesus told them this story:

A rich man's farm produced a big crop, ¹⁷and he said to himself, "What can I do? I don't have a place large enough to store everything."

¹⁸Later, he said, "Now I know what I'll do. I'll tear down my barns and build bigger ones, where I can store all my grain and other goods. ¹⁹Then I'll say to myself, 'You have stored up enough good things to last for years to come. Live it up! Eat, drink, and enjoy yourself.'"

²⁰But God said to him, "You fool! Tonight you will die. Then who will get what you have stored up?"

²¹"This is what happens to people who store up everything for themselves, but are poor in the sight of God."

## Worry
*(Matthew 6.25-34)*

²²Jesus said to his disciples:

I tell you not to worry about your life! Don't worry about having something to eat or wear. ²³Life is more than food or clothing. ²⁴Look at the crows! They don't plant or harvest, and they don't have storehouses or barns. But God takes care of them. You are much more important than any birds. ²⁵Can worry make you live longer?[i] ²⁶If you don't have power over small things, why worry about everything else?

²⁷Look how the wild flowers grow! They don't work hard to make their clothes. But I tell you that

Solomon with all his wealth[j] wasn't as well clothed as one of these flowers. 28 God gives such beauty to everything that grows in the fields, even though it is here today and thrown into a fire tomorrow. Won't he do even more for you? You have such little faith!

29 Don't keep worrying about having something to eat or drink. 30 Only people who don't know God are always worrying about such things. Your Father knows what you need. 31 But put God's work first, and these things will be yours as well.

## Treasures in Heaven
### (Matthew 6.19-21)

32 My little group of disciples, don't be afraid! Your Father wants to give you the kingdom. 33 Sell what you have and give the money to the poor. Make yourselves moneybags that never wear out. Make sure your treasure is safe in heaven, where thieves cannot steal it and moths cannot destroy it. 34 Your heart will always be where your treasure is.

## Faithful and Unfaithful Servants
### (Matthew 24.45-51)

35 Be ready and keep your lamps burning 36 just like those servants who wait up for their master to return from a wedding feast. As soon as he comes and knocks, they open the door for him. 37 Servants are fortunate if their master finds them awake and ready when he comes! I promise you that he will get ready and have his servants sit down so he can serve them. 38 Those servants are really fortunate if their master finds them ready, even though he comes late at night or early in the morning. 39 You would surely not let a thief break into your home, if you knew when the thief was coming. 40 So always be ready! You don't

know when the Son of Man will come.

41 Peter asked Jesus, "Did you say this just for us or for everyone?"

42 The Lord answered:

Who are faithful and wise servants? Who are the ones the master will put in charge of giving the other servants their food supplies at the proper time? 43 Servants are fortunate if their master comes and finds them doing their job. 44 A servant who is always faithful will surely be put in charge of everything the master owns.

45 But suppose one of the servants thinks that the master won't return until late. Suppose that servant starts beating all the other servants and eats and drinks and gets drunk. 46 If that happens, the master will come on a day and at a time when the servant least expects him. That servant will then be punished and thrown out with the servants who cannot be trusted.

47 If servants are not ready or willing to do what their master wants them to do, they will be beaten hard. 48 But servants who don't know what their master wants them to do will not be beaten so hard for doing wrong. If God has been generous with you, he will expect you to serve him well. But if he has been more than generous, he will expect you to serve him even better.

## Not Peace, but Trouble
### (Matthew 10.34-36)

49 I came to set fire to the earth, and I wish it were already on fire! 50 I am going to be put to a hard test. And I will have to suffer a lot of pain until it is over. 51 Do you think that I came to bring peace to earth? No indeed! I came to make people choose sides. 52 A family of five will be divided, with two of them against the other three. 53 Fathers and sons will turn against one another, and mothers and daughters will do the same. Mothers-in-law and

j 12.27 Solomon with all his wealth: The Jewish people thought that Solomon was the richest person who had ever lived.

daughters-in-law will also turn against each other.

## Knowing What To Do
### (Matthew 16.2, 3; 5.25, 26)

54 Jesus said to all the people:

As soon as you see a cloud coming up in the west, you say, "It's going to rain," and it does. 55 When the south wind blows, you say, "It's going to get hot," and it does. 56 Are you trying to fool someone? You can predict the weather by looking at the earth and sky, but you don't really know what's going on right now. 57 Why don't you understand the right thing to do? 58 When someone accuses you of something, try to settle things before you are taken to court. If you don't, you will be dragged before the judge. Then the judge will hand you over to the jailer, and you will be locked up. 59 You won't get out until you have paid the last cent you owe.

## Turn Back to God

**13** About this same time Jesus was told that Pilate had given orders for some people from Galilee to be killed while they were offering sacrifices. 2 Jesus replied:

Do you think that these people were worse sinners than everyone else in Galilee just because of what happened to them? 3 Not at all! But you can be sure that if you don't turn back to God, every one of you will also be killed. 4 What about those eighteen people who died when the tower in Siloam fell on them? Do you think they were worse than everyone else in Jerusalem? 5 Not at all! But you can be sure that if you don't turn back to God, every one of you will also die.

## A Story about a Fig Tree

6 Jesus then told them this story:

A man had a fig tree growing in his vineyard. One day he went out to pick some figs, but he didn't find any. 7 So he said to the gardener, "For three years I have come looking for figs on this tree, and I haven't found any yet. Chop it down! Why should it take up space?"

8 The gardener answered, "Master, leave it for another year. I'll dig around it and put some manure on it to make it grow. 9 Maybe it will have figs on it next year. If it doesn't, you can have it cut down."

## Healing a Woman on the Sabbath

10 One Sabbath, Jesus was teaching in a Jewish meeting place, 11 and a woman was there who had been crippled by an evil spirit for eighteen years. She was completely bent over and could not straighten up. 12 When Jesus saw the woman, he called her over and said, "You are now well." 13 He placed his hands on her, and right away she stood up straight and praised God.

14 The man in charge of the meeting place was angry because Jesus had healed someone on the Sabbath. So he said to the people, "Each week has six days when we can work. Come and be healed on one of those days, but not on the Sabbath."

15 The Lord replied, "Are you trying to fool someone? Won't any one of you untie your ox or donkey and lead it out to drink on a Sabbath? 16 This woman belongs to the family of Abraham, but Satan has kept her bound for eighteen years. Isn't it right to set her free on the Sabbath?" 17 Jesus' words made his enemies ashamed. But everyone else in the crowd was happy about the wonderful things he was doing.

## A Mustard Seed and Yeast
### (Matthew 13.31-33; Mark 4.30-32)

18 Jesus said, "What is God's kingdom like? What can I compare it with? 19 It is like what happens when someone plants a mustard seed in a garden. The seed grows as big as a tree, and birds nest in its branches."

20 Then Jesus said, "What can I compare God's kingdom with? 21 It is like what happens when a woman mixes

yeast into three batches of flour. Finally, all the dough rises."

### The Narrow Door
#### (Matthew 7.13, 14, 21-23)

²²As Jesus was on his way to Jerusalem, he taught the people in the towns and villages. ²³Someone asked him, "Lord, are only a few people going to be saved?"

Jesus answered:

²⁴Do all you can to go in by the narrow door! A lot of people will try to get in, but will not be able to. ²⁵Once the owner of the house gets up and locks the door, you will be left standing outside. You will knock on the door and say, "Sir, open the door for us!"

But the owner will answer, "I don't know a thing about you!"

²⁶Then you will start saying, "We dined with you, and you taught in our streets."

²⁷But he will say, "I really don't know who you are! Get away from me, you evil people!"

²⁸Then when you have been thrown outside, you will weep and grit your teeth because you will see Abraham and Isaac and all the prophets in God's kingdom. ²⁹People will come from all directions and sit down to feast in God's kingdom. ³⁰There the ones who are now least important will be the most important, and those who are now most important will be least important.

### Jesus and Herod

³¹At that time some Pharisees came to Jesus and said, "You had better get away from here! Herod*k* wants to kill you."

³²Jesus said to them:

Go tell that fox, "I am going to force out demons and heal people today and tomorrow, and three days later I'll be through." ³³But I am going on my way today and tomorrow and the next day. After all, Jerusa-

lem is the place where prophets are killed.

### Jesus Loves Jerusalem
#### (Matthew 23.37-39)

³⁴Jerusalem, Jerusalem! Your people have killed the prophets and have stoned the messengers who were sent to you. I have often wanted to gather your people, as a hen gathers her chicks under her wings. But you wouldn't let me. ³⁵Now your temple will be deserted. You won't see me again until the time when you say,

"Blessed is the one who comes
in the name of the Lord."

### Jesus Heals a Sick Man

**14** One Sabbath, Jesus was having dinner in the home of an important Pharisee, and everyone was carefully watching Jesus. ²All of a sudden a man with swollen legs stood up in front of him. ³Jesus turned and asked the Pharisees and the teachers of the Law of Moses, "Is it right to heal on the Sabbath?" ⁴But they did not say a word.

Jesus took hold of the man. Then he healed him and sent him away. ⁵Afterwards, Jesus asked the people, "If your son or ox falls into a well, wouldn't you pull him out right away, even on the Sabbath?" ⁶There was nothing they could say.

### How To Be a Guest

⁷Jesus saw how the guests had tried to take the best seats. So he told them: ⁸When you are invited to a wedding feast, don't sit in the best place. Someone more important may have been invited. ⁹Then the one who invited you will come and say, "Give your place to this other guest!" You will be embarrassed and will have to sit in the worst place.

¹⁰When you are invited to be a guest, go and sit in the worst place. Then the one who invited you may

come and say, "My friend, take a better seat!" You will then be honored in front of all the other guests. [11] If you put yourself above others, you will be put down. But if you humble yourself, you will be honored.

[12] Then Jesus said to the man who had invited him:

When you give a dinner or a banquet, don't invite your friends and family and relatives and rich neighbors. If you do, they will invite you in return, and you will be paid back. [13] When you give a feast, invite the poor, the crippled, the lame, and the blind. [14] They cannot pay you back. But God will bless you and reward you when his people rise from death.

## The Great Banquet
### (Matthew 22.1-10)

[15] After Jesus had finished speaking, one of the guests said, "The greatest blessing of all is to be at the banquet in God's kingdom!"

[16] Jesus told him:

A man once gave a great banquet and invited a lot of guests. [17] When the banquet was ready, he sent a servant to tell the guests, "Everything is ready! Please come."

[18] One guest after another started making excuses. The first one said, "I bought some land, and I've got to look it over. Please excuse me."

[19] Another guest said, "I bought five teams of oxen, and I need to try them out. Please excuse me."

[20] Still another guest said, "I have just gotten married, and I can't be there."

[21] The servant told his master what happened, and the master became so angry that he said, "Go as fast as you can to every street and alley in town! Bring in everyone who is poor or crippled or blind or lame."

[22] When the servant returned, he said, "Master, I've done what you told me, and there is still plenty of room for more people."

[23] His master then told him, "Go out along the back roads and fence rows and make people come in, so that my house will be full. [24] Not one of the guests I first invited will get even a bite of my food!"

## Being a Disciple
### (Matthew 10.37, 38)

[25] Large crowds were walking along with Jesus, when he turned and said:

[26] You cannot be my disciple, unless you love me more than you love your father and mother, your wife and children, and your brothers and sisters. You cannot come with me unless you love me more than you love your own life.

[27] You cannot be my disciple unless you carry your own cross and come with me.

[28] Suppose one of you wants to build a tower. What is the first thing you will do? Won't you sit down and figure out how much it will cost and if you have enough money to pay for it? [29] Otherwise, you will start building the tower, but not be able to finish. Then everyone who sees what is happening will laugh at you. [30] They will say, "You started building, but could not finish the job."

[31] What will a king do if he has only ten thousand soldiers to defend himself against a king who is about to attack him with twenty thousand soldiers? Before he goes out to battle, won't he first sit down and decide if he can win? [32] If he thinks he won't be able to defend himself, he will send messengers and ask for peace while the other king is still a long way off. [33] So then, you cannot be my disciple unless you give away everything you own.

## Salt and Light
### (Matthew 5.13; Mark 9.50)

[34] Salt is good, but if it no longer tastes like salt, how can it be made to taste salty again? [35] It is no longer good for the soil or even for the manure pile. People simply throw it out. If you have ears, pay attention!

## One Sheep
### (Matthew 18.12-14)

**15** Tax collectors[l] and sinners were all crowding around to listen to Jesus. [2] So the Pharisees and the teachers of the Law of Moses started grumbling, "This man is friendly with sinners. He even eats with them."

[3] Then Jesus told them this story:

[4] If any of you has a hundred sheep, and one of them gets lost, what will you do? Won't you leave the ninety-nine in the field and go look for the lost sheep until you find it? [5] And when you find it, you will be so glad that you will put it on your shoulder [6] and carry it home. Then you will call in your friends and neighbors and say, "Let's celebrate! I've found my lost sheep."

[7] Jesus said, "In the same way there is more happiness in heaven because of one sinner who turns to God than over ninety-nine good people who don't need to."

## One Coin

[8] Jesus told the people another story: What will a woman do if she has ten silver coins and loses one of them? Won't she light a lamp, sweep the floor, and look carefully until she finds it? [9] Then she will call in her friends and neighbors and say, "Let's celebrate! I've found the coin I lost."

[10] Jesus said, "In the same way God's angels are happy when even one person turns to him."

## Two Sons

[11] Jesus also told them another story: Once a man had two sons. [12] The younger son said to his father, "Give me my share of the property." So the father divided his property between his two sons.

[13] Not long after that, the younger son packed up everything he owned and left for a foreign country, where he wasted all his money in wild living. [14] He had spent everything, when a bad famine spread through that whole land. Soon he had nothing to eat.

[15] He went to work for a man in that country, and the man sent him out to take care of his pigs.[m] [16] He would have been glad to eat what the pigs were eating,[n] but no one gave him a thing.

[17] Finally, he came to his senses and said, "My father's workers have plenty to eat, and here I am, starving to death! [18] I will go to my father and say to him, 'Father, I have sinned against God in heaven and against you. [19] I am no longer good enough to be called your son. Treat me like one of your workers.' "

[20] The younger son got up and started back to his father. But when he was still a long way off, his father saw him and felt sorry for him. He ran to his son and hugged and kissed him.

[21] The son said, "Father, I have sinned against God in heaven and against you. I am no longer good enough to be called your son."

[22] But his father said to the servants, "Hurry and bring the best clothes and put them on him. Give him a ring for his finger and sandals[o] for his feet. [23] Get the best calf and prepare it, so we can eat and celebrate. [24] This son of mine was dead, but has now come back to life. He was lost and has now been found." And they began to celebrate.

[25] The older son had been out in the field. But when he came near the house, he heard the music and danc-

---

[l]**15.1** *Tax collectors*: See the note at 3.12.   [m]**15.15** *pigs*: The Jewish religion taught that pigs were not fit to eat or even to touch. A Jewish man would have felt terribly insulted if he had to feed pigs, much less eat with them.   [n]**15.16** *what the pigs were eating*: The Greek text has "(bean) pods," which came from a tree in Palestine. These were used to feed animals. Poor people sometimes ate them too.   [o]**15.22** *ring ... sandals*: These show that the young man's father fully accepted him as his son. A ring was a sign of high position in the family. Sandals showed that he was a son instead of a slave, since slaves did not usually wear sandals.

ing. 26 So he called one of the servants over and asked, "What's going on here?"
27 The servant answered, "Your
brother has come home safe and
sound, and your father ordered us
to kill the best calf." 28 The older
brother got so angry that he would
not even go into the house.
His father came out and begged
him to go in. 29 But he said to his
father, "For years I have worked for
you like a slave and have always
obeyed you. But you have never
even given me a little goat, so that
I could give a dinner for my friends.
30 This other son of yours wasted
your money on prostitutes. And
now that he has come home, you
ordered the best calf to be killed
for a feast."
31 His father replied, "My son, you
are always with me, and everything
I have is yours. 32 But we should be
glad and celebrate! Your brother
was dead, but he is now alive. He
was lost and has now been found."

### A Dishonest Manager

**16** Jesus said to his disciples:
A rich man once had a man-
ager to take care of his business. But
he was told that his manager was
wasting money. 2 So the rich man
called him in and said, "What is this
I hear about you? Tell me what you
have done! You are no longer going
to work for me."
3 The manager said to himself,
"What shall I do now that my master
is going to fire me? I can't dig
ditches, and I'm ashamed to beg. 4 I
know what I'll do, so that people will
welcome me into their homes after
I've lost my job."
5 Then one by one he called in the
people who were in debt to his master. He asked the first one, "How
much do you owe my master?"
6 "A hundred barrels of olive oil,"
the man answered.
So the manager said, "Take your
bill and sit down and quickly write
'fifty'."
7 The manager asked someone
else who was in debt to his master,
"How much do you owe?"
"A thousand bushels[p] of wheat,"
the man replied.
The manager said, "Take your bill
and write 'eight hundred'."
8 The master praised his dishonest
manager for looking out for himself
so well. That's how it is! The people
of this world look out for themselves
better than the people who belong
to the light.
9 My disciples, I tell you to use
wicked wealth to make friends for
yourselves. Then when it is gone,
you will be welcomed into an eternal
home. 10 Anyone who can be trusted
in little matters can also be trusted
in important matters. But anyone
who is dishonest in little matters will
be dishonest in important matters.
11 If you cannot be trusted with this
wicked wealth, who will trust you
with true wealth? 12 And if you cannot be trusted with what belongs to
someone else, who will give you
something that will be your own?
13 You cannot be the slave of two
masters. You will like one more than
the other or be more loyal to one
than to the other. You cannot serve
God and money.

### Some Sayings of Jesus

*(Matthew 11.12, 13; 5.31, 32; Mark 10.11, 12)*

14 The Pharisees really loved money.
So when they heard what Jesus said,
they made fun of him. 15 But Jesus told
them:
You are always making yourselves look good, but God sees what
is in your heart. The things that
most people think are important
are worthless as far as God is
concerned.
16 Until the time of John the Baptist, people had to obey the Law of
Moses and the Books of the Prophets.[q] But since God's kingdom

[p] **16.7** *A thousand bushels*: The Greek text has "A hundred measures," and each measure is about ten or twelve bushels. [q] **16.16** *the Law of Moses and the Books of the Prophets*: The Jewish Scriptures, that is, the Old Testament.

has been preached, everyone is trying hard to get in. [17] Heaven and earth will disappear before the smallest letter of the Law does.

[18] It is a terrible sin[r] for a man to divorce his wife and marry another woman. It is also a terrible sin for a man to marry a divorced woman.

### Lazarus and the Rich Man

[19] There was once a rich man who wore expensive clothes and every day ate the best food. [20] But a poor beggar named Lazarus was brought to the gate of the rich man's house. [21] He was happy just to eat the scraps that fell from the rich man's table. His body was covered with sores, and dogs kept coming up to lick them. [22] The poor man died, and angels took him to the place of honor next to Abraham.[s]

The rich man also died and was buried. [23] He went to hell[t] and was suffering terribly. When he looked up and saw Abraham far off and Lazarus at his side, [24] he said to Abraham, "Have pity on me! Send Lazarus to dip his finger in water and touch my tongue. I'm suffering terribly in this fire."

[25] Abraham answered, "My friend, remember that while you lived, you had everything good, and Lazarus had everything bad. Now he is happy, and you are in pain. [26] And besides, there is a deep ditch between us, and no one from either side can cross over."

[27] But the rich man said, "Abraham, then please send Lazarus to my father's home. [28] Let him warn my five brothers, so they won't come to this horrible place."

[29] Abraham answered, "Your brothers can read what Moses and the prophets[u] wrote. They should pay attention to that."

[30] Then the rich man said, "No, that's not enough! If only someone from the dead would go to them, they would listen and turn to God."

[31] So Abraham said, "If they won't pay attention to Moses and the prophets, they won't listen even to someone who comes back from the dead."

### Faith and Service
(Matthew 18.6, 7, 21, 22; Mark 9.42)

**17** Jesus said to his disciples:
There will always be something that causes people to sin. But anyone who causes them to sin is in for trouble. A person who causes even one of my little followers to sin [2] would be better off thrown into the ocean with a heavy stone tied around their neck. [3] So be careful what you do.

Correct any followers[v] of mine who sin, and forgive the ones who say they are sorry. [4] Even if one of them mistreats you seven times in one day and says, "I am sorry," you should still forgive that person.

[5] The apostles said to the Lord, "Make our faith stronger!"

[6] Jesus replied:
If you had faith no bigger than a tiny mustard seed, you could tell this mulberry tree to pull itself up, roots and all, and to plant itself in the ocean. And it would!

[7] If your servant comes in from plowing or from taking care of the sheep, would you say, "Welcome! Come on in and have something to eat"? [8] No, you wouldn't say that. You would say, "Fix me something to eat. Get ready to serve me, so I can have my meal. Then later on you

[r] 16.18 *a terrible sin*: The Greek text uses a word that means the sin of being unfaithful in marriage. [s] 16.22 *the place of honor next to Abraham*: The Jewish people thought that heaven would be a banquet that God would give for them. Abraham would be the most important person there, and the guest of honor would sit next to him. [t] 16.23 *hell*: The Greek text has "hades," which the Jewish people often thought of as the place where the dead wait for the final judgment. [u] 16.29 *Moses and the prophets*: The Jewish Scriptures, that is, the Old Testament. [v] 17.3 *followers*: The Greek text has "brothers," which is often used in the New Testament for followers of Jesus.

can eat and drink." [9] Servants don't deserve special thanks for doing what they are supposed to do. [10] And that's how it should be with you. When you've done all you should, then say, "We are merely servants, and we have simply done our duty."

### Ten Men with Leprosy

[11] On his way to Jerusalem, Jesus went along the border between Samaria and Galilee. [12] As he was going into a village, ten men with leprosy[w] came toward him. They stood at a distance [13] and shouted, "Jesus, Master, have pity on us!"

[14] Jesus looked at them and said, "Go show yourselves to the priests."[x]

On their way they were healed. [15] When one of them discovered that he was healed, he came back, shouting praises to God. [16] He bowed down at the feet of Jesus and thanked him. The man was from the country of Samaria.

[17] Jesus asked, "Weren't ten men healed? Where are the other nine? [18] Why was this foreigner the only one who came back to thank God?" [19] Then Jesus told the man, "You may get up and go. Your faith has made you well."

### God's Kingdom
(Matthew 24.23-28, 37-41)

[20] Some Pharisees asked Jesus when God's kingdom would come. He answered, "God's kingdom isn't something you can see. [21] There is no use saying, 'Look! Here it is' or 'Look! There it is.' God's kingdom is here with you."[y]

[22] Jesus said to his disciples:

The time will come when you will long to see one of the days of the Son of Man, but you will not. [23] When people say to you, "Look there," or "Look here," don't go looking for him. [24] The day of the Son of Man will be like lightning flashing across the sky. [25] But first he must suffer terribly and be rejected by the people of today. [26] When the Son of Man comes, things will be just as they were when Noah lived. [27] People were eating, drinking, and getting married right up to the day when Noah went into the big boat. Then the flood came and drowned everyone on earth.

[28] When Lot[z] lived, people were also eating and drinking. They were buying, selling, planting, and building. [29] But on the very day Lot left Sodom, fiery flames poured down from the sky and killed everyone. [30] The same will happen on the day when the Son of Man appears.

[31] At that time no one on a rooftop[a] should go down into the house to get anything. No one in a field should go back to the house for anything. [32] Remember what happened to Lot's wife.[b]

[33] People who try to save their lives will lose them, and those who lose their lives will save them. [34] On that night two people will be sleeping in the same bed, but only one will be taken. The other will be left. [35-36] Two women will be together grinding wheat, but only one will be taken. The other will be left.[c]

[37] Then Jesus' disciples spoke up, "But where will this happen, Lord?"

Jesus said, "Where there is a corpse, there will always be buzzards."[d]

---

[w] 17.12 leprosy: See the note at 4.27.   [x] 17.14 show yourselves to the priests: See the note at 5.14.   [y] 17.21 here with you: Or "in your hearts."   [z] 17.27,28 Noah . . . Lot: When God destroyed the earth by a flood, he saved Noah and his family. And when God destroyed the cities of Sodom and Gomorrah and the evil people who lived there, he rescued Lot and his family (see Genesis 19.1-29).   [a] 17.31 rooftop: See the note at 5.19.   [b] 17.32 what happened to Lot's wife: She turned to a block of salt when she disobeyed God (see Genesis 19.26).   [c] 17.35,36 will be left: Some manuscripts add, "Two men will be in the same field, but only one will be taken. The other will be left."   [d] 17.37 Where there is a corpse, there will always be buzzards: This saying may mean that when anything important happens, people soon know about it. Or the saying may mean that whenever something bad happens, curious people gather around and stare. But the word translated "buzzard" also means "eagle" and may refer to the Roman army, which had an eagle as its symbol.

## A Widow and a Judge

**18** Jesus told his disciples a story about how they should keep on praying and never give up:

² In a town there was once a judge who didn't fear God or care about people. ³ In that same town there was a widow who kept going to the judge and saying, "Make sure that I get fair treatment in court."

⁴ For a while the judge refused to do anything. Finally, he said to himself, "Even though I don't fear God or care about people, ⁵ I will help this widow because she keeps on bothering me. If I don't help her, she will wear me out."

⁶ The Lord said:

Think about what that crooked judge said. ⁷ Won't God protect his chosen ones who pray to him day and night? Won't he be concerned for them? ⁸ He will surely hurry and help them. But when the Son of Man comes, will he find on this earth anyone with faith?

## A Pharisee and a Tax Collector

⁹ Jesus told a story to some people who thought they were better than others and who looked down on everyone else:

¹⁰ Two men went into the temple to pray.ᵉ One was a Pharisee and the other a tax collector.ᶠ ¹¹ The Pharisee stood over by himself and prayed,ᵍ "God, I thank you that I am not greedy, dishonest, and unfaithful in marriage like other people. And I am really glad that I am not like that tax collector over there. ¹² I go without eatingʰ for two days a week, and I give you one tenth of all I earn."

¹³ The tax collector stood off at a distance and did not think he was good enough even to look up toward heaven. He was so sorry for what

he had done that he pounded his chest and prayed, "God, have pity on me! I am such a sinner."

¹⁴ Then Jesus said, "When the two men went home, it was the tax collector and not the Pharisee who was pleasing to God. If you put yourself above others, you will be put down. But if you humble yourself, you will be honored."

## Jesus Blesses Little Children
### (Matthew 19.13-15; Mark 10.13-16)

¹⁵ Some people brought their little children for Jesus to bless. But when his disciples saw them doing this, they told the people to stop bothering him. ¹⁶ So Jesus called the children over to him and said, "Let the children come to me! Don't try to stop them. People who are like these children belong to God's kingdom.ⁱ ¹⁷ You will never get into God's kingdom unless you enter it like a child!"

## A Rich and Important Man
### (Matthew 19.16-30; Mark 10.17-31)

¹⁸ An important man asked Jesus, "Good Teacher, what must I do to have eternal life?"

¹⁹ Jesus said, "Why do you call me good? Only God is good. ²⁰ You know the commandments: 'Be faithful in marriage. Do not murder. Do not steal. Do not tell lies about others. Respect your father and mother.'"

²¹ He told Jesus, "I have obeyed all these commandments since I was a young man."

²² When Jesus heard this, he said, "There is one thing you still need to do. Go and sell everything you own! Give the money to the poor, and you will have riches in heaven. Then come and be my follower." ²³ When the man heard this, he was sad, because he was very rich.

²⁴ Jesus saw how sad the man was. So he said, "It's terribly hard for rich

---

ᵉ **18.10** *into the temple to pray*: Jewish people usually prayed there early in the morning and late in the afternoon. ᶠ **18.10** *tax collector*: See the note at 3.12. ᵍ **18.11** *stood over by himself and prayed*: Some manuscripts have "stood up and prayed to himself." ʰ **18.12** *without eating*: See the note at 2.37. ⁱ **18.16** *People who are like these children belong to God's kingdom*: Or "God's kingdom belongs to people who are like these children."

people to get into God's kingdom! 25 In fact, it's easier for a camel to go through the eye of a needle than for a rich person to get into God's kingdom."

26 When the crowd heard this, they asked, "How can anyone ever be saved?"

27 Jesus replied, "There are some things that people cannot do, but God can do anything."

28 Peter said, "Remember, we left everything to be your followers!"

29 Jesus answered, "You can be sure that anyone who gives up home or wife or brothers or family or children because of God's kingdom 30 will be given much more in this life. And in the future world they will have eternal life."

## Jesus Again Tells about His Death

*(Matthew 20.17-19; Mark 10.32-34)*

31 Jesus took the twelve apostles aside and said:

We are now on our way to Jerusalem. Everything that the prophets wrote about the Son of Man will happen there. 32 He will be handed over to foreigners,ʲ who will make fun of him, mistreat him, and spit on him. 33 They will beat him and kill him, but three days later he will rise to life.

34 The apostles did not understand what Jesus was talking about. They could not understand, because the meaning of what he said was hidden from them.

## Jesus Heals a Blind Beggar

*(Matthew 20.29-34; Mark 10.46-52)*

35 When Jesus was coming close to Jericho, a blind man sat begging beside the road. 36 The man heard the crowd walking by and asked what was happening. 37 Some people told him that Jesus from Nazareth was passing by. 38 So the blind man shouted, "Jesus, Son of David,ᵏ have pity on me!" 39 The people who were going along with Jesus told the man to be quiet. But he shouted even louder, "Son of David, have pity on me!"

40 Jesus stopped and told some people to bring the blind man over to him. When the blind man was getting near, Jesus asked, 41 "What do you want me to do for you?"

"Lord, I want to see!" he answered.

42 Jesus replied, "Look and you will see! Your eyes are healed because of your faith." 43 Right away the man could see, and he went with Jesus and started thanking God. When the crowds saw what happened, they praised God.

## Zacchaeus

**19** Jesus was going through Jericho, 2 where a man named Zacchaeus lived. He was in charge of collecting taxesˡ and was very rich. 3-4 Jesus was heading his way, and Zacchaeus wanted to see what he was like. But Zacchaeus was a short man and could not see over the crowd. So he ran ahead and climbed up into a sycamore tree.

5 When Jesus got there, he looked up and said, "Zacchaeus, hurry down! I want to stay with you today." 6 Zacchaeus hurried down and gladly welcomed Jesus.

7 Everyone who saw this started grumbling, "This man Zacchaeus is a sinner! And Jesus is going home to eat with him."

8 Later that day Zacchaeus stood up and said to the Lord, "I will give half of my property to the poor. And I will now pay back four times as muchᵐ to everyone I have ever cheated."

9 Jesus said to Zacchaeus, "Today you and your family have been saved,ⁿ

---

ʲ **18.32** *foreigners*: The Romans, who ruled Judea at this time. ᵏ **18.38** *Son of David*: The Jewish people expected the Messiah to be from the family of King David, and for this reason the Messiah was often called the "Son of David." ˡ **19.2** *in charge of collecting taxes*: See the note at 3.12. ᵐ **19.8** *pay back four times as much*: Both Jewish and Roman law said that a person must pay back four times the amount that was taken. ⁿ **19.9** *saved*: Zacchaeus was Jewish, but it is only now that he is rescued from sin and placed under God's care.

because you are a true son of Abraham.[o] [10] The Son of Man came to look for and to save people who are lost."

## A Story about Ten Servants
### (Matthew 25.14-30)

[11] The crowd was still listening to Jesus as he was getting close to Jerusalem. Many of them thought that God's kingdom would soon appear, [12] and Jesus told them this story:

A prince once went to a foreign country to be crowned king and then to return. [13] But before leaving, he called in ten servants and gave each of them some money. He told them, "Use this to earn more money until I get back."

[14] But the people of his country hated him, and they sent messengers to the foreign country to say, "We don't want this man to be our king."

[15] After the prince had been made king, he returned and called in his servants. He asked them how much they had earned with the money they had been given.

[16] The first servant came and said, "Sir, with the money you gave me I have earned ten times as much."

[17] "That's fine, my good servant!" the king said. "Since you have shown that you can be trusted with a small amount, you will be given ten cities to rule."

[18] The second one came and said, "Sir, with the money you gave me, I have earned five times as much."

[19] The king said, "You will be given five cities."

[20] Another servant came and said, "Sir, here is your money. I kept it safe in a handkerchief. [21] You are a hard man, and I was afraid of you. You take what isn't yours, and you harvest crops you didn't plant."

[22] "You worthless servant!" the king told him. "You have condemned yourself by what you have just said. You knew that I am a hard man, taking what isn't mine and harvesting what I've not planted. [23] Why didn't you put my money in the bank? On my return, I could have had the money together with interest."

[24] Then he said to some other servants standing there, "Take the money away from him and give it to the servant who earned ten times as much."

[25] But they said, "Sir, he already has ten times as much!"

[26] The king replied, "Those who have something will be given more. But everything will be taken away from those who don't have anything. [27] Now bring me the enemies who didn't want me to be their king. Kill them while I watch!"

## Jesus Enters Jerusalem
### (Matthew 21.1-11; Mark 11.1-11; John 12.12-19)

[28] When Jesus had finished saying all this, he went on toward Jerusalem. [29] As he was getting near Bethphage and Bethany on the Mount of Olives, he sent two of his disciples on ahead. [30] He told them, "Go into the next village, where you will find a young donkey that has never been ridden. Untie the donkey and bring it here. [31] If anyone asks why you are doing that, just say, 'The Lord[p] needs it.' "

[32] They went off and found everything just as Jesus had said. [33] While they were untying the donkey, its owners asked, "Why are you doing that?"

[34] They answered, "The Lord[p] needs it."

[35] Then they led the donkey to Jesus. They put some of their clothes on its back and helped Jesus get on. [36] And as he rode along, the people spread clothes on the road[q] in front of him. [37] When Jesus was starting down the Mount of Olives, his large crowd of disciples were happy and praised God because of all the miracles they had seen. [38] They shouted,

---

[o] 19.9 *son of Abraham*: As used in this verse, the words mean that Zacchaeus is truly one of God's special people.   [p] 19.31 *The Lord*: Or "The master of the donkey."   [p] 19.34 *The Lord*: Or "The master of the donkey."   [q] 19.36 *spread clothes on the road*: This was one way that the Jewish people welcomed a famous person.

"Blessed is the king who comes
in the name of the Lord!
Peace in heaven
and glory to God."

**39** Some Pharisees in the crowd said to Jesus, "Teacher, make your disciples stop shouting!"

**40** But Jesus answered, "If they keep quiet, these stones will start shouting."

**41** When Jesus came closer and could see Jerusalem, he cried **42** and said:

It is too bad that today your people don't know what will bring them peace! Now it is hidden from them. **43** Jerusalem, the time will come when your enemies will build walls around you to attack you. Armies will surround you and close in on you from every side. **44** They will level you to the ground and kill your people. Not one stone in your buildings will be left on top of another. This will happen because you did not see that God had come to save you.*r*

### Jesus in the Temple
(Matthew 21.12-17; Mark 11.15-19; John 2.13-22)

**45** When Jesus entered the temple, he started chasing out the people who were selling things. **46** He told them, "The Scriptures say, 'My house should be a place of worship.' But you have made it a place where robbers hide!"

**47** Each day, Jesus kept on teaching in the temple. So the chief priests, the teachers of the Law of Moses, and some other important people tried to have him killed. **48** But they could not find a way to do it, because everyone else was eager to listen to him.

### A Question about Jesus' Authority
(Matthew 21.23-27; Mark 11.27-33)

**20** One day, Jesus was teaching in the temple and telling the good news. So the chief priests, the teachers, and the nation's leaders **2** asked him, "What right do you have to do these things? Who gave you this authority?"

**3** Jesus replied, "I want to ask you a question. **4** Who gave John the right to baptize? Was it God in heaven or merely some human being?"

**5** They talked this over and said to each other, "We can't say that God gave John this right. Jesus will ask us why we didn't believe John. **6** And we can't say that it was merely some human who gave John the right to baptize. The crowd will stone us to death, because they think John was a prophet."

**7** So they told Jesus, "We don't know who gave John the right to baptize."

**8** Jesus replied, "Then I won't tell you who gave me the right to do what I do."

### Renters of a Vineyard
(Matthew 21.33-46; Mark 12.1-12)

**9** Jesus told the people this story:

A man once planted a vineyard and rented it out. Then he left the country for a long time. **10** When it was time to harvest the crop, he sent a servant to ask the renters for his share of the grapes. But they beat up the servant and sent him away without anything. **11** So the owner sent another servant. The renters also beat him up. They insulted him terribly and sent him away without a thing. **12** The owner sent a third servant. He was also beaten terribly and thrown out of the vineyard.

**13** The owner then said to himself, "What am I going to do? I know what. I'll send my son, the one I love so much. They will surely respect him!"

**14** When the renters saw the owner's son, they said to one another, "Someday he will own the vineyard. Let's kill him! Then we can have it all for ourselves." **15** So they threw him out of the vineyard and killed him.

Jesus asked, "What do you think the owner of the vineyard will do? **16** I'll tell you what. He will come and kill those renters and let someone else have his vineyard."

---

*r*19.44 *that God had come to save you*: The Jewish people looked for the time when God would come and rescue them from their enemies. But when Jesus came, many of them refused to obey him.

When the people heard this, they said, "This must never happen!" [17] But Jesus looked straight at them and said, "Then what do the Scriptures mean when they say, 'The stone that the builders tossed aside is now the most important stone of all'? [18] Anyone who stumbles over this stone will get hurt, and anyone it falls on will be smashed to pieces."

[19] The chief priests and the teachers of the Law of Moses knew that Jesus was talking about them when he was telling this story. They wanted to arrest him right then, but they were afraid of the people.

## Paying Taxes
*(Matthew 22.15-22; Mark 12.13-17)*

[20] Jesus' enemies kept watching him closely, because they wanted to hand him over to the Roman governor. So they sent some men who pretended to be good. But they were really spies trying to catch Jesus saying something wrong. [21] The spies said to him, "Teacher, we know that you teach the truth about what God wants people to do. And you treat everyone with the same respect, no matter who they are. [22] Tell us, should we pay taxes to the Emperor or not?"

[23] Jesus knew that they were trying to trick him. So he told them, [24] "Show me a coin." Then he asked, "Whose picture and name are on it?"

"The Emperor's," they answered.

[25] Then he told them, "Give the Emperor what belongs to him and give God what belongs to God." [26] Jesus' enemies could not catch him saying anything wrong there in front of the people. They were amazed at his answer and kept quiet.

## Life in the Future World
*(Matthew 22.23-33; Mark 12.18-27)*

[27] The Sadducees did not believe that people would rise to life after death. So some of them came to Jesus [28] and said:

Teacher, Moses wrote that if a married man dies and has no children, his brother should marry the widow. Their first son would then be thought of as the son of the dead brother.

[29] There were once seven brothers. The first one married, but died without having any children. [30] The second one married his brother's widow, and he also died without having any children. [31] The same thing happened to the third one. Finally, all seven brothers married that woman and died without having any children. [32] At last the woman died. [33] When God raises people from death, whose wife will this woman be? All seven brothers had married her.

[34] Jesus answered:

The people in this world get married. [35] But in the future world no one who is worthy to rise from death will either marry [36] or die. They will be like the angels and will be God's children, because they have been raised to life.

[37] In the story about the burning bush, Moses clearly shows that people will live again. He said, "The Lord is the God worshiped by Abraham, Isaac, and Jacob."[s] [38] So the Lord isn't the God of the dead, but of the living. This means that everyone is alive as far as God is concerned.

[39] Some of the teachers of the Law of Moses said, "Teacher, you have given a good answer!" [40] From then on, no one dared to ask Jesus any questions.

## About David's Son
*(Matthew 22.41-46; Mark 12.35-37)*

[41] Jesus asked, "Why do people say that the Messiah will be the son of King David?[t] [42] In the book of Psalms, David himself says,

'The Lord said to my Lord,
    Sit at my right side[u]

[s] 20.37 *"The Lord is the God worshiped by Abraham, Isaac, and Jacob"*: Jesus argues that if God is worshiped by these three, they must be alive, because he is the God of the living. [t] 20.41 *the son of King David*: See the note at 18.38. [u] 20.42 *right side*: The place of power and honor.

43 until I make your enemies
into a footstool for you.'

44 David spoke of the Messiah as his
Lord, so how can the Messiah be
his son?''

## Jesus and the Teachers
## of the Law of Moses
(Matthew 23.1-36; Mark 12.38-40; Luke 11.37-54)

45 While everyone was listening to
Jesus, he said to his disciples:

46 Guard against the teachers of
the Law of Moses! They love to walk
around in long robes, and they like
to be greeted in the market. They
want the front seats in the meeting
places and the best seats at banquets. 47 But they cheat widows out
of their homes and then pray long
prayers just to show off. These
teachers will be punished most
of all.

## A Widow's Offering
(Mark 12.41-44)

**21** Jesus looked up and saw some
rich people tossing their gifts
into the offering box. 2 He also saw a
poor widow putting in two pennies.
3 And he said, "I tell you that this poor
woman has put in more than all the others. 4 Everyone else gave what they
didn't need. But she is very poor and
gave everything she had.''

## The Temple Will Be Destroyed
(Matthew 24.1, 2; Mark 13.1, 2)

5 Some people were talking about the
beautiful stones used to build the temple and about the gifts that had been
placed in it. Jesus said, 6 "Do you see
these stones? The time is coming when
not one of them will be left in place.
They will all be knocked down.''

## Warning about Trouble
(Matthew 24.3-14; Mark 13.3-13)

7 Some people asked, "Teacher, when
will all this happen? How can we know
when these things are about to take
place?''

8 Jesus replied:
Don't be fooled by those who will
come and claim to be me. They will
say, "I am Christ!" and "Now is the
time!'' But don't follow them.
9 When you hear about wars and
riots, don't be afraid. These things
will have to happen first, but that
isn't the end.

10 Nations will go to war against
one another, and kingdoms will attack each other. 11 There will be
great earthquakes, and in many
places people will starve to death
and suffer terrible diseases. All sorts
of frightening things will be seen in
the sky.

12 Before all this happens, you will
be arrested and punished. You will
be tried in your meeting places and
put in jail. Because of me you will
be placed on trial before kings and
governors. 13 But this will be your
chance to tell about your faith.

14 Don't worry about what you will
say to defend yourselves. 15 I will
give you the wisdom to know what
to say. None of your enemies will
be able to oppose you or to say that
you are wrong. 16 You will be betrayed by your own parents, brothers, family, and friends. Some of you
will even be killed. 17 Because of me,
you will be hated by everyone. 18 But
don't worry! v 19 You will be saved
by being faithful to me.

## Jerusalem Will Be Destroyed
(Matthew 24.15-21; Mark 13.14-19)

20 When you see Jerusalem surrounded by soldiers, you will know
that it will soon be destroyed. 21 If
you are living in Judea at that time,
run to the mountains. If you are in
the city, leave it. And if you are out
in the country, don't go back into
the city. 22 This time of punishment
is what is written about in the Scriptures. 23 It will be an awful time for
women who are expecting babies or
nursing young children! Everywhere in the land people will suffer
horribly and be punished. 24 Some

v 21.18 *But don't worry*: The Greek text has "Not a hair of your head will be lost," which
means, "There's no need to worry."

of them will be killed by swords. Others will be carried off to foreign countries. Jerusalem will be overrun by foreign nations until their time comes to an end.

### When the Son of Man Appears
*(Matthew 24.29-31; Mark 13.24-27)*

25 Strange things will happen to the sun, moon, and stars. The nations on earth will be afraid of the roaring sea and tides, and they won't know what to do. 26 People will be so frightened that they will faint because of what is happening to the world. Every power in the sky will be shaken.w 27 Then the Son of Man will be seen, coming in a cloud with great power and glory. 28 When all of this starts happening, stand up straight and be brave. You will soon be set free.

### A Lesson from a Fig Tree
*(Matthew 24.32-35; Mark 13.28-31)*

29 Then Jesus told them a story: When you see a fig tree or any other tree 30 putting out leaves, you know that summer will soon come. 31 So, when you see these things happening, you know that God's kingdom will soon be here. 32 You can be sure that some of the people of this generation will still be alive when all of this takes place. 33 The sky and the earth won't last forever, but my words will.

### A Warning

34 Don't spend all of your time thinking about eating or drinking or worrying about life. If you do, the final day will suddenly catch you 35 like a trap. That day will surprise everyone on earth. 36 Watch out and keep praying that you can escape all that is going to happen and that the Son of Man will be pleased with you.

37 Jesus taught in the temple each day, and he spent each night on the Mount of Olives. 38 Everyone got up early and came to the temple to hear him teach.

### A Plot To Kill Jesus
*(Matthew 26.1-5, 14, 16; Mark 14.1, 2, 10, 11; John 11.45-53)*

**22** The Festival of Thin Bread, also called Passover, was near. 2 The chief priests and the teachers of the Law of Moses were looking for a way to get rid of Jesus, because they were afraid of what the people might do. 3 Then Satan entered the heart of Judas Iscariot,x who was one of the twelve apostles.
4 Judas went to talk with the chief priests and the officers of the temple police about how he could help them arrest Jesus. 5 They were very pleased and offered to pay Judas some money. 6 He agreed and started looking for a good chance to betray Jesus when the crowds were not around.

### Jesus Eats with His Disciples
*(Matthew 26.17-25; Mark 14.12-21; John 13.21-30)*

7 The day had come for the Festival of Thin Bread, and it was time to kill the Passover lambs. 8 So Jesus said to Peter and John, "Go and prepare the Passover meal for us to eat."
9 But they asked, "Where do you want us to prepare it?"
10 Jesus told them, "As you go into the city, you will meet a man carrying a jar of water.y Follow him into the house 11 and say to the owner, 'Our teacher wants to know where he can eat the Passover meal with his disciples.' 12 The owner will take you upstairs and show you a large room ready for you to use. Prepare the meal there."
13 Peter and John left. They found everything just as Jesus had told them, and they prepared the Passover meal.

w21.26 *Every power in the sky will be shaken*: In ancient times people thought that the stars were spiritual powers. x22.3 *Iscariot*: See the note at 6.16. y22.10 *a man carrying a jar of water*: A male slave carrying water would probably mean that the family was rich.

## The Lord's Supper
*(Matthew 26.26-30; Mark 14.22-26;*
*1 Corinthians 11.23-25)*

14 When the time came for Jesus and the apostles to eat, 15 he said to them, "I have very much wanted to eat this Passover meal with you before I suffer. 16 I tell you that I will not eat another Passover meal until it is finally eaten in God's kingdom."

17 Jesus took a cup of wine in his hands and gave thanks to God. Then he told the apostles, "Take this wine and share it with each other. 18 I tell you that I will not drink any more wine until God's kingdom comes."

19 Jesus took some bread in his hands and gave thanks for it. He broke the bread and handed it to his apostles. Then he said, "This is my body, which is given for you. Eat this as a way of remembering me!"

20 After the meal he took another cup of wine in his hands. Then he said, "This is my blood. It is poured out for you, and with it God makes his new agreement. 21 The one who will betray me is here at the table with me! 22 The Son of Man will die in the way that has been decided for him, but it will be terrible for the one who betrays him!"

23 Then the apostles started arguing about who would ever do such a thing.

## An Argument about Greatness

24 The apostles got into an argument about which one of them was the greatest. 25 So Jesus told them:

Foreign kings order their people around, and powerful rulers call themselves everyone's friends. z 26 But don't be like them. The most important one of you should be like the least important, and your leader should be like a servant. 27 Who do people think is the greatest, a person who is served or one who serves? Isn't it the one who is served? But I have been with you as a servant.

28 You have stayed with me in all my troubles. 29 So I will give you the right to rule as kings, just as my Father has given me the right to rule as a king. 30 You will eat and drink with me in my kingdom, and you will each sit on a throne to judge the twelve tribes of Israel.

## Jesus' Disciples Will Be Tested
*(Matthew 26.31-35; Mark 14.27-31; John 13.36-38)*

31 Jesus said, "Simon, listen to me! Satan has demanded the right to test each one of you, as a farmer does when he separates wheat from the husks. a 32 But Simon, I have prayed that your faith will be strong. And when you have come back to me, help the others."

33 Peter said, "Lord, I am ready to go with you to jail and even to die with you."

34 Jesus replied, "Peter, I tell you that before a rooster crows tomorrow morning, you will say three times that you don't know me."

## Moneybags, Traveling Bags, and Swords

35 Jesus asked his disciples, "When I sent you out without a moneybag or a traveling bag or sandals, did you need anything?"

"No!" they answered.

36 Jesus told them, "But now, if you have a moneybag, take it with you. Also take a traveling bag, and if you don't have a sword, b sell some of your clothes and buy one. 37 Do this because the Scriptures say, 'He was considered a criminal.' This was written about me, and it will soon come true."

38 The disciples said, "Lord, here are two swords!"

"Enough of that!" Jesus replied.

z 22.25 everyone's friends: This translates a Greek word that rulers sometimes used as a title for themselves or for special friends. a 22.31 separates wheat from the husks: See the note at 3.17. b 22.36 moneybag . . . traveling bag . . . sword: These were things that someone would take on a dangerous journey. Jesus was telling his disciples to be ready for anything that might happen. They seem to have understood what he meant (see 22.49-51).

## Jesus Prays

*(Matthew 26.36-46; Mark 14.32-42)*

<sup>39</sup> Jesus went out to the Mount of Olives, as he often did, and his disciples went with him. <sup>40</sup> When they got there, he told them, "Pray that you won't be tested."

<sup>41</sup> Jesus walked on a little way before he knelt down and prayed, <sup>42</sup> "Father, if you will, please don't make me suffer by having me drink from this cup.<sup>c</sup> But do what you want, and not what I want."

<sup>43</sup> Then an angel from heaven came to help him. <sup>44</sup> Jesus was in great pain and prayed so sincerely that his sweat fell to the ground like drops of blood.<sup>d</sup>

<sup>45</sup> Jesus got up from praying and went over to his disciples. They were asleep and worn out from being so sad. <sup>46</sup> He said to them, "Why are you asleep? Wake up and pray that you won't be tested."

## Jesus Is Arrested

*(Matthew 26.47-56; Mark 14.43-50; John 18.3-11)*

<sup>47</sup> While Jesus was still speaking, a crowd came up. It was led by Judas, one of the twelve apostles. He went over to Jesus and greeted him with a kiss.<sup>e</sup>

<sup>48</sup> Jesus asked Judas, "Are you betraying the Son of Man with a kiss?"

<sup>49</sup> When Jesus' disciples saw what was about to happen, they asked, "Lord, should we attack them with a sword?" <sup>50</sup> One of the disciples even struck at the high priest's servant with his sword and cut off the servant's right ear.

<sup>51</sup> "Enough of that!" Jesus said. Then he touched the servant's ear and healed it.

<sup>52</sup> Jesus spoke to the chief priests, the temple police, and the leaders who had come to arrest him. He said, "Why do you come out with swords and clubs and treat me like a criminal? <sup>53</sup> I was with you every day in the temple, and

you didn't arrest me. But this is your time, and darkness<sup>f</sup> is in control."

## Peter Says He Doesn't Know Jesus

*(Matthew 26.57, 58, 67-75; Mark 14.53, 54, 66-72; John 18.12-18, 25-27)*

<sup>54</sup> Jesus was arrested and led away to the house of the high priest, while Peter followed at a distance. <sup>55</sup> Some people built a fire in the middle of the courtyard and were sitting around it. Peter sat there with them, <sup>56</sup> and a servant girl saw him. Then after she had looked at him carefully, she said, "This man was with Jesus!"

<sup>57</sup> Peter said, "Woman, I don't even know that man!"

<sup>58</sup> A little later someone else saw Peter and said, "You are one of them!"

"No, I'm not!" Peter replied.

<sup>59</sup> About an hour later another man insisted, "This man must have been with Jesus. They both come from Galilee."

<sup>60</sup> Peter replied, "I don't know what you are talking about!" Right then, while Peter was still speaking, a rooster crowed.

<sup>61</sup> The Lord turned and looked at Peter. And Peter remembered that the Lord had said, "Before a rooster crows tomorrow morning, you will say three times that you don't know me." <sup>62</sup> Then Peter went out and cried hard.

<sup>63</sup> The men who were guarding Jesus made fun of him and beat him. <sup>64</sup> They put a blindfold on him and said, "Tell us who struck you!" <sup>65</sup> They kept on insulting Jesus in many other ways.

## Jesus Is Questioned by the Council

*(Matthew 26.59-66; Mark 14.55-64; John 18.19-24)*

<sup>66</sup> At daybreak the nation's leaders, the chief priests, and the teachers of the Law of Moses got together and brought Jesus before their council. <sup>67</sup> They said, "Tell us! Are you the Messiah?"

Jesus replied, "If I said so, you wouldn't believe me. <sup>68</sup> And if I asked

---

<sup>c</sup>**22.42** *having me drink from this cup*: In the Scriptures "to drink from a cup" sometimes means to suffer. <sup>d</sup>**22.43, 44** *Then an angel . . . like drops of blood*: Verses 43, 44 are not in some manuscripts. <sup>e</sup>**22.47** *greeted him with a kiss*: It was the custom for people to greet each other with a kiss on the cheek. <sup>f</sup>**22.53** *darkness*: Darkness stands for the power of the devil.

you a question, you wouldn't answer. ⁶⁹ But from now on, the Son of Man will be seated at the right side of God All-Powerful."

⁷⁰ Then they asked, "Are you the Son of God?" *g*

Jesus answered, "You say I am!" *h*

⁷¹ They replied, "Why do we need more witnesses? He said it himself!"

## Pilate Questions Jesus
*(Matthew 27.1, 2, 11-14; Mark 15.1-5; John 18.28-38)*

**23** Everyone in the council got up and led Jesus off to Pilate. ² They started accusing him and said, "We caught this man trying to get our people to riot and to stop paying taxes to the Emperor. He also claims that he is the Messiah, our king."

³ Pilate asked Jesus, "Are you the king of the Jews?"

"Those are your words," Jesus answered.

⁴ Pilate told the chief priests and the crowd, "I don't find him guilty of anything."

⁵ But they all kept on saying, "He has been teaching and causing trouble all over Judea. He started in Galilee and has now come all the way here."

## Jesus Is Brought before Herod

⁶ When Pilate heard this, he asked, "Is this man from Galilee?" ⁷ After Pilate learned that Jesus came from the region ruled by Herod,*i* he sent him to Herod, who was in Jerusalem at that time.

⁸ For a long time Herod had wanted to see Jesus and was very happy because he finally had this chance. He had heard many things about Jesus and hoped to see him work a miracle.

⁹ Herod asked him a lot of questions, but Jesus did not answer. ¹⁰ Then the chief priests and the teachers of the Law of Moses stood up and accused him of all kinds of bad things. ¹¹ Herod and his soldiers made fun of Jesus and insulted him. They put a fine robe on him and sent him back to Pilate. ¹² That same day Herod and Pilate became friends, even though they had been enemies before this.

## The Death Sentence
*(Matthew 27.15-26; Mark 15.6-15; John 18.39—19.16)*

¹³ Pilate called together the chief priests, the leaders, and the people. ¹⁴ He told them, "You brought Jesus to me and said he was a troublemaker. But I have questioned him here in front of you, and I have not found him guilty of anything that you say he has done. ¹⁵ Herod didn't find him guilty either and sent him back. This man doesn't deserve to be put to death! ¹⁶⁻¹⁷ I will just have him beaten with a whip and set free." *i*

¹⁸ But the whole crowd shouted, "Kill Jesus! Give us Barabbas!" ¹⁹ Now Barabbas was in jail because he had started a riot in the city and had murdered someone.

²⁰ Pilate wanted to set Jesus free, so he spoke again to the crowds. ²¹ But they kept shouting, "Nail him to a cross! Nail him to a cross!"

²² Pilate spoke to them a third time, "But what crime has he done? I have not found him guilty of anything for which he should be put to death. I will have him beaten with a whip and set free."

²³ The people kept on shouting as loud as they could for Jesus to be put to death. ²⁴ Finally, Pilate gave in. ²⁵ He freed the man who was in jail for rioting and murder, because he was the one the crowd wanted to be set free. Then Pilate handed Jesus over for them to do what they wanted with him.

## Jesus Is Nailed to a Cross
*(Matthew 27.31-44; Mark 15.21-32; John 19.17-27)*

²⁶ As Jesus was being led away, some soldiers grabbed hold of a man from

---

*g* **22.70** *Son of God:* This was one of the titles used for the kings of Israel.   *h* **22.70** *You say I am:* Or "That's what you say."   *i* **23.7** *Herod:* Herod Antipas, the son of Herod the Great.
*j* **23.16,17** *set free:* Some manuscripts add, "Pilate said this, because at every Passover he was supposed to set one prisoner free for the Jewish people."

Cyrene named Simon. He was coming in from the fields, but they put the cross on him and made him carry it behind Jesus.

27 A large crowd was following Jesus, and in the crowd a lot of women were crying and weeping for him. 28 Jesus turned to the women and said:

Women of Jerusalem, don't cry for me! Cry for yourselves and for your children. 29 Someday people will say, "Women who never had children are really fortunate!" 30 At that time everyone will say to the mountains, "Fall on us!" They will say to the hills, "Hide us!" 31 If this can happen when the wood is green, what do you think will happen when it is dry?k

32 Two criminals were led out to be put to death with Jesus. 33 When the soldiers came to the place called "The Skull,"l they nailed Jesus to a cross. They also nailed the two criminals to crosses, one on each side of Jesus.

34-35 Jesus said, "Father, forgive these people! They don't know what they're doing."m

While the crowd stood there watching Jesus, the soldiers gambled for his clothes. The leaders insulted him by saying, "He saved others. Now he should save himself, if he really is God's chosen Messiah!"

36 The soldiers made fun of Jesus and brought him some wine. 37 They said, "If you are the king of the Jews, save yourself!"

38 Above him was a sign that said, "This is the King of the Jews."

39 One of the criminals hanging there also insulted Jesus by saying, "Aren't you the Messiah? Save yourself and save us!"

40 But the other criminal told the first one off, "Don't you fear God? Aren't you getting the same punishment as this man? 41 We got what was coming to us, but he didn't do anything wrong." 42 Then he said to Jesus, "Remember me when you come into power!"

43 Jesus replied, "I promise that today you will be with me in paradise."n

## The Death of Jesus
(Matthew 27.45-56; Mark 15.33-41; John 19.28-30)

44 Around noon the sky turned dark and stayed that way until the middle of the afternoon. 45 The sun stopped shining, and the curtain in the templeo split down the middle. 46 Jesus shouted, "Father, I put myself in your hands!" Then he died.

47 When the Roman officer saw what had happened, he praised God and said, "Jesus must really have been a good man!"

48 A crowd had gathered to see the terrible sight. Then after they had seen it, they felt brokenhearted and went home. 49 All of Jesus' close friends and the women who had come with him from Galilee stood at a distance and watched.

## Jesus Is Buried
(Matthew 27.57-61; Mark 15.42-47; John 19.38-42)

50-51 There was a man named Joseph, who was from Arimathea in Judea. Joseph was a good and honest man, and he was eager for God's kingdom to come. He was also a member of the council, but he did not agree with what they had decided. 52 Joseph went to Pilate and asked for Jesus' body. 53 He took the body down

k 23.31 If this can happen when the wood is green, what do you think will happen when it is dry?: This saying probably means, "If this can happen to an innocent person, what do you think will happen to one who is guilty?" l 23.33 "The Skull": The place was probably given this name because it was near a large rock in the shape of a human skull. m 23.34,35 Jesus said, "Father, forgive these people! They don't know what they're doing.": These words are not in some manuscripts. n 23.43 paradise: In the Greek translation of the Old Testament, this word is used for the Garden of Eden. In New Testament times it was sometimes used for the place where God's people are happy and at rest, as they wait for the final judgment. o 23.45 curtain in the temple: There were two curtains in the temple. One was at the entrance, and the other separated the holy place from the most holy place that the Jewish people thought of as God's home on earth. The second curtain is probably the one which is meant.

from the cross and wrapped it in fine cloth. Then he put it in a tomb that had been cut out of solid rock and had never been used. 54 It was Friday, and the Sabbath was about to begin.[p]

55 The women who had come with Jesus from Galilee followed Joseph and watched how Jesus' body was placed in the tomb. 56 Then they went to prepare some sweet-smelling spices for his burial. But on the Sabbath they rested, as the Law of Moses commands.

### *Jesus Is Alive*

*(Matthew 28.1-10; Mark 16.1-8; John 20.1-10)*

**24** Very early on Sunday morning the women went to the tomb, carrying the spices that they had prepared. 2 When they found the stone rolled away from the entrance, 3 they went in. But they did not find the body of the Lord[q] Jesus, 4 and they did not know what to think.

Suddenly two men in shining white clothes stood beside them. 5 The women were afraid and bowed to the ground. But the men said, "Why are you looking in the place of the dead for someone who is alive? 6 Jesus isn't here! He has been raised from death. Remember that while he was still in Galilee, he told you, 7 'The Son of Man will be handed over to sinners who will nail him to a cross. But three days later he will rise to life.' " 8 Then they remembered what Jesus had said.

9-10 Mary Magdalene, Joanna, Mary the mother of James, and some other women were the ones who had gone to the tomb. When they returned, they told the eleven apostles and the others what had happened. 11 The apostles thought it was all nonsense, and they would not believe.

12 But Peter ran to the tomb. And when he stooped down and looked in, he saw only the burial clothes. Then he returned, wondering what had happened.[r]

### *Jesus Appears to Two Disciples*

*(Mark 16.12, 13)*

13 That same day two of Jesus' disciples were going to the village of Emmaus, which was about seven miles from Jerusalem. 14 As they were talking and thinking about what had happened, 15 Jesus came near and started walking along beside them. 16 But they did not know who he was.

17 Jesus asked them, "What were you talking about as you walked along?"

The two of them stood there looking sad and gloomy. 18 Then the one named Cleopas asked Jesus, "Are you the only person from Jerusalem who didn't know what was happening there these last few days?"

19 "What do you mean?" Jesus asked.

They answered:

> Those things that happened to Jesus from Nazareth. By what he did and said he showed that he was a powerful prophet, who pleased God and all the people. 20 Then the chief priests and our leaders had him arrested and sentenced to die on a cross. 21 We had hoped that he would be the one to set Israel free! But it has already been three days since all this happened.
>
> 22 Some women in our group surprised us. They had gone to the tomb early in the morning, 23 but did not find the body of Jesus. They came back, saying that they had seen a vision of angels who told them that he is alive. 24 Some men from our group went to the tomb and found it just as the women had said. But they didn't see Jesus either.

25 Then Jesus asked the two disciples, "Why can't you understand? How can you be so slow to believe all that the prophets said? 26 Didn't you know that the Messiah would have to suffer before he was given his glory?" 27 Jesus then explained everything written about himself in the Scriptures, beginning with the Law of Moses and the Books of the Prophets.[s]

[p] **23.54** *the Sabbath was about to begin*: The Sabbath begins at sunset on Friday. [q] **24.3** *the Lord*: These words are not in some manuscripts. [r] **24.12** *what had happened*: Verse 12 is not in some manuscripts. [s] **24.27** *the Law of Moses and the Books of the Prophets*: The Jewish Scriptures, that is, the Old Testament.

28 When the two of them came near the village where they were going, Jesus seemed to be going farther. 29 They begged him, "Stay with us! It's already late, and the sun is going down." So Jesus went into the house to stay with them.

30 After Jesus sat down to eat, he took some bread. He blessed it and broke it. Then he gave it to them. 31 At once they knew who he was, but he disappeared. 32 They said to each other, "When he talked with us along the road and explained the Scriptures to us, didn't it warm our hearts?" 33 So they got right up and returned to Jerusalem.

The two disciples found the eleven apostles and the others gathered together. 34 And they learned from the group that the Lord was really alive and had appeared to Peter. 35 Then the disciples from Emmaus told what happened on the road and how they knew he was the Lord when he broke the bread.

### What Jesus' Followers Must Do
*(Matthew 28.16-20; Mark 16.14-18; John 20.19-23; Acts 1.6-8)*

36 While Jesus' disciples were talking about what had happened, Jesus appeared and greeted them. 37 They were frightened and terrified because they thought they were seeing a ghost. 38 But Jesus said, "Why are you so frightened? Why do you doubt? 39 Look at my hands and my feet and see who I am! Touch me and find out for yourselves. Ghosts don't have flesh and bones as you see I have."

40 After Jesus said this, he showed them his hands and his feet. 41 The disciples were so glad and amazed that they could not believe it. Jesus then asked them, "Do you have something to eat?" 42 They gave him a piece of baked fish. 43 He took it and ate it as they watched.

44 Jesus said to them, "While I was still with you, I told you that everything written about me in the Law of Moses, the Books of the Prophets, and in the Psalms t had to happen."

45 Then he helped them understand the Scriptures. 46 He told them:

The Scriptures say that the Messiah must suffer, then three days later he will rise from death. 47 They also say that all people of every nation must be told in my name to turn to God, in order to be forgiven. So beginning in Jerusalem, 48 you must tell everything that has happened. 49 I will send you the one my Father has promised, u but you must stay in the city until you are given power from heaven.

### Jesus Returns to Heaven
*(Mark 16.19, 20; Acts 1.9-11)*

50 Jesus led his disciples out to Bethany, where he raised his hands and blessed them. 51 As he was doing this, he left and was taken up to heaven. v 52 After his disciples had worshiped him, w they returned to Jerusalem and were very happy. 53 They spent their time in the temple, praising God.

---

t 24.44 *Psalms*: The Jewish Scriptures were made up of three parts: (1) the Law of Moses, (2) the Books of the Prophets, (3) and the Writings, which included the Psalms. Sometimes the Scriptures were just called the Law or the Law (of Moses) and the Books of the Prophets. u 24.49 *the one my Father has promised*: Jesus means the Holy Spirit. v 24.51 *and was taken up to heaven*: These words are not in some manuscripts. w 24.52 *After his disciples had worshiped him*: These words are not in some manuscripts.

# JOHN

## ABOUT THIS BOOK

Who is Jesus Christ? John answers this question in the first chapter of his Gospel. Using the words of an early Christian hymn, he calls Jesus the "Word" by which God created everything and by which he gave life to everyone (1.3, 4) He shows how John the Baptist announced Jesus' coming, "Here is the Lamb of God who takes away the sin of the world" (1.29). When Philip met Jesus he knew Jesus was "the one that Moses and the Prophets wrote about" (1.45). And, in the words of Nathanael, Jesus is "the Son of God and the King of Israel" (1.49).

In John's Gospel we learn a lot about who Jesus is by observing what he said and did when he was with other people. These include a Samaritan woman who received Jesus' offer of life-giving water, a woman who had been caught in sin, his friend Lazarus who was brought back to life by Jesus, and his follower Thomas who doubted that Jesus was raised from death. Jesus also refers to himself as "I am", a phrase which translates the most holy name for God in the Hebrew Scriptures. He uses this name for himself when he makes his claim to be the life-giving bread, the light of the world, the good shepherd, and the true vine.

Jesus performs seven miracles that are more than miracles. Each of them is a "sign" that tells us something about Jesus as the Son of God. For example, by healing a lame man (5.1-8), Jesus shows that he is just like his Father, who never stops working (5.17). This sign also teaches that the Son does only what he sees his Father doing (5.19), and that like the Father "the Son gives life to anyone he wants to" (5.21).

The way John tells the story of Jesus is quite different from the other three Gospels. Here, Jesus has long conversations with people about who he is and what God sent him to do. In these conversations he teaches many important things—for example, that he is the way, the truth and the life.

Why did John write? John himself tells us, "So that you will put your faith in Jesus as the Messiah and the Son of God" (20.31). How is this possible? Jesus answers that question in his words to Nicodemus:

> God loved the people of this world so much that he gave his only Son, so that everyone who has faith in him will have eternal life and never really die. (3.16)

## A QUICK LOOK AT THIS BOOK

119

### The Word of Life

**1** In the beginning was the one
who is called the Word.
The Word was with God
and was truly God.
² From the very beginning
the Word was with God.

³ And with this Word,
God created all things.
Nothing was made
without the Word.
Everything that was created
⁴ received its life from him,
and his life gave light
to everyone.
⁵ The light keeps shining
in the dark,
and darkness has never
put it out.ᵃ

⁶ God sent a man named John,
⁷ who came to tell
about the light
and to lead all people
to have faith.
⁸ John wasn't that light.
He came only to tell
about the light.

⁹ The true light that shines
on everyone
was coming into the world.
¹⁰ The Word was in the world,
but no one knew him,
though God had made the world
with his Word.
¹¹ He came into his own world,
but his own nation
did not welcome him.
¹² Yet some people accepted him
and put their faith in him.
So he gave them the right
to be the children of God.
¹³ They were not God's children
by nature or because
of any human desires.
God himself was the one
who made them his children.

¹⁴ The Word became
a human being
and lived here with us.

We saw his true glory,
the glory of the only Son
of the Father.
From him all the kindness
and all the truth of God
have come down to us.

¹⁵ John spoke about him and shouted, "This is the one I told you would come! He is greater than I am, because he was alive before I was born."

¹⁶ Because of all that the Son is, we have been given one blessing after another.ᵇ ¹⁷ The Law was given by Moses, but Jesus Christ brought us undeserved kindness and truth. ¹⁸ No one has ever seen God. The only Son, who is truly God and is closest to the Father, has shown us what God is like.

### John the Baptist Tells about Jesus
*(Matthew 3.1-12; Mark 1.1-8; Luke 3.15-17)*

¹⁹⁻²⁰ The leaders in Jerusalem sent priests and temple helpers to ask John who he was. He told them plainly, "I am not the Messiah." ²¹ Then when they asked him if he were Elijah, he said, "No, I am not!" And when they asked if he were the Prophet,ᶜ he also said "No!"

²² Finally, they said, "Who are you then? We have to give an answer to the ones who sent us. Tell us who you are!"

²³ John answered in the words of the prophet Isaiah, "I am only someone shouting in the desert, 'Get the road ready for the Lord!'"

²⁴ Some Pharisees had also been sent to John. ²⁵ They asked him, "Why are you baptizing people, if you are not the Messiah or Elijah or the Prophet?"

²⁶ John told them, "I use water to baptize people. But here with you is someone you don't know. ²⁷ Even though I came first, I am not good enough to untie his sandals." ²⁸ John said this as was baptizing east of the Jordan River in Bethany.ᵈ

ᵃ**1.5** *put it out*: Or "understood it." ᵇ**1.16** *one blessing after another*: Or "one blessing in place of another." ᶜ**1.21** *the Prophet*: Many of the Jewish people expected God to send them a prophet who would be like Moses, but with even greater power (see Deuteronomy 18.15, 18). ᵈ**1.28** *Bethany*: An unknown village east of the Jordan with the same name as the village near Jerusalem.

### The Lamb of God

29 The next day, John saw Jesus coming toward him and said:

Here is the Lamb of God who takes away the sin of the world! 30 He is the one I told you about when I said, "Someone else will come. He is greater than I am, because he was alive before I was born." 31 I didn't know who he was. But I came to baptize you with water, so that everyone in Israel would see him.

32 I was there and saw the Spirit come down on him like a dove from heaven. And the Spirit stayed on him. 33 Before this I didn't know who he was. But the one who sent me to baptize with water had told me, "You will see the Spirit come down and stay on someone. Then you will know that he is the one who will baptize with the Holy Spirit." 34 I saw this happen, and I tell you that he is the Son of God.

### The First Disciples of Jesus

35 The next day, John was there again, and two of his followers were with him. 36 When he saw Jesus walking by, he said, "Here is the Lamb of God!" 37 John's two followers heard him, and they went with Jesus.

38 When Jesus turned and saw them, he asked, "What do you want?"

They answered, "Rabbi, where do you live?" The Hebrew word "Rabbi" means "Teacher."

39 Jesus replied, "Come and see!" It was already about four o'clock in the afternoon when they went with him and saw where he lived. So they stayed on for the rest of the day.

40 One of the two men who had heard John and had gone with Jesus was Andrew, the brother of Simon Peter. 41 The first thing Andrew did was to find his brother and tell him, "We have found the Messiah!" The Hebrew word "Messiah" means the same as the Greek word "Christ."

42 Andrew brought his brother to Jesus. And when Jesus saw him, he said, "Simon son of John, you will be called Cephas." This name can be translated as "Peter." e

### Jesus Chooses Philip and Nathanael

43-44 The next day Jesus decided to go to Galilee. There he met Philip, who was from Bethsaida, the hometown of Andrew and Peter. Jesus said to Philip, "Come with me."

45 Philip then found Nathanael and said, "We have found the one that Moses and the Prophets f wrote about. He is Jesus, the son of Joseph from Nazareth."

46 Nathanael asked, "Can anything good come from Nazareth?"

Philip answered, "Come and see."

47 When Jesus saw Nathanael coming toward him, he said, "Here is a true descendant of our ancestor Israel. And he isn't deceitful." g

48 "How do you know me?" Nathanael asked.

Jesus answered, "Before Philip called you, I saw you under the fig tree."

49 Nathanael said, "Rabbi, you are the Son of God and the King of Israel!"

50 Jesus answered, "Did you believe me just because I said that I saw you under the fig tree? You will see something even greater. 51 I tell you for certain that you will see heaven open and God's angels going up and coming down on the Son of Man." h

### Jesus at a Wedding in Cana

2 Three days later Mary, the mother of Jesus, was at a wedding feast in the village of Cana in Galilee. 2 Jesus

---

e 1.42 Peter: The Aramaic name "Cephas" and the Greek name "Peter" each mean "rock."
f 1.45 Moses and the Prophets: The Jewish Scriptures, that is, the Old Testament.
g 1.47 Israel . . . isn't deceitful: Israel (meaning "a man who wrestled with God" or "a prince of God") was the name that the Lord gave to Jacob (meaning "cheater" or "deceiver"), the famous ancestor of the Jewish people. h 1.51 going up and coming down on the Son of Man: When Jacob (see the note at verse 47) was running from his brother Esau, he had a dream in which he saw angels going up and down on a ladder from earth to heaven (see Genesis 32.22-32).

and his disciples had also been invited and were there.

³ When the wine was all gone, Mary said to Jesus, "They don't have any more wine."

⁴ Jesus replied, "Mother, my time hasn't yet come!ⁱ You must not tell me what to do."

⁵ Mary then said to the servants, "Do whatever Jesus tells you to do."

⁶ At the feast there were six stone water jars that were used by the people for washing themselves in the way that their religion said they must. Each jar held about twenty or thirty gallons. ⁷ Jesus told the servants to fill them to the top with water. Then after the jars had been filled, ⁸ he said, "Now take some water and give it to the man in charge of the feast."

The servants did as Jesus told them, ⁹ and the man in charge drank some of the water that had now turned into wine. He did not know where the wine had come from, but the servants did. He called the bridegroom over ¹⁰ and said, "The best wine is always served first. Then after the guests have had plenty, the other wine is served. But you have kept the best until last!"

¹¹ This was Jesus' first miracle,ʲ and he did it in the village of Cana in Galilee. There Jesus showed his glory, and his disciples put their faith in him. ¹² After this, he went with his mother, his brothers, and his disciples to the town of Capernaum, where they stayed for a few days.

### Jesus in the Temple
*(Matthew 21.12, 13; Mark 11.15-17; Luke 19.45, 46)*

¹³ Not long before the Jewish festival of Passover, Jesus went to Jerusalem. ¹⁴ There he found people selling cattle, sheep, and doves in the temple. He also saw moneychangers sitting at their tables. ¹⁵ So he took some rope and made a whip. Then he chased everyone out of the temple, together with their sheep and cattle. He turned over the tables of the moneychangers and scattered their coins.

¹⁶ Jesus said to the people who had been selling doves, "Get those doves out of here! Don't make my Father's house a marketplace."

¹⁷ The disciples then remembered that the Scriptures say, "My love for your house burns in me like a fire."

¹⁸ The Jewish leaders asked Jesus, "What miracleʲ will you work to show us why you have done this?"

¹⁹ "Destroy this temple," Jesus answered, "and in three days I will build it again!"

²⁰ The leaders replied, "It took forty-six years to build this temple. What makes you think you can rebuild it in three days?"

²¹ But Jesus was talking about his body as a temple. ²² And when he was raised from death, his disciples remembered what he had told them. Then they believed the Scriptures and the words of Jesus.

### Jesus Knows What People Are Like

²³ In Jerusalem during Passover many people put their faith in Jesus, because they saw him work miracles.ʲ ²⁴ But Jesus knew what was in their hearts, and he would not let them have power over him. ²⁵ No one had to tell him what people were like. He already knew.

### Jesus and Nicodemus

**3** There was a man named Nicodemus who was a Pharisee and a Jewish leader. ² One night he went to Jesus and said, "Sir, we know that God has sent you to teach us. You could not work these miracles, unless God were with you."

³ Jesus replied, "I tell you for certain that you must be born from aboveᵏ before you can see God's kingdom!"

---

ⁱ**2.4** *my time hasn't yet come!*: The time when the true glory of Jesus would be seen, and he would be recognized as God's Son (see 12.23).   ʲ**2.11** *miracle*: The Greek text has "sign." In the Gospel of John the word "sign" is used for the miracle itself and as a way of pointing to Jesus as the Son of God.   ʲ**2.18** *miracle*: See the note at 2.11.   ʲ**2.23** *miracles*: See the note at 2.11.   ᵏ**3.3** *from above*: Or "in a new way." The same Greek word is used in verses 7, 31.

4 Nicodemus asked, "How can a grown man ever be born a second time?"

5 Jesus answered:

I tell you for certain that before you can get into God's kingdom, you must be born not only by water, but by the Spirit. 6 Humans give life to their children. Yet only God's Spirit can change you into a child of God. 7 Don't be surprised when I say that you must be born from above. 8 Only God's Spirit gives new life. The Spirit is like the wind that blows wherever it wants to. You can hear the wind, but you don't know where it comes from or where it is going. 9 "How can this be?" Nicodemus asked.

10 Jesus replied:

How can you be a teacher of Israel and not know these things? 11 I tell you for certain that we know what we are talking about because we have seen it ourselves. But none of you will accept what we say. 12 If you don't believe when I talk to you about things on earth, how can you possibly believe if I talk to you about things in heaven?

13 No one has gone up to heaven except the Son of Man, who came down from there. 14 And the Son of Man must be lifted up, just as that metal snake was lifted up by Moses in the desert.l 15 Then everyone who has faith in the Son of Man will have eternal life.

16 God loved the people of this world so much that he gave his only Son, so that everyone who has faith in him will have eternal life and never really die. 17 God did not send his Son into the world to condemn its people. He sent him to save them! 18 No one who has faith in God's Son will be condemned. But everyone who doesn't have faith in him has already been condemned for not having faith in God's only Son.

19 The light has come into the world, and people who do evil things are judged guilty because they love the dark more than the light. 20 People who do evil hate the light and won't come to the light, because it clearly shows what they have done. 21 But everyone who lives by the truth will come to the light, because they want others to know that God is really the one doing what they do.

### Jesus and John the Baptist

22 Later, Jesus and his disciples went to Judea, where he stayed with them for a while and was baptizing people. 23-24 John had not yet been put in jail. He was at Aenon near Salim, where there was a lot of water, and people were coming there for John to baptize them.

25 John's followers got into an argument with a Jewish manm about a ceremony of washing.n 26 They went to John and said, "Rabbi, you spoke about a man when you were with him east of the Jordan. He is now baptizing people, and everyone is going to him."

27 John replied:

No one can do anything unless God in heaven allows it. 28 You surely remember how I told you that I am not the Messiah. I am only the one sent ahead of him.

29 At a wedding the groom is the one who gets married. The best man is glad just to be there and to hear the groom's voice. That's why I am so glad. 30 Jesus must become more important, while I become less important.

### The One Who Comes from Heaven

31 God's Son comes from heaven and is above all others. Everyone who comes from the earth belongs to the earth and speaks about

l3.14 just as that metal snake was lifted up by Moses in the desert: When the Lord punished the people of Israel by sending snakes to bite them, he told Moses to hold a metal snake up on a pole. Everyone who looked at the snake was cured of the snake bites (see Numbers 21.4-9). m3.25 a Jewish man: Some manuscripts have "some Jewish men." n3.25 about a ceremony of washing: The Jewish people had many rules about washing themselves and their dishes, in order to make themselves fit to worship God.

earthly things. The one who comes from heaven is above all others. [32] He speaks about what he has seen and heard, and yet no one believes him. [33] But everyone who does believe him has shown that God is truthful. [34] The Son was sent to speak God's message, and he has been given the full power of God's Spirit.

[35] The Father loves the Son and has given him everything. [36] Everyone who has faith in the Son has eternal life. But no one who rejects him will ever share in that life, and God will be angry with them forever.

4 Jesus knew that the Pharisees had heard that he was winning and baptizing more followers than John was. [2] But Jesus' disciples were really the ones doing the baptizing, and not Jesus himself.

### Jesus and the Samaritan Woman

[3] Jesus left Judea and started for Galilee again. [4] This time he had to go through Samaria, [5] and on his way he came to the town of Sychar. It was near the field that Jacob had long ago given to his son Joseph. [6-8] The well that Jacob had dug was still there, and Jesus sat down beside it because he was tired from traveling. It was noon, and after Jesus' disciples had gone into town to buy some food, a Samaritan woman came to draw water from the well.

Jesus asked her, "Would you please give me a drink of water?"

[9] "You are a Jew," she replied, "and I am a Samaritan woman. How can you ask me for a drink of water when Jews and Samaritans won't have anything to do with each other?"[o]

[10] Jesus answered, "You don't know what God wants to give you, and you don't know who is asking you for a drink. If you did, you would ask me for the water that gives life."

[11] "Sir," the woman said, "you don't even have a bucket, and the well is deep. Where are you going to get this life-giving water? [12] Our ancestor Jacob dug this well for us, and his family and animals got water from it. Are you greater than Jacob?"

[13] Jesus answered, "Everyone who drinks this water will get thirsty again. [14] But no one who drinks the water I give will ever be thirsty again. The water I give is like a flowing fountain that gives eternal life."

[15] The woman replied, "Sir, please give me a drink of that water! Then I won't get thirsty and have to come to this well again."

[16] Jesus told her, "Go and bring your husband."

[17-18] The woman answered, "I don't have a husband."

"That's right," Jesus replied, "you're telling the truth. You don't have a husband. You have already been married five times, and the man you are now living with isn't your husband."

[19] The woman said, "Sir, I can see that you are a prophet. [20] My ancestors worshiped on this mountain,[p] but you Jews say Jerusalem is the only place to worship."

[21] Jesus said to her:

Believe me, the time is coming when you won't worship the Father either on this mountain or in Jerusalem. [22] You Samaritans don't really know the one you worship. But we Jews do know the God we worship, and by using us, God will save the world. [23] But a time is coming, and it is already here! Even now the true worshipers are being led by the Spirit to worship the Father according to the truth. These are the ones the Father is seeking to worship him. [24] God is Spirit, and those who worship God must be led by the Spirit to worship him according to the truth.

[25] The woman said, "I know that the Messiah will come. He is the one we call Christ. When he comes, he will explain everything to us."

---

o4.9 *won't have anything to do with each other*: Or "won't use the same cups." The Samaritans lived in the land between Judea and Galilee. They worshiped God differently from the Jews and did not get along with them.   p4.20 *this mountain*: Mount Gerizim, near the city of Shechem.

26 "I am that one," Jesus told her, "and I am speaking to you now."

27 The disciples returned about this time and were surprised to find Jesus talking with a woman. But none of them asked him what he wanted or why he was talking with her.

28 The woman left her water jar and ran back into town. She said to the people, 29 "Come and see a man who told me everything I have ever done! Could he be the Messiah?" 30 Everyone in town went out to see Jesus.

31 While this was happening, Jesus' disciples were saying to him, "Teacher, please eat something."

32 But Jesus told them, "I have food that you don't know anything about."

33 His disciples started asking each other, "Has someone brought him something to eat?"

34 Jesus said:

My food is to do what God wants! He is the one who sent me, and I must finish the work that he gave me to do. 35 You may say that there are still four months until harvest time. But I tell you to look, and you will see that the fields are ripe and ready to harvest.

36 Even now the harvest workers are receiving their reward by gathering a harvest that brings eternal life. Then everyone who planted the seed and everyone who harvests the crop will celebrate together. 37 So the saying proves true, "Some plant the seed, and others harvest the crop." 38 I am sending you to harvest crops in fields where others have done all the hard work.

39 A lot of Samaritans in that town put their faith in Jesus because the woman had said, "This man told me everything I have ever done." 40 They came and asked him to stay in their town, and he stayed on for two days.

41 Many more Samaritans put their faith in Jesus because of what they heard him say. 42 They told the woman, "We no longer have faith in Jesus just because of what you told us. We have heard him ourselves, and we are

certain that he is the Savior of the world!"

## Jesus Heals an Official's Son
### (Matthew 8.5-13; Luke 7.1-10)

43-44 Jesus had said, "Prophets are honored everywhere, except in their own country." Then two days later he left 45 and went to Galilee. The people there welcomed him, because they had gone to the festival in Jerusalem and had seen everything he had done.

46 While Jesus was in Galilee, he returned to the village of Cana, where he had turned the water into wine. There was an official in Capernaum whose son was sick. 47 And when the man heard that Jesus had come from Judea, he went and begged him to keep his son from dying.

48 Jesus told the official, "You won't have faith unless you see miracles and wonders!"

49 The man replied, "Lord, please come before my son dies!"

50 Jesus then said, "Your son will live. Go on home to him." The man believed Jesus and started back home.

51 Some of the official's servants met him along the road and told him, "Your son is better!" 52 He asked them when the boy got better, and they answered, "The fever left him yesterday at one o'clock."

53 The boy's father realized that at one o'clock the day before, Jesus had told him, "Your son will live!" So the man and everyone in his family put their faith in Jesus.

54 This was the second miracle q that Jesus worked after he left Judea and went to Galilee.

## Jesus Heals a Sick Man

5 Later, Jesus went to Jerusalem for another Jewish festival. r 2 In the city near the sheep gate was a pool with five porches, and its name in Hebrew was Bethzatha. s

---

q 4.54 *miracle*: See the note at 2.11. r 5.1 *another Jewish festival*: Either the Festival of Shelters or Passover. s 5.2 *Bethzatha*: Some manuscripts have "Bethesda" and others have "Bethsaida."

**3-4** Many sick, blind, lame, and crippled people were lying close to the pool. *t*

**5** Beside the pool was a man who had been sick for thirty-eight years. **6** When Jesus saw the man and realized that he had been crippled for a long time, he asked him, "Do you want to be healed?"

**7** The man answered, "Lord, I don't have anyone to put me in the pool when the water is stirred up. I try to get in, but someone else always gets there first."

**8** Jesus told him, "Pick up your mat and walk!" **9** Right then the man was healed. He picked up his mat and started walking around. The day on which this happened was a Sabbath.

**10** When the Jewish leaders saw the man carrying his mat, they said to him, "This is the Sabbath! No one is allowed to carry a mat on the Sabbath."

**11** But he replied, "The man who healed me told me to pick up my mat and walk."

**12** They asked him, "Who is this man that told you to pick up your mat and walk?" **13** But he did not know who Jesus was, and Jesus had left because of the crowd.

**14** Later, Jesus met the man in the temple and told him, "You are now well. But don't sin anymore or something worse might happen to you." **15** The man left and told the leaders that Jesus was the one who had healed him. **16** They started making a lot of trouble for Jesus because he did things like this on the Sabbath.

**17** But Jesus said, "My Father has never stopped working, and that is why I keep on working." **18** Now the leaders wanted to kill Jesus for two reasons. First, he had broken the law of the Sabbath. But even worse, he had said that God was his Father, which made him equal with God.

### The Son's Authority

**19** Jesus told the people:

I tell you for certain that the Son cannot do anything on his own. He can do only what he sees the Father doing, and he does exactly what he sees the Father do. **20** The Father loves the Son and has shown him everything he does. The Father will show him even greater things, and you will be amazed. **21** Just as the Father raises the dead and gives life, so the Son gives life to anyone he wants to.

**22** The Father doesn't judge anyone, but he has made his Son the judge of everyone. **23** The Father wants all people to honor the Son as much as they honor him. When anyone refuses to honor the Son, that is the same as refusing to honor the Father who sent him. **24** I tell you for certain that everyone who hears my message and has faith in the one who sent me has eternal life and will never be condemned. They have already gone from death to life.

**25** I tell you for certain that the time will come, and it is already here, when all of the dead will hear the voice of the Son of God. And those who listen to it will live! **26** The Father has the power to give life, and he has given that same power to the Son. **27** And he has given his Son the right to judge everyone, because he is the Son of Man.

**28** Don't be surprised! The time will come when all of the dead will hear the voice of the Son of Man, **29** and they will come out of their graves. Everyone who has done good things will rise to life, but everyone who has done evil things will rise and be condemned.

**30** I cannot do anything on my own. The Father sent me, and he is the one who told me to judge. I judge with fairness, because I obey him, and I don't just try to please myself.

### Witnesses to Jesus

**31** If I speak for myself, there is no way to prove I am telling the truth. **32** But there is someone else who

*t* **5.3,4** *pool*: Some manuscripts add, "They were waiting for the water to be stirred, because an angel from the Lord would sometimes come down and stir it. The first person to get into the pool after that would be healed."

speaks for me, and I know what he says is true. <sup>33</sup> You sent messengers to John, and he told them the truth. <sup>34</sup> I don't depend on what people say about me, but I tell you these things so that you may be saved. <sup>35</sup> John was a lamp that gave a lot of light, and you were glad to enjoy his light for a while.

<sup>36</sup> But something more important than John speaks for me. I mean the things that the Father has given me to do! All of these speak for me and prove that the Father sent me.

<sup>37</sup> The Father who sent me also speaks for me, but you have never heard his voice or seen him face to face. <sup>38</sup> You have not believed his message, because you refused to have faith in the one he sent.

<sup>39</sup> You search the Scriptures, because you think you will find eternal life in them. The Scriptures tell about me, <sup>40</sup> but you refuse to come to me for eternal life.

<sup>41</sup> I don't care about human praise, <sup>42</sup> but I do know that none of you love God. <sup>43</sup> I have come with my Father's authority, and you have not welcomed me. But you will welcome people who come on their own. <sup>44</sup> How could you possibly believe? You like to have your friends praise you, and you don't care about praise that the only God can give!

<sup>45</sup> Don't think that I will be the one to accuse you to the Father. You have put your hope in Moses, yet he is the very one who will accuse you. <sup>46</sup> Moses wrote about me, and if you had believed Moses, you would have believed me. <sup>47</sup> But if you don't believe what Moses wrote, how can you believe what I say?

### Feeding Five Thousand
(Matthew 14.13-21; Mark 6.30-44; Luke 9.10-17)

**6** Jesus crossed Lake Galilee, which was also known as Lake Tiberias. <sup>2</sup> A large crowd had seen him work mir-

acles to heal the sick, and those people went with him. <sup>3-4</sup> It was almost time for the Jewish festival of Passover, and Jesus went up on a mountain with his disciples and sat down. <sup>u</sup>

<sup>5</sup> When Jesus saw the large crowd coming toward him, he asked Philip, "Where will we get enough food to feed all these people?" <sup>6</sup> He said this to test Philip, since he already knew what he was going to do.

<sup>7</sup> Philip answered, "Don't you know that it would take almost a year's wages<sup>v</sup> just to buy only a little bread for each of these people?"

<sup>8</sup> Andrew, the brother of Simon Peter, was one of the disciples. He spoke up and said, <sup>9</sup> "There is a boy here who has five small loaves<sup>w</sup> of barley bread and two fish. But what good is that with all these people?"

<sup>10</sup> The ground was covered with grass, and Jesus told his disciples to have everyone sit down. About five thousand men were in the crowd. <sup>11</sup> Jesus took the bread in his hands and gave thanks to God. Then he passed the bread to the people, and he did the same with the fish, until everyone had plenty to eat.

<sup>12</sup> The people ate all they wanted, and Jesus told his disciples to gather up the leftovers, so that nothing would be wasted. <sup>13</sup> The disciples gathered them up and filled twelve large baskets with what was left over from the five barley loaves.

<sup>14</sup> After the people had seen Jesus work this miracle,<sup>x</sup> they began saying, "This must be the Prophet<sup>y</sup> who is to come into the world!" <sup>15</sup> Jesus realized that they would try to force him to be their king. So he went up on a mountain, where he could be alone.

### Jesus Walks on the Water
(Matthew 14.22-27; Mark 6.45-52)

<sup>16</sup> That evening, Jesus' disciples went down to the lake. <sup>17</sup> They got into a boat

---

<sup>u</sup>**6.3,4** *sat down*: Possibly to teach. Teachers in the ancient world, including Jewish teachers, usually sat down to teach. <sup>v</sup>**6.7** *almost a year's wages*: The Greek text has "two hundred silver coins." Each coin was worth the average day's wages for a worker. <sup>w</sup>**6.9** *small loaves*: These would have been flat and round or in the shape of a bun. <sup>x</sup>**6.14** *miracle*: See the note at 2.11. <sup>y</sup>**6.14** *the Prophet*: See the note at 1.21.

and started across for Capernaum. Later that evening Jesus had still not come to them, [18] and a strong wind was making the water rough.

[19] When the disciples had rowed for three or four miles, they saw Jesus walking on the water. He kept coming closer to the boat, and they were terrified. [20] But he said, "I am Jesus![z] Don't be afraid!" [21] The disciples wanted to take him into the boat, but suddenly the boat reached the shore where they were headed.

### The Bread That Gives Life

[22] The people who had stayed on the east side of the lake knew that only one boat had been there. They also knew that Jesus had not left in it with his disciples. But the next day [23] some boats from Tiberias sailed near the place where the crowd had eaten the bread for which the Lord had given thanks. [24] They saw that Jesus and his disciples had left. Then they got into the boats and went to Capernaum to look for Jesus. [25] They found him on the west side of the lake and asked, "Rabbi, when did you get here?"

[26] Jesus answered, "I tell you for certain that you are not looking for me because you saw the miracles,[a] but because you ate all the food you wanted. [27] Don't work for food that spoils. Work for food that gives eternal life. The Son of Man will give you this food, because God the Father has given him the right to do so."

[28] "What exactly does God want us to do?" the people asked.

[29] Jesus answered, "God wants you to have faith in the one he sent."

[30] They replied, "What miracle will you work, so that we can have faith in you? What will you do? [31] For example, when our ancestors were in the desert, they were given manna[b] to eat. It happened just as the Scriptures say, 'God gave them bread from heaven to eat.' "

[32] Jesus then told them, "I tell you for certain that Moses wasn't the one who gave you bread from heaven. My Father is the one who gives you the true bread from heaven. [33] And the bread that God gives is the one who came down from heaven to give life to the world."

[34] The people said, "Lord, give us this bread and don't ever stop!"

[35] Jesus replied:

I am the bread that gives life! No one who comes to me will ever be hungry. No one who has faith in me will ever be thirsty. [36] I have told you already that you have seen me and still do not have faith in me. [37] Everything and everyone that the Father has given me will come to me, and I won't turn any of them away.

[38] I didn't come from heaven to do what I want! I came to do what the Father wants me to do. He sent me, [39] and he wants to make certain that none of the ones he has given me will be lost. Instead, he wants me to raise them to life on the last day.[c] [40] My Father wants everyone who sees the Son to have faith in him and to have eternal life. Then I will raise them to life on the last day.

[41] The people started grumbling because Jesus had said he was the bread that had come down from heaven. [42] They were asking each other, "Isn't he Jesus, the son of Joseph? Don't we know his father and mother? How can he say that he has come down from heaven?"

[43] Jesus told them:

Stop grumbling! [44] No one can come to me, unless the Father who sent me makes them want to come. But if they do come, I will raise them to life on the last day. [45] One of the prophets wrote, "God will teach all of them." And so everyone who listens to the Father and learns from him will come to me.

[46] The only one who has seen the Father is the one who has come from

him. No one else has ever seen the Father. ⁴⁷I tell you for certain that everyone who has faith in me has eternal life.

⁴⁸I am the bread that gives life! ⁴⁹Your ancestors ate manna ᵈ in the desert, and later they died. ⁵⁰But the bread from heaven has come down, so that no one who eats it will ever die. ⁵¹I am that bread from heaven! Everyone who eats it will live forever. My flesh is the life-giving bread that I give to the people of this world.

⁵²They started arguing with each other and asked, "How can he give us his flesh to eat?"

⁵³Jesus answered:

I tell you for certain that you won't live unless you eat the flesh and drink the blood of the Son of Man. ⁵⁴But if you do eat my flesh and drink my blood, you will have eternal life, and I will raise you to life on the last day. ⁵⁵My flesh is the true food, and my blood is the true drink. ⁵⁶If you eat my flesh and drink my blood, you are one with me, and I am one with you.

⁵⁷The living Father sent me, and I have life because of him. Now everyone who eats my flesh will live because of me. ⁵⁸The bread that comes down from heaven isn't like what your ancestors ate. They died, but whoever eats this bread will live forever.

⁵⁹Jesus was teaching in a Jewish place of worship in Capernaum when he said these things.

### The Words of Eternal Life

⁶⁰Many of Jesus' disciples heard him and said, "This is too hard for anyone to understand."

⁶¹Jesus knew that his disciples were grumbling. So he asked, "Does this bother you? ⁶²What if you should see the Son of Man go up to heaven where he came from? ⁶³The Spirit is the one who gives life! Human strength can do

nothing. The words that I have spoken to you are from that life-giving Spirit. ⁶⁴But some of you refuse to have faith in me." Jesus said this, because from the beginning he knew who would have faith in him. He also knew which one would betray him.

⁶⁵Then Jesus said, "You cannot come to me, unless the Father makes you want to come. That is why I have told these things to all of you."

⁶⁶Because of what Jesus said, many of his disciples turned their backs on him and stopped following him. ⁶⁷Jesus then asked his twelve disciples if they were going to leave him. ⁶⁸Simon Peter answered, "Lord, there is no one else that we can go to! Your words give eternal life. ⁶⁹We have faith in you, and we are sure that you are God's Holy One."

⁷⁰Jesus told his disciples, "I chose all twelve of you, but one of you is a demon!" ⁷¹Jesus was talking about Judas, the son of Simon Iscariot.ᵉ He would later betray Jesus, even though he was one of the twelve disciples.

### Jesus' Brothers Don't Have Faith in Him

7 Jesus decided to leave Judea and to start going through Galilee because the leaders of the people wanted to kill him. ²It was almost time for the Festival of Shelters, ³and Jesus' brothers said to him, "Why don't you go to Judea? Then your disciples can see what you are doing. ⁴No one does anything in secret, if they want others to know about them. So let the world know what you are doing!" ⁵Even Jesus' own brothers had not yet become his followers.

⁶Jesus answered, "My time hasn't yet come,ᶠ but your time is always here. ⁷The people of this world cannot hate you. They hate me, because I tell them that they do evil things. ⁸Go on to the festival. My time hasn't yet come, and I am not going." ⁹Jesus said this and stayed on in Galilee.

ᵈ6.49 *manna*: See the note at 6.31. ᵉ6.71 *Iscariot*: This may mean "a man from Kerioth" (a place in Judea). But more probably it means "a man who was a liar" or "a man who was a betrayer." ᶠ7.6 *My time hasn't yet come*: See the note at 2.4.

## Jesus at the Festival of Shelters

10 After Jesus' brothers had gone to the festival, he went secretly, without telling anyone.

11 During the festival the leaders looked for Jesus and asked, "Where is he?" 12 The crowds even got into an argument about him. Some were saying, "Jesus is a good man," while others were saying, "He is lying to everyone." 13 But the people were afraid of their leaders, and none of them talked in public about him.

14 When the festival was about half over, Jesus went into the temple and started teaching. 15 The leaders were surprised and said, "How does this man know so much? He has never been taught!"

16 Jesus replied:

I am not teaching something that I thought up. What I teach comes from the one who sent me. 17 If you really want to obey God, you will know if what I teach comes from God or from me. 18 If I wanted to bring honor to myself, I would speak for myself. But I want to honor the one who sent me. That is why I tell the truth and not a lie. 19 Didn't Moses give you the Law? Yet none of you obey it! So why do you want to kill me?

20 The crowd replied, "You're crazy! What makes you think someone wants to kill you?"

21 Jesus answered:

I worked one miracle,g and it amazed you. 22 Moses commanded you to circumcise your sons. But it wasn't really Moses who gave you this command. It was your ancestors, and even on the Sabbath you circumcise your sons 23 in order to obey the Law of Moses. Why are you angry with me for making someone completely well on the Sabbath? 24 Don't judge by appearances. Judge by what is right.

25 Some of the people from Jerusalem were saying, "Isn't this the man they want to kill? 26 Yet here he is, speaking for everyone to hear. And no one is arguing with him. Do you suppose the authorities know that he is the Messiah? 27 But how could that be? No one knows where the Messiah will come from, but we know where this man comes from."

28 As Jesus was teaching in the temple, he shouted, "Do you really think you know me and where I came from? I didn't come on my own! The one who sent me is truthful, and you don't know him. 29 But I know the one who sent me, because I came from him."

30 Some of the people wanted to arrest Jesus right then. But no one even laid a hand on him, because his time had not yet come.h 31 A lot of people in the crowd put their faith in him and said, "When the Messiah comes, he surely won't perform more miraclesi than this man has done!"

## Officers Sent To Arrest Jesus

32 When the Pharisees heard the crowd arguing about Jesus, they got together with the chief priests and sent some temple police to arrest him. 33 But Jesus told them, "I will be with you a little while longer, and then I will return to the one who sent me. 34 You will look for me, but you won't find me. You cannot go where I am going."

35 The people asked each other, "Where can he go to keep us from finding him? Is he going to some foreign country where our people live? Is he going there to teach the Greeks?j 36 What did he mean by saying that we will look for him, but won't find him? Why can't we go where he is going?"

## Streams of Life-Giving Water

37 On the last and most important day of the festival, Jesus stood up and shouted, "If you are thirsty, come to me and drink! 38 Have faith in me, and you will have life-giving water flowing from deep inside you, just as the Scriptures say." 39 Jesus was talking about the

g 7.21 one miracle: The healing of the lame man (5.1-18) (see the note at 2.11).   h 7.30 his time had not yet come: See the note at 2.4.   i 7.31 miracles: See the note at 2.11.
j 7.35 Greeks: Perhaps Gentiles or Jews who followed Greek customs.

Holy Spirit, who would be given to everyone that had faith in him. The Spirit had not yet been given to anyone, since Jesus had not yet been given his full glory. *k*

## The People Take Sides

**40** When the crowd heard Jesus say this, some of them said, "He must be the Prophet!" *l* **41** Others said, "He is the Messiah!" Others even said, "Can the Messiah come from Galilee? **42** The Scriptures say that the Messiah will come from the family of King David. Doesn't this mean that he will be born in David's hometown of Bethlehem?" **43** The people started taking sides against each other because of Jesus. **44** Some of them wanted to arrest him, but no one laid a hand on him.

## The Leaders Refuse To Have Faith in Jesus

**45** When the temple police returned to the chief priests and Pharisees, they were asked, "Why didn't you bring Jesus here?"

**46** They answered, "No one has ever spoken like that man!"

**47** The Pharisees said to them, "Have you also been fooled? **48** Not one of the chief priests or the Pharisees has faith in him. **49** And these people who don't know the Law are under God's curse anyway."

**50** Nicodemus was there at the time. He was a member of the council, and was the same one who had earlier come to see Jesus. *m* He said, **51** "Our Law doesn't let us condemn people before we hear what they have to say. We cannot judge them before we know what they have done."

**52** Then they said, "Nicodemus, you must be from Galilee! Read the Scriptures, and you will find that no prophet is to come from Galilee."

## A Woman Caught in Sin

**8** **53** Everyone else went home, **1** but Jesus walked out to the Mount of Olives. **2** Then early the next morning he went to the temple. The people came to him, and he sat down *n* and started teaching them.

**3** The Pharisees and the teachers of the Law of Moses brought in a woman who had been caught in bed with a man who wasn't her husband. They made her stand in the middle of the crowd. **4** Then they said, "Teacher, this woman was caught sleeping with a man who isn't her husband. **5** The Law of Moses teaches that a woman like this should be stoned to death! What do you say?"

**6** They asked Jesus this question, because they wanted to test him and bring some charge against him. But Jesus simply bent over and started writing on the ground with his finger.

**7** They kept on asking Jesus about the woman. Finally, he stood up and said, "If any of you have never sinned, then go ahead and throw the first stone at her!" **8** Once again he bent over and began writing on the ground. **9** The people left one by one, beginning with the oldest. Finally, Jesus and the woman were there alone.

**10** Jesus stood up and asked her, "Where is everyone? Isn't there anyone left to accuse you?"

**11** "No sir," the woman answered.

Then Jesus told her, "I am not going to accuse you either. You may go now, but don't sin anymore." *o*

## Jesus Is the Light for the World

**12** Once again Jesus spoke to the people. This time he said, "I am the light for the world! Follow me, and you won't be walking in the dark. You will have the light that gives life."

**13** The Pharisees objected, "You are the only one speaking for yourself, and what you say isn't true!"

---

*k* 7.39 *had not yet been given his full glory*: In the Gospel of John, Jesus is given his full glory both when he is nailed to the cross and when he is raised from death to sit beside his Father in heaven. *l* 7.40 *the Prophet*: See the note at 1.21. *m* 7.50 *who had earlier come to see Jesus*: See 3.1-21. *n* 8.2 *sat down*: See the note at 6.3, 4. *o* 8.11 *don't sin anymore*: Verses 1-11 are not in some manuscripts. In other manuscripts these verses are placed after 7.36 or after 21.25 or after Luke 21.38, with some differences in the text.

14 Jesus replied:

Even if I do speak for myself, what I say is true! I know where I came from and where I am going. But you don't know where I am from or where I am going. 15 You judge in the same way that everyone else does, but I don't judge anyone. 16 If I did judge, I would judge fairly, because I would not be doing it alone. The Father who sent me is here with me. 17 Your Law requires two witnesses to prove that something is true. 18 I am one of my witnesses, and the Father who sent me is the other one.

19 "Where is your Father?" they asked.

"You don't know me or my Father!" Jesus answered. "If you knew me, you would know my Father."

20 Jesus said this while he was still teaching in the place where the temple treasures were stored. But no one arrested him, because his time had not yet come.[p]

### *You Cannot Go Where I Am Going*

21 Jesus also told them, "I am going away, and you will look for me. But you cannot go where I am going, and you will die with your sins unforgiven."

22 The people asked, "Does he intend to kill himself? Is that what he means by saying we cannot go where he is going?"

23 Jesus answered, "You are from below, but I am from above. You belong to this world, but I don't. 24 That is why I said you will die with your sins unforgiven. If you don't have faith in me for who I am,[q] you will die, and your sins will not be forgiven."

25 "Who are you?" they asked Jesus.

Jesus answered, "I am exactly who I told you at the beginning. 26 There is a lot more I could say to condemn you. But the one who sent me is truthful, and I tell the people of this world only what I have heard from him."

27 No one understood that Jesus was talking to them about the Father.

28 Jesus went on to say, "When you have lifted up the Son of Man,[r] you will know who I am. You will also know that I don't do anything on my own. I say only what my Father taught me. 29 The one who sent me is with me. I always do what pleases him, and he will never leave me."

30 After Jesus said this, many of the people put their faith in him.

### *The Truth Will Set You Free*

31 Jesus told the people who had faith in him, "If you keep on obeying what I have said, you truly are my disciples. 32 You will know the truth, and the truth will set you free."

33 They answered, "We are Abraham's children! We have never been anyone's slaves. How can you say we will be set free?"

34 Jesus replied:

I tell you for certain that anyone who sins is a slave of sin! 35 And slaves don't stay in the family forever, though the Son will always remain in the family. 36 If the Son gives you freedom, you are free! 37 I know that you are from Abraham's family. Yet you want to kill me, because my message isn't really in your hearts. 38 I am telling you what my Father has shown me, just as you are doing what your father has taught you.

### *Your Father Is the Devil*

39 The people said to Jesus, "Abraham is our father!"

Jesus replied, "If you were Abraham's children, you would do what Abraham did. 40 Instead, you want to kill me for telling you the truth that God gave me. Abraham never did anything like that. 41 But you are doing exactly what your father does."

"Don't accuse us of having someone

[p] **8.20** *his time had not yet come*: See the note at 2.4. [q] **8.24** *I am*: For the Jewish people the most holy name of God is "Yahweh," which may be translated "I am." In the Gospel of John "I am" is sometimes used by Jesus to show that he is that one. [r] **8.28** *lifted up the Son of Man*: See the note at 7.39.

else as our father!" they said. "We just have one father, and he is God."

42 Jesus answered:

If God were your Father, you would love me, because I came from God and only from him. He sent me. I did not come on my own. 43 Why can't you understand what I am talking about? Can't you stand to hear what I am saying? 44 Your father is the devil, and you do exactly what he wants. He has always been a murderer and a liar. There is nothing truthful about him. He speaks on his own, and everything he says is a lie. Not only is he a liar himself, but he is also the father of all lies.

45 Everything I have told you is true, and you still refuse to have faith in me. 46 Can any of you accuse me of sin? If you cannot, why won't you have faith in me? After all, I am telling you the truth. 47 Anyone who belongs to God will listen to his message. But you refuse to listen, because you don't belong to God.

### Jesus and Abraham

48 The people told Jesus, "We were right to say that you are a Samaritans and that you have a demon in you!"

49 Jesus answered, "I don't have a demon in me. I honor my Father, and you refuse to honor me. 50 I don't want honor for myself. But there is one who wants me to be honored, and he is also the one who judges. 51 I tell you for certain that if you obey my words, you will never die."

52 Then the people said, "Now we are sure that you have a demon. Abraham is dead, and so are the prophets. How can you say that no one who obeys your words will ever die? 53 Are you greater than our father Abraham? He died, and so did the prophets. Who do you think you are?"

54 Jesus replied, "If I honored myself, it would mean nothing. My Father is the one who honors me. You claim that he is your God, 55 even though you

don't really know him. If I said I didn't know him, I would be a liar, just like all of you. But I know him, and I do what he says. 56 Your father Abraham was really glad to see me."

57 "You are not even fifty years old!" they said. "How could you have seen Abraham?"

58 Jesus answered, "I tell you for certain that even before Abraham was, I was, and I am."t 59 The people picked up stones to kill Jesus, but he hid and left the temple.

### Jesus Heals a Man Born Blind

**9** As Jesus walked along, he saw a man who had been blind since birth. 2 Jesus' disciples asked, "Teacher, why was this man born blind? Was it because he or his parents sinned?"

3 "No, it wasn't!" Jesus answered. "But because of his blindness, you will see God work a miracle for him. 4 As long as it is day, we must do what the one who sent me wants me to do. When night comes, no one can work. 5 While I am in the world, I am the light for the world."

6 After Jesus said this, he spit on the ground. He made some mud and smeared it on the man's eyes. 7 Then he said, "Go and wash off the mud in Siloam Pool." The man went and washed in Siloam, which means "One Who Is Sent." When he had washed off the mud, he could see.

8 The man's neighbors and the people who had seen him begging wondered if he really could be the same man. 9 Some of them said he was the same beggar, while others said he only looked like him. But he told them, "I am that man."

10 "Then how can you see?" they asked.

11 He answered, "Someone named Jesus made some mud and smeared it on my eyes. He told me to go and wash it off in Siloam Pool. When I did, I could see."

12 "Where is he now?" they asked.

"I don't know," he answered.

---

s8.48 Samaritan: See 4.9 and the note there.   t8.58 I am: See the note at 8.24.

## The Pharisees Try To Find Out What Happened

**13-14** The day when Jesus made the mud and healed the man was a Sabbath. So the people took the man to the Pharisees. **15** They asked him how he was able to see, and he answered, "Jesus made some mud and smeared it on my eyes. Then after I washed it off, I could see."

**16** Some of the Pharisees said, "This man Jesus doesn't come from God. If he did, he would not break the law of the Sabbath."

Others asked, "How could someone who is a sinner work such a miracle?" *u*

Since the Pharisees could not agree among themselves, **17** they asked the man, "What do you say about this one who healed your eyes?"

"He is a prophet!" the man told them.

**18** But the Jewish leaders would not believe that the man had once been blind. They sent for his parents **19** and asked them, "Is this the son that you said was born blind? How can he now see?"

**20** The man's parents answered, "We are certain that he is our son, and we know that he was born blind. **21** But we don't know how he got his sight or who gave it to him. Ask him! He is old enough to speak for himself."

**22-23** The man's parents said this because they were afraid of their leaders. The leaders had already agreed that no one was to have anything to do with anyone who said Jesus was the Messiah.

**24** The leaders called the man back and said, "Swear by God to tell the truth! We know that Jesus is a sinner."

**25** The man replied, "I don't know if he is a sinner or not. All I know is that I used to be blind, but now I can see!"

**26** "What did he do to you?" they asked. "How did he heal your eyes?"

**27** The man answered, "I have already told you once, and you refused to listen. Why do you want me to tell you again? Do you also want to become his disciples?"

**28** The leaders insulted the man and said, "You are his follower! We are fol-lowers of Moses. **29** We are sure that God spoke to Moses, but we don't even know where Jesus comes from."

**30** "How strange!" the man replied. "He healed my eyes, and yet you don't know where he comes from. **31** We know that God listens only to people who love and obey him. God doesn't listen to sinners. **32** And this is the first time in history that anyone has ever given sight to someone born blind. **33** Jesus could not do anything unless he came from God."

**34** The leaders told the man, "You have been a sinner since the day you were born! Do you think you can teach us anything?" Then they said, "You can never come back into any of our meeting places!"

**35** When Jesus heard what had happened, he went and found the man. Then Jesus asked, "Do you have faith in the Son of Man?"

**36** He replied, "Sir, if you will tell me who he is, I will put my faith in him."

**37** "You have already seen him," Jesus answered, "and right now he is talking with you."

**38** The man said, "Lord, I put my faith in you!" Then he worshiped Jesus.

**39** Jesus told him, "I came to judge the people of this world. I am here to give sight to the blind and to make blind everyone who can see."

**40** When the Pharisees heard Jesus say this, they asked, "Are we blind?"

**41** Jesus answered, "If you were blind, you would not be guilty. But now that you claim to see, you will keep on being guilty."

## A Story about Sheep

**10** Jesus said:
I tell you for certain that only thieves and robbers climb over the fence instead of going in through the gate to the sheep pen. **2-3** But the gatekeeper opens the gate for the shepherd, and he goes in through it. The sheep know their shepherd's voice. He calls each of them by name and leads them out.

**4** When he has led out all of his sheep, he walks in front of them, and they follow, because they know his voice. [5] The sheep will not follow strangers. They don't recognize a stranger's voice, and they run away. [6] Jesus told the people this story. But they did not understand what he was talking about.

## Jesus Is the Good Shepherd

[7] Jesus said:

I tell you for certain that I am the gate for the sheep. [8] Everyone who came before me was a thief or a robber, and the sheep did not listen to any of them. [9] I am the gate. All who come in through me will be saved. Through me they will come and go and find pasture.

[10] A thief comes only to rob, kill, and destroy. I came so that everyone would have life, and have it in its fullest. [11] I am the good shepherd, and the good shepherd gives up his life for his sheep. [12] Hired workers are not like the shepherd. They don't own the sheep, and when they see a wolf coming, they run off and leave the sheep. Then the wolf attacks and scatters the flock. [13] Hired workers run away because they don't care about the sheep.

[14] I am the good shepherd. I know my sheep, and they know me. [15] Just as the Father knows me, I know the Father, and I give up my life for my sheep. [16] I have other sheep that are not in this sheep pen. I must bring them together too, when they hear my voice. Then there will be one flock of sheep and one shepherd.

[17] The Father loves me, because I give up my life, so that I may receive it back again. [18] No one takes my life from me. I give it up willingly! I have the power to give it up and the power to receive it back again, just as my Father commanded me to do.

[19] The people took sides because of what Jesus had told them. [20] Many of them said, "He has a demon in him! He is crazy! Why listen to him?"

[21] But others said, "How could anyone with a demon in him say these things? No one like that could give sight to a blind person!"

## Jesus Is Rejected

[22] That winter, Jesus was in Jerusalem for the Temple Festival. [23] One day he was walking in that part of the temple known as Solomon's Porch,[v] [24] and the people gathered all around him. They said, "How long are you going to keep us guessing? If you are the Messiah, tell us plainly!"

[25] Jesus answered:

I have told you, and you refused to believe me. The things I do by my Father's authority show who I am. [26] But since you are not my sheep, you don't believe me. [27] My sheep know my voice, and I know them. They follow me, [28] and I give them eternal life, so that they will never be lost. No one can snatch them out of my hand. [29] My Father gave them to me, and he is greater than all others.[w] No one can snatch them from his hands, [30] and I am one with the Father.

[31] Once again the people picked up stones in order to kill Jesus. [32] But he said, "I have shown you many good things that my Father sent me to do. Which one are you going to stone me for?"

[33] They answered, "We are not stoning you because of any good thing you did. We are stoning you because you did a terrible thing. You are just a man, and here you are claiming to be God!"

[34] Jesus replied:

In your Scriptures doesn't God say, "You are gods"? [35] You can't argue with the Scriptures, and God spoke to those people and called them gods. [36] So why do you accuse me of a terrible sin for saying that I am the Son of God? After all, it is the Father who prepared me for this work. He is also the one who sent me into the world. [37] If I don't do as

---

[v] 10.23 *Solomon's Porch*: A public place with tall columns along the east side of the temple.
[w] 10.29 *he is greater than all others*: Some manuscripts have "they are greater than all others."

my Father does, you should not believe me. [38] But if I do what my Father does, you should believe because of that, even if you don't have faith in me. Then you will know for certain that the Father is one with me, and I am one with the Father.

[39] Again they wanted to arrest Jesus. But he escaped [40] and crossed the Jordan to the place where John had earlier been baptizing. While Jesus was there, [41] many people came to him. They were saying, "John didn't work any miracles, but everything he said about Jesus is true." [42] A lot of those people also put their faith in Jesus.

## The Death of Lazarus

**11** [1-2] A man by the name of Lazarus was sick in the village of Bethany. He had two sisters, Mary and Martha. This was the same Mary who later poured perfume on the Lord's head and wiped his feet with her hair. [3] The sisters sent a message to the Lord and told him that his good friend Lazarus was sick.

[4] When Jesus heard this, he said, "His sickness won't end in death. It will bring glory to God and his Son."

[5] Jesus loved Martha and her sister and brother. [6] But he stayed where he was for two more days. [7] Then he said to his disciples, "Now we will go back to Judea."

[8] "Teacher," they said, "the people there want to stone you to death! Why do you want to go back?"

[9] Jesus answered, "Aren't there twelve hours in each day? If you walk during the day, you will have light from the sun, and you won't stumble. [10] But if you walk during the night, you will stumble, because you don't have any light." [11] Then he told them, "Our friend Lazarus is asleep, and I am going there to wake him up."

[12] They replied, "Lord, if he is asleep, he will get better." [13] Jesus really meant that Lazarus was dead, but they thought he was talking only about sleep.

[14] Then Jesus told them plainly, "Lazarus is dead! [15] I am glad that I wasn't there, because now you will have a chance to put your faith in me. Let's go to him."

[16] Thomas, whose nickname was "Twin," said to the other disciples, "Come on. Let's go, so we can die with him."

## Jesus Brings Lazarus to Life

[17] When Jesus got to Bethany, he found that Lazarus had already been in the tomb four days. [18] Bethany was only about two miles from Jerusalem, [19] and many people had come from the city to comfort Martha and Mary because their brother had died.

[20] When Martha heard that Jesus had arrived, she went out to meet him, but Mary stayed in the house. [21] Martha said to Jesus, "Lord, if you had been here, my brother would not have died. [22] Yet even now I know that God will do anything you ask."

[23] Jesus told her, "Your brother will live again!"

[24] Martha answered, "I know that he will be raised to life on the last day,[x] when all the dead are raised."

[25] Jesus then said, "I am the one who raises the dead to life! Everyone who has faith in me will live, even if they die. [26] And everyone who lives because of faith in me will never really die. Do you believe this?"

[27] "Yes, Lord!" she replied. "I believe that you are Christ, the Son of God. You are the one we hoped would come into the world."

[28] After Martha said this, she went and privately said to her sister Mary, "The Teacher is here, and he wants to see you." [29] As soon as Mary heard this, she got up and went out to Jesus. [30] He was still outside the village where Martha had gone to meet him. [31] Many people had come to comfort Mary, and when they saw her quickly leave the house, they thought she was going out to the tomb to cry. So they followed her.

[32] Mary went to where Jesus was.

x **11.24** *the last day*: When God will judge all people.

Then as soon as she saw him, she knelt at his feet and said, "Lord, if you had been here, my brother would not have died."

33 When Jesus saw that Mary and the people with her were crying, he was terribly upset 34 and asked, "Where have you put his body?"

They replied, "Lord, come and you will see."

35 Jesus started crying, 36 and the people said, "See how much he loved Lazarus."

37 Some of them said, "He gives sight to the blind. Why couldn't he have kept Lazarus from dying?"

38 Jesus was still terribly upset. So he went to the tomb, which was a cave with a stone rolled against the entrance. 39 Then he told the people to roll the stone away. But Martha said, "Lord, you know that Lazarus has been dead four days, and there will be a bad smell."

40 Jesus replied, "Didn't I tell you that if you had faith, you would see the glory of God?"

41 After the stone had been rolled aside, Jesus looked up toward heaven and prayed, "Father, I thank you for answering my prayer. 42 I know that you always answer my prayers. But I said this, so that the people here would believe that you sent me."

43 When Jesus had finished praying, he shouted, "Lazarus, come out!" 44 The man who had been dead came out. His hands and feet were wrapped with strips of burial cloth, and a cloth covered his face.

Jesus then told the people, "Untie him and let him go."

## The Plot To Kill Jesus

(Matthew 26.1-5; Mark 14.1, 2; Luke 22.1, 2)

45 Many of the people who had come to visit Mary saw the things that Jesus did, and they put their faith in him. 46 Others went to the Pharisees and told what Jesus had done. 47 Then the chief priests and the Pharisees called the council together and said, "What should we do? This man is working a lot of miracles.y 48 If we don't stop him now, everyone will put their faith in him. Then the Romans will come and destroy our temple and our nation."z

49 One of the council members was Caiaphas, who was also high priest that year. He spoke up and said, "You people don't have any sense at all! 50 Don't you know it is better for one person to die for the people than for the whole nation to be destroyed?" 51 Caiaphas did not say this on his own. As high priest that year, he was prophesying that Jesus would die for the nation. 52 Yet Jesus would not die just for the Jewish nation. He would die to bring together all of God's scattered people. 53 From that day on, the council started making plans to put Jesus to death.

54 Because of this plot against him, Jesus stopped going around in public. He went to the town of Ephraim, which was near the desert, and he stayed there with his disciples.

55 It was almost time for Passover. Many of the Jewish people who lived out in the country had come to Jerusalem to get themselves readya for the festival. 56 They looked around for Jesus. Then when they were in the temple, they asked each other, "You don't think he will come here for Passover, do you?"

57 The chief priests and the Pharisees told the people to let them know if any of them saw Jesus. That is how they hoped to arrest him.

## At Bethany

(Matthew 26.6-13; Mark 14.3-9)

12 Six days before Passover Jesus went back to Bethany, where he had raised Lazarus from death. 2 A meal had been prepared for Jesus. Martha was doing the serving, and Lazarus himself was there.

---

y 11.47 miracles: See the note at 2.11.   z 11.48 destroy our temple and our nation: The Jewish leaders were afraid that Jesus would lead his followers to rebel against Rome and that the Roman army would then destroy their nation.   a 11.55 get themselves ready: The Jewish people had to do certain things to prepare themselves to worship God.

3 Mary took a very expensive bottle of perfume b and poured it on Jesus' feet. She wiped them with her hair, and the sweet smell of the perfume filled the house.

4 A disciple named Judas Iscariot c was there. He was the one who was going to betray Jesus, and he asked, 5 "Why wasn't this perfume sold for three hundred silver coins and the money given to the poor?" 6 Judas did not really care about the poor. He asked this because he carried the moneybag and sometimes would steal from it.

7 Jesus replied, "Leave her alone! She has kept this perfume for the day of my burial. 8 You will always have the poor with you, but you won't always have me."

### A Plot To Kill Lazarus

9 A lot of people came when they heard that Jesus was there. They also wanted to see Lazarus, because Jesus had raised him from death. 10 So the chief priests made plans to kill Lazarus. 11 He was the reason that many of the people were turning from them and putting their faith in Jesus.

### Jesus Enters Jerusalem
(Matthew 21.1-11; Mark 11.1-11; Luke 19.28-40)

12 The next day a large crowd was in Jerusalem for Passover. When they heard that Jesus was coming for the festival, 13 they took palm branches and went out to greet him. d They shouted,

"Hooray! e
God bless the one who comes
  in the name of the Lord!
God bless the King
  of Israel!"

14 Jesus found a donkey and rode on it, just as the Scriptures say,

15 "People of Jerusalem,
  don't be afraid!
Your King is now coming,
and he is riding
  on a donkey."

16 At first, Jesus' disciples did not understand. But after he had been given his glory, f they remembered all this. Everything had happened exactly as the Scriptures said it would.

17-18 A crowd had come to meet Jesus because they had seen him call Lazarus out of the tomb. They kept talking about him and this miracle. g 19 But the Pharisees said to each other, "There is nothing that can be done! Everyone in the world is following Jesus."

### Some Greeks Want To Meet Jesus

20 Some Greeks h had gone to Jerusalem to worship during Passover. 21 Philip from Bethsaida in Galilee was there too. So they went to him and said, "Sir, we would like to meet Jesus." 22 Philip told Andrew. Then the two of them went to Jesus and told him.

### The Son of Man Must Be Lifted Up

23 Jesus said:
The time has come for the Son of Man to be given his glory. i 24 I tell you for certain that a grain of wheat that falls on the ground will never be more than one grain unless it dies. But if it dies, it will produce lots of wheat. 25 If you love your life, you will lose it. If you give it up in this world, you will be given eternal life. 26 If you serve me, you must go with me. My servants will be with me wherever I am. If you serve me, my Father will honor you.

27 Now I am deeply troubled, and I don't know what to say. But I must not ask my Father to keep me from this time of suffering. In fact, I came

b 12.3 very expensive bottle of perfume: The Greek text has "expensive perfume made of pure spikenard," a plant used to make perfume.   c 12.4 Iscariot: See the note at 6.71.
d 12.13 took palm branches and went out to greet him: This was one way that the Jewish people welcomed a famous person.   e 12.13 Hooray: This translates a word that can mean "please save us." But it is most often used as a shout of praise to God.   f 12.16 had been given his glory: See the note at 7.39.   g 12.17,18 miracle: See the note at 2.11.
h 12.20 Greeks: Perhaps Gentiles who worshiped with the Jews. See the note at 7.35.
i 12.23 be given his glory: See the note at 7.39.

into the world to suffer. [28] So Father, bring glory to yourself.

A voice from heaven then said, "I have already brought glory to myself, and I will do it again!" [29] When the crowd heard the voice, some of them thought it was thunder. Others thought an angel had spoken to Jesus.

[30] Then Jesus told the crowd, "That voice spoke to help you, not me. [31] This world's people are now being judged, and the ruler of this world[j] is already being thrown out! [32] If I am lifted up above the earth, I will make everyone want to come to me." [33] Jesus was talking about the way he would be put to death.

[34] The crowd said to Jesus, "The Scriptures teach that the Messiah will live forever. How can you say that the Son of Man must be lifted up? Who is this Son of Man?"

[35] Jesus answered, "The light will be with you for only a little longer. Walk in the light while you can. Then you won't be caught walking blindly in the dark. [36] Have faith in the light while it is with you, and you will be children of the light."

### The People Refuse To Have Faith in Jesus

After Jesus had said these things, he left and went into hiding. [37] He had worked a lot of miracles[k] among the people, but they were still not willing to have faith in him. [38] This happened so that what the prophet Isaiah had said would come true,

"Lord, who has believed
    our message?
And who has seen
    your mighty strength?"

[39] The people could not have faith in Jesus, because Isaiah had also said,

[40] "The Lord has blinded
    the eyes of the people,
and he has made
    the people stubborn.

He did this so that they
    could not see
    or understand,
and so that they
    would not turn to the Lord
    and be healed."

[41] Isaiah said this, because he saw the glory of Jesus and spoke about him.[l] [42] Even then, many of the leaders put their faith in Jesus, but they did not tell anyone about it. The Pharisees had already given orders for the people not to have anything to do with anyone who had faith in Jesus. [43] And besides, the leaders liked praise from others more than they liked praise from God.

### Jesus Came To Save the World

[44] In a loud voice Jesus said:

Everyone who has faith in me also has faith in the one who sent me. [45] And everyone who has seen me has seen the one who sent me. [46] I am the light that has come into the world. No one who has faith in me will stay in the dark.

[47] I am not the one who will judge those who refuse to obey my teachings. I came to save the people of this world, not to be their judge. [48] But everyone who rejects me and my teachings will be judged on the last day[m] by what I have said. [49] I don't speak on my own. I say only what the Father who sent me has told me to say. [50] I know that his commands will bring eternal life. That is why I tell you exactly what the Father has told me.

### Jesus Washes the Feet of His Disciples

**13** It was before Passover, and Jesus knew that the time had come for him to leave this world and to return to the Father. He had always loved his followers in this world, and he loved them to the very end.

[2] Even before the evening meal

---

[j] **12.31** *world*: In the Gospel of John "world" sometimes refers to the people who live in this world and to the evil forces that control their lives. [k] **12.37** *miracles*: See the note at 2.11. [l] **12.41** *he saw the glory of Jesus and spoke about him*: Or "he saw the glory of God and spoke about Jesus." [m] **12.48** *the last day*: When God will judge all people.

started, the devil had made Judas, the son of Simon Iscariot,[n] decide to betray Jesus.

[3] Jesus knew that he had come from God and would go back to God. He also knew that the Father had given him complete power. [4] So during the meal Jesus got up, removed his outer garment, and wrapped a towel around his waist. [5] He put some water into a large bowl. Then he began washing his disciples' feet and drying them with the towel he was wearing.

[6] But when he came to Simon Peter, that disciple asked, "Lord, are you going to wash my feet?"

[7] Jesus answered, "You don't really know what I am doing, but later you will understand."

[8] "You will never wash my feet!" Peter replied.

"If I don't wash you," Jesus told him, "you don't really belong to me."

[9] Peter said, "Lord, don't wash just my feet. Wash my hands and my head."

[10] Jesus answered, "People who have bathed and are clean all over need to wash just their feet. And you, my disciples, are clean, except for one of you." [11] Jesus knew who would betray him. That is why he said, "except for one of you."

[12] After Jesus had washed his disciples' feet and had put his outer garment back on, he sat down again.[o] Then he said:

Do you understand what I have done? [13] You call me your teacher and Lord, and you should, because that is who I am. [14] And if your Lord and teacher has washed your feet, you should do the same for each other. [15] I have set the example, and you should do for each other exactly what I have done for you. [16] I tell you for certain that servants are not greater than their master, and messengers are not greater than the one who sent them. [17] You know these things, and God will bless you, if you do them.

[18] I am not talking about all of you.

I know the ones I have chosen. But what the Scriptures say must come true. And they say, "The man who ate with me has turned against me!" [19] I am telling you this before it all happens. Then when it does happen, you will believe who I am.[p] [20] I tell you for certain that anyone who welcomes my messengers also welcomes me, and anyone who welcomes me welcomes the one who sent me.

### Jesus Tells What Will Happen to Him
(Matthew 26.20-25; Mark 14.17-21; Luke 22.21-23)

[21] After Jesus had said these things, he was deeply troubled and told his disciples, "I tell you for certain that one of you will betray me." [22] They were confused about what he meant. And they just stared at each other.

[23] Jesus' favorite disciple was sitting next to him at the meal, [24] and Simon motioned for that disciple to find out which one Jesus meant. [25] So the disciple leaned toward Jesus and asked, "Lord, which one of us are you talking about?"

[26] Jesus answered, "I will dip this piece of bread in the sauce and give it to the one I was talking about."

Then Jesus dipped the bread and gave it to Judas, the son of Simon Iscariot.[q] [27] Right then Satan took control of Judas.

Jesus said, "Judas, go quickly and do what you have to do." [28] No one at the meal understood what Jesus meant. [29] But because Judas was in charge of the money, some of them thought that Jesus had told him to buy something they needed for the festival. Others thought that Jesus had told him to give some money to the poor. [30] Judas took the piece of bread and went out.

It was already night.

### The New Command

[31] After Judas had gone, Jesus said:
Now the Son of Man will be given glory, and he will bring glory to

[n] 13.2 Iscariot: See the note at 6.71.   [o] 13.12 sat down again: On special occasions the Jewish people followed the Greek and Roman custom of lying down on their left side and leaning on their left elbow, while eating with their right hand.   [p] 13.19 I am: See the note at 8.24.
[q] 13.26 Iscariot: See the note at 6.71.

God. ³²Then, after God is given glory because of him, God will bring glory to him, and God will do it very soon.

³³My children, I will be with you for a little while longer. Then you will look for me, but you won't find me. I tell you just as I told the people, "You cannot go where I am going." ³⁴But I am giving you a new command. You must love each other, just as I have loved you. ³⁵If you love each other, everyone will know that you are my disciples.

### Peter's Promise
*(Matthew 26.31-35; Mark 14.27-31; Luke 22.31-34)*

³⁶Simon Peter asked, "Lord, where are you going?"

Jesus answered, "You can't go with me now, but later on you will."

³⁷Peter asked, "Lord, why can't I go with you now? I would die for you!"

³⁸"Would you really die for me?" Jesus asked. "I tell you for certain that before a rooster crows, you will say three times that you don't even know me."

### Jesus Is the Way to the Father

**14** Jesus said to his disciples, "Don't be worried! Have faith in God and have faith in me.ʳ ²There are many rooms in my Father's house. I wouldn't tell you this, unless it was true. I am going there to prepare a place for each of you. ³After I have done this, I will come back and take you with me. Then we will be together. ⁴You know the way to where I am going."

⁵Thomas said, "Lord, we don't even know where you are going! How can we know the way?"

⁶"I am the way, the truth, and the life!" Jesus answered. "Without me, no one can go to the Father. ⁷If you had known me, you would have known the Father. But from now on, you do know him, and you have seen him."

⁸Philip said, "Lord, show us the Father. That is all we need."

⁹Jesus replied:

Philip, I have been with you for a long time. Don't you know who I am? If you have seen me, you have seen the Father. How can you ask me to show you the Father? ¹⁰Don't you believe that I am one with the Father and that the Father is one with me? What I say isn't said on my own. The Father who lives in me does these things.

¹¹Have faith in me when I say that the Father is one with me and that I am one with the Father. Or else have faith in me simply because of the things I do. ¹²I tell you for certain that if you have faith in me, you will do the same things that I am doing. You will do even greater things, now that I am going back to the Father. ¹³Ask me, and I will do whatever you ask. This way the Son will bring honor to the Father. ¹⁴I will do whatever you ask me to do.

### The Holy Spirit Is Promised

¹⁵Jesus said to his disciples:

If you love me, you will do as I command. ¹⁶Then I will ask the Father to send you the Holy Spirit who will helpˢ you and always be with you. ¹⁷The Spirit will show you what is true. The people of this world cannot accept the Spirit, because they don't see or know him. But you know the Spirit, who is with you and will keep on living in you.

¹⁸I won't leave you like orphans. I will come back to you. ¹⁹In a little while the people of this world won't be able to see me, but you will see me. And because I live, you will live. ²⁰Then you will know that I am one with the Father. You will know that you are one with me, and I am one with you. ²¹If you love me, you will do what I have said, and my Father will love you. I will also love you and show you what I am like.

ʳ**14.1** *Have faith in God and have faith in me*: Or "You have faith in God, so have faith in me." ˢ**14.16** *help*: The Greek word may mean "comfort," "encourage," or "defend."

²²The other Judas, not Judas Iscariot,[t] then spoke up and asked, "Lord, what do you mean by saying that you will show us what you are like, but you will not show the people of this world?" ²³Jesus replied:

If anyone loves me, they will obey me. Then my Father will love them, and we will come to them and live in them. ²⁴But anyone who doesn't love me, won't obey me. What they have heard me say doesn't really come from me, but from the Father who sent me.

²⁵I have told you these things while I am still with you. ²⁶But the Holy Spirit will come and help[u] you, because the Father will send the Spirit to take my place. The Spirit will teach you everything and will remind you of what I said while I was with you.

²⁷I give you peace, the kind of peace that only I can give. It isn't like the peace that this world can give. So don't be worried or afraid. ²⁸You have already heard me say that I am going and that I will also come back to you. If you really love me, you should be glad that I am going back to the Father, because he is greater than I am.

²⁹I am telling you this before I leave, so that when it does happen, you will have faith in me. ³⁰I cannot speak with you much longer, because the ruler of this world is coming. But he has no power over me. ³¹I obey my Father, so that everyone in the world might know that I love him.

It is time for us to go now.

### Jesus Is the True Vine

**15** Jesus said to his disciples:
I am the true vine, and my Father is the gardener. ²He cuts away every branch of mine that doesn't produce fruit. But he trims clean every branch that does produce fruit, so that it will produce even more fruit. ³You are already clean because of what I have said to you.

⁴Stay joined to me, and I will stay joined to you. Just as a branch cannot produce fruit unless it stays joined to the vine, you cannot produce fruit unless you stay joined to me. ⁵I am the vine, and you are the branches. If you stay joined to me, and I stay joined to you, then you will produce lots of fruit. But you cannot do anything without me. ⁶If you don't stay joined to me, you will be thrown away. You will be like dry branches that are gathered up and burned in a fire.

⁷Stay joined to me and let my teachings become part of you. Then you can pray for whatever you want, and your prayer will be answered. ⁸When you become fruitful disciples of mine, my Father will be honored. ⁹I have loved you, just as my Father has loved me. So remain faithful to my love for you. ¹⁰If you obey me, I will keep loving you, just as my Father keeps loving me, because I have obeyed him.

¹¹I have told you this to make you as completely happy as I am. ¹²Now I tell you to love each other, as I have loved you. ¹³The greatest way to show love for friends is to die for them. ¹⁴And you are my friends, if you obey me. ¹⁵Servants don't know what their master is doing, and so I don't speak to you as my servants. I speak to you as my friends, and I have told you everything that my Father has told me.

¹⁶You did not choose me. I chose you and sent you out to produce fruit, the kind of fruit that will last. Then my Father will give you whatever you ask for in my name.[v] ¹⁷So I command you to love each other.

### The World's Hatred

¹⁸If the people of this world[w] hate you, just remember that they hated me first. ¹⁹If you belonged to the

---

[t] **14.22** *Iscariot:* See the note at 6.71.   [u] **14.26** *help:* See the note at 14.16.   [v] **15.16** *in my name:* Or "because you are my followers."   [w] **15.18** *world:* See the note at 12.31.

world, its people would love you. But you don't belong to the world. I have chosen you to leave the world behind, and that is why its people hate you. 20 Remember how I told you that servants are not greater than their master. So if people mistreat me, they will mistreat you. If they do what I say, they will do what you say.

21 People will do to you exactly what they did to me. They will do it because you belong to me, and they don't know the one who sent me. 22 If I had not come and spoken to them, they would not be guilty of sin. But now they have no excuse for their sin.

23 Everyone who hates me also hates my Father. 24 I have done things that no one else has ever done. If they had not seen me do these things, they would not be guilty. But they did see me do these things, and they still hate me and my Father too. 25 That is why the Scriptures are true when they say, "People hated me for no reason."

26 I will send you the Spirit who comes from the Father and shows what is true. The Spirit will help[x] you and will tell you about me. 27 Then you will also tell others about me, because you have been with me from the beginning.

**16** I am telling you this to keep you from being afraid. 2 You will be chased out of the Jewish meeting places. And the time will come when people will kill you and think they are doing God a favor. 3 They will do these things because they don't know either the Father or me. 4 I am saying this to you now, so that when the time comes, you will remember what I have said.

### The Work of the Holy Spirit

I was with you at the first, and so I didn't tell you these things. 5 But now I am going back to the Father who sent me, and none of you asks me where I am going. 6 You are very

sad from hearing all of this. 7 But I tell you that I am going to do what is best for you. That is why I am going away. The Holy Spirit cannot come to help[x] you until I leave. But after I am gone, I will send the Spirit to you.

8 The Spirit will come and show the people of this world the truth about sin and God's justice and the judgment. 9 The Spirit will show them that they are wrong about sin, because they didn't have faith in me. 10 They are wrong about God's justice, because I am going to the Father, and you won't see me again. 11 And they are wrong about the judgment, because God has already judged the ruler of this world.

12 I have much more to say to you, but right now it would be more than you could understand. 13 The Spirit shows what is true and will come and guide you into the full truth. The Spirit doesn't speak on his own. He will tell you only what he has heard from me, and he will let you know what is going to happen. 14 The Spirit will bring glory to me by taking my message and telling it to you. 15 Everything that the Father has is mine. That is why I have said that the Spirit takes my message and tells it to you.

### Sorrow Will Turn into Joy

16 Jesus told his disciples, "For a little while you won't see me, but after a while you will see me."

17 They said to each other, "What does Jesus mean by saying that for a little while we won't see him, but after a while we will see him? What does he mean by saying that he is going to the Father? 18 What is this 'little while' that he is talking about? We don't know what he means."

19 Jesus knew that they had some questions, so he said:

You are wondering what I meant when I said that for a little while you won't see me, but after a while you will see me. [20] I tell you for certain that you will cry and be sad, but the world will be happy. You will be sad, but later you will be happy.

[21] When a woman is about to give birth, she is in great pain. But after it is all over, she forgets the pain and is happy, because she has brought a child into the world. [22] You are now very sad. But later I will see you, and you will be so happy that no one will be able to change the way you feel. [23] When that time comes, you won't have to ask me about anything. I tell you for certain that the Father will give you whatever you ask for in my name. [24] You have not asked for anything in this way before, but now you must ask in my name.ʸ Then it will be given to you, so that you will be completely happy.

[25] I have used examples to explain to you what I have been talking about. But the time will come when I will speak to you plainly about the Father and will no longer use examples like these. [26] You will ask the Father in my name,ᶻ and I won't have to ask him for you. [27] God the Father loves you because you love me, and you believe that I have come from him. [28] I came from the Father into the world, but I am leaving the world and returning to the Father.

[29] The disciples said, "Now you are speaking plainly to us! You are not using examples. [30] At last we know that you understand everything, and we don't have any more questions. Now we believe that you truly have come from God."

[31] Jesus replied:

Do you really believe me? [32] The time will come and is already here when all of you will be scattered. Each of you will go back home and leave me by myself. But the Father will be with me, and I won't be alone. [33] I have told you this, so that you might have peace in your hearts because of me. While you are in the world, you will have to suffer. But cheer up! I have defeated the world.ᵃ

## Jesus Prays

**17** After Jesus had finished speaking to his disciples, he looked up toward heaven and prayed:

Father, the time has come for you to bring glory to your Son, in order that he may bring glory to you. [2] And you gave him power over all people, so that he would give eternal life to everyone you give him. [3] Eternal life is to know you, the only true God, and to know Jesus Christ, the one you sent. [4] I have brought glory to you here on earth by doing everything you gave me to do. [5] Now, Father, give me back the glory that I had with you before the world was created.

[6] You have given me some followers from this world, and I have shown them what you are like. They were yours, but you gave them to me, and they have obeyed you. [7] They know that you gave me everything I have. [8] I told my followers what you told me, and they accepted it. They know that I came from you, and they believe that you are the one who sent me. [9] I am praying for them, but not for those who belong to this world.ᵃ My followers belong to you, and I am praying for them. [10] All that I have is yours, and all that you have is mine, and they will bring glory to me.

[11] Holy Father, I am no longer in the world. I am coming to you, but my followers are still in the world. So keep them safe by the power of the name that you have given me. Then they will be one with each other, just as you and I are one. [12] While I was with them, I kept them safe by the power you have given me. I guarded them, and not one of them was lost, except the one who had to be lost. This happened

---

ʸ**16.23,24** *in my name . . . in my name*: Or "as my disciples . . . as my disciples." ᶻ**16.26** *in my name*: Or "because you are my followers." ᵃ**16.33** *world*: See the note at 12.31. ᵃ**17.9** *world*: See the note at 12.31.

145

JOHN 17, 18

so that what the Scriptures say would come true.

¹³ I am on my way to you. But I say these things while I am still in the world, so that my followers will have the same complete joy that I do. ¹⁴ I have told them your message. But the people of this world hate them, because they don't belong to this world, just as I don't.

¹⁵ Father, I don't ask you to take my followers out of the world, but keep them safe from the evil one. ¹⁶ They don't belong to this world, and neither do I. ¹⁷ Your word is the truth. So let this truth make them completely yours. ¹⁸ I am sending them into the world, just as you sent me. ¹⁹ I have given myself completely for their sake, so that they may belong completely to the truth.

²⁰ I am not praying just for these followers. I am also praying for everyone else who will have faith because of what my followers will say about me. ²¹ I want all of them to be one with each other, just as I am one with you and you are one with me. I also want them to be one with us. Then the people of this world will believe that you sent me.

²² I have honored my followers in the same way that you honored me, in order that they may be one with each other, just as we are one. ²³ I am one with them, and you are one with me, so that they may become completely one. Then this world's people will know that you sent me. They will know that you love my followers as much as you love me.

²⁴ Father, I want everyone you have given me to be with me, wherever I am. Then they will see the glory that you have given me, because you loved me before the world was created. ²⁵ Good Father, the people of this world don't know you. But I know you, and my followers know that you sent me. ²⁶ I told them what you are like, and I will tell them even more. Then the love that

you have for me will become part of them, and I will be one with them.

### Jesus Is Betrayed and Arrested
(Matthew 26.47-56; Mark 14.43-50; Luke 22.47-53)

**18** When Jesus had finished praying, he and his disciples crossed the Kidron Valley and went into a garden.ᵇ ² Jesus had often met there with his disciples, and Judas knew where the place was.

³⁻⁵ Judas had promised to betray Jesus. So he went to the garden with some Roman soldiers and temple police, who had been sent by the chief priests and the Pharisees. They carried torches, lanterns, and weapons. Jesus already knew everything that was going to happen, but he asked, "Who are you looking for?"

They answered, "We are looking for Jesus from Nazareth!"

Jesus told them, "I am Jesus!"ᶜ ⁶ At once they all backed away and fell to the ground.

⁷ Jesus again asked, "Who are you looking for?"

"We are looking for Jesus from Nazareth," they answered.

⁸ This time Jesus replied, "I have already told you that I am Jesus. If I am the one you are looking for, let these others go. ⁹ Then everything will happen, just as the Scriptures say, 'I did not lose anyone you gave me.'"

¹⁰ Simon Peter had brought along a sword. He now pulled it out and struck at the servant of the high priest. The servant's name was Malchus, and Peter cut off his right ear. ¹¹ Jesus told Peter, "Put your sword away. I must drink from the cupᵈ that the Father has given me."

### Jesus Is Brought to Annas
(Matthew 26.57, 58; Mark 14.53, 54; Luke 22.54)

¹² The Roman officer and his men, together with the temple police, arrested Jesus and tied him up. ¹³ They took him

---

ᵇ 18.1 *garden*: The Greek word is usually translated "garden," but probably referred to an olive orchard.   ᶜ 18.3-5 *I am Jesus*: The Greek text has "I am" (see the note at 8.24).   ᵈ 18.11 *drink from the cup*: In the Scriptures a cup is sometimes used as a symbol of suffering. To "drink from the cup" is to suffer.

first to Annas, who was the father-in-law of Caiaphas, the high priest that year. [14] This was the same Caiaphas who had told the Jewish leaders, "It is better if one person dies for the people."

## Peter Says He Doesn't Know Jesus
*(Matthew 26.69, 70; Mark 14.66-68; Luke 22.55-57)*

[15] Simon Peter and another disciple followed Jesus. That disciple knew the high priest, and he followed Jesus into the courtyard of the high priest's house. [16] Peter stayed outside near the gate. But the other disciple came back out and spoke to the girl at the gate. She let Peter go in, [17] but asked him, "Aren't you one of that man's followers?"

"No, I am not!" Peter answered.

[18] It was cold, and the servants and temple police had made a charcoal fire. They were warming themselves around it, when Peter went over and stood near the fire to warm himself.

## Jesus Is Questioned by the High Priest
*(Matthew 26.59-66; Mark 14.55-64; Luke 22.66-71)*

[19] The high priest questioned Jesus about his followers and his teaching. [20] But Jesus told him, "I have spoken freely in front of everyone. And I have always taught in our meeting places and in the temple, where all of our people come together. I have not said anything in secret. [21] Why are you questioning me? Why don't you ask the people who heard me? They know what I have said."

[22] As soon as Jesus said this, one of the temple police hit him and said, "That's no way to talk to the high priest!"

[23] Jesus answered, "If I have done something wrong, say so. But if not, why did you hit me?" [24] Jesus was still tied up, and Annas sent him to Caiaphas the high priest.

## Peter Again Denies that He Knows Jesus
*(Matthew 26.71-75; Mark 14.69-72; Luke 22.58-62)*

[25] While Simon Peter was standing there warming himself, someone asked him, "Aren't you one of Jesus' followers?"

Again Peter denied it and said, "No, I am not!"

[26] One of the high priest's servants was there. He was a relative of the servant whose ear Peter had cut off, and he asked, "Didn't I see you in the garden with that man?"

[27] Once more Peter denied it, and right then a rooster crowed.

## Jesus Is Tried by Pilate
*(Matthew 27.1, 2, 11-14; Mark 15.1-5; Luke 23.1-5)*

[28] It was early in the morning when Jesus was taken from Caiaphas to the building where the Roman governor stayed. But the crowd waited outside. Any of them who had gone inside would have become unclean and would not be allowed to eat the Passover meal.[e]

[29] Pilate came out and asked, "What charges are you bringing against this man?"

[30] They answered, "He is a criminal! That's why we brought him to you."

[31] Pilate told them, "Take him and judge him by your own laws."

The crowd replied, "We are not allowed to put anyone to death." [32] And so what Jesus said about his death[f] would soon come true.

[33] Pilate then went back inside. He called Jesus over and asked, "Are you the king of the Jews?"

[34] Jesus answered, "Are you asking this on your own or did someone tell you about me?"

[35] "You know I'm not a Jew!" Pilate said. "Your own people and the chief priests brought you to me. What have you done?"

---

*e* **18.28** *would have become unclean and would not be allowed to eat the Passover meal*: Jewish people who came in close contact with foreigners right before Passover were not allowed to eat the Passover meal.  *f* **18.32** *about his death*: Jesus had said that he would die by being "lifted up," which meant that he would die on a cross. The Romans killed criminals by nailing them on a cross, but they did not let the Jews kill anyone in this way.

36 Jesus answered, "My kingdom doesn't belong to this world. If it did, my followers would have fought to keep me from being handed over to our leaders. No, my kingdom doesn't belong to this world."

37 "So you are a king," Pilate replied.

"You are saying that I am a king," Jesus told him. "I was born into this world to tell about the truth. And everyone who belongs to the truth knows my voice."

38 Pilate asked Jesus, "What is truth?"

## Jesus Is Sentenced to Death
*(Matthew 27.15-31; Mark 15.6-20; Luke 23.13-25)*

Pilate went back out and said, "I don't find this man guilty of anything! 39 And since I usually set a prisoner free for you at Passover, would you like for me to set free the king of the Jews?"

40 They shouted, "No, not him! We want Barabbas." Now Barabbas was a terrorist.g

**19** Pilate gave orders for Jesus to be beaten with a whip. 2 The soldiers made a crown out of thorn branches and put it on Jesus. Then they put a purple robe on him. 3 They came up to him and said, "Hey, you king of the Jews!" They also hit him with their fists.

4 Once again Pilate went out. This time he said, "I will have Jesus brought out to you again. Then you can see for yourselves that I have not found him guilty."

5 Jesus came out, wearing the crown of thorns and the purple robe. Pilate said, "Here is the man!"h

6 When the chief priests and the temple police saw him, they yelled, "Nail him to a cross! Nail him to a cross!"

Pilate told them, "You take him and nail him to a cross! I don't find him guilty of anything."

7 The crowd replied, "He claimed to be the Son of God! Our Law says that he must be put to death."

8 When Pilate heard this, he was terrified. 9 He went back inside and asked Jesus, "Where are you from?" But Jesus did not answer.

10 "Why won't you answer my question?" Pilate asked. "Don't you know that I have the power to let you go free or to nail you to a cross?"

11 Jesus replied, "If God had not given you the power, you couldn't do anything at all to me. But the one who handed me over to you did something even worse."

12 Then Pilate wanted to set Jesus free. But the crowd again yelled, "If you set this man free, you are no friend of the Emperor! Anyone who claims to be a king is an enemy of the Emperor."

13 When Pilate heard this, he brought Jesus out. Then he sat down on the judge's bench at the place known as "The Stone Pavement." In Aramaic this pavement is called "Gabbatha." 14 It was about noon on the day before Passover, and Pilate said to the crowd, "Look at your king!"

15 "Kill him! Kill him!" they yelled. "Nail him to a cross!"

"So you want me to nail your king to a cross?" Pilate asked.

The chief priests replied, "The Emperor is our king!" 16 Then Pilate handed Jesus over to be nailed to a cross.

## Jesus Is Nailed to a Cross
*(Matthew 27.32-44; Mark 15.21-32; Luke 23.26-43)*

Jesus was taken away, 17 and he carried his cross to a place known as "The Skull."i In Aramaic this place is called "Golgotha." 18 There Jesus was nailed to the cross, and on each side of him a man was also nailed to a cross.

19 Pilate ordered the charge against Jesus to be written on a board and put above the cross. It read, "Jesus of Nazareth, King of the Jews." 20 The words were written in Hebrew, Latin, and Greek.

The place where Jesus was taken wasn't far from the city, and many of

g 18.40 *terrorist*: Someone who stirred up trouble against the Romans in the hope of gaining freedom for the Jewish people. h 19.5 *"Here is the man!"*: Or "Look at the man!" i 19.17 *The Skull*: The place was probably given this name because it was near a large rock in the shape of a human skull.

the people read the charge against him. ²¹ So the chief priests went to Pilate and said, "Why did you write that he is King of the Jews? You should have written, 'He claimed to be King of the Jews.' "

²² But Pilate told them, "What is written will not be changed!"

²³ After the soldiers had nailed Jesus to the cross, they divided up his clothes into four parts, one for each of them. But his outer garment was made from a single piece of cloth, and it did not have any seams. ²⁴ The soldiers said to each other, "Let's not rip it apart. We will gamble to see who gets it." This happened so that the Scriptures would come true, which say,

> "They divided up my clothes
> and gambled
>   for my garments."

The soldiers then did what they had decided.

²⁵ Jesus' mother stood beside his cross with her sister and Mary the wife of Clopas. Mary Magdalene was standing there too.ⁱ ²⁶ When Jesus saw his mother and his favorite disciple with her, he said to his mother, "This man is now your son." ²⁷ Then he said to the disciple, "She is now your mother." From then on, that disciple took her into his own home.

## The Death of Jesus
(Matthew 27.45-56; Mark 15.33-41; Luke 23.44-49)

²⁸ Jesus knew that he had now finished his work. And in order to make the Scriptures come true, he said, "I am thirsty!" ²⁹ A jar of cheap wine was there. Someone then soaked a sponge with the wine and held it up to Jesus' mouth on the stem of a hyssop plant.

³⁰ After Jesus drank the wine, he said, "Everything is done!" He bowed his head and died.

## A Spear Is Stuck in Jesus' Side

³¹ The next day would be both a Sabbath and the Passover. It was a special day for the Jewish people,ᵏ and they did not want the bodies to stay on the crosses during that day. So they asked Pilate to break the men's legsˡ and take their bodies down. ³² The soldiers first broke the legs of the other two men who were nailed there. ³³ But when they came to Jesus, they saw that he was already dead, and they did not break his legs.

³⁴ One of the soldiers stuck his spear into Jesus' side, and blood and water came out. ³⁵ We know this is true, because it was told by someone who saw it happen. Now you can have faith too. ³⁶ All this happened so that the Scriptures would come true, which say, "No bone of his body will be broken" ³⁷ and, "They will see the one in whose side they stuck a spear."

## Jesus Is Buried
(Matthew 27.57-61; Mark 15.42-47; Luke 23.50-56)

³⁸ Joseph from Arimathea was one of Jesus' disciples. He had kept it secret though, because he was afraid of the Jewish leaders. But now he asked Pilate to let him have Jesus' body. Pilate gave him permission, and Joseph took it down from the cross. ³⁹ Nicodemus also came with about seventy-five pounds of spices made from myrrh and aloes. This was the same Nicodemus who had visited Jesus one night.ᵐ ⁴⁰ The two men wrapped the body in a linen cloth, together with

---

ⁱ **19.25** *Jesus' mother stood beside his cross with her sister and Mary the wife of Clopas. Mary Magdalene was standing there too*: The Greek text may also be understood to include only three women ("Jesus' mother stood beside the cross with her sister, Mary the mother of Clopas. Mary Magdalene was standing there too.") or merely two women ("Jesus' mother was standing there with her sister Mary of Clopas, that is Mary Magdalene."). "Of Clopas" may mean "daughter of" or "mother of." ᵏ **19.31** *a special day for the Jewish people*: Passover could be any day of the week. But according to the Gospel of John, Passover was on a Sabbath in the year that Jesus was nailed to a cross. ˡ **19.31** *break the men's legs*: This was the way that the Romans sometimes speeded up the death of a person who had been nailed to a cross. ᵐ **19.39** *Nicodemus who had visited Jesus one night*: See 3.1-21.

the spices, which was how the Jewish people buried their dead. [41] In the place where Jesus had been nailed to a cross, there was a garden with a tomb that had never been used. [42] The tomb was nearby, and since it was the time to prepare for the Sabbath, they were in a hurry to put Jesus' body there.

## Jesus Is Alive
*(Matthew 28.1-10; Mark 16.1-8; Luke 24.1-12)*

**20** On Sunday morning while it was still dark, Mary Magdalene went to the tomb and saw that the stone had been rolled away from the entrance. [2] She ran to Simon Peter and to Jesus' favorite disciple and said, "They have taken the Lord from the tomb! We don't know where they have put him."

[3] Peter and the other disciple started for the tomb. [4] They ran side by side, until the other disciple ran faster than Peter and got there first. [5] He bent over and saw the strips of linen cloth lying inside the tomb, but he did not go in. [6] When Simon Peter got there, he went into the tomb and saw the strips of cloth. [7] He also saw the piece of cloth that had been used to cover Jesus' face. It was rolled up and in a place by itself. [8] The disciple who got there first then went into the tomb, and when he saw it, he believed. [9] At that time Peter and the other disciple did not know that the Scriptures said Jesus would rise to life. [10] So the two of them went back to the other disciples.

## Jesus Appears to Mary Magdalene
*(Mark 16.9-11)*

[11] Mary Magdalene stood crying outside the tomb. She was still weeping, when she stooped down [12] and saw two angels inside. They were dressed in white and were sitting where Jesus' body had been. One was at the head and the other was at the foot. [13] The angels asked Mary, "Why are you crying?"

She answered, "They have taken away my Lord's body! I don't know where they have put him."

[14] As soon as Mary said this, she turned around and saw Jesus standing there. But she did not know who he was. [15] Jesus asked her, "Why are you crying? Who are you looking for?"

She thought he was the gardener and said, "Sir, if you have taken his body away, please tell me, so I can go and get him."

[16] Then Jesus said to her, "Mary!"

She turned and said to him, "Rabboni." The Aramaic word "Rabboni" means "Teacher."

[17] Jesus told her, "Don't hold on to me! I have not yet gone to the Father. But tell my disciples that I am going to the one who is my Father and my God, as well as your Father and your God." [18] Mary Magdalene then went and told the disciples that she had seen the Lord. She also told them what he had said to her.

## Jesus Appears to His Disciples
*(Matthew 28.16-20; Mark 16.14-18; Luke 24.36-49)*

[19] The disciples were afraid of the Jewish leaders, and on the evening of that same Sunday they locked themselves in a room. Suddenly, Jesus appeared in the middle of the group. He greeted them [20] and showed them his hands and his side. When the disciples saw the Lord, they became very happy.

[21] After Jesus had greeted them again, he said, "I am sending you, just as the Father has sent me." [22] Then he breathed on them and said, "Receive the Holy Spirit. [23] If you forgive anyone's sins, they will be forgiven. But if you don't forgive their sins, they will not be forgiven."

## Jesus and Thomas

[24] Although Thomas the Twin was one of the twelve disciples, he wasn't with the others when Jesus appeared to them. [25] So they told him, "We have seen the Lord!"

But Thomas said, "First, I must see the nail scars in his hands and touch them with my finger. I must put my hand where the spear went into his side. I won't believe unless I do this!"

[26] A week later the disciples were together again. This time, Thomas was with them. Jesus came in while the doors were still locked and stood in the

middle of the group. He greeted his disciples [27] and said to Thomas, "Put your finger here and look at my hands! Put your hand into my side. Stop doubting and have faith!"

[28] Thomas replied, "You are my Lord and my God!"

[29] Jesus said, "Thomas, do you have faith because you have seen me? The people who have faith in me without seeing me are the ones who are really blessed!"

### Why John Wrote His Book

[30] Jesus worked many other miracles[n] for his disciples, and not all of them are written in this book. [31] But these are written so that you will put your faith in Jesus as the Messiah and the Son of God. If you have faith in[o] him, you will have true life.

### Jesus Appears to Seven Disciples

**21** Jesus later appeared to his disciples along the shore of Lake Tiberias. [2] Simon Peter, Thomas the Twin, Nathanael from Cana in Galilee, and the brothers James and John,[p] were there, together with two other disciples. [3] Simon Peter said, "I'm going fishing!"

The others said, "We will go with you." They went out in their boat. But they didn't catch a thing that night.

[4] Early the next morning Jesus stood on the shore, but the disciples did not realize who he was. [5] Jesus shouted, "Friends, have you caught anything?"

"No!" they answered.

[6] So he told them, "Let your net down on the right side of your boat, and you will catch some fish."

They did, and the net was so full of fish that they could not drag it up into the boat.

[7] Jesus' favorite disciple told Peter, "It's the Lord!" When Simon heard that it was the Lord, he put on the clothes that he had taken off while he was working. Then he jumped into the wa-

ter. [8] The boat was only about a hundred yards from shore. So the other disciples stayed in the boat and dragged in the net full of fish.

[9] When the disciples got out of the boat, they saw some bread and a charcoal fire with fish on it. [10] Jesus told his disciples, "Bring some of the fish you just caught." [11] Simon Peter got back into the boat and dragged the net to shore. In it were one hundred fifty-three large fish, but still the net did not rip.

[12] Jesus said, "Come and eat!" But none of the disciples dared ask who he was. They knew he was the Lord. [13] Jesus took the bread in his hands and gave some of it to his disciples. He did the same with the fish. [14] This was the third time that Jesus appeared to his disciples after he was raised from death.

### Jesus and Peter

[15] When Jesus and his disciples had finished eating, he asked, "Simon son of John, do you love me more than the others do?"[q]

Simon Peter answered, "Yes, Lord, you know I do!"

"Then feed my lambs," Jesus said.

[16] Jesus asked a second time, "Simon son of John, do you love me?"

Peter answered, "Yes, Lord, you know I love you!"

"Then take care of my sheep," Jesus told him.

[17] Jesus asked a third time, "Simon son of John, do you love me?"

Peter was hurt because Jesus had asked him three times if he loved him. So he told Jesus, "Lord, you know everything. You know I love you."

Jesus replied, "Feed my sheep. [18] I tell you for certain that when you were a young man, you dressed yourself and went wherever you wanted to go. But when you are old, you will hold out your hands. Then others will wrap your belt around you and lead you where you don't want to go."

---

[n]**20.30** *miracles*: See the note at 2.11.   [o]**20.31** *put your faith in ... have faith in*: Some manuscripts have "keep on having faith in ... keep on having faith in."   [p]**21.2** *the brothers James and John*: Greek "the two sons of Zebedee."   [q]**21.15** *more than the others do?*: Or "more than you love these things?"

19 Jesus said this to tell how Peter would die and bring honor to God. Then he said to Peter, "Follow me!"

## Jesus and His Favorite Disciple

20 Peter turned and saw Jesus' favorite disciple following them. He was the same one who had sat next to Jesus at the meal and had asked, "Lord, who is going to betray you?" 21 When Peter saw that disciple, he asked Jesus, "Lord, what about him?"

22 Jesus answered, "What is it to you, if I want him to live until I return? You must follow me." 23 So the rumor spread among the other disciples that this disciple would not die. But Jesus did not say he would not die. He simply said, "What is it to you, if I want him to live until I return?"

24 This disciple is the one who told all of this. He wrote it, and we know he is telling the truth.

25 Jesus did many other things. If they were all written in books, I don't suppose there would be room enough in the whole world for all the books.

# ACTS

## ABOUT THIS BOOK

This is the second book written by Luke. His first one is commonly known as the Gospel of Luke. In it he told "all that Jesus did and taught from the very first until he was taken up to heaven" (1.1, 2). In this book Luke continues the story by describing some of the struggles the disciples faced as they tried to obey the command of Jesus: "You will tell everyone about me in Jerusalem, in all Judea, in Samaria, and everywhere in the world" (1.8).

So many different countries are mentioned in Acts that the book may seem to have been written only to tell about the spread of the Christian message. But that is only part of the story. After Jesus was taken up to heaven, one of the big problems for his followers was deciding who could belong to God's people. And since Jesus and his first followers were Jews, it was only natural for many of them to think that his message was only for Jews. But in Acts the Spirit is always present to show that Jesus came to save both Jews and Gentiles, and that God wants followers from every nation and race to be part of his people.

The first conflict between Christians and Jews took place when some of the Jewish religious leaders rejected the message about Jesus (4.1-31; 7.1-59). But the most serious problems for the early church happened because the disciples at first failed to understand that anyone could become a follower of Jesus without first becoming a Jew. This began to change when Philip dared to take the message to the Samaritans (8.7-25), and when Peter went to the home of Cornelius, a captain in the Roman army (10.1-48).

Finally, Peter reported to the church in Jerusalem (11.1-18) and a meeting was held there (15.3-35) to discuss the question of who could become followers of Christ. Before the meeting was over, everyone agreed that the Spirit of God was leading them to reach out to Gentiles as well as Jews with the good news of Jesus.

The one who did the most for the spread of the faith was a man named Paul, and much of the book tells about his preaching among the Gentiles. Finally, he took the message to Rome, the world's most important city at that time (28.16-31). One of Luke's main reasons for writing was to show that nothing could keep the Christian message from spreading everywhere:

> For two years Paul stayed in a rented house and welcomed
> everyone who came to see him. He bravely preached about
> God's kingdom and taught about the Lord Jesus Christ, and
> no one tried to stop him.                              (28.30, 31)

## A QUICK LOOK AT THIS BOOK

152

---

**1** Theophilus, I first wrote to you[a] about all that Jesus did and taught from the very first [2] until he was taken up to heaven. But before he was taken up, he gave orders to the apostles he had chosen with the help of the Holy Spirit.

[3] For forty days after Jesus had suffered and died, he proved in many ways that he had been raised from death. He appeared to his apostles and spoke to them about God's kingdom. [4] While he was still with them, he said:

Don't leave Jerusalem yet. Wait here for the Father to give you the Holy Spirit, just as I told you he has promised to do. [5] John baptized with water, but in a few days you will be baptized with the Holy Spirit.

### Jesus Is Taken to Heaven

[6] While the apostles were still with Jesus, they asked him, "Lord, are you now going to give Israel its own king again?"[b]

[7] Jesus said to them, "You don't need to know the time of those events that only the Father controls. [8] But the Holy Spirit will come upon you and give you power. Then you will tell everyone about me in Jerusalem, in all Judea, in Samaria, and everywhere in the world." [9] After Jesus had said this and while they were watching, he was taken up into a cloud. They could not see him, [10] but as he went up, they kept looking up into the sky.

Suddenly two men dressed in white clothes were standing there beside them. [11] They said, "Why are you men from Galilee standing here and looking up into the sky? Jesus has been taken to heaven. But he will come back in the same way that you have seen him go."

### Someone To Take the Place of Judas

[12-13] The Mount of Olives was about half a mile from Jerusalem. The apostles who had gone there were Peter, John, James, Andrew, Philip, Thomas, Bartholomew, Matthew, James the son of Alphaeus, Simon, known as the Eager One,[c] and Judas the son of James.

After the apostles returned to the city, they went upstairs to the room where they had been staying.

[14] The apostles often met together and prayed with a single purpose in mind.[d] The women and Mary the mother of Jesus would meet with them, and so would his brothers. [15] One day there were about one hundred twenty of the Lord's followers meeting together, and Peter stood up to speak to them. [16-17] He said:

My friends, long ago by the power of the Holy Spirit, David said something about Judas, and what he said has now happened. Judas was one of us and had worked with us, but he brought the mob to arrest Jesus. [18] Then Judas bought some land with the money he was given for doing that evil thing. He fell headfirst into the field. His body burst open, and all his insides came out. [19] When the people of Jerusalem found out about this, they called the place Akeldama, which in the local language means "Field of Blood."

[20] In the book of Psalms it says,

---

[a] **1.1** *I first wrote to you*: The Gospel of Luke.   [b] **1.6** *are you now going to give Israel its own king again?*: Or "Are you now going to rule Israel as its king?"   [c] **1.12,13** *known as the Eager One*: The Greek text has "Cananaean," which probably comes from a Hebrew word meaning "zealous" (see Luke 6.15). "Zealot" was the name later given to the members of a Jewish group which resisted and fought against the Romans.   [d] **1.14** *met together and prayed with a single purpose in mind*: Or "met together in a special place for prayer."

"Leave his house empty,
and don't let anyone
live there."

It also says,

"Let someone else
have his job."

**21-22** So we need someone else to help us tell others that Jesus has been raised from death. He must also be one of the men who was with us from the very beginning. He must have been with us from the time the Lord Jesus was baptized by John until the day he was taken to heaven. **23** Two men were suggested: One of them was Joseph Barsabbas, known as Justus, and the other was Matthias. **24** Then they all prayed, "Lord, you know what everyone is like! Show us the one you have chosen **25** to be an apostle and to serve in place of Judas, who got what he deserved." **26** They drew names, and Matthias was chosen to join the group of the eleven apostles.

### The Coming of the Holy Spirit

**2** On the day of Pentecost[e] all the Lord's followers were together in one place. **2** Suddenly there was a noise from heaven like the sound of a mighty wind! It filled the house where they were meeting. **3** Then they saw what looked like fiery tongues moving in all directions, and a tongue came and settled on each person there. **4** The Holy Spirit took control of everyone, and they began speaking whatever languages the Spirit let them speak.

**5** Many religious Jews from every country in the world were living in Jerusalem. **6** And when they heard this noise, a crowd gathered. But they were surprised, because they were hearing everything in their own languages. **7** They were excited and amazed, and said:

Don't all these who are speaking come from Galilee? **8** Then why do we hear them speaking our very own languages? **9** Some of us are from Parthia, Media, and Elam. Others are from Mesopotamia, Judea, Cappadocia, Pontus, Asia, **10** Phrygia, Pamphylia, Egypt, parts of Libya near Cyrene, Rome, **11** Crete, and Arabia. Some of us were born Jews, and others of us have chosen to be Jews. Yet we all hear them using our own languages to tell the wonderful things God has done.

**12** Everyone was excited and confused. Some of them even kept asking each other, "What does all this mean?" **13** Others made fun of the Lord's followers and said, "They are drunk."

### Peter Speaks to the Crowd

**14** Peter stood with the eleven apostles and spoke in a loud and clear voice to the crowd:

Friends and everyone else living in Jerusalem, listen carefully to what I have to say! **15** You are wrong to think that these people are drunk. After all, it is only nine o'clock in the morning. **16** But this is what God had the prophet Joel say,

**17** "When the last days come,
I will give my Spirit
to everyone.
Your sons and daughters
will prophesy.
Your young men
will see visions,
and your old men
will have dreams.
**18** In those days I will give
my Spirit to my servants,
both men and women,
and they will prophesy.

**19** I will work miracles
in the sky above
and wonders
on the earth below.
There will be blood and fire
and clouds of smoke.
**20** The sun will turn dark,

[e]**2.1** *Pentecost*: A Jewish festival that came fifty days after Passover and celebrated the wheat harvest. Jews later celebrated Pentecost as the time when they were given the Law of Moses.

and the moon
> will be as red as blood
before the great
and wonderful day
> of the Lord appears.
21 Then the Lord
> will save everyone
> who asks for his help."

22 Now, listen to what I have to say about Jesus from Nazareth. God proved that he sent Jesus to you by having him work miracles, wonders, and signs. All of you know this. 23 God had already planned and decided that Jesus would be handed over to you. So you took him and had evil men put him to death on a cross. 24 But God set him free from death and raised him to life. Death could not hold him in its power. 25 What David said are really the words of Jesus,

> "I always see the Lord
> near me,
> and I will not be afraid
> with him at my right side.
26 Because of this,
> my heart will be glad,
> my words will be joyful,
> and I will live in hope.
27 The Lord won't leave me
> in the grave.
> I am his holy one,
> and he won't let
> my body decay.
28 He has shown me
> the path to life,
> and he makes me glad
> by being near me."

29 My friends, it is right for me to speak to you about our ancestor David. He died and was buried, and his tomb is still here. 30 But David was a prophet, and he knew that God had made a promise he would not break. He had told David that someone from his own family would someday be king. 31 David knew this would happen, and so he told us that Christ would be raised to life. He said that God would not leave him in the grave or let his body decay. 32 All of us can tell you that God has raised Jesus to life!

33 Jesus was taken up to sit at the right side[f] of God, and he was given the Holy Spirit, just as the Father had promised. Jesus is also the one who has given the Spirit to us, and that is what you are now seeing and hearing.

34 David didn't go up to heaven. So he wasn't talking about himself when he said, "The Lord told my Lord to sit at his right side, 35 until he made my Lord's enemies into a footstool for him." 36 Everyone in Israel should then know for certain that God has made Jesus both Lord and Christ, even though you put him to death on a cross.

37 When the people heard this, they were very upset. They asked Peter and the other apostles, "Friends, what shall we do?"

38 Peter said, "Turn back to God! Be baptized in the name of Jesus Christ, so that your sins will be forgiven. Then you will be given the Holy Spirit. 39 This promise is for you and your children. It is for everyone our Lord God will choose, no matter where they live."

40 Peter told them many other things as well. Then he said, "I beg you to save yourselves from what will happen to all these evil people." 41 On that day about three thousand believed his message and were baptized. 42 They spent their time learning from the apostles, and they were like family to each other. They also broke bread[g] and prayed together.

### Life among the Lord's Followers

43 Everyone was amazed by the many miracles and wonders that the apostles worked. 44 All the Lord's followers often met together, and they shared everything they had. 45 They would sell their property and possessions and give the money to whoever needed it. 46 Day after day they met together in the temple. They broke bread[g] together in

---

f2.33 right side: The place of honor and power.   g2.42 broke bread: They ate together and celebrated the Lord's Supper.   g2.46 broke bread: They ate together and celebrated the Lord's Supper.

different homes and shared their food happily and freely, [47] while praising God. Everyone liked them, and each day the Lord added to their group others who were being saved.

## Peter and John Heal a Lame Man

**3** The time of prayer[h] was about three o'clock in the afternoon, and Peter and John were going into the temple. [2] A man who had been born lame was being carried to the temple door. Each day he was placed beside this door, known as the Beautiful Gate. He sat there and begged from the people who were going in.

[3] The man saw Peter and John entering the temple, and he asked them for money. [4] But they looked straight at him and said, "Look up at us!"

[5] The man stared at them and thought he was going to get something. [6] But Peter said, "I don't have any silver or gold! But I will give you what I do have. In the name of Jesus Christ from Nazareth, get up and start walking." [7] Peter then took him by the right hand and helped him up.

At once the man's feet and ankles became strong, [8] and he jumped up and started walking. He went with Peter and John into the temple, walking and jumping and praising God. [9] Everyone saw him walking around and praising God. [10] They knew that he was the beggar who had been lying beside the Beautiful Gate, and they were completely surprised. They could not imagine what had happened to the man.

## Peter Speaks in the Temple

[11] While the man kept holding on to Peter and John, the whole crowd ran to them in amazement at the place known as Solomon's Porch.[i] [12] Peter saw that a crowd had gathered, and he said:

Friends, why are you surprised at what has happened? Why are you staring at us? Do you think we have

some power of our own? Do you think we were able to make this man walk because we are so religious? [13] The God that Abraham, Isaac, Jacob, and our other ancestors worshiped has brought honor to his Servant[j] Jesus. He is the one you betrayed. You turned against him when he was being tried by Pilate, even though Pilate wanted to set him free.

[14] You rejected Jesus, who was holy and good. You asked for a murderer to be set free, [15] and you killed the one who leads people to life. But God raised him from death, and all of us can tell you what he has done. [16] You see this man, and you know him. He put his faith in the name of Jesus and was made strong. Faith in Jesus made this man completely well while everyone was watching.

[17] My friends, I am sure that you and your leaders didn't know what you were doing. [18] But God had his prophets tell that his Messiah would suffer, and now he has kept that promise. [19] So turn to God! Give up your sins, and you will be forgiven. [20] Then that time will come when the Lord will give you fresh strength. He will send you Jesus, his chosen Messiah. [21] But Jesus must stay in heaven until God makes all things new, just as his holy prophets promised long ago.

[22] Moses said, "The Lord your God will choose one of your own people to be a prophet, just as he chose me. Listen to everything he tells you. [23] No one who disobeys that prophet will be one of God's people any longer."

[24] Samuel and all the other prophets who came later also spoke about what is now happening. [25] You are really the ones God told his prophets to speak to. And you were given the promise that God made to your ancestors. He said to Abraham, "All nations on earth will be blessed because of someone from your fam-

---

[h] **3.1** *The time of prayer*: Many of the Jewish people prayed in their homes at regular times each day (see Daniel 6.11), and on special occasions they prayed in the temple.
[i] **3.11** *Solomon's Porch*: A public place with tall columns along the east side of the temple.
[j] **3.13** *Servant*: Or "Son."

ily." ²⁶ God sent his chosen Son ᵏ to you first, because God wanted to bless you and make each one of you turn away from your sins.

## Peter and John Are Brought in Front of the Council

4 The apostles were still talking to the people, when some priests, the captain of the temple guard, and some Sadducees arrived. ² These men were angry because the apostles were teaching the people that the dead would be raised from death, just as Jesus had been raised from death. ³ It was already late in the afternoon, and they arrested Peter and John and put them in jail for the night. ⁴ But a lot of people who had heard the message believed it. So by now there were about five thousand followers of the Lord.

⁵ The next morning the leaders, the elders, and the teachers of the Law of Moses met in Jerusalem. ⁶ The high priest Annas was there, as well as Caiaphas, John, Alexander, and other members of the high priest's family. ⁷ They brought in Peter and John and made them stand in the middle while they questioned them. They asked, "By what power and in whose name have you done this?"

⁸ Peter was filled with the Holy Spirit and told the nation's leaders and the elders:

⁹ You are questioning us today about a kind deed in which a crippled man was healed. ¹⁰ But there is something we must tell you and everyone else in Israel. This man is standing here completely well because of the power of Jesus Christ from Nazareth. You put Jesus to death on a cross, but God raised him to life. ¹¹ He is the stone that you builders thought was worthless, and now he is the most important stone of all. ¹² Only Jesus has the power to save! His name is the only one in all the world that can save anyone.

¹³ The officials were amazed to see how brave Peter and John were, and they knew that these two apostles were only ordinary men and not well educated. The officials were certain that these men had been with Jesus. ¹⁴ But they could not deny what had happened. The man who had been healed was standing there with the apostles. ¹⁵ The officials commanded them to leave the council room. Then the officials said to each other, ¹⁶ "What can we do with these men? Everyone in Jerusalem knows about this miracle, and we cannot say it didn't happen. ¹⁷ But to keep this thing from spreading, we will warn them never again to speak to anyone about the name of Jesus." ¹⁸ So they called the two apostles back in and told them that they must never, for any reason, teach anything about the name of Jesus.

¹⁹ Peter and John answered, "Do you think God wants us to obey you or to obey him? ²⁰ We cannot keep quiet about what we have seen and heard."

²¹⁻²² The officials could not find any reason to punish Peter and John. So they threatened them and let them go. The man who was healed by this miracle was more than forty years old, and everyone was praising God for what had happened.

## Peter and Others Pray for Courage

²³ As soon as Peter and John had been set free, they went back and told the others everything that the chief priests and the leaders had said to them. ²⁴ When the rest of the Lord's followers heard this, they prayed together and said:

Master, you created heaven and earth, the sea, and everything in them. ²⁵ And by the Holy Spirit you spoke to our ancestor David. He was your servant, and you told him to say:

"Why are all the Gentiles
    so furious?
Why do people
    make foolish plans?
²⁶ The kings of earth
    prepare for war,
and the rulers
    join together

ᵏ3.26 Son: Or "Servant."

against the Lord
and his Messiah."

27 Here in Jerusalem, Herod[1] and Pontius Pilate got together with the Gentiles and the people of Israel. Then they turned against your holy Servant[m] Jesus, your chosen Messiah. 28 They did what you in your power and wisdom had already decided would happen.

29 Lord, listen to their threats! We are your servants. So make us brave enough to speak your message. 30 Show your mighty power, as we heal people and work miracles and wonders in the name of your holy Servant[m] Jesus.

31 After they had prayed, the meeting place shook. They were all filled with the Holy Spirit and bravely spoke God's message.

### Sharing Possessions

32 The group of followers all felt the same way about everything. None of them claimed that their possessions were their own, and they shared everything they had with each other. 33 In a powerful way the apostles told everyone that the Lord Jesus was now alive. God greatly blessed his followers,[n] 34 and no one went in need of anything. Everyone who owned land or houses would sell them and bring the money 35 to the apostles. Then they would give the money to anyone who needed it.

36-37 Joseph was one of the followers who had sold a piece of property and brought the money to the apostles. He was a Levite from Cyprus, and the apostles called him Barnabas, which means, "one who encourages others."

### Peter Condemns Ananias and Sapphira

5 Ananias and his wife Sapphira also sold a piece of property. 2 But they agreed to cheat and keep some of the money for themselves.

So when Ananias took the rest of the money to the apostles, 3 Peter said, "Why has Satan made you keep back some of the money from the sale of the property? Why have you lied to the Holy Spirit? 4 The property was yours before you sold it, and even after you sold it, the money was still yours. What made you do such a thing? You didn't lie to people. You lied to God!"

5 As soon as Ananias heard this, he dropped dead, and everyone who heard about it was frightened. 6 Some young men came in and wrapped up his body. Then they took it out and buried it.

7 Three hours later Sapphira came in, but she did not know what had happened to her husband. 8 Peter asked her, "Tell me, did you sell the property for this amount?"

"Yes," she answered, "that's the amount."

9 Then Peter said, "Why did the two of you agree to test the Lord's Spirit? The men who buried Ananias are by the door, and they will carry you out!" 10 At once she fell at Peter's feet and died.

When the young men came back in, they found Sapphira lying there dead. So they carried her out and buried her beside her husband. 11 The church members were afraid, and so was everyone else who heard what had happened.

### Peter's Unusual Power

12 The apostles worked many miracles and wonders among the people. All of the Lord's followers often met in the part of the temple known as Solomon's Porch.[o] 13 No one outside their group dared join them, even though everyone liked them very much.

14 Many men and women started having faith in the Lord. 15 Then sick people were brought out to the road and placed on cots and mats. It was hoped that Peter would walk by, and his shadow would fall on them and heal

[1]4.27 Herod: Herod Antipas, the son of Herod the Great.   [m]4.27 Servant: See the note at 3.13.   [m]4.30 Servant: See the note at 3.13.   [n]4.33 God greatly blessed his followers: Or "Everyone highly respected his followers."   [o]5.12 Solomon's Porch: See the note at 3.11.

them. ¹⁶ A lot of people living in the towns near Jerusalem brought those who were sick or troubled by evil spirits, and they were all healed.

### Trouble for the Apostles

¹⁷ The high priest and all the other Sadducees who were with him became jealous. ¹⁸ They arrested the apostles and put them in the city jail. ¹⁹ But that night an angel from the Lord opened the doors of the jail and led the apostles out. The angel said, ²⁰ "Go to the temple and tell the people everything about this new life." ²¹ So they went into the temple before sunrise and started teaching.

The high priest and his men called together their council, which included all of Israel's leaders. Then they ordered the apostles to be brought to them from the jail. ²² The temple police who were sent to the jail did not find the apostles. They returned and said, ²³ "We found the jail locked tight and the guards standing at the doors. But when we opened the doors and went in, we didn't find anyone there." ²⁴ The captain of the temple police and the chief priests listened to their report, but they did not know what to think about it. ²⁵ Just then someone came in and said, "Right now those men you put in jail are in the temple, teaching the people!" ²⁶ The captain went with some of the temple police and brought the apostles back. But they did not use force. They were afraid that the people might start throwing stones at them.

²⁷ When the apostles were brought before the council, the high priest said to them, ²⁸ "We told you plainly not to teach in the name of Jesus. But look what you have done! You have been teaching all over Jerusalem, and you are trying to blame us for his death."

²⁹ Peter and the apostles replied:

We don't obey people. We obey God. ³⁰ You killed Jesus by nailing him to a cross. But the God our ancestors worshiped raised him to life ³¹ and made him our Leader and Savior. Then God gave him a place at his right side,ᵖ so that the people of Israel would turn back to him and be forgiven. ³² We are here to tell you about all this, and so is the Holy Spirit, who is God's gift to everyone who obeys God.

³³ When the council members heard this, they became so angry that they wanted to kill the apostles. ³⁴ But one of the members was the Pharisee Gamaliel, a highly respected teacher. He ordered the apostles to be taken out of the room for a little while. ³⁵ Then he said to the council:

Be careful what you do with these men. ³⁶ Not long ago Theudas claimed to be someone important, and about four hundred men joined him. But he was killed. All his followers were scattered, and that was the end of that.

³⁷ Later, when the people of our nation were being counted, Judas from Galilee showed up. A lot of people followed him, but he was killed, and all his followers were scattered.

³⁸ So I advise you to stay away from these men. Leave them alone. If what they are planning is something of their own doing, it will fail. ³⁹ But if God is behind it, you cannot stop it anyway, unless you want to fight against God.

The council members agreed with what he said, ⁴⁰ and they called the apostles back in. They had them beaten with a whip and warned them not to speak in the name of Jesus. Then they let them go.

⁴¹ The apostles left the council and were happy, because God had considered them worthy to suffer for the sake of Jesus. ⁴² Every day they spent time in the temple and in one home after another. They never stopped teaching and telling the good news that Jesus is the Messiah.

### Seven Leaders for the Church

**6** A lot of people were now becoming followers of the Lord. But some of the ones who spoke Greek started complaining about the ones who spoke

p**5.31** *right side*: See the note at 2.33.

Aramaic. They complained that the Greek-speaking widows were not given their share when the food supplies were handed out each day.

2 The twelve apostles called the whole group of followers together and said, "We should not give up preaching God's message in order to serve at tables.q 3 My friends, choose seven men who are respected and wise and filled with God's Spirit. We will put them in charge of these things. 4 We can spend our time praying and serving God by preaching."

5 This suggestion pleased everyone, and they began by choosing Stephen. He had great faith and was filled with the Holy Spirit. Then they chose Philip, Prochorus, Nicanor, Timon, Parmenas, and also Nicolaus, who worshiped with the Jewish peopler in Antioch. 6 These men were brought to the apostles. Then the apostles prayed and placed their hands on the men to show that they had been chosen to do this work. 7 God's message spread, and many more people in Jerusalem became followers. Even a large number of priests put their faith in the Lord.

### Stephen Is Arrested

8 God gave Stephen the power to work great miracles and wonders among the people. 9 But some men from Cyrene and Alexandria were members of a group who called themselves "Free Men."s They started arguing with Stephen. Some others from Cilicia and Asia also argued with him. 10 But they were no match for Stephen, who spoke with the great wisdom that the Spirit gave him. 11 So they talked some men into saying, "We heard Stephen say terrible things against Moses and God!"

12 They turned the people and their leaders and the teachers of the Law of Moses against Stephen. Then they all grabbed Stephen and dragged him in front of the council.

13 Some men agreed to tell lies about Stephen, and they said, "This man keeps on saying terrible things about this holy temple and the Law of Moses. 14 We have heard him claim that Jesus from Nazareth will destroy this place and change the customs that Moses gave us." 15 Then all the council members stared at Stephen. They saw that his face looked like the face of an angel.

### Stephen's Speech

7 The high priest asked Stephen, "Are they telling the truth about you?"

2 Stephen answered:

Friends, listen to me. Our glorious God appeared to our ancestor Abraham while he was still in Mesopotamia, before he had moved to Haran. 3 God told him, "Leave your country and your relatives and go to a land that I will show you." 4 Then Abraham left the land of the Chaldeans and settled in Haran.

After his father died, Abraham came and settled in this land where you now live. 5 God didn't give him any part of it, not even a square foot. But God did promise to give it to him and his family forever, even though Abraham didn't have any children. 6 God said that Abraham's descendants would live for a while in a foreign land. There they would be slaves and would be mistreated four hundred years. 7 But he also said, "I will punish the nation that makes them slaves. Then later they will come and worship me in this place."

8 God said to Abraham, "Every son in each family must be circumcised to show that you have kept your agreement with me." So when Isaac was eight days old, Abraham circumcised him. Later, Isaac circumcised his son Jacob, and Jacob circumcised his twelve sons. 9 These men were our ancestors.

Joseph was also one of our fa-

q6.2 to serve at tables: This may mean either that they were in charge of handing out food to the widows or that they were in charge of the money, since the Greek word "table" may also mean "bank." r6.5 worshiped with the Jewish people: This translates the Greek word "proselyte" that means a Gentile who had accepted the Jewish religion. s6.9 Free Men: A group of Jewish men who had once been slaves, but had been freed.

mous ancestors. His brothers were jealous of him and sold him as a slave to be taken to Egypt. But God was with him <sup>10</sup> and rescued him from all his troubles. God made him so wise that the Egyptian king thought highly of him. The king even made Joseph governor over Egypt and put him in charge of everything he owned. <sup>11</sup> Everywhere in Egypt and Canaan the grain crops failed. There was terrible suffering, and our ancestors could not find enough to eat. <sup>12</sup> But when Jacob heard that there was grain in Egypt, he sent our ancestors there for the first time. <sup>13</sup> It was on their second trip that Joseph told his brothers who he was, and the king learned about Joseph's family. <sup>14</sup> Joseph sent for his father and his relatives. In all, there were seventy-five of them. <sup>15</sup> His father went to Egypt and died there, just as our ancestors did. <sup>16</sup> Later their bodies were taken back to Shechem and placed in the tomb that Abraham had bought from the sons of Hamor. <sup>17</sup> Finally, the time came for God to do what he had promised Abraham. By then the number of our people in Egypt had greatly increased. <sup>18</sup> Another king was ruling Egypt, and he didn't know anything about Joseph. <sup>19</sup> He tricked our ancestors and was cruel to them. He even made them leave their babies outside, so they would die.

<sup>20</sup> During this time Moses was born. He was a very beautiful child, and for three months his parents took care of him in their home. <sup>21</sup> Then when they were forced to leave him outside, the king's daughter found him and raised him as her own son. <sup>22</sup> Moses was given the best education in Egypt. He was a strong man and a powerful speaker. <sup>23</sup> When Moses was forty years old, he wanted to help the Israelites because they were his own people.

<sup>24</sup> One day he saw an Egyptian mistreating one of them. So he rescued the man and killed the Egyptian. <sup>25</sup> Moses thought the rest of his people would realize that God was going to use him to set them free. But they didn't understand.

<sup>26</sup> The next day Moses saw two of his own people fighting, and he tried to make them stop. He said, "Men, you are both Israelites. Why are you so cruel to each other?"

<sup>27</sup> But the man who had started the fight pushed Moses aside and asked, "Who made you our ruler and judge? <sup>28</sup> Are you going to kill me, just as you killed that Egyptian yesterday?" <sup>29</sup> When Moses heard this, he ran away to live in the country of Midian. His two sons were born there.

<sup>30</sup> Forty years later, an angel appeared to Moses from a burning bush in the desert near Mount Sinai. <sup>31</sup> Moses was surprised by what he saw. He went closer to get a better look, and the Lord said, <sup>32</sup> "I am the God who was worshiped by your ancestors, Abraham, Isaac, and Jacob." Moses started shaking all over and didn't dare to look at the bush.

<sup>33</sup> The Lord said to him, "Take off your sandals. The place where you are standing is holy. <sup>34</sup> With my own eyes I have seen the suffering of my people in Egypt. I have heard their groans and have come down to rescue them. Now I am sending you back to Egypt."

<sup>35</sup> This was the same Moses that the people rejected by saying, "Who made you our leader and judge?" God's angel had spoken to Moses from the bush. And God had even sent the angel to help Moses rescue the people and be their leader.

<sup>36</sup> In Egypt and at the Red Sea<sup>t</sup> and in the desert, Moses rescued the people by working miracles and wonders for forty years. <sup>37</sup> Moses is the one who told the people of Israel, "God will choose one of your people

<sup>t</sup>7.36 *Red Sea*: This name comes from the Bible of the early Christians, a translation made into Greek about 200 B.C. It refers to the body of water that the Israelites crossed and was one of the marshes or fresh water lakes near the eastern part of the Nile Delta, where they lived and where the towns of Exodus 13.17—14.9 were located.

to be a prophet, just as he chose me." [38] Moses brought our people together in the desert, and the angel spoke to him on Mount Sinai. There he was given these life-giving words to pass on to us. [39] But our ancestors refused to obey Moses. They rejected him and wanted to go back to Egypt.

[40] The people said to Aaron, "Make some gods to lead us! Moses led us out of Egypt, but we don't know what's happened to him now." [41] Then they made an idol in the shape of a calf. They offered sacrifices to the idol and were pleased with what they had done.

[42] God turned his back on his people and left them. Then they worshiped the stars in the sky, just as it says in the Book of the Prophets, "People of Israel, you didn't offer sacrifices and offerings to me during those forty years in the desert. [43] Instead, you carried the tent where the god Molech is worshiped, and you took along the star of your god Rephan. You made those idols and worshiped them. So now I will have you carried off beyond Babylonia."

[44] The tent where our ancestors worshiped God was with them in the desert. This was the same tent that God had commanded Moses to make. And it was made like the model that Moses had seen. [45] Later it was given to our ancestors, and they took it with them when they went with Joshua. They carried the tent along as they took over the land from those people that God had chased out for them. Our ancestors used this tent until the time of King David. [46] He pleased God and asked him if he could build a house of worship for the people[u] of Israel. [47] And it was finally King Solomon who built a house for God.[v]

[48] But the Most High God doesn't live in houses made by humans. It is just as the prophet said, when he spoke for the Lord,

[49] "Heaven is my throne,
and the earth
  is my footstool.
What kind of house
  will you build for me?
In what place will I rest?
[50]   I have made everything."

[51] You stubborn and hardheaded people! You are always fighting against the Holy Spirit, just as your ancestors did. [52] Is there one prophet that your ancestors didn't mistreat? They killed the prophets who told about the coming of the One Who Obeys God.[w] And now you have turned against him and killed him. [53] Angels gave you God's Law, but you still don't obey it.

### Stephen Is Stoned to Death

[54] When the council members heard Stephen's speech, they were angry and furious. [55] But Stephen was filled with the Holy Spirit. He looked toward heaven, where he saw our glorious God and Jesus standing at his right side.[x] [56] Then Stephen said, "I see heaven open and the Son of Man standing at the right side of God!"

[57] The council members shouted and covered their ears. At once they all attacked Stephen [58] and dragged him out of the city. Then they started throwing stones at him. The men who had brought charges against him put their coats at the feet of a young man named Saul.[y] [59] As Stephen was being stoned to death, he called out, "Lord Jesus, please welcome me!" [60] He knelt down and shouted, "Lord, don't blame them for what they have done." Then he died.

**8** [1-2] Saul approved the stoning of Stephen. Some faithful followers of the Lord buried Stephen and mourned very much for him.

---

[u]7.46 *the people*: Some manuscripts have "God." [v]7.47 *God*: Or "the people." [w]7.52 *One Who Obeys God*: That is, Jesus. [x]7.55 *standing at his right side*: The "right side" is the place of honor and power. "Standing" may mean that Jesus is welcoming Stephen (see verse 59). [y]7.58 *Saul*: Better known as Paul, who became a famous follower of Jesus.

## Saul Makes Trouble for the Church

At that time the church in Jerusalem suffered terribly. All of the Lord's followers, except the apostles, were scattered everywhere in Judea and Samaria. ³ Saul started making a lot of trouble for the church. He went from house to house, arresting men and women and putting them in jail.

## The Good News Is Preached in Samaria

⁴ The Lord's followers who had been scattered went from place to place, telling the good news. ⁵ Philip went to the city of Samaria and told the people about Christ. ⁶ They crowded around Philip because they were eager to hear what he was saying and to see him work miracles. ⁷ Many people with evil spirits were healed, and the spirits went out of them with a shout. A lot of crippled and lame people were also healed. ⁸ Everyone in that city was very glad because of what was happening.

⁹ For some time a man named Simon had lived in the city of Samaria and had amazed the people. He practiced witchcraft and claimed to be somebody great. ¹⁰ Everyone, rich and poor, crowded around him. They said, "This man is the power of God called 'The Great Power.'"

¹¹ For a long time, Simon had used witchcraft to amaze the people, and they kept crowding around him. ¹² But when they believed what Philip was saying about God's kingdom and about the name of Jesus Christ, they were all baptized. ¹³ Even Simon believed and was baptized. He stayed close to Philip, because he marveled at all the miracles and wonders.

¹⁴ The apostles in Jerusalem heard that some people in Samaria had accepted God's message, and they sent Peter and John. ¹⁵ When the two apostles arrived, they prayed that the people would be given the Holy Spirit. ¹⁶ Before this, the Holy Spirit had not been given to anyone in Samaria, though some of them had been baptized in the name of the Lord Jesus. ¹⁷ Peter and John then placed their hands on everyone who had faith in the Lord, and they were given the Holy Spirit.

¹⁸ Simon noticed that the Spirit was given only when the apostles placed their hands on the people. So he brought money ¹⁹ and said to Peter and John, "Let me have this power too! Then anyone I place my hands on will also be given the Holy Spirit."

²⁰ Peter said to him, "You and your money will both end up in hell if you think you can buy God's gift! ²¹ You don't have any part in this, and God sees that your heart isn't right. ²² Get rid of these evil thoughts and ask God to forgive you. ²³ I can see that you are jealous and bound by your evil ways."

²⁴ Simon said, "Please pray to the Lord, so that what you said won't happen to me."

²⁵ After Peter and John had preached about the Lord, they returned to Jerusalem. On their way they told the good news in many villages of Samaria.

## Philip and an Ethiopian Official

²⁶ The Lord's angel said to Philip, "Go south $z$ along the desert road that leads from Jerusalem to Gaza." $a$ ²⁷ So Philip left.

An important Ethiopian official happened to be going along that road in his chariot. He was the chief treasurer for Candace, the Queen of Ethiopia. The official had gone to Jerusalem to worship ²⁸ and was now on his way home. He was sitting in his chariot, reading the book of the prophet Isaiah. ²⁹ The Spirit told Philip to catch up with the chariot. ³⁰ Philip ran up close and heard the man reading aloud from the book of Isaiah. Philip asked him, "Do you understand what you are reading?"

³¹ The official answered, "How can I understand unless someone helps me?" He then invited Philip to come up and sit beside him.

³² The man was reading the passage that said,

---

$z$ 8.26 *Go south*: Or "About noon go." $a$ 8.26 *the desert road that leads from Jerusalem to Gaza*: Or "the road that leads from Jerusalem to Gaza in the desert."

"He was led like a sheep
on its way to be killed.
He was silent as a lamb
whose wool
is being cut off,
and he did not say
a word.
33 He was treated like a nobody
and did not receive
a fair trial.
How can he have children,
if his life
is snatched away?"

34 The official said to Philip, "Tell me, was the prophet talking about himself or about someone else?" 35 So Philip began at this place in the Scriptures and explained the good news about Jesus.

36-37 As they were going along the road, they came to a place where there was some water. The official said, "Look! Here is some water. Why can't I be baptized?" b 38 He ordered the chariot to stop. Then they both went down into the water, and Philip baptized him.

39 After they had come out of the water, the Lord's Spirit took Philip away. The official never saw him again, but he was very happy as he went on his way.

40 Philip later appeared in Azotus. He went from town to town, all the way to Caesarea, telling people about Jesus.

## Saul Becomes a Follower of the Lord
(Acts 22.6-16; 26.12-18)

9 Saul kept on threatening to kill the Lord's followers. He even went to the high priest 2 and asked for letters to their leaders in Damascus. He did this because he wanted to arrest and take to Jerusalem any man or woman who had accepted the Lord's Way. c 3 When Saul had almost reached Damascus, a bright light from heaven suddenly flashed around him. 4 He fell to the ground and heard a voice that said, "Saul! Saul! Why are you so cruel to me?"

5 "Who are you?" Saul asked.
"I am Jesus," the Lord answered. "I am the one you are so cruel to. 6 Now get up and go into the city, where you will be told what to do."

7 The men with Saul stood there speechless. They had heard the voice, but they had not seen anyone. 8 Saul got up from the ground, and when he opened his eyes, he could not see a thing. Someone then led him by the hand to Damascus, 9 and for three days he was blind and did not eat or drink.

10 A follower named Ananias lived in Damascus, and the Lord spoke to him in a vision. Ananias answered, "Lord, here I am."

11 The Lord said to him, "Get up and go to the house of Judas on Straight Street. When you get there, you will find a man named Saul from the city of Tarsus. Saul is praying, 12 and he has seen a vision. He saw a man named Ananias coming to him and putting his hands on him, so that he could see again."

13 Ananias replied, "Lord, a lot of people have told me about the terrible things this man has done to your followers in Jerusalem. 14 Now the chief priests have given him the power to come here and arrest anyone who worships in your name."

15 The Lord said to Ananias, "Go! I have chosen him to tell foreigners, kings, and the people of Israel about me. 16 I will show him how much he must suffer for worshiping in my name."

17 Ananias left and went into the house where Saul was staying. Ananias placed his hands on him and said, "Saul, the Lord Jesus has sent me. He is the same one who appeared to you along the road. He wants you to be able to see and to be filled with the Holy Spirit."

18 Suddenly something like fish scales fell from Saul's eyes, and he could see. He got up and was baptized. 19 Then he ate and felt much better.

b 8.36,37 Why can't I be baptized: Some manuscripts add, "Philip replied, 'You can, if you believe with all your heart.' "The official answered, 'I believe that Jesus Christ is the Son of God.' " c 9.2 accepted the Lord's Way: In the book of Acts, this means to become a follower of the Lord Jesus.

## Saul Preaches in Damascus

For several days Saul stayed with the Lord's followers in Damascus. <sup>20</sup> Soon he went to the Jewish meeting places and started telling people that Jesus is the Son of God. <sup>21</sup> Everyone who heard Saul was amazed and said, "Isn't this the man who caused so much trouble for those people in Jerusalem who worship in the name of Jesus? Didn't he come here to arrest them and take them to the chief priests?"

<sup>22</sup> Saul preached with such power that he completely confused the Jewish people in Damascus, as he tried to show them that Jesus is the Messiah. <sup>23</sup> Later some of them made plans to kill Saul, <sup>24</sup> but he found out about it. He learned that they were guarding the gates of the city day and night in order to kill him. <sup>25</sup> Then one night his followers let him down over the city wall in a large basket.

## Saul in Jerusalem

<sup>26</sup> When Saul arrived in Jerusalem, he tried to join the followers. But they were all afraid of him, because they did not believe he was a true follower. <sup>27</sup> Then Barnabas helped him by taking him to the apostles. He explained how Saul had seen the Lord and how the Lord had spoken to him. Barnabas also said that when Saul was in Damascus, he had spoken bravely in the name of Jesus.

<sup>28</sup> Saul moved about freely with the followers in Jerusalem and told everyone about the Lord. <sup>29</sup> He was always arguing with the Jews who spoke Greek, and so they tried to kill him. <sup>30</sup> But the followers found out about this and took Saul to Caesarea. From there they sent him to the city of Tarsus.

<sup>31</sup> The church in Judea, Galilee, and Samaria now had a time of peace and kept on worshiping the Lord. The church became stronger, as the Holy Spirit encouraged it and helped it grow.

## Peter Heals Aeneas

<sup>32</sup> While Peter was traveling from place to place, he visited the Lord's followers who lived in the town of Lydda. <sup>33</sup> There he met a man named Aeneas, who for eight years had been sick in bed and could not move. <sup>34</sup> Peter said to Aeneas, "Jesus Christ has healed you! Get up and make up your bed."<sup>d</sup> Right away he stood up.

<sup>35</sup> Many people in the towns of Lydda and Sharon saw Aeneas and became followers of the Lord.

## Peter Brings Dorcas Back to Life

<sup>36</sup> In Joppa there was a follower named Tabitha. Her Greek name was Dorcas, which means "deer." She was always doing good things for people and had given much to the poor. <sup>37</sup> But she got sick and died, and her body was washed and placed in an upstairs room. <sup>38</sup> Joppa wasn't far from Lydda, and the followers heard that Peter was there. They sent two men to say to him, "Please come with us as quickly as you can!" <sup>39</sup> Right away, Peter went with them.

The men took Peter upstairs into the room. Many widows were there crying. They showed him the coats and clothes that Dorcas had made while she was still alive.

<sup>40</sup> After Peter had sent everyone out of the room, he knelt down and prayed. Then he turned to the body of Dorcas and said, "Tabitha, get up!" The woman opened her eyes, and when she saw Peter, she sat up. <sup>41</sup> He took her by the hand and helped her to her feet.

Peter called in the widows and the other followers and showed them that Dorcas had been raised from death. <sup>42</sup> Everyone in Joppa heard what had happened, and many of them put their faith in the Lord. <sup>43</sup> Peter stayed on for a while in Joppa in the house of a man named Simon, who made leather.

## Peter and Cornelius

**10** In Caesarea there was a man named Cornelius, who was the captain of a group of soldiers called "The Italian Unit." <sup>2</sup> Cornelius was a very religious man. He worshiped God, and so did everyone else who lived in

<sup>d</sup>**9.34** and make up your bed: Or "and fix something to eat."

his house. He had given a lot of money to the poor and was always praying to God.

³One afternoon at about three o'clock,ᵉ Cornelius had a vision. He saw an angel from God coming to him and calling him by name. ⁴Cornelius was surprised and stared at the angel. Then he asked, "What is this all about?"

The angel answered, "God has heard your prayers and knows about your gifts to the poor. ⁵Now send some men to Joppa for a man named Simon Peter. ⁶He is visiting with Simon the leather maker, who lives in a house near the sea." ⁷After saying this, the angel left.

Cornelius called in two of his servants and one of his soldiers who worshiped God. ⁸He explained everything to them and sent them off to Joppa.

⁹The next day about noon these men were coming near Joppa. Peter went up on the roofᶠ of the house to pray ¹⁰and became very hungry. While the food was being prepared, he fell sound asleep and had a vision. ¹¹He saw heaven open, and something came down like a huge sheet held up by its four corners. ¹²In it were all kinds of animals, snakes, and birds. ¹³A voice said to him, "Peter, get up! Kill these and eat them."

¹⁴But Peter said, "Lord, I can't do that! I've never eaten anything that is unclean and not fit to eat."ᵍ

¹⁵The voice spoke to him again, "When God says that something can be used for food, don't say it isn't fit to eat."

¹⁶This happened three times before the sheet was suddenly taken back to heaven.

¹⁷Peter was still wondering what all of this meant, when the men sent by Cornelius came and stood at the gate. They had found their way to Simon's house ¹⁸and were asking if Simon Peter was staying there.

¹⁹While Peter was still thinking about the vision, the Holy Spirit said

to him, "Threeʰ men are here looking for you. ²⁰Hurry down and go with them. Don't worry, I sent them."

²¹Peter went down and said to the men, "I am the one you are looking for. Why have you come?"

²²They answered, "Captain Cornelius sent us. He is a good man who worships God and is liked by the Jewish people. One of God's holy angels told Cornelius to send for you, so he could hear what you have to say." ²³Peter invited them to spend the night.

The next morning, Peter and some of the Lord's followers in Joppa left with the men who had come from Cornelius. ²⁴The next day they arrived in Caesarea where Cornelius was waiting for them. He had also invited his relatives and close friends.

²⁵When Peter arrived, Cornelius greeted him. Then he knelt at Peter's feet and started worshiping him. ²⁶But Peter took hold of him and said, "Stand up! I am nothing more than a human."

²⁷As Peter entered the house, he was still talking with Cornelius. Many people were there, ²⁸and Peter said to them, "You know that we Jews are not allowed to have anything to do with other people. But God has shown me that he doesn't think anyone is unclean or unfit. ²⁹I agreed to come here, but I want to know why you sent for me."

³⁰Cornelius answered:

Four days ago at about three o'clock in the afternoon I was praying at home. Suddenly a man in bright clothes stood in front of me. ³¹He said, "Cornelius, God has heard your prayers, and he knows about your gifts to the poor. ³²Now send to Joppa for Simon Peter. He is visiting in the home of Simon the leather maker, who lives near the sea."

³³I sent for you right away, and you have been good enough to come. All of us are here in the presence of the Lord God, so that we can hear what he has to say.

34 Peter then said:

Now I am certain that God treats all people alike. 35 God is pleased with everyone who worships him and does right, no matter what nation they come from. 36 This is the same message that God gave to the people of Israel, when he sent Jesus Christ, the Lord of all, to offer peace to them.

37 You surely know what happened[i] everywhere in Judea. It all began in Galilee after John had told everyone to be baptized. 38 God gave the Holy Spirit and power to Jesus from Nazareth. He was with Jesus, as he went around doing good and healing everyone who was under the power of the devil. 39 We all saw what Jesus did both in Israel and in the city of Jerusalem.

Jesus was put to death on a cross. 40 But three days later, God raised him to life and let him be seen. 41 Not everyone saw him. He was seen only by us, who ate and drank with him after he was raised from death. We were the ones God chose to tell others about him.

42 God told us to announce clearly to the people that Jesus is the one he has chosen to judge the living and the dead. 43 Every one of the prophets has said that all who have faith in Jesus will have their sins forgiven in his name.

44 While Peter was still speaking, the Holy Spirit took control of everyone who was listening. 45 Some Jewish followers of the Lord had come with Peter, and they were surprised that the Holy Spirit had been given to Gentiles. 46 Now they were hearing Gentiles speaking unknown languages and praising God.

Peter said, 47 "These Gentiles have been given the Holy Spirit, just as we have! I am certain that no one would dare stop us from baptizing them." 48 Peter ordered them to be baptized in the name of Jesus Christ, and they asked him to stay on for a few days.

## Peter Reports to the Church in Jerusalem

11 The apostles and the followers in Judea heard that Gentiles had accepted God's message. 2 So when Peter came to Jerusalem, some of the Jewish followers started arguing with him. They wanted Gentile followers to be circumcised, and 3 they said, "You stayed in the homes of Gentiles, and you even ate with them!"

4 Then Peter told them exactly what had happened:

5 I was in the town of Joppa and was praying when I fell sound asleep and had a vision. I saw heaven open, and something like a huge sheet held by its four corners came down to me. 6 When I looked in it, I saw animals, wild beasts, snakes, and birds. 7 I heard a voice saying to me, "Peter, get up! Kill these and eat them."

8 But I said, "Lord, I can't do that! I've never taken a bite of anything that is unclean and not fit to eat."[i]

9 The voice from heaven spoke to me again, "When God says that something can be used for food, don't say it isn't fit to eat." 10 This happened three times before it was all taken back into heaven.

11 Suddenly three men from Caesarea stood in front of the house where I was staying. 12 The Holy Spirit told me to go with them and not to worry. Then six of the Lord's followers went with me to the home of a man 13 who told us that an angel had appeared to him. The angel had ordered him to send to Joppa for someone named Simon Peter. 14 Then Peter would tell him how he and everyone in his house could be saved.

15 After I started speaking, the Holy Spirit was given to them, just as the Spirit had been given to us at the beginning. 16 I remembered that the Lord had said, "John baptized with water, but you will be baptized with the Holy Spirit." 17 God gave those Gentiles the same

---

[i] 10.37 what happened: Or "the message that went." [i] 11.8 unclean and not fit to eat: See the note at 10.14.

gift that he gave us when we put our faith in the Lord Jesus Christ. So how could I have gone against God?

18 When they heard Peter say this, they stopped arguing and started praising God. They said, "God has now let Gentiles turn to him, and he has given life to them!"

### The Church in Antioch

19 Some of the Lord's followers had been scattered because of the terrible trouble that started when Stephen was killed. They went as far as Phoenicia, Cyprus, and Antioch, but they told the message only to the Jews. 20 Some of the followers from Cyprus and Cyrene went to Antioch and started telling Gentiles k the good news about the Lord Jesus. 21 The Lord's power was with them, and many people turned to the Lord and put their faith in him. 22 News of what was happening reached the church in Jerusalem. Then they sent Barnabas to Antioch.

23 When Barnabas got there and saw what God had been kind enough to do for them, he was very glad. So he begged them to remain faithful to the Lord with all their hearts. 24 Barnabas was a good man of great faith, and he was filled with the Holy Spirit. Many more people turned to the Lord.

25 Barnabas went to Tarsus to look for Saul. 26 He found Saul and brought him to Antioch, where they met with the church for a whole year and taught many of its people. There in Antioch the Lord's followers were first called Christians.

27 During this time some prophets from Jerusalem came to Antioch. 28 One of them was Agabus. Then with the help of the Spirit, he told that there would be a terrible famine everywhere in the world. And it happened when Claudius was Emperor.l 29 The followers in Antioch decided to send whatever help they could to the followers in Judea. 30 So they had Barnabas and Saul take their gifts to the church leaders in Jerusalem.

### Herod Causes Trouble for the Church

**12** At that time King Herod m caused terrible suffering for some members of the church. 2 He ordered soldiers to cut off the head of James, the brother of John. 3 When Herod saw that this pleased the Jewish people, he had Peter arrested during the Festival of Thin Bread. 4 He put Peter in jail and ordered four squads of soldiers to guard him. Herod planned to put him on trial in public after the festival.

5 While Peter was being kept in jail, the church never stopped praying to God for him.

### Peter Is Rescued

6 The night before Peter was to be put on trial, he was asleep and bound by two chains. A soldier was guarding him on each side, and two other soldiers were guarding the entrance to the jail. 7 Suddenly an angel from the Lord appeared, and light flashed around in the cell. The angel poked Peter in the side and woke him up. Then he said, "Quick! Get up!"

The chains fell off his hands, 8 and the angel said, "Get dressed and put on your sandals." Peter did what he was told. Then the angel said, "Now put on your coat and follow me." 9 Peter left with the angel, but he thought everything was only a dream. 10 They went past the two groups of soldiers, and when they came to the iron gate to the city, it opened by itself. They went out and were going along the street, when all at once the angel disappeared.

11 Peter now realized what had happened, and he said, "I am certain that the Lord sent his angel to rescue me from Herod and from everything the Jewish leaders planned to do to me."

k 11.20 Gentiles: This translates a Greek word that may mean "people who speak Greek" or "people who live as Greeks do." Here the word seems to mean "people who are not Jews." Some manuscripts have "Greeks," which also seems to mean "people who are not Jews." l 11.28 when Claudius was Emperor: A.D. 41-54. m 12.1 Herod: Herod Agrippa I, the grandson of Herod the Great.

12 Then Peter went to the house of Mary the mother of John whose other name was Mark. Many of the Lord's followers had come together there and were praying.

13 Peter knocked on the gate, and a servant named Rhoda came to answer. 14 When she heard Peter's voice, she was too excited to open the gate. She ran back into the house and said that Peter was standing there.

15 "You are crazy!" everyone told her. But she kept saying that it was Peter. Then they said, "It must be his angel."[n] 16 But Peter kept on knocking, until finally they opened the gate. They saw him and were completely amazed.

17 Peter motioned for them to keep quiet. Then he told how the Lord had led him out of jail. He also said, "Tell James[o] and the others what has happened." After that, he left and went somewhere else.

18 The next morning the soldiers who had been on guard were terribly worried and wondered what had happened to Peter. 19 Herod ordered his own soldiers to search for him, but they could not find him. Then he questioned the guards and had them put to death. After this, Herod left Judea to stay in Caesarea for a while.

### Herod Dies

20 Herod and the people of Tyre and Sidon were very angry with each other. But their country got its food supply from the region that he ruled. So a group of them went to see Blastus, who was one of Herod's high officials. They convinced Blastus that they wanted to make peace between their cities and Herod, 21 and a day was set for them to meet with him.

Herod came dressed in his royal robes. He sat down on his throne and made a speech. 22 The people shouted, "You speak more like a god than a man!" 23 At once an angel from the Lord struck him down because he took

the honor that belonged to God. Later, Herod was eaten by worms and died.

24 God's message kept spreading. 25 And after Barnabas and Saul had done the work they were sent to do, they went back to Jerusalem[p] with John, whose other name was Mark.

### Barnabas and Saul Are Chosen and Sent

13 The church at Antioch had several prophets and teachers. They were Barnabas, Simeon, also called Niger, Lucius from Cyrene, Manaen, who was Herod's[q] close friend, and Saul. 2 While they were worshiping the Lord and going without eating,[r] the Holy Spirit told them, "Appoint Barnabas and Saul to do the work for which I have chosen them." 3 Everyone prayed and went without eating for a while longer. Next, they placed their hands on Barnabas and Saul to show that they had been appointed to do this work. Then everyone sent them on their way.

### Barnabas and Saul in Cyprus

4 After Barnabas and Saul had been sent by the Holy Spirit, they went to Seleucia. From there they sailed to the island of Cyprus. 5 They arrived at Salamis and began to preach God's message in the Jewish meeting places. They also had John[s] as a helper.

6 Barnabas and Saul went all the way to the city of Paphos on the other end of the island, where they met a Jewish man named Bar-Jesus. He practiced witchcraft and was a false prophet. 7 He also worked for Sergius Paulus, who was very smart and was the governor of the island. Sergius Paulus wanted to hear God's message, and he sent for Barnabas and Saul. 8 But Bar-Jesus, whose other name was Elymas, was against them. He even tried to keep the governor from having faith in the Lord. 9 Then Saul, better known as Paul, was filled with the Holy Spirit. He

looked straight at Elymas [10] and said, "You son of the devil! You are a liar, a crook, and an enemy of everything that is right. When will you stop speaking against the true ways of the Lord? [11] The Lord is going to punish you by making you completely blind for a while."

Suddenly the man's eyes were covered by a dark mist, and he went around trying to get someone to lead him by the hand. [12] When the governor saw what had happened, he was amazed at this teaching about the Lord. So he put his faith in the Lord.

### Paul and Barnabas in Antioch of Pisidia

[13] Paul and the others left Paphos and sailed to Perga in Pamphylia. But John[s] left them and went back to Jerusalem. [14] The rest of them went on from Perga to Antioch in Pisidia. Then on the Sabbath they went to the Jewish meeting place and sat down.

[15] After the reading of the Law and the Prophets,[t] the leaders sent someone over to tell Paul and Barnabas, "Friends, if you have anything to say that will help the people, please say it."

[16] Paul got up. He motioned with his hand and said:

People of Israel, and everyone else who worships God, listen! [17] The God of Israel chose our ancestors, and he let our people prosper while they were living in Egypt. Then with his mighty power he led them out, [18] and for about forty years he took care of[u] them in the desert. [19] He destroyed seven nations in the land of Canaan and gave their land to our people. [20] All this happened in about 450 years.

Then God gave our people judges until the time of the prophet Samuel, [21] but the people demanded a king. So for forty years God gave them King Saul, the son of Kish from the tribe of Benjamin. [22] Later, God removed Saul and let David rule in his place. God said about him, "David the son of Jesse is the kind of person who pleases me most! He does everything I want him to do."

[23] God promised that someone from David's family would come to save the people of Israel, and that one is Jesus. [24] But before Jesus came, John was telling everyone in Israel to turn back to God and be baptized. [25] Then, when John's work was almost done, he said, "Who do you people think I am? Do you think I am the Promised One? He will come later, and I am not good enough to untie his sandals."

[26] Now listen, you descendants of Abraham! Pay attention, all of you Gentiles who are here to worship God! Listen to this message about how to be saved, because it is for everyone. [27] The people of Jerusalem and their leaders didn't realize who Jesus was. And they didn't understand the words of the prophets that they read each Sabbath. So they condemned Jesus just as the prophets had said.

[28-29] They did exactly what the Scriptures said they would. Even though they couldn't find any reason to put Jesus to death, they still asked Pilate to have him killed.

After Jesus had been put to death, he was taken down from the cross[v] and placed in a tomb. [30] But God raised him from death! [31] Then for many days Jesus appeared to his followers who had gone with him from Galilee to Jerusalem. Now they are telling our people about him.

[32] God made a promise to our ancestors. And we are here to tell you the good news [33] that he has kept this promise to us. It is just as the second Psalm says about Jesus,

"You are my son because today I have become your Father."

**34** God raised Jesus from death and will never let his body decay. It is just as God said,

"I will make to you
the same holy promise
   that I made to David."

**35** And in another psalm it says, "God will never let the body of his Holy One decay."
**36** When David was alive, he obeyed God. Then after he died, he was buried in the family grave, and his body decayed. **37** But God raised Jesus from death, and his body did not decay.
**38** My friends, the message is that Jesus can forgive your sins! The Law of Moses could not set you free from all your sins. **39** But everyone who has faith in Jesus is set free.
**40** Make sure that what the prophets have said doesn't happen to you. They said,

**41** "Look, you people
   who make fun of God!
Be amazed
   and disappear.
I will do something today
   that you won't believe,
even if someone
   tells you about it!"

**42** As Paul and Barnabas were leaving the meeting, the people begged them to say more about these same things on the next Sabbath. **43** After the service, many Jews and a lot of Gentiles who worshiped God went with them. Paul and Barnabas begged them all to remain faithful to God, who had been so kind to them.
**44** The next Sabbath almost everyone in town came to hear the message about the Lord.ʷ **45** When the Jewish people saw the crowds, they were very jealous. They insulted Paul and spoke against everything he said.
**46** But Paul and Barnabas bravely said:

We had to tell God's message to you before we told it to anyone else. But you rejected the message! This proves that you don't deserve eternal life. Now we are going to the Gentiles. **47** The Lord has given us this command,

"I have placed you here
as a light
   for the Gentiles.
You are to take
   the saving power of God
to people everywhere on earth."

**48** This message made the Gentiles glad, and they praised what they had heard about the Lord.ʷ Everyone who had been chosen for eternal life then put their faith in the Lord.
**49** The message about the Lord spread all over that region. **50** But the Jewish leaders went to some of the important men in the town and to some respected women who were religious. They turned them against Paul and Barnabas and started making trouble for them. They even chased them out of that part of the country.
**51** Paul and Barnabas shook the dust from that place off their feetˣ and went on to the city of Iconium.
**52** But the Lord's followers in Antioch were very happy and were filled with the Holy Spirit.

### Paul and Barnabas in Iconium

**14** Paul and Barnabas spoke in the Jewish meeting place in Iconium, just as they had done at Antioch, and many Jews and Gentilesʸ put their faith in the Lord. **2** But the Jews who did not have faith in him made the other Gentiles angry and turned them against the Lord's followers.
**3** Paul and Barnabas stayed there for a while, having faith in the Lord and bravely speaking his message. The Lord gave them the power to work miracles and wonders, and he showed that their message about his great kindness was true.
**4** The people of Iconium did not know what to think. Some of them believed the Jewish group, and others believed the apostles. **5** Finally, some Gentiles

and Jews, together with their leaders, decided to make trouble for Paul and Barnabas and to stone them to death.

6-7 But when the two apostles found out what was happening, they escaped to the region of Lycaonia. They preached the good news there in the towns of Lystra and Derbe and in the nearby countryside.

### Paul and Barnabas in Lystra

8 In Lystra there was a man who had been born with crippled feet and had never been able to walk. 9 The man was listening to Paul speak, when Paul saw that he had faith in Jesus and could be healed. So he looked straight at the man 10 and shouted, "Stand up!" The man jumped up and started walking around.

11 When the crowd saw what Paul had done, they yelled out in the language of Lycaonia, "The gods have turned into humans and have come down to us!" 12 The people then gave Barnabas the name Zeus, and they gave Paul the name Hermes, z because he did the talking.

13 The temple of Zeus was near the entrance to the city. Its priest and the crowds wanted to offer a sacrifice to Barnabas and Paul. So the priest brought some bulls and flowers to the city gates. 14 When the two apostles found out about this, they tore their clothes in horror and ran to the crowd, shouting:

15 Why are you doing this? We are humans just like you. Please give up all this foolishness. Turn to the living God, who made the sky, the earth, the sea, and everything in them. 16 In times past, God let each nation go its own way. 17 But he showed that he was there by the good things he did. God sends rain from heaven and makes your crops grow. He gives food to you and makes your hearts glad.

18 Even after Paul and Barnabas had said all this, they could hardly keep the people from offering a sacrifice to them.

19 Some Jewish leaders from Antioch and Iconium came and turned the crowds against Paul. They hit him with stones and dragged him out of the city, thinking he was dead. 20 But when the Lord's followers gathered around Paul, he stood up and went back into the city. The next day he and Barnabas went to Derbe.

### Paul and Barnabas Return to Antioch in Syria

21 Paul and Barnabas preached the good news in Derbe and won some people to the Lord. Then they went back to Lystra, Iconium, and Antioch in Pisidia. 22 They encouraged the followers and begged them to remain faithful. They told them, "We have to suffer a lot before we can get into God's kingdom." 23 Paul and Barnabas chose some leaders for each of the churches. Then they went without eating a and prayed that the Lord would take good care of these leaders.

24 Paul and Barnabas went on through Pisidia to Pamphylia, 25 where they preached in the town of Perga. Then they went down to Attalia 26 and sailed to Antioch in Syria. It was there that they had been placed in God's care for the work they had now completed. b

27 After arriving in Antioch, they called the church together. They told the people what God had helped them do and how he had made it possible for the Gentiles to believe. 28 Then they stayed there with the followers for a long time.

15 Some people came from Judea and started teaching the Lord's followers that they could not be saved, unless they were circumcised as Moses had taught. 2 This caused trouble, and Paul and Barnabas argued with them about this teaching. So it was decided to send Paul and Barnabas and a few others to Jerusalem to discuss this problem with the apostles and the church leaders.

z 14.12 Hermes: The Greeks thought of Hermes as the messenger of the other gods, especially of Zeus, their chief god.   a 14.23 went without eating: See the note at 13.2.
b 14.26 the work they had now completed: See 13.1-3.

## The Church Leaders Meet in Jerusalem

³ The men who were sent by the church went through Phoenicia and Samaria, telling how the Gentiles had turned to God. This news made the Lord's followers very happy. ⁴ When the men arrived in Jerusalem, they were welcomed by the church, including the apostles and the leaders. They told them everything God had helped them do. ⁵ But some Pharisees had become followers of the Lord. They stood up and said, "Gentiles who have faith in the Lord must be circumcised and told to obey the Law of Moses."

⁶ The apostles and church leaders met to discuss this problem about Gentiles. ⁷ They had talked it over for a long time, when Peter got up and said:

My friends, you know that God decided long ago to let me be the one from your group to preach the good news to the Gentiles. God did this so that they would hear and obey him. ⁸ He knows what is in everyone's heart. And he showed that he had chosen the Gentiles, when he gave them the Holy Spirit, just as he had given his Spirit to us. ⁹ God treated them in the same way that he treated us. They put their faith in him, and he made their hearts pure.

¹⁰ Now why are you trying to make God angry by placing a heavy burden on these followers? This burden was too heavy for us or our ancestors. ¹¹ But our Lord Jesus is kind to us, and we are saved by faith in him, just as the Gentiles are.

¹² Everyone kept quiet and listened as Barnabas and Paul told how God had given them the power to work a lot of miracles and wonders for the Gentiles. ¹³ After they had finished speaking, James<sup>c</sup> said:

My friends, listen to me! ¹⁴ Simon Peter<sup>d</sup> has told how God first came to the Gentiles and made some of them his own people. ¹⁵ This agrees with what the prophets wrote,

¹⁶ "I, the Lord, will return
and rebuild
   David's fallen house.
I will build it from its ruins
   and set it up again,
¹⁷ Then other nations
will turn to me
   and be my chosen ones.
I, the Lord, say this.
¹⁸    I promised it long ago."

¹⁹ And so, my friends, I don't think we should place burdens on the Gentiles who are turning to God. ²⁰ We should simply write and tell them not to eat anything that has been offered to idols. They should be told not to eat the meat of any animal that has been strangled or that still has blood in it. They must also not commit any terrible sexual sins.<sup>e</sup>

²¹ We must remember that the Law of Moses has been preached in city after city for many years, and every Sabbath it is read at our meeting.

## A Letter to Gentiles Who Had Faith in the Lord

²² The apostles, the leaders, and all the church members decided to send some men to Antioch along with Paul and Barnabas. They chose Silas and Judas Barsabbas,<sup>f</sup> who were two leaders of the Lord's followers. ²³ They wrote a letter that said:

We apostles and leaders send friendly greetings to all of you Gentiles who are followers of the Lord in Antioch, Syria, and Cilicia.

²⁴ We have heard that some people from here have terribly upset you by what they said. But we did not send them! ²⁵ So we met together

<hr/>

c 15.13 *James*: The Lord's brother.  d 15.14 *Simon Peter*: The Greek text has "Simeon," which is another form of the name "Simon." The apostle Peter is meant.  e 15.20 *not commit any terrible sexual sins*: This probably refers to the laws about the wrong kind of marriages that are forbidden in Leviticus 18.6-18 or to some serious sexual sin.  f 15.22 *Judas Barsabbas*: He may have been a brother of Joseph Barsabbas (see 1.23), but the name "Barsabbas" was often used by the Jewish people.

and decided to choose some men and to send them to you along with our good friends Barnabas and Paul. [26] These men have risked their lives for our Lord Jesus Christ. [27] We are also sending Judas and Silas, who will tell you in person the same things that we are writing.

[28] The Holy Spirit has shown us that we should not place any extra burden on you. [29] But you should not eat anything offered to idols. You should not eat any meat that still has the blood in it or any meat of any animal that has been strangled. You must also not commit any terrible sexual sins. If you follow these instructions, you will do well.

We send our best wishes.

[30] The four men left Jerusalem and went to Antioch. Then they called the church members together and gave them the letter. [31] When the letter was read, everyone was pleased and greatly encouraged. [32] Judas and Silas were prophets, and they spoke a long time, encouraging and helping the Lord's followers.

[33] The men from Jerusalem stayed on in Antioch for a while. And when they left to return to the ones who had sent them, the followers wished them well. [34-35] But Paul and Barnabas stayed on in Antioch, where they and many others taught and preached about the Lord. g

### Paul and Barnabas Go Their Separate Ways

[36] Sometime later Paul said to Barnabas, "Let's go back and visit the Lord's followers in the cities where we preached his message. Then we will know how they are doing." [37] Barnabas wanted to take along John, whose other name was Mark. [38] But Paul did not want to, because Mark had left them in Pamphylia and had stopped working with them.

[39] Paul and Barnabas argued, then each of them went his own way. Barna-

bas took Mark and sailed to Cyprus, [40] but Paul took Silas and left after the followers had placed them in God's care. [41] They traveled through Syria and Cilicia, encouraging the churches.

### Timothy Works with Paul and Silas

**16** Paul and Silas went back to Derbe and Lystra, where there was a follower named Timothy. His mother was also a follower. She was Jewish, and his father was Greek. [2] The Lord's followers in Lystra and Iconium said good things about Timothy, [3] and Paul wanted him to go with them. But Paul first had him circumcised, because all the Jewish people around there knew that Timothy's father was Greek. h

[4] As Paul and the others went from city to city, they told the followers what the apostles and leaders in Jerusalem had decided, and they urged them to follow these instructions. [5] The churches became stronger in their faith, and each day more people put their faith in the Lord.

### Paul's Vision in Troas

[6] Paul and his friends went through Phrygia and Galatia, but the Holy Spirit would not let them preach in Asia. [7] After they arrived in Mysia, they tried to go into Bithynia, but the Spirit of Jesus would not let them. [8] So they went on through i Mysia until they came to Troas.

[9] During the night, Paul had a vision of someone from Macedonia who was standing there and begging him, "Come over to Macedonia and help us!" [10] After Paul had seen the vision, we began looking for a way to go to Macedonia. We were sure that God had called us to preach the good news there.

### Lydia Becomes a Follower of the Lord

[11] We sailed straight from Troas to Samothrace, and the next day we ar-

---

g 15.34,35 Verse 34, which says that Silas decided to stay on in Antioch, is not in some manuscripts. h 16.3 *had him circumcised . . . Timothy's father was Greek*: Timothy would not have been acceptable to the Jews unless he had been circumcised, and Greeks did not circumcise their sons. i 16.8 *went on through*: Or "passed by."

rived in Neapolis. [12] From there we went to Philippi, which is a Roman colony in the first district of Macedonia.[j]

We spent several days in Philippi. [13] Then on the Sabbath we went outside the city gate to a place by the river, where we thought there would be a Jewish meeting place for prayer. We sat down and talked with the women who came. [14] One of them was Lydia, who was from the city of Thyatira and sold expensive purple cloth. She was a worshiper of the Lord God, and he made her willing to accept what Paul was saying. [15] Then after she and her family were baptized, she kept on begging us, "If you think I really do have faith in the Lord, come stay in my home." Finally, we accepted her invitation.

### Paul and Silas Are Put in Jail

[16] One day on our way to the place of prayer, we were met by a slave girl. She had a spirit in her that gave her the power to tell the future. By doing this she made a lot of money for her owners. [17] The girl followed Paul and the rest of us and kept yelling, "These men are servants of the Most High God! They are telling you how to be saved."

[18] This went on for several days. Finally, Paul got so upset that he turned and said to the spirit, "In the name of Jesus Christ, I order you to leave this girl alone!" At once the evil spirit left her.

[19] When the girl's owners realized that they had lost all chances for making more money, they grabbed Paul and Silas and dragged them into court. [20] They told the officials, "These Jews are upsetting our city! [21] They are telling us to do things we Romans are not allowed to do."

[22] The crowd joined in the attack on Paul and Silas. Then the officials tore the clothes off the two men and ordered them to be beaten with a whip. [23] After they had been badly beaten, they were put in jail, and the jailer was told to guard them carefully. [24] The jailer did

as he was told. He put them deep inside the jail and chained their feet to heavy blocks of wood.

[25] About midnight Paul and Silas were praying and singing praises to God, while the other prisoners listened. [26] Suddenly a strong earthquake shook the jail to its foundations. The doors opened, and the chains fell from all the prisoners.

[27] When the jailer woke up and saw that the doors were open, he thought that the prisoners had escaped. He pulled out his sword and was about to kill himself. [28] But Paul shouted, "Don't harm yourself! No one has escaped."

[29] The jailer asked for a torch and went into the jail. He was shaking all over as he knelt down in front of Paul and Silas. [30] After he had led them out of the jail, he asked, "What must I do to be saved?"

[31] They replied, "Have faith in the Lord Jesus and you will be saved! This is also true for everyone who lives in your home."

[32] Then Paul and Silas told him and everyone else in his house about the Lord. [33] While it was still night, the jailer took them to a place where he could wash their cuts and bruises. Then he and everyone in his home were baptized. [34] They were very glad that they had put their faith in God. After this, the jailer took Paul and Silas to his home and gave them something to eat.

[35] The next morning the officials sent some police with orders for the jailer to let Paul and Silas go. [36] The jailer told Paul, "The officials have ordered me to set you free. Now you can leave in peace."

[37] But Paul told the police, "We are Roman citizens,[k] and the Roman officials had us beaten in public without giving us a trial. They threw us into jail. Now do they think they can secretly send us away? No, they cannot! They will have to come here themselves and let us out."

[38] When the police told the officials that Paul and Silas were Roman citizens, the officials were afraid. [39] So

---

[j] 16.12 *in the first district of Macedonia*: Some manuscripts have "and the leading city of Macedonia." [k] 16.37 *Roman citizens*: Only a small number of the people living in the Roman Empire were citizens, and they had special rights and privileges.

they came and apologized. They led them out of the jail and asked them to please leave town. ⁴⁰ But Paul and Silas went straight to the home of Lydia, where they saw the Lord's followers and encouraged them. Then they left.

## Trouble in Thessalonica

**17** After Paul and his friends had traveled through Amphipolis and Apollonia, they went on to Thessalonica. A Jewish meeting place was in that city. ² So as usual, Paul went there to worship, and on three Sabbaths he spoke to the people. He used the Scriptures ³ to show them that the Messiah had to suffer, but that he would rise from death. Paul also told them that Jesus is the Messiah he was preaching about. ⁴ Some of them believed what Paul had said, and they became followers with Paul and Silas. Some Gentiles*l* and many important women also believed the message.

⁵ The Jewish leaders were jealous and got some worthless bums who hung around the marketplace to start a riot in the city. They wanted to drag Paul and Silas out to the mob, and so they went straight to Jason's home. ⁶ But when they did not find them there, they dragged out Jason and some of the Lord's followers. They took them to the city authorities and shouted, "Paul and Silas have been upsetting things everywhere. Now they have come here, ⁷ and Jason has welcomed them into his home. All of them break the laws of the Roman Emperor by claiming that someone named Jesus is king."

⁸ The officials and the people were upset when they heard this. ⁹ So they made Jason and the other followers pay bail before letting them go.

## People in Berea Welcome the Message

¹⁰ That same night the Lord's followers sent Paul and Silas on to Berea, and after they arrived, they went to the Jewish meeting place. ¹¹ The people in Berea were much nicer than those in Thessalonica, and they gladly accepted the message. Day after day they studied the Scriptures to see if these things were true. ¹² Many of them put their faith in the Lord, including some important Greek women and several men.

¹³ When the Jewish leaders in Thessalonica heard that Paul had been preaching God's message in Berea, they went there and caused trouble by turning the crowds against Paul.

¹⁴ Right away the followers sent Paul down to the coast, but Silas and Timothy stayed in Berea. ¹⁵ Some men went with Paul as far as Athens, and then returned with instructions for Silas and Timothy to join him as soon as possible.

## Paul in Athens

¹⁶ While Paul was waiting in Athens, he was upset to see all the idols in the city. ¹⁷ He went to the Jewish meeting place to speak to the Jews and to anyone who worshiped with them. Day after day he also spoke to everyone he met in the market. ¹⁸ Some of them were Epicureans*m* and some were Stoics,*n* and they started arguing with him.

People were asking, "What is this know-it-all trying to say?"

Some even said, "Paul must be preaching about foreign gods! That's what he means when he talks about Jesus and about people rising from death."*o*

¹⁹ They brought Paul before a council called the Areopagus, and said, "Tell us what your new teaching is all about. ²⁰ We have heard you say some strange things, and we want to know what you mean."

²¹ More than anything else the people of Athens and the foreigners living there loved to hear and to talk about

---

*l* 17.4 *Gentiles*: See the note at 14.1.   *m* 17.18 *Epicureans*: People who followed the teaching of a man named Epicurus, who taught that happiness should be the main goal in life. *n* 17.18 *Stoics*: Followers of a man named Zeno, who taught that people should learn self-control and be guided by their consciences.   *o* 17.18 *people rising from death*: Or "a goddess named 'Rising from Death.'"

anything new. [22]So Paul stood up in front of the council and said:

People of Athens, I see that you are very religious. [23]As I was going through your city and looking at the things you worship, I found an altar with the words, "To an Unknown God." You worship this God, but you don't really know him. So I want to tell you about him. [24]This God made the world and everything in it. He is Lord of heaven and earth, and he doesn't live in temples built by human hands. [25]He doesn't need help from anyone. He gives life, breath, and everything else to all people. [26]From one person God made all nations who live on earth, and he decided when and where every nation would be.

[27]God has done all this, so that we will look for him and reach out and find him. He isn't far from any of us, [28]and he gives us the power to live, to move, and to be who we are. "We are his children," just as some of your poets have said.

[29]Since we are God's children, we must not think that he is like an idol made out of gold or silver or stone. He isn't like anything that humans have thought up and made. [30]In the past, God forgave all this because people did not know what they were doing. But now he says that everyone everywhere must turn to him. [31]He has set a day when he will judge the world's people with fairness. And he has chosen the man Jesus to do the judging for him. God has given proof of this to all of us by raising Jesus from death.

[32]As soon as the people heard Paul say that a man had been raised from death, some of them started laughing. Others said, "We will hear you talk about this some other time." [33]When Paul left the council meeting, [34]some of the men put their faith in the Lord and went with Paul. One of them was a council member named Dionysius. A woman named Damaris and several others also put their faith in the Lord.

### *Paul in Corinth*

**18** Paul left Athens and went to Corinth, [2]where he met Aquila, a Jewish man from Pontus. Not long before this, Aquila had come from Italy with his wife Priscilla, because Emperor Claudius had ordered the Jewish people to leave Rome.[p] Paul went to see Aquila and Priscilla [3]and found out that they were tent makers. Paul was a tent maker too. So he stayed with them, and they worked together.

[4]Every Sabbath, Paul went to the Jewish meeting place. He spoke to Jews and Gentiles[q] and tried to win them over. [5]But after Silas and Timothy came from Macedonia, he spent all his time preaching to the Jews about Jesus the Messiah. [6]Finally, they turned against him and insulted him. So he shook the dust from his clothes[r] and told them, "Whatever happens to you will be your own fault! I am not to blame. From now on I am going to preach to the Gentiles."

[7]Paul then moved into the house of a man named Titius Justus, who worshiped God and lived next door to the meeting place. [8]Crispus was the leader of the meeting place. He and everyone in his family put their faith in the Lord. Many others in Corinth also heard the message, and all the people who had faith in the Lord were baptized.

[9]One night, Paul had a vision, and in it the Lord said, "Don't be afraid to keep on preaching. Don't stop! [10]I am with you, and you won't be harmed. Many people in this city belong to me." [11]Paul stayed on in Corinth for a year and a half, teaching God's message to the people.

[12]While Gallio was governor of Achaia, some of the Jewish leaders got together and grabbed Paul. They brought him into court [13]and said, "This man is trying to make our people

[p] **18.2** *Emperor Claudius had ordered all the Jewish people to leave Rome*: Probably A.D. 49, though it may have been A.D. 41. [q] **18.4** *Gentiles*: Here the word is "Greeks." But see the note at 14.1. [r] **18.6** *shook the dust from his clothes*: This means the same as shaking dust from the feet (see the note at 13.51).

worship God in a way that is against our Law!"

¹⁴Even before Paul could speak, Gallio said, "If you were charging this man with a crime or some other wrong, I would have to listen to you. ¹⁵But since this concerns only words, names, and your own law, you will have to take care of it. I refuse to judge such matters." ¹⁶Then he sent them out of the court. ¹⁷The crowd grabbed Sosthenes, the Jewish leader, and beat him up in front of the court. But none of this mattered to Gallio.

## Paul Returns to Antioch in Syria

¹⁸After Paul had stayed for a while with the Lord's followers in Corinth, he told them good-by and sailed on to Syria with Aquila and Priscilla. But before he left, he had his head shaved<sup>s</sup> at Cenchreae because he had made a promise to God.

¹⁹The three of them arrived in Ephesus, where Paul left Priscilla and Aquila. He then went into the Jewish meeting place to talk with the people there. ²⁰They asked him to stay longer, but he refused. ²¹He told them good-by and said, "If God lets me, I will come back."

²²Paul sailed to Caesarea, where he greeted the church. Then he went on to Antioch. ²³After staying there for a while, he left and visited several places in Galatia and Phrygia. He helped the followers there to become stronger in their faith.

## Apollos in Ephesus

²⁴A Jewish man named Apollos came to Ephesus. Apollos had been born in the city of Alexandria. He was a very good speaker and knew a lot about the Scriptures. ²⁵He also knew much about the Lord's Way,<sup>t</sup> and he spoke about it with great excitement. What he taught about Jesus was right, but all

he knew was John's message about baptism.

²⁶Apollos started speaking bravely in the Jewish meeting place. But when Priscilla and Aquila heard him, they took him to their home and helped him understand God's Way even better.

²⁷Apollos decided to travel through Achaia. So the Lord's followers wrote letters, encouraging the followers there to welcome him. After Apollos arrived in Achaia, he was a great help to everyone who had put their faith in the Lord Jesus because of God's kindness. ²⁸He got into fierce arguments with the Jewish people, and in public he used the Scriptures to prove that Jesus is the Messiah.

## Paul in Ephesus *

**19** While Apollos was in Corinth, Paul traveled across the hill country to Ephesus, where he met some of the Lord's followers. ²He asked them, "When you put your faith in Jesus, were you given the Holy Spirit?"

"No!" they answered. "We have never even heard of the Holy Spirit."

³"Then why were you baptized?" Paul asked.

They answered, "Because of what John taught."<sup>u</sup>

⁴Paul replied, "John baptized people so that they would turn to God. But he also told them that someone else was coming, and that they should put their faith in him. Jesus is the one that John was talking about." ⁵After the people heard Paul say this, they were baptized in the name of the Lord Jesus. ⁶Then Paul placed his hands on them. The Holy Spirit was given to them, and they spoke unknown languages and prophesied. ⁷There were about twelve men in this group.

⁸For three months Paul went to the Jewish meeting place and talked bravely with the people about God's kingdom. He tried to win them over, ⁹but some of them were stubborn and

<sup>s</sup>**18.18** *he had his head shaved*: Paul had promised to be a "Nazirite" for a while. This meant that for the time of the promise, he could not cut his hair or drink wine. When the time was over, he would have to cut his hair and offer a sacrifice to God. <sup>t</sup>**18.25** *the Lord's Way*: See the note at 9.2. <sup>u</sup>**19.3** *Then why were you baptized? . . . Because of what John taught*: Or "In whose name were you baptized? . . . We were baptized in John's name."

refused to believe. In front of everyone they said terrible things about God's Way. Paul left and took the followers with him to the lecture hall of Tyrannus. He spoke there every day <sup>10</sup> for two years, until every Jew and Gentile<sup>v</sup> in Asia had heard the Lord's message.

### The Sons of Sceva

<sup>11</sup> God gave Paul the power to work great miracles. <sup>12</sup> People even took handkerchiefs and aprons that had touched Paul's body, and they carried them to everyone who was sick. All of the sick people were healed, and the evil spirits went out.

<sup>13</sup> Some Jewish men started going around trying to force out evil spirits by using the name of the Lord Jesus. They said to the spirits, "Come out in the name of that same Jesus that Paul preaches about!"

<sup>14</sup> Seven sons of a high priest named Sceva were doing this, <sup>15</sup> when an evil spirit said to them, "I know Jesus! And I have heard about Paul. But who are you?" <sup>16</sup> Then the man with the evil spirit jumped on them and beat them up. They ran out of the house, naked and bruised.

<sup>17</sup> When the Jews and Gentiles<sup>v</sup> in Ephesus heard about this, they were so frightened that they praised the name of the Lord Jesus. <sup>18</sup> Many who were followers now started telling everyone about the evil things they had been doing. <sup>19</sup> Some who had been practicing witchcraft even brought their books and burned them in public. These books were worth about fifty thousand silver coins. <sup>20</sup> So the Lord's message spread and became even more powerful.

### The Riot in Ephesus

<sup>21</sup> After all of this had happened, Paul decided<sup>w</sup> to visit Macedonia and Achaia on his way to Jerusalem. Paul had said, "From there I will go on to Rome." <sup>22</sup> So he sent his two helpers, Timothy and Erastus, to Macedonia. But he stayed on in Asia for a while.

<sup>23</sup> At that time there was serious trouble because of the Lord's Way.<sup>x</sup> <sup>24</sup> A silversmith named Demetrius had a business that made silver models of the temple of the goddess Artemis. Those who worked for him earned a lot of money. <sup>25</sup> Demetrius brought together everyone who was in the same business and said.

Friends, you know that we make a good living at this. <sup>26</sup> But you have surely seen and heard how this man Paul is upsetting a lot of people, not only in Ephesus, but almost everywhere in Asia. He claims that the gods we humans make are not really gods at all. <sup>27</sup> Everyone will start saying terrible things about our business. They will stop respecting the temple of the goddess Artemis, who is worshiped in Asia and all over the world. Our great goddess will be forgotten!

<sup>28</sup> When the workers heard this, they got angry and started shouting, "Great is Artemis, the goddess of the Ephesians!" <sup>29</sup> Soon the whole city was in a riot, and some men grabbed Gaius and Aristarchus, who had come from Macedonia with Paul. Then everyone in the crowd rushed to the place where the town meetings were held.

<sup>30</sup> Paul wanted to go out and speak to the people, but the Lord's followers would not let him. <sup>31</sup> A few of the local officials were friendly to Paul, and they sent someone to warn him not to go.

<sup>32</sup> Some of the people in the meeting were shouting one thing, and others were shouting something else. Everyone was completely confused, and most of them did not even know why they were there.

<sup>33</sup> Several of the Jewish leaders pushed a man named Alexander to the front of the crowd and started telling him what to say. He motioned with his hand and tried to explain what was going on. <sup>34</sup> But when the crowd saw that he was Jewish, they all shouted for two hours, "Great is Artemis, the goddess of the Ephesians!"

<sup>v</sup>**19.10** *Gentile(s)*: The text has "Greek(s)" (see the note at 14.1).   <sup>v</sup>**19.17** *Gentile(s)*: The text has "Greek(s)" (see the note at 14.1).   <sup>w</sup>**19.21** *Paul decided*: Or "Paul was led by the Holy Spirit."   <sup>x</sup>**19.23** *the Lord's Way*: See the note at 9.2.

[35] Finally, a town official made the crowd be quiet. Then he said:

People of Ephesus, who in the world doesn't know that our city is the center for worshiping the great goddess Artemis? Who doesn't know that her image which fell from heaven is right here? [36] No one can deny this, and so you should calm down and not do anything foolish. [37] You have brought men in here who have not robbed temples or spoken against our goddess.

[38] If Demetrius and his workers have a case against these men, we have courts and judges. Let them take their complaints there. [39] But if you want to do more than that, the matter will have to be brought before the city council. [40] We could easily be accused of starting a riot today. There is no excuse for it! We cannot even give a reason for this uproar.

[41] After saying this, he told the people to leave.

## Paul Goes through Macedonia and Greece

**20** When the riot was over, Paul sent for the followers and encouraged them. He then told them good-by and left for Macedonia. [2] As he traveled from place to place, he encouraged the followers with many messages. Finally, he went to Greece[y] [3] and stayed there for three months.

Paul was about to sail to Syria. But some of the Jewish leaders plotted against him, so he decided to return by way of Macedonia. [4] With him were Sopater, son of Pyrrhus from Berea, and Aristarchus and Secundus from Thessalonica. Gaius from Derbe was also with him, and so were Timothy and the two Asians, Tychicus and Trophimus. [5] They went on ahead to Troas and waited for us there. [6] After the Festival of Thin Bread, we sailed from Philippi. Five days later we met them in Troas and stayed there for a week.

## Paul's Last Visit to Troas

[7] On the first day of the week[z] we met to break bread together.[a] Paul spoke to the people until midnight because he was leaving the next morning. [8] In the upstairs room where we were meeting, there were a lot of lamps. [9] A young man by the name of Eutychus was sitting on a window sill. While Paul was speaking, the young man got very sleepy. Finally, he went to sleep and fell three floors all the way down to the ground. When they picked him up, he was dead.

[10] Paul went down and bent over Eutychus. He took him in his arms and said, "Don't worry! He's alive." [11] After Paul had gone back upstairs, he broke bread, and ate with us. He then spoke until dawn and left. [12] Then the followers took the young man home alive and were very happy.

## The Voyage from Troas to Miletus

[13] Paul decided to travel by land to Assos. The rest of us went on ahead by ship, and we were to take him aboard there. [14] When he met us in Assos, he came aboard, and we sailed on to Mitylene. [15] The next day we came to a place near Chios, and the following day we reached Samos. The day after that we sailed to Miletus. [16] Paul had decided to sail on past Ephesus, because he did not want to spend too much time in Asia. He was in a hurry and wanted to be in Jerusalem in time for Pentecost.[b]

## Paul Says Good-by to the Church Leaders of Ephesus

[17] From Miletus, Paul sent a message for the church leaders at Ephesus to come and meet with him. [18] When they got there, he said:

You know everything I did during the time I was with you when I first came to Asia. [19] Some of the Jews plotted against me and caused me

[y] **20.2** *Greece*: Probably Corinth.  [z] **20.7** *On the first day of the week*: Since the Jewish day began at sunset, the meeting would have begun in the evening.  [a] **20.7** *break bread together*: See the note at 2.46.  [b] **20.16** *in time for Pentecost*: The Jewish people liked to be in Jerusalem for this festival (see the note at 2.1).

a lot of sorrow and trouble. But I served the Lord and was humble. 20 When I preached in public or taught in your homes, I didn't hold back from telling anything that would help you. 21 I told Jews and Gentiles to turn to God and have faith in our Lord Jesus.

22 I don't know what will happen to me in Jerusalem, but I must obey God's Spirit and go there. 23 In every city I visit, I am told by the Holy Spirit that I will be put in jail and will be in trouble in Jerusalem. 24 But I don't care what happens to me, as long as I finish the work that the Lord Jesus gave me to do. And that work is to tell the good news about God's great kindness.

25 I have gone from place to place, preaching to you about God's kingdom, but now I know that none of you will ever see me again. 26 I tell you today that I am no longer responsible for any of you! 27 I have told you everything God wants you to know. 28 Look after yourselves and everyone the Holy Spirit has placed in your care. Be like shepherds to God's church. It is the flock that he bought with the blood of his own Son. c

29 I know that after I am gone, others will come like fierce wolves to attack you. 30 Some of your own people will tell lies to win over the Lord's followers. 31 Be on your guard! Remember how day and night for three years I kept warning you with tears in my eyes.

32 I now place you in God's care. Remember the message about his great kindness! This message can help you and give you what belongs to you as God's people. 33 I have never wanted anyone's money or clothes. 34 You know how I have worked with my own hands to make a living for myself and my friends. 35 By everything I did, I showed how you should work to help everyone who is weak. Remember that our Lord Jesus said, "More bless-

ings come from giving than from receiving."

36 After Paul had finished speaking, he knelt down with all of them and prayed. 37 Everyone cried and hugged and kissed him. 38 They were especially sad because Paul had told them, "You will never see me again."

Then they went with him to the ship.

## Paul Goes to Jerusalem

21 After saying good-by, we sailed straight to Cos. The next day we reached Rhodes and from there sailed on to Patara. 2 We found a ship going to Phoenicia, so we got on board and sailed off.

3 We came within sight of Cyprus and then sailed south of it on to the port of Tyre in Syria, where the ship was going to unload its cargo. 4 We looked up the Lord's followers and stayed with them for a week. The Holy Spirit had told them to warn Paul not to go on to Jerusalem. 5 But when the week was over, we started on our way again. All the men, together with their wives and children, walked with us from the town to the seashore. We knelt on the beach and prayed. 6 Then after saying good-by to each other, we got into the ship, and they went back home.

7 We sailed from Tyre to Ptolemais, where we greeted the followers and stayed with them for a day. 8 The next day we went to Caesarea and stayed with Philip, the preacher. He was one of the seven men who helped the apostles, 9 and he had four unmarried d daughters who prophesied.

10 We had been in Caesarea for several days, when the prophet Agabus came to us from Judea. 11 He took Paul's belt, and with it he tied up his own hands and feet. Then he told us, "The Holy Spirit says that some of the Jewish leaders in Jerusalem will tie up the man who owns this belt. They will also hand him over to the Gentiles." 12 After Agabus said this, we and the followers living there begged Paul not to go to Jerusalem. 13 But Paul answered, "Why are you

---

c 20.28 the blood of his own Son: Or "his own blood."   d 21.9 unmarried: Or "virgin."

crying and breaking my heart? I am not only willing to be put in jail for the Lord Jesus. I am even willing to die for him in Jerusalem!"

¹⁴ Since we could not get Paul to change his mind, we gave up and prayed, "Lord, please make us willing to do what you want."

¹⁵ Then we got ready to go to Jerusalem. ¹⁶ Some of the followers from Caesarea went with us and took us to stay in the home of Mnason. He was from Cyprus and had been a follower from the beginning.

## Paul Visits James

¹⁷ When we arrived in Jerusalem, the Lord's followers gladly welcomed us. ¹⁸ Paul went with us to see James*e* the next day, and all the church leaders were present. ¹⁹ Paul greeted them and told how God had used him to help the Gentiles. ²⁰ Everyone who heard this praised God and said to Paul:

My friend, you can see how many tens of thousands of our people have become followers! And all of them are eager to obey the Law of Moses. ²¹ But they have been told that you are teaching those who live among the Gentiles to disobey this Law. They claim that you are telling them not to circumcise their sons or to follow our customs.

²² What should we do now that our people have heard that you are here? ²³ Please do what we ask, because four of our men have made special promises to God. ²⁴ Join with them and prepare yourself for the ceremony that goes with the promises. Pay the cost for their heads to be shaved. Then everyone will learn that the reports about you are not true. They will know that you do obey the Law of Moses.

²⁵ Some while ago we told the Gentile followers what we think they should do. We instructed them not to eat anything offered to idols. They were told not to eat any meat with blood still in it or the meat of

an animal that has been strangled. They were also told not to commit any terrible sexual sins.*f*

²⁶ The next day Paul took the four men with him and got himself ready at the same time they did. Then he went into the temple and told when the final ceremony would take place and when an offering would be made for each of them.

## Paul Is Arrested

²⁷ When the period of seven days for the ceremony was almost over, some of the Jewish people from Asia saw Paul in the temple. They got a large crowd together and started attacking him. ²⁸ They were shouting, "Friends, help us! This man goes around everywhere, saying bad things about our nation and about the Law of Moses and about this temple. He has even brought shame to this holy temple by bringing in Gentiles." ²⁹ Some of them thought that Paul had brought Trophimus from Ephesus into the temple, because they had seen them together in the city.

³⁰ The whole city was in an uproar, and the people turned into a mob. They grabbed Paul and dragged him out of the temple. Then suddenly the doors were shut. ³¹ The people were about to kill Paul when the Roman army commander heard that all Jerusalem was starting to riot. ³² So he quickly took some soldiers and officers and ran to where the crowd had gathered.

As soon as the mob saw the commander and soldiers, they stopped beating Paul. ³³ The army commander went over and arrested him and had him bound with two chains. Then he tried to find out who Paul was and what he had done. ³⁴ Part of the crowd shouted one thing, and part of them shouted something else. But they were making so much noise that the commander could not find out a thing. Then he ordered Paul to be taken into the fortress. ³⁵ As they reached the steps, the crowd became so wild that the soldiers had to lift Paul up and carry him.

*e* 21.18 *James*: The Lord's brother. *f* 21.25 *not to commit any terrible sexual sins*: See the note at 15.20.

36 The crowd followed and kept shouting, "Kill him! Kill him!"

## Paul Speaks to the Crowd

37 When Paul was about to be taken into the fortress, he asked the commander, "Can I say something to you?"

"How do you know Greek?" the commander asked. 38 "Aren't you that Egyptian who started a riot not long ago and led four thousand terrorists into the desert?"

39 "No!" Paul replied. "I am a Jew from Tarsus, an important city in Cilicia. Please let me speak to the crowd."

40 The commander told him he could speak, so Paul stood on the steps and motioned to the people. When they were quiet, he spoke to them in Aramaic:

**22** "My friends and leaders of our nation, listen as I explain what happened!" 2 When the crowd heard Paul speak to them in Aramaic, they became even quieter. Then Paul said:

3 I am a Jew, born and raised in the city of Tarsus in Cilicia. I was a student of Gamaliel and was taught to follow every single law of our ancestors. In fact, I was just as eager to obey God as any of you are today.

4 I made trouble for everyone who followed the Lord's Way, g and I even had some of them killed. I had others arrested and put in jail. I didn't care if they were men or women. 5 The high priest and all the council members can tell you that this is true. They even gave me letters to the Jewish leaders in Damascus, so that I could arrest people there and bring them to Jerusalem to be punished.

6 One day about noon I was getting close to Damascus, when a bright light from heaven suddenly flashed around me. 7 I fell to the ground and heard a voice asking, "Saul, Saul, why are you so cruel to me?"

8 "Who are you?" I answered.

The Lord replied, "I am Jesus from Nazareth! I am the one you are so cruel to." 9 The men who were traveling with me saw the light, but did not hear the voice.

10 I asked, "Lord, what do you want me to do?"

Then he told me, "Get up and go to Damascus. When you get there, you will be told what to do." 11 The light had been so bright that I couldn't see. And the other men had to lead me by the hand to Damascus.

12 In that city there was a man named Ananias, who faithfully obeyed the Law of Moses and was well liked by all the Jewish people living there. 13 He came to me and said, "Saul, my friend, you can now see again!"

At once I could see. 14 Then Ananias told me, "The God that our ancestors worshiped has chosen you to know what he wants done. He has chosen you to see the One Who Obeys God h and to hear his voice. 15 You must tell everyone what you have seen and heard. 16 What are you waiting for? Get up! Be baptized, and wash away your sins by praying to the Lord."

17 After this I returned to Jerusalem and went to the temple to pray. There I had a vision 18 of the Lord who said to me, "Hurry and leave Jerusalem! The people won't listen to what you say about me."

19 I replied, "Lord, they know that in many of our meeting places I arrested and beat people who had faith in you. 20 Stephen was killed because he spoke for you, and I stood there and cheered them on. I even guarded the clothes of the men who murdered him."

21 But the Lord told me to go, and he promised to send me far away to the Gentiles.

22 The crowd listened until Paul said this. Then they started shouting, "Get rid of this man! He doesn't deserve to live." 23 They kept shouting. They waved their clothes around and threw dust into the air.

g 22.4 *followed the Lord's Way*: See the note at 9.2.   h 22.14 *One Who Obeys God*: See the note at 7.52.

## Paul and the Roman Army Commander

24 The Roman commander ordered Paul to be taken into the fortress and beaten with a whip. He did this to find out why the people were screaming at Paul.

25 While the soldiers were tying Paul up to be beaten, he asked the officer standing there, "Is it legal to beat a Roman citizen before he has been tried in court?"

26 When the officer heard this, he went to the commander and said, "What are you doing? This man is a Roman citizen!"

27 The commander went to Paul and asked, "Tell me, are you a Roman citizen?"

"Yes," Paul answered.

28 The commander then said, "I paid a lot of money to become a Roman citizen."[i]

But Paul replied, "I was born a Roman citizen."

29 The men who were about to beat and question Paul quickly backed off. And the commander himself was frightened when he realized that he had put a Roman citizen in chains.

## Paul Is Tried by the Council

30 The next day the commander wanted to know the real reason why the Jewish leaders had brought charges against Paul. So he had Paul's chains removed, and he ordered the chief priests and the whole council to meet. Then he had Paul led in and made him stand in front of them.

23 Paul looked straight at the council members and said, "My friends, to this day I have served God with a clear conscience!"

2 Then Ananias the high priest ordered the men standing beside Paul to hit him on the mouth. 3 Paul turned to the high priest and said, "You whitewashed wall![j] God will hit you. You sit there to judge me by the Law of Moses. But at the same time you order

men to break the Law by hitting me."

4 The men standing beside Paul asked, "Don't you know you are insulting God's high priest?"

5 Paul replied, "Oh! I didn't know he was the high priest. The Scriptures do tell us not to speak evil about a leader of our people."

6 When Paul saw that some of the council members were Sadducees and others were Pharisees, he shouted, "My friends, I am a Pharisee and the son of a Pharisee. I am on trial simply because I believe that the dead will be raised to life."

7 As soon as Paul said this, the Pharisees and the Sadducees got into a big argument, and the council members started taking sides. 8 The Sadducees do not believe in angels or spirits or that the dead will rise to life. But the Pharisees believe in all of these, 9 and so there was a lot of shouting. Some of the teachers of the Law of Moses were Pharisees. Finally, they became angry and said, "We don't find anything wrong with this man. Maybe a spirit or an angel really did speak to him."

10 The argument became fierce, and the commander was afraid that Paul would be pulled apart. So he ordered the soldiers to go in and rescue Paul. Then they took him back into the fortress.

11 That night the Lord stood beside Paul and said, "Don't worry! Just as you have told others about me in Jerusalem, you must also tell about me in Rome."

## A Plot To Kill Paul

12-13 The next morning more than forty Jewish men got together and vowed that they would not eat or drink anything until they had killed Paul. 14 Then some of them went to the chief priests and the nation's leaders and said, "We have promised God that we would not eat a thing until we have killed Paul. 15 You and everyone in the council must go to the commander and pretend that you want to find out more

---

[i]22.28 *Roman citizen*: See the note at 16.37.   [j]23.3 *whitewashed wall*: Someone who pretends to be good, but really isn't.

about the charges against Paul. Ask for him to be brought before your court. Meanwhile, we will be waiting to kill him before he gets there."

¹⁶ When Paul's nephew heard about the plot, he went to the fortress and told Paul about it. ¹⁷ So Paul said to one of the army officers, "Take this young man to the commander. He has something to tell him."

¹⁸ The officer took him to the commander and said, "The prisoner named Paul asked me to bring this young man to you, because he has something to tell you."

¹⁹ The commander took the young man aside and asked him in private, "What do you want to tell me?"

²⁰ He answered, "Some men are planning to ask you to bring Paul down to the Jewish council tomorrow. They will claim that they want to find out more about him. ²¹ But please don't do what they say. More than forty men are going to attack Paul. They have made a vow not to eat or drink anything until they have killed him. Even now they are waiting to hear what you decide."

²² The commander sent the young man away after saying to him, "Don't let anyone know that you told me this."

### Paul Is Sent to Felix the Governor

²³ The commander called in two of his officers and told them, "By nine o'clock tonight have two hundred soldiers ready to go to Caesarea. Take along seventy men on horseback and two hundred foot soldiers with spears. ²⁴ Get a horse ready for Paul and make sure that he gets safely through to Felix the governor."

²⁵ The commander wrote a letter that said:

²⁶ Greetings from Claudius Lysias to the Honorable Governor Felix:

²⁷ Some Jews grabbed this man and were about to kill him. But when I found out that he was a Roman citizen, I took some soldiers and rescued him.

²⁸ I wanted to find out what they had against him. So I brought him before their council ²⁹ and learned that the charges concern only their religious laws. This man isn't guilty of anything for which he should die or even be put in jail.

³⁰ As soon as I learned that there was a plot against him, I sent him to you and told their leaders to bring charges against him in your court.

³¹ The soldiers obeyed the commander's orders, and that same night they took Paul to the city of Antipatris. ³² The next day the foot soldiers returned to the fortress and let the soldiers on horseback take him the rest of the way. ³³ When they came to Caesarea, they gave the letter to the governor and handed Paul over to him.

³⁴ The governor read the letter. Then he asked Paul and found out that he was from Cilicia. ³⁵ The governor said, "I will listen to your case as soon as the people come to bring their charges against you." After saying this, he gave orders for Paul to be kept as a prisoner in Herod's palace. ᵏ

### Paul Is Accused in the Court of Felix

24 Five days later Ananias the high priest, together with some of their leaders and a lawyer named Tertullus, went to the governor to present their case against Paul. ² So Paul was called in, and Tertullus stated the case against him: ˡ

Honorable Felix, you have brought our people a long period of peace, and because of your concern our nation is much better off. ³ All of us are always grateful for what you have done. ⁴ I don't want to bother you, but please be patient with us and listen to me for just a few minutes.

⁵ This man has been found to be a real pest and troublemaker for our people all over the world. He is also a leader of a group called Nazarenes. ⁶⁻⁸ When he tried to disgrace

---

ᵏ 23.35 *Herod's palace*: The palace built by Herod the Great and used by the Roman governors of Palestine. ˡ 24.2 *Paul was called in, and Tertullus stated the case against him*: Or "Tertullus was called in and stated the case against Paul."

the temple, we arrested him. *m* If you question him, you will find out for yourself that our charges are true. [9] The Jewish crowd spoke up and agreed with what Tertullus had said.

### Paul Defends Himself

[10] The governor motioned for Paul to speak, and he began:

I know that you have judged the people of our nation for many years, and I am glad to defend myself in your court. [11] It was no more than twelve days ago that I went to worship in Jerusalem. You can find this out easily enough. [12] Never once did the Jews find me arguing with anyone in the temple. I didn't cause trouble in their meeting places or in the city itself. [13] There is no way that they can prove these charges that they are now bringing against me.

[14] I admit that their leaders think that the Lord's Way *n* which I follow is based on wrong beliefs. But I still worship the same God that my ancestors worshiped. And I believe everything written in the Law of Moses and in the Prophets. *o* [15] I am just as sure as these people are that God will raise from death everyone who is good or evil. [16] And because I am sure, I try my best to have a clear conscience in whatever I do for God or for people.

[17] After being away for several years, I returned here to bring gifts for the poor people of my nation and to offer sacrifices. [18] This is what I was doing when I was found going through a ceremony in the temple. I wasn't with a crowd, and there was no uproar. [19] Some Jews from Asia were there at that time, and if they have anything to say against me, they should be here now. [20] Or ask the ones who are here. They can tell you that they didn't find me guilty of anything when I was tried by their own council. [21] The only charge they can bring against me is what I shouted out in court, when I said, "I am on trial today because I believe that the dead will be raised to life!"

[22] Felix knew a lot about the Lord's Way. *p* But he brought the trial to an end and said, "I will make my decision after Lysias the commander arrives." [23] He then ordered the army officer to keep Paul under guard, but not to lock him up or to stop his friends from helping him.

### Paul Is Kept under Guard

[24] Several days later Felix and his wife Drusilla, who was Jewish, went to the place where Paul was kept under guard. They sent for Paul and listened while he spoke to them about having faith in Christ Jesus. [25] But Felix was frightened when Paul started talking to them about doing right, about self-control, and about the coming judgment. So he said to Paul, "That's enough for now. You may go. But when I have time I will send for you." [26] After this, Felix often sent for Paul and talked with him, because he hoped that Paul would offer him a bribe.

[27] Two years later Porcius Festus became governor in place of Felix. But since Felix wanted to do the Jewish leaders a favor, he kept Paul in jail.

### Paul Asks To Be Tried by the Roman Emperor

**25** Three days after Festus had become governor, he went from Caesarea to Jerusalem. [2] There the chief priests and some Jewish leaders told him about their charges against Paul. They also asked Festus [3] if he would be willing to bring Paul to Jerusalem. They begged him to do this because they were planning to attack and kill Paul on the way. [4] But Festus told

*m* **24.6-8** *we arrested him*: Some manuscripts add, "We wanted to judge him by our own laws. But Lysias the commander took him away from us by force. Then Lysias ordered us to bring our charges against this man in your court." *n* **24.14** *the Lord's Way*: See the note at 9.2. *o* **24.14** *Law of Moses . . . the Prophets*: The Jewish Scriptures, that is, the Old Testament. *p* **24.22** *the Lord's Way*: See the note at 9.2.

them, "Paul will be kept in Caesarea, and I am soon going there myself. [5] If he has done anything wrong, let your leaders go with me and bring charges against him there."

[6] Festus stayed in Jerusalem for eight or ten more days before going to Caesarea. Then the next day he took his place as judge and had Paul brought into court. [7] As soon as Paul came in, the leaders from Jerusalem crowded around him and said he was guilty of many serious crimes. But they could not prove anything. [8] Then Paul spoke in his own defense, "I have not broken the Law of my people. And I have not done anything against either the temple or the Emperor."

[9] Festus wanted to please the leaders. So he asked Paul, "Are you willing to go to Jerusalem and be tried by me on these charges?"

[10] Paul replied, "I am on trial in the Emperor's court, and that's where I should be tried. You know very well that I have not done anything to harm the Jewish nation. [11] If I had done something deserving death, I would not ask to escape the death penalty. But I am not guilty of any of these crimes, and no one has the right to hand me over to these people. I now ask to be tried by the Emperor himself."

[12] After Festus had talked this over with members of his council, he told Paul, "You have asked to be tried by the Emperor, and to the Emperor you will go!"

## Paul Speaks to Agrippa and Bernice

[13] A few days later King Agrippa and Bernice came to Caesarea to visit Festus. [14] They had been there for several days, when Festus told the king about the charges against Paul. He said:

Felix left a man here in jail, [15] and when I went to Jerusalem, the chief priests and the Jewish leaders came and asked me to find him guilty. [16] I told them that it isn't the Roman custom to hand a man over to people who are bringing charges against him. He must first have the chance to meet them face to face and to defend himself against their charges. [17] So when they came here with

me, I wasted no time. On the very next day I took my place on the judge's bench and ordered him to be brought in. [18] But when the men stood up to make their charges against him, they did not accuse him of any of the crimes that I thought they would. [19] Instead, they argued with him about some of their beliefs and about a dead man named Jesus, who Paul said was alive.

[20] Since I did not know how to find out the truth about all this, I asked Paul if he would be willing to go to Jerusalem and be put on trial there. [21] But Paul asked to be kept in jail until the Emperor could decide his case. So I ordered him to be kept here until I could send him to the Emperor.

[22] Then Agrippa said to Festus, "I would also like to hear what this man has to say."

Festus answered, "You can hear him tomorrow."

[23] The next day Agrippa and Bernice made a big show as they came into the meeting room. High ranking army officers and leading citizens of the town were also there. Festus then ordered Paul to be brought in [24] and said:

King Agrippa and other guests, look at this man! Every Jew from Jerusalem and Caesarea has come to me, demanding for him to be put to death. [25] I have not found him guilty of any crime deserving death. But because he has asked to be judged by the Emperor, I have decided to send him to Rome. [26] I have to write some facts about this man to the Emperor. So I have brought him before all of you, but especially before you, King Agrippa. After we have talked about his case, I will then have something to write. [27] It makes no sense to send a prisoner to the Emperor without stating the charges against him.

## Paul's Defense before Agrippa

**26** Agrippa told Paul, "You may now speak for yourself."

Paul stretched out his hand and said: [2] King Agrippa, I am glad for this chance to defend myself before you today on all these charges that my own people have brought against me. ³ You know a lot about our religious customs and the beliefs that divide us. So I ask you to listen patiently to me.

⁴⁻⁵ All the Jews have known me since I was a child. They know what kind of life I have lived in my own country and in Jerusalem. And if they were willing, they could tell you that I was a Pharisee, a member of a group that is stricter than any other. ⁶ Now I am on trial because I believe the promise God made to our people long ago.

⁷ Day and night our twelve tribes have earnestly served God, waiting for his promised blessings. King Agrippa, because of this hope, some of their leaders have brought charges against me. ⁸ Why should any of you doubt that God raises the dead to life?

⁹ I once thought that I should do everything I could to oppose Jesus from Nazareth. ¹⁰ I did this first in Jerusalem, and with the authority of the chief priests I put many of God's people in jail. I even voted for them to be killed. ¹¹ I often had them punished in our meeting places, and I tried to make them give up their faith. In fact, I was so angry with them, that I went looking for them in foreign cities.

¹² King Agrippa, one day I was on my way to Damascus with the authority and permission of the chief priests. ¹³ About noon I saw a light brighter than the sun. It flashed from heaven on me and on everyone traveling with me. ¹⁴ We all fell to the ground. Then I heard a voice say to me in Aramaic, "Saul, Saul, why are you so cruel to me? It's foolish to fight against me!"

¹⁵ "Who are you?" I asked.

Then the Lord answered, "I am Jesus! I am the one you are so cruel to. ¹⁶ Now stand up. I have appeared to you, because I have chosen you to be my servant. You are to tell others what you have learned about me and what I will show you later."

¹⁷ The Lord also said, "I will protect you from the Jews and from the Gentiles that I am sending you to. ¹⁸ I want you to open their eyes, so that they will turn from darkness to light and from the power of Satan to God. Then their sins will be forgiven, and by faith in me they will become part of God's holy people."

¹⁹ King Agrippa, I obeyed this vision from heaven. ²⁰ First I preached to the people in Damascus, and then I went to Jerusalem and all over Judea. Finally, I went to the Gentiles and said, "Stop sinning and turn to God! Then prove what you have done by the way you live."

²¹ That is why some men grabbed me in the temple and tried to kill me. ²² But all this time God has helped me, and I have preached both to the rich and to the poor. I have told them only what the prophets and Moses said would happen. ²³ I told them how the Messiah would suffer and be the first to be raised from death, so that he could bring light to his own people and to the Gentiles.

²⁴ Before Paul finished defending himself, Festus shouted, "Paul, you're crazy! Too much learning has driven you out of your mind."

²⁵ But Paul replied, "Honorable Festus, I am not crazy. What I am saying is true, and it makes sense. ²⁶ None of these things happened off in a corner somewhere. I am sure that King Agrippa knows what I am talking about. That's why I can speak so plainly to him."

²⁷ Then Paul said to Agrippa, "Do you believe what the prophets said? I know you do."

²⁸ Agrippa asked Paul, "In such a short time do you think you can talk me into being a Christian?"

²⁹ Paul answered, "Whether it takes a short time or a long time, I wish you and everyone else who hears me today would become just like me! Except, of course, for these chains."

³⁰ Then King Agrippa, Governor Festus, Bernice, and everyone who was with them got up. ³¹ But before they left, they said, "This man isn't guilty of anything. He doesn't deserve to die or to be put in jail."

³² Agrippa told Festus, "Paul could

have been set free, if he had not asked to be tried by the Roman Emperor."

### Paul Is Taken to Rome

**27** When it was time for us to sail to Rome, Captain Julius from the Emperor's special troops was put in charge of Paul and the other prisoners. [2] We went aboard a ship from Adramyttium that was about to sail to some ports along the coast of Asia. Aristarchus from Thessalonica in Macedonia sailed on the ship with us.

[3] The next day we came to shore at Sidon. Captain Julius was very kind to Paul. He even let him visit his friends, so they could give him whatever he needed. [4] When we left Sidon, the winds were blowing against us, and we sailed close to the island of Cyprus to be safe from the wind. [5] Then we sailed south of Cilicia and Pamphylia until we came to the port of Myra in Lycia. [6] There the army captain found a ship from Alexandria that was going to Italy. So he ordered us to board that ship.

[7] We sailed along slowly for several days and had a hard time reaching Cnidus. The wind would not let us go any farther in that direction, so we sailed past Cape Salmone, where the island of Crete would protect us from the wind. [8] We went slowly along the coast and finally reached a place called Fair Havens, not far from the town of Lasea.

[9] By now we had already lost a lot of time, and sailing was no longer safe. In fact, even the Great Day of Forgiveness[q] was past. [10] Then Paul spoke to the crew of the ship, "Men, listen to me! If we sail now, our ship and its cargo will be badly damaged, and many lives will be lost." [11] But Julius listened to the captain of the ship and its owner, rather than to Paul.

[12] The harbor at Fair Havens wasn't a good place to spend the winter. Because of this, almost everyone agreed that we should at least try to sail along the coast of Crete as far as Phoenix. It had a harbor that opened toward the southwest and northwest,[r] and we could spend the winter there.

### The Storm at Sea

[13] When a gentle wind from the south started blowing, the men thought it was a good time to do what they had planned. So they pulled up the anchor, and we sailed along the coast of Crete. [14] But soon a strong wind called "The Northeaster" blew against us from the island. [15] The wind struck the ship, and we could not sail against it. So we let the wind carry the ship.

[16] We went along the island of Cauda on the side that was protected from the wind. We had a hard time holding the lifeboat in place, [17] but finally we got it where it belonged. Then the sailors wrapped ropes around the ship to hold it together. They lowered the sail and let the ship drift along, because they were afraid it might hit the sandbanks in the gulf of Syrtis.

[18] The storm was so fierce that the next day they threw some of the ship's cargo overboard. [19] Then on the third day, with their bare hands they threw overboard some of the ship's gear. [20] For several days we could not see either the sun or the stars. A strong wind kept blowing, and we finally gave up all hope of being saved.

[21] Since none of us had eaten anything for a long time, Paul stood up and told the men:

You should have listened to me! If you had stayed on in Crete, you would not have had this damage and loss. [22] But now I beg you to cheer up, because you will be safe. Only the ship will be lost.

[23] I belong to God, and I worship him. Last night he sent an angel [24] to tell me, "Paul, don't be afraid! You will stand trial before the Emperor. And because of you, God will save the lives of everyone on the ship." [25] Cheer up! I am sure that God will do exactly what he promised. [26] But

---

q27.9 *Great Day of Forgiveness*: This Jewish festival took place near the end of September. The sailing season was dangerous after the middle of September, and it was stopped completely between the middle of November and the middle of March.   r27.12 *southwest and northwest*: Or "northeast and southeast."

we will first be shipwrecked on some island.

27 For fourteen days and nights we had been blown around over the Mediterranean Sea. But about midnight the sailors realized that we were getting near land. 28 They measured and found that the water was about one hundred twenty feet deep. A little later they measured again and found it was only about ninety feet. 29 The sailors were afraid that we might hit some rocks, and they let down four anchors from the back of the ship. Then they prayed for daylight.

30 The sailors wanted to escape from the ship. So they lowered the lifeboat into the water, pretending that they were letting down an anchor from the front of the ship. 31 But Paul said to Captain Julius and the soldiers, "If the sailors don't stay on the ship, you won't have any chance to save your lives." 32 The soldiers then cut the ropes that held the lifeboat and let it fall into the sea.

33 Just before daylight Paul begged the people to eat something. He told them, "For fourteen days you have been so worried that you haven't eaten a thing. 34 I beg you to eat something. Your lives depend on it. Do this and not one of you will be hurt."

35 After Paul had said this, he took a piece of bread and gave thanks to God. Then in front of everyone, he broke the bread and ate some. 36 They all felt encouraged, and each of them ate something. 37 There were 276 people on the ship, 38 and after everyone had eaten, they threw the cargo of wheat into the sea to make the ship lighter.

### The Shipwreck

39 Morning came, and the ship's crew saw a coast that they did not recognize. But they did see a cove with a beach. So they decided to try to run the ship aground on the beach. 40 They cut the anchors loose and let them sink into the sea. At the same time they untied the ropes that were holding the rudders. Next, they raised the sail at the front of the ship and let the wind carry the ship toward the beach. 41 But it ran aground on a sandbank. The front of the ship stuck firmly in the sand, and the rear was being smashed by the force of the waves.

42 The soldiers decided to kill the prisoners to keep them from swimming away and escaping. 43 But Captain Julius wanted to save Paul's life, and he did not let the soldiers do what they had planned. Instead, he ordered everyone who could swim to dive into the water and head for shore. 44 Then he told the others to hold on to planks of wood or parts of the ship. At last, everyone safely reached shore.

### On the Island of Malta

28 When we came ashore, we learned that the island was called Malta. 2 The local people were very friendly, and they welcomed us by building a fire, because it was rainy and cold.

3 After Paul had gathered some wood and had put it on the fire, the heat caused a snake to crawl out, and it bit him on the hand. 4 When the local people saw the snake hanging from Paul's hand, they said to each other, "This man must be a murderer! He didn't drown in the sea, but the goddess of justice will kill him anyway."

5 Paul shook the snake off into the fire and wasn't harmed. 6 The people kept thinking that Paul would either swell up or suddenly drop dead. They watched him for a long time, and when nothing happened to him, they changed their minds and said, "This man is a god."

7 The governor of the island was named Publius, and he owned some of the land around there. Publius was very friendly and welcomed us into his home for three days. 8 His father was in bed, sick with fever and stomach trouble, and Paul went to visit him. Paul healed the man by praying and placing his hands on him.

9 After this happened, everyone on the island brought their sick people to Paul, and they were all healed. 10 The people were very respectful to us, and when we sailed, they gave us everything we needed.

## From Malta to Rome

¹¹ Three months later we sailed in a ship that had been docked at Malta for the winter. The ship was from Alexandria in Egypt and was known as "The Twin Gods."ˢ ¹² We arrived in Syracuse and stayed for three days. ¹³ From there we sailed to Rhegium. The next day a south wind began to blow, and two days later we arrived in Puteoli. ¹⁴ There we found some of the Lord's followers, who begged us to stay with them. A week later we left for the city of Rome.

¹⁵ Some of the followers in Rome heard about us and came to meet us at the Market of Appius and at the Three Inns. When Paul saw them, he thanked God and was encouraged.

## Paul in Rome

¹⁶ We arrived in Rome, and Paul was allowed to live in a house by himself with a soldier to guard him.

¹⁷ Three days after we got there, Paul called together some of the Jewish leaders and said:

My friends, I have never done anything to hurt our people, and I have never gone against the customs of our ancestors. But in Jerusalem I was handed over as a prisoner to the Romans. ¹⁸ They looked into the charges against me and wanted to release me. They found that I had not done anything deserving death. ¹⁹ The Jewish leaders disagreed, so I asked to be tried by the Emperor. But I don't have anything to say against my own nation. ²⁰ I am bound by these chains because of what we people of Israel hope for. That's why I have called you here to talk about this hope of ours. ²¹ The leaders replied, "No one from Judea has written us a letter about you. And not one of them has come here to report on you or to say anything against you. ²² But we would like to hear what you have to say. We understand that people everywhere are against this new group."

²³ They agreed on a time to meet with Paul, and many of them came to his house. From early morning until late in the afternoon, Paul talked to them about God's kingdom. He used the Law of Moses and the Books of the Prophetsᵗ to try to win them over to Jesus.

²⁴ Some of the leaders agreed with what Paul said, but others did not. ²⁵ Since they could not agree among themselves, they started leaving. But Paul said, "The Holy Spirit said the right thing when he sent Isaiah the prophet ²⁶ to tell our ancestors,

'Go to these people
    and tell them:
You will listen and listen,
    but never understand.
You will look and look,
    but never see.
²⁷ All of you
    have stubborn hearts.
Your ears are stopped up,
    and your eyes are covered.
You cannot see or hear
    or understand.
If you could,
you would turn to me,
    and I would heal you.' "

²⁸⁻²⁹ Paul said, "You may be sure that God wants to save the Gentiles! And they will listen."ᵘ

³⁰ For two years Paul stayed in a rented house and welcomed everyone who came to see him. ³¹ He bravely preached about God's kingdom and taught about the Lord Jesus Christ, and no one tried to stop him.

---

ˢ 28.11 *known as "The Twin Gods"*: Or "carried on its bow a wooden carving of the Twin Gods." These gods were Castor and Pollux, two of the favorite gods among sailors.
ᵗ 28.23 *Law of Moses and the Books of the Prophets*: The Jewish Bible, that is, the Old Testament.   ᵘ 28.28,29 *And they will listen*: Some manuscripts add, "After Paul said this, the people left, but they got into a fierce argument among themselves."

# ROMANS

## ABOUT THIS LETTER

Paul wrote this letter to introduce himself and his message to the church at Rome. He had never been to this important city, although he knew the names of many Christians there and hoped to visit them soon (15.22—16.21). Paul tells them that he is an apostle, chosen to preach the good news (1.1). And the message he proclaims "is God's powerful way of saving all people who have faith, whether they are Jews or Gentiles" (1.16).

Paul reminds his readers, "All of us have sinned and fallen short of God's glory" (3.23). But how can we be made acceptable to God? This is the main question that Paul answers in this letter. He begins by showing how everyone has failed to do what God requires. The Jews have not obeyed the Law of Moses, and the Gentiles have refused even to think about God, although God has spoken to them in many different ways (1.18—3.20).

Now we see how God does make us acceptable to him
... He accepts people only because they have faith in Jesus
Christ ... God treats us much better than we deserve, and
because of Jesus Christ, he freely accepts us and sets us free
from our sins. (3.21a-24)

God gave Jesus to die for our sins, and he raised him to life,
so that we would be made acceptable to God. (4.25)

## A QUICK LOOK AT THIS LETTER

Paul and His Message of Good News (1.1-17)
Everyone Is Guilty (1.18—3.20)
God's Way of Accepting People (3.21—4.25)
A New Life for God's People (5.1—8.39)
What about the People of Israel? (9.1—11.36)
How to Live the New Life of Love (12.1—15.13)
Paul's Plans and Personal Greetings (15.14—16.27)

---

**1** From Paul, a servant of Christ Jesus.

God chose me to be an apostle, and he appointed me to preach the good news ²that he promised long ago by what his prophets said in the holy Scriptures. ³⁻⁴This good news is about his Son, our Lord Jesus Christ! As a human, he was from the family of David. But the Holy Spirit[a] proved that Jesus is the powerful Son of God,[b] because he was raised from death.

⁵Jesus was kind to me and chose me to be an apostle,[c] so that people of all nations would obey and have faith. ⁶You are some of those people chosen by Jesus Christ.

⁷This letter is to all of you in Rome. God loves you and has chosen you to be his very own people.

---

a 1.4 the Holy Spirit: Or "his own spirit of holiness." b 1.4 proved that Jesus is the powerful Son of God: Or "proved in a powerful way that Jesus is the Son of God." c 1.5 Jesus was kind to me and chose me to be an apostle: Or "Jesus was kind to us and chose us to be his apostles."

I pray that God our Father and our Lord Jesus Christ will be kind to you and will bless you with peace!

## A Prayer of Thanks

8 First, I thank God in the name of Jesus Christ for all of you. I do this because people everywhere in the world are talking about your faith. 9 God has seen how I never stop praying for you, while I serve him with all my heart and tell the good news about his Son.

10 In all my prayers, I ask God to make it possible for me to visit you. 11 I want to see you and share with you the same blessings that God's Spirit has given me. Then you will grow stronger in your faith. 12 What I am saying is that we can encourage each other by the faith that is ours.

13 My friends, I want you to know that I have often planned to come for a visit. But something has always kept me from doing it. I want to win followers to Christ in Rome, as I have done in many other places. 14-15 It doesn't matter if people are civilized and educated, or if they are uncivilized and uneducated. I must tell the good news to everyone. That's why I am eager to visit all of you in Rome.

## The Power of the Good News

16 I am proud of the good news! It is God's powerful way of saving all people who have faith, whether they are Jews or Gentiles. 17 The good news tells how God accepts everyone who has faith, but only those who have faith. d It is just as the Scriptures say, "The people God accepts because of their faith will live." e

## Everyone Is Guilty

18 From heaven God shows how angry he is with all the wicked and evil things that sinful people do to crush the truth. 19 They know everything that can be known about God, because God has shown it all to them. 20 God's eternal power and character cannot be seen. But from the beginning of creation, God has shown what these are like by all he has made. That's why those people don't have any excuse. 21 They know about God, but they don't honor him or even thank him. Their thoughts are useless, and their stupid minds are in the dark. 22 They claim to be wise, but they are fools. 23 They don't worship the glorious and eternal God. Instead, they worship idols that are made to look like humans who cannot live forever, and like birds, animals, and reptiles.

24 So God let these people go their own way. They did what they wanted to do, and their filthy thoughts made them do shameful things with their bodies. 25 They gave up the truth about God for a lie, and they worshiped God's creation instead of God, who will be praised forever. Amen.

26 God let them follow their own evil desires. Women no longer wanted to have sex in a natural way, and they did things with each other that were not natural. 27 Men behaved in the same way. They stopped wanting to have sex with women and had strong desires for sex with other men. They did shameful things with each other, and what has happened to them is punishment for their foolish deeds.

28 Since these people refused even to think about God, he let their useless minds rule over them. That's why they do all sorts of indecent things. 29 They are evil, wicked, and greedy, as well as mean in every possible way. They want what others have, and they murder, argue, cheat, and are hard to get along with. They gossip, 30 say cruel things about others, and hate God. They are proud, conceited, and boastful, always thinking up new ways to do evil.

These people don't respect their parents. 31 They are stupid, unreliable, and don't have any love or pity for others. 32 They know God has said that anyone

---

d 1.17 *but only those who have faith*: Or "and faith is all that matters."   e 1.17 *The people God accepts because of their faith will live*: Or "The people God accepts will live because of their faith."

who acts this way deserves to die. But they keep on doing evil things, and they even encourage others to do them.

## God's Judgment Is Fair

**2** Some of you accuse others of doing wrong. But there is no excuse for what you do. When you judge others, you condemn yourselves, because you are guilty of doing the very same things. [2] We know that God is right to judge everyone who behaves in this way. [3] Do you really think God won't punish you, when you behave exactly like the people you accuse? [4] You surely don't think much of God's wonderful goodness or of his patience and willingness to put up with you. Don't you know that the reason God is good to you is because he wants you to turn to him?

[5] But you are stubborn and refuse to turn to God. So you are making things even worse for yourselves on that day when he will show how angry he is and will judge the world with fairness. [6] God will reward each of us for what we have done. [7] He will give eternal life to everyone who has patiently done what is good in the hope of receiving glory, honor, and life that lasts forever. [8] But he will show how angry and furious he can be with every selfish person who rejects the truth and wants to do evil. [9] All who are wicked will be punished with trouble and suffering. It doesn't matter if they are Jews or Gentiles. [10] But all who do right will be rewarded with glory, honor, and peace, whether they are Jews or Gentiles. [11] God doesn't have any favorites!

[12] Those people who don't know about God's Law will still be punished for what they do wrong. And the Law will be used to judge everyone who knows what it says. [13] God accepts those who obey his Law, but not those who simply hear it.

[14] Some people naturally obey the Law's commands, even though they don't have the Law. [15] This proves that the conscience is like a law written in the human heart. And it will show whether we are forgiven or condemned, [16] when God has Jesus Christ judge everyone's secret thoughts, just as my message says.

## The Jews and the Law

[17] Some of you call yourselves Jews. You trust in the Law and take pride in God. [18] By reading the Scriptures you learn how God wants you to behave, and you discover what is right. [19] You are sure that you are a guide for the blind and a light for all who are in the dark. [20] And since there is knowledge and truth in God's Law, you think you can instruct fools and teach young people.

[21] But how can you teach others when you refuse to learn? You preach that it is wrong to steal. But do you steal? [22] You say people should be faithful in marriage. But are you faithful? You hate idols, yet you rob their temples. [23] You take pride in the Law, but you disobey the Law and bring shame to God. [24] It is just as the Scriptures tell us, "You have made foreigners say insulting things about God."

[25] Being circumcised is worthwhile, if you obey the Law. But if you don't obey the Law, you are no better off than people who are not circumcised. [26] In fact, if they obey the Law, they are as good as anyone who is circumcised. [27] So everyone who obeys the Law, but has never been circumcised, will condemn you. Even though you are circumcised and have the Law, you still don't obey its teachings.

[28] Just because you live like a Jew and are circumcised doesn't make you a real Jew. [29] To be a real Jew you must obey the Law. True circumcision is something that happens deep in your heart, not something done to your body. And besides, you should want praise from God and not from humans.

**3** What good is it to be a Jew? What good is it to be circumcised? [2] It is good in a lot of ways! First of all, God's messages were spoken to the Jews. [3] It is true that some of them did not believe the message. But does this mean that God cannot be trusted, just because they did not have faith? [4] No, indeed! God tells the truth, even if everyone else is a liar. The Scriptures say about God,

"Your words
    will be proven true,
and in court
    you will win your case."

⁵ If our evil deeds show how right
God is, then what can we say? Is it
wrong for God to become angry and
punish us? What a foolish thing to ask.
⁶ But the answer is, "No." Otherwise,
how could God judge the world? ⁷ Since
your lies bring great honor to God by
showing how truthful he is, you may
ask why God still says you are a sinner.
⁸ You might as well say, "Let's do something evil, so that something good will
come of it!" Some people even claim
that we are saying this. But God is fair
and will judge them as well.

### No One Is Good

⁹ What does all this mean? Does it
mean that we Jews are better off ᶠ than
the Gentiles? No, it doesn't! Jews, as
well as Gentiles, are ruled by sin, just
as I have said. ¹⁰ The Scriptures tell us,

"No one is acceptable to God!
¹¹ Not one of them understands
    or even searches for God.
¹² They have all turned away
    and are worthless.
    There isn't one person
    who does right.
¹³ Their words are like
    an open pit,
and their tongues are good
    only for telling lies.
Each word is as deadly
    as the fangs of a snake,
¹⁴ and they say nothing
    but bitter curses.
¹⁵ These people quickly
    become violent.
¹⁶ Wherever they go,
    they leave ruin
    and destruction.
¹⁷ They don't know how
    to live in peace.
¹⁸     They don't even fear God."

¹⁹ We know that everything in the
Law was written for those who are un-

der its power. The Law says these
things to stop anyone from making excuses and to let God show that the
whole world is guilty. ²⁰ God doesn't accept people simply because they obey
the Law. No, indeed! All the Law does
is to point out our sin.

### God's Way of Accepting People

²¹ Now we see how God does make
us acceptable to him. The Law and the
Prophets ᵍ tell how we become acceptable, and it isn't by obeying the Law of
Moses. ²² God treats everyone alike. He
accepts people only because they have
faith in Jesus Christ. ²³ All of us have
sinned and fallen short of God's glory.
²⁴ But God treats us much better than
we deserve, ʰ and because of Christ
Jesus, he freely accepts us and sets us
free from our sins. ²⁵⁻²⁶ God sent Christ
to be our sacrifice. Christ offered his
life's blood, so that by faith in him we
could come to God. And God did this
to show that in the past he was right
to be patient and forgive sinners. This
also shows that God is right when he
accepts people who have faith in Jesus.
²⁷ What is left for us to brag about?
Not a thing! Is it because we obeyed
some law? No! It is because of faith.
²⁸ We see that people are acceptable to
God because they have faith, and not
because they obey the Law. ²⁹ Does
God belong only to the Jews? Isn't he
also the God of the Gentiles? Yes, he
is! ³⁰ There is only one God, and he accepts Gentiles as well as Jews, simply
because of their faith. ³¹ Do we destroy
the Law by our faith? Not at all! We
make it even more powerful.

### The Example of Abraham

4 Well then, what can we say about
our ancestor Abraham? ² If he became acceptable to God because of
what he did, then he would have something to brag about. But he would
never be able to brag about it to God.
³ The Scriptures say, "God accepted

---

ᶠ**3.9** *better off*: Or "worse off."   ᵍ**3.21** *The Law and the Prophets*: The Jewish Scriptures,
that is, the Old Testament.   ʰ**3.24** *treats us much better than we deserve*: The Greek word
*charis*, traditionally rendered "grace," is translated here and other places in the CEV to
express the overwhelming kindness of God.

Abraham because Abraham had faith in him."

⁴ Money paid to workers isn't a gift. It is something they earn by working. ⁵ But you cannot make God accept you because of something you do. God accepts sinners only because they have faith in him. ⁶ In the Scriptures David talks about the blessings that come to people who are acceptable to God, even though they don't do anything to deserve these blessings. David says,

⁷ "God blesses people
   whose sins are forgiven
and whose evil deeds
   are forgotten.
⁸ The Lord blesses people
   whose sins are erased
   from his book."

⁹ Are these blessings meant for circumcised people or for those who are not circumcised? Well, the Scriptures say that God accepted Abraham because Abraham had faith in him. ¹⁰ But when did this happen? Was it before or after Abraham was circumcised? Of course, it was before.

¹¹ Abraham let himself be circumcised to show that he had been accepted because of his faith even before he was circumcised. This makes Abraham the father of all who are acceptable to God because of their faith, even though they are not circumcised. ¹² This also makes Abraham the father of everyone who is circumcised and has faith in God, as Abraham did before he was circumcised.

### The Promise Is for All Who Have Faith

¹³ God promised Abraham and his descendants that he would give them the world. This promise wasn't made because Abraham had obeyed a law, but because his faith in God made him acceptable. ¹⁴ If Abraham and his descendants were given this promise because they had obeyed a law, then faith would mean nothing, and the promise would be worthless.

¹⁵ God becomes angry when his Law is broken. But where there isn't a law, it cannot be broken. ¹⁶ Everything depends on having faith in God, so that God's promise is assured by his great kindness. This promise isn't only for Abraham's descendants who have the Law. It is for all who are Abraham's descendants because they have faith, just as he did. Abraham is the ancestor of us all. ¹⁷ The Scriptures say that Abraham would become the ancestor of many nations. This promise was made to Abraham because he had faith in God, who raises the dead to life and creates new things.

¹⁸ God promised Abraham a lot of descendants. And when it all seemed hopeless, Abraham still had faith in God and became the ancestor of many nations. ¹⁹ Abraham's faith never became weak, not even when he was nearly a hundred years old. He knew that he was almost dead and that his wife Sarah could not have children. ²⁰ But Abraham never doubted or questioned God's promise. His faith made him strong, and he gave all the credit to God.

²¹ Abraham was certain that God could do what he had promised. ²² So God accepted him, ²³ just as we read in the Scriptures. But these words were not written only for Abraham. ²⁴ They were written for us, since we will also be accepted because of our faith in God, who raised our Lord Jesus to life. ²⁵ God gave Jesus to die for our sins, and he raised him to life, so that we would be made acceptable to God.

### What It Means To Be Acceptable to God

**5** By faith we have been made acceptable to God. And now, because of our Lord Jesus Christ, we live at peace[i] with God. ² Christ has also introduced us[j] to God's undeserved kindness, on which we take our stand. So we are happy, as we look forward to sharing in the glory of God. ³ But that's not all! We gladly suffer,[k] because we know that suffering helps us to endure. ⁴ And

---

[i]**5.1** *we live at peace*: Some manuscripts have "let us live at peace." [j]**5.2** *introduced us*: Some manuscripts add "by faith." [k]**5.3** *We gladly suffer*: Or "Let us gladly suffer."

endurance builds character, which gives us a hope [5]that will never disappoint us. All of this happens because God has given us the Holy Spirit, who fills our hearts with his love.

[6]Christ died for us at a time when we were helpless and sinful. [7]No one is really willing to die for an honest person, though someone might be willing to die for a truly good person. [8]But God showed how much he loved us by having Christ die for us, even though we were sinful.

[9]But there is more! Now that God has accepted us because Christ sacrificed his life's blood, we will also be kept safe from God's anger. [10]Even when we were God's enemies, he made peace with us, because his Son died for us. Yet something even greater than friendship is ours. Now that we are at peace with God, we will be saved by his Son's life. [11]And in addition to everything else, we are happy because God sent our Lord Jesus Christ to make peace with us.

### Adam and Christ

[12]Adam sinned, and that sin brought death into the world. Now everyone has sinned, and so everyone must die. [13]Sin was in the world before the Law came. But no record of sin was kept, because there was no Law. [14]Yet death still had power over all who lived from the time of Adam to the time of Moses. This happened, though not everyone disobeyed a direct command from God, as Adam did.

In some ways Adam is like Christ who came later. [15]But the gift that God was kind enough to give was very different from Adam's sin. That one sin brought death to many others. Yet in an even greater way, Jesus Christ alone brought God's gift of kindness to many people.

[16]There is a lot of difference between Adam's sin and God's gift. That one sin led to punishment. But God's gift made it possible for us to be acceptable to him, even though we have sinned many times. [17]Death ruled like a king because Adam had sinned. But that cannot compare with what Jesus Christ has done. God has been so kind to us,

and he has accepted us because of Jesus. And so we will live and rule like kings.

[18]Everyone was going to be punished because Adam sinned. But because of the good thing that Christ has done, God accepts us and gives us the gift of life. [19]Adam disobeyed God and caused many others to be sinners. But Jesus obeyed him and will make many people acceptable to God.

[20]The Law came, so that the full power of sin could be seen. Yet where sin was powerful, God's kindness was even more powerful. [21]Sin ruled by means of death. But God's kindness now rules, and God has accepted us because of Jesus Christ our Lord. This means that we will have eternal life.

### Dead to Sin but Alive because of Christ

**6** What should we say? Should we keep on sinning, so that God's wonderful kindness will show up even better? [2]No, we should not! If we are dead to sin, how can we go on sinning? [3]Don't you know that all who share in Christ Jesus by being baptized also share in his death? [4]When we were baptized, we died and were buried with Christ. We were baptized, so that we would live a new life, as Christ was raised to life by the glory of God the Father.

[5]If we shared in Jesus' death by being baptized, we will be raised to life with him. [6]We know that the persons we used to be were nailed to the cross with Jesus. This was done, so that our sinful bodies would no longer be the slaves of sin. [7]We know that sin doesn't have power over dead people.

[8]As surely as we died with Christ, we believe we will also live with him. [9]We know that death no longer has any power over Christ. He died and was raised to life, never again to die. [10]When Christ died, he died for sin once and for all. But now he is alive, and he lives only for God. [11]In the same way, you must think of yourselves as dead to the power of sin. But Christ Jesus has given life to you, and you live for God.

[12]Don't let sin rule your body. After

all, your body is bound to die, so don't obey its desires [13] or let any part of it become a slave of evil. Give yourselves to God, as people who have been raised from death to life. Make every part of your body a slave that pleases God. [14] Don't let sin keep ruling your lives. You are ruled by God's kindness and not by the Law.

### Slaves Who Do What Pleases God

[15] What does all this mean? Does it mean we are free to sin, because we are ruled by God's wonderful kindness and not by the Law? Certainly not! [16] Don't you know that you are slaves of anyone you obey? You can be slaves of sin and die, or you can be obedient slaves of God and be acceptable to him. [17] You used to be slaves of sin. But I thank God that with all your heart you obeyed the teaching you received from me. [18] Now you are set free from sin and are slaves who please God.

[19] I am using these everyday examples, because in some ways you are still weak. You used to let the different parts of your body be slaves of your evil thoughts. But now you must make every part of your body serve God, so that you will belong completely to him. [20] When you were slaves of sin, you didn't have to please God. [21] But what good did you receive from the things you did? All you have to show for them is your shame, and they lead to death. [22] Now you have been set free from sin, and you are God's slaves. This will make you holy and will lead you to eternal life. [23] Sin pays off with death. But God's gift is eternal life given by Jesus Christ our Lord.

### An Example from Marriage

**7** My friends, you surely understand enough about law to know that laws only have power over people who are alive. [2] For example, the Law says that a man's wife must remain his wife as long as he lives. But once her husband is dead, she is free [3] to marry someone else. However, if she goes off with another man while her husband is still alive, she is said to be unfaithful. [4] That is how it is with you, my friends. You are now part of the body of Christ and are dead to the power of the Law. You are free to belong to Christ, who was raised to life so that we could serve God. [5] When we thought only of ourselves, the Law made us have sinful desires. It made every part of our bodies into slaves who are doomed to die. [6] But the Law no longer rules over us. We are like dead people, and it cannot have any power over us. Now we can serve God in a new way by obeying his Spirit, and not in the old way by obeying the written Law.

### The Battle with Sin

[7] Does this mean that the Law is sinful? Certainly not! But if it had not been for the Law, I would not have known what sin is really like. For example, I would not have known what it means to want something that belongs to someone else, unless the Law had told me not to do that. [8] It was sin that used this command as a way of making me have all kinds of desires. But without the Law, sin is dead.

[9] Before I knew about the Law, I was alive. But as soon as I heard that command, sin came to life, [10] and I died. The very command that was supposed to bring life to me, instead brought death. [11] Sin used this command to trick me, and because of it I died. [12] Still, the Law and its commands are holy and correct and good.

[13] Am I saying that something good caused my death? Certainly not! It was sin that killed me by using something good. Now we can see how terrible and evil sin really is. [14] We know that the Law is spiritual. But I am merely a human, and I have been sold as a slave to sin. [15] In fact, I don't understand why I act the way I do. I don't do what I know is right. I do the things I hate. [16] Although I don't do what I know is right, I agree that the Law is good. [17] So I am not the one doing these evil things. The sin that lives in me is what does them.

[18] I know that my selfish desires won't let me do anything that is good. Even when I want to do right, I cannot. [19] Instead of doing what I know is right, I do wrong. [20] And so, if I don't do what

I know is right, I am no longer the one doing these evil things. The sin that lives in me is what does them.

21 The Law has shown me that something in me keeps me from doing what I know is right. 22 With my whole heart I agree with the Law of God. 23 But in every part of me I discover something fighting against my mind, and it makes me a prisoner of sin that controls everything I do. 24 What a miserable person I am. Who will rescue me from this body that is doomed to die? 25 Thank God! Jesus Christ will rescue me.

So with my mind I serve the Law of God, although my selfish desires make me serve the law of sin.

### Living by the Power of God's Spirit

8 If you belong to Christ Jesus, you won't be punished. 2 The Holy Spirit will give you life that comes from Christ Jesus and will set you[l] free from sin and death. 3 The Law of Moses cannot do this, because our selfish desires make the Law weak. But God set you free when he sent his own Son to be like us sinners and to be a sacrifice for our sin. God used Christ's body to condemn sin. 4 He did this, so that we would do what the Law commands by obeying the Spirit instead of our own desires.

5 People who are ruled by their desires think only of themselves. Everyone who is ruled by the Holy Spirit thinks about spiritual things. 6 If our minds are ruled by our desires, we will die. But if our minds are ruled by the Spirit, we will have life and peace. 7 Our desires fight against God, because they do not and cannot obey God's laws. 8 If we follow our desires, we cannot please God.

9 You are no longer ruled by your desires, but by God's Spirit, who lives in you. People who don't have the Spirit of Christ in them don't belong to him. 10 But Christ lives in you. So you are alive because God has accepted you,

even though your bodies must die because of your sins. 11 Yet God raised Jesus to life! God's Spirit now lives in you, and he will raise you to life by his Spirit.

12 My dear friends, we must not live to satisfy our desires. 13 If you do, you will die. But you will live, if by the help of God's Spirit you say "No" to your desires. 14 Only those people who are led by God's Spirit are his children. 15 God's Spirit doesn't make us slaves who are afraid of him. Instead, we become his children and call him our Father.[m] 16 God's Spirit makes us sure that we are his children. 17 His Spirit lets us know that together with Christ we will be given what God has promised. We will also share in the glory of Christ, because we have suffered with him.

### A Wonderful Future for God's People

18 I am sure that what we are suffering now cannot compare with the glory that will be shown to us. 19 In fact, all creation is eagerly waiting for God to show who his children are. 20 Meanwhile, creation is confused, but not because it wants to be confused. God made it this way in the hope 21 that creation would be set free from decay and would share in the glorious freedom of his children. 22 We know that all creation is still groaning and is in pain, like a woman about to give birth.

23 The Spirit makes us sure about what we will be in the future. But now we groan silently, while we wait for God to show that we are his children.[n] This means that our bodies will also be set free. 24 And this hope is what saves us. But if we already have what we hope for, there is no need to keep on hoping. 25 However, we hope for something we have not yet seen, and we patiently wait for it.

26 In certain ways we are weak, but the Spirit is here to help us. For example, when we don't know what to pray

---

[l]8.2 you: Some manuscripts have "me." [m]8.15 our Father: The Greek text uses the Aramaic word "Abba" (meaning "father"), which shows the close relation between the children and their father. [n]8.23 to show that we are his children: These words are not in some manuscripts. The translation of the remainder of the verse would then read, "while we wait for God to set our bodies free."

for, the Spirit prays for us in ways that cannot be put into words. 27 All of our thoughts are known to God. He can understand what is in the mind of the Spirit, as the Spirit prays for God's people. 28 We know that God is always at work for the good of everyone who loves him. o They are the ones God has chosen for his purpose, 29 and he has always known who his chosen ones would be. He had decided to let them become like his own Son, so that his Son would be the first of many children. 30 God then accepted the people he had already decided to choose, and he has shared his glory with them.

## God's Love

31 What can we say about all this? If God is on our side, can anyone be against us? 32 God did not keep back his own Son, but he gave him for us. If God did this, won't he freely give us everything else? 33 If God says his chosen ones are acceptable to him, can anyone bring charges against them? 34 Or can anyone condemn them? No indeed! Christ died and was raised to life, and now he is at God's right side, p speaking to him for us. 35 Can anything separate us from the love of Christ? Can trouble, suffering, and hard times, or hunger and nakedness, or danger and death? 36 It is exactly as the Scriptures say,

"For you we face death
all day long.
We are like sheep
on their way
to be butchered."

37 In everything we have won more than a victory because of Christ who loves us. 38 I am sure that nothing can separate us from God's love—not life or death, not angels or spirits, not the present or the future, 39 and not powers above or powers below. Nothing in all

creation can separate us from God's love for us in Christ Jesus our Lord!

## God's Choice of Israel

**9** I am a follower of Christ, and the Holy Spirit is a witness to my conscience. So I tell the truth and I am not lying when I say 2 my heart is broken and I am in great sorrow. 3 I would gladly be placed under God's curse and be separated from Christ for the good of my own people. 4 They are the descendants of Israel, and they are also God's chosen people. God showed them his glory. He made agreements with them and gave them his Law. The temple is theirs and so are the promises that God made to them. 5 They have those famous ancestors, who were also the ancestors of Jesus Christ. I pray that God, who rules over all, will be praised forever! q Amen.

6 It cannot be said that God broke his promise. After all, not all of the people of Israel are the true people of God. 7-8 In fact, when God made the promise to Abraham, he meant only Abraham's descendants by his son Isaac. God was talking only about Isaac when he promised 9 Sarah, "At this time next year I will return, and you will already have a son."

10 Don't forget what happened to the twin sons of Isaac and Rebecca. 11-12 Even before they were born or had done anything good or bad, the Lord told Rebecca that her older son would serve the younger one. The Lord said this to show that he makes his own choices and that it wasn't because of anything either of them had done. 13 That's why the Scriptures say that the Lord liked Jacob more than Esau. 14 Are we saying that God is unfair? Certainly not! 15 The Lord told Moses that he has pity and mercy on anyone he wants to. 16 Everything then depends on God's mercy and not on what people want or do. 17 In the Scriptures the Lord

o**8.28** *God is always at work for the good of everyone who loves him*: Or "All things work for the good of everyone who loves God" or "God's Spirit always works for the good of everyone who loves God." p**8.34** *right side*: The place of power and honor. q**9.5** *Christ. I pray that God, who rules over all, will be praised forever*: Or "Christ, who rules over all. I pray that God will be praised forever" or "Christ. And I pray that Christ, who is God and rules over all, will be praised forever."

says to the king of Egypt, "I let you become king, so that I could show you my power and be praised by all people on earth." [18] Everything depends on what God decides to do, and he can either have pity on people or make them stubborn.

## God's Anger and Mercy

[19] Someone may ask, "How can God blame us, if he makes us behave in the way he wants us to?" [20] But, my friend, I ask, "Who do you think you are to question God? Does the clay have the right to ask the potter why he shaped it the way he did? [21] Doesn't a potter have the right to make a fancy bowl and a plain bowl out of the same lump of clay?"

[22] God wanted to show his anger and reveal his power against everyone who deserved to be destroyed. But instead, he patiently put up with them. [23] He did this by showing how glorious he is when he has pity on the people he has chosen to share in his glory. [24] Whether Jews or Gentiles, we are those chosen ones, [25] just as the Lord says in the book of Hosea,

"Although they are not
my people,
  I will make them my people.
I will treat with love
those nations
  that have never been loved.

[26] "Once they were told,
  'You are not my people.'
But in that very place
they will be called
  children of the living God."

[27] And this is what the prophet Isaiah said about the people of Israel,

"The people of Israel
are as many
as the grains of sand
  along the beach.
But only a few who are left
  will be saved.

[28] The Lord will be quick
  and sure to do on earth
what he has warned
  he will do."

[29] Isaiah also said,

"If the Lord All-Powerful
had not spared some
  of our descendants,
we would have been destroyed
like the cities of Sodom
  and Gomorrah." [r]

## Israel and the Good News

[30] What does all of this mean? It means that the Gentiles were not trying to be acceptable to God, but they found that he would accept them if they had faith. [31-32] It also means that the people of Israel were not acceptable to God. And why not? It was because they were trying [s] to be acceptable by obeying the Law instead of by having faith in God. The people of Israel fell over the stone that makes people stumble, [33] just as God says in the Scriptures,

"Look! I am placing in Zion
a stone to make people
  stumble and fall.
But those who have faith
in that one will never
  be disappointed."

**10** Dear friends, my greatest wish and my prayer to God is for the people of Israel to be saved. [2] I know they love God, but they don't understand [3] what makes people acceptable to him. So they refuse to trust God, and they try to be acceptable by obeying the Law. [4] But Christ makes the Law no longer necessary [t] for those who become acceptable to God by faith.

## Anyone Can Be Saved

[5] Moses said that a person could become acceptable to God by obeying the Law. He did this when he wrote, "If you want to live, you must do all that the Law commands."

[r]9.29 *Sodom and Gomorrah*: During the time of Abraham the Lord destroyed these two cities because their people were so sinful.   [s]9.31 *because they were trying*: Or "while they were trying" or "even though they were trying."   [t]10.4 *But Christ makes the Law no longer necessary*: Or "But Christ gives the full meaning to the Law."

⁶But people whose faith makes them acceptable to God will never ask, "Who will go up to heaven to bring Christ down?" ⁷Neither will they ask, "Who will go down into the world of the dead to raise him to life?"

⁸All who are acceptable because of their faith simply say, "The message is as near as your mouth or your heart." And this is the same message we preach about faith. ⁹So you will be saved, if you honestly say, "Jesus is Lord," and if you believe with all your heart that God raised him from death. ¹⁰God will accept you and save you, if you truly believe this and tell it to others.

¹¹The Scriptures say that no one who has faith will be disappointed, ¹²no matter if that person is a Jew or a Gentile. There is only one Lord, and he is generous to everyone who asks for his help. ¹³All who call out to the Lord will be saved.

¹⁴How can people have faith in the Lord and ask him to save them, if they have never heard about him? And how can they hear, unless someone tells them? ¹⁵And how can anyone tell them without being sent by the Lord? The Scriptures say it is a beautiful sight to see even the feet of someone coming to preach the good news. ¹⁶Yet not everyone has believed the message. For example, the prophet Isaiah asked, "Lord, has anyone believed what we said?"

¹⁷No one can have faith without hearing the message about Christ. ¹⁸But am I saying that the people of Israel did not hear? No, I am not! The Scriptures say,

"The message was told
    everywhere on earth.
It was announced
    all over the world."

¹⁹Did the people of Israel understand or not? Moses answered this question when he told that the Lord had said,

"I will make Israel jealous
    of people
who are a nation
    of nobodies.
I will make them angry
    at people

who don't understand
    a thing."

²⁰Isaiah was fearless enough to tell that the Lord had said,

"I was found by people
who were not looking
    for me.
I appeared to the ones
who were not asking
    about me."

²¹And Isaiah said about the people of Israel,

"All day long the Lord
    has reached out
to people who are stubborn
    and refuse to obey."

## God Has Not Rejected His People

**11** Am I saying that God has turned his back on his people? Certainly not! I am one of the people of Israel, and I myself am a descendant of Abraham from the tribe of Benjamin. ²God did not turn his back on his chosen people. Don't you remember reading in the Scriptures how Elijah complained to God about the people of Israel? ³He said, "Lord, they killed your prophets and destroyed your altars. I am the only one left, and now they want to kill me."

⁴But the Lord told Elijah, "I still have seven thousand followers who have not worshiped Baal." ⁵It is the same way now. God was kind to the people of Israel, and so a few of them are still his followers. ⁶This happened because of God's undeserved kindness and not because of anything they have done. It could not have happened except for God's kindness.

⁷This means that only a chosen few of the people of Israel found what all of them were searching for. And the rest of them were stubborn, ⁸just as the Scriptures say,

"God made them so stupid
    that their eyes are blind,
and their ears
    are still deaf."

⁹Then David said,

"Turn their meals
    into bait for a trap,

so that they will stumble
and be given
    what they deserve.
10 Blindfold their eyes!
    Don't let them see.
Bend their backs
beneath a burden
    that will never be lifted."

### Gentiles Will Be Saved

11 Do I mean that the people of Israel fell, never to get up again? Certainly not! Their failure made it possible for the Gentiles to be saved, and this will make the people of Israel jealous. 12 But if the rest of the world's people were helped so much by Israel's sin and loss, they will be helped even more by their full return.

13 I am now speaking to you Gentiles, and as long as I am an apostle to you, I will take pride in my work. 14 I hope in this way to make some of my own people jealous enough to be saved. 15 When Israel rejected God,ᵘ the rest of the people in the world were able to turn to him. So when God makes friends with Israel, it will be like bringing the dead back to life. 16 If part of a batch of dough is made holy by being offered to God, then all of the dough is holy. If the roots of a tree are holy, the rest of the tree is holy too.

17 You Gentiles are like branches of a wild olive tree that were made to be part of a cultivated olive tree. You have taken the place of some branches that were cut away from it. And because of this, you enjoy the blessings that come from being part of that cultivated tree. 18 But don't think you are better than the branches that were cut away. Just remember that you are not supporting the roots of that tree. Its roots are supporting you.

19 Maybe you think those branches were cut away, so that you could be put in their place. 20 That's true enough. But they were cut away because they did not have faith, and you are where you are because you do have faith. So don't be proud, but be afraid.

21 If God cut away those natural branches, couldn't he do the same to you?

22 Now you see both how kind and how hard God can be. He was hard on those who fell, but he was kind to you. And he will keep on being kind to you, if you keep on trusting in his kindness. Otherwise, you will be cut away too.

23 If those other branches will start having faith, they will be made a part of that tree again. God has the power to put them back. 24 After all, it wasn't natural for branches to be cut from a wild olive tree and to be made part of a cultivated olive tree. So it is much more likely that God will join the natural branches back to the cultivated olive tree.

### The People of Israel Will Be Brought Back

25 My friends, I don't want you Gentiles to be too proud of yourselves. So I will explain the mystery of what has happened to the people of Israel. Some of them have become stubborn, and they will stay like that until the complete number of you Gentiles has come in. 26 In this way all of Israel will be saved, as the Scriptures say,

"From Zion someone will come
    to rescue us.
Then Jacob's descendants
    will stop being evil.
27 This is what the Lord
    has promised to do
when he forgives their sins."

28 The people of Israel are treated as God's enemies, so that the good news can come to you Gentiles. But they are still the chosen ones, and God loves them because of their famous ancestors. 29 God doesn't take back the gifts he has given or forget about the people he has chosen.

30 At one time you Gentiles rejected God. But now Israel has rejected God, and you have been shown mercy. 31 And because of the mercy shown to

ᵘ11.15 *When Israel rejected God:* Or "When Israel was rejected."

you, they will also be shown mercy.
<sup></sup>³²All people have disobeyed God, and
that's why he treats them as prisoners.
But he does this, so that he can have
mercy on all of them.

³³Who can measure the wealth and
wisdom and knowledge of God? Who
can understand his decisions or explain
what he does?

³⁴ "Has anyone known
the thoughts of the Lord
or given him advice?
³⁵ Has anyone loaned
something to the Lord
that must be repaid?"

³⁶Everything comes from the Lord. All
things were made because of him and
will return to him. Praise the Lord forever! Amen.

### Christ Brings New Life

**12** Dear friends, God is good. So I
beg you to offer your bodies to
him as a living sacrifice, pure and
pleasing. That's the most sensible way
to serve God. ²Don't be like the people
of this world, but let God change the
way you think. Then you will know
how to do everything that is good and
pleasing to him.

³I realize how kind God has been to
me, and so I tell each of you not to think
you are better than you really are. Use
good sense and measure yourself by
the amount of faith that God has given
you. ⁴A body is made up of many parts,
and each of them has its own use.
⁵That's how it is with us. There are
many of us, but we each are part of
the body of Christ, as well as part of
one another.

⁶God has also given each of us different gifts to use. If we can prophesy, we
should do it according to the amount
of faith we have. ⁷If we can serve others, we should serve. If we can teach,
we should teach. ⁸If we can encourage
others, we should encourage them. If
we can give, we should be generous.
If we are leaders, we should do our
best. If we are good to others, we
should do it cheerfully.

### Rules for Christian Living

⁹Be sincere in your love for others.
Hate everything that is evil and hold
tight to everything that is good. ¹⁰Love
each other as brothers and sisters and
honor others more than you do yourself. ¹¹Never give up. Eagerly follow
the Holy Spirit and serve the Lord.
¹²Let your hope make you glad. Be patient in time of trouble and never stop
praying. ¹³Take care of God's needy
people and welcome strangers into
your home.

¹⁴Ask God to bless everyone who
mistreats you. Ask him to bless them
and not to curse them. ¹⁵When others
are happy, be happy with them, and
when they are sad, be sad. ¹⁶Be
friendly with everyone. Don't be proud
and feel that you are smarter than others. Make friends with ordinary peo-
ple.ᵛ ¹⁷Don't mistreat someone who
has mistreated you. But try to earn the
respect of others, ¹⁸and do your best
to live at peace with everyone.

¹⁹Dear friends, don't try to get even.
Let God take revenge. In the Scriptures
the Lord says,

"I am the one to take revenge
and pay them back."

²⁰The Scriptures also say,

"If your enemies are hungry,
give them something to eat.
And if they are thirsty,
give them something
to drink.
This will be the same
as piling burning coals
on their heads."

²¹Don't let evil defeat you, but defeat
evil with good.

### Obey Rulers

**13** Obey the rulers who have authority over you. Only God can
give authority to anyone, and he puts
these rulers in their places of power.
²People who oppose the authorities are
opposing what God has done, and they
will be punished. ³Rulers are a threat
to evil people, not to good people.

ᵛ **12.16** *Make friends with ordinary people*: Or "Do ordinary jobs."

There is no need to be afraid of the authorities. Just do right, and they will praise you for it. ⁴After all, they are God's servants, and it is their duty to help you.

If you do something wrong, you ought to be afraid, because these rulers have the right to punish you. They are God's servants who punish criminals to show how angry God is. ⁵But you should obey the rulers because you know it is the right thing to do, and not just because of God's anger.

⁶You must also pay your taxes. The authorities are God's servants, and it is their duty to take care of these matters. ⁷Pay all that you owe, whether it is taxes and fees or respect and honor.

## Love

⁸Let love be your only debt! If you love others, you have done all that the Law demands. ⁹In the Law there are many commands, such as, "Be faithful in marriage. Do not murder. Do not steal. Do not want what belongs to others." But all of these are summed up in the command that says, "Love others as much as you love yourself." ¹⁰No one who loves others will harm them. So love is all that the Law demands.

## The Day When Christ Returns

¹¹You know what sort of times we live in, and so you should live properly. It is time to wake up. You know that the day when we will be saved is nearer now than when we first put our faith in the Lord. ¹²Night is almost over, and day will soon appear. We must stop behaving as people do in the dark and be ready to live in the light. ¹³So behave properly, as people do in the day. Don't go to wild parties or get drunk or be vulgar or indecent. Don't quarrel or be jealous. ¹⁴Let the Lord Jesus Christ be as near to you as the clothes you wear. Then you won't try to satisfy your selfish desires.

## Don't Criticize Others

**14** Welcome all the Lord's followers, even those whose faith is weak. Don't criticize them for having

beliefs that are different from yours. ²Some think it is all right to eat anything, while those whose faith is weak will eat only vegetables. ³But you should not criticize others for eating or for not eating. After all, God welcomes everyone. ⁴What right do you have to criticize someone else's servants? Only their Lord can decide if they are doing right, and the Lord will make sure that they do right.

⁵Some of the Lord's followers think one day is more important than another. Others think all days are the same. But each of you should make up your own mind. ⁶Any followers who count one day more important than another day do it to honor their Lord. And any followers who eat meat give thanks to God, just like the ones who don't eat meat.

⁷Whether we live or die, it must be for God, rather than for ourselves. ⁸Whether we live or die, it must be for the Lord. Alive or dead, we still belong to the Lord. ⁹This is because Christ died and rose to life, so that he would be the Lord of the dead and of the living. ¹⁰Why do you criticize other followers of the Lord? Why do you look down on them? The day is coming when God will judge all of us. ¹¹In the Scriptures God says,

"I swear by my very life
that everyone will kneel down
and praise my name!"

¹²And so, each of us must give an account to God for what we do.

## Don't Cause Problems for Others

¹³We must stop judging others. We must also make up our minds not to upset anyone's faith. ¹⁴The Lord Jesus has made it clear to me that God considers all foods fit to eat. But if you think some foods are unfit to eat, then for you they are not fit.

¹⁵If you are hurting others by the foods you eat, you are not guided by love. Don't let your appetite destroy someone Christ died for. ¹⁶Don't let your right to eat bring shame to Christ. ¹⁷God's kingdom isn't about eating and drinking. It is about pleasing God, about living in peace, and about true

happiness. All this comes from the Holy Spirit. [18] If you serve Christ in this way, you will please God and be respected by people. [19] We should try[w] to live at peace and help each other have a strong faith.

[20] Don't let your appetite destroy what God has done. All foods are fit to eat, but it is wrong to cause problems for others by what you eat. [21] It is best not to eat meat or drink wine or do anything else that causes problems for other followers of the Lord. [22] What you believe about these things should be kept between you and God. You are fortunate, if your actions don't make you have doubts. [23] But if you do have doubts about what you eat, you are going against your beliefs. And you know that is wrong, because anything you do against your beliefs is sin.

## Please Others and Not Yourself

**15** If our faith is strong, we should be patient with the Lord's followers whose faith is weak. We should try to please them instead of ourselves. [2] We should think of their good and try to help them by doing what pleases them. [3] Even Christ did not try to please himself. But as the Scriptures say, "The people who insulted you also insulted me." [4] And the Scriptures were written to teach and encourage us by giving us hope. [5] God is the one who makes us patient and cheerful. I pray that he will help you live at peace with each other, as you follow Christ. [6] Then all of you together will praise God, the Father of our Lord Jesus Christ.

## The Good News Is for Jews and Gentiles

[7] Honor God by accepting each other, as Christ has accepted you. [8] I tell you that Christ came as a servant of the Jews to show that God has kept the promises he made to their famous ancestors. Christ also came, [9] so that the Gentiles would praise God for being kind to them. It is just as the Scriptures say,

"I will tell the nations
  about you,
and I will sing praises
  to your name."

[10] The Scriptures also say to the Gentiles, "Come and celebrate with God's people."

[11] Again the Scriptures say,

"Praise the Lord,
  all you Gentiles.
All you nations, come
  and worship him."

[12] Isaiah says,

"Someone from David's family
  will come to power.
He will rule the nations,
  and they will put their hope
  in him."

[13] I pray that God, who gives hope, will bless you with complete happiness and peace because of your faith. And may the power of the Holy Spirit fill you with hope.

## Paul's Work as a Missionary

[14] My friends, I am sure that you are very good and that you have all the knowledge you need to teach each other. [15] But I have spoken to you plainly and have tried to remind you of some things. God was so kind to me! [16] He chose me to be a servant of Christ Jesus for the Gentiles and to do the work of a priest in the service of his good news. God did this so that the Holy Spirit could make the Gentiles into a holy offering, pleasing to him.

[17] Because of Christ Jesus, I can take pride in my service for God. [18] In fact, all I will talk about is how Christ let me speak and work, so that the Gentiles would obey him. [19] Indeed, I will tell how Christ worked miracles and wonders by the power of the Holy Spirit. I have preached the good news about him all the way from Jerusalem to Illyricum. [20] But I have always tried to preach where people have never heard about Christ. I am like a builder who doesn't build on anyone else's

---

w 14.19 *We should try*: Some manuscripts have "We try."

foundation. [21] It is just as the Scriptures say,

"All who haven't been told about him
will see him,
and those who haven't heard about him
will understand."

## Paul's Plan To Visit Rome

[22] My work has always kept me from coming to see you. [23] Now there is nothing left for me to do in this part of the world, and for years I have wanted to visit you. [24] So I plan to stop off on my way to Spain. Then after a short, but refreshing, visit with you, I hope you will quickly send me on. [25-26] I am now on my way to Jerusalem to deliver the money that the Lord's followers in Macedonia and Achaia collected for God's needy people. [27] This is something they really wanted to do. But sharing their money with the Jews was also like paying back a debt, because the Jews had already shared their spiritual blessings with the Gentiles. [28] After I have safely delivered this money, I will visit you and then go on to Spain. [29] And when I do arrive in Rome, I know it will be with the full blessings of Christ.

[30] My friends, by the power of the Lord Jesus Christ and by the love that comes from the Holy Spirit, I beg you to pray sincerely with me and for me. [31] Pray that God will protect me from the unbelievers in Judea, and that his people in Jerusalem will be pleased with what I am doing. [32] Ask God to let me come to you and have a pleasant and refreshing visit. [33] I pray that God, who gives peace, will be with all of you. Amen.

## Personal Greetings

**16** I have good things to say about Phoebe, who is a leader in the church at Cenchreae. [2] Welcome her in a way that is proper for someone who has faith in the Lord and is one of God's own people. Help her in any way you can. After all, she has proved to be a respected leader for many others, including me.

[3] Give my greetings to Priscilla and Aquila. They have not only served Christ Jesus together with me, [4] but they have even risked their lives for me. I am grateful for them and so are all the Gentile churches. [5] Greet the church that meets in their home.

Greet my dear friend Epaenetus, who was the first person in Asia to have faith in Christ.

[6] Greet Mary, who has worked so hard for you.

[7] Greet my relatives[x] Andronicus and Junias, who were in jail with me. They are highly respected by the apostles and were followers of Christ before I was.

[8] Greet Ampliatus, my dear friend whose faith is in the Lord.

[9] Greet Urbanus, who serves Christ along with us.

Greet my dear friend Stachys.

[10] Greet Apelles, a faithful servant of Christ.

Greet Aristobulus and his family.

[11] Greet Herodion, who is a relative[x] of mine.

Greet Narcissus and the others in his family, who have faith in the Lord.

[12] Greet Tryphaena and Tryphosa, who work hard for the Lord.

Greet my dear friend Persis. She also works hard for the Lord.

[13] Greet Rufus, that special servant of the Lord, and greet his mother, who has been like a mother to me.

[14] Greet Asyncritus, Phlegon, Hermes, Patrobas, and Hermas, as well as our friends who are with them.

[15] Greet Philologus, Julia, Nereus and his sister, and Olympas, and all of God's people who are with them.

[16] Be sure to give each other a warm greeting.

All of Christ's churches greet you.

[17] My friends, I beg you to watch out for anyone who causes trouble and divides the church by refusing to do what all of you were taught. Stay away from them! [18] They want to serve themselves and not Christ the Lord. Their flattery and fancy talk fool people who don't

x **16.7** *relative(s)*: Or "Jewish friend(s)." x **16.11** *relative(s)*: Or "Jewish friend(s)."

know any better. [19] I am glad that everyone knows how well you obey the Lord. But still, I want you to understand what is good and not have anything to do with evil. [20] Then God, who gives peace, will soon crush Satan under your feet. I pray that our Lord Jesus will be kind to you.

[21] Timothy, who works with me, sends his greetings, and so do my relatives,[x] Lucius, Jason, and Sosipater.

[22] I, Tertius, also send my greetings. I am a follower of the Lord, and I wrote this letter.[y]

[23-24] Gaius welcomes me and the whole church into his home, and he sends his greetings.

Erastus, the city treasurer, and our dear friend Quartus send their greetings too.[z]

### Paul's Closing Prayer

[25] Praise God! He can make you strong by means of my good news, which is the message about[a] Jesus Christ. For ages and ages this message was kept secret, [26] but now at last it has been told. The eternal God commanded his prophets to write about the good news, so that all nations would obey and have faith. [27] And now, because of Jesus Christ, we can praise the only wise God forever! Amen.[b]

[x] 16.21 *relative(s)*: Or "Jewish friend(s)."   [y] 16.22 *I wrote this letter*: Paul probably dictated this letter to Tertius.   [z] 16.23,24 *send their greetings too*: Some manuscripts add, "I pray that our Lord Jesus Christ will always be kind to you. Amen."   [a] 16.25 *about*: Or "from."   [b] 16.27 *Amen*: Some manuscripts have verses 25-27 after 14.23. Others have the verses here and after 14.23, and one manuscript has them after 15.33.

# 1 CORINTHIANS

## ABOUT THIS LETTER

Although this letter is called the First Letter to the Corinthians, it is not really the first one that Paul wrote to this church. We know this because he mentions in this letter that he had written one before (5.9). The Christians in Corinth had also written to him (7.1), and part of First Corinthians contains Paul's answers to questions they had asked.

Corinth is a large port city in southern Greece. Paul began his work there in a Jewish meeting place, but he had to move next door to the home of a Gentile who had become a follower of Jesus (Acts 18.1-17). Most of the followers in Corinth were poor people (1 Corinthians 1.26-29), though some of them were wealthy (1 Corinthians 11.18-21), and one was even the city treasurer (Romans 16.23). While he was in Corinth, Paul worked as a tentmaker to earn a living (Acts 18.3; 1 Corinthians 4.12; 9.1-18).

Paul was especially concerned about the way the Corinthian Christians were always arguing and dividing themselves into groups (1.10—4.21) and about the way they treated one another (5.1—6.20). These are two of Paul's main concerns as he writes this letter. But he also wants to answer the questions they asked him about marriage (7.1-40) and food offered to idols (8.1-13). Paul encourages them to worship God the right way (10.1—14.40) and to be firm in their belief that God has given them victory over death (15.1-58).

Love, Paul tells them, is even more important than faith or hope. All of the problems in the church could be solved, if all the members would love one another, as Christians should:

> Love is kind and patient,
> never jealous, boastful,
>     proud, or rude.
> Love rejoices in the truth,
>     but not in evil.
> Love is always supportive,
> loyal, hopeful,
>     and trusting.
> Love never fails!
>                     (13.4, 5, 6-8)

## A QUICK LOOK AT THIS LETTER

**1** From Paul, chosen by God to be an apostle of Christ Jesus, and from Sosthenes, who is also a follower.

² To God's church in Corinth. Christ Jesus chose you to be his very own people, and you worship in his name, as we and all others do who call him Lord.

³ My prayer is that God our Father and the Lord Jesus Christ will be kind to you and will bless you with peace!

⁴ I never stop thanking my God for being kind enough to give you Christ Jesus, ⁵ who helps you speak and understand so well. ⁶ Now you are certain that everything we told you about our Lord Christ Jesus is true. ⁷ You are not missing out on any blessings, as you wait for him to return. ⁸ And until the day Christ does return, he will keep you completely innocent. ⁹ God can be trusted, and he chose you to be partners with his Son, our Lord Jesus Christ.

### Taking Sides

¹⁰ My dear friends, as a follower of our Lord Jesus Christ, I beg you to get along with each other. Don't take sides. Always try to agree in what you think. ¹¹ Several people from Chloe's family*a* have already reported to me that you keep arguing with each other. ¹² They have said that some of you claim to follow me, while others claim to follow Apollos or Peter*b* or Christ.

¹³ Has Christ been divided up? Was I nailed to a cross for you? Were you baptized in my name? ¹⁴ I thank God*c* that I didn't baptize any of you except Crispus and Gaius. ¹⁵ Not one of you can say that you were baptized in my name. ¹⁶ I did baptize the family*d* of Stephanas, but I don't remember if I baptized anyone else. ¹⁷ Christ did not send me to baptize. He sent me to tell the good news without using big words that would make the cross of Christ lose its power.

### Christ Is God's Power and Wisdom

¹⁸ The message about the cross doesn't make any sense to lost people. But for those of us who are being saved, it is God's power at work. ¹⁹ As God says in the Scriptures,

"I will destroy the wisdom
of all who claim
  to be wise.
I will confuse those
who think they know
  so much."

²⁰ What happened to those wise people? What happened to those experts in the Scriptures? What happened to the ones who think they have all the answers? Didn't God show that the wisdom of this world is foolish? ²¹ God was wise and decided not to let the people of this world use their wisdom to learn about him.

Instead, God chose to save only those who believe the foolish message we preach. ²² Jews ask for miracles, and Greeks want something that sounds wise. ²³ But we preach that Christ was nailed to a cross. Most Jews have problems with this, and most Gentiles think it is foolish. ²⁴ Our message is God's power and wisdom for the Jews and the Greeks that he has chosen. ²⁵ Even when God is foolish, he is wiser than everyone else, and even when God is weak, he is stronger than everyone else.

²⁶ My dear friends, remember what you were when God chose you. The people of this world didn't think that many of you were wise. Only a few of you were in places of power, and not many of you came from important families. ²⁷ But God chose the foolish things of this world to put the wise to shame. He chose the weak things of this world to put the powerful to shame. ²⁸ What the world thinks is worthless, useless, and nothing at all is what God has used to destroy what the world considers important. ²⁹ God did all this to keep anyone from bragging to him.

---

*a* **1.11** *family*: Family members and possibly slaves and others who may have lived in the house. *b* **1.12** *Peter*: The Greek text has "Cephas," which is an Aramaic name meaning "rock." Peter is the Greek name with the same meaning. *c* **1.14** *I thank God*: Some manuscripts have "I thank my God." *d* **1.16** *family*: See the note at 1.11.

[30] You are God's children. He sent Christ Jesus to save us and to make us wise, acceptable, and holy. [31] So if you want to brag, do what the Scriptures say and brag about the Lord.

## Telling about Christ and the Cross

2 Friends, when I came and told you the mystery[e] that God had shared with us, I didn't use big words or try to sound wise. [2] In fact, while I was with you, I made up my mind to speak only about Jesus Christ, who had been nailed to a cross.

[3] At first, I was weak and trembling with fear. [4] When I talked with you or preached, I didn't try to prove anything by sounding wise. I simply let God's Spirit show his power. [5] That way you would have faith because of God's power and not because of human wisdom.

[6] We do use wisdom when speaking to people who are mature in their faith. But it isn't the wisdom of this world or of its rulers, who will soon disappear. [7] We speak of God's hidden and mysterious wisdom that God decided to use for our glory long before the world began. [8] The rulers of this world didn't know anything about this wisdom. If they had known about it, they would not have nailed the glorious Lord to a cross. [9] But it is just as the Scriptures say,

"What God has planned
   for people who love him
is more than eyes have seen
   or ears have heard.
It has never even
   entered our minds!"

[10] God's Spirit has shown you everything. His Spirit finds out everything, even what is deep in the mind of God. [11] You are the only one who knows what is in your own mind, and God's Spirit is the only one who knows what is in God's mind. [12] But God has given us his Spirit. That's why we don't think the same way that the people of this world think. That's also why we can recognize the blessings that God has given us.

[13] Every word we speak was taught to us by God's Spirit, not by human wisdom. And this same Spirit helps us teach spiritual things to spiritual people.[f] [14] That's why only someone who has God's Spirit can understand spiritual blessings. Anyone who doesn't have God's Spirit thinks these blessings are foolish. [15] People who are guided by the Spirit can make all kinds of judgments, but they cannot be judged by others. [16] The Scriptures ask,

"Has anyone ever known
   the thoughts of the Lord
   or given him advice?"

But we understand what Christ is thinking.[g]

## Working Together for God

3 My friends, you are acting like the people of this world. That's why I could not speak to you as spiritual people. You are like babies as far as your faith in Christ is concerned. [2] So I had to treat you like babies and feed you milk. You could not take solid food, and you still cannot, [3] because you are not yet spiritual. You are jealous and argue with each other. This proves that you are not spiritual and that you are acting like the people of this world.

[4] Some of you say that you follow me, and others claim to follow Apollos. Isn't that how ordinary people behave? [5] Apollos and I are merely servants who helped you to have faith. It was the Lord who made it all happen. [6] I planted the seeds, Apollos watered them, but God made them sprout and grow. [7] What matters isn't those who planted or watered, but God who made the plants grow. [8] The one who plants is just as important as the one who waters. And each one will be paid for what they do. [9] Apollos and I work together for God, and you are God's garden and God's building.

---

[e]2.1 *mystery*: Some manuscripts have "testimony." [f]2.13 *teach spiritual things to spiritual people*: Or "compare spiritual things with spiritual things." [g]2.16 *we understand what Christ is thinking*: Or "we think as Christ does."

## Only One Foundation

¹⁰ God was kind and let me become an expert builder. I laid a foundation on which others have built. But we must each be careful how we build, ¹¹ because Christ is the only foundation. ¹²⁻¹³ Whatever we build on that foundation will be tested by fire on the day of judgment. Then everyone will find out if we have used gold, silver, and precious stones, or wood, hay, and straw. ¹⁴ We will be rewarded if our building is left standing. ¹⁵ But if it is destroyed by the fire, we will lose everything. Yet we ourselves will be saved, like someone escaping from flames.

¹⁶ All of you surely know that you are God's temple and that his Spirit lives in you. ¹⁷ Together you are God's holy temple, and God will destroy anyone who destroys his temple.

¹⁸ Don't fool yourselves! If any of you think you are wise in the things of this world, you will have to become foolish before you can be truly wise. ¹⁹ This is because God considers the wisdom of this world to be foolish. It is just as the Scriptures say, "God catches the wise when they try to outsmart him." ²⁰ The Scriptures also say, "The Lord knows that the plans made by wise people are useless." ²¹⁻²² So stop bragging about what anyone has done. Paul and Apollos and Peter[h] all belong to you. In fact, everything is yours, including the world, life, death, the present, and the future. Everything belongs to you, ²³ and you belong to Christ, and Christ belongs to God.

## The Work of the Apostles

4 Think of us as servants of Christ who have been given the work of explaining God's mysterious ways. ² And since our first duty is to be faithful to the one we work for, ³ it doesn't matter to me if I am judged by you or even by a court of law. In fact, I don't judge myself. ⁴ I don't know of anything against me, but that doesn't prove that I am right. The Lord is my judge. ⁵ So don't judge anyone until the Lord re-turns. He will show what is hidden in the dark and what is in everyone's heart. Then God will be the one who praises each of us.

⁶ Friends, I have used Apollos and myself as examples to teach you the meaning of the saying, "Follow the rules." I want you to stop saying that one of us is better than the other. ⁷ What is so special about you? What do you have that you were not given? And if it was given to you, how can you brag? ⁸ Are you already satisfied? Are you now rich? Have you become kings while we are still nobodies? I wish you were kings. Then we could have a share in your kingdom.

⁹ It seems to me that God has put us apostles in the worst possible place. We are like prisoners on their way to death. Angels and the people of this world just laugh at us. ¹⁰ Because of Christ we are thought of as fools, but Christ has made you wise. We are weak and hated, but you are powerful and respected. ¹¹ Even today we go hungry and thirsty and don't have anything to wear except rags. We are mistreated and don't have a place to live. ¹² We work hard with our own hands, and when people abuse us, we wish them well. When we suffer, we are patient. ¹³ When someone curses us, we answer with kind words. Until now we are thought of as nothing more than the trash and garbage of this world.

¹⁴ I am not writing to embarrass you. I want to help you, just as parents help their own dear children. ¹⁵ Ten thousand people may teach you about Christ, but I am your only father. You became my children when I told you about Christ Jesus, ¹⁶ and I want you to be like me. ¹⁷ That's why I sent Timothy to you. I love him like a son, and he is a faithful servant of the Lord. Timothy will tell you what I do to follow Christ and how it agrees with what I always teach about Christ in every church.

¹⁸ Some of you think I am not coming for a visit, and so you are bragging. ¹⁹ But if the Lord lets me come, I will soon be there. Then I will find out if the ones who are doing all this brag-

h **3.21,22** *Peter*: See the note at 1.12.

ging really have any power. [20] God's kingdom isn't just a lot of words. It is power. [21] What do you want me to do when I arrive? Do you want me to be hard on you or to be kind and gentle?

## Immoral Followers

**5** I have heard terrible things about some of you. In fact, you are behaving worse than the Gentiles. A man is even sleeping with his own stepmother.[i] [2] You are proud, when you ought to feel bad enough to chase away anyone who acts like that.

[3-4] I am with you only in my thoughts. But in the name of our Lord Jesus I have already judged this man, as though I were with you in person. So when you meet together and the power of the Lord Jesus is with you, I will be there too. [5] You must then hand that man over to Satan. His body will be destroyed, but his spirit will be saved when the Lord Jesus returns.

[6] Stop being proud! Don't you know how a little yeast can spread through the whole batch of dough? [7] Get rid of the old yeast! Then you will be like fresh bread made without yeast, and that is what you are. Our Passover lamb is Christ, who has already been sacrificed. [8] So don't celebrate the festival by being evil and sinful, which is like serving bread made with yeast. Be pure and truthful and celebrate by using bread made without yeast.

[9] In my other letter[j] I told you not to have anything to do with immoral people. [10] But I wasn't talking about the people of this world. You would have to leave this world to get away from everyone who is immoral or greedy or who cheats or worships idols. [11] I was talking about your own people who are immoral or greedy or worship idols or curse others or get drunk or cheat. Don't even eat with them! [12] Why should I judge outsiders? Aren't we supposed to judge only church members? [13] God judges everyone else. The

Scriptures say, "Chase away any of your own people who are evil."

## Taking Each Other to Court

**6** When one of you has a complaint against another, do you take your complaint to a court of sinners? Or do you take it to God's people? [2] Don't you know that God's people will judge the world? And if you are going to judge the world, can't you settle small problems? [3] Don't you know that we will judge angels? And if that is so, we can surely judge everyday matters. [4] Why do you take everyday complaints to judges who are not respected by the church? [5] I say this to your shame. Aren't any of you wise enough to act as a judge between one follower and another? [6] Why should one of you take another to be tried by unbelievers?

[7] When one of you takes another to court, all of you lose. It would be better to let yourselves be cheated and robbed. [8] But instead, you cheat and rob other followers.

[9] Don't you know that evil people won't have a share in the blessings of God's kingdom? Don't fool yourselves! No one who is immoral or worships idols or is unfaithful in marriage or is a pervert or behaves like a homosexual [10] will share in God's kingdom. Neither will any thief or greedy person or drunkard or anyone who curses and cheats others. [11] Some of you used to be like that. But now the name of our Lord Jesus Christ and the power of God's Spirit have washed you and made you holy and acceptable to God.

## Honor God with Your Body

[12] Some of you say, "We can do anything we want to." But I tell you that not everything is good for us. So I refuse to let anything have power over me. [13] You also say, "Food is meant for our bodies, and our bodies are meant for food." But I tell you that God will destroy them both. We are not supposed to do indecent things with our

---

[i]**5.1** *is even sleeping with his own stepmother*: Or "has even married his own stepmother." [j]**5.9** *other letter*: An unknown letter that Paul wrote to the Christians at Corinth before he wrote this one.

bodies. We are to use them for the Lord who is in charge of our bodies. ¹⁴ God will raise us from death by the same power that he used when he raised our Lord to life.

¹⁵ Don't you know that your bodies are part of the body of Christ? Is it right for me to join part of the body of Christ to a prostitute? No, it isn't! ¹⁶ Don't you know that a man who does that becomes part of her body? The Scriptures say, "The two of them will be like one person." ¹⁷ But anyone who is joined to the Lord is one in spirit with him.

¹⁸ Don't be immoral in matters of sex. That is a sin against your own body in a way that no other sin is. ¹⁹ You surely know that your body is a temple where the Holy Spirit lives. The Spirit is in you and is a gift from God. You are no longer your own. ²⁰ God paid a great price for you. So use your body to honor God.

## Questions about Marriage

**7** Now I will answer the questions that you asked in your letter. You asked, "Is it best for people not to marry?"ᵏ ² Well, having your own husband or wife should keep you from doing something immoral. ³ Husbands and wives should be fair with each other about having sex. ⁴ A wife belongs to her husband instead of to herself, and a husband belongs to his wife instead of to himself. ⁵ So don't refuse sex to each other, unless you agree not to have sex for a little while, in order to spend time in prayer. Then Satan won't be able to tempt you because of your lack of self-control. ⁶ In my opinion that is what should be done, though I don't know of anything the Lord said about this matter. ⁷ I wish that all of you were like me, but God has given different gifts to each of us.

⁸ Here is my advice for people who have never been married and for widows. You should stay single, just as I am. ⁹ But if you don't have enough self-control, then go ahead and get married. After all, it is better to marry than to burn with desire.ˡ

¹⁰ I instruct married couples to stay together, and this is exactly what the Lord himself taught. A wife who leaves her husband ¹¹ should either stay single or go back to her husband. And a husband should not leave his wife.

¹² I don't know of anything else the Lord said about marriage. All I can do is to give you my own advice. If your wife isn't a follower of the Lord, but is willing to stay with you, don't divorce her. ¹³ If your husband isn't a follower, but is willing to stay with you, don't divorce him. ¹⁴ Your husband or wife who isn't a follower is made holy by having you as a mate. This also makes your children holy and keeps them from being unclean in God's sight.

¹⁵ If your husband or wife isn't a follower of the Lord and decides to divorce you, then you should agree to it. You are no longer bound to that person. After all, God chose you and wants you to live at peace. ¹⁶ And besides, how do you know if you will be able to save your husband or wife who isn't a follower?

## Obeying the Lord at All Times

¹⁷ In every church I tell the people to stay as they were when the Lord Jesus chose them and God called them to be his own. Now I say the same thing to you. ¹⁸ If you are already circumcised, don't try to change it. If you are not circumcised, don't get circumcised. ¹⁹ Being circumcised or uncircumcised isn't really what matters. The important thing is to obey God's commands. ²⁰ So don't try to change what you were when God chose you. ²¹ Are you a slave? Don't let that bother you. But if you can win your freedom, you should. ²² When the Lord chooses slaves, they become his free people. And when he chooses free people, they become slaves of Christ. ²³ God paid a great price for you. So don't become slaves of anyone else. ²⁴ Stay what you were when God chose you.

ᵏ7.1 *people not to marry*: Or "married couples not to have sex."  ˡ7.9 *with desire*: Or "in the flames of hell."

## Unmarried People

25 I don't know of anything that the Lord said about people who have never been married.[m] But I will tell you what I think. And you can trust me, because the Lord has treated me with kindness. 26 We are now going through hard times, and I think it is best for you to stay as you are. 27 If you are married, stay married. If you are not married, don't try to get married. 28 It isn't wrong to marry, even if you have never been married before. But those who marry will have a lot of trouble, and I want to protect you from that.

29 My friends, what I mean is that the Lord will soon come,[n] and it won't matter if you are married or not. 30 It will be all the same if you are crying or laughing, or if you are buying or are completely broke. 31 It won't make any difference how much good you are getting from this world or how much you like it. This world as we know it is now passing away.

32 I want all of you to be free from worry. An unmarried man worries about how to please the Lord. 33 But a married man has more worries. He must worry about the things of this world, because he wants to please his wife. 34 So he is pulled in two directions. Unmarried women and women who have never been married[o] worry only about pleasing the Lord, and they keep their bodies and minds pure. But a married woman worries about the things of this world, because she wants to please her husband. 35 What I am saying is for your own good—it isn't to limit your freedom. I want to help you to live right and to love the Lord above all else.

36 But suppose you are engaged to someone old enough to be married, and you want her so much that all you can think about is getting married. Then go ahead and marry.[p] There is nothing

wrong with that. 37 But it is better to have self-control and to make up your mind not to marry. 38 It is perfectly all right to marry, but it is better not to get married at all.

39 A wife should stay married to her husband until he dies. Then she is free to marry again, but only to a man who is a follower of the Lord. 40 However, I think I am obeying God's Spirit when I say she would be happier to stay single.

## Food Offered to Idols

8 In your letter you asked me about food offered to idols. All of us know something about this subject. But knowledge makes us proud of ourselves, while love makes us helpful to others. 2 In fact, people who think they know so much don't know anything at all. 3 But God has no doubts about who loves him.

4 Even though food is offered to idols, we know that none of the idols in this world are alive. After all, there is only one God. 5 Many things in heaven and on earth are called gods and lords, but none of them really are gods or lords. 6 We have only one God, and he is the Father. He created everything, and we live for him. Jesus Christ is our only Lord. Everything was made by him, and by him life was given to us.

7 Not everyone knows these things. In fact, many people have grown up with the belief that idols have life in them. So when they eat meat offered to idols, they are bothered by a weak conscience. 8 But food doesn't bring us any closer to God. We are no worse off if we don't eat, and we are no better off if we do.

9 Don't cause problems for someone with a weak conscience, just because you have the right to eat anything. 10 You know all this, and so it doesn't bother you to eat in the temple of an

m 7.25 people who have never been married: Or "virgins." n 7.29 the Lord will soon come: Or "there's not much time left" or "the time for decision comes quickly." o 7.34 women who have never been married: Or "virgins." p 7.36 But suppose you are engaged . . . go ahead and marry: Verses 36-38 may also be translated: 36"If you feel that you are not treating your grown daughter right by keeping her from getting married, then let her marry. You won't be doing anything wrong. 37But it is better to have self-control and make up your mind not to let your daughter get married. 38It is all right for you to let her marry. But it is better if you don't let her marry at all."

idol. But suppose a person with a weak conscience sees you and decides to eat food that has been offered to idols. [11] Then what you know has destroyed someone Christ died for. [12] When you sin by hurting a follower with a weak conscience, you sin against Christ. [13] So if I hurt one of the Lord's followers by what I eat, I will never eat meat as long as I live.

## The Rights of an Apostle

**9** I am free. I am an apostle. I have seen the Lord Jesus and have led you to have faith in him. [2] Others may think that I am not an apostle, but you are proof that I am an apostle to you.

[3] When people question me, I tell them [4] that Barnabas and I have the right to our food and drink. [5] We each have the right to marry one of the Lord's followers and to take her along with us, just as the other apostles and the Lord's brothers and Peter[q] do. [6] Are we the only ones who have to support ourselves by working at another job? [7] Do soldiers pay their own salaries? Don't people who raise grapes eat some of what they grow? Don't shepherds get milk from their own goats?

[8-9] I am not saying this on my own authority. The Law of Moses tells us not to muzzle an ox when it is grinding grain. But was God concerned only about an ox? [10] No, he wasn't! He was talking about us. This was written in the Scriptures so that all who plow and all who grind the grain will look forward to sharing in the harvest. [11] When we told the message to you, it was like planting spiritual seed. So we have the right to accept material things as our harvest from you. [12] If others have the right to do this, we have an even greater right. But we haven't used this right of ours. We are willing to put up with anything to keep from causing trouble for the message about Christ.

[13] Don't you know that people who work in the temple make their living from what is brought to the temple?

Don't you know that a person who serves at the altar is given part of what is offered? [14] In the same way, the Lord wants everyone who preaches the good news to make a living from preaching this message.

[15] But I have never used these privileges of mine, and I am not writing this because I want to start now. I would rather die than have someone rob me of the right to take pride in this. [16] I don't have any reason to brag about preaching the good news. Preaching is something God told me to do, and if I don't do it, I am doomed. [17] If I preach because I want to, I will be paid. But even if I don't want to, it is still something God has sent me to do. [18] What pay am I given? It is the chance to preach the good news free of charge and not to use the privileges that are mine because I am a preacher.

[19] I am not anyone's slave. But I have become a slave to everyone, so that I can win as many people as possible. [20] When I am with the Jews, I live like a Jew to win Jews. They are ruled by the Law of Moses, and I am not. But I live by the Law to win them. [21] And when I am with people who are not ruled by the Law, I forget about the Law to win them. Of course, I never really forget about the law of God. In fact, I am ruled by the law of Christ. [22] When I am with people whose faith is weak, I live as they do to win them. I do everything I can to win everyone I possibly can. [23] I do all this for the good news, because I want to share in its blessings.

## A Race and a Fight

[24] You know that many runners enter a race, and only one of them wins the prize. So run to win! [25] Athletes work hard to win a crown that cannot last, but we do it for a crown that will last forever. [26] I don't run without a goal. And I don't box by beating my fists in the air. [27] I keep my body under control and make it my slave, so I won't lose out after telling the good news to others.

q9.5 *Peter*: See the note at 1.12.

## Don't Worship Idols

**10** Friends, I want to remind you that all of our ancestors walked under the cloud and went through the sea. ²This was like being baptized and becoming followers of Moses. ³All of them also ate the same spiritual food ⁴and drank the same spiritual drink, which flowed from the spiritual rock that followed them. That rock was Christ. ⁵But most of them did not please God. So they died, and their bodies were scattered all over the desert.

⁶What happened to them is a warning to keep us from wanting to do the same evil things. ⁷They worshiped idols, just as the Scriptures say, "The people sat down to eat and drink. Then they got up to dance around." So don't worship idols. ⁸Some of those people did shameful things, and in a single day about twenty-three thousand of them died. Don't do shameful things as they did. ⁹And don't try to test Christ,ʳ as some of them did and were later bitten by poisonous snakes. ¹⁰Don't even grumble, as some of them did and were killed by the destroying angel. ¹¹These things happened to them as a warning to us. All this was written in the Scriptures to teach us who live in these last days.

¹²Even if you think you can stand up to temptation, be careful not to fall. ¹³You are tempted in the same way that everyone else is tempted. But God can be trusted not to let you be tempted too much, and he will show you how to escape from your temptations.

¹⁴My friends, you must keep away from idols. ¹⁵I am speaking to you as people who have enough sense to know what I am talking about. ¹⁶When we drink from the cup that we ask God to bless, isn't that sharing in the blood of Christ? When we eat the bread that we break, isn't that sharing in the body of Christ? ¹⁷By sharing in the same loaf of bread, we become one body, even though there are many of us.

¹⁸Aren't the people of Israel sharing in the worship when they gather around the altar and eat the sacrifices offered there? ¹⁹Am I saying that either the idols or the food sacrificed to them is anything at all? ²⁰No, I am not! That food is really sacrificed to demons and not to God. I don't want you to have anything to do with demons. ²¹You cannot drink from the cup of demons and still drink from the Lord's cup. You cannot eat at the table of demons and still eat at the Lord's table. ²²We would make the Lord jealous if we did that. And we are not stronger than the Lord.

## Always Honor God

²³Some of you say, "We can do whatever we want to!" But I tell you that not everything may be good or helpful. ²⁴We should think about others and not about ourselves. ²⁵However, when you buy meat in the market, go ahead and eat it. Keep your conscience clear by not asking where the meat came from. ²⁶The Scriptures say, "The earth and everything in it belong to the Lord."

²⁷If an unbeliever invites you to dinner, and you want to go, then go. Eat whatever you are served. Don't cause a problem for someone's conscience by asking where the food came from. ²⁸⁻²⁹But if you are told that it has been sacrificed to idols, don't cause a problem by eating it. I don't mean a problem for yourself, but for the one who told you. Why should my freedom be limited by someone else's conscience? ³⁰If I give thanks for what I eat, why should anyone accuse me of doing wrong?

³¹When you eat or drink or do anything else, always do it to honor God. ³²Don't cause problems for Jews or Greeks or anyone else who belongs to God's church. ³³I always try to please others instead of myself, in the hope

**11** that many of them will be saved. ¹You must follow my example, as I follow the example of Christ.

## Rules for Worship

²I am proud of you, because you always remember me and obey the teachings I gave you. ³Now I want you to

---

ʳ **10.9** *Christ*: Some manuscripts have "the Lord."

know that Christ is the head over all men, and a man is the head over a woman. But God is the head over Christ. [4] This means that any man who prays or prophesies with something on his head brings shame to his head.

[5] But any woman who prays or prophesies without something on her head brings shame to her head. In fact, she may as well shave her head.[s] [6] A woman should wear something on her head. It is a disgrace for a woman to shave her head or cut her hair. But if she refuses to wear something on her head, let her cut off her hair.

[7] Men were created to be like God and to bring honor to God. This means that a man should not wear anything on his head. Women were created to bring honor to men. [8] It was the woman who was made from a man, and not the man who was made from a woman. [9] He wasn't created for her. She was created for him. [10] And so, because of this, and also because of the angels, a woman ought to wear something on her head, as a sign of her authority.[t]

[11] As far as the Lord is concerned, men and women need each other. [12] It is true that the first woman came from a man, but all other men have been given birth by women. Yet God is the one who created everything. [13] Ask yourselves if it is proper for a woman to pray without something on her head. [14] Isn't it unnatural and disgraceful for men to have long hair? [15] But long hair is a beautiful way for a woman to cover her head. [16] This is how things are done in all of God's churches,[u] and that's why none of you should argue about what I have said.

### Rules for the Lord's Supper

[17] Your worship services do you more harm than good. I am certainly not going to praise you for this. [18] I am told that you can't get along with each other when you worship, and I am sure that some of what I have heard is true.

[19] You are bound to argue with each other, but it is easy to see which of you have God's approval.

[20] When you meet together, you don't really celebrate the Lord's Supper. [21] You even start eating before everyone gets to the meeting, and some of you go hungry, while others get drunk. [22] Don't you have homes where you can eat and drink? Do you hate God's church? Do you want to embarrass people who don't have anything? What can I say to you? I certainly cannot praise you.

### The Lord's Supper
*(Matthew 26.26-29; Mark 14.22-25; Luke 22.14-20)*

[23] I have already told you what the Lord Jesus did on the night he was betrayed. And it came from the Lord himself.

He took some bread in his hands. [24] Then after he had given thanks, he broke it and said, "This is my body, which is given for you. Eat this and remember me."

[25] After the meal, Jesus took a cup of wine in his hands and said, "This is my blood, and with it God makes his new agreement with you. Drink this and remember me."

[26] The Lord meant that when you eat this bread and drink from this cup, you tell about his death until he comes.

[27] But if you eat the bread and drink the wine in a way that isn't worthy of the Lord, you sin against his body and blood. [28] That's why you must examine the way you eat and drink. [29] If you fail to understand that you are the body of the Lord, you will condemn yourselves by the way you eat and drink. [30] That's why many of you are sick and weak and why a lot of others have died. [31] If we carefully judge ourselves, we won't be punished. [32] But when the Lord judges and punishes us, he does it to keep us from being condemned with the rest of the world.

[33] My dear friends, you should wait

---

[s] **11.5** *she may as well shave her head:* A woman's hair was a mark of beauty, and it was shameful for a woman to cut her hair short or to shave her head, so that she looked like a man.   [t] **11.10** *as a sign of her authority:* Or "as a sign that she is under someone's authority."   [u] **11.16** *This is how things are done in all of God's churches:* Or "There is no set rule for this in any of God's churches."

until everyone gets there before you start eating. [34] If you really are hungry, you can eat at home. Then you won't condemn yourselves when you meet together.

After I arrive, I will instruct you about the other matters.

### Spiritual Gifts

**12** My friends, you asked me about spiritual gifts. [2] I want you to remember that before you became followers of the Lord, you were led in all the wrong ways by idols that cannot even talk. [3] Now I want you to know that if you are led by God's Spirit, you will say that Jesus is Lord, and you will never curse Jesus.

[4] There are different kinds of spiritual gifts, but they all come from the same Spirit. [5] There are different ways to serve the same Lord, [6] and we can each do different things. Yet the same God works in all of us and helps us in everything we do.

[7] The Spirit has given each of us a special way of serving others. [8] Some of us can speak with wisdom, while others can speak with knowledge, but these gifts come from the same Spirit. [9] To others the Spirit has given great faith or the power to heal the sick [10] or the power to work mighty miracles. Some of us are prophets, and some of us recognize when God's Spirit is present.[v] Others can speak different kinds of languages, and still others can tell what these languages mean. [11] But it is the Spirit who does all this and decides which gifts to give to each of us.

### One Body with Many Parts

[12] The body of Christ has many different parts, just as any other body does. [13] Some of us are Jews, and others are Gentiles. Some of us are slaves, and others are free. But God's Spirit baptized each of us and made us part of the body of Christ. Now we each drink from that same Spirit.[w]

[14] Our bodies don't have just one part. They have many parts. [15] Suppose a foot says, "I'm not a hand, and so I'm not part of the body." Wouldn't the foot still belong to the body? [16] Or suppose an ear says, "I'm not an eye, and so I'm not part of the body." Wouldn't the ear still belong to the body? [17] If our bodies were only an eye, we couldn't hear a thing. And if they were only an ear, we couldn't smell a thing. [18] But God has put all parts of our body together in the way that he decided is best.

[19] A body isn't really a body, unless there is more than one part. [20] It takes many parts to make a single body. [21] That's why the eyes cannot say they don't need the hands. That's also why the head cannot say it doesn't need the feet. [22] In fact, we cannot get along without the parts of the body that seem to be the weakest. [23] We take special care to dress up some parts of our bodies. We are modest about our personal parts, [24] but we don't have to be modest about other parts.

God put our bodies together in such a way that even the parts that seem the least important are valuable. [25] He did this to make all parts of the body work together smoothly, with each part caring about the others. [26] If one part of our body hurts, we hurt all over. If one part of our body is honored, the whole body will be happy.

[27] Together you are the body of Christ. Each one of you is part of his body. [28] First, God chose some people to be apostles and prophets and teachers for the church. But he also chose some to work miracles or heal the sick or help others or be leaders or speak different kinds of languages. [29] Not everyone is an apostle. Not everyone is a prophet. Not everyone is a teacher. Not everyone can work miracles. [30] Not everyone can heal the sick. Not everyone can speak different kinds of languages. Not everyone can tell what these languages mean. [31] I want you to

---

[v]**12.10** *and some of us ... present:* Or "and some of us recognize the difference between God's Spirit and other spirits." [w]**12.13** *Some of us are Jews ... that same Spirit:* Verse 13 may also be translated, "God's Spirit is inside each of us, and all around us as well. So it doesn't matter that some of us are Jews and others are Gentiles and that some are slaves and others are free. Together we are one body."

desire the best gifts.ˣ So I will show
you a much better way.

## Love

**13** What if I could speak
all languages of humans
and of angels?
If I did not love others,
I would be nothing more
than a noisy gong
or a clanging cymbal.
² What if I could prophesy
and understand all secrets
and all knowledge?
And what if I had faith
that moved mountains?
I would be nothing,
unless I loved others.
³ What if I gave away all
that I owned
and let myself
be burned alive?ʸ
I would gain nothing,
unless I loved others.
⁴ Love is kind and patient,
never jealous, boastful,
proud, or ⁵ rude.
Love isn't selfish
or quick tempered.
It doesn't keep a record
of wrongs that others do.
⁶ Love rejoices in the truth,
but not in evil.
⁷ Love is always supportive,
loyal, hopeful,
and trusting.
⁸ Love never fails!

Everyone who prophesies
will stop,
and unknown languages
will no longer
be spoken.
All that we know
will be forgotten.
⁹ We don't know everything,
and our prophecies
are not complete.
¹⁰ But what is perfect
will someday appear,
and what isn't perfect
will then disappear.

¹¹ When we were children,
we thought and reasoned
as children do.
But when we grew up,
we quit our childish ways.
¹² Now all we can see of God
is like a cloudy picture
in a mirror.
Later we will see him
face to face.
We don't know everything,
but then we will,
just as God completely
understands us.
¹³ For now there are faith,
hope, and love.
But of these three,
the greatest is love.

## Speaking Unknown Languages and Prophesying

**14** Love should be your guide. Be
eager to have the gifts that come
from the Holy Spirit, especially the gift
of prophecy. ² If you speak languages
that others don't know, God will understand what you are saying, though no
one else will know what you mean. You
will be talking about mysteries that
only the Spirit understands. ³ But when
you prophesy, you will be understood,
and others will be helped. They will be
encouraged and made to feel better.

⁴ By speaking languages that others
don't know, you help only yourself. But
by prophesying you help everyone in
the church. ⁵ I am glad for you to speak
unknown languages, although I had
rather for you to prophesy. In fact,
prophesying does much more good
than speaking unknown languages, unless someone can help the church by
explaining what you mean.

⁶ My friends, what good would it do,
if I came and spoke unknown languages to you and didn't explain what
I meant? How would I help you, unless
I told you what God had shown me or
gave you some knowledge or prophecy
or teaching? ⁷ If all musical instruments
sounded alike, how would you know
the difference between a flute and a

harp? ⁸ If a bugle call isn't clear, how would you know to get ready for battle? ⁹ That's how it is when you speak unknown languages. If no one can understand what you are talking about, you will only be talking to the wind. ¹⁰ There are many different languages in this world, and all of them make sense. ¹¹ But if I don't understand the language that someone is using, we will be like foreigners to each other. ¹² If you really want spiritual gifts, choose the ones that will be most helpful to the church.

¹³ When we speak languages that others don't know, we should pray for the power to explain what we mean. ¹⁴ For example, if I use an unknown language in my prayers, my spirit prays but my mind is useless. ¹⁵ Then what should I do? There are times when I should pray with my spirit, and times when I should pray with my mind. Sometimes I should sing with my spirit, and at other times I should sing with my mind.

¹⁶ Suppose some strangers are in your worship service, when you are praising God with your spirit. If they don't understand you, how will they know to say, "Amen"? ¹⁷ You may be worshiping God in a wonderful way, but no one else will be helped. ¹⁸ I thank God that I speak unknown languages more than any of you. ¹⁹ But words that make sense can help the church. That's why in church I had rather speak five words that make sense than to speak ten thousand words in a language that others don't know.

²⁰ My friends, stop thinking like children. Think like mature people and be as innocent as tiny babies. ²¹ In the Scriptures the Lord says,

"I will use strangers
who speak unknown languages
  to talk to my people.
They will speak to them
  in foreign languages,
but still my people
  won't listen to me."

²² Languages that others don't know may mean something to unbelievers, but not to the Lord's followers. Prophecy, on the other hand, is for followers, not for unbelievers. ²³ Suppose everyone in your worship service started speaking unknown languages, and some outsiders or some unbelievers come in. Won't they think you are crazy? ²⁴ But suppose all of you are prophesying when those unbelievers and outsiders come in. They will realize that they are sinners, and they will want to change their ways because of what you are saying. ²⁵ They will tell what is hidden in their hearts. Then they will kneel down and say to God, "We are certain that you are with these people."

### Worship Must Be Orderly

²⁶ My friends, when you meet to worship, you must do everything for the good of everyone there. That's how it should be when someone sings or teaches or tells what God has said or speaks an unknown language or explains what the language means. ²⁷ No more than two or three of you should speak unknown languages during the meeting. You must take turns, and someone should always be there to explain what you mean. ²⁸ If no one can explain, you must keep silent in church and speak only to yourself and to God.

²⁹ Two or three persons may prophesy, and everyone else must listen carefully. ³⁰ If someone sitting there receives a message from God, the speaker must stop and let the other person speak. ³¹ Let only one person speak at a time, then all of you will learn something and be encouraged. ³² A prophet should be willing to stop and let someone else speak. ³³ God wants everything to be done peacefully and in order.

When God's people meet in church, ³⁴ the women must not be allowed to speak. They must keep quiet and listen, as the Law of Moses teaches. ³⁵ If there is something they want to know, they can ask their husbands when they get home. It is disgraceful for women to speak in church. ³⁶ God's message did not start with you people, and you are not the only ones it has reached.

³⁷ If you think of yourself as a prophet or a spiritual person, you will know that I am writing only what the Lord has commanded. ³⁸ So don't pay attention to anyone who ignores what I am

writing. [39] My friends, be eager to prophesy and don't stop anyone from speaking languages that others don't know. [40] But do everything properly and in order.

## Christ Was Raised to Life

**15** My friends, I want you to remember the message that I preached and that you believed and trusted. [2] You will be saved by this message, if you hold firmly to it. But if you don't, your faith was all for nothing.

[3] I told you the most important part of the message exactly as it was told to me. That part is:

Christ died for our sins,
    as the Scriptures say.
[4] He was buried,
    and three days later
he was raised to life,
    as the Scriptures say.
[5] Christ appeared to Peter, [z]
    then to the twelve.
[6] After this, he appeared
    to more than five hundred
    other followers.
Most of them are still alive,
    but some have died.
[7] He also appeared to James,
    and then to all
        of the apostles.

[8] Finally, he appeared to me, even though I am like someone who was born at the wrong time. [a]

[9] I am the least important of all the apostles. In fact, I caused so much trouble for God's church that I don't even deserve to be called an apostle. [10] But God was kind! He made me what I am, and his wonderful kindness wasn't wasted. I worked much harder than any of the other apostles, although it was really God's kindness at work and not me. [11] But it doesn't matter if I preached or if they preached. All of you believed the message just the same.

## God's People Will Be Raised to Life

[12] If we preach that Christ was raised from death, how can some of you say

that the dead will not be raised to life? [13] If they won't be raised to life, Christ himself wasn't raised to life. [14] And if Christ wasn't raised to life, our message is worthless, and so is your faith. [15] If the dead won't be raised to life, we have told lies about God by saying that he raised Christ to life, when he really did not.

[16] So if the dead won't be raised to life, Christ wasn't raised to life. [17] Unless Christ was raised to life, your faith is useless, and you are still living in your sins. [18] And those people who died after putting their faith in him are completely lost. [19] If our hope in Christ is good only for this life, we are worse off than anyone else.

[20] But Christ has been raised to life! And he makes us certain that others will also be raised to life. [21] Just as we will die because of Adam, we will be raised to life because of Christ. [22] Adam brought death to all of us, and Christ will bring life to all of us. [23] But we must each wait our turn. Christ was the first to be raised to life, and his people will be raised to life when he returns. [24] Then after Christ has destroyed all powers and forces, the end will come, and he will give the kingdom to God the Father.

[25] Christ will rule until he puts all his enemies under his power, [26] and the last enemy he destroys will be death. [27] When the Scriptures say that he will put everything under his power, they don't include God. It was God who put everything under the power of Christ. [28] After everything is under the power of God's Son, he will put himself under the power of God, who put everything under his Son's power. Then God will mean everything to everyone.

[29] If the dead are not going to be raised to life, what will people do who are being baptized for them? Why are they being baptized for those dead people? [30] And why do we always risk our lives [31] and face death every day? The pride that I have in you because of Christ Jesus our Lord is what makes me say this. [32] What do you think I gained by fighting wild animals in

---

[z] 15.5 *Peter*: See the note at 1.12.    [a] 15,8 *who was born at the wrong time*: The meaning of these words in Greek is not clear.

Ephesus? If the dead are not raised to life,

"Let's eat and drink.
Tomorrow we die."

33 Don't fool yourselves. Bad friends will destroy you. 34 Be sensible and stop sinning. You should be embarrassed that some people still don't know about God.

### What Our Bodies Will Be Like

35 Some of you have asked, "How will the dead be raised to life? What kind of bodies will they have?" 36 Don't be foolish. A seed must die before it can sprout from the ground. 37 Wheat seeds and all other seeds look different from the sprouts that come up. 38 This is because God gives everything the kind of body he wants it to have. 39 People, animals, birds, and fish are each made of flesh, but none of them are alike. 40 Everything in the heavens has a body, and so does everything on earth. But each one is very different from all the others. 41 The sun isn't like the moon, the moon isn't like the stars, and each star is different.

42 That's how it will be when our bodies are raised to life. These bodies will die, but the bodies that are raised will live forever. 43 These ugly and weak bodies will become beautiful and strong. 44 As surely as there are physical bodies, there are spiritual bodies. And our physical bodies will be changed into spiritual bodies.

45 The first man was named Adam, and the Scriptures tell us that he was a living person. But Jesus, who may be called the last Adam, is a life-giving spirit. 46 We see that the one with a spiritual body did not come first. He came after the one who had a physical body. 47 The first man was made from the dust of the earth, but the second man came from heaven. 48 Everyone on earth has a body like the body of the one who was made from the dust of the earth. And everyone in heaven has a body like the body of the one who came from heaven. 49 Just as we are like the one who was made out of earth, we will be like the one who came from heaven.

50 My friends, I want you to know that our bodies of flesh and blood will decay. This means that they cannot share in God's kingdom, which lasts forever. 51 I will explain a mystery to you. Not every one of us will die, but we will all be changed. 52 It will happen suddenly, quicker than the blink of an eye. At the sound of the last trumpet the dead will be raised. We will all be changed, so that we will never die again. 53 Our dead and decaying bodies will be changed into bodies that won't die or decay. 54 The bodies we now have are weak and can die. But they will be changed into bodies that are eternal. Then the Scriptures will come true,

"Death has lost the battle!
55 Where is its victory?
Where is its sting?"

56 Sin is what gives death its sting, and the Law is the power behind sin. 57 But thank God for letting our Lord Jesus Christ give us the victory!

58 My dear friends, stand firm and don't be shaken. Always keep busy working for the Lord. You know that everything you do for him is worthwhile.

### A Collection for God's People

**16** When you collect money for God's people, I want you to do exactly what I told the churches in Galatia to do. 2 That is, each Sunday each of you must put aside part of what you have earned. If you do this, you won't have to take up a collection when I come. 3 Choose some followers to take the money to Jerusalem. I will send them on with the money and with letters which show that you approve of them. 4 If you think I should go along, they can go with me.

### Paul's Travel Plans

5 After I have gone through Macedonia, I hope to see you 6 and visit with you for a while. I may even stay all winter, so that you can help me on my way to wherever I will be going next. 7 If the Lord lets me, I would rather come later for a longer visit than to stop off now for only a short visit. 8 I will stay in Ephesus until Pentecost, 9 because

there is a wonderful opportunity for me to do some work here. But there are also many people who are against me.

[10] When Timothy arrives, give him a friendly welcome. He is doing the Lord's work, just as I am. [11] Don't let anyone mistreat him. I am looking for him to return to me together with the other followers. So when he leaves, send him off with your blessings.

[12] I have tried hard to get our friend Apollos to visit you with the other followers. He doesn't want to come just now, but he will come when he can.

### Personal Concerns and Greetings

[13] Keep alert. Be firm in your faith. Stay brave and strong. [14] Show love in everything you do.

[15] You know that Stephanas and his family were the first in Achaia to have faith in the Lord. They have done all they can for God's people. My friends, I ask you [16] to obey leaders like them

and to do the same for all others who work hard with you.

[17] I was glad to see Stephanas and Fortunatus and Achaicus. Having them here was like having you. [18] They made me feel much better, just as they made you feel better. You should appreciate people like them.

[19] Greetings from the churches in Asia.

Aquila and Priscilla, together with the church that meets in their house, send greetings in the name of the Lord.

[20] All of the Lord's followers send their greetings.

Give each other a warm greeting.

[21] I am signing this letter myself: PAUL.

[22] I pray that God will put a curse on everyone who doesn't love the Lord. And may the Lord come soon.

[23] I pray that the Lord Jesus will be kind to you.

[24] I love everyone who belongs to Christ Jesus.

# 2 CORINTHIANS

## ABOUT THIS LETTER

*In the beginning of this letter Paul answers the concerns of the Christians in Corinth who accused him of not living up to his promise to visit them. Paul had changed his mind for a good reason. He had stayed away from Corinth so that he would not seem to be too hard and demanding (1.23). He also wanted to see if they would follow his instructions about forgiving and comforting people who had sinned (2.5-11).*

*Paul reminds the Corinthians that God is generous and wants them to be just as generous in their giving to help God's people in Jerusalem and Judea (8.1—9.15).*

*Paul is a servant of God's new agreement (3.1-17). He is faithful in trying to bring people to God, even if it means terrible suffering for himself (4.1—6.13; 10.1—12.10). And what has God done to make it possible for us to come to him?*

God has done it all! He sent Christ to make peace between himself and us, and he has given us the work of making peace between himself and others.

What we mean is that God was in Christ, offering peace and forgiveness to the people of this world. And he has given us the work of sharing his message about peace.     (5.18, 19)

## A QUICK LOOK AT THIS LETTER

*Paul Gives Thanks to God (1.1-11)*
*The Work of an Apostle for God's People (1.12—2.17)*
*Guided by the Love of Christ (3.1—7.16)*
*Gifts for the Poor (8.1—9.15)*
*Paul Is a True Apostle (10.1—13.10)*
*Final Greetings (13.11-13)*

---

**1** From Paul, chosen by God to be an apostle of Jesus Christ, and from Timothy, who is also a follower.

To God's church in Corinth and to all of God's people in Achaia.

²I pray that God our Father and the Lord Jesus Christ will be kind to you and will bless you with peace!

### Paul Gives Thanks

³Praise God, the Father of our Lord Jesus Christ! The Father is a merciful God, who always gives us comfort. ⁴He comforts us when we are in trouble, so that we can share that same comfort with others in trouble. ⁵We share in the terrible sufferings of Christ, but also in the wonderful comfort he gives. ⁶We suffer in the hope that you will be comforted and saved. And because we are comforted, you will also be comforted, as you patiently endure suffering like ours. ⁷You never disappoint us. You suffered as much as we did, and we know that you will be comforted as we were.

⁸My friends, I want you to know what a hard time we had in Asia. Our sufferings were so horrible and so

225

unbearable that death seemed certain. [9] In fact, we felt sure that we were going to die. But this made us stop trusting in ourselves and start trusting God, who raises the dead to life. [10] God saved us from the threat of death,[a] and we are sure that he will do it again and again. [11] Please help us by praying for us. Then many people will give thanks for the blessings we receive in answer to all these prayers.

## Paul's Change of Plans

[12] We can be proud of our clear conscience. We have always lived honestly and sincerely, especially when we were with you. And we were guided by God's wonderful kindness instead of by the wisdom of this world. [13] I am not writing anything you cannot read and understand. I hope you will understand it completely, [14] just as you already partly understand us. Then when our Lord Jesus returns, you can be as proud of us as we are of you.

[15] I was so sure of your pride in us that I had planned to visit you first of all. In this way you would have the blessing of two visits from me. [16] Once on my way to Macedonia and again on my return from there. Then you could send me on to Judea. [17] Do you think I couldn't make up my mind about what to do? Or do I seem like someone who says "Yes" or "No" simply to please others? [18] God can be trusted, and so can I, when I say that our answer to you has always been "Yes" and never "No." [19] This is because Jesus Christ the Son of God is always "Yes" and never "No." And he is the one that Silas,[b] Timothy, and I told you about. [20] Christ says "Yes" to all of God's promises. That's why we have Christ to say "Amen"[c] for us to the glory of God. [21] And so God makes it possible for you and us to stand firmly together with Christ. God is also the one who chose us [22] and put his Spirit in our hearts to show that we belong only to him.

[23] God is my witness that I stayed away from Corinth, just to keep from being hard on you. [24] We are not bosses who tell you what to believe. We are working with you to make you glad, because your faith is strong.

**2** I have decided not to make my next visit with you so painful. [2] If I make you feel bad, who would be left to cheer me up, except the people I had made to feel bad? [3] The reason I want to be happy is to make you happy. I wrote as I did because I didn't want to visit you and be made to feel bad, when you should make me feel happy. [4] At the time I wrote, I was suffering terribly. My eyes were full of tears, and my heart was broken. But I didn't want to make you feel bad. I only wanted to let you know how much I cared for you.

## Forgiveness

[5] I don't want to be hard on you. But if one of you has made someone feel bad, I am not really the one who has been made to feel bad. Some of you are the ones. [6] Most of you have already pointed out the wrong that person did, and that is punishment enough for what was done. [7] When people sin, you should forgive and comfort them, so they won't give up in despair. [8] You should make them sure of your love for them.

[9] I also wrote because I wanted to test you and find out if you would follow my instructions. [10] I will forgive anyone you forgive. Yes, for your sake and with Christ as my witness, I have forgiven whatever needed to be forgiven. [11] I have done this to keep Satan from getting the better of us. We all know what goes on in his mind.

[12] When I went to Troas to preach the good news about Christ, I found that the Lord had already prepared the way. [13] But I was worried when I didn't find my friend Titus there. So I left the other followers and went on to Macedonia. [14] I am grateful that God always makes it possible for Christ to lead us

to victory. God also helps us spread the knowledge about Christ everywhere, and this knowledge is like the smell of perfume. [15-16] In fact, God thinks of us as a perfume that brings Christ to everyone. For people who are being saved, this perfume has a sweet smell and leads them to a better life. But for people who are lost, it has a bad smell and leads them to a horrible death.

No one really has what it takes to do this work. [17] A lot of people try to get rich from preaching God's message. But we are God's sincere messengers, and by the power of Christ we speak our message with God as our witness.

## God's New Agreement·

**3** Are we once again bragging about ourselves? Do we need letters to you or from you to tell others about us? Some people do need letters that tell about them. [2] But you are our letter, and you are in our[d] hearts for everyone to read and understand. [3] You are like a letter written by Christ and delivered by us. But you are not written with pen and ink or on tablets made of stone. You are written in our hearts by the Spirit of the living God.

[4] We are sure about all this. Christ makes us sure in the very presence of God. [5] We don't have the right to claim that we have done anything on our own. God gives us what it takes to do all that we do. [6] He makes us worthy to be the servants of his new agreement that comes from the Holy Spirit and not from a written Law. After all, the Law brings death, but the Spirit brings life.

[7] The Law of Moses brought only the promise of death, even though it was carved on stones and given in a wonderful way. Still the Law made Moses' face shine so brightly that the people of Israel could not look at it, even though it was a fading glory. [8] So won't the agreement that the Spirit brings to us be even more wonderful? [9] If something that brings the death sentence is glorious, won't something that makes us acceptable to God be even more glorious? [10] In fact, the new agreement is

so wonderful that the Law is no longer glorious at all. [11] The Law was given with a glory that faded away. But the glory of the new agreement is much greater, because it will never fade away.

[12] This wonderful hope makes us feel like speaking freely. [13] We are not like Moses. His face was shining, but he covered it to keep the people of Israel from seeing the brightness fade away. [14] The people were stubborn, and something still keeps them from seeing the truth when the Law is read. Only Christ can take away the covering that keeps them from seeing.

[15] When the Law of Moses is read, they have their minds covered over [16] with a covering that is removed only for those who turn to the Lord. [17] The Lord and the Spirit are one and the same, and the Lord's Spirit sets us free. [18] So our faces are not covered. They show the bright glory of the Lord, as the Lord's Spirit makes us more and more like our glorious Lord.

## Treasure in Clay Jars

**4** God has been kind enough to trust us with this work. That's why we never give up. [2] We don't do shameful things that must be kept secret. And we don't try to fool anyone or twist God's message around. God is our witness that we speak only the truth, so others will be sure that we can be trusted. [3] If there is anything hidden about our message, it is hidden only to someone who is lost.

[4] The god who rules this world has blinded the minds of unbelievers. They cannot see the light, which is the good news about our glorious Christ, who shows what God is like. [5] We are not preaching about ourselves. Our message is that Jesus Christ is Lord. He also sent us to be your servants. [6] The Scriptures say, "God commanded light to shine in the dark." Now God is shining in our hearts to let you know that his glory is seen in Jesus Christ.

[7] We are like clay jars in which this treasure is stored. The real power

---

[d]**3.2** *our*: Some manuscripts have "your."

comes from God and not from us. 8 We often suffer, but we are never crushed. Even when we don't know what to do, we never give up. 9 In times of trouble, God is with us, and when we are knocked down, we get up again. 10-11 We face death every day because of Jesus. Our bodies show what his death was like, so that his life can also be seen in us. 12 This means that death is working in us, but life is working in you.

13 In the Scriptures it says, "I spoke because I had faith." We have that same kind of faith. So we speak 14 because we know that God raised the Lord Jesus to life. And just as God raised Jesus, he will also raise us to life. Then he will bring us into his presence together with you. 15 All of this has been done for you, so that more and more people will know how kind God is and will praise and honor him.

### Faith in the Lord

16 We never give up. Our bodies are gradually dying, but we ourselves are being made stronger each day. 17 These little troubles are getting us ready for an eternal glory that will make all our troubles seem like nothing. 18 Things that are seen don't last forever, but things that are not seen are eternal. That's why we keep our minds on the things that cannot be seen.

5 Our bodies are like tents that we live in here on earth. But when these tents are destroyed, we know that God will give each of us a place to live. These homes will not be buildings that someone has made, but they are in heaven and will last forever. 2 While we are here on earth, we sigh because we want to live in that heavenly home. 3 We want to put it on like clothes and not be naked.

4 These tents we now live in are like a heavy burden, and we groan. But we don't do this just because we want to leave these bodies that will die. It is because we want to change them for bodies that will never die. 5 God is the one who makes all of this possible. He has given us his Spirit to make us certain that he will do it. 6 So always be cheerful!

As long as we are in these bodies, we are away from the Lord. 7 But we live by faith, not by what we see. 8 We should be cheerful, because we would rather leave these bodies and be at home with the Lord. 9 But whether we are at home with the Lord or away from him, we still try our best to please him. 10 After all, Christ will judge each of us for the good or the bad that we do while living in these bodies.

### Bringing People to God

11 We know what it means to respect the Lord, and we encourage everyone to turn to him. God himself knows what we are like, and I hope you also know what kind of people we are. 12 We are not trying once more to brag about ourselves. But we want you to be proud of us, when you are with those who are not sincere and brag about what others think of them.

13 If we seem out of our minds, it is between God and us. But if we are in our right minds, it is for your good. 14 We are ruled by Christ's love for us. We are certain that if one person died for everyone else, then all of us have died. 15 And Christ did die for all of us. He died so we would no longer live for ourselves, but for the one who died and was raised to life for us.

16 We are careful not to judge people by what they seem to be, though we once judged Christ in that way. 17 Anyone who belongs to Christ is a new person. The past is forgotten, and everything is new. 18 God has done it all! He sent Christ to make peace between himself and us, and he has given us the work of making peace between himself and others.

19 What we mean is that God was in Christ, offering peace and forgiveness to the people of this world. And he has given us the work of sharing his message about peace. 20 We were sent to speak for Christ, and God is begging you to listen to our message. We speak for Christ and sincerely ask you to make peace with God. 21 Christ never sinned! But God treated him as a sinner, so that Christ could make us acceptable to God.

---

**6** We work together with God, and we beg you to make good use of God's kindness to you. ² In the Scriptures God says,

"When the time came,
I listened to you,
and when you needed help,
I came to save you."

That time has come. This is the day for you to be saved.

³ We don't want anyone to find fault with our work, and so we try hard not to cause problems. ⁴ But in everything and in every way we show that we truly are God's servants. We have always been patient, though we have had a lot of trouble, suffering, and hard times. ⁵ We have been beaten, put in jail, and hurt in riots. We have worked hard and have gone without sleep or food. ⁶ But we have kept ourselves pure and have been understanding, patient, and kind. The Holy Spirit has been with us, and our love has been real. ⁷ We have spoken the truth, and God's power has worked in us. In all our struggles we have said and done only what is right.

⁸ Whether we were honored or dishonored or praised or cursed, we always told the truth about ourselves. But some people said we did not. ⁹ We are unknown to others, but well known to you. We seem to be dying, and yet we are still alive. We have been punished, but never killed, ¹⁰ and we are always happy, even in times of suffering. Although we are poor, we have made many people rich. And though we own nothing, everything is ours.

¹¹ Friends in Corinth, we are telling the truth when we say that there is room in our hearts for you. ¹² We are not holding back on our love for you, but you are holding back on your love for us. ¹³ I speak to you as I would speak to my own children. Please make room in your hearts for us.

### The Temple of the Living God

¹⁴ Stay away from people who are not followers of the Lord! Can someone who is good get along with someone who is evil? Are light and darkness the same? ¹⁵ Is Christ a friend of Satan?ᵉ Can people who follow the Lord have anything in common with those who don't? ¹⁶ Do idols belong in the temple of God? We are the temple of the living God, as God himself says,

"I will live with these people
and walk among them.
I will be their God,
and they will be
my people."

¹⁷ The Lord also says,

"Leave them and stay away!
Don't touch anything
that isn't clean.
Then I will welcome you
¹⁸ and be your Father.
You will be my sons
and my daughters,
as surely as I am God,
the All-Powerful."

**7** My friends, God has made us these promises. So we should stay away from everything that keeps our bodies and spirits from being clean. We should honor God and try to be completely like him.

### The Church Makes Paul Happy

² Make a place for us in your hearts! We haven't mistreated or hurt anyone. We haven't cheated anyone. ³ I am not saying this to be hard on you. But, as I have said before, you will always be in our thoughts, whether we live or die. ⁴ I trust you completely.ᶠ I am always proud of you, and I am greatly encouraged. In all my trouble I am still very happy.

⁵ After we came to Macedonia, we didn't have any chance to rest. We were faced with all kinds of problems. We were troubled by enemies and troubled by fears. ⁶ But God cheers up people in need, and that is what he did when he sent Titus to us. ⁷ Of course, we were glad to see Titus, but what really made us glad is the way you cheered him up.

ᵉ**6.15** *Satan*: The Greek text has "Beliar," which is another form of the Hebrew word "Belial," meaning "wicked" or "useless." The Jewish people sometimes used this as a name for Satan. ᶠ**7.4** *I trust you completely*: Or "I have always spoken the truth to you" or "I can speak freely to you."

He told how sorry you were and how concerned you were about me. And this made me even happier.

⁸ I don't feel bad anymore, even though my letter<sup>g</sup> hurt your feelings. I did feel bad at first, but I don't now. I know that the letter hurt you for a while. ⁹ Now I am happy, but not because I hurt your feelings. It is because God used your hurt feelings to make you turn back to him, and none of you were harmed by us. ¹⁰ When God makes you feel sorry enough to turn to him and be saved, you don't have anything to feel bad about. But when this world makes you feel sorry, it can cause your death.

¹¹ Just look what God has done by making you feel sorry! You sincerely want to prove that you are innocent. You are angry. You are shocked. You are eager to see that justice is done. You have proved that you were completely right in this matter. ¹² When I wrote you, it wasn't to accuse the one who was wrong or to take up for the one who was hurt. I wrote, so that God would show you how much you do care for us. ¹³ And we were greatly encouraged.

Although we were encouraged, we felt even better when we saw how happy Titus was, because you had shown that he had nothing to worry about. ¹⁴ We had told him how much we thought of you, and you did not disappoint us. Just as we have always told you the truth, so everything we told him about you has also proved to be true. ¹⁵ Titus loves all of you very much, especially when he remembers how you obeyed him and how you trembled with fear when you welcomed him. ¹⁶ It makes me really glad to know that I can depend on you.

### Generous Giving

**8** My friends, we want you to know that the churches in Macedonia<sup>h</sup> have shown others how kind God is.

² Although they were going through hard times and were very poor, they were glad to give generously. ³ They gave as much as they could afford and even more, simply because they wanted to. ⁴ They even asked and begged us to let them have the joy of giving their money for God's people. ⁵ And they did more than we had hoped. They gave themselves first to the Lord and then to us, just as God wanted them to do.

⁶ Titus was the one who got you started doing this good thing, so we begged him to have you finish what you had begun. ⁷ You do everything better than anyone else. You have stronger faith. You speak better and know more. You are eager to give, and you love us better.<sup>i</sup> Now you must give more generously than anyone else.

⁸ I am not ordering you to do this. I am simply testing how real your love is by comparing it with the concern that others have shown. ⁹ You know that our Lord Jesus Christ was kind enough to give up all his riches and become poor, so that you could become rich.

¹⁰ A year ago you were the first ones to give, and you gave because you wanted to. So listen to my advice. ¹¹ I think you should finish what you started. If you give according to what you have, you will prove that you are as eager to give as you were to think about giving. ¹² It doesn't matter how much you have. What matters is how much you are willing to give from what you have.

¹³ I am not trying to make life easier for others by making life harder for you. But it is only fair ¹⁴ for you to share with them when you have so much, and they have so little. Later, when they have more than enough, and you are in need, they can share with you. Then everyone will have a fair share, ¹⁵ just as the Scriptures say,

"Those who gathered
too much
    had nothing left.

ᵍ7.8 *my letter*: There is no copy of this letter that Paul wrote to the church at Corinth. ʰ8.1 *churches in Macedonia*: The churches that Paul had started in Philippi and Thessalonica. The church in Berea is probably also meant. ⁱ8.7 *you love us better*: Some manuscripts have "we love you better."

Those who gathered
only a little
    had all they needed."

## Titus and His Friends

¹⁶ I am grateful that God made Titus care as much about you as we do. ¹⁷ When we begged Titus to visit you, he said he would. He wanted to because he cared so much for you. ¹⁸ With Titus we are also sending one of the Lord's followers who is well known in every church for spreading the good news. ¹⁹ The churches chose this follower to travel with us while we carry this gift that will bring praise to the Lord and show how much we hope to help. ²⁰ We don't want anyone to find fault with the way we handle your generous gift. ²¹ But we want to do what pleases the Lord and what people think is right.

²² We are also sending someone else with Titus and the other follower. We approve of this man. In fact, he has already shown us many times that he wants to help. And now he wants to help even more than ever, because he trusts you so much. ²³ Titus is my partner, who works with me to serve you. The other two followers are sent by the churches, and they bring honor to Christ. ²⁴ Treat them in such a way that the churches will see your love and will know why we bragged about you.

## The Money for God's People

**9** I don't need to write you about the money you plan to give for God's people. ² I know how eager you are to give. And I have proudly told the Lord's followers in Macedonia that you people in Achaia have been ready for a whole year. Now your desire to give has made them want to give. ³ That's why I am sending Titus and the two others to you. I want you to be ready, just as I promised. This will prove that we were not wrong to brag about you.

⁴ Some followers from Macedonia may come with me, and I want them to find that you have the money ready. If you don't, I would be embarrassed for trusting you to do this. But you would be embarrassed even more. ⁵ So I have decided to ask Titus and the oth-

ers to spend some time with you before I arrive. This way they can arrange to collect the money you have promised. Then you will have the chance to give because you want to, and not because you feel forced to. ⁶ Remember this saying,

"A few seeds make
    a small harvest,
but a lot of seeds make
    a big harvest."

⁷ Each of you must make up your own mind about how much to give. But don't feel sorry that you must give and don't feel that you are forced to give. God loves people who love to give. ⁸ God can bless you with everything you need, and you will always have more than enough to do all kinds of good things for others. ⁹ The Scriptures say,

"God freely gives his gifts
to the poor,
    and always does right."

¹⁰ God gives seed to farmers and provides everyone with food. He will increase what you have, so that you can give even more to those in need. ¹¹ You will be blessed in every way, and you will be able to keep on being generous. Then many people will thank God when we deliver your gift. ¹² What you are doing is much more than a service that supplies God's people with what they need. It is something that will make many others thank God. ¹³ The way in which you have proved yourselves by this service will bring honor and praise to God. You believed the message about Christ, and you obeyed it by sharing generously with God's people and with everyone else. ¹⁴ Now they are praying for you and want to see you, because God used you to bless them so very much. ¹⁵ Thank God for his gift that is too wonderful for words!

## Paul Defends His Work for Christ

**10** Do you think I am a coward when I am with you and brave when I am far away? Well, I ask you to listen, because Christ himself was humble and gentle. ² Some people have said that we act like the people of this world. So when I arrive, I expect I will have to be firm and forceful in what I say to them. Please don't make me treat you that way. ³ We live in this world, but we don't act like its people ⁴ or fight our battles with the weapons of this world. Instead, we use God's power that can destroy fortresses. We destroy arguments ⁵ and every bit of pride that keeps anyone from knowing God. We capture people's thoughts and make them obey Christ. ⁶ And when you completely obey him, we will punish anyone who refuses to obey.

⁷ You judge by appearances.ⁱ If any of you think you are the only ones who belong to Christ, then think again. We belong to Christ as much as you do. ⁸ Maybe I brag a little too much about the authority that the Lord gave me to help you and not to hurt you. Yet I am not embarrassed to brag. ⁹ And I am not trying to scare you with my letters. ¹⁰ Some of you are saying, "Paul's letters are harsh and powerful. But in person, he is a weakling and has nothing worth saying." ¹¹ Those people had better understand that when I am with you, I will do exactly what I say in my letters.

¹² We won't dare compare ourselves with those who think so much of themselves. But they are foolish to compare themselves with themselves. ¹³ We won't brag about something we don't have a right to brag about. We will only brag about the work that God has sent us to do, and you are part of that work. ¹⁴ We are not bragging more than we should. After all, we did bring the message about Christ to you.

¹⁵ We don't brag about what others have done, as if we had done those things ourselves. But I hope that as you become stronger in your faith, we will be able to reach many more of the people around you.ᵏ That has always been our goal. ¹⁶ Then we will be able to preach the good news in other lands where we cannot take credit for work someone else has already done. ¹⁷ The Scriptures say, "If you want to brag, then brag about the Lord." ¹⁸ You may

brag about yourself, but the only approval that counts is the Lord's approval.

### Paul and the False Apostles

**11** Please put up with a little of my foolishness. ² I am as concerned about you as God is. You were like a virgin bride I had chosen only for Christ. ³ But now I fear that you will be tricked, just as Eve was tricked by that lying snake. I am afraid that you might stop thinking about Christ in an honest and sincere way. ⁴ We told you about Jesus, and you received the Holy Spirit and accepted our message. But you let some people tell you about another Jesus. Now you are ready to receive another spirit and accept a different message. ⁵ I think I am as good as any of those super apostles. ⁶ I may not speak as well as they do, but I know as much. And this has already been made perfectly clear to you.

⁷ Was it wrong for me to lower myself and honor you by preaching God's message free of charge? ⁸ I robbed other churches by taking money from them to serve you. ⁹ Even when I was in need, I still didn't bother you. In fact, some of the Lord's followers from Macedonia brought me what I needed. I have not been a burden to you in the past, and I will never be a burden. ¹⁰ As surely as I speak the truth about Christ, no one in Achaia can stop me from bragging about this. ¹¹ And it isn't because I don't love you. God himself knows how much I do love you.

¹² I plan to go on doing just what I have always done. Then those people won't be able to brag about doing the same things we are doing. ¹³ Anyway, they are no more than false apostles and dishonest workers. They only pretend to be apostles of Christ. ¹⁴ And it is no wonder. Even Satan tries to make himself look like an angel of light. ¹⁵ So why does it seem strange for Satan's servants to pretend to do what is right? Someday they will get exactly what they deserve.

---

ⁱ 10.7 *You judge by appearances*: Or "Take a close look at yourselves."   ᵏ 10.15 *we will be able to reach many more of the people around you*: Or "you will praise us even more because of our work among you."

## Paul's Sufferings for Christ

[16] I don't want any of you to think that I am a fool. But if you do, then let me be a fool and brag a little. [17] When I do all this bragging, I do it as a fool and not for the Lord. [18] Yet if others want to brag about what they have done, so will I. [19] And since you are so smart, you will gladly put up with a fool. [20] In fact, you let people make slaves of you and cheat you and steal from you. Why, you even let them strut around and slap you in the face. [21] I am ashamed to say that we are too weak to behave in such a way.

If they can brag, so can I, but it is a foolish thing to do. [22] Are they Hebrews? So am I. Are they Jews? So am I. Are they from the family of Abraham? Well, so am I. [23] Are they servants of Christ? I am a fool to talk this way, but I serve him better than they do. I have worked harder and have been put in jail more times. I have been beaten with whips more and have been in danger of death more often.

[24] Five times my own people gave me thirty-nine lashes with a whip. [25] Three times the Romans beat me with a big stick, and once my enemies stoned me. I have been shipwrecked three times, and I even had to spend a night and a day in the sea. [26] During my many travels, I have been in danger from rivers, robbers, my own people, and foreigners. My life has been in danger in cities, in deserts, at sea, and with people who only pretended to be the Lord's followers.

[27] I have worked and struggled and spent many sleepless nights. I have gone hungry and thirsty and often had nothing to eat. I have been cold from not having enough clothes to keep me warm. [28] Besides everything else, each day I am burdened down, worrying about all the churches. [29] When others are weak, I am weak too. When others are tricked into sin, I get angry.[l]

[30] If I have to brag, I will brag about how weak I am. [31] God, the Father of our Lord Jesus, knows I am not lying. And God is to be praised forever! [32] The governor of Damascus at the time of King Aretas had the city gates guarded, so that he could capture me. [33] But I escaped by being let down in a basket through a window in the city wall.

## Visions from the Lord

**12** I have to brag. There is nothing to be gained by it, but I must brag about the visions and other things that the Lord has shown me. [2] I know about one of Christ's followers who was taken up into the third heaven fourteen years ago. I don't know if the man was still in his body when it happened, but God certainly knows.

[3] As I said, only God really knows if this man was in his body at the time. [4] But he was taken up into paradise,[m] where he heard things that are too wonderful to tell. [5] I will brag about that man, but not about myself, except to say how weak I am.

[6] Yet even if I did brag, I would not be foolish. I would simply be speaking the truth. But I will try not to say too much. That way, none of you will think more highly of me than you should because of what you have seen me do and say. [7] Of course, I am now referring to the wonderful things I saw. One of Satan's angels was sent to make me suffer terribly, so that I would not feel too proud.[n]

[8] Three times I begged the Lord to make this suffering go away. [9] But he replied, "My kindness is all you need. My power is strongest when you are weak." So if Christ keeps giving me his power, I will gladly brag about how weak I am. [10] Yes, I am glad to be weak or insulted or mistreated or to have troubles and sufferings, if it is for Christ. Because when I am weak, I am strong.

---

[l] **11.29** *When others are tricked into sin, I get angry*: Or "When others stumble into sin, I hurt for them." [m] **12.4** *paradise*: In the Greek translation of the Old Testament, this word is used for the Garden of Eden. In New Testament times it was sometimes used for the place where God's people are happy and at rest, as they wait for the final judgment. [n] **12.7** *Of course . . . too proud*: Or "Because of the wonderful things that I saw, one of Satan's angels was sent to make me suffer terribly, so that I would not feel too proud."

## Paul's Concern
## for the Lord's Followers at Corinth

¹¹ I have been making a fool of my-self. But you forced me to do it, when you should have been speaking up for me. I may be nothing at all, but I am as good as those super apostles. ¹² When I was with you, I was patient and worked all the powerful miracles and signs and wonders of a true apostle. ¹³ You missed out on only one blessing that the other churches received. That is, you didn't have to support me. Forgive me for doing you wrong.

¹⁴ I am planning to visit you for the third time. But I still won't make a burden of myself. What I really want is you, and not what you have. Children are not supposed to save up for their parents, but parents are supposed to take care of their children. ¹⁵ So I will gladly give all that I have and all that I am. Will you love me less for loving you too much? ¹⁶ You agree that I wasn't a burden to you. Maybe that's because I was trying to catch you off guard and trick you. ¹⁷ Were you cheated by any of those I sent to you? ¹⁸ I urged Titus to visit you, and I sent another follower with him. But Titus didn't cheat you, and we felt and behaved the same way he did.

¹⁹ Have you been thinking all along that we have been defending ourselves to you? Actually, we have been speaking to God as followers of Christ. But, my friends, we did it all for your good.

²⁰ I am afraid that when I come, we won't be pleased with each other. I fear that some of you may be arguing or jealous or angry or selfish or gossiping or insulting each other. I even fear that you may be proud and acting like a mob. ²¹ I am afraid God will make me ashamed when I visit you again. I will feel like crying because many of you have never given up your old sins. You are still doing things that are immoral, indecent, and shameful.

## Final Warnings and Greetings

**13** I am on my way to visit you for the third time. And as the Scriptures say, "Any charges must be proved true by at least two or three witnesses." ² During my second visit I warned you that I would punish you and anyone else who doesn't stop sinning. I am far away from you now, but I give you the same warning. ³ This should prove to you that I am speaking for Christ. When he corrects you, he won't be weak. He will be powerful! ⁴ Although he was weak when he was nailed to the cross, he now lives by the power of God. We are weak, just as Christ was. But you will see that we will live by the power of God, just as Christ does.

⁵ Test yourselves and find out if you really are true to your faith. If you pass the test, you will discover that Christ is living in you. But if Christ isn't living in you, you have failed. ⁶ I hope you will discover that we have not failed. ⁷ We pray that you will stop doing evil things. We don't pray like this to make ourselves look good, but to get you to do right, even if we are failures.

⁸ All we can do is to follow the truth and not fight against it. ⁹ Even though we are weak, we are glad that you are strong, and we pray that you will do even better. ¹⁰ I am writing these things to you before I arrive. This way I won't have to be hard on you when I use the authority that the Lord has given me. I was given this authority, so that I could help you and not destroy you.

¹¹ Good-by, my friends. Do better and pay attention to what I have said. Try to get along and live peacefully with each other.

Now I pray that God, who gives love and peace, will be with you. ¹² Give each other a warm greeting. All of God's people send their greetings.

¹³ I pray that the Lord Jesus Christ will bless you and be kind to you! May God bless you with his love, and may the Holy Spirit join all your hearts together.

# GALATIANS

## ABOUT THIS LETTER

*From the very beginning of this letter to the churches in the region of Galatia (in central Asia Minor), Paul makes two things clear to his readers: he is a true apostle, and his message is the only true message (1.1-10). These statements were very important, because some people claimed that Paul was a false apostle with a false message.*

*Paul was indeed a true apostle, and his mission to the Gentiles was given to him by the Lord and approved by the apostles in Jerusalem (1.18—2.10). Paul had even corrected the apostle Peter, when he had stopped eating with Gentile followers who were not obeying the Law of Moses (2.1-18).*

*Faith is the only way to be saved. Paul insists that this was true already for Abraham, who had received God's promise by faith. And Paul leaves no doubt about what his own faith means to him:*

> I have been nailed to the cross with Christ. I have died, but
> Christ lives in me. And I now live by faith in the Son of God,
> who loved me and gave his life for me.          (2.19b, 20)

## A QUICK LOOK AT THIS LETTER

*A True Apostle and the True Message (1.1-10)*
*God Chose Paul To Be an Apostle (1.11-24)*
*Paul Defends His Message (2.1-21)*
*Faith Is the Only Way To Be Saved (3.1—4.31)*
*Guided by the Spirit and Love (5.1—6.10)*
*Final Warnings (6.11-18)*

---

**1** **1-2** From the apostle Paul and from all the Lord's followers with me.

I was chosen to be an apostle by Jesus Christ and by God the Father, who raised him from death. No mere human chose or appointed me to this work.

To the churches in Galatia.

**3** I pray that God the Father and our Lord Jesus Christ will be kind to you and will bless you with peace! **4** Christ obeyed God our Father and gave himself as a sacrifice for our sins to rescue us from this evil world. **5** God will be given glory forever and ever. Amen.

### The Only True Message

**6** I am shocked that you have so quickly turned from God, who chose you because of his wonderful kindness.[a] You have believed another message, **7** when there is really only one true message. But some people are causing you trouble and want to make you turn away from the good news about Christ. **8** I pray that God will punish anyone who preaches anything different from our message to you! It doesn't matter if that person is one of us or an angel from heaven. **9** I have said it before, and I will say it again. I hope God will punish anyone who preaches anything different from what you have already believed.

**10** I am not trying to please people. I want to please God. Do you think I am trying to please people? If I were doing that, I would not be a servant of Christ.

---

*a* **1.6** *his wonderful kindness:* Some manuscripts have "the wonderful kindness of Christ."

## How Paul Became an Apostle

[11] My friends, I want you to know that no one made up the message I preach. [12] It wasn't given or taught to me by some mere human. My message came directly from Jesus Christ when he appeared to me.

[13] You know how I used to live as a Jew. I was cruel to God's church and even tried to destroy it. [14] I was a much better Jew than anyone else my own age, and I obeyed every law that our ancestors had given us. [15] But even before I was born, God had chosen me. He was kind and had decided [16] to show me his Son, so that I would announce his message to the Gentiles. I didn't talk this over with anyone. [17] I didn't say a word, not even to the men in Jerusalem who were apostles before I was. Instead, I went at once to Arabia, and afterwards I returned to Damascus.

[18] Three years later I went to visit Peter[b] in Jerusalem and stayed with him for fifteen days. [19] The only other apostle I saw was James, the Lord's brother. [20] And in the presence of God I swear I am telling the truth.

[21] Later, I went to the regions of Syria and Cilicia. [22] But no one who belonged to Christ's churches in Judea had ever seen me in person. [23] They had only heard that the one who had been cruel to them was now preaching the message that he had once tried to destroy. [24] And because of me, they praised God.

**2** Fourteen years later I went to Jerusalem with Barnabas. I also took along Titus. [2] But I went there because God had told me to go, and I explained the good news that I had been preaching to the Gentiles. Then I met privately with the ones who seemed to be the most important leaders. I wanted to make sure that my work in the past and my future work would not be for nothing.

[3] Titus went to Jerusalem with me. He was a Greek, but still he wasn't forced to be circumcised. [4] We went there because of those who pretended to be fol-lowers and had sneaked in among us as spies. They had come to take away the freedom that Christ Jesus had given us, and they were trying to make us their slaves. [5] But we wanted you to have the true message. That's why we didn't give in to them, not even for a second.

[6] Some of them were supposed to be important leaders, but I didn't care who they were. God doesn't have any favorites! None of these so-called special leaders added anything to my message. [7] They realized that God had sent me with the good news for Gentiles, and that he had sent Peter with the same message for Jews. [8] God, who had sent Peter on a mission to the Jews, was now using me to preach to the Gentiles.

[9] James, Peter,[b] and John realized that God had given me the message about his undeserved kindness. And these men are supposed to be the backbone of the church. They even gave Barnabas and me a friendly hand-shake. This was to show that we would work with Gentiles and that they would work with Jews. [10] They only asked us to remember the poor, and that was something I had always been eager to do.

## Paul Corrects Peter at Antioch

[11] When Peter came to Antioch, I told him face-to-face that he was wrong. [12] He used to eat with Gentile followers of the Lord, until James sent some Jewish followers. Peter was afraid of the Jews and soon stopped eating with Gentiles. [13] He and the others hid their true feelings so well that even Barnabas was fooled. [14] But when I saw that they were not really obeying the truth that is in the good news, I corrected Peter in front of everyone and said:

Peter, you are a Jew, but you live like a Gentile. So how can you force Gentiles to live like Jews?

[15] We are Jews by birth and are not sinners like Gentiles. [16] But we know that God accepts only those

who have faith in Jesus Christ. No one can please God by simply obeying the Law. So we put our faith in Christ Jesus, and God accepted us because of our faith.

17 When we Jews started looking for a way to please God, we discovered that we are sinners too. Does this mean that Christ is the one who makes us sinners? No, it doesn't! 18 But if I tear down something and then build it again, I prove that I was wrong at first. 19 It was the Law itself that killed me and freed me from its power, so that I could live for God.

I have been nailed to the cross with Christ. 20 I have died, but Christ lives in me. And I now live by faith in the Son of God, who loved me and gave his life for me. 21 I don't turn my back on God's undeserved kindness. If we can be acceptable to God by obeying the Law, it was useless for Christ to die.

### Faith Is the Only Way

3 You stupid Galatians! I told you exactly how Jesus Christ was nailed to a cross. Has someone now put an evil spell on you? 2 I want to know only one thing. How were you given God's Spirit? Was it by obeying the Law of Moses or by hearing about Christ and having faith in him? 3 How can you be so stupid? Do you think that by yourself you can complete what God's Spirit started in you? 4 Have you gone through all of this for nothing? Is it all really for nothing? 5 God gives you his Spirit and works miracles in you. But does he do this because you obey the Law of Moses or because you have heard about Christ and have faith in him?

6 The Scriptures say that God accepted Abraham because Abraham had faith. 7 And so, you should understand that everyone who has faith is a child of Abraham. c 8 Long ago the Scriptures said that God would accept the Gentiles because of their faith. That's why God told Abraham the good news that all nations would be blessed because of him. 9 This means that everyone who has faith will share in the blessings that were given to Abraham because of his faith.

10 Anyone who tries to please God by obeying the Law is under a curse. The Scriptures say, "Everyone who doesn't obey everything in the Law is under a curse." 11 No one can please God by obeying the Law. The Scriptures also say, "The people God accepts because of their faith will live." d

12 The Law isn't based on faith. It promises life only to people who obey its commands. 13 But Christ rescued us from the Law's curse, when he became a curse in our place. This is because the Scriptures say that anyone who is nailed to a tree is under a curse. 14 And because of what Jesus Christ has done, the blessing that was promised to Abraham was taken to the Gentiles. This happened so that by faith we would be given the promised Holy Spirit.

### The Law and the Promise

15 My friends, I will use an everyday example to explain what I mean. Once someone agrees to something, no one else can change or cancel the agreement. e 16 That is how it is with the promises God made to Abraham and his descendant. f The promises were not made to many descendants, but only to one, and that one is Christ. 17 What I am saying is that the Law cannot change or cancel God's promise that was made 430 years before the Law was given. 18 If we have to obey the Law in order to receive God's blessings, those blessings don't really come to us because of God's promise. But God was

---

c3.7 a child of Abraham: God chose Abraham, and so it was believed that anyone who was a child of Abraham was also a child of God (see the note at 3.29). d3.11 The people God accepts because of their faith will live: Or "The people God accepts will live because of their faith." e3.15 Once someone . . . cancel the agreement: Or "Once a person makes out a will, no one can change or cancel it." f3.16 descendant: The Greek text has "seed," which may mean one or many descendants. In this verse Paul says it means Christ.

kind to Abraham and made him a promise.

19 What is the use of the Law? It was given later to show that we sin. But it was only supposed to last until the coming of that descendant[g] who was given the promise. In fact, angels gave the Law to Moses, and he gave it to the people. 20 There is only one God, and the Law did not come directly from him.

### Slaves and Children

21 Does the Law disagree with God's promises? No, it doesn't! If any law could give life to us, we could become acceptable to God by obeying that law. 22 But the Scriptures say that sin controls everyone, so that God's promises will be for anyone who has faith in Jesus Christ.

23 The Law controlled us and kept us under its power until the time came when we would have faith. 24 In fact, the Law was our teacher. It was supposed to teach us until we had faith and were acceptable to God. 25 But once a person has learned to have faith, there is no more need to have the Law as a teacher.

26 All of you are God's children because of your faith in Christ Jesus. 27 And when you were baptized, it was as though you had put on Christ in the same way you put on new clothes. 28 Faith in Christ Jesus is what makes each of you equal with each other, whether you are a Jew or a Greek, a slave or a free person, a man or a woman. 29 So if you belong to Christ, you are now part of Abraham's family,[h] and you will be given what God

4 has promised. 1 Children who are under age are no better off than slaves, even though everything their parents own will someday be theirs. 2 This is because children are placed in the care of guardians and teachers until the time their parents have set. 3 That is how it was with us. We were like children ruled by the powers of this world.

4 But when the time was right, God sent his Son, and a woman gave birth to him. His Son obeyed the Law, 5 so he could set us free from the Law, and we could become God's children. 6 Now that we are his children, God has sent the Spirit of his Son into our hearts. And his Spirit tells us that God is our Father. 7 You are no longer slaves. You are God's children, and you will be given what he has promised.

### Paul's Concern for the Galatians

8 Before you knew God, you were slaves of gods that are not real. 9 But now you know God, or better still, God knows you. How can you turn back and become the slaves of those weak and pitiful powers?[i] 10 You even celebrate certain days, months, seasons, and years. 11 I am afraid I have wasted my time working with you.

12 My friends, I beg you to be like me, just as I once tried to be like you. Did you mistreat me 13 when I first preached to you? No you didn't, even though you knew I had come there because I was sick. 14 My illness must have caused you some trouble, but you didn't hate me or turn me away because of it. You welcomed me as though I were one of God's angels or even Christ Jesus himself. 15 Where is that good feeling now? I am sure that if it had been possible, you would have taken out your own eyes and given them to me. 16 Am I now your enemy, just because I told you the truth?

17 Those people may be paying you a lot of attention, but it isn't for your good. They only want to keep you away from me, so you will pay them a lot of attention. 18 It is always good to give your attention to something worthwhile, even when I am not with you. 19 My children, I am in terrible pain until Christ may be seen living in you. 20 I wish I were with you now. Then I would

---

[g]3.19 *that descendant*: Jesus.   [h]3.29 *you are now part of Abraham's family*: Paul tells the Galatians that faith in Jesus Christ is what makes someone a true child of Abraham and of God (see the note at 3.7).   [i]4.9 *powers*: Spirits were thought to control human lives and were believed to be connected with the movements of the stars.

not have to talk this way. You really have me puzzled.

### Hagar and Sarah

21 Some of you would like to be under the rule of the Law of Moses. But do you know what the Law says? 22 In the Scriptures we learn that Abraham had two sons. The mother of one of them was a slave, while the mother of the other one had always been free. 23 The son of the slave woman was born in the usual way. But the son of the free woman was born because of God's promise.

24 All of this has another meaning as well. Each of the two women stands for one of the agreements God made with his people. Hagar, the slave woman, stands for the agreement that was made at Mount Sinai. Everyone born into her family is a slave. 25 Hagar also stands for Mount Sinai in Arabia*j* and for the present city of Jerusalem. She*k* and her children are slaves. 26 But our mother is the city of Jerusalem in heaven above, and she isn't a slave. 27 The Scriptures say about her,

"You have never had children,
  but now you can be glad.
You have never given birth,
  but now you can shout.
Once you had no children,
  but now you will have
more children than a woman
  who has been married
    for a long time."

28 My friends, you were born because of this promise, just as Isaac was. 29 But the child who was born in the natural way made trouble for the child who was born because of the Spirit. The same thing is happening today. 30 The Scriptures say, "Get rid of the slave woman and her son! He won't be given anything. The son of the free woman will receive everything." 31 My friends, we are children of the free woman and not of the slave.

### Christ Gives Freedom

**5** Christ has set us free! This means we are really free. Now hold on to your freedom and don't ever become slaves of the Law again.

2 I, Paul, promise you that Christ won't do you any good if you get circumcised. 3 If you do, you must obey the whole Law. 4 And if you try to please God by obeying the Law, you have cut yourself off from Christ and his wonderful kindness. 5 But the Spirit makes us sure that God will accept us because of our faith in Christ. 6 If you are a follower of Christ Jesus, it makes no difference whether you are circumcised or not. All that matters is your faith that makes you love others.

7 You were doing so well until someone made you turn from the truth. 8 And that person was certainly not sent by the one who chose you. 9 A little yeast can change a whole batch of dough, 10 but you belong to the Lord. That makes me certain that you will do what I say, instead of what someone else tells you to do. Whoever is causing trouble for you will be punished.

11 My friends, if I still preach that people need to be circumcised, why am I in so much trouble? The message about the cross would no longer be a problem, if I told people to be circumcised. 12 I wish that everyone who is upsetting you would not only get circumcised, but would cut off much more!

13 My friends, you were chosen to be free. So don't use your freedom as an excuse to do anything you want. Use it as an opportunity to serve each other with love. 14 All that the Law says can be summed up in the command to love others as much as you love yourself. 15 But if you keep attacking each other like wild animals, you had better watch out or you will destroy yourselves.

### God's Spirit and Our Own Desires

16 If you are guided by the Spirit, you won't obey your selfish desires. 17 The Spirit and your desires are enemies of

*j***4.25** *Hagar also stands for Mount Sinai in Arabia*: Some manuscripts have "Sinai is a mountain in Arabia." This sentence would then be translated: "Sinai is a mountain in Arabia, and Hagar stands for the present city of Jerusalem." *k***4.25** *She*: "Hagar" or "Jerusalem."

each other. They are always fighting each other and keeping you from doing what you feel you should. [18]But if you obey the Spirit, the Law of Moses has no control over you.

[19]People's desires make them give in to immoral ways, filthy thoughts, and shameful deeds. [20]They worship idols, practice witchcraft, hate others, and are hard to get along with. People become jealous, angry, and selfish. They not only argue and cause trouble, but they are [21]envious. They get drunk, carry on at wild parties, and do other evil things as well. I told you before, and I am telling you again: No one who does these things will share in the blessings of God's kingdom.

[22]God's Spirit makes us loving, happy, peaceful, patient, kind, good, faithful, [23]gentle, and self-controlled. There is no law against behaving in any of these ways. [24]And because we belong to Christ Jesus, we have killed our selfish feelings and desires. [25]God's Spirit has given us life, and so we should follow the Spirit. [26]But don't be conceited or make others jealous by claiming to be better than they are.

## Help Each Other

6 My friends, you are spiritual. So if someone is trapped in sin, you should gently lead that person back to the right path. But watch out, and don't be tempted yourself. [2]You obey the law of Christ when you offer each other a helping hand.

[3]If you think you are better than others, when you really aren't, you are wrong. [4]Do your own work well, and then you will have something to be proud of. But don't compare yourself with others. [5]We each must carry our own load.

[6]Share every good thing you have with anyone who teaches you what God has said.

[7]You cannot fool God, so don't make a fool of yourself! You will harvest what you plant. [8]If you follow your selfish desires, you will harvest destruction, but if you follow the Spirit, you will harvest eternal life. [9]Don't get tired of helping others. You will be rewarded when the time is right, if you don't give up. [10]We should help people whenever we can, especially if they are followers of the Lord.

## Final Warnings

[11]You can see what big letters I make when I write with my own hand. [12]Those people who are telling you to get circumcised are only trying to show how important they are. And they don't want to get into trouble for preaching about the cross of Christ. [13]They are circumcised, but they don't obey the Law of Moses. All they want is to brag about having you circumcised. [14]But I will never brag about anything except the cross of our Lord Jesus Christ. Because of his cross, the world is dead as far as I am concerned, and I am dead as far as the world is concerned. [15]It doesn't matter if you are circumcised or not. All that matters is that you are a new person. [16]If you follow this rule, you will belong to God's true people. God will treat you with undeserved kindness and will bless you with peace. [17]On my own body are scars that prove I belong to Christ Jesus. So I don't want anyone to bother me anymore. [18]My friends, I pray that the Lord Jesus Christ will be kind to you! Amen.

# EPHESIANS

## ABOUT THIS LETTER

"Praise the God and Father of our Lord Jesus Christ for the spiritual blessings that Christ has brought us from heaven!" (1.3). Paul begins his letter to the Christians in Ephesus with a powerful reminder of the main theme of his message. Christ died on the cross to set us free (1.7, 8). But God raised Christ from death, and he now sits at God's right side in heaven, where he rules over this world. And he will rule over the future world as well (1.20, 21).

Christ brought Jews and Gentiles together by "breaking down the wall of hatred" that separated them (2.14) and he united them all as part of that holy temple where God's Spirit lives (2.22). This was according to God's eternal plan (3.11).

There is only one Lord, one Spirit of God, and one God, who is the Father of all people (4.4, 5). This means that Christians must let the Spirit keep their hearts united, so they can live at peace with each other (4.3). The idea of all Christians being one with Christ is so central to this letter that it occurs twenty times. There is one faith and one baptism by which believers become one body.

Ephesus was a port city on the western shore of Asia Minor (modern-day Turkey). In Paul's time this was the fourth largest city in the Roman empire. It was also an ancient center of nature religion where the goddess Artemis was widely worshiped (Acts 19).

Paul lets the Ephesians know that much is expected of people who are called to a new life (4.17—5.20). Followers of the Lord are God's dear children, and they must do as God does (5.1). They used to live in the dark, but they must now live in the light and make their light shine (5.8, 9).

Paul then teaches husbands and wives, children and parents, and slaves and masters how to live as Christians (5.21—6.9).

Paul never forgets how kind God is:

> God was merciful! We were dead because of our sins, but God loved us so much that he made us alive with Christ, and God's wonderful kindness is what saves you. . . . You were saved by faith in God, who treats us much better than we deserve. This is God's gift to you, and not anything you have done on your own. (2.4, 5, 8)

## A QUICK LOOK AT THIS LETTER

Greetings (1.1, 2)
Christ Brings Spiritual Blessings (1.3—3.21)
A New Life in Unity with Christ (4.1—6.20)
Final Greetings (6.21-24)

# 1
From Paul, chosen by God to be an apostle of Christ Jesus.

To God's people who live in Ephesus and[a] are faithful followers of Christ Jesus.

[2] I pray that God our Father and our Lord Jesus Christ will be kind to you and will bless you with peace!

## Christ Brings
## Spiritual Blessings

[3] Praise the God and Father of our Lord Jesus Christ for the spiritual blessings that Christ has brought us from heaven! [4] Before the world was created, God had Christ choose us to live with him and to be his holy and innocent and loving people. [5] God was kind[b] and decided that Christ would choose us to be God's own adopted children. [6] God was very kind to us because of the Son he dearly loves, and so we should praise God.

[7-8] Christ sacrificed his life's blood to set us free, which means that our sins are now forgiven. Christ did this because God was so kind to us. God has great wisdom and understanding, [9] and by what Christ has done, God has shown us his own mysterious ways. [10] Then when the time is right, God will do all that he has planned, and Christ will bring together everything in heaven and on earth.

[11] God always does what he plans, and that's why he had Christ choose us. [12] He did this so that we Jews would bring honor to him and be the first ones to have hope because of him. [13] Christ also brought you the truth, which is the good news about how you can be saved. You put your faith in Christ and were given the promised Holy Spirit to show that you belong to God. [14] The Spirit also makes us sure that we will be given what God has stored up for his people. Then we will be set free, and God will be honored and praised.

## Paul's Prayer

[15] I have heard about your faith in the Lord Jesus and your love for all of God's people. [16] So I never stop being grateful for you, as I mention you in my prayers. [17] I ask the glorious Father and God of our Lord Jesus Christ to give you his Spirit. The Spirit will make you wise and let you understand what it means to know God. [18] My prayer is that light will flood your hearts and that you will understand the hope that was given to you when God chose you. Then you will discover the glorious blessings that will be yours together with all of God's people.

[19] I want you to know about the great and mighty power that God has for us followers. It is the same wonderful power he used [20] when he raised Christ from death and let him sit at his right side[c] in heaven. [21] There Christ rules over all forces, authorities, powers, and rulers. He rules over all beings in this world and will rule in the future world as well. [22] God has put all things under the power of Christ, and for the good of the church he has made him the head of everything. [23] The church is Christ's body and is filled with Christ who completely fills everything.[d]

## From Death to Life

# 2
In the past you were dead because you sinned and fought against God. [2] You followed the ways of this world and obeyed the devil. He rules the world, and his spirit has power over everyone who doesn't obey God. [3] Once we were also ruled by the selfish desires of our bodies and minds. We had made God angry, and we were going to be punished like everyone else.

[4-5] But God was merciful! We were dead because of our sins, but God loved us so much that he made us alive with Christ, and God's wonderful kindness is what saves you. [6] God raised us from death to life with Christ Jesus, and he

---

[a] **1.1** *live in Ephesus and*: Some manuscripts do not have these words.   [b] **1.4,5** *holy and innocent and loving people.* [5] *God was kind*: Or "holy and innocent people. God was loving [5] and kind."   [c] **1.20** *right side*: The place of power and honor.   [d] **1.23** *and is filled with Christ who completely fills everything*: Or "which completely fills Christ and fully completes his work."

has given us a place beside Christ in heaven. [7] God did this so that in the future world he could show how truly good and kind he is to us because of what Christ Jesus has done. [8] You were saved by faith in God, who treats us much better than we deserve.[e] This is God's gift to you, and not anything you have done on your own. [9] It isn't something you have earned, so there is nothing you can brag about. [10] God planned for us to do good things and to live as he has always wanted us to live. That's why he sent Christ to make us what we are.

### United by Christ

[11] Don't forget that you are Gentiles. In fact, you used to be called "uncircumcised" by those who take pride in being circumcised. [12] At that time you did not know about Christ. You were foreigners to the people of Israel, and you had no part in the promises that God had made to them. You were living in this world without hope and without God, [13] and you were far from God. But Christ offered his life's blood as a sacrifice and brought you near God.

[14] Christ has made peace between Jews and Gentiles, and he has united us by breaking down the wall of hatred that separated us. Christ gave his own body [15] to destroy the Law of Moses with all its rules and commands. He even brought Jews and Gentiles together as though we were only one person, when he united us in peace. [16] On the cross Christ did away with our hatred for each other. He also made peace[f] between us and God by uniting Jews and Gentiles in one body. [17] Christ came and preached peace to you Gentiles, who were far from God, and peace to us Jews, who were near God. [18] And because of Christ, all of us can come to the Father by the same Spirit.

[19] You Gentiles are no longer strangers and foreigners. You are citizens with everyone else who belongs to the family of God. [20] You are like a building with the apostles and prophets as the foundation and with Christ as the most important stone. [21] Christ is the one who holds the building together and makes it grow into a holy temple for the Lord. [22] And you are part of that building Christ has built as a place for God's own Spirit to live.

### Paul's Mission to the Gentiles

**3** Christ Jesus made me his prisoner, so that I could help you Gentiles. [2] You have surely heard about God's kindness in choosing me to help you. [3] In fact, this letter tells you a little about how God has shown me his mysterious ways. [4] As you read the letter, you will also find out how well I really do understand the mystery about Christ. [5] No one knew about this mystery until God's Spirit told it to his holy apostles and prophets. [6] And the mystery is this: Because of Christ Jesus, the good news has given the Gentiles a share in the promises that God gave to the Jews. God has also let the Gentiles be part of the same body.

[7] God treated me with kindness. His power worked in me, and it became my job to spread the good news. [8] I am the least important of all God's people. But God was kind and chose me to tell the Gentiles that because of Christ there are blessings that cannot be measured. [9] God, who created everything, wanted me to help everyone understand the mysterious plan that had always been hidden in his mind. [10] Then God would use the church to show the powers and authorities in the spiritual world that he has many different kinds of wisdom.

[11] God did this according to his eternal plan. And he was able to do what he had planned because of all that Christ Jesus our Lord had done. [12] Christ now gives us courage and confidence, so that we can come to God by faith. [13] That's why you should not be discouraged when I suffer for you. After all, it will bring honor to you.

---

[e] **2.8** *treats us much better than we deserve*: The Greek word *charis*, traditionally rendered "grace," is translated here and other places in the CEV to express the overwhelming kindness of God. [f] **2.16** *He also made peace*: Or "The cross also made peace."

### Christ's Love for Us

**14** I kneel in prayer to the Father. **15** All beings in heaven and on earth receive their life from him.*g* **16** God is wonderful and glorious. I pray that his Spirit will make you become strong followers **17** and that Christ will live in your hearts because of your faith. Stand firm and be deeply rooted in his love. **18** I pray that you and all of God's people will understand what is called wide or long or high or deep.*h* **19** I want you to know all about Christ's love, although it is too wonderful to be measured. Then your lives will be filled with all that God is.

**20-21** I pray that Christ Jesus and the church will forever bring praise to God. His power at work in us can do far more than we dare ask or imagine. Amen.

### Unity with Christ

**4** As a prisoner of the Lord, I beg you to live in a way that is worthy of the people God has chosen to be his own. **2** Always be humble and gentle. Patiently put up with each other and love each other. **3** Try your best to let God's Spirit keep your hearts united. Do this by living at peace. **4** All of you are part of the same body. There is only one Spirit of God, just as you were given one hope when you were chosen to be God's people. **5** We have only one Lord, one faith, and one baptism. **6** There is one God who is the Father of all people. Not only is God above all others, but he works by using all of us, and he lives in all of us.

**7** Christ has generously divided out his gifts to us. **8** As the Scriptures say,

"When he went up
  to the highest place,
 he led away many prisoners
 and gave gifts to people."

**9** When it says, "he went up," it means that Christ had been deep in the earth. **10** This also means that the one who went deep into the earth is the same one who went into the highest heaven, so that he would fill the whole universe.

**11** Christ chose some of us to be apostles, prophets, missionaries, pastors, and teachers, **12** so that his people would learn to serve and his body would grow strong. **13** This will continue until we are united by our faith and by our understanding of the Son of God. Then we will be mature, just as Christ is, and we will be completely like him.*i*

**14** We must stop acting like children. We must not let deceitful people trick us by their false teachings, which are like winds that toss us around from place to place. **15** Love should always make us tell the truth. Then we will grow in every way and be more like Christ, the head **16** of the body. Christ holds it together and makes all of its parts work perfectly, as it grows and becomes strong because of love.

### The Old Life and the New Life

**17** As a follower of the Lord, I order you to stop living like stupid, godless people. **18** Their minds are in the dark, and they are stubborn and ignorant and have missed out on the life that comes from God. They no longer have any feelings about what is right, **19** and they are so greedy that they do all kinds of indecent things.

**20-21** But that isn't what you were taught about Jesus Christ. He is the truth, and you heard about him and learned about him. **22** You were told that your foolish desires will destroy you and that you must give up your old way of life with all its bad habits. **23** Let the Spirit change your way of thinking **24** and make you into a new person. You were created to be like God, and so you must please him and be truly holy.

### Rules for the New Life

**25** We are part of the same body. Stop lying and start telling each other the

---

*g***3.15** *receive their life from him*: Or "know who they really are because of him."
*h***3.18** *what is called wide or long or high or deep*: This may refer to the heavenly Jerusalem or to God's love or wisdom or to the meaning of the cross. *i***4.13** *and we will be completely like him*: Or "and he is completely perfect."

truth. <sup>26</sup>Don't get so angry that you sin. Don't go to bed angry <sup>27</sup>and don't give the devil a chance.

<sup>28</sup>If you are a thief, quit stealing. Be honest and work hard, so you will have something to give to people in need.

<sup>29</sup>Stop all your dirty talk. Say the right thing at the right time and help others by what you say.

<sup>30</sup>Don't make God's Spirit sad. The Spirit makes you sure that someday you will be free from your sins.

<sup>31</sup>Stop being bitter and angry and mad at others. Don't yell at one another or curse each other or ever be rude. <sup>32</sup>Instead, be kind and merciful, and forgive others, just as God forgave you because of Christ.

**5** Do as God does. After all, you are his dear children. <sup>2</sup>Let love be your guide. Christ loved us<sup>j</sup> and offered his life for us as a sacrifice that pleases God.

<sup>3</sup>You are God's people, so don't let it be said that any of you are immoral or indecent or greedy. <sup>4</sup>Don't use dirty or foolish or filthy words. Instead, say how thankful you are. <sup>5</sup>Being greedy, indecent, or immoral is just another way of worshiping idols. You can be sure that people who behave in this way will never be part of the kingdom that belongs to Christ and to God.

### Living as People of Light

<sup>6</sup>Don't let anyone trick you with foolish talk. God punishes everyone who disobeys him and says<sup>k</sup> foolish things. <sup>7</sup>So don't have anything to do with anyone like that.

<sup>8</sup>You used to be like people living in the dark, but now you are people of the light because you belong to the Lord. So act like people of the light <sup>9</sup>and make your light shine. Be good and honest and truthful, <sup>10</sup>as you try to please the Lord. <sup>11</sup>Don't take part in doing those worthless things that are done in the dark. Instead, show how wrong they are. <sup>12</sup>It is disgusting even to talk about what is done in the dark. <sup>13</sup>But the light will show what these

things are really like. <sup>14</sup>Light shows up everything,<sup>l</sup> just as the Scriptures say,

"Wake up from your sleep
and rise from death.
Then Christ will shine on you."

<sup>15</sup>Act like people with good sense and not like fools. <sup>16</sup>These are evil times, so make every minute count. <sup>17</sup>Don't be stupid. Instead, find out what the Lord wants you to do. <sup>18</sup>Don't destroy yourself by getting drunk, but let the Spirit fill your life. <sup>19</sup>When you meet together, sing psalms, hymns, and spiritual songs, as you praise the Lord with all your heart. <sup>20</sup>Always use the name of our Lord Jesus Christ to thank God the Father for everything.

### Wives and Husbands

<sup>21</sup>Honor Christ and put others first. <sup>22</sup>A wife should put her husband first, as she does the Lord. <sup>23</sup>A husband is the head of his wife, as Christ is the head and the Savior of the church, which is his own body. <sup>24</sup>Wives should always put their husbands first, as the church puts Christ first.

<sup>25</sup>A husband should love his wife as much as Christ loved the church and gave his life for it. <sup>26</sup>He made the church holy by the power of his word, and he made it pure by washing it with water. <sup>27</sup>Christ did this, so that he would have a glorious and holy church, without faults or spots or wrinkles or any other flaws.

<sup>28</sup>In the same way, a husband should love his wife as much as he loves himself. A husband who loves his wife shows that he loves himself. <sup>29</sup>None of us hate our own bodies. We provide for them and take good care of them, just as Christ does for the church, <sup>30</sup>because we are each part of his body. <sup>31</sup>As the Scriptures say, "A man leaves his father and mother to get married, and he becomes like one person with his wife." <sup>32</sup>This is a great mystery, but I understand it to mean Christ and his church. <sup>33</sup>So each husband should love his wife as much as he loves himself,

---

<sup>j</sup>**5.2** *us*: Some manuscripts have "you." <sup>k</sup>**5.6** *says*: Or "does." <sup>l</sup>**5.14** *Light shows up everything*: Or "Everything that is seen in the light becomes light itself."

and each wife should respect her husband.

## Children and Parents

**6** Children, you belong to the Lord, and you do the right thing when you obey your parents. The first commandment with a promise says, ² "Obey your father and your mother, ³ and you will have a long and happy life."

⁴ Parents, don't be hard on your children. Raise them properly. Teach them and instruct them about the Lord.

## Slaves and Masters

⁵ Slaves, you must obey your earthly masters. Show them great respect and be as loyal to them as you are to Christ. ⁶ Try to please them at all times, and not just when you think they are watching. You are slaves of Christ, so with your whole heart you must do what God wants you to do. ⁷ Gladly serve your masters, as though they were the Lord himself, and not simply people. ⁸ You know that you will be rewarded for any good things you do, whether you are slaves or free.

⁹ Slave owners, you must treat your slaves with this same respect. Don't threaten them. They have the same Master in heaven that you do, and he doesn't have any favorites.

## The Fight against Evil

¹⁰ Finally, let the mighty strength of the Lord make you strong. ¹¹ Put on all the armor that God gives, so you can defend yourself against the devil's tricks. ¹² We are not fighting against humans. We are fighting against forces and authorities and against rulers of darkness and powers in the spiritual world. ¹³ So put on all the armor that God gives. Then when that evil day*m* comes, you will be able to defend yourself. And when the battle is over, you will still be standing firm.

¹⁴ Be ready! Let the truth be like a belt around your waist, and let God's justice protect you like armor. ¹⁵ Your desire to tell the good news about peace should be like shoes on your feet. ¹⁶ Let your faith be like a shield, and you will be able to stop all the flaming arrows of the evil one. ¹⁷ Let God's saving power be like a helmet, and for a sword use God's message that comes from the Spirit.

¹⁸ Never stop praying, especially for others. Always pray by the power of the Spirit. Stay alert and keep praying for God's people. ¹⁹ Pray that I will be given the message to speak and that I may fearlessly explain the mystery about the good news. ²⁰ I was sent to do this work, and that's the reason I am in jail. So pray that I will be brave and will speak as I should.

## Final Greetings

²¹⁻²² I want you to know how I am getting along and what I am doing. That's why I am sending Tychicus to you. He is a dear friend, as well as a faithful servant of the Lord. He will tell you how I am doing, and he will cheer you up.

²³ I pray that God the Father and the Lord Jesus Christ will give peace, love, and faith to every follower! ²⁴ May God be kind to everyone who keeps on loving our Lord Jesus Christ.

*m* **6.13** *that evil day:* Either the present (see 5.16) or "the day of death" or "the day of judgment."

# PHILIPPIANS

## ABOUT THIS LETTER

Paul wrote this letter from jail (1.7) to thank the Lord's followers at Philippi for helping him with their gifts and prayers (1.5; 4.10-19). He hopes to be set free, so that he can continue preaching the good news (3.17-19). But he knows that he might be put to death (1.21; 2.17; 3.10).

The city of Philippi is in the part of northern Greece known as Macedonia. It was at Philippi that Paul had entered Europe for the first time, and there he preached the good news and began a church (Acts 16). He now warns the Christians at Philippi that they may have to suffer, just as Christ suffered and Paul is now suffering. If this happens, the Philippians should count it a blessing that comes from having faith in Christ (1.28-30).

There were problems in the church at Philippi, because some of the members claimed that people must obey the law of Moses, or they could not be saved. But Paul has no patience with such members and warns the church, "Watch out for those people who behave like dogs!" (3.2-11). This letter is also filled with joy. Even in jail, Paul is happy because he has discovered how to make the best of a bad situation and because he remembers all the kindness shown to him by the people in the church at Philippi.

Paul reminds them that God's people are to live in harmony (2.2; 4.2, 3) and to think the same way that Christ Jesus did:

> Christ was truly God.
> But he did not try to remain
>   equal with God.
> He gave up everything
>   and became a slave,
> when he became
>   like one of us.        (2.6, 7)

## A QUICK LOOK AT THIS LETTER

Greetings and a Prayer (1.1-11)
What Life Means to Paul (1.12-30)
Christ's Example of True Humility (2.1-18)
News about Paul's Friends (2.19-30)
Being Acceptable to God (3.1—4.9)
Paul Thanks the Philippians (4.10-20)
Final Greetings (4.21-23)

---

1 From Paul and Timothy, servants of Christ Jesus.

To all of God's people who belong to Christ Jesus at Philippi and to all of your church officials and officers.[a] ²I pray that God our Father and the Lord Jesus Christ will be kind to you and will bless you with peace!

---

[a] 1.1 church officials and officers: Or "bishops and deacons."

## Paul's Prayer for the Church in Philippi

³ Every time I think of you, I thank my God. ⁴ And whenever I mention you in my prayers, it makes me happy. ⁵ This is because you have taken part with me in spreading the good news from the first day you heard about it. ⁶ God is the one who began this good work in you, and I am certain that he won't stop before it is complete on the day that Christ Jesus returns.

⁷ You have a special place in my heart. So it is only natural for me to feel the way I do. All of you have helped in the work that God has given me, as I defend the good news and tell about it here in jail. ⁸ God himself knows how much I want to see you. He knows that I care for you in the same way that Christ Jesus does.

⁹ I pray that your love will keep on growing and that you will fully know and understand ¹⁰ how to make the right choices. Then you will still be pure and innocent when Christ returns. And until that day, ¹¹ Jesus Christ will keep you busy doing good deeds that bring glory and praise to God.

## What Life Means to Paul

¹² My dear friends, I want you to know that what has happened to me has helped to spread the good news. ¹³ The Roman guards and all the others know that I am here in jail because I serve Christ. ¹⁴ Now most of the Lord's followers have become brave and are fearlessly telling the message.ᵇ

¹⁵ Some are preaching about Christ because they are jealous and envious of us. Others are preaching because they want to help. ¹⁶ They love Christ and know that I am here to defend the good news about him. ¹⁷ But the ones who are jealous of us are not sincere. They just want to cause trouble for me while I am in jail. ¹⁸ But that doesn't matter. All that matters is that people are telling about Christ, whether they

are sincere or not. That is what makes me glad.

I will keep on being glad, ¹⁹ because I know that your prayers and the help that comes from the Spirit of Christ Jesus will keep me safe. ²⁰ I honestly expect and hope that I will never do anything to be ashamed of. Whether I live or die, I always want to be as brave as I am now and bring honor to Christ.

²¹ If I live, it will be for Christ, and if I die, I will gain even more. ²² I don't know what to choose. I could keep on living and doing something useful. ²³ It is a hard choice to make. I want to die and be with Christ, because that would be much better. ²⁴⁻²⁵ But I know that all of you still need me. That's why I am sure I will stay on to help you grow and be happy in your faith. ²⁶ Then, when I visit you again, you will have good reason to take great pride in Christ Jesus because of me.ᶜ

²⁷ Above all else, you must live in a way that brings honor to the good news about Christ. Then, whether I visit you or not, I will hear that all of you think alike. I will know that you are working together and that you are struggling side by side to get others to believe the good news.

²⁸ Be brave when you face your enemies. Your courage will show them that they are going to be destroyed, and it will show you that you will be saved. God will make all of this happen, ²⁹ and he has blessed you. Not only do you have faith in Christ, but you suffer for him. ³⁰ You saw me suffer, and you still hear about my troubles. Now you must suffer in the same way.

## True Humility

**2** Christ encourages you, and his love comforts you. God's Spirit unites you, and you are concerned for others. ² Now make me completely happy! Live in harmony by showing love for each other. Be united in what you think, as if you were only one person. ³ Don't be jealous or proud, but be humble and

---

ᵇ **1.14** *the message*: Some manuscripts have "the Lord's message," and others have "God's message." ᶜ **1.26** *take great pride in Christ Jesus because of me*: Or "take great pride in me because of Christ Jesus."

consider others more important than
yourselves. ⁴Care about them as much
as you care about yourselves ⁵and
think the same way that Christ Jesus
thought:ᵈ

⁶ Christ was truly God.
But he did not try to remainᵉ
equal with God.
⁷ He gave up everythingᶠ
and became a slave,
when he became
like one of us.

⁸ Christ was humble.
He obeyed God and even died
on a cross.
⁹ Then God gave Christ
the highest place
and honored his name
above all others.

¹⁰ So at the name of Jesus
everyone will bow down,
those in heaven, on earth,
and under the earth.
¹¹ And to the glory
of God the Father
everyone will openly agree,
"Jesus Christ is Lord!"

### Lights in the World

¹² My dear friends, you always
obeyed when I was with you. Now that
I am away, you should obey even more.
So work with fear and trembling to discover what it really means to be saved.
¹³ God is working in you to make you
willing and able to obey him.
¹⁴ Do everything without grumbling
or arguing. ¹⁵ Then you will be the pure
and innocent children of God. You live
among people who are crooked and
evil, but you must not do anything that
they can say is wrong. Try to shine as
lights among the people of this world,
¹⁶ as you hold firmly toᵍ the message
that gives life. Then on the day when
Christ returns, I can take pride in you.
I can also know that my work and ef-
forts were not useless.

¹⁷Your faith in the Lord and your
service are like a sacrifice offered to
him. And my own blood may have to
be poured out with the sacrifice.ʰ If
this happens, I will be glad and rejoice
with you. ¹⁸In the same way, you
should be glad and rejoice with me.

### Timothy and Epaphroditus

¹⁹I want to be encouraged by news
about you. So I hope the Lord Jesus
will soon let me send Timothy to you.
²⁰I don't have anyone else who cares
about you as much as he does. ²¹The
others think only about what interests
them and not about what concerns
Christ Jesus. ²²But you know what
kind of person Timothy is. He has
worked with me like a son in spreading
the good news. ²³I hope to send him
to you, as soon as I find out what is
going to happen to me. ²⁴And I feel
sure that the Lord will also let me come
soon.
²⁵I think I ought to send my dear
friend Epaphroditus back to you. He is
a follower and a worker and a soldier
of the Lord, just as I am. You sent him
to look after me, ²⁶but now he is eager
to see you. He is worried, because you
heard he was sick. ²⁷In fact, he was
very sick and almost died. But God was
kind to him, and also to me, and he kept
me from being burdened down with
sorrow.
²⁸Now I am more eager than ever to
send Epaphroditus back again. You
will be glad to see him, and I won't have
to worry any longer. ²⁹Be sure to give
him a cheerful welcome, just as people
who serve the Lord deserve. ³⁰He almost died working for Christ, and he
risked his own life to do for me what
you could not.

### Being Acceptable to God

**3** Finally, my dear friends, be glad
that you belong to the Lord. It
doesn't bother me to write the same

ᵈ2.5 *think the same way that Christ Jesus thought*: Or "think the way you should because
you belong to Christ Jesus." ᵉ2.6 *remain*: Or "become." ᶠ2.7 *He gave up everything*:
Greek, "He emptied himself." ᵍ2.16 *hold firmly to*: Or "offer them." ʰ2.17 *my own blood
may have to be poured out with the sacrifice*: Offerings of water or wine were sometimes
poured out when animals were sacrificed on the altar.

things to you that I have written before. In fact, it is for your own good.

<sup>2</sup> Watch out for those people who behave like dogs! They are evil and want to do more than just circumcise you. <sup>3</sup> But we are the ones who are truly circumcised, because we worship by the power of God's Spirit<sup>i</sup> and take pride in Christ Jesus. We don't brag about what we have done, <sup>4</sup> although I could. Others may brag about themselves, but I have more reason to brag than anyone else. <sup>5</sup> I was circumcised when I was eight days old,<sup>j</sup> and I am from the nation of Israel and the tribe of Benjamin. I am a true Hebrew. As a Pharisee, I strictly obeyed the Law of Moses. <sup>6</sup> And I was so eager that I even made trouble for the church. I did everything the Law demands in order to please God.

<sup>7</sup> But Christ has shown me that what I once thought was valuable is worthless. <sup>8</sup> Nothing is as wonderful as knowing Christ Jesus my Lord. I have given up everything else and count it all as garbage. All I want is Christ <sup>9</sup> and to know that I belong to him. I could not make myself acceptable to God by obeying the Law of Moses. God accepted me simply because of my faith in Christ. <sup>10</sup> All I want is to know Christ and the power that raised him to life. I want to suffer and die as he did, <sup>11</sup> so that somehow I also may be raised to life.

### Running toward the Goal

<sup>12</sup> I have not yet reached my goal, and I am not perfect. But Christ has taken hold of me. So I keep on running and struggling to take hold of the prize. <sup>13</sup> My friends, I don't feel that I have already arrived. But I forget what is behind, and I struggle for what is ahead. <sup>14</sup> I run toward the goal, so that I can win the prize of being called to heaven. This is the prize that God offers because of what Christ Jesus has done. <sup>15</sup> All of us who are mature should think in this same way. And if any of you think differently, God will make it clear

to you. <sup>16</sup> But we must keep going in the direction that we are now headed.

<sup>17</sup> My friends, I want you to follow my example and learn from others who closely follow the example we set for you. <sup>18</sup> I often warned you that many people are living as enemies of the cross of Christ. And now with tears in my eyes, I warn you again <sup>19</sup> that they are headed for hell! They worship their stomachs and brag about the disgusting things they do. All they can think about are the things of this world.

<sup>20</sup> But we are citizens of heaven and are eagerly waiting for our Savior to come from there. Our Lord Jesus Christ <sup>21</sup> has power over everything, and he will make these poor bodies of ours like his own glorious body.

**4** Dear friends, I love you and long to see you. Please keep on being faithful to the Lord. You are my pride and joy.

### Paul Encourages the Lord's Followers

<sup>2</sup> Euodia and Syntyche, you belong to the Lord, so I beg you to stop arguing with each other. <sup>3</sup> And, my true partner,<sup>k</sup> I ask you to help them. These women have worked together with me and with Clement and with the others in spreading the good news. Their names are now written in the book of life.<sup>l</sup>

<sup>4</sup> Always be glad because of the Lord! I will say it again: Be glad. <sup>5</sup> Always be gentle with others. The Lord will soon be here. <sup>6</sup> Don't worry about anything, but pray about everything. With thankful hearts offer up your prayers and requests to God. <sup>7</sup> Then, because you belong to Christ Jesus, God will bless you with peace that no one can completely understand. And this peace will control the way you think and feel.

<sup>8</sup> Finally, my friends, keep your minds on whatever is true, pure, right, holy, friendly, and proper. Don't ever stop thinking about what is truly worthwhile and worthy of praise. <sup>9</sup> You know the teachings I gave you, and you

---

<sup>i</sup>**3.3** *by the power of God's Spirit:* Or "sincerely." <sup>j</sup>**3.5** *when I was eight days old:* Jewish boys are circumcised eight days after birth. <sup>k</sup>**4.3** *partner:* Or "Syzygus," a person's name. <sup>l</sup>**4.3** *the book of life:* A book in which the names of God's people are written.

know what you heard me say and saw me do. So follow my example. And God, who gives peace, will be with you.

## Paul Gives Thanks for the Gifts He Was Given

[10] The Lord has made me very grateful that at last you have thought about me once again. Actually, you were thinking about me all along, but you didn't have any chance to show it. [11] I am not complaining about having too little. I have learned to be satisfied with[m] whatever I have. [12] I know what it is to be poor or to have plenty, and I have lived under all kinds of conditions. I know what it means to be full or to be hungry, to have too much or too little. [13] Christ gives me the strength to face anything.

[14] It was good of you to help me when I was having such a hard time. [15] My friends at Philippi, you remember what it was like when I started preaching the good news in Macedonia.[n] After I left there, you were the only church that became my partner by giving blessings and by receiving them in return. [16] Even when I was in Thessalonica, you helped me more than once. [17] I am not trying to get something from you, but I want you to receive the blessings that come from giving.

[18] I have been paid back everything, and with interest. I am completely satisfied with the gifts that you had Epaphroditus bring me. They are like a sweet-smelling offering or like the right kind of sacrifice that pleases God. [19] I pray that God will take care of all your needs with the wonderful blessings that come from Christ Jesus! [20] May God our Father be praised forever and ever. Amen.

## Final Greetings

[21] Give my greetings to all who are God's people because of Christ Jesus. The Lord's followers here with me send you their greetings.

[22] All of God's people send their greetings, especially those in the service of the Emperor.

[23] I pray that our Lord Jesus Christ will be kind to you and will bless your life!

[m]**4.11** *be satisfied with*: Or "get by on."   [n]**4.15** *when I started preaching the good news in Macedonia*: Paul is talking about his first visit to Philippi (see Acts 16.12-40).

# COLOSSIANS

## ABOUT THIS LETTER

Colossae was an important city in western Asia Minor, about 100 miles east of the port city of Ephesus. Paul had never been to Colossae, but he was pleased to learn that the Christians there were strong in their faith (1.3-7; 2.6, 7). They had heard the good news from a man named Epaphras who had lived there (1.7; 4.12, 13), but was in jail with Paul (Philemon 23) at the time that Paul wrote this letter (1.14; 4.3, 10, 18).

Many of the church members in Colossae were Gentiles (1.27), and some of them were influenced by strange religious ideas and practices (2.16-23). They thought that to obey God fully they must give up certain physical desires and worship angels and other spiritual powers. But Paul wanted them to know that Christ was with God in heaven, ruling over all powers in the universe (3.1). And so, their worship should be directed to Christ.

Paul quotes a beautiful hymn that explains who Christ is:

> Christ is exactly like God,
>     who cannot be seen.
> He is the first-born Son,
>     superior to all creation.
>
> God himself was pleased
>     to live fully in his Son.
> And God was pleased
>     for him to make peace
> by sacrificing his blood
>     on the cross.
>                     (1.15, 19, 20a)

## A QUICK LOOK AT THIS LETTER

Greetings (1.1, 2)
A Prayer of Thanks (1.3-8)
The Person and Work of Christ (1.9—2.19)
New Life with Christ (2.20—4.6)
Final Greetings (4.7-18)

---

**1** From Paul, chosen by God to be an apostle of Christ Jesus, and from Timothy, who is also a follower. ²To God's people who live in Colossae and are faithful followers of Christ.

I pray that God our Father will be kind to you and will bless you with peace!

### A Prayer of Thanks

³Each time we pray for you, we thank God, the Father of our Lord Jesus Christ. ⁴We have heard of your faith in Christ and of your love for all of God's people, ⁵because what you hope for is kept safe for you in heaven. You first heard about this hope when you

believed the true message, which is the good news.

⁶ The good news is spreading all over the world with great success. It has spread in that same way among you, ever since the first day you learned the truth about God's wonderful kindness ⁷ from our good friend Epaphras. He works together with us for Christ and is a faithful worker for you.ᵃ ⁸ He is also the one who told us about the love that God's Spirit has given you.

### The Person and Work of Christ

⁹ We have not stopped praying for you since the first day we heard about you. In fact, we always pray that God will show you everything he wants you to do and that you may have all the wisdom and understanding that his Spirit gives. ¹⁰ Then you will live a life that honors the Lord, and you will always please him by doing good deeds. You will come to know God even better. ¹¹ His glorious power will make you patient and strong enough to endure anything, and you will be truly happy.

¹² I pray that you will be grateful to God for letting youᵃ have part in what he has promised his people in the kingdom of light. ¹³ God rescued us from the dark power of Satan and brought us into the kingdom of his dear Son, ¹⁴ who forgives our sins and sets us free.

¹⁵ Christ is exactly like God,
   who cannot be seen.
He is the first-born Son,
   superior to all creation.
¹⁶ Everything was created by him,
   everything in heaven
      and on earth,
   everything seen and unseen,
   including all forces
      and powers,
   and all rulers
      and authorities.
All things were created
   by God's Son,
and everything was made
   for him.

¹⁷ God's Son was before all else,
   and by him everything
      is held together.
¹⁸ He is the head of his body,
   which is the church.
He is the very beginning,
   the first to be raised
      from death,
   so that he would be
      above all others.

¹⁹ God himself was pleased
   to live fully in his Son.
²⁰ And God was pleased
   for him to make peace
by sacrificing his blood
   on the cross,
so that all beings in heaven
   and on earth
   would be brought back to God.

²¹ You used to be far from God. Your thoughts made you his enemies, and you did evil things. ²² But his Son became a human and died. So God made peace with you, and now he lets you stand in his presence as people who are holy and faultless and innocent. ²³ But you must stay deeply rooted and firm in your faith. You must not give up the hope you received when you heard the good news. It was preached to everyone on earth, and I myself have become a servant of this message.

### Paul's Service to the Church

²⁴ I am glad that I can suffer for you. I am pleased also that in my own body I can continueᵇ the suffering of Christ for his body, the church. ²⁵ God's plan was to make me a servant of his church and to send me to preach his complete message to you. ²⁶ For ages and ages this message was kept secret from everyone, but now it has been explained to God's people. ²⁷ God did this because he wanted you Gentiles to understand his wonderful and glorious mystery. And the mystery is that Christ lives in you, and he is your hope of sharing in God's glory.

²⁸ We announce the message about Christ, and we use all our wisdom to

---

ᵃ 1.7 you: Some manuscripts have "us."   ᵃ 1.12 you: Some manuscripts have "us."
ᵇ 1.24 continue: Or "complete."

warn and teach everyone, so that all of Christ's followers will grow and become mature. [29] That's why I work so hard and use the mighty power he gives me.

**2** I want you to know what a struggle I am going through for you, for God's people at Laodicea, and for all of those followers who have never met me. [2] I do it to encourage them. Then as their hearts are joined together in love, they will be wonderfully blessed with complete understanding. And they will truly know Christ. Not only is he the key to God's mystery, [3] but all wisdom and knowledge are hidden away in him. [4] I tell you these things to keep you from being fooled by fancy talk. [5] Even though I am not with you, I keep thinking about you. I am glad to know that you are living as you should and that your faith in Christ is strong.

### Christ Brings Real Life

[6] You have accepted Christ Jesus as your Lord. Now keep on following him. [7] Plant your roots in Christ and let him be the foundation for your life. Be strong in your faith, just as you were taught. And be grateful.

[8] Don't let anyone fool you by using senseless arguments. These arguments may sound wise, but they are only human teachings. They come from the powers of this world[c] and not from Christ.

[9] God lives fully in Christ. [10] And you are fully grown because you belong to Christ, who is over every power and authority. [11] Christ has also taken away your selfish desires, just as circumcision removes flesh from the body. [12] And when you were baptized, it was the same as being buried with Christ. Then you were raised to life because you had faith in the power of God, who raised Christ from death. [13] You were dead, because you were sinful and were not God's people. But God let Christ

make you[d] alive, when he forgave all our sins.

[14] God wiped out the charges that were against us for disobeying the Law of Moses. He took them away and nailed them to the cross. [15] There Christ defeated all powers and forces. He let the whole world see them being led away as prisoners when he celebrated his victory.

[16] Don't let anyone tell you what you must eat or drink. Don't let them say that you must celebrate the New Moon festival, the Sabbath, or any other festival. [17] These things are only a shadow of what was to come. But Christ is real!

[18] Don't be cheated by people who make a show of acting humble and who worship angels.[e] They brag about seeing visions. But it is all nonsense, because their minds are filled with selfish desires. [19] They are no longer part of Christ, who is the head of the whole body. Christ gives the body its strength, and he uses its joints and muscles to hold it together, as it grows by the power of God.

### Christ Brings New Life

[20] You died with Christ. Now the forces of the universe[f] don't have any power over you. Why do you live as if you had to obey such rules as, [21] "Don't handle this. Don't taste that. Don't touch this."? [22] After these things are used, they are no longer good for anything. So why be bothered with the rules that humans have made up? [23] Obeying these rules may seem to be the smart thing to do. They appear to make you love God more and to be very humble and to have control over your body. But they don't really have any power over our desires.

**3** You have been raised to life with Christ. Now set your heart on what is in heaven, where Christ rules at God's right side.[g] [2] Think about what

---

[c]**2.8** *powers of this world:* Spirits and unseen forces were thought to control human lives and were believed to be connected with the movements of the stars.   [d]**2.13** *you:* See the note at 1.7.   [e]**2.18** *worship angels:* Or "worship with angels (in visions of heaven)."   [f]**2.20** *forces of the universe:* See the note at 2.8.   [g]**3.1** *right side:* The place of power and honor.

is up there, not about what is here on earth. [3] You died, which means that your life is hidden with Christ, who sits beside God. [4] Christ gives meaning to your[h] life, and when he appears, you will also appear with him in glory.

[5] Don't be controlled by your body. Kill every desire for the wrong kind of sex. Don't be immoral or indecent or have evil thoughts. Don't be greedy, which is the same as worshiping idols. [6] God is angry with people who disobey him by doing[i] these things. [7] And that is exactly what you did, when you lived among people who behaved in this way. [8] But now you must stop doing such things. You must quit being angry, hateful, and evil. You must no longer say insulting or cruel things about others. [9] And stop lying to each other. You have given up your old way of life with its habits.

[10] Each of you is now a new person. You are becoming more and more like your Creator, and you will understand him better. [11] It doesn't matter if you are a Greek or a Jew, or if you are circumcised or not. You may even be a barbarian or a Scythian,[j] and you may be a slave or a free person. Yet Christ is all that matters, and he lives in all of us.

[12] God loves you and has chosen you as his own special people. So be gentle, kind, humble, meek, and patient. [13] Put up with each other, and forgive anyone who does you wrong, just as Christ has forgiven you. [14] Love is more important than anything else. It is what ties everything completely together.

[15] Each one of you is part of the body of Christ, and you were chosen to live together in peace. So let the peace that comes from Christ control your thoughts. And be grateful. [16] Let the message about Christ completely fill your lives, while you use all your wisdom to teach and instruct each other. With thankful hearts, sing psalms, hymns, and spiritual songs to God. [17] Whatever you say or do should be done in the name of the Lord Jesus, as you give thanks to God the Father because of him.

## Some Rules for Christian Living

[18] A wife must put her husband first. This is her duty as a follower of the Lord.

[19] A husband must love his wife and not abuse her.

[20] Children must always obey their parents. This pleases the Lord.

[21] Parents, don't be hard on your children. If you are, they might give up.

[22] Slaves, you must always obey your earthly masters. Try to please them at all times, and not just when you think they are watching. Honor the Lord and serve your masters with your whole heart. [23] Do your work willingly, as though you were serving the Lord himself, and not just your earthly master. [24] In fact, the Lord Christ is the one you are really serving, and you know that he will reward you. [25] But Christ has no favorites! He will punish evil people, just as they deserve.

4 Slave owners, be fair and honest with your slaves. Don't forget that you have a Master in heaven.

[2] Never give up praying. And when you pray, keep alert and be thankful. [3] Be sure to pray that God will make a way for us to spread his message and explain the mystery about Christ, even though I am in jail for doing this. [4] Please pray that I will make the message as clear as possible.

[5] When you are with unbelievers, always make good use of the time. [6] Be pleasant and hold their interest when you speak the message. Choose your words carefully and be ready to give answers to anyone who asks questions.

## Final Greetings

[7] Tychicus is the dear friend, who faithfully works and serves the Lord with us, and he will give you the news about me. [8] I am sending him to cheer

---

[h] 3.4 *your*: Some manuscripts have "our." [i] 3.6 *people who disobey him by doing*: Some manuscripts do not have these words. [j] 3.11 *a barbarian or a Scythian*: Barbarians were people who could not speak Greek and would be in the lower class of society. Scythians were people who were known for their cruelty.

you up by telling you how we are getting along. ⁹Onesimus, that dear and faithful follower from your own group, is coming with him. The two of them will tell you everything that has happened here.

¹⁰Aristarchus is in jail with me. He sends greetings to you, and so does Mark, the cousin of Barnabas. You have already been told to welcome Mark, if he visits you. ¹¹Jesus, who is known as Justus, sends his greetings. These three men are the only Jewish followers who have worked with me for the kingdom of God. They have given me much comfort.

¹²Your own Epaphras, who serves Christ Jesus, sends his greetings. He always prays hard that you may fully know what the Lord wants you to do and that you may do it completely. ¹³I have seen how much trouble he has gone through for you and for the followers in Laodicea and Hierapolis.

¹⁴Our dear doctor Luke sends you his greetings, and so does Demas.

¹⁵Give my greetings to the followers at Laodicea, especially to Nympha and the church that meets in her home.

¹⁶After this letter has been read to your people, be sure to have it read in the church at Laodicea. And you should read the letter that I have sent to them.ᵏ

¹⁷Remind Archippus to do the work that the Lord has given him to do.

¹⁸I am signing this letter myself: PAUL.

Don't forget that I am in jail.

I pray that God will be kind to you.

ᵏ4.16 *the letter that I have sent to them*: This is the only mention of the letter to the church at Laodicea.

# 1 THESSALONIANS

## ABOUT THIS LETTER

Paul started the church in Thessalonica (2.13, 14), while working hard to support himself (2.9). In this important city of northern Greece, many of the followers had worshiped idols before becoming Christians (1.9). But they were faithful to the Lord, and because of them the Lord's message had spread everywhere in that region (1.8). This letter may have been the first one that Paul wrote, and maybe even the first of all the New Testament writings.

Some people in Thessalonica began to oppose Paul, and he had to escape to Athens. But he sent his young friend Timothy to find out how the Christians were doing (3.1-5). When Timothy returned, he gave Paul good reports of their faith and love (3.6-10).

The church itself had problems. Some of its members had quit working, since they thought that the Lord would soon return (4.11, 12). Others were worried because relatives and friends had already died before Christ's return. So Paul tried to explain to them more clearly what would happen when the Lord returns (4.13-15), and then told them how they should live in the meanwhile (5.1-11).

Paul's final instructions are well worth remembering:

> Always be joyful and never stop praying. Whatever happens, keep thanking God because of Jesus Christ. This is what God wants you to do.　　　　　　　　　　　　　　(5.16-18)

## A QUICK LOOK AT THIS LETTER

Greetings (1.1-3)
The Thessalonians' Faith and Example (1.4—3.13)
A Life That Pleases God (4.1-12)
What to Expect When the Lord Returns (4.13—5.11)
Final Instructions and Greetings (5.12-28)

---

**1** From Paul, Silas,[a] and Timothy.

To the church in Thessalonica, the people of God the Father and of the Lord Jesus Christ.

I pray that God will be kind to you and will bless you with peace!

² We thank God for you and always mention you in our prayers. Each time we pray, ³ we tell God our Father about your faith and loving work and about your firm hope in our Lord Jesus Christ.

### The Thessalonians' Faith and Example

⁴ My dear friends, God loves you, and we know he has chosen you to be his people. ⁵ When we told you the good news, it was with the power and assurance that come from the Holy Spirit, and not simply with words. You knew what kind of people we were and how we helped you. ⁶ So, when you accepted the message, you followed our example and the example of the Lord. You

---

a 1.1 *Silas*: The Greek text has "Silvanus," another form of the name Silas.

suffered, but the Holy Spirit made you glad. ⁷You became an example for all the Lord's followers in Macedonia and Achaia. ⁸And because of you, the Lord's message has spread everywhere in those regions. Now the news of your faith in God is known all over the world, and we don't have to say a thing about it. ⁹Everyone is talking about how you welcomed us and how you turned away from idols to serve the true and living God. ¹⁰They also tell how you are waiting for his Son Jesus to come from heaven. God raised him from death, and on the day of judgment Jesus will save us from God's anger.

### Paul's Work in Thessalonica

**2** My friends, you know that our time with you wasn't wasted. ²As you remember, we had been mistreated and insulted at Philippi. But God gave us the courage to tell you the good news about him, even though many people caused us trouble. ³We didn't have any hidden motives when we won you over, and we didn't try to fool or trick anyone. ⁴God was pleased to trust us with his message. We didn't speak to please people, but to please God who knows our motives.

⁵You also know that we didn't try to flatter anyone. God himself knows that what we did wasn't a cover-up for greed. ⁶We were not trying to get you or anyone else to praise us. ⁷But as apostles, we could have demanded help from you. After all, Christ is the one who sent us. We chose to be like children or like a mother ᵇ nursing her baby. ⁸We cared so much for you, and you became so dear to us, that we were willing to give our lives for you when we gave you God's message.

⁹My dear friends, you surely haven't forgotten our hard work and hardships. You remember how night and day we struggled to make a living, so that we could tell you God's message without being a burden to anyone. ¹⁰Both you and God are witnesses that we were pure and honest and innocent in our

dealings with you followers of the Lord. ¹¹You also know we did everything for you that parents would do for their own children. ¹²We begged, encouraged, and urged each of you to live in a way that would honor God. He is the one who chose you to share in his own kingdom and glory.

¹³We always thank God that you believed the message we preached. It came from him, and it isn't something made up by humans. You accepted it as God's message, and now he is working in you. ¹⁴My friends, you did just like God's churches in Judea and like the other followers of Christ Jesus there. And so, you were mistreated by your own people, in the same way they were mistreated by their people. ¹⁵Those evil people killed the Lord Jesus and the prophets, and they even chased us away. God doesn't like what they do and neither does anyone else. ¹⁶They keep us from speaking his message to the Gentiles and from leading them to be saved. They have always gone too far with their sins. Now God has finally become angry and will punish them.

### Paul Wants To Visit the Church Again

¹⁷My friends, we were kept from coming to you for a while, but we never stopped thinking about you. We were eager to see you and tried our best to visit you in person. ¹⁸We really wanted to come. I myself tried several times, but Satan always stopped us. ¹⁹After all, when the Lord Jesus appears, who else but you will give us hope and joy and be like a glorious crown for us? ²⁰You alone are our glory and joy!

**3** Finally, we couldn't stand it any longer. We decided to stay in Athens by ourselves ²and send our friend Timothy to you. He works with us as God's servant and preaches the good news about Christ. We wanted him to make you strong in your faith and to encourage you. ³We didn't want any of you to be discouraged by all these troubles. You knew we would have to suffer, ⁴because when we were with

---

ᵇ**2.7** *like children or like a mother*: Some manuscripts have "as gentle as a mother."

you, we told you this would happen.
And we did suffer, as you well know.
⁵ At last, when I could not wait any
longer, I sent Timothy to find out about
your faith. I hoped that Satan had not
tempted you and made all our work
useless.

⁶ Timothy has come back from his
visit with you and has told us about
your faith and love. He also said that
you always have happy memories of us
and that you want to see us as much
as we want to see you.

⁷ My friends, even though we have a
lot of trouble and suffering, your faith
makes us feel better about you. ⁸ Your
strong faith in the Lord is like a breath
of new life. ⁹ How can we possibly
thank God enough for all the happiness
you have brought us? ¹⁰ Day and night
we sincerely pray that we will see you
again and help you to have an even
stronger faith.

¹¹ We pray that God our Father and
our Lord Jesus will let us visit you.
¹² May the Lord make your love for
each other and for everyone else grow
by leaps and bounds. That's how our
love for you has grown. ¹³ And when
our Lord comes with all of his people,
I pray that he will make your hearts
pure and innocent in the sight of God
the Father.

### A Life That Pleases God

4 Finally, my dear friends, since you
belong to the Lord Jesus, we beg
and urge you to live as we taught you.
Then you will please God. You are already living that way, but try even
harder. ² Remember the instructions we
gave you as followers of the Lord Jesus.
³ God wants you to be holy, so don't
be immoral in matters of sex. ⁴ Respect
and honor your wife.ᶜ ⁵ Don't be a slave
of your desires or live like people who
don't know God. ⁶ You must not cheat
any of the Lord's followers in matters
of sex.ᵈ Remember, we warned you
that he punishes everyone who does
such things. ⁷ God didn't choose you to
be filthy, but to be pure. ⁸ So if you don't

obey these rules, you are not really
disobeying us. You are disobeying
God, who gives you his Holy Spirit.

⁹ We don't have to write you about
the need to love each other. God has
taught you to do this, ¹⁰ and you already
have shown your love for all of his people in Macedonia. But, my dear friends,
we ask you to do even more. ¹¹ Try your
best to live quietly, to mind your own
business, and to work hard, just as we
taught you to do. ¹² Then you will be
respected by people who are not followers of the Lord, and you won't have
to depend on anyone.

### The Lord's Coming

¹³ My friends, we want you to understand how it will be for those followers
who have already died. Then you won't
grieve over them and be like people
who don't have any hope. ¹⁴ We believe
that Jesus died and was raised to life.
We also believe that when God brings
Jesus back again, he will bring with
him all who had faith in Jesus before
they died. ¹⁵ Our Lord Jesus told us that
when he comes, we won't go up to meet
him ahead of his followers who have
already died.

¹⁶ With a loud command and with the
shout of the chief angel and a blast of
God's trumpet, the Lord will return
from heaven. Then those who had faith
in Christ before they died will be raised
to life. ¹⁷ Next, all of us who are still
alive will be taken up into the clouds
together with them to meet the Lord
in the sky. From that time on we will
all be with the Lord forever. ¹⁸ Encourage each other with these words.

5 I don't need to write you about the
time or date when all this will happen. ² You surely know that the Lord's
returnᵉ will be as a thief coming at
night. ³ People will think they are safe
and secure. But destruction will suddenly strike them like the pains of a
woman about to give birth. And they
won't escape.

⁴ My dear friends, you don't live in
darkness, and so that day won't sur-

ᶜ4.4 *your wife*: Or "your body." ᵈ4.6 *in matters of sex*: Or "in business." ᵉ5.2 *the Lord's
return*: The Greek text has "the day of the Lord."

prise you like a thief. ⁵You belong to the light and live in the day. We don't live in the night or belong to the dark. ⁶Others may sleep, but we should stay awake and be alert. ⁷People sleep during the night, and some even get drunk. ⁸But we belong to the day. So we must stay sober and let our faith and love be like a suit of armor. Our firm hope that we will be saved is our helmet.

⁹God doesn't intend to punish us, but to have our Lord Jesus Christ save us. ¹⁰Christ died for us, so that we could live with him, whether we are alive or dead when he comes. ¹¹That's why you must encourage and help each other, just as you are already doing.

### Final Instructions and Greetings

¹²My friends, we ask you to be thoughtful of your leaders who work hard and tell you how to live for the Lord. ¹³Show them great respect and love because of their work. Try to get along with each other. ¹⁴My friends, we beg you to warn anyone who isn't living right. Encourage anyone who feels left out, help all who are weak, and be patient with everyone. ¹⁵Don't be hateful to people, just because they are hateful to you. Rather, be good to each other and to everyone else.

¹⁶Always be joyful ¹⁷and never stop praying. ¹⁸Whatever happens, keep thanking God because of Jesus Christ. This is what God wants you to do.

¹⁹Don't turn away God's Spirit ²⁰or ignore prophecies. ²¹Put everything to the test. Accept what is good ²²and don't have anything to do with evil.

²³I pray that God, who gives peace, will make you completely holy. And may your spirit, soul, and body be kept healthy and faultless until our Lord Jesus Christ returns. ²⁴The one who chose you can be trusted, and he will do this.

²⁵Friends, please pray for us.

²⁶Give the Lord's followers a warm greeting.

²⁷In the name of the Lord I beg you to read this letter to all his followers.

²⁸I pray that our Lord Jesus Christ will be kind to you!

# 2 THESSALONIANS

## ABOUT THIS LETTER

*In this letter to the believers in Thessalonica, Paul begins by thanking God that their faith and love keep growing all the time (1.3). They were going through a lot of troubles, but Paul insists that this is God's way of testing their faith, not a way of punishing them (1.4, 5).*

*Someone in Thessalonica claimed to have a letter from Paul, saying that the Lord had already returned (2.2). But Paul warns the church not to be fooled! The Lord will not return until after the "wicked one" has appeared (2.3).*

*Paul also warns against laziness (3.6-10), and he tells the church to guard against any followers who refuse to obey what he has written in this letter.*

*The letter closes with a prayer:*

> I pray that the Lord, who gives peace, will always bless you with peace. May the Lord be with all of you. (3.16)

## A QUICK LOOK AT THIS LETTER

*Greetings (1.1, 2)*
*The Lord's Return Will Bring Justice (1.3-12)*
*The Lord Has Not Returned Yet (2.1-12)*
*Be Faithful (2.13-17)*
*Pray and Work (3.1-15)*
*A Final Prayer (3.16-18)*

---

**1** From Paul, Silas,[a] and Timothy.
    To the church in Thessalonica, the people of God our Father and of the Lord Jesus Christ.
    [2] I pray that God our Father and the Lord Jesus Christ will be kind to you and will bless you with peace!

### When Christ Returns

[3] My dear friends, we always have good reason to thank God for you, because your faith in God and your love for each other keep growing all the time. [4] That's why we brag about you to all of God's churches. We tell them how patient you are and how you keep on having faith, even though you are going through a lot of trouble and suffering.

[5] All of this shows that God judges fairly and that he is making you fit to share in his kingdom for which you are suffering. [6] It is only right for God to punish everyone who is causing you trouble, [7] but he will give you relief from your troubles. He will do the same for us, when the Lord Jesus comes from heaven with his powerful angels [8] and with a flaming fire.

Our Lord Jesus will punish anyone who doesn't know God and won't obey his message. [9] Their punishment will be eternal destruction, and they will be kept far from the presence of our Lord and his glorious strength. [10] This will

---

[a] **1.1** *Silas:* The Greek text has "Silvanus," which is another form of the name Silas.

261

happen on that day when the Lord returns to be praised and honored by all who have faith in him and belong to him. This includes you, because you believed what we said.

<sup>11</sup> God chose you, and we keep praying that God will make you worthy of being his people. We pray for God's power to help you do all the good things that you hope to do and that your faith makes you want to do. <sup>12</sup> Then, because God and our Lord Jesus Christ are so kind, you will bring honor to the name of our Lord Jesus, and he will bring honor to you.

### The Lord's Return

**2** When our Lord Jesus returns, we will be gathered up to meet him. So I ask you, my friends, <sup>2</sup> not to be easily upset or disturbed by people who claim that the Lord<sup>b</sup> has already come. They may say that they heard this directly from the Holy Spirit, or from someone else, or even that they read it in one of our letters. <sup>3</sup> But don't be fooled! People will rebel against God. Then before the Lord returns, the wicked<sup>c</sup> one who is doomed to be destroyed will appear. <sup>4</sup> He will brag and oppose everything that is holy or sacred. He will even sit in God's temple and claim to be God. <sup>5</sup> Don't you remember that I told you this while I was still with you? <sup>6</sup> You already know what is holding this wicked one back until it is time for him to come. <sup>7</sup> His mysterious power is already at work, but someone is holding him back. And the wicked one won't appear until that someone is out of the way. <sup>8</sup> Then he will appear, but the Lord Jesus will kill him simply by breathing on him. He will be completely destroyed by the Lord's glorious return.

<sup>9</sup> When the wicked one appears, Satan will pretend to work all kinds of miracles, wonders, and signs. <sup>10</sup> Lost people will be fooled by his evil deeds. They could be saved, but they will refuse to love the truth and accept it.

<sup>11</sup> So God will make sure that they are fooled into believing a lie. <sup>12</sup> All of them will be punished, because they would rather do evil than believe the truth.

### Be Faithful

<sup>13</sup> My friends, the Lord loves you, and it is only natural for us to thank God for you. God chose you to be the first ones to be saved.<sup>d</sup> His Spirit made you holy, and you put your faith in the truth. <sup>14</sup> God used our preaching as his way of inviting you to share in the glory of our Lord Jesus Christ. <sup>15</sup> My friends, that's why you must remain faithful and follow closely what we taught you in person and by our letters.

<sup>16</sup> God our Father loves us. He is kind and has given us eternal comfort and a wonderful hope. We pray that our Lord Jesus Christ and God our Father <sup>17</sup> will encourage you and help you always to do and say the right thing.

### Pray for Us

**3** Finally, our friends, please pray for us. This will help the message about the Lord to spread quickly, and others will respect it, just as you do. <sup>2</sup> Pray that we may be kept safe from worthless and evil people. After all, not everyone has faith. <sup>3</sup> But the Lord can be trusted to make you strong and protect you from harm. <sup>4</sup> He has made us sure that you are obeying what we taught you and that you will keep on obeying. <sup>5</sup> I pray that the Lord will guide you to be as loving as God and as patient as Christ.

### Warnings against Laziness

<sup>6</sup> My dear friends, in the name of<sup>e</sup> the Lord Jesus, I beg you not to have anything to do with any of your people who loaf around and refuse to obey the instructions we gave you. <sup>7</sup> You surely know that you should follow our example. We didn't waste our time loafing,

---

<sup>b</sup>**2.2** *Lord*: The Greek text has "day of the Lord." <sup>c</sup>**2.3** *wicked*: Some manuscripts have "sinful." <sup>d</sup>**2.13** *God chose you to be the first ones to be saved*: Some manuscripts have "From the beginning God chose you to be saved." <sup>e</sup>**3.6** *in the name of*: Or "as a follower of."

8 and we didn't accept food from anyone without paying for it. We didn't want to be a burden to any of you, so night and day we worked as hard as we could.

9 We had the right not to work, but we wanted to set an example for you. 10 We also gave you the rule that if you don't work, you don't eat. 11 Now we learn that some of you just loaf around and won't do any work, except the work of a busybody. 12 So, for the sake of our Lord Jesus Christ, we ask and beg these people to settle down and start working for a living. 13 Dear friends, you must never become tired of doing right.

14 Be on your guard against any followers who refuse to obey what we have written in this letter. Put them to shame by not having anything to do with them. 15 Don't consider them your enemies, but speak kindly to them as you would to any other follower.

### Final Prayer

16 I pray that the Lord, who gives peace, will always bless you with peace. May the Lord be with all of you.

17 I always sign my letters as I am now doing: PAUL.

18 I pray that our Lord Jesus Christ will be kind to all of you.

# 1 TIMOTHY

## ABOUT THIS LETTER

Timothy traveled and worked with Paul (Romans 16.21; 1 Corinthians 16.10; Philippians 2.19), and because of their shared faith, Timothy was like a son to Paul (1.2). Timothy became one of Paul's most faithful co-workers, and Paul mentions Timothy in five of his letters.

Although this letter is addressed to Timothy personally, it actually addresses many of the concerns Paul had with the life of the entire church. Guidelines are given for choosing church officials (3.1-7), officers (3.8-13), and leaders (5.17-20).

Christians are to pray for everyone and to remember:

There is only one God,
and Christ Jesus
is the only one
who can bring us
to God.        (2.5)

## A QUICK LOOK AT THIS LETTER

Greetings (1.1, 2)
Instructions for Church Life (1.3—3.13)
The Mystery of Our Religion (3.14—4.5)
Paul's Advice to Timothy (4.6—6.21)

**1** From Paul.
God our Savior and Christ Jesus commanded me to be an apostle of Christ Jesus, who gives us hope.

[2] Timothy, because of our faith, you are like a son to me. I pray that God our Father and our Lord Jesus Christ will be kind and merciful to you. May they bless you with peace!

### Warning against False Teaching

[3] When I was leaving for Macedonia, I asked you to stay on in Ephesus and warn certain people there to stop spreading their false teachings. [4] You needed to warn them to stop wasting their time on senseless stories and endless lists of ancestors. Such things only cause arguments. They don't help anyone to do God's work that can only be done by faith.

[5] You must teach people to have genuine love, as well as a good conscience and true faith. [6] There are some who have given up these for nothing but empty talk. [7] They want to be teachers of the Law of Moses. But they don't know what they are talking about, even though they think they do.

[8] We know that the Law is good, if it is used in the right way. [9] We also understand that it wasn't given to control people who please God, but to control lawbreakers, criminals, godless people, and sinners. It is for wicked and evil people, and for murderers, who would even kill their own parents. [10] The Law was written for people who are sexual perverts or who live as homosexuals or are kidnappers or liars or won't tell the truth in court. It is for anything else that opposes the correct teaching [11] of the good news that the glorious and wonderful God has given me.

### Being Thankful for God's Kindness

[12] I thank Christ Jesus our Lord. He has given me the strength for my work because he knew that he could trust me. [13] I used to say terrible and insulting things about him, and I was cruel. But he had mercy on me because I didn't know what I was doing, and I had not yet put my faith in him. [14] Christ Jesus our Lord was very kind to me. He has greatly blessed my life with faith and love just like his own.

[15] "Christ Jesus came into the world to save sinners." This saying is true, and it can be trusted. I was the worst sinner of all! [16] But since I was worse than anyone else, God had mercy on me and let me be an example of the endless patience of Christ Jesus. He did this so that others would put their faith in Christ and have eternal life. [17] I pray that honor and glory will always be given to the only God, who lives forever and is the invisible and eternal King! Amen.

[18] Timothy, my son, the instructions I am giving you are based on what some prophets[a] once said about you. If you follow these instructions, you will fight like a good soldier. [19] You will be faithful and have a clear conscience. Some people have made a mess of their faith because they didn't listen to their consciences. [20] Two of them are Hymenaeus and Alexander. I have given these men over to the power of Satan, so they will learn not to oppose God.

### How To Pray

**2** First of all, I ask you to pray for everyone. Ask God to help and bless them all, and tell God how thankful you are for each of them. [2] Pray for kings and others in power, so that we may live quiet and peaceful lives as we worship and honor God. [3] This kind of prayer is good, and it pleases God our Savior. [4] God wants everyone to be saved and to know the whole truth, which is,

[5] There is only one God,
and Christ Jesus
is the only one
who can bring us
to God.
Jesus was truly human,
and he gave himself
to rescue all of us.
[6] God showed us this
at the right time.

---

[a] **1.18** *prophets:* Probably the Christian prophets referred to in 4.14.

7 This is why God chose me to be a preacher and an apostle of the good news. I am telling the truth. I am not lying. God sent me to teach the Gentiles about faith and truth.

8 I want everyone everywhere to lift innocent hands toward heaven and pray, without being angry or arguing with each other.

9 I would like for women to wear modest and sensible clothes. They should not have fancy hairdos, or wear expensive clothes, or put on jewelry made of gold or pearls. 10 Women who claim to love God should do helpful things for others, 11 and they should learn by being quiet and paying attention. 12 They should be silent and not be allowed to teach or to tell men what to do. 13 After all, Adam was created before Eve, 14 and the man Adam wasn't the one who was fooled. It was the woman Eve who was completely fooled and sinned. 15 But women will be saved by having children,b if they stay faithful, loving, holy, and modest.

### Church Officials

**3** It is true thatc anyone who desires to be a church officiald wants to be something worthwhile. 2 That's why officials must have a good reputation and be faithful in marriage.e They must be self-controlled, sensible, well-behaved, friendly to strangers, and able to teach. 3 They must not be heavy drinkers or troublemakers. Instead, they must be kind and gentle and not love money.

4 Church officials must be in control of their own families, and they must see that their children are obedient and always respectful. 5 If they don't know how to control their own families, how can they look after God's people? 6 They must not be new followers of the Lord. If they are, they might be-

come proud and be doomed along with the devil. 7 Finally, they must be well-respected by people who are not followers. Then they won't be trapped and disgraced by the devil.

### Church Officers

8 Church officersf should be serious. They must not be liars, heavy drinkers, or greedy for money. 9 And they must have a clear conscience and hold firmly to what God has shown us about our faith. 10 They must first prove themselves. Then if no one has anything against them, they can serve as officers. 11 Womeng must also be serious. They must not gossip or be heavy drinkers, and they must be faithful in everything they do. 12 Church officers must be faithful in marriage.h They must be in full control of their children and everyone else in their home. 13 Those who serve well as officers will earn a good reputation and will be highly respected for their faith in Christ Jesus.

### The Mystery of Our Religion

14 I hope to visit you soon. But I am writing these instructions, 15 so that if I am delayed, you will know how everyone who belongs to God's family ought to behave. After all, the church of the living God is the strong foundation of truth.

16 Here is the great mystery of our religion:

Christi came as a human.
The Spirit proved
that he pleased God,
and he was seen by angels.

Christ was preached
to the nations.

b2.15 saved by having children: Or "brought safely through childbirth" or "saved by the birth of a child" (that is, by the birth of Jesus) or "saved by being good mothers." c3.1 It is true that: These words may be taken with 2.15. If so, that verse would be translated: "It is true that women will be saved . . . holy, and modest." And 3.1 would be translated, "Anyone who desires . . . something worthwhile." d3.1 church official: Or "bishop." e3.2 be faithful in marriage: Or "be the husband of only one wife" or "have never been divorced." f3.8 Church officers: Or "Deacons." g3.11 Women: Either church officers or the wives of church officers. h3.12 be faithful in marriage: See the note at 3.2. i3.16 Christ: The Greek text has "he," probably meaning "Christ." Some manuscripts have "God."

People in this world
put their faith in him,
and he was taken up to glory.

## People Will Turn from Their Faith

**4** God's Spirit clearly says that in the last days many people will turn from their faith. They will be fooled by evil spirits and by teachings that come from demons. [2] They will also be fooled by the false claims of liars whose consciences have lost all feeling. These liars [3] will forbid people to marry or to eat certain foods. But God created these foods to be eaten with thankful hearts by his followers who know the truth. [4] Everything God created is good. And if you give thanks, you may eat anything. [5] What God has said and your prayer will make it fit to eat.

## Paul's Advice to Timothy

[6] If you teach these things to other followers, you will be a good servant of Christ Jesus. You will show that you have grown up on the teachings about our faith and on the good instructions you have obeyed. [7] Don't have anything to do with worthless, senseless stories. Work hard to be truly religious. [8-9] As the saying goes,

"Exercise is good
    for your body,
but religion helps you
    in every way.
It promises life
    now and forever."

These words are worthwhile and should not be forgotten. [10] We have put our hope in the living God, who is the Savior of everyone, but especially of those who have faith. That's why we work and struggle so hard. [j]
[11] Teach these things and tell everyone to do what you say. [12] Don't let anyone make fun of you, just because you are young. Set an example for other followers by what you say and do, as well as by your love, faith, and purity.

[13] Until I arrive, be sure to keep on reading the Scriptures in worship, and don't stop preaching and teaching. [14] Use the gift you were given when the prophets spoke and the group of church leaders [k] blessed you by placing their hands on you. [15] Remember these things and think about them, so everyone can see how well you are doing. [16] Be careful about the way you live and about what you teach. Keep on doing this, and you will save not only yourself, but the people who hear you.

## How To Act toward Others

**5** Don't correct an older man. Encourage him, as you would your own father. Treat younger men as you would your own brother, [2] and treat older women as you would your own mother. Show the same respect to younger women that you would to your sister.
[3] Take care of any widow who is really in need. [4] But if a widow has children or grandchildren, they should learn to serve God by taking care of her, as she once took care of them. This is what God wants them to do. [5] A widow who is really in need is one who doesn't have any relatives. She has faith in God, and she keeps praying to him night and day, asking for his help. [6] A widow who thinks only about having a good time is already dead, even though she is still alive. [7] Tell all of this to everyone, so they will do the right thing. [8] People who don't take care of their relatives, and especially their own families, have given up their faith. They are worse than someone who doesn't have faith in the Lord.
[9] For a widow to be put on the list of widows, she must be at least sixty years old, and she must have been faithful in marriage. [l] [10] She must also be well-known for doing all sorts of good things, such as raising children, giving food to strangers, welcoming God's

---

[j]**4.10** *struggle so hard*: Some manuscripts have "are treated so badly." [k]**4.14** *group of church leaders*: Or "group of elders" or "group of presbyters" or "group of priests." This translates one Greek word, and it is related to the one used in 5.17, 19. [l]**5.9** *been faithful in marriage*: Or "been the wife of only one husband" or "never been divorced."

people into her home,[m] helping people in need, and always making herself useful.

[11] Don't put young widows on the list. They may later have a strong desire to get married. Then they will turn away from Christ [12] and become guilty of breaking their promise to him. [13] Besides, they will become lazy and get into the habit of going from house to house. Next, they will start gossiping and become busybodies, talking about things that are none of their business.

[14] I would prefer that young widows get married, have children, and look after their families. Then the enemy won't have any reason to say insulting things about us. [15] Look what's already happened to some of the young widows! They have turned away to follow Satan.

[16] If a woman who is a follower has any widows in her family, she[n] should help them. This will keep the church from having that burden, and then the church can help widows who are really in need.

## Church Leaders

[17] Church leaders[o] who do their job well deserve to be paid[p] twice as much, especially if they work hard at preaching and teaching. [18] It is just as the Scriptures say, "Don't muzzle an ox when you are using it to grind grain." You also know the saying, "Workers are worth their pay."

[19] Don't listen to any charge against a church leader, unless at least two or three people bring the same charges. [20] But if any of the leaders should keep on sinning, they must be corrected in front of the whole group, as a warning to everyone else.

[21] In the presence of God and Christ Jesus and their chosen angels, I order you to follow my instructions! Be fair with everyone, and don't have any favorites.

[22] Don't be too quick to accept people into the service of the Lord[q] by placing your hands on them.

Don't sin because others do, but stay close to God.

[23] Stop drinking only water. Take a little wine to help your stomach trouble and the other illnesses you always have.

[24] Some people get caught in their sins right away, even before the time of judgment. But other people's sins don't show up until later. [25] It is the same with good deeds. Some are easily seen, but none of them can be hidden.

**6** If you are a slave, you should respect and honor your owner. This will keep people from saying bad things about God and about our teaching. [2] If any of you slaves have owners who are followers, you should show them respect. After all, they are also followers of Christ, and he loves them. So you should serve and help them the best you can.

## False Teaching and True Wealth

These are the things you must teach and tell the people to do. [3] Anyone who teaches something different disagrees with the correct and godly teaching of our Lord Jesus Christ. [4] Those people who disagree are proud of themselves, but they don't really know a thing. Their minds are sick, and they like to argue over words. They cause jealousy, disagreements, unkind words, evil suspicions, [5] and nasty quarrels. They have wicked minds and have missed out on the truth.

These people think religion is supposed to make you rich. [6] And religion does make your life rich, by making you content with what you have. [7] We didn't bring anything into this world, and we won't[r] take anything with us

---

[m]**5.10** *welcoming God's people into her home*: The Greek text has "washing the feet of God's people." In New Testament times most people either went barefoot or wore sandals, and a host would often wash the feet of special guests.   [n]**5.16** *woman . . . she*: Some manuscripts have "man . . . he," and others have "man or woman . . . that person."   [o]**5.17** *leaders*: Or "elders" or "presbyters" or "priests."   [p]**5.17** *paid*: Or "honored" or "respected."   [q]**5.22** *to accept people into the service of the Lord*: Or "to forgive people."   [r]**6.7** *we won't*: Some manuscripts have "we surely won't."

when we leave. ⁸ So we should be satisfied just to have food and clothes. ⁹ People who want to be rich fall into all sorts of temptations and traps. They are caught by foolish and harmful desires that drag them down and destroy them. ¹⁰ The love of money causes all kinds of trouble. Some people want money so much that they have given up their faith and caused themselves a lot of pain.

### Fighting a Good Fight for the Faith

¹¹ Timothy, you belong to God, so keep away from all these evil things. Try your best to please God and to be like him. Be faithful, loving, dependable, and gentle. ¹² Fight a good fight for the faith and claim eternal life. God offered it to you when you clearly told about your faith, while so many people listened. ¹³ Now I ask you to make a promise. Make it in the presence of God, who gives life to all, and in the presence of Jesus Christ, who openly told Pontius Pilate about his faith. ¹⁴ Promise to obey completely and fully all that you have been told until our Lord Jesus Christ returns.

¹⁵ The glorious God
  is the only Ruler,
  the King of kings
and Lord of lords.
At the time that God
  has already decided,
he will send Jesus Christ
  back again.

¹⁶ Only God lives forever!
And he lives in light
  that no one can come near.
No human has ever seen God
  or ever can see him.
God will be honored,
and his power
  will last forever. Amen.

¹⁷ Warn the rich people of this world not to be proud or to trust in wealth that is easily lost. Tell them to have faith in God, who is rich and blesses us with everything we need to enjoy life. ¹⁸ Instruct them to do as many good deeds as they can and to help everyone. Remind the rich to be generous and share what they have. ¹⁹ This will lay a solid foundation for the future, so that they will know what true life is like.

²⁰ Timothy, guard what God has placed in your care! Don't pay any attention to that godless and stupid talk that sounds smart but really isn't. ²¹ Some people have even lost their faith by believing this talk.

I pray that the Lord will be kind to all of you!

# 2 TIMOTHY

## ABOUT THIS LETTER

*In his second letter to Timothy, Paul is more personal than in his first one. Timothy is like a "dear child" to Paul, and Paul always mentions him in his prayers (1.2, 3) because he wants Timothy to be a "good soldier" of Christ Jesus and to learn to endure suffering (2.1, 3). Paul mentions Timothy's mother and grandmother by name in this letter and reminds Timothy how he had placed his hands on him as a special sign that the Spirit was guiding his work.*

*Some who claimed to be followers of the Lord had already been trapped by the devil, and Paul warns Timothy to run from those temptations that often catch young people (2.20-26; 3.1-9). He tells Timothy to keep preaching God's message, even if it is not the popular thing to do (4.2). He should also beware of false teachers.*

*Paul knows that he will soon die for his faith, but he will be rewarded for his faithfulness (4.6-8), and he reminds Timothy of the true message:*

> If we died with Christ,
>     we will live with him.
> If we don't give up,
>     we will rule with him.
>         (2.11, 12a)

## A QUICK LOOK AT THIS LETTER

*Greetings and Prayer for Timothy (1.1, 2)*
*Do Not Be Ashamed of the Lord (1.3-18)*
*How To Be a Good Soldier of Christ (2.1-26)*
*What People Will Be Like in the Last Days (3.1-9)*
*Keep Being Faithful (3.10—4.8)*
*Personal Instructions and Final Greetings (4.9-22)*

---

**1** From Paul, an apostle of Christ Jesus.

God himself chose me to be an apostle, and he gave me the promised life that Jesus Christ makes possible.

² Timothy, you are like a dear child to me. I pray that God our Father and our Lord Christ Jesus will be kind and merciful to you and will bless you with peace!

### Do Not Be Ashamed of the Lord

³ Night and day I mention you in my prayers. I am always grateful for you, as I pray to the God my ancestors and I have served with a clear conscience. ⁴ I remember how you cried, and I want to see you, because that will make me truly happy. ⁵ I also remember the genuine faith of your mother Eunice. Your grandmother Lois had the same sort of faith, and I am sure that you have it as well. ⁶ So I ask you to make full use of the gift that God gave you when I placed my hands on you.ᵃ Use it well. ⁷ God's Spiritᵇ doesn't make cowards out of us. The Spirit gives us power, love, and self-control.

ᵃ **1.6** *when I placed my hands on you:* Church leaders placed their hands on people who were being appointed to preach or teach (see 1 Timothy 4.14). ᵇ **1.7** *God's Spirit:* Or "God."

8 Don't be ashamed to speak for our Lord. And don't be ashamed of me, just because I am in jail for serving him. Use the power that comes from God and join with me in suffering for telling the good news.

9 God saved us and chose us
  to be his holy people.
We did nothing
  to deserve this,
but God planned it
  because he is so kind.
Even before time began
God planned for Christ Jesus
  to show kindness to us.

10 Now Christ Jesus has come
  to show us the kindness
  of God.
Christ our Savior defeated death
  and brought us
  the good news.
It shines like a light
  and offers life
  that never ends.

11 My work is to be a preacher, an apostle, and a teacher.c 12 That's why I am suffering now. But I am not ashamed! I know the one I have faith in, and I am sure that he can guard until the last day what he has trusted me with.d 13 Now follow the example of the correct teaching I gave you, and let the faith and love of Christ Jesus be your model. 14 You have been trusted with a wonderful treasure. Guard it with the help of the Holy Spirit, who lives within you.

15 You know that everyone in Asia has turned against me, especially Phygelus and Hermogenes. 16 I pray that the Lord will be kind to the family of Onesiphorus. He often cheered me up and wasn't ashamed of me when I was put in jail. 17 Then after he arrived in Rome, he searched everywhere until he found me. 18 I pray that the Lord Jesus will ask God to show mercy to Onesiphorus on the day of judgment. You know how much he helped me in Ephesus.

## A Good Soldier of Christ Jesus

2 Timothy, my child, Christ Jesus is kind, and you must let him make you strong. 2 You have often heard me teach. Now I want you to tell these same things to followers who can be trusted to tell others.

3 As a good soldier of Christ Jesus you must endure your share of suffering. 4 Soldiers on duty don't work at outside jobs. They try only to please their commanding officer. 5 No one wins an athletic contest without obeying the rules. 6 And farmers who work hard are the first to eat what grows in their field. 7 If you keep in mind what I have told you, the Lord will help you understand completely.

8 Keep your mind on Jesus Christ! He was from the family of David and was raised from death, just as my good news says. 9 And because of this message, I am locked up in jail and treated like a criminal. But God's good news isn't locked in jail, 10 and so I am willing to put up with anything. Then God's special people will be saved. They will be given eternal glory because they belong to Christ Jesus. 11 Here is a true message:

"If we died with Christ,
  we will live with him.
12 If we don't give up,
  we will rule with him.
If we deny
  that we know him,
he will deny
  that he knows us.
13 If we are not faithful,
  he will still be faithful.
Christ cannot deny
  who he is."

## An Approved Worker

14 Don't let anyone forget these things. And with Gode as your witness, you must warn them not to argue about words. These arguments don't help anyone. In fact, they ruin everyone who listens to them. 15 Do your best to win

c 1.11 teacher: Some manuscripts add "of the Gentiles." d 1.12 what he has trusted me with: Or "what I have trusted him with." e 2.14 God: Some manuscripts have "the Lord," and others have "Christ."

God's approval as a worker who doesn't need to be ashamed and who teaches only the true message.

¹⁶ Keep away from worthless and useless talk. It only leads people farther away from God. ¹⁷ That sort of talk is like a sore that won't heal. And Hymenaeus and Philetus have been talking this way ¹⁸ by teaching that the dead have already been raised to life. This is far from the truth, and it is destroying the faith of some people.

¹⁹ But the foundation that God has laid is solid. On it is written, "The Lord knows who his people are. So everyone who worships the Lord must turn away from evil."

²⁰ In a large house some dishes are made of gold or silver, while others are made of wood or clay. Some of these are special, and others are not. ²¹ That's also how it is with people. The ones who stop doing evil and make themselves pure will become special. Their lives will be holy and pleasing to their Master, and they will be able to do all kinds of good deeds.

²² Run from temptations that capture young people. Always do the right thing. Be faithful, loving, and easy to get along with. Worship with people whose hearts are pure. ²³ Stay away from stupid and senseless arguments. These only lead to trouble, ²⁴ and God's servants must not be troublemakers. They must be kind to everyone, and they must be good teachers and very patient.

²⁵ Be humble when you correct people who oppose you. Maybe God will lead them to turn to him and learn the truth. ²⁶ They have been trapped by the devil, and he makes them obey him, but God may help them escape.

### What People Will Be Like in the Last Days

**3** You can be certain that in the last days there will be some very hard times. ² People will love only themselves and money. They will be proud, stuck-up, rude, and disobedient to their parents. They will also be ungrateful, godless, ³ heartless, and hateful. Their words will be cruel, and they will have no self-control or pity. These people will hate everything that is good. ⁴ They will be sneaky, reckless, and puffed up with pride. Instead of loving God, they will love pleasure. ⁵ Even though they will make a show of being religious, their religion won't be real. Don't have anything to do with such people.

⁶ Some men fool whole families, just to get power over those women who are slaves of sin and are controlled by all sorts of desires. ⁷ These women always want to learn something new, but they never can discover the truth. ⁸ Just as Jannes and Jambres[f] opposed Moses, these people are enemies of the truth. Their minds are sick, and their faith isn't real. ⁹ But they won't get very far with their foolishness. Soon everyone will know the truth about them, just as Jannes and Jambres were found out.

### Paul's Last Instructions to Timothy

¹⁰ Timothy, you know what I teach and how I live. You know what I want to do and what I believe. You have seen how patient and loving I am, and how in the past I put up with ¹¹ trouble and suffering in the cities of Antioch, Iconium, and Lystra. Yet the Lord rescued me from all those terrible troubles. ¹² Anyone who belongs to Christ Jesus and wants to live right will have trouble from others. ¹³ But evil people who pretend to be what they are not will become worse than ever, as they fool others and are fooled themselves.

¹⁴ Keep on being faithful to what you were taught and to what you believed. After all, you know who taught you these things. ¹⁵ Since childhood, you have known the Holy Scriptures that are able to make you wise enough to have faith in Christ Jesus and be saved. ¹⁶ Everything in the Scriptures is God's Word. All of it is useful for teaching

---

ᶠ3.8 *Jannes and Jambres*: These names are not found in the Old Testament. But many believe these were the names of the two Egyptian magicians who opposed Moses when he wanted to lead the people of Israel out of Egypt (see Exodus 7.11, 22).

and helping people and for correcting them and showing them how to live. [17] The Scriptures train God's servants to do all kinds of good deeds.

4 When Christ Jesus comes as king, he will be the judge of everyone, whether they are living or dead. So with God and Christ as witnesses, I command you [2] to preach God's message. Do it willingly, even if it isn't the popular thing to do. You must correct people and point out their sins. But also cheer them up, and when you instruct them, always be patient. [3] The time is coming when people won't listen to good teaching. Instead, they will look for teachers who will please them by telling them only what they are itching to hear. [4] They will turn from the truth and eagerly listen to senseless stories. [5] But you must stay calm and be willing to suffer. You must work hard to tell the good news and to do your job well.

[6] Now the time has come for me to die. My life is like a drink offering[g] being poured out on the altar. [7] I have fought well. I have finished the race, and I have been faithful. [8] So a crown will be given to me for pleasing the Lord. He judges fairly, and on the day of judgment he will give a crown to me and to everyone else who wants him to appear with power.

### Personal Instructions

[9] Come to see me as soon as you can. [10] Demas loves the things of this world so much that he left me and went to Thessalonica. Crescens has gone to Ga-

latia, and Titus has gone to Dalmatia. [11] Only Luke has stayed with me.

Mark can be very helpful to me, so please find him and bring him with you. [12] I sent Tychicus to Ephesus. [13] When you come, bring the coat I left at Troas with Carpus. Don't forget to bring the scrolls, especially the ones made of leather.[h]

[14] Alexander, the metalworker, has hurt me in many ways. But the Lord will pay him back for what he has done. [15] Alexander opposes what we preach. You had better watch out for him. [16] When I was first put on trial, no one helped me. In fact, everyone deserted me. I hope it won't be held against them. [17] But the Lord stood beside me. He gave me the strength to tell his full message, so that all Gentiles would hear it. And I was kept safe from hungry lions. [18] The Lord will always keep me from being harmed by evil, and he will bring me safely into his heavenly kingdom. Praise him forever and ever! Amen.

### Final Greetings

[19] Give my greetings to Priscilla and Aquila and to the family of Onesiphorus. [20] Erastus stayed at Corinth.

Trophimus was sick when I left him at Miletus. [21] Do your best to come before winter.

Eubulus, Pudens, Linus, and Claudia send you their greetings, and so do the rest of the Lord's followers. [22] I pray that the Lord will bless your life and will be kind to you.

---

[g] **4.6** *drink offering*: Water or wine was sometimes poured out as an offering when an animal sacrifice was made.   [h] **4.13** *the ones made of leather*: A scroll was a kind of rolled up book, and it could be made out of paper (called "papyrus") or leather (that is, animal skin) or even copper.

# TITUS

## ABOUT THIS LETTER

*Paul mentions Titus several times in his letters as someone who worked with him in Asia Minor and Greece (2 Corinthians 2.13; 7.6, 13; 8.6, 16, 23; 12.18; Galatians 2.3). He is told by Paul to appoint church leaders and officials in Crete.*

*Paul instructs Titus to make sure that church leaders and officials have good reputations (1.5-9) and that all of the Lord's followers keep themselves pure and avoid arguments (1.10—2.9).*

*Paul includes special instructions for the different groups within the church in Crete. He reminds Titus that a new way of life is possible because of what God has done by sending Jesus Christ: God has saved them, washed them by the power of the Holy Spirit, and given them a fresh start and the hope of eternal life.*

*Paul also tells how we are saved:*

> God our Savior showed us
>   how good and kind he is.
> He saved us because
>   of his mercy,
> and not because
> of any good things
>   that we have done.
>
>                                    (3.4, 5)

## A QUICK LOOK AT THIS LETTER

*Greetings and a Prayer for Titus (1.1-4)*
*Instructions for Church Officials (1.5-16)*
*Instructions for Church People (2.1—3.11)*
*Personal Advice and Final Greetings (3.12-15)*

---

**1** From Paul, a servant of God and an apostle of Jesus Christ.

I encourage God's own people to have more faith and to understand the truth about religion. ² Then they will have the hope of eternal life that God promised long ago. And God never tells a lie! ³ So, at the proper time, God our Savior gave this message and told me to announce what he had said.

⁴ Titus, because of our faith, you are like a son to me. I pray that God our Father and Christ Jesus our Savior will be kind to you and will bless you with peace!

### What Titus Was To Do in Crete

⁵ I left you in Crete to do what had been left undone and to appoint leaders*a* for the churches in each town. As I told you, ⁶ they must have a good reputation and be faithful in marriage.*b* Their children must be followers of the Lord and not have a reputation for being wild and disobedient.

*a* **1.5** *leaders*: Or "elders" or "presbyters" or "priests." *b* **1.6** *be faithful in marriage*: Or "be the husband of only one wife" or "have never been divorced."

273

[7] Church officials[c] are in charge of God's work, and so they must also have a good reputation. They must not be bossy, quick-tempered, heavy drinkers, bullies, or dishonest in business. [8] Instead, they must be friendly to strangers and enjoy doing good things. They must also be sensible, fair, pure, and self-controlled. [9] They must stick to the true message they were taught, so that their good teaching can help others and correct everyone who opposes it.

[10] There are many who don't respect authority, and they fool others by talking nonsense. This is especially true of some Jewish followers. [11] But you must make them be quiet. They are after money, and they upset whole families by teaching what they should not. [12] It is like one of their own prophets once said,

"The people of Crete
    always tell lies.
They are greedy and lazy
    like wild animals."

[13] That surely is a true saying. And you should be hard on such people, so you can help them grow stronger in their faith. [14] Don't pay any attention to any of those senseless Jewish stories and human commands. These are made up by people who won't obey the truth.

[15] Everything is pure for someone whose heart is pure. But nothing is pure for an unbeliever with a dirty mind. That person's mind and conscience are destroyed. [16] Such people claim to know God, but their actions prove that they really don't. They are disgusting. They won't obey God, and they are too worthless to do anything good.

## Instructions for Different Groups of People

**2** Titus, you must teach only what is correct. [2] Tell the older men to have self-control and to be serious and sensible. Their faith, love, and patience must never fail.

[3] Tell the older women to behave as those who love the Lord should. They must not gossip about others or be slaves of wine. They must teach what is proper, [4] so the younger women will be loving wives and mothers. [5] Each of the younger women must be sensible and kind, as well as a good homemaker, who puts her own husband first. Then no one can say insulting things about God's message.

[6] Tell the young men to have self-control in everything.

[7] Always set a good example for others. Be sincere and serious when you teach. [8] Use clean language that no one can criticize. Do this, and your enemies will be too ashamed to say anything against you.

[9] Tell slaves always to please their owners by obeying them in everything. Slaves must not talk back to their owners [10] or steal from them. They must be completely honest and trustworthy. Then everyone will show great respect for what is taught about God our Savior.

## God's Kindness and the New Life

[11] God has shown us how kind he is by coming to save all people. [12] He taught us to give up our wicked ways and our worldly desires and to live decent and honest lives in this world. [13] We are filled with hope, as we wait for the glorious return of our great God and Savior Jesus Christ.[d] [14] He gave himself to rescue us from everything that is evil and to make our hearts pure. He wanted us to be his own people and to be eager to do right.

[15] Teach these things, as you use your full authority to encourage and correct people. Make sure you earn everyone's respect.

## Doing Helpful Things

**3** Remind your people to obey the rulers and authorities and not to be rebellious. They must always be ready to do something helpful [2] and not say cruel things or argue. They should be gentle and kind to everyone. ³We used to be stupid, disobedient, and foolish, as well as slaves of all sorts of desires and pleasures. We were evil and jealous. Everyone hated us, and we hated everyone.

⁴ God our Savior showed us
how good and kind he is.
⁵ He saved us because
of his mercy,
and not because
of any good things
that we have done.

God washed us by the power
of the Holy Spirit.
He gave us new birth
and a fresh beginning.
⁶ God sent Jesus Christ
our Savior
to give us his Spirit.

⁷ Jesus treated us much better
than we deserve.
He made us acceptable to God
and gave us the hope
of eternal life.

⁸This message is certainly true. These teachings are useful and helpful for everyone. I want you to insist that the people follow them, so that all who have faith in God will be sure to do good deeds. ⁹But don't have anything to do with stupid arguments about ancestors. And stay away from disagreements and quarrels about the Law of Moses. Such arguments are useless and senseless.

¹⁰Warn troublemakers once or twice. Then don't have anything else to do with them. ¹¹You know that their minds are twisted, and their own sins show how guilty they are.

## Personal Instructions and Greetings

¹²I plan to send Artemas or Tychicus to you. After he arrives, please try your best to meet me at Nicopolis. I have decided to spend the winter there.

¹³When Zenas the lawyer and Apollos get ready to leave, help them as much as you can, so they won't have need of anything.

¹⁴Our people should learn to spend their time doing something useful and worthwhile.

¹⁵Greetings to you from everyone here. Greet all of our friends who share in our faith.

I pray that the Lord will be kind to all of you!

# PHILEMON

## ABOUT THIS LETTER

Philemon was a wealthy man who owned slaves and who used his large house for church meetings (2). He probably lived in Colossae, since Paul's letter to the Colossians mentions Onesimus, a slave of Philemon, and Archippus (Colossians 4.9, 17).

Paul is writing from jail on behalf of Onesimus, a runaway slave owned by Philemon. Onesimus had become a follower of the Lord and a valuable friend to Paul, and Paul is writing to encourage Philemon to accept Onesimus also as a friend and follower of the Lord.

This letter is an excellent example of the art of letter-writing in the Roman world, and it is the most personal of all Paul's letters. The way the letter is written suggests that Paul and Philemon were close friends.

## A QUICK LOOK AT THIS LETTER

Greetings to Philemon (1-3)
Paul Speaks to Philemon about Onesimus (4-22)
Final Greetings and a Prayer (23-25)

---

[1] From Paul, who is in jail for serving Christ Jesus, and from Timothy, who is like a brother because of our faith.

Philemon, you work with us and are very dear to us. This letter is to you [2] and to the church that meets in your home. It is also to our dear friend Apphia and to Archippus, who serves the Lord as we do.

[3] I pray that God our Father and our Lord Jesus Christ will be kind to you and will bless you with peace!

### Philemon's Love and Faith

[4] Philemon, each time I mention you in my prayers, I thank God. [5] I hear about your faith in our Lord Jesus and about your love for all of God's people. [6] As you share your faith with others, I pray that they may come to know all the blessings Christ has given us. [7] My friend, your love has made me happy and has greatly encouraged me. It has also cheered the hearts of God's people.

### Paul Speaks to Philemon about Onesimus

[8] Christ gives me the courage to tell you what to do. [9] But I would rather ask you to do it simply because of love. Yes, as someone[a] in jail for Christ, [10] I beg you to help Onesimus![b] He is like a son to me because I led him to Christ here in jail. [11] Before this, he was useless to you, but now he is useful both to you and to me.

[12] Sending Onesimus back to you makes me very sad. [13] I would like to keep him here with me, where he could take your place in helping me while I am here in prison for preaching the good news. [14] But I won't do anything unless you agree to it first. I want your act of kindness to come from your heart, and not be something you feel forced to do.

[15] Perhaps Onesimus was taken from you for a little while so that you could have him back for good, [16] but not as a slave. Onesimus is much more than a slave. To me he is a dear friend, but

---

[a] 9 someone: Greek "a messenger" or "an old man."   [b] 10 Onesimus: In Greek this name means "useful."

276

to you he is even more, both as a person and as a follower of the Lord.

¹⁷ If you consider me a friend because of Christ, then welcome Onesimus as you would welcome me. ¹⁸ If he has cheated you or owes you anything, charge it to my account. ¹⁹ With my own hand I write: I, PAUL, WILL PAY YOU BACK. But don't forget that you owe me your life. ²⁰ My dear friend and follower of Christ our Lord, please cheer me up by doing this for me.

²¹ I am sure you will do all I have asked, and even more. ²² Please get a room ready for me. I hope your prayers will be answered, and I can visit you.

²³ Epaphras is also here in jail for being a follower of Christ Jesus. He sends his greetings, ²⁴ and so do Mark, Aristarchus, Demas, and Luke, who work together with me.

²⁵ I pray that the Lord Jesus Christ will be kind to you!

# HEBREWS

## ABOUT THIS LETTER

Many religious people in the first century after Jesus' birth, both Jews and Gentiles, had questions about the religion of the early Christians. They were looking for evidence that this new faith was genuine. Jews had the miracle of crossing the Red Sea and the agreement made with God at Mount Sinai to support their faith. But what miracles did Christians have? Jews had beautiful worship ceremonies and a high priest who offered sacrifices in the temple so that the people would be forgiven. But what did Christians have? How could this new Christian faith, centered in Jesus, offer forgiveness of sins and friendship with God?

The letter to the Hebrews was written to answer exactly these kinds of questions. In it the author tells the readers how important Jesus really is. He is greater than any of God's angels (1.5-14), greater than any prophet, and greater even than Moses and Joshua (2.1—4.14). Jesus is the perfect high priest because he never sinned, and by offering his own life he has made the perfect sacrifice for sin once for all time (9.23—10.18). By his death and return from death he has opened the way for all people to come to God (4.14—5.10; 7.1—8.13).

This letter has much to say about the importance of faith. The writer points out that what Jesus offers comes only by faith. And this faith makes his followers sure of what they hope for and gives them proof of things that cannot be seen. The writer praises God's faithful people of the past (11.1-40) and encourages those who follow Jesus now to keep their eyes on him as they run the race (12.1-3).

What does it mean to have a high priest like Jesus?

> Jesus understands every weakness of ours, because he was tempted in every way that we are. But he did not sin! So whenever we are in need, we should come bravely before the throne of our merciful God. There we will be treated with undeserved kindness, and we will find help. (4.15, 16)

## A QUICK LOOK AT THIS LETTER

The Greatness of God's Son (1.1-4)
Jesus Is Greater than Angels (1.5—2.18)
Jesus Is Greater than Moses and Joshua (3.1—4.13)
Jesus Is the Great High Priest (4.14—7.28)
Jesus Brings a Better Agreement (8.1—9.22)
Jesus' Sacrifice Is Once and for All (9.23—10.31)
Some of God's People Who Had Great Faith (11.1-40)
Follow the Example of Jesus (12.1—13.19)
Final Prayers and Greetings (13.20-25)

**1** Long ago in many ways and at many times God's prophets spoke his message to our ancestors. ² But now at last, God sent his Son to bring his message to us. God created the universe by his Son, and everything will someday belong to the Son. ³ God's Son has all the brightness of God's own glory and is like him in every way. By his own mighty word, he holds the universe together.

After the Son had washed away our sins, he sat down at the right side[a] of the glorious God in heaven. ⁴ He had become much greater than the angels, and the name he was given is far greater than any of theirs.

### God's Son Is Greater than Angels

⁵ God has never said
to any of the angels,
"You are my Son, because today
I have become your Father!"
Neither has God said
to any of them,
"I will be his Father,
and he will be my Son!"

⁶ When God brings his first-born Son[b] into the world, he commands all of his angels to worship him. ⁷ And when God speaks about the angels, he says,

"I change my angels into wind
and my servants
into flaming fire."

⁸ But God says about his Son,

"You are God,
and you will rule
as King forever!
Your[c] royal power
brings about justice.
⁹ You loved justice
and hated evil,
and so I, your God,
have chosen you.
I appointed you
and made you happier
than any of your friends."

¹⁰ The Scriptures also say,

"In the beginning, Lord,
you were the one
who laid the foundation
of the earth
and created the heavens.
¹¹ They will all disappear
and wear out like clothes,
but you will last forever.
¹² You will roll them up
like a robe
and change them
like a garment.
But you are always the same,
and you will live forever."

¹³ God never said to any
of the angels,
"Sit at my right side
until I make your enemies
into a footstool for you!"

¹⁴ Angels are merely spirits sent to serve people who are going to be saved.

### This Great Way of Being Saved

**2** We must give our full attention to what we were told, so that we won't drift away. ² The message spoken by angels proved to be true, and all who disobeyed or rejected it were punished as they deserved. ³ So if we refuse this great way of being saved, how can we hope to escape? The Lord himself was the first to tell about it, and people who heard the message proved to us that it was true. ⁴ God himself showed that his message was true by working all kinds of powerful miracles and wonders. He also gave his Holy Spirit to anyone he chose to.

### The One Who Leads Us To Be Saved

⁵ We know that God did not put the future world under the power of angels. ⁶ Somewhere in the Scriptures someone says to God,

"What makes you care
about us humans?

Why are you concerned
for weaklings such as we?
⁷ You made us lower
than the angels
for a while.
Yet you have crowned us
with glory and honor.ᵈ
⁸ And you have put everything
under our power!"

God has put everything under our
power and has not left anything out
of our power. But we still don't see
it all under our power. ⁹What we
do see is Jesus, who for a little while
was made lower than the angels.
Because of God's wonderful kindness,
Jesus died for everyone. And now that
Jesus has suffered and died, he is
crowned with glory and honor!
¹⁰Everything belongs to God, and all
things were created by his power. So
God did the right thing when he made
Jesus perfect by suffering, as Jesus led
many of God's children to be saved and
to share in his glory. ¹¹Jesus and
the people he makes holy all belong
to the same family. That is why
he isn't ashamed to call them his
brothers and sisters. ¹²He even said
to God,

"I will tell them your name
and sing your praises
when they come together
to worship."

¹³He also said,

"I will trust God."

Then he said,

"Here I am with the children
God has given me."

¹⁴We are people of flesh and blood.
That is why Jesus became one of us.
He died to destroy the devil, who had
power over death. ¹⁵But he also died
to rescue all of us who live each day
in fear of dying. ¹⁶Jesus clearly did not
come to help angels, but he did come
to help Abraham's descendants. ¹⁷He
had to be one of us, so that he could
serve God as our merciful and faithful

high priest and sacrifice himself for the
forgiveness of our sins. ¹⁸And now that
Jesus has suffered and was tempted,
he can help anyone else who is
tempted.

## Jesus Is Greater than Moses

**3** My friends, God has chosen you to
be his holy people. So think about
Jesus, the one we call our apostle and
high priest! ² Jesus was faithful to God,
who appointed him, just as Moses was
faithful in serving all ofᵉ God's people.
³But Jesus deserves more honor than
Moses, just as the builder of a house
deserves more honor than the house.
⁴Of course, every house is built by
someone, and God is really the one who
built everything.
⁵Moses was a faithful servant and
told God's people what would be said
in the future. ⁶But Christ is the Son in
charge of God's people. And we are
those people, if we keep on being brave
and don't lose hope.

## A Rest for God's People

⁷It is just as the Holy Spirit says,

"If you hear God's voice today,
⁸    don't be stubborn!
Don't rebel like those people
who were tested
in the desert.
*⁹ For forty years your ancestors
tested God and saw
the things he did.

¹⁰ "Then God got tired of them
and said,
'You people never
show good sense,
and you don't understand
what I want you to do.'
¹¹ God became angry
and told the people,
'You will never enter
my place of rest!' "

¹²My friends, watch out! Don't let
evil thoughts or doubts make any of
you turn from the living God. ¹³You

---

ᵈ2.7 and honor: Some manuscripts add "and you have placed us in charge of all you
created." ᵉ3.2 all of: Some manuscripts do not have these words.

must encourage one another each day. And you must keep on while there is still a time that can be called "today." If you don't, then sin may fool some of you and make you stubborn. <sup>14</sup> We were sure about Christ when we first became his people. So let's hold tightly to our faith until the end. <sup>15</sup> The Scriptures say,

"If you hear his voice today,
don't be stubborn
like those who rebelled."

<sup>16</sup> Who were those people that heard God's voice and rebelled? Weren't they the same ones that came out of Egypt with Moses? <sup>17</sup> Who were the people that made God angry for forty years? Weren't they the ones that sinned and died in the desert? <sup>18</sup> And who did God say would never enter his place of rest? Weren't they the ones that disobeyed him? <sup>19</sup> We see that those people did not enter the place of rest because they did not have faith.

**4** The promise to enter the place of rest is still good, and we must take care that none of you miss out. <sup>2</sup> We have heard the message, just as they did. But they failed to believe what they heard, and the message did not do them any good. <sup>3</sup> Only people who have faith will enter the place of rest. It is just as the Scriptures say,

"God became angry
and told the people,
'You will never enter
my place of rest!' "

God said this, even though everything has been ready from the time of creation. <sup>4</sup> In fact, somewhere the Scriptures say that by the seventh day, God had finished his work, and so he rested. <sup>5</sup> We also read that he later said, "You people will never enter my place of rest!" <sup>6</sup> This means that the promise to enter is still good, because those who first heard about it disobeyed and did not enter. <sup>7</sup> Much later God told David to make the promise again, just as I have already said,

"If you hear his voice today,
don't be stubborn!"

<sup>8</sup> If Joshua had really given the people rest, there would not be any need

for God to talk about another day of rest. <sup>9</sup> But God has promised us a Sabbath when we will rest, even though it has not yet come. <sup>10</sup> On that day God's people will rest from their work, just as God rested from his work.

<sup>11</sup> We should do our best to enter that place of rest, so that none of us will disobey and miss going there, as they did. <sup>12</sup> What God has said isn't only alive and active! It is sharper than any double-edged sword. His word can cut through our spirits and souls and through our joints and marrow, until it discovers the desires and thoughts of our hearts. <sup>13</sup> Nothing is hidden from God! He sees through everything, and we will have to tell him the truth.

## Jesus Is the Great High Priest

<sup>14</sup> We have a great high priest, who has gone into heaven, and he is Jesus the Son of God. That is why we must hold on to what we have said about him. <sup>15</sup> Jesus understands every weakness of ours, because he was tempted in every way that we are. But he did not sin! <sup>16</sup> So whenever we are in need, we should come bravely before the throne of our merciful God. There we will be treated with undeserved kindness, and we will find help.

**5** Every high priest is appointed to help others by offering gifts and sacrifices to God because of their sins. <sup>2</sup> A high priest has weaknesses of his own, and he feels sorry for foolish and sinful people. <sup>3</sup> That is why he must offer sacrifices for his own sins and for the sins of others. <sup>4</sup> But no one can have the honor of being a high priest simply by wanting to be one. Only God can choose a priest, and God is the one who chose Aaron.

<sup>5</sup> That is how it was with Christ. He became a high priest, but not just because he wanted the honor of being one. It was God who told him,

"You are my Son, because today
I have become your Father!"

<sup>6</sup> In another place, God says,

"You are a priest forever
just like Melchizedek."[f]

· [7] God had the power to save Jesus from death. And while Jesus was on earth, he begged God with loud crying and tears to save him. He truly worshiped God, and God listened to his prayers. [8] Jesus is God's own Son, but still he had to suffer before he could learn what it really means to obey God. [9] Suffering made Jesus perfect, and now he can save forever all who obey him. [10] This is because God chose him to be a high priest like Melchizedek.

### Warning against Turning Away

[11] Much more could be said about this subject. But it is hard to explain, and all of you are slow to understand. [12] By now you should have been teachers, but once again you need to be taught the simplest things about what God has said. You need milk instead of solid food. [13] People who live on milk are like babies who don't really know what is right. [14] Solid food is for mature people who have been trained to know right from wrong.

**6** We must try to become mature and start thinking about more than just the basic things we were taught about Christ. We shouldn't need to keep talking about why we ought to turn from deeds that bring death and why we ought to have faith in God. [2] And we shouldn't need to keep teaching about baptisms[g] or about the laying on of hands[h] or about people being raised from death and the future judgment. [3] Let's grow up, if God is willing.

[4-6] But what about people who turn away after they have already seen the light and have received the gift from heaven and have shared in the Holy Spirit? What about those who turn away after they have received the good message of God and the powers of the

future world? There is no way to bring them back. What they are doing is the same as nailing the Son of God to a cross and insulting him in public!

[7] A field is useful to farmers, if there is enough rain to make good crops grow. In fact, God will bless that field. [8] But land that produces only thornbushes is worthless. It is likely to fall under God's curse, and in the end it will be set on fire.

[9] My friends, we are talking this way. But we are sure that you are doing those really good things that people do when they are being saved. [10] God is always fair. He will remember how you helped his people in the past and how you are still helping them. You belong to God, and he won't forget the love you have shown his people. [11] We wish that each of you would always be eager to show how strong and lasting your hope really is. [12] Then you would never be lazy. You would be following the example of those who had faith and were patient until God kept his promise to them.

### God's Promise Is Sure

[13] No one is greater than God. So he made a promise in his own name when he said to Abraham, [14] "I, the Lord, will bless you with many descendants!" [15] Then after Abraham had been very patient, he was given what God had promised. [16] When anyone wants to settle an argument, they make a vow by using the name of someone or something greater than themselves. [17] So when God wanted to prove for certain that his promise to his people could not be broken, he made a vow. [18] God cannot tell lies! And so his promises and vows are two things that can never be changed.

We have run to God for safety. Now his promises should greatly encourage us to take hold of the hope that is right in front of us. [19] This hope is like a firm and steady anchor for our souls. In

---

[f]**5.6** *Melchizedek*: When Melchizedek is mentioned in the Old Testament, he is described as a priest who lived before Aaron. Nothing is said about his ancestors or his death (see 7.3 and Genesis 14.17-20).   [g]**6.2** *baptisms*: Or "ceremonies of washing."   [h]**6.2** *laying on of hands*: This was a ceremony in which church leaders and others put their hands on people to show that those people were chosen to do some special kind of work.

fact, hope reaches behind the curtain[i] and into the most holy place. [20] Jesus has gone there ahead of us, and he is our high priest forever, just like Melchizedek.[j]

## The Priestly Family of Melchizedek

**7** Melchizedek was both king of Salem and priest of God Most High. He was the one who went out and gave Abraham his blessing, when Abraham returned from killing the kings. [2] Then Abraham gave him a tenth of everything he had.

The meaning of the name Melchizedek is "King of Justice." But since Salem means "peace," he is also "King of Peace." [3] We are not told that he had a father or mother or ancestors or beginning or end. He is like the Son of God and will be a priest forever.[k]

[4] Notice how great Melchizedek is! Our famous ancestor Abraham gave him a tenth of what he had taken from his enemies. [5] The Law teaches that even Abraham's descendants must give a tenth of what they possess. And they are to give this to their own relatives, who are the descendants of Levi and are priests. [6] Although Melchizedek wasn't a descendant of Levi, Abraham gave him a tenth of what he had. Then Melchizedek blessed Abraham, who had been given God's promise. [7] Everyone agrees that a person who gives a blessing is greater than the one who receives the blessing.

[8] Priests are given a tenth of what people earn. But all priests die, except Melchizedek, and the Scriptures teach that he is alive. [9] Levi's descendants are now the ones who receive a tenth from people. We could even say that when Abraham gave Melchizedek a tenth, Levi also gave him a tenth. [10] This is because Levi was born later into the family of Abraham, who gave a tenth to Melchizedek.

[11] Even though the Law of Moses says that the priests must be descendants of Levi, those priests cannot make anyone perfect. So there needs to be a priest like Melchizedek, rather than one from the priestly family of Aaron.[l] [12] And when the rules for selecting a priest are changed, the Law must also be changed.

[13] The person we are talking about is our Lord, who came from a tribe that had never had anyone to serve as a priest at the altar. [14] Everyone knows he came from the tribe of Judah, and Moses never said that priests would come from that tribe.

[15] All of this becomes clearer, when someone who is like Melchizedek is appointed to be a priest. [16] That person wasn't appointed because of his ancestors, but because his life can never end. [17] The Scriptures say about him,

"You are a priest forever,
    just like Melchizedek."

[18] In this way a weak and useless command was put aside, [19] because the Law cannot make anything perfect. At the same time, we are given a much better hope, and it can bring us close to God.

[20-21] God himself made a promise when this priest was appointed. But he did not make a promise like this when the other priests were appointed. The promise he made is,

"I, the Lord, promise that you
    will be a priest forever!
And I will never
    change my mind!"

[22] This means that Jesus guarantees us a better agreement with God. [23] There have been a lot of other priests, and all of them have died. [24] But Jesus will never die, and so he will be a priest forever! [25] He is forever able to save[m] the people he leads to God, because he always lives to speak to God for them.

[26] Jesus is the high priest we need. He is holy and innocent and faultless, and not at all like us sinners. Jesus is

---

[i] 6.19 *behind the curtain*: In the tent that was used for worship, a curtain separated the "holy place" from the "most holy place," which only the high priest could enter.
[j] 6.20 *Melchizedek*: See the note at 5.6.   [k] 7.3 *will be a priest forever*: See the note at 5.6.
[l] 7.11 *descendants of Levi . . . from the priestly family of Aaron*: Levi was the ancestor of the tribe from which priests and their helpers (called "Levites") were chosen. Aaron was the first high priest.   [m] 7.25 *forever able to save*: Or "able to save forever."

honored above all beings in heaven, [27] and he is better than any other high priest. Jesus doesn't need to offer sacrifices each day for his own sins and then for the sins of the people. He offered a sacrifice once for all, when he gave himself. [28] The Law appoints priests who have weaknesses. But God's promise, which came later than the Law, appoints his Son. And he is the perfect high priest forever.

## A Better Promise

**8** What I mean is that we have a high priest who sits at the right side[n] of God's great throne in heaven. [2] He also serves as the priest in the most holy place[o] inside the real tent there in heaven. This tent of worship was set up by the Lord, not by humans. [3] Since all priests must offer gifts and sacrifices, Christ also needed to have something to offer. [4] If he were here on earth, he would not be a priest at all, because here the Law appoints other priests to offer sacrifices. [5] But the tent where they serve is just a copy and a shadow of the real one in heaven. Before Moses made the tent, he was told, "Be sure to make it exactly like the pattern you were shown on the mountain!" [6] Now Christ has been appointed to serve as a priest in a much better way, and he has given us much assurance of a better agreement.

[7] If the first agreement with God had been all right, there would not have been any need for another one. [8] But the Lord found fault with it and said,

"I tell you the time will come,
when I will make
  a new agreement
with the people of Israel
  and the people of Judah.
[9] It won't be like the agreement
  that I made
  with their ancestors,

when I took them by the hand
  and led them out of Egypt.
They broke their agreement
  with me,
and I stopped caring
  about them!

[10] "But now I tell the people
of Israel
  this is my new agreement:
'The time will come
  when I, the Lord,
will write my laws
  on their minds and hearts.
I will be their God,
and they will be
  my people.
[11] Not one of them
will have to teach another
  to know me, their Lord.'

"All of them will know me,
  no matter who they are.
[12] I will treat them with kindness,
  even though they are wicked.
I will forget their sins."

[13] When the Lord talks about a new agreement, he means that the first one is out of date. And anything that is old and useless will soon disappear.

## The Tent in Heaven

**9** The first promise that was made included rules for worship and a tent for worship here on earth. [2] The first part of the tent was called the holy place, and a lampstand, a table, and the sacred loaves of bread were kept there.

[3] Behind the curtain was the most holy place. [4] The gold altar that was used for burning incense was in this holy place. The gold-covered sacred chest was also there, and inside it were three things. First, there was a gold jar filled with manna.[p] Then there was Aaron's walking stick that sprouted.[q] Finally, there were the flat stones with

the Ten Commandments written on them. ⁵On top of the chest were the glorious creatures with wings^r opened out above the place of mercy.^s

Now isn't the time to go into detail about these things. ⁶But this is how everything was when the priests went each day into the first part of the tent to do their duties. ⁷However, only the high priest could go into the second part of the tent, and he went in only once a year. Each time he carried blood to offer for his sins and for any sins that the people had committed without meaning to.

⁸All of this is the Holy Spirit's way of saying that no one could enter the most holy place while the tent was still the place of worship. ⁹This also has a meaning for today. It shows that we cannot make our consciences clear by offering gifts and sacrifices. ¹⁰These rules are merely about such things as eating and drinking and ceremonies for washing ourselves. And rules about physical things will last only until the time comes to change them for something better.

¹¹Christ came as the high priest of the good things that are now here.^t He also went into a much better tent that wasn't made by humans and that doesn't belong to this world. ¹²Then Christ went once for all into the most holy place and freed us from sin forever. He did this by offering his own blood instead of the blood of goats and bulls.

¹³According to the Law of Moses, those people who become unclean are not fit to worship God. Yet they will be considered clean, if they are sprinkled with the blood of goats and bulls and with the ashes of a sacrificed calf. ¹⁴But Christ was sinless, and he offered himself as an eternal and spiritual sacrifice to God. That's why his blood is much more powerful and makes our^u consciences clear. Now we can serve

the living God and no longer do things that lead to death.

¹⁵Christ died to rescue those who had sinned and broken the old agreement. Now he brings his chosen ones a new agreement with its guarantee of God's eternal blessings! ¹⁶In fact, making an agreement of this kind is like writing a will. This is because the one who makes the will must die before it is of any use. ¹⁷In other words, a will doesn't go into effect as long as the one who made it is still alive.

¹⁸Blood was also used^v to put the first agreement into effect. ¹⁹Moses told the people all that the Law said they must do. Then he used red wool and a hyssop plant to sprinkle the people and the book of the Law with the blood of bulls and goats^w and with water. ²⁰He told the people, "With this blood God makes his agreement with you." ²¹Moses also sprinkled blood on the tent and on everything else that was used in worship. ²²The Law says that almost everything must be sprinkled with blood, and no sins can be forgiven unless blood is offered.

### Christ's Great Sacrifice

²³These things are only copies of what is in heaven, and so they had to be made holy by these ceremonies. But the real things in heaven must be made holy by something better. ²⁴This is why Christ did not go into a tent that had been made by humans and was only a copy of the real one. Instead, he went into heaven and is now there with God to help us.

²⁵Christ did not have to offer himself many times. He wasn't like a high priest who goes into the most holy place each year to offer the blood of an animal. ²⁶If he had offered himself every year, he would have suffered many times since the creation of the world. But instead, near the end of time

^r9.5 glorious creatures with wings: Two of these creatures (called "cherubim" in Hebrew and Greek) with outspread wings were on top of the sacred chest and were symbols of God's throne. ^s9.5 place of mercy: The lid of the sacred chest, which was thought to be God's throne on earth. ^t9.11 that are now here: Some manuscripts have "that were coming." ^u9.14 our: Some manuscripts have "your," and others have "their." ^v9.18 Blood was also used: Or "There also had to be a death." ^w9.19 blood of bulls and goats: Some manuscripts do not have "and goats."

he offered himself once and for all, so that he could be a sacrifice that does away with sin.

27 We die only once, and then we are judged. 28 So Christ died only once to take away the sins of many people. But when he comes again, it will not be to take away sin. He will come to save everyone who is waiting for him.

**10** The Law of Moses is like a shadow of the good things to come. This shadow isn't the good things themselves, because it cannot free people from sin by the sacrifices that are offered year after year. 2 If there were worshipers who already have their sins washed away and their consciences made clear, there would not be any need to go on offering sacrifices. 3-4 But the blood of bulls and goats cannot take away sins. It only reminds people of their sins from one year to the next.

5 When Christ came into the world, he said to God,

"Sacrifices and offerings
    are not what you want,
but you have given me
    my body.
6 No, you are not pleased
with animal sacrifices
    and offerings for sin."

7 Then Christ said,

"And so, my God,
    I have come to do
what you want,
    as the Scriptures say."

8 The Law teaches that offerings and sacrifices must be made because of sin. But why did Christ mention these things and say that God did not want them? 9 Well, it was to do away with offerings and sacrifices and to replace them. That is what he meant by saying to God, "I have come to do what you want." 10 So we are made holy because Christ obeyed God and offered himself once for all.

11 The priests do their work each day, and they keep on offering sacrifices that can never take away sins. 12 But Christ offered himself as a sacrifice that is good forever. Now he is sitting at God's right side,ˣ 13 and he will stay there until his enemies are put under his power. 14 By his one sacrifice he has forever set free from sin the people he brings to God.

15 The Holy Spirit also speaks of this by telling us that the Lord said,

16. "When the time comes,
    I will make an agreement
        with them.
I will write my laws
    on their minds and hearts.
17 Then I will forget
    about their sins
and no longer remember
    their evil deeds."

18 When sins are forgiven, there is no more need to offer sacrifices.

### Encouragement and Warning

19 My friends, the blood of Jesus gives us courage to enter the most holy place 20 by a new way that leads to life! And this way takes us through the curtain that is Christ himself.

21 We have a great high priest who is in charge of God's house. 22 So let's come near God with pure hearts and a confidence that comes from having faith. Let's keep our hearts pure, our consciences free from evil, and our bodies washed with clean water. 23 We must hold tightly to the hope that we say is ours. After all, we can trust the one who made the agreement with us. 24 We should keep on encouraging each other to be thoughtful and to do helpful things. 25 Some people have gotten out of the habit of meeting for worship, but we must not do that. We should keep on encouraging each other, especially since you know that the day of the Lord's coming is getting closer.

26 No sacrifices can be made for people who decide to sin after they find out about the truth. 27 They are God's enemies, and all they can look forward to is a terrible judgment and a furious fire. 28 If two or more witnesses accused someone of breaking the Law of Moses,

ˣ 10.12 *right side*: See the note at 1.3.

that person could be put to death. <sup>29</sup>But it is much worse to dishonor God's Son and to disgrace the blood of the promise that made us holy. And it is just as bad to insult the Holy Spirit, who shows us mercy. <sup>30</sup>We know that God has said he will punish and take revenge. We also know that the Scriptures say the Lord will judge his people. <sup>31</sup>It is a terrible thing to fall into the hands of the living God!

<sup>32</sup>Don't forget all the hard times you went through when you first received the light. <sup>33</sup>Sometimes you were abused and mistreated in public, and at other times you shared in the sufferings of others. <sup>34</sup>You were kind to people in jail. And you gladly let your possessions be taken away, because you knew you had something better, something that would last forever.

<sup>35</sup>Keep on being brave! It will bring you great rewards. <sup>36</sup>Learn to be patient, so that you will please God and be given what he has promised. <sup>37</sup>As the Scriptures say,

"God is coming soon!
   It won't be very long.
<sup>38</sup> The people God accepts
   will live because
      of their faith.*y*
But he isn't pleased
   with anyone
      who turns back."

<sup>39</sup>We are not like those people who turn back and get destroyed. We will keep on having faith until we are saved.

### The Great Faith of God's People

**11** Faith makes us sure of what we hope for and gives us proof of what we cannot see. <sup>2</sup>It was their faith that made our ancestors pleasing to God.

<sup>3</sup>Because of our faith, we know that the world was made at God's command. We also know that what can be seen was made out of what cannot be seen.

<sup>4</sup>Because Abel had faith, he offered God a better sacrifice than Cain did.

God was pleased with him and his gift, and even though Abel is now dead, his faith still speaks for him.

<sup>5</sup>Enoch had faith and did not die. He pleased God, and God took him up to heaven. That's why his body was never found. <sup>6</sup>But without faith no one can please God. We must believe that God is real and that he rewards everyone who searches for him.

<sup>7</sup>Because Noah had faith, he was warned about something that had not yet happened. He obeyed and built a boat that saved him and his family. In this way the people of the world were judged, and Noah was given the blessings that come to everyone who pleases God.

<sup>8</sup>Abraham had faith and obeyed God. He was told to go to the land that God had said would be his, and he left for a country he had never seen. <sup>9</sup>Because Abraham had faith, he lived as a stranger in the promised land. He lived there in a tent, and so did Isaac and Jacob, who were later given the same promise. <sup>10</sup>Abraham did this, because he was waiting for the eternal city that God had planned and built.

<sup>11</sup>Even when Sarah was too old to have children, she had faith that God would do what he had promised, and she had a son. <sup>12</sup>Her husband Abraham was almost dead, but he became the ancestor of many people. In fact, there are as many of them as there are stars in the sky or grains of sand along the beach.

<sup>13</sup>Every one of those people died. But they still had faith, even though they had not received what they had been promised. They were glad just to see these things from far away, and they agreed that they were only strangers and foreigners on this earth. <sup>14</sup>When people talk this way, it is clear that they are looking for a place to call their own. <sup>15</sup>If they had been talking about the land where they had once lived, they could have gone back at any time. <sup>16</sup>But they were looking forward to a better home in heaven. That's why God wasn't ashamed for them to call him

---

*y* **10.38** *The people God accepts will live because of their faith*: Or "The people God accepts because of their faith will live."

their God. He even built a city for them.
[17-18] Abraham had been promised that Isaac, his only son,[z] would continue his family. But when Abraham was tested, he had faith and was willing to sacrifice Isaac, [19] because he was sure that God could raise people to life. This was just like getting Isaac back from death.

[20] Isaac had faith, and he promised blessings to Jacob and Esau. [21] Later, when Jacob was about to die, he leaned on his walking stick and worshiped. Then because of his faith he blessed each of Joseph's sons. [22] And right before Joseph died, he had faith that God would lead the people of Israel out of Egypt. So he told them to take his bones with them.

[23] Because Moses' parents had faith, they kept him hidden until he was three months old. They saw that he was a beautiful child, and they were not afraid to disobey the king's orders.[a] [24] Then after Moses grew up, his faith made him refuse to be called the king's grandson. [25] He chose to be mistreated with God's people instead of having the good time that sin could bring for a little while. [26] Moses knew that the treasures of Egypt were not as wonderful as what he would receive from suffering for the Messiah,[b] and he looked forward to his reward.

[27] Because of his faith, Moses left Egypt. Moses had seen the invisible God and wasn't afraid of the king's anger. [28] His faith also made him celebrate Passover. He sprinkled the blood of animals on the doorposts, so that the firstborn sons of the people of Israel would not be killed by the destroying angel.

[29] Because of their faith, the people walked through the Red Sea[c] on dry land. But when the Egyptians tried to do it, they were drowned.

[30] God's people had faith, and when they had walked around the city of Jeri-

cho for seven days, its walls fell down.
[31] Rahab had been a prostitute, but she had faith and welcomed the spies. So she wasn't killed with the people who disobeyed.

[32] What else can I say? There isn't enough time to tell about Gideon, Barak, Samson, Jephthah, David, Samuel, and the prophets. [33] Their faith helped them conquer kingdoms, and because they did right, God made promises to them. They closed the jaws of lions [34] and put out raging fires and escaped from the swords of their enemies. Although they were weak, they were given the strength and power to chase foreign armies away.

[35] Some women received their loved ones back from death. Many of these people were tortured, but they refused to be released. They were sure that they would get a better reward when the dead are raised to life. [36] Others were made fun of and beaten with whips, and some were chained in jail. [37] Still others were stoned to death or sawed in two[d] or killed with swords. Some had nothing but sheep skins or goat skins to wear. They were poor, mistreated, and tortured. [38] The world did not deserve these good people, who had to wander in deserts and on mountains and had to live in caves and holes in the ground.

[39] All of them pleased God because of their faith! But still they died without being given what had been promised. [40] This was because God had something better in store for us. And he did not want them to reach the goal of their faith without us.

## A Large Crowd of Witnesses

**12** Such a large crowd of witnesses is all around us! So we must get rid of everything that slows us down,

---

[z] 11.17,18 *his only son*: Although Abraham had a son by a slave woman, his son Isaac was considered his only son, because he was born as a result of God's promise to Abraham.
[a] 11.23 *the king's orders*: The king of Egypt ordered all Israelite baby boys to be left outside of their homes, so they would die or be killed. [b] 11.26 *the Messiah*: Or "Christ."
[c] 11.29 *Red Sea*: This name comes from the Bible of the early Christians, a translation made into Greek about 200 B.C. It refers to the body of water that the Israelites crossed and was one of the marshes or fresh water lakes near the eastern part of the Nile Delta, where they lived and where the towns of Exodus 13.17—14.9 were located. [d] 11.37 *sawed in two*: Some manuscripts have "tested" or "tempted."

especially the sin that just won't let go. And we must be determined to run the race that is ahead of us. ² We must keep our eyes on Jesus, who leads us and makes our faith complete. He endured the shame of being nailed to a cross, because he knew that later on he would be glad he did. Now he is seated at the right side*e* of God's throne! ³ So keep your mind on Jesus, who put up with many insults from sinners. Then you won't get discouraged and give up.

⁴ None of you have yet been hurt*f* in your battle against sin. ⁵ But you have forgotten that the Scriptures say to God's children,

"When the Lord punishes you,
    don't make light of it,
and when he corrects you,
    don't be discouraged.
⁶ The Lord corrects the people
    he loves
and disciplines those
    he calls his own."

⁷ Be patient when you are being corrected! This is how God treats his children. Don't all parents correct their children? ⁸ God corrects all of his children, and if he doesn't correct you, then you don't really belong to him. ⁹ Our earthly fathers correct us, and we still respect them. Isn't it even better to be given true life by letting our spiritual Father correct us?

¹⁰ Our human fathers correct us for a short time, and they do it as they think best. But God corrects us for our own good, because he wants us to be holy, as he is. ¹¹ It is never fun to be corrected. In fact, at the time it is always painful. But if we learn to obey by being corrected, we will do right and live at peace.

¹² Now stand up straight! Stop your knees from shaking ¹³ and walk a straight path. Then lame people will be healed, instead of getting worse.

## Warning against Turning from God

¹⁴ Try to live at peace with everyone! Live a clean life. If you don't, you will never see the Lord. ¹⁵ Make sure that no one misses out on God's wonderful kindness. Don't let anyone become bitter and cause trouble for the rest of you. ¹⁶ Watch out for immoral and ungodly people like Esau, who sold his future blessing*g* for only one meal. ¹⁷ You know how he later wanted it back. But there was nothing he could do to change things, even though he begged his father and cried.

¹⁸ You have not come to a place like Mount Sinai*h* that can be seen and touched. There is no flaming fire or dark cloud or storm ¹⁹ or trumpet sound. The people of Israel heard a voice speak. But they begged it to stop, ²⁰ because they could not obey its commands. They were even told to kill any animal that touched the mountain. ²¹ The sight was so frightening that Moses said he shook with fear.

²² You have now come to Mount Zion and to the heavenly Jerusalem. This is the city of the living God, where thousands and thousands of angels have come to celebrate. ²³ Here you will find all of God's dearest children,*i* whose names are written in heaven. And you will find God himself, who judges everyone. Here also are the spirits of those good people who have been made perfect. ²⁴ And Jesus is here! He is the one who makes God's new agreement with us, and his sprinkled blood says much better things than the blood of Abel.*j*

²⁵ Make sure that you obey the one who speaks to you. The people did not

*e* **12.2** *right side*: See the note at 1.3. *f* **12.4** *hurt*: Or "killed." *g* **12.16** *sold his future blessing*: As the first-born son, Esau had certain privileges that were known as a "birthright." *h* **12.18** *a place like Mount Sinai*: The Greek text has "a place," but the writer is referring to the time that the Lord spoke to the people of Israel from Mount Sinai (see Exodus 19.16-25). *i* **12.23** *all of God's dearest children*: The Greek text has "the gathering of the first-born children" (see the note at 1.6). *j* **12.24** *blood of Abel*: Cain and Abel were the two sons of Adam and Eve. Cain murdered Abel (see Genesis 4.1-16).

escape, when they refused to obey the one who spoke to them at Mount Sinai. Do you think you can possibly escape, if you refuse to obey the one who speaks to you from heaven? 26 When God spoke the first time, his voice shook only the earth. This time he has promised to shake the earth once again, and heaven too.

27 The words "once again" mean that these created things will someday be shaken and removed. Then what cannot be shaken will last. 28 We should be grateful that we were given a kingdom that cannot be shaken. And in this kingdom we please God by worshiping him and by showing him great honor and respect. 29 Our God is like a destructive fire!

## Service That Pleases God

**13** Keep being concerned about each other as the Lord's followers should.

2 Be sure to welcome strangers into your home. By doing this, some people have welcomed angels as guests, without even knowing it.

3 Remember the Lord's people who are in jail and be concerned for them. Don't forget those who are suffering, but imagine that you are there with them.

4 Have respect for marriage. Always be faithful to your partner, because God will punish anyone who is immoral or unfaithful in marriage.

5 Don't fall in love with money. Be satisfied with what you have. The Lord has promised that he will not leave us or desert us. 6 That should make you feel like saying,

"The Lord helps me!
Why should I be afraid
    of what people
    can do to me?"

7 Don't forget about your leaders who taught you God's message. Remember what kind of lives they lived and try to have faith like theirs.

8 Jesus Christ never changes! He is the same yesterday, today, and forever. 9 Don't be fooled by any kind of strange teachings. It is better to receive strength from God's undeserved kindness than to depend on certain foods. After all, these foods don't really help the people who eat them. 10 But we have an altar where even the priests who serve in the place of worship have no right to eat.

11 After the high priest offers the blood of animals as a sin offering, the bodies of those animals are burned outside the camp. 12 Jesus himself suffered outside the city gate, so that his blood would make people holy. 13 That's why we should go outside the camp to Jesus and share in his disgrace. 14 On this earth we don't have a city that lasts forever, but we are waiting for such a city.

15 Our sacrifice is to keep offering praise to God in the name of Jesus. 16 But don't forget to help others and to share your possessions with them. This too is like offering a sacrifice that pleases God.

17 Obey your leaders and do what they say. They are watching over you, and they must answer to God. So don't make them sad as they do their work. Make them happy. Otherwise, they won't be able to help you at all.

18 Pray for us. Our consciences are clear, and we always try to live right. 19 I especially want you to pray that I can visit you again soon.

## Final Prayers and Greetings

20 God gives peace, and he raised our Lord Jesus Christ from death. Now Jesus is like a Great Shepherd whose blood was used to make God's eternal agreement with his flock.k 21 I pray that God will make you ready to obey him and that you will always be eager to do right. May Jesus help you do what pleases God. To Jesus Christ be glory forever and ever! Amen.

22 My friends, I have written only a

---

k 13.20 whose blood was used to make God's eternal agreement with his flock: See 9.18-22.

short letter to encourage you, and I beg you to pay close attention to what I have said.

²³ By now you surely must know that our friend Timothy is out of jail. If he gets here in time, I will bring him with me when I come to visit you.

²⁴ Please give my greetings to your leaders and to the rest of the Lord's people.

His followers from Italy send you their greetings.

²⁵ I pray that God will be kind to all of you![1]

---

[1] **13.25** *to all of you!*: Some manuscripts add "Amen."

# JAMES

## ABOUT THIS LETTER

*This is a good example of a general letter, because it is addressed to Christians scattered throughout the Roman empire. Though written as a letter, it is more like a short book of instructions for daily living.*

*For James faith means action! In fact, the entire book is a series of examples that show faith in action in wise and practical ways.*

*His advice was clear and to the point: If you are poor, don't despair! Don't give up when your faith is being tested. Don't get angry quickly. Don't favor the rich over the poor. Do good things for others. Control your tongue and desires. Surrender to God and rely on his wisdom. Resist the devil. Don't brag about what you are going to do. If you are rich, use your money to help the poor. Be patient and kind, and pray for those who need God's help.*

## A QUICK LOOK AT THIS LETTER

*Greetings (1.1)*
*A Life of Faith and Wisdom (1.2-18)*
*Hearing and Obeying God's Message (1.19-27)*
*Don't Favor the Rich and Powerful (2.1-13)*
*Faith and Works (2.14-26)*
*Wisdom and Words (3.1-18)*
*Warning against Friendship with the World (4.1—5.6)*
*Patience, Kindness, and Prayer (5.7-20)*

---

**1** From James, a servant of God and of our Lord Jesus Christ.

Greetings to the twelve tribes scattered all over the world. *a*

### Faith and Wisdom

² My friends, be glad, even if you have a lot of trouble. ³ You know that you learn to endure by having your faith tested. ⁴ But you must learn to endure everything, so that you will be completely mature and not lacking in anything.

⁵ If any of you need wisdom, you should ask God, and it will be given to you. God is generous and won't correct you for asking. ⁶ But when you ask for something, you must have faith and not doubt. Anyone who doubts is like an ocean wave tossed around in a storm. ⁷⁻⁸ If you are that kind of person, you can't make up your mind, and you surely can't be trusted. So don't expect the Lord to give you anything at all.

### Poor People and Rich People

⁹ Any of God's people who are poor should be glad that he thinks so highly of them. ¹⁰ But any who are rich should be glad when God makes them humble. Rich people will disappear like wild flowers ¹¹ scorched by the burning heat of the sun. The flowers lose their blossoms, and their beauty is destroyed. That is how the rich will disappear, as they go about their business.

*a* **1.1** *twelve tribes scattered all over the world:* James is saying that the Lord's followers are like the tribes of Israel that were scattered everywhere by their enemies.

292

### Trials and Temptations

¹² God will bless you, if you don't give up when your faith is being tested. He will reward you with a glorious life,ᵇ just as he rewards everyone who loves him.
¹³ Don't blame God when you are tempted! God cannot be tempted by evil, and he doesn't use evil to tempt others. ¹⁴ We are tempted by our own desires that drag us off and trap us. ¹⁵ Our desires make us sin, and when sin is finished with us, it leaves us dead.
¹⁶ Don't be fooled, my dear friends. ¹⁷ Every good and perfect gift comes down from the Father who created all the lights in the heavens. He is always the same and never makes dark shadows by changing. ¹⁸ He wanted us to be his own special people,ᶜ and so he sent the true message to give us new birth.

### Hearing and Obeying

¹⁹ My dear friends, you should be quick to listen and slow to speak or to get angry. ²⁰ If you are angry, you cannot do any of the good things that God wants done. ²¹ You must stop doing anything immoral or evil. Instead be humble and accept the message that is planted in you to save you.
²² Obey God's message! Don't fool yourselves by just listening to it. ²³ If you hear the message and don't obey it, you are like people who stare at themselves in a mirror ²⁴ and forget what they look like as soon as they leave. ²⁵ But you must never stop looking at the perfect law that sets you free. God will bless you in everything you do, if you listen and obey, and don't just hear and forget.
²⁶ If you think you are being religious, but can't control your tongue, you are fooling yourself, and everything you do is useless. ²⁷ Religion that pleases God the Father must be pure and spotless.

You must help needy orphans and widows and not let this world make you evil.

### Warning against Having Favorites

**2** My friends, if you have faith in our glorious Lord Jesus Christ, you won't treat some people better than others. ² Suppose a rich person wearing fancy clothes and a gold ring comes to one of your meetings. And suppose a poor person dressed in worn-out clothes also comes. ³ You must not give the best seat to the one in fancy clothes and tell the one who is poor to stand at the side or sit on the floor. ⁴ That is the same as saying that some people are better than others, and you would be acting like a crooked judge.
⁵ My dear friends, pay attention. God has given a lot of faith to the poor people in this world. He has also promised them a share in his kingdom that he will give to everyone who loves him. ⁶ You mistreat the poor. But isn't it the rich who boss you around and drag you off to court? ⁷ Aren't they the ones who make fun of your Lord?
⁸ You will do all right, if you obey the most important lawᵈ in the Scriptures. It is the law that commands us to love others as much as we love ourselves. ⁹ But if you treat some people better than others, you have done wrong, and the Scriptures teach that you have sinned.
¹⁰ If you obey every law except one, you are still guilty of breaking them all. ¹¹ The same God who told us to be faithful in marriage also told us not to murder. So even if you are faithful in marriage, but murder someone, you still have broken God's Law.
¹² Speak and act like people who will be judged by the law that sets us free. ¹³ Do this, because on the day of judgment there will be no pity for those who have not had pity on others. But even in judgment, God is merciful!ᵉ

---

ᵇ1.12 *a glorious life*: The Greek text has "the crown of life." In ancient times an athlete who had won a contest was rewarded with a crown of flowers as a sign of victory.   ᶜ1.18 *his own special people*: The Greek text has "the first of his creatures." The Law of Moses taught that the first-born of all animals and the first part of the harvest were special and belonged to the Lord.   ᵈ2.8 *most important law*: The Greek text has "royal law," meaning the one given by the king (that is, God).   ᵉ2.13 *But even in judgment, God is merciful!*: Or "So be merciful, and you will be shown mercy on the day of judgment."

### Faith and Works

14 My friends, what good is it to say you have faith, when you don't do anything to show that you really do have faith? Can that kind of faith save you? 15 If you know someone who doesn't have any clothes or food, 16 you shouldn't just say, "I hope all goes well for you. I hope you will be warm and have plenty to eat." What good is it to say this, unless you do something to help? 17 Faith that doesn't lead us to do good deeds is all alone and dead!

18 Suppose someone disagrees and says, "It is possible to have faith without doing kind deeds."

I would answer, "Prove that you have faith without doing kind deeds, and I will prove that I have faith by doing them." 19 You surely believe there is only one God. That's fine. Even demons believe this, and it makes them shake with fear.

20 Does some stupid person want proof that faith without deeds is useless? 21 Well, our ancestor Abraham pleased God by putting his son Isaac on the altar to sacrifice him. 22 Now you see how Abraham's faith and deeds worked together. He proved that his faith was real by what he did. 23 This is what the Scriptures mean by saying, "Abraham had faith in God, and God was pleased with him." That's how Abraham became God's friend.

24 You can now see that we please God by what we do and not only by what we believe. 25 For example, Rahab had been a prostitute. But she pleased God when she welcomed the spies and sent them home by another way.

26 Anyone who doesn't breathe is dead, and faith that doesn't do anything is just as dead!

### The Tongue

3 My friends, we should not all try to become teachers. In fact, teachers will be judged more strictly than others. 2 All of us do many wrong things. But if you can control your tongue, you are mature and able to control your whole body.

3 By putting a bit into the mouth of a horse, we can turn the horse in different directions. 4 It takes strong winds to move a large sailing ship, but the captain uses only a small rudder to make it go in any direction. 5 Our tongues are small too, and yet they brag about big things.

It takes only a spark to start a forest fire! 6 The tongue is like a spark. It is an evil power that dirties the rest of the body and sets a person's entire life on fire with flames that come from hell itself. 7 All kinds of animals, birds, reptiles, and sea creatures can be tamed and have been tamed. 8 But our tongues get out of control. They are restless and evil, and always spreading deadly poison.

9-10 My dear friends, with our tongues we speak both praises and curses. We praise our Lord and Father, and we curse people who were created to be like God, and this isn't right. 11 Can clean water and dirty water both flow from the same spring? 12 Can a fig tree produce olives or a grapevine produce figs? Does fresh water come from a well full of salt water?

### Wisdom from Above

13 Are any of you wise or sensible? Then show it by living right and by being humble and wise in everything you do. 14 But if your heart is full of bitter jealousy and selfishness, don't brag or lie to cover up the truth. 15 That kind of wisdom doesn't come from above. It is earthly and selfish and comes from the devil himself. 16 Whenever people are jealous or selfish, they cause trouble and do all sorts of cruel things. 17 But the wisdom that comes from above leads us to be pure, friendly, gentle, sensible, kind, helpful, genuine, and sincere. 18 When peacemakers plant seeds of peace, they will harvest justice.

### Friendship with the World

4 Why do you fight and argue with each other? Isn't it because you are full of selfish desires that fight to control your body? 2 You want something you don't have, and you will do anything to get it. You will even kill! But you still cannot get what you want, and you won't get it by fighting and argu-

ing. You should pray for it. ³Yet even when you do pray, your prayers are not answered, because you pray just for selfish reasons.

⁴You people aren't faithful to God! Don't you know that if you love the world, you are God's enemies? And if you decide to be a friend of the world, you make yourself an enemy of God. ⁵Do you doubt the Scriptures that say, "God truly cares about the Spirit he has put in us"?ᶠ ⁶In fact, God treats us with even greater kindness, just as the Scriptures say,

> "God opposes everyone
>     who is proud,
> but he is kind to everyone
>     who is humble."

⁷Surrender to God! Resist the devil, and he will run from you. ⁸Come near to God, and he will come near to you. Clean up your lives, you sinners. Purify your hearts, you people who can't make up your mind. ⁹Be sad and sorry and weep. Stop laughing and start crying. Be gloomy instead of glad. ¹⁰Be humble in the Lord's presence, and he will honor you.

### Saying Cruel Things about Others

¹¹My friends, don't say cruel things about others! If you do, or if you condemn others, you are condemning God's Law. And if you condemn the Law, you put yourself above the Law and refuse to obey either it ¹²or God who gave it. God is our judge, and he can save or destroy us. What right do you have to condemn anyone?

### Warning against Bragging

¹³You should know better than to say, "Today or tomorrow we will go to the city. We will do business there for a year and make a lot of money!" ¹⁴What do you know about tomorrow? How can you be so sure about your life? It is nothing more than mist that appears for only a little while before it disappears. ¹⁵You should say, "If the Lord lets us live, we will do these things." ¹⁶Yet you are stupid enough to brag, and it is wrong to be so proud. ¹⁷If you don't do what you know is right, you have sinned.

### Warning to the Rich

5 You rich people should cry and weep! Terrible things are going to happen to you. ²Your treasures have already rotted, and moths have eaten your clothes. ³Your money has rusted, and the rust will be evidence against you, as it burns your body like fire. Yet you keep on storing up wealth in these last days. ⁴You refused to pay the people who worked in your fields, and now their unpaid wages are shouting out against you. The Lord All-Powerful has surely heard the cries of the workers who harvested your crops.

⁵While here on earth, you have thought only of filling your own stomachs and having a good time. But now you are like fat cattle on their way to be butchered. ⁶You have condemned and murdered innocent people, who couldn't even fight back.

### Be Patient and Kind

⁷My friends, be patient until the Lord returns. Think of farmers who wait patiently for the spring and summer rains to make their valuable crops grow. ⁸Be patient like those farmers and don't give up. The Lord will soon be here! ⁹Don't grumble about each other or you will be judged, and the judge is right outside the door.

¹⁰My friends, follow the example of the prophets who spoke for the Lord. They were patient, even when they had to suffer. ¹¹In fact, we praise the ones who endured the most. You remember how patient Job was and how the Lord finally helped him. The Lord did this because he is so merciful and kind.

¹²My friends, above all else, don't take an oath. You must not swear by heaven or by earth or by anything else. "Yes" or "No" is all you need to say.

ᶠ4.5 *God truly cares about the Spirit he has put in us*: One possible meaning for the difficult Greek text; other translations are possible, such as, "the Spirit that God put in us truly cares."

If you say anything more, you will be condemned.

**13** If you are having trouble, you should pray. And if you are feeling good, you should sing praises. **14** If you are sick, ask the church leaders<sup>g</sup> to come and pray for you. Ask them to put olive oil<sup>h</sup> on you in the name of the Lord. **15** If you have faith when you pray for sick people, they will get well. The Lord will heal them, and if they have sinned, he will forgive them.

**16** If you have sinned, you should tell each other what you have done. Then you can pray for one another and be healed. The prayer of an innocent person is powerful, and it can help a lot. **17** Elijah was just as human as we are, and for three and a half years his prayers kept the rain from falling. **18** But when he did pray for rain, it fell from the skies and made the crops grow.

**19** My friends, if any followers have wandered away from the truth, you should try to lead them back. **20** If you turn sinners from the wrong way, you will save them from death, and many of their sins will be forgiven.

*g***5.14** *church leaders*: Or "elders" or "presbyters" or "priests." *h***5.14** *olive oil*: The Jewish people used olive oil for healing.

# 1 PETER

## ABOUT THIS LETTER

*In this letter Peter has much to say about suffering. He shows how it can be a way of serving the Lord, of sharing the faith, and of being tested. The letter was written to Christians scattered all over the northern part of Asia Minor. In this part of the Roman empire many Christians had already suffered unfair treatment from people who did not believe in Jesus. And they could expect to suffer even more.*

*Peter was quick to offer encouragement. His letter reminds the readers that some of the Lord's followers may have to go through times of hard testing. But this should make them glad, Peter declares, because it will strengthen their faith and bring them honor on the day when Jesus Christ returns (1.6, 7).*

*Peter reminds them that Christ suffered here on earth, and when his followers suffer for doing right they are sharing his sufferings (2.18-25; 4.12-17). In fact, Christians should expect to suffer for their faith (3.8—4.19).*

*But because of who God is and because of what God has done by raising Jesus Christ from death, Christians can have hope in the future. Just as Christ suffered before he received honor from God, so will Christians be tested by suffering before they receive honor when the Lord returns. Peter uses poetic language to remind his readers of what Christ has done:*

> Christ died once for our sins.
> An innocent person died
>     for those who are guilty.
> Christ did this
>     to bring you to God,

when his body
was put to death
and his spirit
was made alive.      (3.18)

## A QUICK LOOK AT THIS LETTER

*Greetings and Prayer (1.1, 2)*
*A Real Reason for Hope (1.3-12)*
*Living as God's Holy People (1.13—2.17)*
*The Example of Christ's Suffering (2.18-25)*
*Being a Christian and Suffering (3.1—4.19)*
*Advice for Church Leaders (5.1-11)*
*Final Greetings (5.12-14)*

1 From Peter, an apostle of Jesus Christ.
To God's people who are scattered like foreigners in Pontus, Galatia, Cappadocia, Asia, and Bithynia. ²God the Father decided to choose you as his people, and his Spirit has made you holy. You have obeyed Jesus Christ and are sprinkled with his blood.ᵃ
I pray that God will be kind to you and will keep on giving you peace!

### A Real Reason for Hope

³Praise God, the Father of our Lord Jesus Christ. God is so good, and by raising Jesus from death, he has given us new life and a hope that lives on. ⁴God has something stored up for you in heaven, where it will never decay or be ruined or disappear.
⁵You have faith in God, whose power will protect you until the last day.ᵇ Then he will save you, just as he has always planned to do. ⁶On that day you will be glad, even if you have to go through many hard trials for a while. ⁷Your faith will be like gold that has been tested in a fire. And these trials will prove that your faith is worth much more than gold that can be destroyed. They will show that you will be given

praise and honor and glory when Jesus Christ returns.
⁸You have never seen Jesus, and you don't see him now. But still you love him and have faith in him, and no words can tell how glad and happy ⁹you are to be saved. That's why you have faith.
¹⁰Some prophets told how kind God would be to you, and they searched hard to find out more about the way you would be saved. ¹¹The Spirit of Christ was in them and was telling them how Christ would suffer and would then be given great honor. So they searched to find out exactly who Christ would be and when this would happen. ¹²But they were told that they were serving you and not themselves. They preached to you by the power of the Holy Spirit, who was sent from heaven. And their message was only for you, even though angels would like to know more about it.

### Chosen To Live a Holy Life

¹³Be alert and think straight. Put all your hope in how kind God will be to you when Jesus Christ appears. ¹⁴Behave like obedient children. Don't let your lives be controlled by your desires, as they used to be. ¹⁵Always live

---

ᵃ**1.2** *sprinkled with his blood*: According to Exodus 24.3-8 the people of Israel were sprinkled with the blood of cows to show they would keep their agreement with God. Peter says that it is the blood of Jesus that seals the agreement between God and his people (see Hebrews 9.18-21).   ᵇ**1.5** *the last day*: When God will judge all people.

as God's holy people should, because God is the one who chose you, and he is holy. [16] That's why the Scriptures say, "I am the holy God, and you must be holy too."

[17] You say that God is your Father, but God doesn't have favorites! He judges all people by what they do. So you must honor God while you live as strangers here on earth. [18] You were rescued[c] from the useless way of life that you learned from your ancestors. But you know that you were not rescued by such things as silver or gold that don't last forever. [19] You were rescued by the precious blood of Christ, that spotless and innocent lamb. [20] Christ was chosen even before the world was created, but because of you, he did not come until these last days. [21] And when he did come, it was to lead you to have faith in God, who raised him from death and honored him in a glorious way. That's why you have put your faith and hope in God.

[22] You obeyed the truth,[d] and your souls were made pure. Now you sincerely love each other. But you must keep on loving with all your heart. [23] Do this because God has given you new birth by his message that lives on forever. [24] The Scriptures say,

"Humans wither like grass,
and their glory fades
    like wild flowers.
Grass dries up,
and flowers fall
    to the ground.
[25] But what the Lord has said
    will stand forever."

Our good news to you is what the Lord has said.

## A Living Stone and a Holy Nation

**2** Stop being hateful! Quit trying to fool people, and start being sincere. Don't be jealous or say cruel things about others. [2] Be like newborn babies who are thirsty for the pure spiritual milk that will help you grow and be saved. [3] You have already found out how good the Lord really is.

[4] Come to Jesus Christ. He is the living stone that people have rejected, but which God has chosen and highly honored. [5] And now you are living stones that are being used to build a spiritual house. You are also a group of holy priests, and with the help of Jesus Christ you will offer sacrifices that please God. [6] It is just as God says in the Scriptures,

"Look! I am placing in Zion
a choice and precious
    cornerstone.
No one who has faith
in that one
    will be disappointed."

[7] You are followers of the Lord, and that stone is precious to you. But it isn't precious to those who refuse to follow him. They are the builders who tossed aside the stone that turned out to be the most important one of all. [8] They disobeyed the message and stumbled and fell over that stone, because they were doomed.

[9] But you are God's chosen and special people. You are a group of royal priests and a holy nation. God has brought you out of darkness into his marvelous light. Now you must tell all the wonderful things that he has done. The Scriptures say,

[10] "Once you were nobody.
    Now you are God's people.
At one time no one
    had pity on you.
Now God has treated you
    with kindness.

## Live as God's Servants Should

[11] Dear friends, you are foreigners and strangers on this earth. So I beg you not to surrender to those desires that fight against you. [12] Always let others see you behaving properly, even

---

[c]**1.18** *rescued*: The Greek word often, though not always, means payment of a price to free a slave or prisoner.  [d]**1.22** *You obeyed the truth*: Some manuscripts add "by the power of the Spirit."

though they may still accuse you of doing wrong. Then on the day of judgment, they will honor God by telling the good things they saw you do. ¹³ The Lord wants you to obey all human authorities, especially the Emperor, who rules over everyone. ¹⁴ You must also obey governors, because they are sent by the Emperor to punish criminals and to praise good citizens. ¹⁵ God wants you to silence stupid and ignorant people by doing right. ¹⁶ You are free, but still you are God's servants, and you must not use your freedom as an excuse for doing wrong. ¹⁷ Respect everyone and show special love for God's people. Honor God and respect the Emperor.

### The Example of Christ's Suffering

¹⁸ Servants, you must obey your masters and always show respect to them. Do this, not only to those who are kind and thoughtful, but also to those who are cruel. ¹⁹ God will bless you, even if others treat you unfairly for being loyal to him. ²⁰ You don't gain anything by being punished for some wrong you have done. But God will bless you, if you have to suffer for doing something good. ²¹ After all, God chose you to suffer as you follow in the footsteps of Christ, who set an example by suffering for you.

²² Christ did not sin
or ever tell a lie.
²³ Although he was abused,
he never tried to get even.
And when he suffered,
he made no threats.
Instead, he had faith in God,
who judges fairly.
²⁴ Christ carried the burden
of our sins.
He was nailed to the cross,
so that we would stop sinning
and start living right.
By his cuts and bruises
you are healed.
²⁵ You had wandered away
like sheep.
Now you have returned
to the one
who is your shepherd
and protector.

### Wives and Husbands

**3** If you are a wife, you must put your husband first. Even if he opposes our message, you will win him over by what you do. No one else will have to say anything to him, ² because he will see how you honor God and live a pure life. ³ Don't depend on things like fancy hairdos or gold jewelry or expensive clothes to make you look beautiful. ⁴ Be beautiful in your heart by being gentle and quiet. This kind of beauty will last, and God considers it very special.

⁵ Long ago those women who worshiped God and put their hope in him made themselves beautiful by putting their husbands first. ⁶ For example, Sarah obeyed Abraham and called him her master. You are her true children, if you do right and don't let anything frighten you.

⁷ If you are a husband, you should be thoughtful of your wife. Treat her with honor, because she isn't as strong as you are, and she shares with you in the gift of life. Then nothing will stand in the way of your prayers.

### Suffering for Doing Right

⁸ Finally, all of you should agree and have concern and love for each other. You should also be kind and humble. ⁹ Don't be hateful and insult people just because they are hateful and insult you. Instead, treat everyone with kindness. You are God's chosen ones, and he will bless you. The Scriptures say,

¹⁰ "Do you really love life?
Do you want to be happy?
Then stop saying cruel things
and quit telling lies.
¹¹ Give up your evil ways
and do right,
as you find and follow
the road that leads
to peace.
¹² The Lord watches over
everyone who obeys him,
and he listens
to their prayers.
But he opposes everyone
who does evil."

¹³ Can anyone really harm you for being eager to do good deeds? ¹⁴ Even if

you have to suffer for doing good things, God will bless you. So stop being afraid and don't worry about what people might do. <sup>15</sup>Honor Christ and let him be the Lord of your life.

Always be ready to give an answer when someone asks you about your hope. <sup>16</sup>Give a kind and respectful answer and keep your conscience clear. This way you will make people ashamed for saying bad things about your good conduct as a follower of Christ. <sup>17</sup>You are better off to obey God and suffer for doing right than to suffer for doing wrong.

<sup>18</sup> Christ died once for our sins.
An innocent person died
  for those who are guilty.
Christ did this
  to bring you to God,
when his body
  was put to death
and his spirit
  was made alive.

<sup>19</sup>Christ then preached to the spirits that were being kept in prison. <sup>20</sup>They had disobeyed God while Noah was building the boat, but God had been patient with them. Eight people went into that boat and were brought safely through the flood. <sup>21</sup>Those flood waters were like baptism that now saves you. But baptism is more than just washing your body. It means turning to God with a clear conscience, because Jesus Christ was raised from death. <sup>22</sup>Christ is now in heaven, where he sits at the right side<sup>e</sup> of God. All angels, authorities, and powers are under his control.

### Being Faithful to God

**4** Christ suffered here on earth. Now you must be ready to suffer as he did, because suffering shows that you have stopped sinning. <sup>2</sup>It means you have turned from your own desires and want to obey God for the rest of your life. <sup>3</sup>You have already lived long enough like people who don't know God. You were immoral and followed your evil desires. You went around drinking and partying and carrying on. In fact, you even worshiped disgusting idols. <sup>4</sup>Now your former friends wonder why you have stopped running around with them, and they curse you for it. <sup>5</sup>But they will have to answer to God, who judges the living and the dead. <sup>6</sup>The good news has even been preached to the dead,<sup>f</sup> so that after they have been judged for what they have done in this life, their spirits will live with God.

<sup>7</sup>Everything will soon come to an end. So be serious and be sensible enough to pray.

<sup>8</sup>Most important of all, you must sincerely love each other, because love wipes away many sins. <sup>9</sup>Welcome people into your home and don't grumble about it.

<sup>10</sup>Each of you has been blessed with one of God's many wonderful gifts to be used in the service of others. So use your gift well. <sup>11</sup>If you have the gift of speaking, preach God's message. If you have the gift of helping others, do it with the strength that God supplies. Everything should be done in a way that will bring honor to God because of Jesus Christ, who is glorious and powerful forever. Amen.

### Suffering for Being a Christian

<sup>12</sup>Dear friends, don't be surprised or shocked that you are going through testing that is like walking through fire. <sup>13</sup>Be glad for the chance to suffer as Christ suffered. It will prepare you for even greater happiness when he makes his glorious return.

<sup>14</sup>Count it a blessing when you suffer for being a Christian. This shows that God's glorious Spirit is with you. <sup>15</sup>But you deserve to suffer if you are a murderer, a thief, a crook, or a busybody. <sup>16</sup>Don't be ashamed to suffer for being a Christian. Praise God that you belong to him. <sup>17</sup>God has already begun judging his own people. And if his judgment begins with us, imagine how terrible it will be for those who refuse to obey his message. The Scriptures say,

<sup>e</sup>**3.22** *right side*: The place of honor and power. <sup>f</sup>**4.6** *the dead*: Either people who died after becoming followers of Christ or the people of Noah's day (see 3.19).

<sup>18</sup> "If good people barely escape,
what will happen to sinners
and to others
who don't respect God?"

<sup>19</sup> If you suffer for obeying God, you must have complete faith in your faithful Creator and keep on doing right.

### Helping Christian Leaders

5 Church leaders,<sup>g</sup> I am writing to encourage you. I too am a leader, as well as a witness to Christ's suffering, and I will share in his glory when it is shown to us. <sup>2</sup> Just as shepherds watch over their sheep, you must watch over everyone God has placed in your care. Do it willingly in order to please God, and not simply because you think you must. Let it be something you want to do, instead of something you do merely to make money. <sup>3</sup> Don't be bossy to those people who are in your care, but set an example for them. <sup>4</sup> Then when Christ the Chief Shepherd returns, you will be given a crown that will never lose its glory.
<sup>5</sup> All of you young people should obey your elders. In fact, everyone should be humble toward everyone else. The Scriptures say,

"God opposes proud people,
but he helps everyone
who is humble."

<sup>6</sup> Be humble in the presence of God's mighty power, and he will honor you when the time comes. <sup>7</sup> God cares for you, so turn all your worries over to him.
<sup>8</sup> Be on your guard and stay awake. Your enemy, the devil, is like a roaring lion, sneaking around to find someone to attack. <sup>9</sup> But you must resist the devil and stay strong in your faith. You know that all over the world the Lord's followers are suffering just as you are. <sup>10</sup> But God shows undeserved kindness to everyone. That's why he had Christ Jesus choose you to share in his eternal glory. You will suffer for a while, but God will make you complete, steady, strong, and firm. <sup>11</sup> God will be in control forever! Amen.

### Final Greetings

<sup>12</sup> Silvanus helped me write this short letter, and I consider him a faithful follower of the Lord. I wanted to encourage you and tell you how kind God really is, so that you will keep on having faith in him.
<sup>13</sup> Greetings from the Lord's followers in Babylon.<sup>h</sup> They are God's chosen ones.
Mark, who is like a son to me, sends his greetings too.
<sup>14</sup> Give each other a warm greeting. I pray that God will give peace to everyone who belongs to Christ.<sup>i</sup>

---

<sup>g</sup>5.1 *Church leaders*: Or "Elders" or "Presbyters" or "Priests." <sup>h</sup>5.13 *Babylon*: This may be a secret name for the city of Rome. <sup>i</sup>5.14 *Christ*: Some manuscripts add "Amen."

# 2 PETER

## ABOUT THIS LETTER

The writer of this letter wants the readers to know that Christians must live in a way that pleases God (1.3) and hold firmly to the truth they were given (1.12).

He warns them that false prophets and teachers had entered the Christian community and were trying to lead the Lord's followers away from the truth. But they will be punished for their evil deeds (2.1-22). When false teachers are at work, Christians must stick to their faith and be examples for others of right living. They must have understanding, self-control and patience, and they should show love for God and all people.

The readers must never forget that the Lord's return is certain, no matter what others may say (3.1-18):

> Don't forget that for the Lord one day is the same as a thousand years, and a thousand years is the same as one day. The Lord isn't slow about keeping his promises, as some people think he is. In fact, God is patient, because he wants everyone to turn from sin and no one to be lost.          (3.8, 9)

## A QUICK LOOK AT THIS LETTER

Greetings and Prayer (1.1, 2)
How the Lord's Followers Should Live (1.3-15)
The Glory of Christ (1.16-21)
False Prophets and Teachers (2.1-22)
The Lord's Return Is Certain (3.1-18)

---

**1** From Simon Peter, a servant and an apostle of Jesus Christ.

To everyone who shares with us in the privilege of believing that our God and Savior Jesus Christ will do what is just and fair.[a]

²I pray that God will be kind to you and will let you live in perfect peace! May you keep learning more and more about God and our Lord Jesus.

### Living as the Lord's Followers

³We have everything we need to live a life that pleases God. It was all given to us by God's own power, when we learned that he had invited us to share in his wonderful goodness. ⁴God made great and marvelous promises, so that his nature would become part of us. Then we could escape our evil desires and the corrupt influences of this world.

⁵Do your best to improve your faith. You can do this by adding goodness, understanding, ⁶self-control, patience, devotion to God, ⁷concern for others, and love. ⁸If you keep growing in this way, it will show that what you know about our Lord Jesus Christ has made your lives useful and meaningful. ⁹But if you don't grow, you are like someone

---

a **1.1** *To everyone who ... just and fair*: Or "To everyone whose faith in the justice and fairness of our God and Savior Jesus Christ is as precious as our own faith."

who is nearsighted or blind, and you have forgotten that your past sins are forgiven.

¹⁰ My friends, you must do all you can to show that God has really chosen and selected you. If you keep on doing this, you won't stumble and fall. ¹¹ Then our Lord and Savior Jesus Christ will give you a glorious welcome into his kingdom that will last forever.

¹² You are holding firmly to the truth that you were given. But I am still going to remind you of these things. ¹³ In fact, I think I should keep on reminding you until I leave this body. ¹⁴ And our Lord Jesus Christ has already told me that I will soon leave it behind. ¹⁵ That is why I am doing my best to make sure that each of you remembers all of this after I am gone.

### The Message about the Glory of Christ

¹⁶ When we told you about the power and the return of our Lord Jesus Christ, we were not telling clever stories that someone had made up. But with our own eyes we saw his true greatness. ¹⁷ God, our great and wonderful Father, truly honored him by saying, "This is my own dear Son, and I am pleased with him." ¹⁸ We were there with Jesus on the holy mountain and heard this voice speak from heaven.

¹⁹ All of this makes us even more certain that what the prophets said is true. So you should pay close attention to their message, as you would to a lamp shining in some dark place. You must keep on paying attention until daylight comes and the morning star rises in your hearts. ²⁰ But you need to realize that no one alone can understand any of the prophecies in the Scriptures. ²¹ The prophets did not think these things up on their own, but they were guided by the Spirit of God.

### False Prophets and Teachers

2 Sometimes false prophets spoke to the people of Israel. False teachers will also sneak in and speak harmful lies to you. But these teachers don't really belong to the Master who paid a great price for them, and they will quickly destroy themselves. ² Many people will follow their evil ways and cause others to tell lies about the true way. ³ They will be greedy and cheat you with smooth talk. But long ago God decided to punish them, and God doesn't sleep.

⁴ God did not have pity on the angels that sinned. He had them tied up and thrown into the dark pits of hell until the time of judgment. ⁵ And during Noah's time, God did not have pity on the ungodly people of the world. He destroyed them with a flood, though he did save eight people, including Noah, who preached the truth.

⁶ God punished the cities of Sodom and Gomorrah ᵇ by burning them to ashes, and this is a warning to anyone else who wants to sin.

⁷⁻⁸ Lot lived right and was greatly troubled by the terrible way those wicked people were living. He was a good man, and day after day he suffered because of the evil things he saw and heard. So the Lord rescued him. ⁹ This shows that the Lord knows how to rescue godly people from their sufferings and to punish evil people while they wait for the day of judgment.

¹⁰ The Lord is especially hard on people who disobey him and don't think of anything except their own filthy desires. They are reckless and proud and are not afraid of cursing the glorious beings in heaven. ¹¹ Although angels are more powerful than these evil beings, ᶜ even the angels don't dare to accuse them to the Lord.

¹² These people are no better than senseless animals that live by their feelings and are born to be caught and killed. They speak evil of things they don't know anything about. But their own corrupt deeds will destroy them. ¹³ They have done evil, and they will be rewarded with evil.

They think it is fun to have wild parties during the day. They are immoral, and the meals they eat with you are spoiled by the shameful and selfish way they carry on.*d* ¹⁴ All they think about is having sex with someone else's husband or wife. There is no end to their wicked deeds. They trick people who are easily fooled, and their minds are filled with greedy thoughts. But they are headed for trouble!

¹⁵ They have left the true road and have gone down the wrong path by following the example of the prophet Balaam. He was the son of Beor and loved what he got from being a crook. ¹⁶ But a donkey corrected him for this evil deed. It spoke to him with a human voice and made him stop his foolishness.

¹⁷ These people are like dried up water holes and clouds blown by a windstorm. The darkest part of hell is waiting for them. ¹⁸ They brag out loud about their stupid nonsense. And by being vulgar and crude, they trap people who have barely escaped from living the wrong kind of life. ¹⁹ They promise freedom to everyone. But they are merely slaves of filthy living, because people are slaves of whatever controls them.

²⁰ When they learned about our Lord and Savior Jesus Christ, they escaped from the filthy things of this world. But they are again caught up and controlled by these filthy things, and now they are in worse shape than they were at first. ²¹ They would have been better off if they had never known about the right way. Even after they knew what was right, they turned their backs on the holy commandments that they were given. ²² What happened to them is just like the true saying,

"A dog will come back
  to lick up its own vomit.
A pig that has been washed
  will roll in the mud."

## The Lord Will Return

**3** My dear friends, this is the second letter I have written to encourage you to do some honest thinking. I don't want you to forget ² what God's prophets said would happen. You must never forget what the holy prophets taught in the past. And you must remember what the apostles told you our Lord and Savior has commanded us to do.

³ But first you must realize that in the last days some people won't think about anything except their own selfish desires. They will make fun of you ⁴ and say, "Didn't your Lord promise to come back? Yet the first leaders have already died, and the world hasn't changed a bit."

⁵ They will say this because they want to forget that long ago the heavens and the earth were made at God's command. The earth came out of water and was made from water. ⁶ Later it was destroyed by the waters of a mighty flood. ⁷ But God has commanded the present heavens and earth to remain until the day of judgment. Then they will be set on fire, and ungodly people will be destroyed.

⁸ Dear friends, don't forget that for the Lord one day is the same as a thousand years, and a thousand years is the same as one day. ⁹ The Lord isn't slow about keeping his promises, as some people think he is. In fact, God is patient, because he wants everyone to turn from sin and no one to be lost.

¹⁰ The day of the Lord's return will surprise us like a thief. The heavens will disappear with a loud noise, and the heat will melt the whole universe.*e* Then the earth and everything on it will be seen for what they are.*f*

¹¹ Everything will be destroyed. So you should serve and honor God by the way you live. ¹² You should look forward to the day when God judges everyone, and you should try to make

---

*d*2.13 *and the meals they eat with you are spoiled by the shameful and selfish way they carry on*: Some manuscripts have "and the meals they eat with you are spoiled by the shameful way they carry on during your feasts of Christian love." *e*3.10 *the whole universe*: Probably the sun, moon, and stars, or the elements that everything in the universe is made of. *f*3.10 *will be seen for what they are*: Some manuscripts have "will go up in flames."

it come soon.ᵍ On that day the heavens will be destroyed by fire, and everything else will melt in the heat. ¹³ But God has promised us a new heaven and a new earth, where justice will rule. We are really looking forward to that!

¹⁴ My friends, while you are waiting, you should make certain that the Lord finds you pure, spotless, and living at peace. ¹⁵ Don't forget that the Lord is patient because he wants people to be saved. This is also what our dear friend Paul said when he wrote you with the wisdom that God had given him. ¹⁶ Paul talks about these same things in all his letters, but part of what he says is hard to understand. Some ignorant and unsteady people even destroy themselves by twisting what he said. They do the same thing with other Scriptures too.

¹⁷ My dear friends, you have been warned ahead of time! So don't let the errors of evil people lead you down the wrong path and make you lose your balance. ¹⁸ Let the wonderful kindness and the understanding that come from our Lord and Savior Jesus Christ help you to keep on growing. Praise Jesus now and forever! Amen.ʰ

ᵍ**3.12** *and you should try to make it come soon:* Or "and you should eagerly desire for that day to come." ʰ**3.18** *Amen:* Some manuscripts do not have "Amen."

# 1 JOHN

## ABOUT THIS LETTER

*John wants Christian believers to know that when we tell God about our sins, God will forgive us and take them away (1.9).*

*The true test of faith is love for each other (3.11-24). Because God is love, his people must be like him (4.1-21). For a complete victory over sin, we must not only love others, but we must believe that Jesus, the Son of God, is truly Christ, and that his death for us was real (5.1-12).*

*Remember:*

> The Word that gives life
>    was from the beginning,
> and this is the one
>    our message is about.
>          (1.1a)

## A QUICK LOOK AT THIS LETTER

*The Word that Gives Life (1.1-4)*
*God Is Light and Christ Is Our Example (1.5—2.6)*
*The New Commandment (2.7-17)*
*The Enemies of Christ and God's Children (2.18—3.10)*
*God's Love and Our Love (3.11—4.21)*
*Victory Over the World (5.1-21)*

# 1

The Word that gives life
  was from the beginning,
and this is the one
  our message is about.

Our ears have heard,
  our own eyes have seen,
and our hands touched
  this Word.

**2** The one who gives life appeared! We saw it happen, and we are witnesses to what we have seen. Now we are telling you about this eternal life that was with the Father and appeared to us. **3** We are telling you what we have seen and heard, so that you may share in this life with us. And we share in it with the Father and with his Son Jesus Christ. **4** We are writing to tell you these things, because this makes us*a* truly happy.

### God Is Light

**5** Jesus told us that God is light and doesn't have any darkness in him. Now we are telling you.

**6** If we say that we share in life with God and keep on living in the dark, we are lying and are not living by the truth. **7** But if we live in the light, as God does, we share in life with each other. And the blood of his Son Jesus washes all our sins away. **8** If we say that we have not sinned, we are fooling ourselves, and the truth isn't in our hearts. **9** But if we confess our sins to God, he can always be trusted to forgive us and take our sins away.

**10** If we say that we have not sinned, we make God a liar, and his message isn't in our hearts.*b*

### Christ Helps Us

# 2

My children, I am writing this so that you won't sin. But if you do sin, Jesus Christ always does the right thing, and he will speak to the Father for us. **2** Christ is the sacrifice that takes away our sins and the sins of all the world's people.

**3** When we obey God, we are sure that we know him. **4** But if we claim to know him and don't obey him, we are lying and the truth isn't in our hearts. **5** We truly love God only when we obey him as we should, and then we know that we belong to him. **6** If we say we are his, we must follow the example of Christ.

### The New Commandment

**7** My dear friends, I am not writing to give you a new commandment. It is the same one that you were first given, and it is the message you heard. **8** But it really is a new commandment, and you know its true meaning, just as Christ does. You can see the darkness fading away and the true light already shining.

**9** If we claim to be in the light and hate someone, we are still in the dark. **10** But if we love others, we are in the light, and we don't cause problems for them.*c* **11** If we hate others, we are living and walking in the dark. We don't know where we are going, because we can't see in the dark.

**12** Children, I am writing you,
  because your sins
have been forgiven
  in the name of Christ.
**13** Parents, I am writing you,
  because you have known
the one who was there
  from the beginning.
Young people, I am writing you,
because you have defeated
  the evil one.
**14** Children, I am writing you,
because you have known
  the Father.
Parents, I am writing you,
  because you have known
the one who was there
  from the beginning.
Young people, I am writing you,
  because you are strong.
God's message is firm
  in your hearts,

---

*a* **1.4** *us*: Some manuscripts have "you." *b* **1.10** *and his message isn't in our hearts*: Or "because we have not accepted his message." *c* **2.10** *and we don't cause problems for them*: Or "and we can see anything that might make us fall."

and you have defeated
the evil one.

15 Don't love the world or anything that belongs to the world. If you love the world, you cannot love the Father. 16 Our foolish pride comes from this world, and so do our selfish desires and our desire to have everything we see. None of this comes from the Father. 17 The world and the desires it causes are disappearing. But if we obey God, we will live forever.

### The Enemy of Christ

18 Children, this is the last hour. You heard that the enemy of Christ would appear at this time, and many of Christ's enemies have already appeared. So we know that the last hour is here. 19 These people came from our own group, yet they were not part of us. If they had been part of us, they would have stayed with us. But they left, which proves that they did not belong to our group. 20 Christ, the Holy One,*d* has blessed*e* you, and now all of you understand.*f* 21 I did not need to write you about the truth, since you already know it. You also know that liars do not belong to the truth. 22 And a liar is anyone who says that Jesus isn't truly Christ. Anyone who says this is an enemy of Christ and rejects both the Father and the Son. 23 If we reject the Son, we reject the Father. But if we say that we accept the Son, we have the Father. 24 Keep thinking about the message you first heard, and you will always be one in your heart with the Son and with the Father. 25 The Son*g* has promised us*h* eternal life.

26 I am writing to warn you about those people who are misleading you. 27 But Christ has blessed you with the Holy Spirit.*i* Now the Spirit stays in you, and you don't need any teachers. The Spirit is truthful and teaches you everything. So stay one in your heart with Christ, just as the Spirit has taught you to do.

### Children of God

28 Children, stay one in your hearts with Christ. Then when he returns, we will have confidence and won't have to hide in shame. 29 You know that Christ always does right and that everyone who does right is a child of God.

**3** Think how much the Father loves us. He loves us so much that he lets us be called his children, as we truly are. But since the people of this world did not know who Christ*j* is, they don't know who we are. 2 My dear friends, we are already God's children, though what we will be hasn't yet been seen. But we do know that when Christ returns, we will be like him, because we will see him as he truly is. 3 This hope makes us keep ourselves holy, just as Christ*k* is holy.

4 Everyone who sins breaks God's law, because sin is the same as breaking God's law. 5 You know that Christ came to take away sins. He isn't sinful, 6 and people who stay one in their hearts with him won't keep on sinning. If they do keep on sinning, they don't know Christ, and they have never seen him.

7 Children, don't be fooled. Anyone who does right is good, just like Christ

---

*d*2.20 *Christ, the Holy One*: The Greek text has "the Holy One" which may refer either to Christ or to God the Father. *e*2.20 *blessed*: This translates a word which means "to pour olive oil on (someone's head)." In Old Testament times it was the custom to pour olive oil on a person's head when that person was chosen to be a priest or a king. Here the meaning is not clear. It may refer to the ceremony of pouring olive oil on the followers of the Lord right before they were baptized or it may refer to the gift of the Holy Spirit which they were given at baptism (see verse 27). *f*2.20 *now all of you understand*: Some manuscripts have "you understand all things." *g*2.25 *The Son*: The Greek text has "he" and may refer to God the Father. *h*2.25 *us*: Some manuscripts have "you." *i*2.27 *Christ has blessed you with the Holy Spirit*: The Greek text has "You received a pouring on of olive oil from him" (see verse 20). The "pouring on of olive oil" is here taken to refer to the gift of the Holy Spirit, and "he" may refer either to Christ or to the Father. *j*3.1 *Christ*: The Greek text has "he" and may refer to God. *k*3.3 *Christ*: The Greek text has "that one" and may refer to God.

himself. ⁸ Anyone who keeps on sinning belongs to the devil. He has sinned from the beginning, but the Son of God came to destroy all that he has done. ⁹ God's children cannot keep on being sinful. His life-giving power¹ lives in them and makes them his children, so that they cannot keep on sinning. ¹⁰ You can tell God's children from the devil's children, because those who belong to the devil refuse to do right or to love each other.

### Love Each Other

¹¹ From the beginning you were told that we must love each other. ¹² Don't be like Cain, who belonged to the devil and murdered his own brother. Why did he murder him? He did it because his brother was good, and he was evil. ¹³ My friends, don't be surprised if the people of this world hate you. ¹⁴ Our love for each other proves that we have gone from death to life. But if you don't love each other, you are still under the power of death. ¹⁵ If you hate each other, you are murderers, and we know that murderers do not have eternal life. ¹⁶ We know what love is because Jesus gave his life for us. That's why we must give our lives for each other. ¹⁷ If we have all we need and see one of our own people in need, we must have pity on that person, or else we cannot say we love God. ¹⁸ Children, you show love for others by truly helping them, and not merely by talking about it.

¹⁹ When we love others, we know that we belong to the truth, and we feel at ease in the presence of God. ²⁰ But even if we don't feel at ease, God is greater than our feelings, and he knows everything. ²¹ Dear friends, if we feel at ease in the presence of God, we will have the courage to come near him. ²² He will give us whatever we ask, because we obey him and do what pleases him. ²³ God wants us to have faith in his Son Jesus Christ and to love each other. This is also what Jesus taught us to do. ²⁴ If we obey God's commandments, we will stay one in our hearts with him,

and he will stay one with us. The Spirit that he has given us is proof that we are one with him.

### God Is Love

4 Dear friends, don't believe everyone who claims to have the Spirit of God. Test them all to find out if they really do come from God. Many false prophets have already gone out into the world, ² and you can know which ones come from God. His Spirit says that Jesus Christ had a truly human body. ³ But when someone doesn't say this about Jesus, you know that person has a spirit that doesn't come from God and is the enemy of Christ. You knew that this enemy was coming into the world and now is already here.

⁴ Children, you belong to God, and you have defeated these enemies. God's Spirit ᵐ is in you and is more powerful than the one that is in the world. ⁵ These enemies belong to this world, and the world listens to them, because they speak its language. ⁶ We belong to God, and everyone who knows God will listen to us. But the people who don't know God won't listen to us. That is how we can tell the Spirit that speaks the truth from the one that tells lies.

⁷ My dear friends, we must love each other. Love comes from God, and when we love each other, it shows that we have been given new life. We are now God's children, and we know him. ⁸ God is love, and anyone who doesn't love others has never known him. ⁹ God showed his love for us when he sent his only Son into the world to give us life. ¹⁰ Real love isn't our love for God, but his love for us. God sent his Son to be the sacrifice by which our sins are forgiven. ¹¹ Dear friends, since God loved us this much, we must love each other.

¹² No one has ever seen God. But if we love each other, God lives in us, and his love is truly in our hearts.

¹³ God has given us his Spirit. That is how we know that we are one with him, just as he is one with us. ¹⁴ God

---

ˡ**3.9** *His life-giving power*: The Greek text has "his seed." ᵐ**4.4** *God's Spirit*: The Greek text has "he" and may refer to the Spirit or to God or to Jesus.

sent his Son to be the Savior of the world. We saw his Son and are now telling others about him. [15] God stays one with everyone who openly says that Jesus is the Son of God. That's how we stay one with God [16] and are sure that God loves us.

God is love. If we keep on loving others, we will stay one in our hearts with God, and he will stay one with us. [17] If we truly love others and live as Christ did in this world, we won't be worried about the day of judgment. [18] A real love for others will chase those worries away. The thought of being punished is what makes us afraid. It shows that we have not really learned to love.

[19] We love because God loved us first. [20] But if we say we love God and don't love each other, we are liars. We cannot see God. So how can we love God, if we don't love the people we can see? [21] The commandment that God has given us is: "Love God and love each other!"

## Victory over the World

5 If we believe that Jesus is truly Christ, we are God's children. Everyone who loves the Father will also love his children. [2] If we love and obey God, we know that we will love his children. [3] We show our love for God by obeying his commandments, and they are not hard to follow.

[4] Every child of God can defeat the world, and our faith is what gives us this victory. [5] No one can defeat the world without having faith in Jesus as the Son of God.

## Who Jesus Is

[6] Water and blood came out from the side of Jesus Christ. It wasn't just water, but water and blood.[n] The Spirit tells about this, because the Spirit is

truthful. [7] In fact, there are three who tell about it. [8] They are the Spirit, the water, and the blood, and they all agree.

[9] We believe what people tell us. But we can trust what God says even more, and God is the one who has spoken about his Son. [10] If we have faith in God's Son, we have believed what God has said. But if we don't believe what God has said about his Son, it is the same as calling God a liar. [11] God has also said that he gave us eternal life and that this life comes to us from his Son. [12] And so, if we have God's Son, we have this life. But if we don't have the Son, we don't have this life.

## Knowing about Eternal Life

[13] All of you have faith in the Son of God, and I have written to let you know that you have eternal life. [14] We are certain that God will hear our prayers when we ask for what pleases him. [15] And if we know that God listens when we pray, we are sure that our prayers have already been answered.

[16] Suppose you see one of our people commit a sin that isn't a deadly sin. You can pray, and that person will be given eternal life. But the sin must not be one that is deadly. [17] Everything that is wrong is sin, but not all sins are deadly.

[18] We are sure that God's children do not keep on sinning. God's own Son protects them, and the devil cannot harm them.

[19] We are certain that we come from God and that the rest of the world is under the power of the devil.

[20] We know that Jesus Christ the Son of God has come and has shown us the true God. And because of Jesus, we now belong to the true God who gives eternal life.

[21] Children, you must stay away from idols.

---

[n]5.6 Water and blood came out from the side of Jesus Christ. It wasn't just water, but water and blood: See John 19.34. It is also possible to translate, "Jesus Christ came by the water of baptism and by the blood of his death! He was not only baptized, but he bled and died." The purpose of the verse is to tell that Jesus was truly human and that he really died.

# 2 JOHN

## ABOUT THIS LETTER

John writes again about the importance of love in a Christian's life. He points out that truth and love must go together. We must also believe that Christ was truly human, and we must love each other.

## A QUICK LOOK AT THIS LETTER

Greetings and Prayer (1-3)
Truth and Love (4-11)
Final Greetings (12, 13)

---

¹ From the church leader.ᵃ

To a very special woman and her children.ᵇ I truly love all of you, and so does everyone else who knows the truth. ² We love you because the truth is now in our hearts, and it will be there forever.

³ I pray that God the Father and Jesus Christ his Son will be kind and merciful to us! May they give us peace and truth and love.

### Truth and Love

⁴ I was very glad to learn that some of your children are obeying the truth, as the Father told us to do. ⁵ Dear friend, I am not writing to tell you and your children to do something you have not done before. I am writing to tell you to love each other, which is the first thing you were told to do. ⁶ Love means that we do what God tells us. And from the beginning, he told you to love him.

⁷ Many liars have gone out into the world. These deceitful liars are saying that Jesus Christ did not have a truly human body. But they are liars and the enemies of Christ. ⁸ So be sure not to lose what weᶜ have worked for. If you do, you won't be given your full reward. ⁹ Don't keep changing what you were taught about Christ, or else God will no longer be with you. But if you hold firmly to what you were taught, both the Father and the Son will be with you. ¹⁰ If people won't agree to this teaching, don't welcome them into your home or even greet them. ¹¹ Greeting them is the same as taking part in their evil deeds.

### Final Greetings

¹² I have much more to tell you, but I don't want to write it with pen and ink. I want to come and talk to you in person, because that will make usᵈ really happy.

¹³ Greetings from the children of your very special sister.ᵉ

---

ᵃ1 church leader: Or "elder" or "presbyter" or "priest." ᵇ1 very special woman and her children: A group of the Lord's followers who met together for worship. "The children of your ... sister" (see verse 13) is another group of followers. "Very special" (here and verse 13) probably means "chosen (by the Lord)." ᶜ8 we: Some manuscripts have "you." ᵈ12 us: Some manuscripts have "you." ᵉ13 sister: See the note at verse 1.

# 3 JOHN

## ABOUT THIS LETTER

In this letter the writer reminds Christian readers that they should help support those who go to other parts of the world to tell others about the Lord. The letter is written to an important church member named Gaius, who had been very helpful to Christians who traveled around and preached the good news.

## A QUICK LOOK AT THIS LETTER

Greetings to Gaius (1-4)
The Importance of Working Together (5-12)
Final Greetings (13-15)

---

¹ From the church leader.ᵃ
To my dear friend Gaius.
I love you because we follow the truth, ² dear friend, and I pray that all goes well for you. I hope that you are as strong in body, as I know you are in spirit. ³ It makes me very happy when the Lord's followers come by and speak openly of how you obey the truth. ⁴ Nothing brings me greater happiness than to hear that my childrenᵇ are obeying the truth.

### Working Together

⁵ Dear friend, you have always been faithful in helping other followers of the Lord, even the ones you didn't know before. ⁶ They have told the church about your love. They say you were good enough to welcome them and to send them on their mission in a way that God's servants deserve. ⁷ When they left to tell others about the Lord, they decided not to accept help from anyone who wasn't a follower. ⁸ We must support people like them, so that we can take part in what they are doing to spread the truth. ⁹ I wrote to the church. But Diotrephes likes to be the number-one leader, and he won't pay any attention to us. ¹⁰ So if I come, I will remind him of how he has been attacking us with gossip. Not only has he been doing this, but he refuses to welcome any of the Lord's followers who come by. And when other church members want to welcome them, he puts them out of the church.

¹¹ Dear friend, don't copy the evil deeds of others! Follow the example of people who do kind deeds. They are God's children, but those who are always doing evil have never seen God. ¹² Everyone speaks well of Demetrius, and so does the true message that he teaches. I also speak well of him, and you know what I say is true.

### Final Greetings

¹³ I have much more to say to you, but I don't want to write it with pen and ink. ¹⁴ I hope to see you soon, and then we can talk in person. ¹⁵ I pray that God will bless you with peace!
Your friends send their greetings. Please give a personal greeting to each of our friends.

ᵃ1 church leader: Or "elder" or "presbyter" or "priest." ᵇ4 children: Probably persons that the leader had led to be followers of the Lord.

# JUDE

## ABOUT THIS LETTER

*Jude has much to say about false teachers. They are evil! God will punish them, and Christians should not follow their teaching or imitate the way they live.*

*Jude ends with a beautiful prayer-like blessing:*

> Offer praise to God our Savior because of our Lord Jesus Christ! Only God can keep you from falling and make you pure and joyful in his glorious presence. Before time began and now and forevermore, God is worthy of glory, honor, power, and authority. Amen.  (24, 25)

## A QUICK LOOK AT THIS LETTER

Greetings (1, 2)
Defending the Faith against False Teachers (3-23)
Final Prayer (24, 25)

---

¹ From Jude, a servant of Jesus Christ and the brother of James.

To all who are chosen and loved by God the Father and are kept safe by Jesus Christ.

² I pray that God will greatly bless you with kindness, peace, and love!

### False Teachers

³ My dear friends, I really wanted to write you about God's saving power at work in our lives. But instead, I must write and ask you to defend the faith that God has once for all given to his people. ⁴ Some godless people have sneaked in among us and are saying, "God treats us much better than we deserve, and so it is all right to be immoral." They even deny that we must obey Jesus Christ as our only Master and Lord. But long ago the Scriptures warned that these godless people were doomed.

⁵ Don't forget what happened to those people that the Lord rescued from Egypt. Some of them did not have faith, and he later destroyed them. ⁶ You also know about the angels ᵃ who didn't do their work and left their proper places. God chained them with everlasting chains and is now keeping them in dark pits until the great day of judgment. ⁷ We should also be warned by what happened to the cities of Sodom and Gomorrah ᵇ and the nearby towns. Their people became immoral and did all sorts of sexual sins. Then God made an example of them and punished them with eternal fire.

⁸ The people I am talking about are behaving just like those dreamers who destroyed their own bodies. They reject all authority and insult angels. ⁹ Even Michael, the chief angel, didn't dare to insult the devil, when the two of them were arguing about the body of Moses. ᶜ

---

ᵃ 6 *angels*: This may refer to the angels who liked the women on earth so much that they came down and married them (see Genesis 6.2).   ᵇ 7 *Sodom and Gomorrah*: During the time of Abraham the Lord destroyed these cities because the people there were so evil.
ᶜ 9 *Michael . . . the body of Moses*: This refers to what was said in an ancient Jewish book about Moses.

All Michael said was, "The Lord will punish you!"

10 But these people insult powers they don't know anything about. They are like senseless animals that end up getting destroyed, because they live only by their feelings. 11 Now they are in for real trouble. They have followed Cain's exampleᵈ and have made the same mistake that Balaamᵉ did by caring only for money. They have also rebelled against God, just as Korah did.ᶠ Because of all this, they will be destroyed.

12 These people are filthy minded, and by their shameful and selfish actions they spoil the meals you eat together. They are like clouds blown along by the wind, but never bringing any rain. They are like leafless trees, uprooted and dead, and unable to produce fruit. 13 Their shameful deeds show up like foam on wild ocean waves. They are like wandering stars forever doomed to the darkest pits of hell.

14 Enoch was the seventh person after Adam, and he was talking about these people when he said:

Look! The Lord is coming with thousands and thousands of holy angels 15 to judge everyone. He will punish all those ungodly people for all the evil things they have done. The Lord will surely punish those ungodly sinners for every evil thing they have ever said about him.

16 These people grumble and complain and live by their own selfish desires. They brag about themselves and flatter others to get what they want.

## More Warnings

17 My dear friends, remember the warning you were given by the apostles of our Lord Jesus Christ. 18 They told you that near the end of time, selfish and godless people would start making fun of God. 19 And now these people are already making you turn against each other. They think only about this life, and they don't have God's Spirit.

20 Dear friends, keep building on the foundation of your most holy faith, as the Holy Spirit helps you to pray. 21 And keep in step with God's love, as you wait for our Lord Jesus Christ to show how kind he is by giving you eternal life. 22 Be helpful toᵍ all who may have doubts. 23 Rescue any who need to be saved, as you would rescue someone from a fire. Then with fear in your own hearts, have mercy on everyone who needs it. But hate even the clothes of those who have been made dirty by their filthy deeds.

## Final Prayer

24-25 Offer praise to God our Savior because of our Lord Jesus Christ! Only God can keep you from falling and make you pure and joyful in his glorious presence. Before time began and now and forevermore, God is worthy of glory, honor, power, and authority. Amen.

ᵈ11 Cain's example: Cain murdered his brother Abel. ᵉ11 Balaam: According to the biblical account, Balaam refused to curse the people of Israel for profit (see Numbers 22.18; 24.13), though he led them to be unfaithful to the Lord (see Numbers 25.1-3; 31.16). But by New Testament times, some Jewish teachers taught that Balaam was greedy and did accept money to curse them. ᶠ11 just as Korah did: Together with Dathan and Abiram, Korah led a rebellion against Moses and Aaron (see Numbers 16.1-35; 26.9, 10). ᵍ22 Be helpful to: Some manuscripts have "Correct."

# REVELATION

## ABOUT THIS BOOK

This book tells what John had seen in a vision about God's message and about what Jesus Christ had said and done (1.2). The message has three main parts: (1) There are evil forces at work in the world, and Christians may have to suffer and die; (2) Jesus is Lord, and he will conquer all people and powers who oppose God; and (3) God has wonderful rewards in store for his faithful people, who remain faithful to him, especially for those who lose their lives in his service.

This was a powerful message of hope for those early Christians who had to suffer or die for their faith. In this book they learned that, in spite of the cruel power of the Roman Empire, the Lamb of God would win the final victory. And this gave them the courage to be faithful.

Because this book is so full of visions that use ideas and word pictures from the Old Testament, it was like a book with secret messages for the early Christians. The book could be passed around and be understood by Christians, but an official of the Roman Empire would not be able to understand it. For example, when the fall of Babylon is described (chapter 18), the early Christians knew that this pointed to the fall of the Roman Empire. This knowledge gave them hope.

At the beginning of this book there are seven letters to seven churches. These letters show what different groups of the Lord's followers will do in times of persecution (2.1—3.22).

The author uses many powerful images to describe God's power and judgment. The vision of God's throne (4.1-11) and of the scroll and the Lamb (5.1-14) show that God and Christ are in control of all human and supernatural events. Opening seven seals (6.1—8.5), blowing the seven trumpets (8.6—11.19), and emptying the seven bowls (16.1-21) are among the visions that show God's fierce judgment on the world.

After the suffering has ended, God's faithful people will receive the greatest blessing of all:

> God's home is now with his people. He will live with them, and they will be his own. Yes, God will make his home among his people. He will wipe all tears from their eyes, and there will be no more death, suffering, crying, or pain. These things of the past are gone forever. (21.3b, 4)

## A QUICK LOOK AT THIS BOOK

---

**1** This is what God showed to Jesus Christ, so that he could tell his servants what must happen soon. Christ then sent his angel with the message to his servant John. ² And John told everything that he had seen about God's message and about what Jesus Christ had said and done.

³ God will bless everyone who reads this prophecy to others,ᵃ and he will bless everyone who hears and obeys it. The time is almost here.

⁴ From John to the seven churches in Asia.ᵇ

I pray that you
will be blessed
with kindness and peace
from God, who is and was
and is coming.
May you receive
kindness and peace
from the seven spirits
before the throne of God.
⁵ May kindness and peace
be yours
from Jesus Christ,
the faithful witness.

Jesus was the first
to conquer death,
and he is the ruler
of all earthly kings.
Christ loves us,
and by his blood
he set us free
from our sins.
⁶ He lets us rule as kings
and serve God his Father
as priests.
To him be glory and power
forever and ever! Amen.
⁷ Look! He is coming
with the clouds.
Everyone will see him,
even the ones who stuck
a sword through him.
All people on earth
will weep because of him.
Yes, it will happen! Amen.

⁸ The Lord God says, "I am Alpha and Omega,ᶜ the one who is and was and is coming. I am God All-Powerful!"

### A Vision of the Risen Lord

⁹ I am John, a follower together with all of you. We suffer because Jesus is our king, but he gives us the strength to endure. I was sent to Patmos Island,ᵈ because I had preached God's message and had told about Jesus. ¹⁰ On the Lord's day the Spirit took control of me, and behind me I heard a loud voice that sounded like a trumpet. ¹¹ The voice said, "Write in a book what you see. Then send it to the seven churches in Ephesus, Smyrna, Pergamum, Thyatira, Sardis, Philadelphia, and Laodicea."ᵉ ¹² When I turned to see who was speaking to me, I saw seven gold lampstands. ¹³ There with the lampstands was someone who seemed to be the Son of Man.ᶠ He was wearing a robe

---

ᵃ**1.3** *who reads this prophecy to others*: A public reading, in a worship service. ᵇ**1.4** *Asia*: The section 1.4—3.22 is in the form of a letter. Asia was in the eastern part of the Roman Empire and is present day Turkey. ᶜ**1.8** *Alpha and Omega*: The first and last letters of the Greek alphabet, which sometimes mean "first" and "last." ᵈ**1.9** *Patmos Island*: A small island where prisoners were sometimes kept by the Romans. ᵉ**1.11** *Ephesus . . . Laodicea*: Ephesus was in the center with the six other cities forming a half-circle around it. ᶠ**1.13** *Son of Man*: That is, Jesus.

that reached down to his feet, and a gold cloth was wrapped around his chest. ¹⁴His head and his hair were white as wool or snow, and his eyes looked like flames of fire. ¹⁵His feet were glowing like bronze being heated in a furnace, and his voice sounded like the roar of a waterfall. ¹⁶He held seven stars in his right hand, and a sharp double-edged sword was coming from his mouth. His face was shining as bright as the sun at noon.

¹⁷When I saw him, I fell at his feet like a dead person. But he put his right hand on me and said:

Don't be afraid! I am the first, the last, ¹⁸and the living one. I died, but now I am alive forevermore, and I have the keys to death and the world of the dead.ᵍ ¹⁹Write what you have seen and what is and what will happen after these things. ²⁰I will explain the mystery of the seven stars that you saw at my right side and the seven gold lampstands. The seven stars are the angelsʰ of the seven churches, and the lampstands are the seven churches.

### The Letter to Ephesus

**2** This is what you must write to the angel of the church in Ephesus:

I am the one who holds the seven stars in my right hand, and I walk among the seven gold lampstands. Listen to what I say. ²I know everything you have done, including your hard work and how you have endured. I know you won't put up with anyone who is evil. When some people pretended to be apostles, you tested them and found out that they were liars. ³You have endured and gone through hard times because of me, and you have not given up.

⁴But I do have something against you! And it is this: You don't have

as much love as you used to. ⁵Think about where you have fallen from, and then turn back and do as you did at first. If you don't turn back, I will come and take away your lampstand. ⁶But there is one thing you are doing right. You hate what the Nicolaitansⁱ are doing, and so do I.

⁷If you have ears, listen to what the Spirit says to the churches. I will let everyone who wins the victory eat from the life-giving tree in God's wonderful garden.

### The Letter to Smyrna

⁸This is what you must write to the angel of the church in Smyrna:

I am the first and the last. I died, but now I am alive! Listen to what I say.

⁹I know how much you suffer and how poor you are, but you are rich. I also know the cruel things being said about you by people who claim to be God's people. But they are really not. They are a group that belongs to Satan.

¹⁰Don't worry about what you will suffer. The devil will throw some of you into jail, and you will be tested and made to suffer for ten days. But if you are faithful until you die, I will reward you with a glorious life.ʲ

¹¹If you have ears, listen to what the Spirit says to the churches. Whoever wins the victory will not be hurt by the second death.ᵏ

### The Letter to Pergamum

¹²This is what you must write to the angel of the church in Pergamum:

I am the one who has the sharp double-edged sword! Listen to what I say.

¹³I know that you live where Sa-

ᵍ1.18 *keys to death and the world of the dead*: That is, power over death and the world of the dead.  ʰ1.20 *angels*: Perhaps guardian angels that represent the churches, or they may be church leaders or messengers sent to the churches.  ⁱ2.6 *Nicolaitans*: Nothing else is known about these people, though it is possible that they claimed to be followers of Nicolaus from Antioch (see Acts 6.5).  ʲ2.10 *a glorious life*: The Greek text has "a crown of life." In ancient times an athlete who had won a contest was rewarded with a crown of flowers as a sign of victory.  ᵏ2.11 *second death*: The first death is physical death, and the "second death" is eternal death.

tan has his throne.[l] But you have kept true to my name. Right there where Satan lives, my faithful witness Antipas[m] was taken from you and put to death. Even then you did not give up your faith in me.

[14] I do have a few things against you. Some of you are following the teaching of Balaam.[n] Long ago he told Balak to teach the people of Israel to eat food that had been offered to idols and to be immoral. [15] Now some of you are following the teaching of the Nicolaitans.[o] [16] Turn back! If you don't, I will come quickly and fight against these people. And my words will cut like a sword.

[17] If you have ears, listen to what the Spirit says to the churches. To everyone who wins the victory, I will give some of the hidden food.[p] I will also give each one a white stone[q] with a new name[r] written on it. No one will know that name except the one who is given the stone.

### The Letter to Thyatira

[18] This is what you must write to the angel of the church in Thyatira:

I am the Son of God! My eyes are like flames of fire, and my feet are like bronze. Listen to what I say. [19] I know everything about you, including your love, your faith, your service, and how you have endured. I know that you are doing more now than you have ever done before. [20] But I still have something against you because of that woman Jezebel.[s] She calls herself a prophet, and you let her teach and mislead my servants to do immoral things and to eat food offered to idols. [21] I gave her a chance to turn from her sins, but she did not want to stop doing these immoral things.

[22] I am going to strike down Jezebel. Everyone who does these immoral things with her will also be punished, if they don't stop. [23] I will even kill her followers.[t] Then all the churches will see that I know everyone's thoughts and feelings. I will treat each of you as you deserve.

[24] Some of you in Thyatira don't follow Jezebel's teaching. You don't know anything about what her followers call the "deep secrets of Satan." So I won't burden you down with any other commands. [25] But until I come, you must hold firmly to the teaching you have.

[26] I will give power over the nations to everyone who wins the victory and keeps on obeying me until the end. [27-28] I will give each of them the same power that my Father has given me. They will rule the nations with an iron rod and smash those nations to pieces like clay pots. I will also give them the morning star.[u]

[29] If you have ears, listen to what the Spirit says to the churches.

[l]2.13 *where Satan has his throne*: The meaning is uncertain, but it may refer to the city as a center of pagan worship or of Emperor worship.  [m]2.13 *Antipas*: Nothing else is known about this man, who is mentioned only here in the New Testament.  [n]2.14 *Balaam*: According to Numbers 22–24, Balaam refused to disobey the Lord. But in other books of the Old Testament, he is spoken of as evil (see Deuteronomy 23.4, 5; Joshua 13.22; 24.9, 10; Nehemiah 13.2).  [o]2.15 *Nicolaitans*: See the note at 2.6.  [p]2.17 *hidden food*: When the people of Israel were going through the desert, the Lord provided a special food for them. Some of this was placed in a jar and stored in the sacred chest (see Exodus 16). According to later Jewish teaching, the prophet Jeremiah rescued the sacred chest when the temple was destroyed by the Babylonians. He hid the chest in a cave, where it would stay until God came to save his people.  [q]2.17 *white stone*: The meaning of this is uncertain, though it may be the same as a ticket that lets a person into God's banquet where the "hidden food" is eaten. Or it may be a symbol of victory.  [r]2.17 *a new name*: Either the name of Christ or God or the name of the follower who is given the stone.  [s]2.20 *Jezebel*: Nothing else is known about her. This may have been her real name or a name that was given to her because she was like Queen Jezebel, who opposed the Lord (see 1 Kings 19.1, 2; 21.1-26).  [t]2.23 *her followers*: Or "her children."  [u]2.27,28 *the morning star*: Probably thought of as the star that signals the end of night and the beginning of day. In 22.16 Christ is called the "morning star."

### The Letter to Sardis

**3** This is what you must write to the angel of the church in Sardis:

I have the seven spirits of God and the seven stars. Listen to what I say.

I know what you are doing. Everyone may think you are alive, but you are dead. [2] Wake up! You have only a little strength left, and it is almost gone. So try to become stronger. I have found that you are not completely obeying God. [3] Remember the teaching that you were given and that you heard. Hold firmly to it and turn from your sins. If you don't wake up, I will come when you least expect it, just as a thief does.

[4] A few of you in Sardis have not dirtied your clothes with sin. You will walk with me in white clothes, because you are worthy. [5] Everyone who wins the victory will wear white clothes. Their names will not be erased from the book of life,[v] and I will tell my Father and his angels that they are my followers.

[6] If you have ears, listen to what the Spirit says to the churches.

### The Letter to Philadelphia

[7] This is what you must write to the angel of the church in Philadelphia:

I am the one who is holy and true, and I have the keys that belonged to David.[w] When I open a door, no one can close it. And when I close a door, no one can open it. Listen to what I say.

[8] I know everything you have done. And I have placed before you an open door that no one can close. You were not very strong, but you obeyed my message and did not deny that you are my followers.[x] [9] Now you will see what I will do with those people who belong to Satan's group. They claim to be God's people, but they are liars. I will make them come and kneel down at your feet. Then they will know that I love you.

[10] You obeyed my message and endured. So I will protect you from the time of testing that everyone in all the world must go through. [11] I am coming soon. So hold firmly to what you have, and no one will take away the crown that you will be given as your reward.

[12] Everyone who wins the victory will be made into a pillar in the temple of my God, and they will stay there forever. I will write on each of them the name of my God and the name of his city. It is the new Jerusalem that my God will send down from heaven. I will also write on them my own new name.

[13] If you have ears, listen to what the Spirit says to the churches.

### The Letter to Laodicea

[14] This is what you must write to the angel of the church in Laodicea:

I am the one called Amen![y] I am the faithful and true witness and the source[z] of God's creation. Listen to what I say.

[15] I know everything you have done, and you are not cold or hot. I wish you were either one or the other. [16] But since you are lukewarm and neither cold nor hot, I will spit you out of my mouth. [17] You claim to be rich and successful and to have everything you need. But you don't know how bad off you are. You are pitiful, poor, blind, and naked.

[18] Buy your gold from me. It has been refined in a fire, and it will make you rich. Buy white clothes from me. Wear them and you can cover up your shameful nakedness. Buy medicine for your eyes, so that you will be able to see.

[19] I correct and punish everyone I love. So make up your minds to turn away from your sins. [20] Listen! I am standing and knocking at your door. If you hear my voice and open the door, I will come in and we will eat together. [21] Everyone who wins the

---

[v]**3.5** *book of life*: The book in which the names of God's people are written.   [w]**3.7** *the keys that belonged to David*: The keys stand for authority over David's kingdom.   [x]**3.8** *did not deny that you are my followers*: Or "did not say evil things about me."   [y]**3.14** *Amen*: Meaning "Trustworthy."   [z]**3.14** *source*: Or "beginning."

victory will sit with me on my throne, just as I won the victory and sat with my Father on his throne. ²²If you have ears, listen to what the Spirit says to the churches.

## Worship in Heaven

4 After this, I looked and saw a door that opened into heaven. Then the voice that had spoken to me at first and that sounded like a trumpet said, "Come up here! I will show you what must happen next." ²Right then the Spirit took control of me, and there in heaven I saw a throne and someone sitting on it. ³The one who was sitting there sparkled like precious stones of jasper*ᵃ* and carnelian.*ᵇ* A rainbow that looked like an emerald*ᶜ* surrounded the throne.
⁴Twenty-four other thrones were in a circle around that throne. And on each of these thrones there was an elder dressed in white clothes and wearing a gold crown. ⁵Flashes of lightning and roars of thunder came out from the throne in the center of the circle. Seven torches, which are the seven spirits of God, were burning in front of the throne. ⁶Also in front of the throne was something that looked like a glass sea, clear as crystal.
Around the throne in the center were four living creatures covered front and back with eyes. ⁷The first creature was like a lion, the second one was like a bull, the third one had the face of a human, and the fourth was like a flying eagle. ⁸Each of the four living creatures had six wings, and their bodies were covered with eyes. Day and night they never stopped singing,

"Holy, holy, holy is the Lord,
the all-powerful God,
who was and is
and is coming!"

⁹The living creatures kept praising, honoring, and thanking the one who sits on the throne and who lives forever and ever. ¹⁰At the same time the twenty-four elders knelt down before the one sitting on the throne. And as they worshiped the one who lives forever, they placed their crowns in front of the throne and said,

¹¹ "Our Lord and God,
you are worthy
to receive glory,
honor, and power.
You created all things,
and by your decision they are
and were created."

## The Scroll and the Lamb

5 In the right hand of the one sitting on the throne I saw a scroll*ᵈ* that had writing on the inside and on the outside. And it was sealed in seven places. ²I saw a mighty angel ask with a loud voice, "Who is worthy to open the scroll and break its seals?" ³No one in heaven or on earth or under the earth was able to open the scroll or see inside it.
⁴I cried hard because no one was found worthy to open the scroll or see inside it. ⁵Then one of the elders said to me, "Stop crying and look! The one who is called both the 'Lion from the Tribe of Judah'*ᵉ* and 'King David's Great Descendant'*ᶠ* has won the victory. He will open the book and its seven seals."
⁶Then I looked and saw a Lamb standing in the center of the throne that was surrounded by the four living creatures and the elders. The Lamb looked as if it had once been killed. It had seven horns and seven eyes, which are the seven spirits*ᵍ* of God, sent out to all the earth.
⁷The Lamb went over and took the scroll from the right hand of the one

---

ᵃ**4.3** *jasper*: Usually green or clear.  ᵇ**4.3** *carnelian*: Usually deep-red or reddish-white. ᶜ**4.3** *emerald*: A precious stone, usually green.  ᵈ**5.1** *scroll*: A roll of paper or special leather used for writing on. Sometimes a scroll would be sealed on the outside with one or more pieces of wax.  ᵉ**5.5** *'Lion from the Tribe of Judah'*: In Genesis 49.9 the tribe of Judah is called a young lion, and King David was from Judah.  ᶠ**5.5** *'King David's Great Descendant'*: The Greek text has "the root of David" which is a title for the Messiah based on Isaiah 11.1, 10.  ᵍ**5.6** *the seven spirits*: Some manuscripts have "the spirits."

who sat on the throne. [8] After he had taken it, the four living creatures and the twenty-four elders knelt down before him. Each of them had a harp and a gold bowl full of incense, [h] which are the prayers of God's people. [9] Then they sang a new song,

"You are worthy
　　to receive the scroll
and open its seals,
　　because you were killed.
And with your own blood
　　you bought for God
people from every tribe,
　　language, nation, and race.
[10] You let them become kings
　　and serve God as priests,
and they will rule on earth."

[11] As I looked, I heard the voices of a lot of angels around the throne and the voices of the living creatures and of the elders. There were millions and millions of them, [12] and they were saying in a loud voice,

"The Lamb who was killed
　　is worthy to receive power,
riches, wisdom, strength,
　　honor, glory, and praise."

[13] Then I heard all beings in heaven and on the earth and under the earth and in the sea offer praise. Together, all of them were saying,

"Praise, honor, glory,
　　and strength
　　　　forever and ever
to the one who sits
　　on the throne
　　　　and to the Lamb!"

[14] The four living creatures said "Amen," while the elders knelt down and worshiped.

### Opening the Seven Seals

**6** At the same time that I saw the Lamb open the first of the seven seals, I heard one of the four living creatures shout with a voice like thunder. It said, "Come out!" [2] Then I saw a white horse. Its rider carried a bow and was given a crown. He had already won some victories, and he went out to win more.

[3] When the Lamb opened the second seal, I heard the second living creature say, "Come out!" [4] Then another horse came out. It was fiery red. And its rider was given the power to take away all peace from the earth, so that people would slaughter one another. He was also given a big sword.

[5] When the Lamb opened the third seal, I heard the third living creature say, "Come out!" Then I saw a black horse, and its rider had a balance scale in one hand. [6] I heard what sounded like a voice from somewhere among the four living creatures. It said, "A quart of wheat will cost you a whole day's wages! Three quarts of barley will cost you a day's wages too. But don't ruin the olive oil or the wine."

[7] When the Lamb opened the fourth seal, I heard the voice of the fourth living creature say, "Come out!" [8] Then I saw a pale green horse. Its rider was named Death, and Death's Kingdom followed behind. They were given power over one fourth of the earth, and they could kill its people with swords, famines, diseases, and wild animals.

[9] When the Lamb opened the fifth seal, I saw under the altar the souls of everyone who had been killed for speaking God's message and telling about their faith. [10] They shouted, "Master, you are holy and faithful! How long will it be before you judge and punish the people of this earth who killed us?"

[11] Then each of those who had been killed was given a white robe and told to rest for a little while. They had to wait until the complete number of the Lord's other servants and followers would be killed.

[12] When I saw the Lamb open the sixth seal, I looked and saw a great earthquake. The sun turned as dark as sackcloth, [i] and the moon became as red as blood. [13] The stars in the sky fell

---

[h] **5.8** *incense*: A material that produces a sweet smell when burned. Sometimes it is a symbol for the prayers of God's people. [i] **6.12** *sackcloth*: A rough, dark-colored cloth made from goat or camel hair and used to make grain sacks. It was worn in times of trouble or sorrow.

to earth, just like figs shaken loose by a windstorm. [14] Then the sky was rolled up like a scroll,[j] and all mountains and islands were moved from their places.

[15] The kings of the earth, its famous people, and its military leaders hid in caves or behind rocks on the mountains. They hid there together with the rich and the powerful and with all the slaves and free people. [16] Then they shouted to the mountains and the rocks, "Fall on us! Hide us from the one who sits on the throne and from the anger of the Lamb. [17] That terrible day has come! God and the Lamb will show their anger, and who can face it?"

### The 144,000 Are Marked for God

**7** [1-2] After this I saw four angels. Each one was standing on one of the earth's four corners. The angels held back the four winds, so that no wind would blow on the earth or on the sea or on any tree. These angels had also been given the power to harm the earth and the sea. Then I saw another angel come up from where the sun rises in the east, and he was ready to put the mark of the living God on people. He shouted to the four angels, [3] "Don't harm the earth or the sea or any tree! Wait until I have marked the foreheads of the servants of our God."

[4] Then I heard how many people had been marked on the forehead. There were one hundred forty-four thousand, and they came from every tribe of Israel:

[5] 12,000 from Judah,
12,000 from Reuben,
12,000 from Gad,
[6] 12,000 from Asher,
12,000 from Naphtali,
12,000 from Manasseh,
[7] 12,000 from Simeon,
12,000 from Levi,
12,000 from Issachar,
[8] 12,000 from Zebulun,
12,000 from Joseph, and
12,000 from Benjamin.

### People from Every Nation

[9] After this, I saw a large crowd with more people than could be counted. They were from every race, tribe, nation, and language, and they stood before the throne and before the Lamb. They wore white robes and held palm branches in their hands, [10] as they shouted,

"Our God, who sits
  upon the throne,
has the power
to save his people,
  and so does the Lamb."

[11] The angels who stood around the throne knelt in front of it with their faces to the ground. The elders and the four living creatures knelt there with them. Then they all worshiped God [12] and said,

"Amen! Praise, glory, wisdom,
  thanks, honor, power,
and strength belong to our God
  forever and ever! Amen!"

[13] One of the elders asked me, "Do you know who these people are that are dressed in white robes? Do you know where they come from?"
[14] "Sir," I answered, "you must know."
Then he told me:

"These are the ones
who have gone through
  the great suffering.
They have washed their robes
in the blood of the Lamb
  and have made them white.
[15] And so they stand
  before the throne of God
and worship him in his temple
  day and night.
The one who sits on the throne
will spread his tent
  over them.
[16] They will never hunger
  or thirst again,
and they won't be troubled
by the sun
  or any scorching heat.

[j]**6.14** *scroll*: See the note at 5.1.

17 The Lamb in the center
 of the throne
   will be their shepherd.
He will lead them to streams
 of life-giving water,
and God will wipe all tears
 from their eyes."

## The Seventh Seal
## Is Opened

**8** When the Lamb opened the seventh seal, there was silence in heaven for about half an hour. ² I noticed that the seven angels who stood before God were each given a trumpet.

³ Another angel, who had a gold container for incense, *k* came and stood at the altar. This one was given a lot of incense to offer with the prayers of God's people on the gold altar in front of the throne. ⁴ Then the smoke of the incense, together with the prayers of God's people, went up to God from the hand of the angel.

⁵ After this, the angel filled the incense container with fire from the altar and threw it on the earth. Thunder roared, lightning flashed, and the earth shook.

## The Trumpets

⁶ The seven angels now got ready to blow their trumpets.

⁷ When the first angel blew his trumpet, hail and fire mixed with blood were thrown down on the earth. A third of the earth, a third of the trees, and a third of all green plants were burned.

⁸ When the second angel blew his trumpet, something like a great fiery mountain was thrown into the sea. A third of the sea turned to blood, ⁹ a third of the living creatures in the sea died, and a third of the ships were destroyed.

¹⁰ When the third angel blew his trumpet, a great star fell from heaven. It was burning like a torch, and it fell on a third of the rivers and on a third of the springs of water. ¹¹ The name of the star was Bitter, and a third of the

water turned bitter. Many people died because the water was so bitter.

¹² When the fourth angel blew his trumpet, a third of the sun, a third of the moon, and a third of the stars were struck. They each lost a third of their light. So during a third of the day there was no light, and a third of the night was also without light.

¹³ Then I looked and saw a lone eagle flying across the sky. It was shouting, "Trouble, trouble, trouble to everyone who lives on earth! The other three angels are now going to blow their trumpets."

**9** When the fifth angel blew his trumpet, I saw a star *l* fall from the sky to earth. It was given the key to the tunnel that leads down to the deep pit. ² As it opened the tunnel, smoke poured out like the smoke of a great furnace. The sun and the air turned dark because of the smoke. ³ Locusts *m* came out of the smoke and covered the earth. They were given the same power that scorpions have.

⁴ The locusts were told not to harm the grass on the earth or any plant or any tree. They were to punish only those people who did not have God's mark on their foreheads. ⁵ The locusts were allowed to make them suffer for five months, but not to kill them. The suffering they caused was like the sting of a scorpion. ⁶ In those days people will want to die, but they will not be able to. They will hope for death, but it will escape from them.

⁷ These locusts looked like horses ready for battle. On their heads they wore something like gold crowns, and they had human faces. ⁸ Their hair was like a woman's long hair, and their teeth were like those of a lion. ⁹ On their chests they wore armor made of iron. Their wings roared like an army of horse-drawn chariots rushing into battle. ¹⁰ Their tails were like a scorpion's tail with a stinger that had the power to hurt someone for five months. ¹¹ Their king was the angel in charge of the deep pit. In Hebrew his name

---

*k* 8.3 *incense*: See the note at 5.8.   *l* 9.1 *star*: In the ancient world, stars were often thought of as living beings, such as angels.   *m* 9.3 *Locusts*: A type of grasshopper that comes in swarms and causes great damage to crops.

was Abaddon, and in Greek it was Apollyon.[n]

**12** The first horrible thing has now happened! But wait. Two more horrible things will happen soon.

**13** Then the sixth angel blew his trumpet. I heard a voice speak from the four corners of the gold altar that stands in the presence of God. **14** The voice spoke to this angel and said, "Release the four angels who are tied up beside the great Euphrates River." **15** The four angels had been prepared for this very hour and day and month and year. Now they were set free to kill a third of all people.

**16** By listening, I could tell there were more than two hundred million of these war horses. **17** In my vision their riders wore fiery-red, dark-blue, and yellow armor on their chests. The heads of the horses looked like lions, with fire and smoke and sulphur coming out of their mouths. **18** One third of all people were killed by the three terrible troubles caused by the fire, the smoke, and the sulphur. **19** The horses had powerful mouths, and their tails were like poisonous snakes that bite and hurt.

**20** The people who lived through these terrible troubles did not turn away from the idols they had made, and they did not stop worshiping demons. They kept on worshiping idols that were made of gold, silver, bronze, stone, and wood. Not one of these idols could see, hear, or walk. **21** No one stopped murdering or practicing witchcraft or being immoral or stealing.

### The Angel and the Little Scroll

**10** I saw another powerful angel come down from heaven. This one was covered with a cloud, and a rainbow was over his head. His face was like the sun, his legs were like columns of fire, **2** and with his hand he held a little scroll[o] that had been unrolled. He stood there with his right foot on the sea and his left foot on the land. **3** Then he shouted with a voice that sounded like a growling lion. Thunder roared seven times.

**4** After the thunder stopped, I was about to write what it had said. But a voice from heaven shouted, "Keep it secret! Don't write these things."

**5** The angel I had seen standing on the sea and the land then held his right hand up toward heaven. **6** He made a promise in the name of God who lives forever and who created heaven, earth, the sea, and every living creature. The angel said, "You won't have to wait any longer. **7** God told his secret plans to his servants the prophets, and it will all happen by the time the seventh angel sounds his trumpet."

**8** Once again the voice from heaven spoke to me. It said, "Go and take the open scroll from the hand of the angel standing on the sea and the land."

**9** When I went over to ask the angel for the little scroll, the angel said, "Take the scroll and eat it! Your stomach will turn sour, but the taste in your mouth will be as sweet as honey." **10** I took the little scroll from the hand of the angel and ate it. The taste was as sweet as honey, but my stomach turned sour.

**11** Then some voices said, "Keep on telling what will happen to the people of many nations, races, and languages, and also to kings."

### The Two Witnesses

**11** An angel gave me a measuring stick and said:

Measure around God's temple. Be sure to include the altar and everyone worshiping there. **2** But don't measure the courtyard outside the temple building. Leave it out. It has been given to those people who don't know God, and they will trample all over the holy city for forty-two months. **3** My two witnesses will wear sackcloth,[p] while I let them preach for one thousand two hundred sixty days. **4** These two witnesses are the two olive trees and the two lampstands that stand in the presence of the Lord who rules the earth. **5** Any enemy who tries

[n]**9.11** *Abaddon . . . Apollyon*: The Hebrew word "Abaddon" and the Greek word "Apollyon" each mean "destruction." [o]**10.2** *scroll*: See the note at 5.1. [p]**11.3** *sackcloth*: See the note at 6.12.

to harm them will be destroyed by the fire that comes out of their mouths. [6] They have the power to lock up the sky and to keep rain from falling while they are prophesying. And whenever they want to, they can turn water to blood and cause all kinds of terrible troubles on earth.

[7] After the two witnesses have finished preaching God's message, the beast that lives in the deep pit will come up and fight against them. It will win the battle and kill them. [8] Their bodies will be left lying in the streets of the same great city where their Lord was nailed to a cross. And that city is spiritually like the city of Sodom or the country of Egypt.

[9] For three and a half days the people of every nation, tribe, language, and race will stare at the bodies of these two witnesses and refuse to let them be buried. [10] Everyone on earth will celebrate and be happy. They will give gifts to each other, because of what happened to the two prophets who caused them so much trouble. [11] But three and a half days later, God will breathe life into their bodies. They will stand up, and everyone who sees them will be terrified.

[12] The witnesses then heard a loud voice from heaven, saying, "Come up here." And while their enemies were watching, they were taken up to heaven in a cloud. [13] At that same moment there was a terrible earthquake that destroyed a tenth of the city. Seven thousand people were killed, and the rest were frightened and praised the God who rules in heaven.

[14] The second horrible thing has now happened! But the third one will be here soon.

### The Seventh Trumpet

[15] At the sound of the seventh trumpet, loud voices were heard in heaven. They said,

"Now the kingdom
  of this world

belongs to our Lord
  and to his Chosen One!
And he will rule
  forever and ever!"

[16] Then the twenty-four elders, who were seated on thrones in God's presence, knelt down and worshiped him. [17] They said,

"Lord God All-Powerful,
you are and you were,
  and we thank you.
You used your great power
  and started ruling.
[18] When the nations got angry,
  you became angry too!
Now the time has come
for the dead
  to be judged.
It is time for you to reward
  your servants the prophets
and all of your people
who honor your name,
  no matter who they are.
It is time to destroy everyone
who has destroyed
  the earth."

[19] The door to God's temple in heaven was then opened, and the sacred chest [q] could be seen inside the temple. I saw lightning and heard roars of thunder. The earth trembled and huge hailstones fell to the ground.

### The Woman and the Dragon

**12** Something important appeared in the sky. It was a woman whose clothes were the sun. The moon was under her feet, and a crown made of twelve stars was on her head. [2] She was about to give birth, and she was crying because of the great pain.

[3] Something else appeared in the sky. It was a huge red dragon with seven heads and ten horns, and a crown on each of its seven heads. [4] With its tail, it dragged a third of the stars from the sky and threw them down to the earth. Then the dragon turned toward the woman, because it wanted to eat her child as soon as it was born.

[q] **11.19** *sacred chest*: In Old Testament times the sacred chest was kept in the tent used for worship. It was the symbol of God's presence with his people and also of his agreement with them.

⁵ The woman gave birth to a son, who would rule all nations with an iron rod. The boy was snatched away. He was taken to God and placed on his throne. ⁶ The woman ran into the desert to a place that God had prepared for her. There she would be taken care of for one thousand two hundred sixty days.

## Michael Fights the Dragon

⁷ A war broke out in heaven. Michael and his angels were fighting against the dragon and its angels. ⁸ But the dragon lost the battle. It and its angels were forced out of their places in heaven ⁹ and were thrown down to the earth. Yes, that old snake and his angels were thrown out of heaven! That snake, who fools everyone on earth, is known as the devil and Satan. ¹⁰ Then I heard a voice from heaven shout,

"Our God has shown
his saving power,
    and his kingdom has come!
God's own Chosen One
    has shown his authority.
Satan accused our people
in the presence of God
    day and night.
Now he has been thrown out!

¹¹ Our people defeated Satan
    because of the blood*r*
of the Lamb
    and the message of God.
They were willing
    to give up their lives.

¹² The heavens should rejoice,
    together with everyone
        who lives there.
But pity the earth
    and the sea,
because the devil
    was thrown down
        to the earth.
He knows his time is short,
    and he is very angry."

¹³ When the dragon realized that it had been thrown down to the earth, it tried to make trouble for the woman who had given birth to a son. ¹⁴ But the woman was given two wings like those of a huge eagle, so that she could fly into the desert. There she would escape from the snake and be taken care of for a time, two times, and half a time. ¹⁵ The snake then spewed out water like a river to sweep the woman away. ¹⁶ But the earth helped her and swallowed the water that had come from the dragon's mouth. ¹⁷ This made the dragon terribly angry with the woman. So it started a war against the rest of her children. They are the people who obey God and are faithful to what Jesus did and taught. ¹⁸ The dragon*s* stood on the beach beside the sea.

## The Two Beasts

**13** I looked and saw a beast coming up from the sea. This one had ten horns and seven heads, and a crown was on each of its ten horns. On each of its heads were names that were an insult to God. ² The beast that I saw had the body of a leopard, the feet of a bear, and the mouth of a lion. The dragon handed over its own power and throne and great authority to this beast. ³ One of its heads seemed to have been fatally wounded, but now it was well. Everyone on earth marveled at this beast, ⁴ and they worshiped the dragon who had given its authority to the beast. They also worshiped the beast and said, "No one is like this beast! No one can fight against it."

⁵ The beast was allowed to brag and claim to be God, and for forty-two months it was allowed to rule. ⁶ The beast cursed God, and it cursed the name of God. It even cursed the place where God lives, as well as everyone who lives in heaven with God. ⁷ It was allowed to fight against God's people and defeat them. It was also given authority over the people of every tribe, nation, language, and race. ⁸ The beast was worshiped by everyone whose name wasn't written before the time of creation in the book of the Lamb who was killed.*t*

<sup>9</sup> If you have ears,
  then listen!
<sup>10</sup> If you are doomed
  to be captured,
    you will be captured.
  If you are doomed
    to be killed by a sword,
  you will be killed
    by a sword.

This means that God's people must learn to endure and be faithful!

<sup>11</sup> I now saw another beast. This one came out of the ground. It had two horns like a lamb, but spoke like a dragon. <sup>12</sup> It worked for the beast whose fatal wound had been healed. And it used all its authority to force the earth and its people to worship that beast. <sup>13</sup> It worked mighty miracles, and while people watched, it even made fire come down from the sky.

<sup>14</sup> This second beast fooled people on earth by working miracles for the first one. Then it talked them into making an idol in the form of the beast that did not die after being wounded by a sword. <sup>15</sup> It was allowed to put breath into the idol, so that it could speak. Everyone who refused to worship the idol of the beast was put to death. <sup>16</sup> All people were forced to put a mark on their right hand or forehead. Whether they were powerful or weak, rich or poor, free people or slaves, <sup>17</sup> they all had to have this mark, or else they could not buy or sell anything. This mark stood for the name of the beast and for the number of its name.

<sup>18</sup> You need wisdom to understand the number of the beast! But if you are smart enough, you can figure this out. Its number is six hundred sixty-six, and it stands for a person.

## The Lamb and His 144,000 Followers

**14** I looked and saw the Lamb standing on Mount Zion! <sup>u</sup> With him were a hundred forty-four thousand, who had his name and his Father's name written on their foreheads. <sup>2</sup> Then I heard a sound from heaven that was like a roaring flood or loud thunder or even like the music of harps. <sup>3</sup> And a new song was being sung in front of God's throne and in front of the four living creatures and the elders. No one could learn that song, except the one hundred forty-four thousand who had been rescued from the earth. <sup>4</sup> All of these are pure virgins, and they follow the Lamb wherever he leads. They have been rescued to be presented to God and the Lamb as the most precious people <sup>v</sup> on earth. <sup>5</sup> They never tell lies, and they are innocent.

## The Messages of the Three Angels

<sup>6</sup> I saw another angel. This one was flying across the sky and had the eternal good news to announce to the people of every race, tribe, language, and nation on earth. <sup>7</sup> The angel shouted, "Worship and honor God! The time has come for him to judge everyone. Kneel down before the one who created heaven and earth, the oceans, and every stream."

<sup>8</sup> A second angel followed and said, "The great city of Babylon has fallen! This is the city that made all nations drunk and immoral. Now God is angry, and Babylon has fallen."

<sup>9</sup> Finally, a third angel came and shouted:

Here is what will happen if you worship the beast and the idol and have the mark of the beast on your hand or forehead. <sup>10</sup> You will have to drink the wine that God gives to everyone who makes him angry. You will feel his mighty anger, and you will be tortured with fire and burning sulphur, while the holy angels and the Lamb look on.

<sup>11</sup> If you worship the beast and the idol and accept the mark of its name, you will be tortured day and night. The smoke from your torture will go up forever and ever, and you will never be able to rest.

<sup>12</sup> God's people must learn to endure. They must also obey his commands and have faith in Jesus.

---

<sup>u</sup> **14.1** *Mount Zion*: Another name for Jerusalem.   <sup>v</sup> **14.4** *the most precious people*: The Greek text has "the first people." The Law of Moses taught that the first-born of all animals and the first part of the harvest were special and belonged to the Lord.

13 Then I heard a voice from heaven say, "Put this in writing. From now on, the Lord will bless everyone who has faith in him when they die."

The Spirit answered, "Yes, they will rest from their hard work, and they will be rewarded for what they have done."

### The Earth Is Harvested

14 I looked and saw a bright cloud, and someone who seemed to be the Son of Man[w] was sitting on the cloud. He wore a gold crown on his head and held a sharp sickle[x] in his hand. 15 An angel came out of the temple and shouted, "Start cutting with your sickle! Harvest season is here, and all crops on earth are ripe." 16 The one on the cloud swung his sickle and harvested the crops.

17 Another angel with a sharp sickle then came out of the temple in heaven. 18 After this, an angel with power over fire came from the altar and shouted to the angel who had the sickle. He said, "All grapes on earth are ripe! Harvest them with your sharp sickle." 19 The angel swung his sickle on earth and cut off its grapes. He threw them into a pit[y] where they were trampled on as a sign of God's anger. 20 The pit was outside the city, and when the grapes were mashed, blood flowed out. The blood turned into a river that was about two hundred miles long and almost deep enough to cover a horse.

### The Last of the Terrible Troubles

15 After this, I looked at the sky and saw something else that was strange and important. Seven angels were bringing the last seven terrible troubles. When these are ended, God will no longer be angry.

2 Then I saw something that looked like a glass sea mixed with fire, and people were standing on it. They were the ones who had defeated the beast and the idol and the number that tells the name of the beast. God had given

them harps, 3 and they were singing the song that his servant Moses and the Lamb had sung. They were singing,

"Lord God All-Powerful,
you have done great
  and marvelous things.
You are the ruler
  of all nations,
and you do what is
  right and fair.
4 Lord, who doesn't honor
  and praise your name?
You alone are holy,
and all nations will come
  and worship you,
because you have shown
that you judge
  with fairness."

5 After this, I noticed something else in heaven. The sacred tent used for a temple was open. 6 And the seven angels who were bringing the terrible troubles were coming out of it. They were dressed in robes of pure white linen and wore belts made of pure gold. 7 One of the four living creatures gave each of the seven angels a bowl made of gold. These bowls were filled with the anger of God who lives forever and ever. 8 The temple quickly filled with smoke from the glory and power of God. No one could enter it until the seven angels had finished pouring out the seven last troubles.

### The Bowls of God's Anger

16 From the temple I heard a voice shout to the seven angels, "Go and empty the seven bowls of God's anger on the earth."

2 The first angel emptied his bowl on the earth. At once ugly and painful sores broke out on everyone who had the mark of the beast and worshiped the idol.

3 The second angel emptied his bowl on the sea. Right away the sea turned into blood like that of a dead person, and every living thing in the sea died.

w 14.14 *Son of Man*: See the note at 1.13.  x 14.14 *sickle*: A knife with a long curved blade, used to cut grain and other crops.  y 14.19 *pit*: It was the custom to put grapes in a pit (called a wine press) and stomp on them to make juice that would later turn to wine.

4 The third angel emptied his bowl into the rivers and streams. At once they turned to blood. 5 Then I heard the angel, who has power over water, say,

"You have always been,
and you always will be
   the holy God.
You had the right
   to judge in this way.
6 They poured out the blood z
of your people
   and your prophets.
So you gave them blood
   to drink, as they deserve!"
7 After this, I heard
   the altar shout,
"Yes, Lord God All-Powerful,
your judgments are honest
   and fair."

8 The fourth angel emptied his bowl on the sun, and it began to scorch people like fire. 9 Everyone was scorched by its great heat, and all of them cursed the name of God who had power over these terrible troubles. But no one turned to God and praised him.

10 The fifth angel emptied his bowl on the throne of the beast. At once darkness covered its kingdom, and its people began biting their tongues in pain. 11 And because of their painful sores, they cursed the God who rules in heaven. But still they did not stop doing evil things.

12 The sixth angel emptied his bowl on the great Euphrates River, and it completely dried up to make a road for the kings from the east. 13 An evil spirit that looked like a frog came out of the mouth of the dragon. One also came out of the mouth of the beast, and another out of the mouth of the false prophet. 14 These evil spirits had the power to work miracles. They went to every king on earth, to bring them together for a war against God All-Powerful. But that will be the day of God's great victory.

15 Remember that Christ says, "When I come, it will surprise you like a thief! But God will bless you, if you are awake and ready. Then you won't have to walk around naked and be ashamed."

16 Those armies came together in a place that in Hebrew is called Armagedon. a

17 As soon as the seventh angel emptied his bowl in the air, a loud voice from the throne in the temple shouted, "It's done!" 18 There were flashes of lightning, roars of thunder, and the worst earthquake in all history. 19 The great city of Babylon split into three parts, and the cities of other nations fell. So God made Babylon drink from the wine cup that was filled with his anger. 20 Every island ran away, and the mountains disappeared. 21 Hailstones, weighing about a hundred pounds each, fell from the sky on people. Finally, the people cursed God, because the hail was so terrible.

### The Prostitute and the Beast

17 One of the seven angels who had emptied the bowls came over and said to me, "Come on! I will show you how God will punish that shameless prostitute who sits on many oceans. 2 Every king on earth has slept with her, and her shameless ways are like wine that has made everyone on earth drunk."

3 With the help of the Spirit, the angel took me into the desert, where I saw a woman sitting on a red beast. The beast was covered with names that were an insult to God, and it had seven heads and ten horns. 4 The woman was dressed in purple and scarlet robes, and she wore jewelry made of gold, precious stones, and pearls. In her hand she held a gold cup filled with the filthy and nasty things she had done. 5 On her forehead a mysterious name was written:

I AM THE GREAT CITY OF
BABYLON, THE MOTHER
OF EVERY IMMORAL AND FILTHY
THING ON EARTH.

---

z 16.6 *They poured out the blood*: A way of saying, "They murdered." a 16.16 *Armagedon*: The Hebrew form of the name would be "Har Megeddo," meaning "Hill of Megeddo," where many battles were fought in ancient times (see Judges 5.19; 2 Kings 23.29, 30).

6 I could tell that the woman was drunk on the blood of God's people who had given their lives for Jesus. This surprising sight amazed me, 7 and the angel said:

Why are you so amazed? I will explain the mystery about this woman and about the beast she is sitting on, with its seven heads and ten horns. 8 The beast you saw is one that used to be and no longer is. It will come back from the deep pit, but only to be destroyed. Everyone on earth whose names were not written in the book of life b before the time of creation will be amazed. They will see this beast that used to be and no longer is, but will be once more.

9 Anyone with wisdom can figure this out. The seven heads that the woman is sitting on stand for seven hills. These heads are also seven kings. 10 Five of the kings are dead. One is ruling now, and the other one has not yet come. But when he does, he will rule for only a little while.

11 You also saw a beast that used to be and no longer is. That beast is one of the seven kings who will return as the eighth king, but only to be destroyed.

12 The ten horns that you saw are ten more kings, who have not yet come into power, and they will rule with the beast for only a short time. 13 They will all think alike and will give their power and authority to the beast. 14 These kings will go to war against the Lamb. But he will defeat them, because he is Lord over all lords and King over all kings. His followers are chosen and special and faithful.

15 The oceans that you saw the prostitute sitting on are crowds of people from all races and languages. 16 The ten horns and the beast will start hating the shameless woman. They will strip off her clothes and leave her naked. Then they will eat her flesh and throw the rest of her body into a fire. 17 God is the one who made these kings all think alike and decide to give their power to the beast. And they will do this until what God has said comes true.

18 The woman you saw is the great city that rules over all kings on earth.

## The Fall of Babylon

**18** I saw another angel come from heaven. This one had great power, and the earth was bright because of his glory. 2 The angel shouted,

"Fallen! Powerful Babylon
   has fallen
and is now the home
   of demons.
It is the den
   of every filthy spirit
and of all unclean birds,
and every dirty
   and hated animal.
3 Babylon's evil and immoral wine
   has made all nations drunk.
Every king on earth
   has slept with her,
and every merchant on earth
is rich because of
   her evil desires."

4 Then I heard another voice
   from heaven shout,
"My people, you must escape
   from Babylon.
Don't take part in her sins
   and share her punishment.
5 Her sins are piled
   as high as heaven.
God has remembered the evil
   she has done.
6 Treat her as she
   has treated others.
Make her pay double
   for what she has done.
Make her drink twice as much
of what she mixed
   for others.
7 That woman honored herself
   with a life of luxury.
Reward her now
   with suffering and pain.

"Deep in her heart
Babylon said,
   'I am the queen!

b **17.8** *book of life*: See the note at 3.5.

Never will I be a widow
or know what it means
   to be sad.'
8 And so, in a single day
she will suffer the pain
   of sorrow, hunger, and death.
Fire will destroy
   her dead body,
because her judge
   is the powerful Lord God."

9 Every king on earth who slept with her and shared in her luxury will mourn. They will weep, when they see the smoke from that fire. 10 Her sufferings will frighten them, and they will stand at a distance and say,

"Pity that great
   and powerful city!
Pity Babylon!
In a single hour
   her judgment has come."

11 Every merchant on earth will mourn, because there is no one to buy their goods. 12 There won't be anyone to buy their gold, silver, jewels, pearls, fine linen, purple cloth, silk, scarlet cloth, sweet-smelling wood, fancy carvings of ivory and wood, as well as things made of bronze, iron, or marble. 13 No one will buy their cinnamon, spices, incense, myrrh, frankincense,c wine, olive oil, fine flour, wheat, cattle, sheep, horses, chariots, slaves, and other humans.

14 Babylon, the things
   your heart desired
have all escaped
   from you.
Every luxury
and all your glory
   will be lost forever.
You will never
   get them back.

15 The merchants had become rich because of her. But when they saw her sufferings, they were terrified. They stood at a distance, crying and mourning. 16 Then they shouted,

"Pity the great city
   of Babylon!

She dressed in fine linen
and wore purple
   and scarlet cloth.
She had jewelry
   made of gold
and precious stones
   and pearls.
17 Yet in a single hour
   her riches disappeared."

Every ship captain and passenger and sailor stood at a distance, together with everyone who does business by traveling on the sea. 18 When they saw the smoke from her fire, they shouted, "This was the greatest city ever!"
19 They cried loudly, and in their sorrow they threw dust on their heads, as they said,

"Pity the great city
   of Babylon!
Everyone who sailed the seas
became rich
   from her treasures.
But in a single hour
   the city was destroyed.
20 The heavens should be happy
with God's people
   and apostles and prophets.
God has punished her
   for them."

21 A powerful angel then picked up a huge stone and threw it into the sea. The angel said,

"This is how the great city
   of Babylon
will be thrown down,
   never to rise again.
22 The music of harps and singers
and of flutes and trumpets
   will no longer be heard.
No workers will ever
   set up shop in that city,
and the sound
of grinding grain
   will be silenced forever.
23 Lamps will no longer shine
   anywhere in Babylon,
and couples will never again
   say wedding vows there.
Her merchants ruled
   the earth,

c 18.13 myrrh, frankincense: Myrrh was a valuable sweet-smelling powder often used in perfume. Frankincense was a valuable powder that was burned to make a sweet smell.

and by her witchcraft
    she fooled all nations.
²⁴ On the streets of Babylon
    is found the blood
    of God's people
    and of his prophets,
    and everyone else."

**19** After this, I heard what sounded like a lot of voices in heaven, and they were shouting,

"Praise the Lord!
To our God belongs
    the glorious power to save,
² because his judgments
    are honest and fair.
That filthy prostitute
    ruined the earth
    with shameful deeds.
But God has judged her
    and made her pay
the price for murdering
    his servants."

³ Then the crowd shouted,

"Praise the Lord!
Smoke will never stop rising
    from her burning body."

⁴ After this, the twenty-four elders and the four living creatures all knelt before the throne of God and worshiped him. They said, "Amen! Praise the Lord!"

### The Marriage Supper of the Lamb

⁵ From the throne a voice said,

"If you worship
    and fear our God,
give praise to him,
    no matter who you are."

⁶ Then I heard what seemed to be a large crowd that sounded like a roaring flood and loud thunder all mixed together. They were saying,

"Praise the Lord!
Our Lord God All-Powerful
    now rules as king.
⁷ So we will be glad and happy
    and give him praise.
The wedding day of the Lamb

is here,
    and his bride is ready.
⁸ She will be given
    a wedding dress
made of pure
    and shining linen.
This linen stands for
    the good things
God's people have done."

⁹ Then the angel told me, "Put this in writing. God will bless everyone who is invited to the wedding feast of the Lamb." The angel also said, "These things that God has said are true." ¹⁰ I knelt at the feet of the angel and began to worship him. But the angel said, "Don't do that! I am a servant, just like you and everyone else who tells about Jesus. Don't worship anyone but God. Everyone who tells about Jesus does it by the power of the Spirit."

### The Rider on the White Horse

¹¹ I looked and saw that heaven was open, and a white horse was there. Its rider was called Faithful and True, and he is always fair when he judges or goes to war. ¹² He had eyes like flames of fire, and he was wearing a lot of crowns. His name was written on him, but he was the only one who knew what the name meant.

¹³ The rider wore a robe that was covered with*ᵈ* blood, and he was known as "The Word of God." ¹⁴ He was followed by armies from heaven that rode on horses and were dressed in pure white linen. ¹⁵ From his mouth a sharp sword went out to attack the nations. He will rule them with an iron rod and will show the fierce anger of God All-Powerful by trampling the grapes in the pit where wine is made. ¹⁶ On the part of the robe that covered his thigh was written, "KING OF KINGS AND LORD OF LORDS."

¹⁷ I then saw an angel standing on the sun, and he shouted to all the birds flying in the sky, "Come and join in God's great feast! ¹⁸ You can eat the flesh of kings, rulers, leaders, horses, riders,

*ᵈ19.13 covered with:* Some manuscripts have "sprinkled with."

free people, slaves, important people, and everyone else."

¹⁹ I also saw the beast and all kings of the earth come together. They fought against the rider on the white horse and against his army. ²⁰ But the beast was captured and so was the false prophet. This is the same prophet who had worked miracles for the beast, so that he could fool everyone who had the mark of the beast and worshiped the idol. The beast and the false prophet were thrown alive into a lake of burning sulphur. ²¹ But the rest of their army was killed by the sword that came from the mouth of the rider on the horse. Then birds stuffed themselves on the dead bodies.

## The Thousand Years

**20** I saw an angel come down from heaven, carrying the key to the deep pit and a big chain. ² He chained the dragon for a thousand years. It is that old snake, who is also known as the devil and Satan. ³ Then the angel threw the dragon into the pit. He locked and sealed it, so that a thousand years would go by before the dragon could fool the nations again. But after that, it would have to be set free for a little while.

⁴ I saw thrones, and sitting on those thrones were the ones who had been given the right to judge. I also saw the souls of the people who had their heads cut off because they had told about Jesus and preached God's message. They were the same ones who had not worshiped the beast or the idol, and they had refused to let its mark be put on their hands or foreheads. They will come to life and rule with Christ for a thousand years.

⁵⁻⁶ These people are the first to be raised to life, and they are especially blessed and holy. The second death$^e$ has no power over them. They will be priests for God and Christ and will rule with them for a thousand years.

No other dead people were raised to life until a thousand years later.

## Satan Is Defeated

⁷ At the end of the thousand years, Satan will be set free. ⁸ He will fool the countries of Gog and Magog, which are at the far ends of the earth, and their people will follow him into battle. They will have as many followers as there are grains of sand along the beach, ⁹ and they will march all the way across the earth. They will surround the camp of God's people and the city that his people love. But fire will come down from heaven and destroy the whole army. ¹⁰ Then the devil who fooled them will be thrown into the lake of fire and burning sulphur. He will be there with the beast and the false prophet, and they will be in pain day and night forever and ever.

## The Judgment at the Great White Throne

¹¹ I saw a great white throne with someone sitting on it. Earth and heaven tried to run away, but there was no place for them to go. ¹² I also saw all the dead people standing in front of that throne. Every one of them was there, no matter who they had once been. Several books were opened, and then the book of life$^f$ was opened. The dead were judged by what those books said they had done.

¹³ The sea gave up the dead people who were in it, and death and its kingdom also gave up their dead. Then everyone was judged by what they had done. ¹⁴ Afterwards, death and its kingdom were thrown into the lake of fire. This is the second death.$^g$ ¹⁵ Anyone whose name wasn't written in the book of life was thrown into the lake of fire.

## The New Heaven and the New Earth

**21** I saw a new heaven and a new earth. The first heaven and the first earth had disappeared, and so had the sea. ² Then I saw New Jerusalem, that holy city, coming down from God in heaven. It was like a bride dressed

$^e$**20.5,6** *second death:* See the note at 2.11.   $^f$**20.12** *book of life:* See the note at 3.5.
$^g$**20.14** *second death:* See the note at 2.11.

in her wedding gown and ready to meet her husband.

³ I heard a loud voice shout from the throne:

God's home is now with his people. He will live with them, and they will be his own. Yes, God will make his home among his people. ⁴ He will wipe all tears from their eyes, and there will be no more death, suffering, crying, or pain. These things of the past are gone forever.

⁵ Then the one sitting on the throne said:

I am making everything new. Write down what I have said. My words are true and can be trusted. ⁶ Everything is finished! I am Alpha and Omega,ʰ the beginning and the end. I will freely give water from the life-giving fountain to everyone who is thirsty. ⁷ All who win the victory will be given these blessings. I will be their God, and they will be my people.

⁸ But I will tell you what will happen to cowards and to everyone who is unfaithful or dirty-minded or who murders or is sexually immoral or uses witchcraft or worships idols or tells lies. They will be thrown into that lake of fire and burning sulphur. This is the second death.ⁱ

### The New Jerusalem

⁹ I saw one of the seven angels who had the bowls filled with the seven last terrible troubles. The angel came to me and said, "Come on! I will show you the one who will be the bride and wife of the Lamb." ¹⁰ Then with the help of the Spirit, he took me to the top of a very high mountain. There he showed me the holy city of Jerusalem coming down from God in heaven.

¹¹ The glory of God made the city bright. It was dazzling and crystal clear like a precious jasper stone. ¹² The city had a high and thick wall with twelve gates, and each one of them was guarded by an angel. On each of the gates was written the name of one of the twelve tribes of Israel. ¹³ Three of these gates were on the east, three were on the north, three more were on the south, and the other three were on the west. ¹⁴ The city was built on twelve foundation stones. On each of the stones was written the name of one of the Lamb's twelve apostles.

¹⁵ The angel who spoke to me had a gold measuring stick to measure the city and its gates and its walls. ¹⁶ The city was shaped like a cube, because it was just as high as it was wide. When the angel measured the city, it was about fifteen hundred miles high and fifteen hundred miles wide. ¹⁷ Then the angel measured the wall, and by our measurements it was about two hundred sixteen feet high.

¹⁸ The wall was built of jasper, and the city was made of pure gold, clear as crystal. ¹⁹ Each of the twelve foundations was a precious stone. The first was jasper,ʲ the second was sapphire, the third was agate, the fourth was emerald, ²⁰ the fifth was onyx, the sixth was carnelian, the seventh was chrysolite, the eighth was beryl, the ninth was topaz, the tenth was chrysoprase, the eleventh was jacinth, and the twelfth was amethyst. ²¹ Each of the twelve gates was a solid pearl. The streets of the city were made of pure gold, clear as crystal.

²² I did not see a temple there. The Lord God All-Powerful and the Lamb were its temple. ²³ And the city did not need the sun or the moon. The glory of God was shining on it, and the Lamb was its light.

²⁴ Nations will walk by the light of that city, and kings will bring their riches there. ²⁵ Its gates are always open during the day, and night never comes. ²⁶ The glorious treasures of nations will be brought into the city. ²⁷ But nothing unworthy will be allowed to

ʰ21.6 *Alpha and Omega*: See the note at 1.8. ⁱ21.8 *second death*: See the note at 2.11. ʲ21.19 *jasper*: The precious and semi-precious stones mentioned in verses 19, 20 are of different colors. *Jasper* is usually green or clear; *sapphire* is blue; *agate* has circles of brown and white; *emerald* is green; *onyx* has different bands of color; *carnelian* is deepred or reddish-white; *chrysolite* is olive-green; *beryl* is green or bluish-green; *topaz* is yellow; *chrysoprase* is apple-green; *jacinth* is reddish-orange; and *amethyst* is deep purple.

enter. No one who is dirty-minded or who tells lies will be there. Only those whose names are written in the Lamb's book of life[k] will be in the city.

**22** The angel showed me a river that was crystal clear, and its waters gave life. The river came from the throne where God and the Lamb were seated. [2] Then it flowed down the middle of the city's main street. On each side of the river are trees[l] that grow a different kind of fruit each month of the year. The fruit gives life, and the leaves are used as medicine to heal the nations.

[3] God's curse will no longer be on the people of that city. He and the Lamb will be seated there on their thrones, and its people will worship God [4] and will see him face to face. God's name will be written on the foreheads of the people. [5] Never again will night appear, and no one who lives there will ever need a lamp or the sun. The Lord God will be their light, and they will rule forever.

### The Coming of Christ

[6] Then I was told:

These words are true and can be trusted. The Lord God controls the spirits of his prophets, and he is the one who sent his angel to show his servants what must happen right away. [7] Remember, I am coming soon! God will bless everyone who pays attention to the message of this book.

[8] My name is John, and I am the one who heard and saw these things. Then after I had heard and seen all this, I knelt down and began to worship at the feet of the angel who had shown it to me.

[9] But the angel said,

Don't do that! I am a servant, just like you. I am the same as a follower or a prophet or anyone else who obeys what is written in this book. God is the one you should worship.

[10] Don't keep the prophecies in this book a secret. These things will happen soon.

[11] Evil people will keep on being evil, and everyone who is dirty-minded will still be dirty-minded. But good people will keep on doing right, and God's people will always be holy.

[12] Then I was told:

I am coming soon! And when I come, I will reward everyone for what they have done. [13] I am Alpha and Omega,[m] the first and the last, the beginning and the end.

[14] God will bless all who have washed their robes. They will each have the right to eat fruit from the tree that gives life, and they can enter the gates of the city. [15] But outside the city will be dogs, witches, immoral people, murderers, idol worshipers, and everyone who loves to tell lies and do wrong.

[16] I am Jesus! And I am the one who sent my angel to tell all of you these things for the churches. I am David's Great Descendant,[n] and I am also the bright morning star.[o]

[17] The Spirit and the bride say, "Come!"

Everyone who hears this[p] should say, "Come!"

If you are thirsty, come! If you want life-giving water, come and take it. It's free!

[18] Here is my warning for everyone who hears the prophecies in this book:

If you add anything to them, God will make you suffer all the terrible troubles written in this book. [19] If you take anything away from these prophecies, God will not let you have part in the life-giving tree and in the holy city described in this book.

[20] The one who has spoken these things says, "I am coming soon!"

So, Lord Jesus, please come soon!

[21] I pray that the Lord Jesus will be kind to all of you.

---

k21.27 *book of life*: See the note at 3.5.   l22.2 *trees*: The Greek has "tree," which is used in a collective sense of trees on both sides of the heavenly river.   m22.13 *Alpha and Omega*: See the note at 1.8.   n22.16 *David's Great Descendant*: See the note at 5.5.   o22.16 *the bright morning star*: Probably thought of as the brightest star (see 2.27, 28).   p22.17 *who hears this*: The reading of the book of Revelation in a service of worship.

# APPENDICES

## A MINI DICTIONARY OF THE BIBLE

## MAPS

## SPECIAL READER'S HELPS

# A Mini Dictionary for the Bible

This dictionary is divided into 21 sections. The indexes below list all of the sections, and all of the entries in alphabetical order, so that you can find what you are looking for more easily.

## Section Index

## Alphabetical Index

## 1. A Few Basics

**CEV** The *Contemporary English Version* of the Bible.

**Old Testament** This first part of the Bible is made up of the 39 books from Genesis through Malachi. They were written mostly in Hebrew, with a few passages in Aramaic.

**New Testament** This second part of the Bible is made up of the 27 books from Matthew through Revelation. They were written in Greek.

**Chapter and Verse Numbers** These numbers were not part of the original books, but were added hundreds of years later as a way to refer to specific parts of the books of Scripture. For example, Genesis 1.3 means "the book of Genesis, chapter 1, verse 3." Genesis 2.4, 5 means "the book of Genesis, chapter 2, verses 4 through 5." And Genesis 1–2 means, "the book of Genesis, chapters 1 through 2." A few books are so short that they were not divided into chapters, and so these books only have verse numbers. In the text of the CEV, sometimes verse numbers have been combined, for example, 3-4. One reason verse numbers might be combined is that contemporary English says things in a different order than ancient Greek and Hebrew, and so two or more verses are sometimes blended together in the CEV translation. And in lists, the verse numbers are sometimes combined into a single heading to avoid confusion. But all the meaning from the original Greek and Hebrew has been carefully included in the CEV text.

## 2. Scriptures, Manuscripts

**Ancient Translations** The Old Testament was translated into Greek over the period 250–150 B.C. Later, the whole Bible was translated into Latin, Syriac, and some other languages. These ancient translations can sometimes show what the Hebrew or Greek text said at the time they were translated, and so the CEV notes will sometimes refer to them.

**Commandments** God's rules for his people to live by. The most famous are the Ten Commandments (see Exodus 20.1-17; Deuteronomy 5.6-21).

**Dead Sea Scrolls** Manuscripts found near the Dead Sea from 1947–1954. They date from about 250 B.C. to A.D. 68. These manuscripts include at least some parts of nearly all Old Testament books.

**God's Law** God's rules for his people to live by. They are found in the Old Testament, especially in the first five books.

**Law and the Prophets** A term used in New Testament times to refer to the sacred writings of the Jews. The Law and the Prophets were two of the three sections of the Old Testament, but the expression sometimes refers to the entire Old Testament.

**Law of Moses** and **Law of the Lord** Usually refers to the first five books of the Old Testament, but sometimes to the entire Old Testament.

**Manuscript**  In ancient times, all books were copied by hand. A copy made this way is called "a manuscript."

**Proverb**  A wise saying that is short and easy to remember.

**Psalm**  A Hebrew poem. Psalms were often written in such a way that they could be prayed or sung by an individual or a group. Some of the psalms thank and praise God, while others ask God to take away sins or to give protection, comfort, vengeance, or mercy.

**Samaritan Hebrew Text**  The Hebrew text of Genesis through Deuteronomy used and preserved by the Samaritans (see also "Samaria"). This text uses forms of letters and many spellings that are different from the Standard Hebrew Text. It has traditionally been called "the Samaritan Pentateuch."

**Scriptures**  Although this term now refers to the whole Bible, in the New Testament it refers to the Old Testament.

**Standard Hebrew Text**  The Hebrew text that is found in most Hebrew manuscripts of the Old Testament. Almost all of these manuscripts were copied after A.D. 900 (but see also "Dead Sea Scrolls").

**Wisdom**  Often refers to the common sense and practical skill needed to solve everyday problems, but sometimes involves trying to find answers to the hard questions about the meaning of life.

### 3. Languages

**Aramaic**  A language closely related to Hebrew. In New Testament times Aramaic was spoken by many Jews including Jesus. Ezra 4.8—6.18; 7.12-26; and Daniel 2.4b—7.28 were written in Aramaic.

**Greek**  The language used throughout the Mediterranean world in New Testament times, and the language in which the New Testament was written.

**Hebrew**  The language used by most of the people of Israel until the Exile. But after the people returned, more and more people spoke Aramaic instead. Most of the Old Testament was written in Hebrew.

### 4. People

**Aaron**  The brother of Moses. Only he and his descendants were to serve as priests and offer sacrifices for the people of Israel (see Exodus 4.14-16; 28.1; Numbers 16.1—18.7).

**Abel**  The second son of Adam and Eve and the younger brother of Cain. Abel was killed by Cain after God accepted Abel's offering and refused to accept Cain's (see Genesis 4.1-11).

**Abraham**  The first of the three great ancestors of the people of Israel. Abraham was the husband of Sarah and the father of Isaac. At first Abraham's name was Abram, meaning "Great Father." Then, when Abram was ninety-nine years old, God changed Abram's name to Abraham, which means "Father of a Crowd." Abraham trusted God, and so God promised that Abraham and his wife Sarah would have a son and more descendants than could be counted. God also promised that Abraham would be a blessing to everyone on earth (see Genesis 12.1-7; 17.1—18.15).

**Abram**  See "Abraham."

**Adam**  The first man and the husband of Eve (see Genesis 1.26—3.21).

**Agrippa**  (1) Herod Agrippa was king of Judea A.D. 41–44 and mistreated Christians (see Acts 12.1-5). (2) Agrippa II was the son of Herod Agrippa and ruled parts of Palestine from A.D. 53 to A.D. 93 or later. He and his sister Bernice listened to Paul defend himself (see Acts 25.13-26, 32).

*Antipas* (1) Herod Antipas, son of Herod the Great (see "Herod"). (2) An otherwise unknown Christian at Pergamum, who was killed because he was a follower of Christ (see Revelation 2.13).

*Augustus* A title meaning "honored," which was given to Octavian by the Romans when he began ruling the Roman world in 27 B.C. He was the Roman Emperor when Jesus was born.

*Cain* The first son of Adam and Eve; Cain killed his brother Abel after God accepted Abel's offering and refused to accept Cain's (see Genesis 4.1-17).

*David* King of Israel from about 1010–970 B.C. David was the most famous king Israel ever had, and many of the people of Israel hoped that one of his descendants would always be their king (see 1 Samuel 16–30; 2 Samuel; 1 Kings 12).

*Esau* The older son of Isaac and Rebekah, and the brother of Jacob. Esau was also known as Edom and as the ancestor of the Edomites (see Genesis 25.20-34; 26.34-46; 32.1—33.16).

*Eve* The first woman and the wife of Adam (see Genesis 1.26—3.21).

*Felix* The Roman governor of Palestine A.D. 52–60, who listened to Paul speak and kept him in jail (see Acts 23.24—24.27).

*Festus* The Roman governor after Felix, who sent Paul to stand trial in Rome (see Acts 24.27—26.32).

*Hagar* A slave of Sarah, the wife of Abraham. When Sarah could not have any children, she followed the ancient custom of letting her husband have a child by Hagar, her slave. The boy's name was Ishmael (see Genesis 16; 21.8-21).

*Herod* (1) Herod the Great was the king of all Palestine 37–4 B.C., and so he was king at the time Jesus was born (see the note at "A.D."). (2) Herod Antipas was the son of Herod the Great and was the ruler of Galilee 4 B.C.–A.D. 39. (3) Herod Agrippa I, the grandson of Herod the Great, ruled Palestine A.D. 41–44.

*Isaac* The second of the three great ancestors of the people of Israel. He was the son of Abraham and Sarah, and he was the father of Esau and Jacob.

*Ishmael* The son of Abraham and Hagar.

*Israel* See "Jacob."

*Jacob* The third great ancestor of the people of Israel. Jacob was the son of Isaac and Rebekah, and his name was changed to Israel when he struggled with God at Peniel near the Jabbok River (see Genesis 32.22-32).

*Joseph* A son of Jacob and Rachel. Joseph was sold as a slave by his brothers, but later he became governor of Egypt (see Genesis 37.12-36; 41.1-57).

*Lot* A nephew of Abraham and the ancestor of the Moabites and Ammonites (see Genesis 11.27; 13.1-13; 18.16—19.38).

*Noah* When God destroyed the world by a flood, Noah and his family were kept safe in a big boat that God had told him to build (see Genesis 6–8).

*Rebekah* The wife of Isaac, and the mother of Jacob and Esau (see Genesis 24.1-67; 25.19-28).

*Sarah* The wife of Abraham and the mother of Isaac. At first her name was Sarai, but when she was old, God promised her that she would have a son, and he changed her name to Sarah. Both names mean "princess" (see 11.29-30; 17.15-19; 18.9-15; 21.1-7).

*Solomon* A son of King David and Bathsheba. After David's death, Solomon ruled Israel about 970–931 B.C. Solomon built the temple in Jerusalem and was widely known for his wisdom. The Hebrew text indicates that he wrote many of the proverbs and two of the psalms.

## 5. Prophets

**Anna**  A woman prophet who stayed in the temple night and day. Soon after Jesus was born, Mary and Joseph took him to the temple and presented him to the Lord, and Anna talked about the child Jesus to everyone who hoped for Jerusalem to be set free (see Luke 2.36-38).

**Balaam**  A foreign prophet. Balaam was hired by the king of Moab to put a curse on Israel, but instead Balaam blessed Israel (see Numbers 22–24).

**Deborah**  A prophet and judge who helped lead Israel to defeat King Jabin of Hazor (see Judges 4–5).

**Elijah**  A prophet who spoke for God in the early ninth century B.C. and who opposed the evil King Ahab and Queen Jezebel of the northern kingdom. Many Jews in later centuries thought Elijah would return to get everything ready for the day of judgment or for the coming of the Messiah (see 1 Kings 17–21; 2 Kings 1–2; Malachi 4.1-6; Matthew 17.10, 11; Mark 9.11, 12).

**Elisha**  A prophet who assisted Elijah and later took his place. Elisha spoke for God in the late ninth century B.C., and was the prophet who healed Naaman (see 1 Kings 19.19-21; 2 Kings 2–9; 13.14-21).

**Huldah**  A prophet who spoke for God during the late seventh century B.C. After *The Book of God's Law* was found in the temple, King Josiah asked her what the Lord wanted him to do (see 2 Kings 22.14-20).

**Micaiah**  The prophet who told King Ahab that he would die in battle against the Syrian army (see 1 Kings 22.5-38).

**Moses**  The prophet who led the people of Israel when God rescued them from slavery in Egypt. Moses also received laws from God and gave them to Israel (see Exodus 2–12; 19–24; Numbers 12.68).

**Prophesy**  To speak as a prophet (see "Prophet").

**Prophet**  Someone who speaks God's message, which at times included telling what would happen in the future. Sometimes when the Spirit of God took control of prophets, they lost some or all control over their speech and actions or were not aware of what was happening around them.

## 6. Twelve Tribes of Israel

The Bible speaks of all the people in a tribe as having descended from one of the twelve sons of Jacob. The tribes of Ephraim and Manasseh were a little different, because the people in those tribes descended from the two sons of Joseph, who was one of Jacob's sons. That would make a total of thirteen tribes, but the Bible always counts only twelve. In some passages Ephraim and Manasseh are counted as one tribe, and in other passages the Levi tribe is left out, probably because they were designated for priestly service to all the tribes, and as such, were scattered throughout the land belonging to the other tribes. People from other nations were sometimes allowed to become Israelites (see Exodus 12.38; Deuteronomy 23.1-8; and the book of Ruth), and these people would then belong to one of the tribes.

**Asher**  Occupied land along the Mediterranean coast from Mount Carmel to the border with the city of Tyre.

**Benjamin**  Occupied land between Bethel and Jerusalem. When the northern tribes of Israel broke away following the death of Solomon, only the tribes of Benjamin and Judah were left to form the southern kingdom.

**Dan**  First occupied land west of Judah, Benjamin, and Ephraim. But after the Philistines took control of this area, part of the tribe then moved to the northernmost area of Israel.

**Ephraim**  One of the largest tribes. Ephraim occupied the land north of Benjamin and south of West Manasseh.

343

**Gad**  Occupied land east of the Jordan River from the northern end of the Dead Sea north to the Jabbok River.

**Issachar**  Occupied land southwest of Lake Galilee.

**Judah**  Occupied the hill country west of the Dead Sea. When the ten northern tribes of Israel broke away following the death of Solomon, only the tribes of Judah and Benjamin were left to form the southern kingdom, and it was also called "Judah."

**Levi**  The men of this tribe were to be the special servants of the Lord at the sacred tent and later at the temple, and so the people of this tribe were not given tribal land. Instead, they were given towns scattered throughout the other twelve tribes (see also "Levite").

**Manasseh**  Occupied two areas of land: (1) East Manasseh lived east of the Jordan River and north of the Jabbok River in the areas of Bashan and northern Gilead. (2) West Manasseh lived west of the Jordan River and to the north of Ephraim.

**Naphtali**  Occupied land north and west of Lake Galilee.

**Reuben**  Occupied land east of the Dead Sea, from the Arnon River in the south to the northern end of the Dead Sea.

**Simeon**  Occupied land southwest of Judah, and was later practically absorbed into Judah.

**Zebulun**  Occupied land north of Manasseh from the eastern end of Mount Carmel to Mount Tabor.

## 7. Christ's Twelve Apostles

**Apostle**  A person chosen and sent by Christ to take his message to others. Lists of the names of Christ's twelve apostles can be found in Matthew 10.2-4; Mark 3.16-19; Luke 6.14-16; Acts 1.12, 13. Later, others such as Paul and James the brother of Jesus also became known as apostles.

**Simon**  also known as Peter or Cephas

**Andrew**  Simon Peter's brother

**James**  the son of Zebedee

**John**  the son of Zebedee (James and John were also known as "Thunderbolts")

**Philip**  from Bethsaida, the hometown of Simon and Andrew

**Bartholomew**  mentioned in all New Testament lists of the apostles, but nowhere else.

**Thomas**  also known as "The Twin"

**Matthew**  also known as Levi

**James**  the son of Alphaeus

**Thaddeus**  also known as Judas or Jude the son of James

**Simon**  also known as "the Eager One"

**Judas Iscariot**  who betrayed Jesus

**Matthias**  who was chosen to replace Judas Iscariot

## 8. Groups of People, Cities, Nations

**Amalekites**  A nomadic nation living mostly in the area south and east of the Dead Sea. They were enemies of Israel.

**Ammon**  A nation that lived east of Israel. According to Genesis 19.30-38, the people of Ammon descended from Lot, a nephew of Abraham.

**Amorites**  Usually a name for all the non-Israelite nations who lived in Canaan, but in some passages it may refer to one nation scattered in several areas of Canaan.

*Anakim*  Perhaps a group of very large people who lived in Palestine before the Israelites (see Numbers 13.33 and Deuteronomy 2.10, 11, 20, 21).

*Asia*  A Roman province in what is today the nation of Turkey.

*Assyria*  An empire of Old Testament times, whose capital city Nineveh was located in what is today northern Iraq. In 722 B.C. Assyria conquered the kingdom of Israel and took many Israelites as captives. The Assyrians then forced people from other parts of its empire to settle on Israel's land (see 2 Kings 18.9-12).

*Avvites*  A nation that lived along the Mediterranean seacoast before the Philistines came and took their land. The Avvites who survived lived south of the Philistines.

*Babylonia*  A large empire of Old Testament times, whose capital city Babylon was located in south-central Mesopotamia. The Babylonians defeated the southern kingdom of Judah in 586 B.C. and forced many of its people to live in Babylonia (see 2 Kings 25.1-12).

*Canaanites*  The nations who lived in Canaan before the Israelites. Many Canaanites continued to live there even after the Israelites came.

*Cush*  The Hebrew form for Ethiopia (see "Ethiopia" below).

*Disciples*  Those who were followers of Jesus and learned from him. The term often refers to his twelve apostles.

*Edomites*  A nation living in Edom or Seir, an area south and southeast of the Dead Sea. According to Genesis 36.1-43, the Edomites descended from Esau, Jacob's brother.

*Empire*  A number of kingdoms ruled by one strong military power.

*Epicureans*  People who followed the teachings of a man named Epicurus, who taught that happiness should be the main goal in life.

*Ethiopia*  A region south of Egypt that included parts of the present countries of Ethiopia and Sudan.

*Exiles*  Israelites who were taken away as prisoners to Babylonia (see also "Exile").

*Gentiles*  Those people who are not Jews.

*Girgashites*  One of the nations that lived in Canaan before the Israelites.

*Hebrew*  An older term for "Israelite" or "Jewish."

*Hittites*  A nation whose capital city was located in what is now Turkey. The Hittites had an empire that at times controlled some kingdoms in Canaan before 1200 B.C., and many Hittites remained in Canaan even after the Israelites came.

*Hivites*  A nation that lived in Canaan before the Israelites, probably related to the Horites.

*Horites*  A nation that lived in Canaan before the Israelites. The Horites were also known as "Hurrians."

*Israel*  (1) The nation made up of the twelve tribes descended from Jacob (see Section 6, "Twelve Tribes of Israel"). (2) The northern kingdom, after the northern tribes broke away following the death of Solomon (see 1 Kings 12.1-20).

*Jebusites*  A group of Canaanite people who lived at Jebus, also known as Jerusalem (see 2 Samuel 5.6-10).

*Jews*  A name first used in referring to someone belonging to the tribe of Judah. Later, the term came to be used of any Israelite.

*Kadesh*  A town in the desert of Paran southwest of the Dead Sea, near the southern border of Israel and the western border of Edom. Israel camped at Kadesh while the twelve tribal leaders explored Canaan (see Numbers 13–14).

**Levites**  Those Israelites who belonged to the tribe of Levi. God chose the men of one Levite family, the descendants of Aaron, to be Israel's priests. The other men from this tribe helped with the work in the sacred tent and later in the temple (see Numbers 3.5-10).

**Medes**  A nation that lived in what is today northwest Iran. Their kingdom, called "Media," later became one of the most important provinces of the Persian Empire, and Persian laws were referred to as the laws of the Medes and Persians (see Esther 1.19; Daniel 6.8, 12, 15).

**Midianites**  A nomadic nation who lived mainly in the desert along the eastern shore of the Gulf of Aqaba.

**Moab**  A nation that lived east of the Dead Sea. According to Genesis 19.30-38, the people of Moab descended from Lot, the nephew of Abraham.

**Nazarenes**  A name that was sometimes used for the followers of Jesus, who came from the small town of Nazareth (see Acts 24.5).

**Perizzites**  A nation that lived in the central hill country of Canaan, before the Israelites.

**Persia**  A large empire of Old Testament times, whose capital was located in what is now southern Iran. It is sometimes called "the Medo-Persian Empire," because of the importance of the province of Media.

**Pharisees**  A group of Jews who thought they could best serve God by strictly obeying the laws of the Old Testament as well as their own rules, traditions, and teachings.

**Philistines**  The land along the Mediterranean coast controlled by the Philistine people was called "Philistia." There were five main cities, each with its own ruler: Ashdod, Ashkelon, Ekron, Gath, and Gaza. The Philistines were often at war with Israel.

**Phoenicia**  The territory along the Mediterranean Sea controlled by the cities of Tyre, Sidon, Arvad, and Byblos. The coast of modern Lebanon covers about the same area.

**Rapha**  Perhaps a group of very large people who lived in Palestine before the Israelites (see Deuteronomy 2.11, 20).

**Roman Empire**  Controlled the area around the Mediterranean Sea in New Testament times. Its capital was Rome.

**Sadducees**  A small and powerful group of Jews in New Testament times. They were closely connected with the high priests and accepted only the first five books of the Old Testament as their Bible. They also did not believe in life after death.

**Samaria**  (1) The capital city of the northern kingdom of Israel beginning with the rule of King Omri (ruled 885-874 B.C.). (2) In New Testament times, a district between Judea and Galilee, named for the city of Samaria. The people of this district, called "Samaritans," worshiped God differently from the Jews, and these two groups refused to have anything to do with one another.

**Sidon**  See "Phoenicia."

**Stoics**  Followers of a man named Zeno, who taught that people should learn self-control and be guided by their consciences.

**Tyre**  See "Phoenicia."

## 9. Places

**Bashan**  The flat highlands and wooded hills of southern Syria. Bashan was just north of the region of Gilead and was known for its fat cattle and fine grain.

**Canaan** The area now covered by Israel plus Gaza, the West Bank of Jordan, Lebanon, and southern Syria (see Numbers 34.1-12). Many passages use the term to refer only to the area south of Lebanon.

**Gethsemane** A garden or olive orchard on the Mount of Olives (see "Mount of Olives").

**Gilead** A region east of the Jordan River. Moab lay to the south of Gilead, and Bashan was to the north.

**Hinnom Valley** A valley west and south of Jerusalem, where human sacrifice was sometimes made in Old Testament times (see "Molech").

**Mount of Olives** A mountain just east of Jerusalem, across Kidron Valley from the temple. Gethsemane, a place where Jesus and his disciples often went to pray, was on this mountain, and so were the villages of Bethany, Bethphage, and Bahurim (see Matthew 26.36; Mark 14.32; Luke 22.39; John 18.1, 2).

**Palestine** The area now covered by Israel, Gaza, and Jordan.

**Peniel** A place near the Jabbok River where Jacob wrestled with God. Then God changed Jacob's name to Israel (see Genesis 32.22-32).

**Zion** Another name for Jerusalem. Zion can also refer to the hill in Jerusalem where the temple was built.

## 10. Objects

**Chariot** A two-wheeled cart that was open at the back and that was pulled by horses.

**Cistern** A hole or pit used for storing rainwater. Cisterns were sometimes dug in the ground and lined with stones and plaster, and at other times they were cut into the rock. The CEV sometimes translates "cistern" as "well."

**Cross** A device used by the Romans to put people to death. It was made of two pieces of lumber crossed in a "T," "†," or "X" shape.

**Piece of Silver** In the Old Testament, this usually refers to an amount of silver weighing about 0.4 oz. Coins were not invented until late Old Testament times, so when silver or gold was used to buy things, it was weighed. In traditional translations this amount is called "a shekel." Silver and gold were worth more in biblical times than they are today.

**Sackcloth** A rough, dark-colored cloth made from goat or camel hair. Sackcloth was usually used to make grain sacks, but clothing made from it was worn in times of trouble or sorrow.

**Scroll** A roll of paper or special thin leather used for writing on.

**Scepter** A decorated rod, often made of gold, that a king held in his hand as a symbol of royal power.

**Sling** A weapon used to throw rocks a little smaller than a tennis ball. A sling was made of a piece of leather that wrapped almost around the rock and had a leather strap at each end. The person would hold the ends of the straps and swing the sling around and around. When the person let go of one strap, the rock would fly out of the sling.

**Tomb** A burial place, often made by cutting a small room out of the rock.

## 11. Festivals and Holy Days

Many of these festivals are still celebrated by Jewish people.

**Festival of Shelters** A festival in the early fall celebrating the period of forty years when the people of Israel walked through the desert and lived in small shelters. This happy celebration began on the fifteenth day of Tishri, and for the next seven days, the people lived in small shelters made of tree branches. The name of this festival in Hebrew is "Sukkoth."

**Festival of Thin Bread**  A seven-day festival right after Passover. During this festival the Israelites ate a thin, flat bread made without yeast to remind themselves how God freed the people of Israel from slavery in Egypt and made them into a nation. The name of this festival in Hebrew is "Mazzoth."

**Festival of Trumpets**  See "New Moon Festival."

**Great Day of Forgiveness**  The tenth day of Tishri in the early fall. On this one day of the year, the high priest was allowed to go into the most holy part of the temple and sprinkle some of the blood of a sacrificed bull on the sacred chest. This was done so that the people's sins would be forgiven. In English this holy day has traditionally been called "the Day of Atonement," and its name in Hebrew is "Yom Kippur."

**Harvest Festival**  See "Pentecost."

**New Moon Festival**  A religious festival held on the day of the new moon, the day when only a thin edge of the moon can be seen. This day was always the first day of the month for the Hebrew calendar. The New Moon Festival was a time for rest from work, and a time for worship, sacrifices, celebration, and eating. The New Moon Festival in the month of Tishri in the early fall was also called "the Festival of Trumpets," and it involved even more sacrifices.

**Passover**  A festival held on the fourteenth day of Abib in the early spring. At Passover the Israelites celebrated the time God rescued them from slavery in Egypt. The name of this festival in Hebrew is "Pesach."

**Pentecost**  A Jewish festival held in mid-spring, fifty days after Passover. At this festival Israelites celebrated the wheat harvest. Pentecost was also known as "the Harvest Festival" and has traditionally been called "the Feast of Weeks"; in Hebrew, its name is "Shavuoth."

**Festival of Purim**  A Jewish festival on the fourteenth and fifteenth of Adar, near the end of winter, when the Jews celebrated how they were saved from Haman, the evil prime minister of Persia who wanted to have them killed (see Esther 9.20-32).

**Sabbath**  The seventh day of the week, from sunset on Friday to sunset on Saturday. Israelites worshiped on the Sabbath and rested from their work in obedience to the third commandment.

**Temple Festival**  In 165 B.C. the Jewish people recaptured the temple in Jerusalem from their enemies and made it fit for worship again. They celebrated this event each year by an eight-day festival that began on the twenty-fifth day of the month of Chislev in the late fall. This festival is traditionally called "the Festival of Dedication," or in Hebrew, "Hanukkah."

## 12. Sacrifice, Temple, Worship

**Altar**  A raised structure where sacrifices and offerings were presented to God or to pagan gods. Altars could be made of rocks, packed earth, metal, or pottery.

**Amen**  A Hebrew word used after a prayer or a blessing and meaning that what had been said was right and true.

**Fire Pan**  A metal pan used for burning incense or carrying hot coals from the altar.

**God's Tent**  See "Sacred Tent."

**High Priest**  See "Priest."

**Holy Place**  The main room of the sacred tent and of the temple. This room contained the sacred bread, the golden incense altar, and the golden lamp stand. A curtain or wall separated the holy place from the most holy place. A priest would go into the holy place once each morning and evening to burn incense on the golden altar (see also "Most Holy Place").

**Incense** A material that makes a sweet smell when burned. It was used in the worship of God.

**Local Shrine** See "Place of Worship."

**Most Holy Place** The inner room of the sacred tent and of the temple. In the sacred tent this room contained only the sacred chest; in Solomon's temple, the most holy place also held statues of winged creatures. Only the high priest could enter the most holy place, and even he could enter it only once a year on the Great Day of Forgiveness. The most holy place has traditionally been called "the holy of holies."

**Offerings** See "Sacrifices."

**Place of Worship** A place to worship God or pagan gods. These places were often on a hill outside of a town and have traditionally been called "high places." In the CEV they are sometimes called "local shrines."

**Priest** A man who led the worship in the sacred tent or in the temple and who offered sacrifices. Some of the more important priests were called "chief priests," and the most important priest was called the "high priest."

**Sacred Chest** The chest or box that contained the two flat stones with the Ten Commandments written on them. The chest was covered with gold, and two golden statues of winged creatures were on the lid of the chest. These winged creatures and the chest represented God's throne on earth. Two wooden poles, one on each side, were put through rings at the corners of the chest, so that the Levites could carry the chest without touching it. The chest was kept in the most holy place (see Exodus 25.10-22).

**Sacred Tent** The tent where the people of Israel worshiped God before the temple was built. It has traditionally been called "the tabernacle" (see Exodus 26).

**Sacrifices** These gifts to God included certain animals, grains, fruits, and sweet-smelling spices. Israelites offered sacrifices to give thanks to God, to ask for his forgiveness and his blessing, and to make a payment for a wrong. Some sacrifices were completely burned on the altar. In the case of other sacrifices, a portion was given to the Lord and burned on the altar, then the rest was eaten by the priests or the worshipers who had offered the sacrifice.

**Sacrifices To Ask the Lord's Blessing** Traditionally called "peace offerings" or "offerings of well-being." A main purpose was to ask for the Lord's blessing, and so in the CEV they are sometimes called "sacrifices to ask the Lord's blessing" (see Leviticus 3).

**Sacrifices To Give Thanks to the Lord** Traditionally called "grain offerings." A main purpose of such sacrifices was to thank the Lord with a gift of grain, and so in the CEV they are sometimes called "sacrifices to give thanks to the Lord" (see Leviticus 2).

**Sacrifices To Make Things Right** Traditionally called "guilt offerings." A main purpose was to make things right when a person had cheated someone or the Lord. These sacrifices were also made when a person had broken certain religious rules (see Leviticus 5.14—6.7).

**Sacrifices To Please the Lord** Traditionally called "whole burnt offerings" because the whole animal was burned on the altar. While these sacrifices did involve forgiveness for sin, a main purpose was to please the Lord with the smell of the smoke from the sacrifice, and so in the CEV they are often called "sacrifices to please the Lord" (see Leviticus 1).

*Snuffer* A small tool used for putting out the flame of an oil lamp, or for trimming off the charred part of the wick.

*Temple* A building used as a place of worship. The god that was worshiped in a particular temple was believed to be present there in a special way. The LORD's temple was in Jerusalem.

## 13. Customs

*Ashes* People put ashes, dust, or dirt on their heads, or they rolled in ash piles or dust or dirt, as a way of showing sorrow.

*Circumcise* To cut off the foreskin from the male organ. This was done for Israelite boys eight days after they were born. God commanded that all newborn Israelite boys be circumcised to show that they belonged to his people (see Genesis 17.9-14).

*Clean* and *Unclean* (1) In Old Testament times, a person who was acceptable to worship God was called "clean." A person who had certain kinds of diseases, who had touched a dead body, or who had broken certain laws became "unclean," and was unacceptable to worship God. If a person was unclean because of disease, the disease would have to be cured before the person could be clean again. And becoming clean involved performing certain ceremonies that sometimes included sacrifices. (2) Animals that were acceptable as food were called "clean." Those that were not acceptable were called "unclean" (see Leviticus 11.1-47; Deuteronomy 14.3-21). (3) Many things including tools, dishes, houses, and land could also become unclean and unusable, especially if they were touched by something unclean. Some unclean objects had to be destroyed, but others could be made clean by being washed or placed in a fire for a short time.

*Going without Eating* This was a way of showing sorrow, or of asking for God's help. It is also called "fasting."

*Tearing Clothes* A way of showing sorrow or anger, or of asking for God's help.

## 14. God, Jesus, Angels

*Angel* A supernatural being who tells God's messages to people or protects those who belong to God.

*Christ* A Greek word meaning "the Chosen One" and used to translate the Hebrew word "Messiah." In New Testament times, many of the Jews believed that God was going to send the Messiah to set them free from the power of their enemies. The term "Christ" is used in the New Testament both as a title and as a name for Jesus.

*Eternal Life* Life that is the gift of God and that never ends.

*Glory* Something seen, heard, or felt that shows a person or thing is important, wonderful, or powerful. When God appeared to people, his glory was often seen as a bright light or as fire and smoke. Jesus' glory was seen when he performed miracles, when he was lifted up on the cross, and when he was raised from death.

*God's Kingdom* God's rule over people, both in this life and in the next.

*Holy One* A name for the Savior that God had promised to send (see "Savior").

*Kingdom of Heaven* See "God's kingdom."

*LORD* In the Old Testament the word "LORD" in capital letters stands for the Hebrew consonants YHWH, the personal name of God. Ancient Hebrew did not have vowel letters, and so anyone reading Hebrew would have to know what vowels to put with the consonants. It is not known for certain what vowel sounds were originally used with the consonants YHWH. The word

"Lord" represents the Hebrew term *Adonai*, the usual word for "lord." By late Old Testament times, Jews considered God's personal name too holy to be pronounced. So they said *Adonai*, "Lord," whenever they read *YHWH*. When the Jewish scribes first translated the Hebrew Scriptures into ancient Greek, they translated the personal name of God as *Kurios*, "Lord." Since that time, most translations, including the *Contemporary English Version*, have followed their example and have avoided using the personal name of God.

**Messiah**   See "Christ."

**Promised One**   A title for the Savior that God promised to send (see "Savior").

**Save**   To rescue people from the power of their enemies or from the power of evil, and to give them new life and place them under God's care (see also "Savior").

**Savior**   The one that God has chosen to rescue or save his people (see also "Save").

**Sin**   Turning away from God and disobeying the teachings or commandments of God.

**Son of Man**   A title often used by Jesus to refer to himself. This title is also found in the Hebrew text of Daniel 7.13 and Psalm 8.4, and God uses it numerous times in the book of Ezekiel to refer to Ezekiel.

**Way**   In the book of Acts the Christian life is sometimes called "the Way" or "the Way of the Lord" or "God's Way."

**Winged Creature**   These supernatural beings represented the presence of God and supported his throne in Ezekiel 1.4-25; 10.1-22. Statues of winged creatures were on top of the sacred chest, and larger ones were in the most holy place in the temple built by Solomon. Wood carvings of winged creatures decorated the inside walls and doors of the temple, and figures of winged creatures were woven into the curtain separating the holy place from the most holy place in the sacred tent. The traditional term for winged creature is "cherub" (or "cherubim" for more than one).

## 15. Foreign Gods, Fortunetellers, Evil Spirits

**Astarte**   A Canaanite goddess. Those who worshiped her believed that she gave them fertile land and many children, and that she helped their animals give birth to lots of young.

**Baal**   A Canaanite god. The Canaanites believed that Baal was the most powerful of all the gods.

**Dagon**   The chief god of the Philistines.

**Demons** and **Evil Spirits**   Supernatural beings that do harmful things to people and sometimes cause them to do bad things. In the New Testament they are sometimes called "unclean spirits," because people under their power were thought to be unclean and unfit to worship God.

**Devil**   The chief of the demons and evil spirits, also known as "Satan."

**Evil Spirits**   See "Demons."

**Fortuneteller**   Fortunetellers thought they could learn secrets or learn about the future by doing such things as watching the flight of birds, looking at the livers of animals, and rolling dice.

**Hermes**   The Greek god of skillful speaking and the messenger of the other Greek gods.

**Molech** or **Milcom**   The national god of the Ammonites. Some Israelites offered human sacrifices to Molech in Hinnom Valley near Jerusalem.

**Satan**   See "Devil."

**Zeus**   The chief god of the Greeks.

## 16. Plants, Animals, and Farming

*Acacia*  A flowering tree that produces a hard, durable wood. The sacred chest, the altars, and certain other wooden objects in the sacred tent were made of acacia wood.

*Aloes*  A sweet-smelling spice that was mixed with myrrh and used as a perfume.

*Barley*  A grain that was used to make bread.

*Cedar*  A tall tree once common in the Lebanon mountains and used for many of the royal building projects in Jerusalem.

*Cumin*  A plant with small seeds used for seasoning food.

*Flax*  The stalks of flax plants were harvested, soaked in water, and dried. Then their fibers were separated and spun into thread, which was woven to make linen cloth.

*Hyssop*  A bush with clusters of small branches. In religious ceremonies, hyssop was sometimes dipped in a liquid and then used to sprinkle people or objects.

*Jackal*  A wild desert animal related to wolves, but smaller.

*Leviathan*  A legendary sea monster representing revolt and evil, also known from Canaanite writings.

*Locust*  A type of grasshopper that comes in huge swarms and causes great damage to plant life.

*Mint*  A garden plant used for seasoning and medicine.

*Mustard*  A large plant with very small seeds, which were ground up and used as a spice.

*Myrrh*  A valuable sweet-smelling powder used in perfume.

*Pomegranate*  A reddish fruit with a hard rind. Figures of pomegranates were used as decorations on the high priest's robe and in the temple.

*Reed*  Several kinds of tall plants related to the grass family can be called "reeds." Some varieties are hollow, and some grow in shallow water. The stems were strong and could be up to 18 feet long and 3 inches across at the base.

*Rue*  A garden plant used for seasoning and medicine.

*Threshing*  The process of separating grain from its husks. Grain was spread out at a "threshing place," a flat area of stone or packed earth. People or animals walked on the grain or dragged heavy boards across it to remove the husks. Then the grain and husks were tossed into the air with a special shovel called a "threshing fork." The wind would blow the light husks away, but the heavy grain would fall back to the surface of the threshing place.

*Wine-pit*  A hollow place cut into the rock where the juice was squeezed from grapes to make wine.

*Yoke*  A strong, heavy, wooden collar that fit around the neck of an ox, so that the ox could pull a plow or a cart.

## 17. Society and Its Leaders

*Citizen*  A person who is given special rights and privileges by a nation or state. In return, a citizen was expected to be loyal to that nation or state.

*Council*  (1) A group of leaders who meet and make decisions for their people. (2) The Old Testament refers to God's council as a group of angels who meet and talk with God in heaven.

*Elders*  Men whose age and wisdom made them respected leaders.

*Emperor*  The person who ruled an empire.

**Generation**  One way of describing a group of people who live during the same period of time. In the Bible the time of one generation is often understood to be about forty years.

**Judges**  Leaders chosen by the Lord for the people of Israel after the time of Joshua and before the time of the kings.

**Tax Collectors**  See "Taxes."

**Taxes**  Special fees collected by rulers. Taxes are usually part of the value of crops, property, or income. Taxes were collected at markets, city gates, ports, and border crossings. In New Testament times, Jews were hired by the Roman government to collect taxes from other Jews, and these tax collectors were hated by their own people.

## 18. Families, Relatives

**Ancestor**  Someone born earlier in a family line, especially several generations earlier.

**Clan**  A group of families who were related to each other and who often lived close to each other. A group of clans made up a tribe.

**Descendant**  Someone born one or more generations later in a family line.

**Tribe**  A large group of people descended from a common ancestor (see also "Clan" and Section 6, "Twelve Tribes of Israel").

## 19. Events

**Exile**  The time in Israel's history (597–539 B.C.) when the Babylonians took away many of the people of Jerusalem and Judah as prisoners of war and made them live in Babylonia. The northern tribes had been taken away by Assyria in 722 B.C.

**Exodus**  The people of Israel leaving Egypt, led by Moses and Aaron. This event is celebrated each year as Passover.

## 20. Dates

**B.C.**  Before Christ. Used to date events that happened before Christ's birth. "B.C." is used after the number of the year.

**A.D.**  *Anno Domini*, Latin for "In the year of the Lord." Used to date events that happened after Christ's birth. "A.D." is often used before the number of the year.[a]

**931 B.C.**  The nation of Israel split into two parts, Israel, the northern kingdom, and Judah, the southern kingdom.

**722 B.C.**  Samaria, the capital of the northern kingdom, was captured by the Assyrian army.

**586 B.C.**  Jerusalem, the capital of the southern kingdom, was captured by the Babylonian army.

**538 B.C.**  Cyrus of Persia allowed the Jews to return to Judah.

**333 B.C.**  Alexander the Great took control of Palestine.

**323 B.C.**  Palestine was taken over by the Ptolemy, who was one of Alexander's generals and who became the ruler of Egypt after Alexander's death.

[a]Note: The numbering system now in use was developed about A.D. 525. The plan was that the year of Christ's birth would be A.D. 1, and then the years would be numbered before and after. But an error was made in assigning A.D. 1, and by the time the error was discovered, the numbering system could not be changed. And so, the correct year of Christ's birth according to the numbering system is probably about 6 B.C.

*198 B.C.*  Palestine was taken over by the Seleucids, the descendants of one of Alexander's generals. They had been the rulers of Syria since Alexander's death.

*166 B.C.*  The Jews revolted, led by Judas Maccabeus and his brothers.

*63 B.C.*  Rome took control of Palestine.

*37 B.C.*  Herod the Great was appointed king of the Jews by the Roman government.

*6 B.C.*  Jesus was born. (See the note following "A.D." above.)

*A.D. 30* (Or possibly A.D. 33) Jesus died and was raised to life.

### 21. The Hebrew Calendar

*Nisan* or *Abib*   first month, about mid-March to mid-April.

*Iyyar* or *Ziv*   second month about mid-April to mid-May.

*Sivan*   third month, about mid-May to mid-June.

*Tammuz*   fourth month, about mid-June to mid-July.

*Ab*   fifth month, about mid-July to mid-August.

*Elul*   sixth month, about mid-August to mid-September.

*Tishri* or *Ethanim*   seventh month, about mid-September to mid-October.

*Marchesvan* or *Bul*   eighth month, about mid-October to mid-November.

*Chislev*   ninth month, about mid-November to mid-December.

*Tebeth*   tenth month, about mid-December to mid-January.

*Shebat*   eleventh month, about mid-January to mid-February.

*Adar*   twelfth month, about mid-February to mid-March.

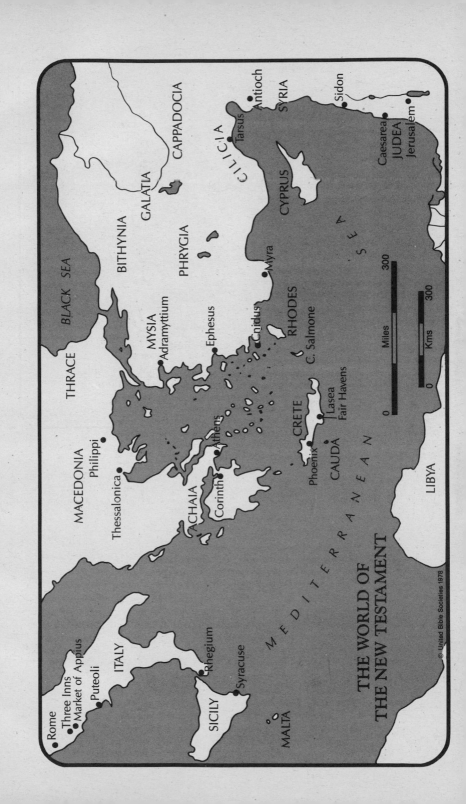

THE WORLD OF
THE NEW TESTAMENT

© United Bible Societies 1978

Antioch
PISIDIA
Iconium
Lystra
Derbe
PAMPHYLIA
CILICIA
Tarsus
Attalia
Perga
LYCIA
Patara
Myra
Seleucia
Antioch
SYRIA
Euphrates R.
CYPRUS
Salamis
Paphos
M E D I T E R R A N E A N

S E A
PHOENICIA
Sidon
Tyre
Damascus
Ptolemais
Caesarea
Samaria
Joppa
Lydda
Jerusalem
Azotus
Gaza
JUDEA

**PALESTINE AND SYRIA**

0     Miles     200

0     Kms     200

Alexandria

© United Bible Societies 1976

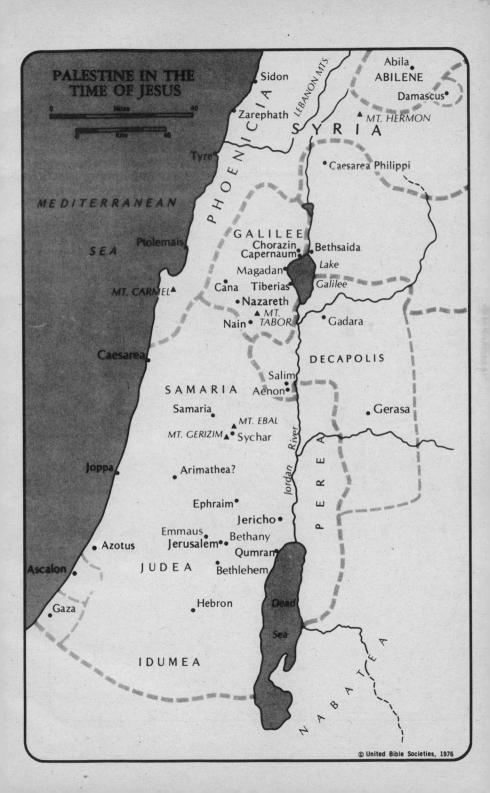

PALESTINE IN THE
TIME OF JESUS

Miles
0          40

Kms
0          40

MEDITERRANEAN

SEA

Sidon

Zarephath

LEBANON MTS.

Abila
ABILENE

Damascus

MT. HERMON

SYRIA

PHOENICIA

Tyre

Caesarea Philippi

Ptolemais

GALILEE
Chorazin
Capernaum          Bethsaida

Magadan                 Lake

MT. CARMEL

Cana    Tiberias           Galilee

Nazareth

Nain        MT.
            TABOR                 Gadara

Caesarea

DECAPOLIS

Salim

SAMARIA     Aenon

Samaria                              Gerasa

MT. EBAL
MT. GERIZIM     Sychar

Jordan River

PEREA

Joppa               Arimathea?

Ephraim

Jericho

Emmaus           Bethany
Azotus   Jerusalem
                 Qumran

JUDEA        Bethlehem

Ascalon

Gaza         Hebron        Dead

                           Sea

IDUMEA

NABATEA

© United Bible Societies, 1976

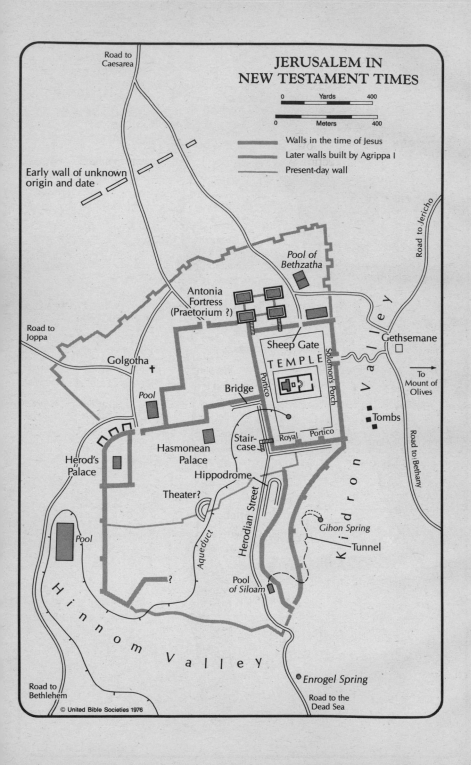

# JERUSALEM IN NEW TESTAMENT TIMES

0 Yards 400

0 Meters 400

Walls in the time of Jesus
Later walls built by Agrippa I
Present-day wall

Road to Caesarea

Early wall of unknown origin and date

Road to Joppa

Road to Jericho

Pool of Bethzatha

Antonia Fortress (Praetorium ?)

Golgotha

Sheep Gate

TEMPLE

Solomon's Porch

Gethsemane

To Mount of Olives

Pool

Bridge

Portico

Tombs

Staircase

Royal Portico

Road to Bethany

Hasmonean Palace

Herod's Palace

Hippodrome

Theater?

Herodian Street

Aqueduct

Pool

?

Gihon Spring

Tunnel

Kidron Valley

Pool of Siloam

Hinnom Valley

Enrogel Spring

Road to Bethlehem

Road to the Dead Sea

© United Bible Societies 1976

# Rejoice!

You have in your hands a message of hope and Good News. It is called the New Testament. It is made up of 27 different books. Each one tells of God's great love and how he has made it possible, through the death and resurrection of Jesus Christ, to unite every person to himself, so that anyone who desires it may discover spiritual guidance and joy.

You are invited to begin reading this Good News today. The section of special helps provided here will help you begin this rewarding journey of discovery.

- *What's in the New Testament* gives you a brief summary of every book in the New Testament along with a handy chart.
- *How to Read the New Testament* provides simple suggestions on how to read the New Testament devotionally and to keep notes on the many lessons you'll learn.
- *Read through the New Testament* is a reading plan that suggests a simple way to read everything the New Testament has to say about Jesus' life, death and resurrection and the spread of the new religion which became known as Christianity.
- *Famous Passages of the New Testament* helps you to quickly locate passages you've heard time and again, but may never have read for yourself.
- *Finding Help in the New Testament* leads you to those passages that can help you when you're facing a difficult problem or special challenge.
- *What the New Testament Says about God's Forgiveness* will lead you to places in the New Testament where you can learn how much God loves each one of us and what he has done to put us right with himself.

So begin your journey of discovery today! Use any one of these special reader's helps to get you started on a daily habit of Scripture reading. And when you finish the New Testament, read the Old Testament, which you will find in any edition of the Bible. Discover for yourself the joy and hope God's Holy Scriptures have to offer.

# The Bible

The New Testament is part of a larger book called the Bible. The word "Bible" comes from the Greek word *biblia*, which means "books." So the Bible is really a collection or library of many books. These books are divided into two main parts, the Old Testament and the New Testament.

## Old Testament

The Old Testament was written in Hebrew and tells the history of the people of Israel. This history is based on their faith in the God of Israel and on their religious life as the people of God. The authors of these books wrote about what God had done for them as a people and how they were to worship and obey God in return. Because most of the authors of the books of the New Testament were Jewish, they were very familiar with the Hebrew Scriptures. The following chart shows the different groups of books that make up the Old Testament. After reading the New Testament you may want to obtain a copy of the Bible so that you can also read these important books.

### The Law
Genesis, Exodus, Leviticus, Numbers, Deuteronomy

### History
Joshua, Judges, Ruth, 1 Samuel, 2 Samuel, 1 Kings, 2 Kings, 1 Chronicles, 2 Chronicles, Ezra, Nehemiah, Esther

### Poetry and Wisdom
Job, Psalms, Proverbs, Ecclesiastes, Song of Songs

### Major Prophets
Isaiah, Jeremiah, Lamentations, Ezekiel, Daniel

### Minor Prophets
Hosea, Joel, Amos, Obadiah, Jonah, Micah, Nahum, Habakkuk, Zephaniah, Haggai, Zechariah, Malachi

## New Testament

The books of the New Testament were written by the followers of Jesus Christ. These followers wanted others to know the Good News about Jesus Christ and the possibility of a "new" life available to them through his death and resurrection. The following chart shows the different groups of books that make up the New Testament. Although scholarly opinion has varied, Paul has traditionally been identified as the author of the letters indicated below.

### The Gospels
Matthew, Mark, Luke, John

### Paul's Letters
Romans, 1 Corinthians, 2 Corinthians, Galatians, Ephesians, Philippians, Colossians, 1 Thessalonians, 2 Thessalonians, 1 Timothy, 2 Timothy, Titus, Philemon

### History
Acts

### General Letters
Hebrews, James, 1 Peter, 2 Peter, 1 John, 2 John, 3 John, Jude

### Prophecy
Revelation

# What's in the New Testament

The following are summaries of each book of the New Testament. It will be obvious from how brief the descriptions are that they are not complete. They should, however, serve as a quick and handy guide to the content of the New Testament. The grouping of the books by sections follows the divisions of the books as they are organized in the English Bible.

## The Gospels

MATTHEW: This Gospel includes many Old Testament quotations, thus appealing to a Jewish audience and presenting Jesus as the Messiah promised in the Hebrew Scriptures. Matthew told the story of Jesus from birth to resurrection and placed emphasis on his teaching.

MARK: Mark wrote a short, action-packed Gospel. He emphasized Jesus' miracles and his life of suffering. His aim was to deepen the faith and commitment of the believers in the community to which he wrote.

LUKE: In this Gospel, the availability of salvation for all people is emphasized. Luke proclaimed this message by showing Jesus' involvement with people who are poor, needy, and on the fringes of society.

JOHN: The Gospel of John stands apart from the others. John organized his message around seven signs that point to Jesus as the Son of God. His writing style is reflective and filled with striking images.

## History

ACTS: When Jesus left his disciples, the Holy Spirit came to abide with them. Written by Luke as the sequel to his Gospel, Acts records key events in the history of the work of the early Christian Church to spread the Gospel throughout the Mediterranean world.

## Paul's Letters

ROMANS: In this important letter, Paul wrote to the Romans about life in the Spirit, which is given to believers in Christ through faith. The apostle tells them about God's great kindness and declares that because of Jesus Christ, God accepts us and sets us free from our sins.

1 CORINTHIANS: This letter deals with the problems the church in Corinth was experiencing: dissension, immorality, public worship, and confusion about spiritual gifts.

1 CORINTHIANS: In this letter, Paul wrote about his relationship with the church of Corinth and the effects of certain false apostles on his ministry.

GALATIANS: This letter addresses freedom from the law through Christ. Paul declares that it is by faith that all who believe are put right with God.

EPHESIANS: A central theme to this letter is that God's eternal purpose is to bring together from many nations and peoples the universal Church of Jesus Christ.

PHILIPPIANS: This letter emphasizes the joy found in any situation when a person believes in Christ. Paul wrote it while in prison.

COLOSSIANS: In this letter Paul tells the people of Colossae to make Christ the center of their faith and to put aside their superstitions.

1 THESSALONIANS: In this letter Paul gives advice to the people of Thessalonica concerning Christ's return.

2 THESSALONIANS: This letter discusses the same topics as the first. Paul teaches the people a way to be ready for the Lord.

1 TIMOTHY: This letter served as a guide for Timothy, a young leader in the church. It contains advice about worship, ministry, and relationships within the church.

2 TIMOTHY: This is Paul's last letter. In it he offers a final challenge to his co-worker.

TITUS: Titus was ministering in Crete. In this letter, Paul gave him advice on how to help Christians follow Christ.

PHILEMON: In this letter, Philemon is urged to forgive his runaway slave, Onesimus, and accept him as a friend in Christ.

## General Letters

HEBREWS: The letter to the Hebrews challenges new Christians to move beyond their traditional rituals and ceremonies and believe that Christ has fulfilled them all.

JAMES: James advises putting beliefs into practice and offers practical ways for Christians to live out their faith.

1 PETER: This letter was written to comfort early Christians who were being persecuted for their faith.

2 PETER: In this letter Peter warns against false teachers and urges Christians to stay loyal to God.

1 JOHN: This letter explains basic truths about the Christian life, with emphasis on the command to love one another.

2 JOHN: This letter, addressed to "the dear Lady and to her children," warns against false teachers.

3 JOHN: In contrast to 2 John, this letter states the need to welcome people who preach Christ.

JUDE: Jude warns against the influence of evil ones outside the fellowship of believers.

## Prophecy

REVELATION: This book was written to encourage persecuted believers and affirm their faith that God will care for them. Using visions and symbols, the writer illustrates the triumph of good over evil and the creation of a new heaven and new earth.

# How to Read the New Testament

Set aside time each day to read from your New Testament. Try to make it the same time each day. Be realistic. Commit yourself only to as much time as you honestly feel that you can stick to on an ongoing basis. Before you begin reading ask for God's guidance and blessing. Some people have found that keeping a daily notebook is helpful. Use the following steps to get the most out of your daily Scripture reading:

1. Select a passage of Scripture (perhaps one from the *Read through the New Testament* section that follows). It is probably best not to try to read more than one to three chapters at one sitting.
2. Examine its context:
   a. What kind of book is it drawn from? A biographical book such as one of the Gospel accounts of Jesus' life; a long historical book, such as *The Acts of the Apostles*; a brief letter to a person (*The Letters of Paul to Timothy*) or to a specific church (*The Letters of Paul to the Corinthians*).
   b. What is the overall purpose/intent of this book? (Do not do lengthy research, but feel free to read the opening and closing paragraphs as well as section headings.)
   c. What occurs or is discussed in the passages immediately preceding and following the passage you chose?
3. Read the passage quickly for sense.
4. Identify key words or phrases. Are there words or thoughts that are repeated throughout the passage? Are any cause and effect relationships established? (These are often signaled by words like *if* and *then*, *therefore*, *because*, *since*, and *so*.) Are any comparisons made or similarities pointed out? Are any two people, things or concepts contrasted?
5. Read the passage again and ask yourself what is the intent or purpose of the passage. Try to find out what the author is saying. Be honest; don't just look for what you want to hear. The New Testament has many strong messages that can change lives!
6. What do you learn about God from this passage? What do you learn about human nature? Ask yourself how this message applies to you. Is there anything you need to change in your life in order to be a more faithful child of God or more loving toward your neighbor? Ask for God's help in making this change.
7. Re-read the passage one more time. Is there one verse you would like to commit to memory? Why not write it on an index card and carry it with you throughout the day as a study aid?
8. Thank God for what he has shown you, and ask for his help as you seek to apply this lesson in your life.
9. Share what you have learned with someone else.

363

# Read through the New Testament

The books of the New Testament were written by the followers of Jesus Christ. The reading plan given here will help you to learn more about Jesus' life and ministry and about what his death and resurrection means to his followers. This Good News was so important to Jesus' first followers that they traveled great distances and took great risks to share it with others. They also wrote many letters to encourage one another to hold fast to their faith in Jesus.

## The Life of Jesus

The New Testament gives four accounts of Jesus' life. They are called Gospels, which means "good news." They tell of his birth, baptism, ministry of teaching and healing, death and resurrection. Although similar in many ways, these books offer four different looks at the life of Jesus. Choose one of the following reading plans to learn more about Jesus and then go on to read the rest of the New Testament.

### Plan A
Read:
  Mark 1-16
  John 1-21
  Luke 1-24
  Matthew 1-28

### Plan B
Read:
The birth of Jesus
  Matthew 1, 2; Luke 1, 2
The public ministry of Jesus
  Matthew 3-20; Mark 1-10; Luke 3.1-19.27; John 1-12
The last days of Jesus' life
  Matthew 21-27; Mark 11-15; Luke 19.28-23.56; John 13-19
The resurrection of Jesus
  Matthew 28; Mark 16; Luke 24; John 20-21

## The Early Church
Jesus speaks to his followers and is taken up to heaven
  Acts 1.1-11
The beginning of the Christian movement in Jerusalem
  Acts 1.12-8.3
The spread of the Christian movement into Judea and Samaria
  Acts 8.4-12.25

## The Ministry of Paul
Paul's first missionary journey
  Acts 13, 14
An important conference in Jerusalem
  Acts 15.1-35
  Also read what Paul had to say about the issues discussed at this conference: Galatians.

364

Paul's second missionary journey
Acts 15.36-18.22
- After Acts 16.5 read 1 Timothy and 2 Timothy to learn more about the young man Timothy who was to become an important assistant to Paul.
- After Acts 18.17 read 1 Thessalonians and 2 Thessalonians.

Paul's third missionary journey
Acts 18.23-21.16
- After Acts 19.41 read 1 Corinthians, Philippians and Philemon.
- After Acts 20.6 read 2 Corinthians and Titus.
- After Acts 20.38 read Romans.

Paul's imprisonments in Jerusalem, Caesarea and Rome
Acts 21.17-28.31
- After Acts 28.31 read Ephesians and Colossians.

## The Spread of Christianity under Roman Persecution

Read:
Hebrews
James
1 Peter
2 Peter
Jude
1 John
2 John
3 John
Revelation

## How to look up a New Testament reference.

Every verse in this New Testament is marked by its own *verse number*. To find any one of the passages listed in these reader's helps, you need to find the book, the chapter in the book, and the verse or verses within that chapter. The chapter number immediately follows the name of the book. This is followed by a period (.) which is followed by the number or range of numbers for the verses you seek. For example: 1 Corinthians 12.1-11 is the First Letter of Paul to the Corinthians, chapter twelve, verses one through eleven.

369

# Famous Passages from the New Testament

## THE LIFE OF JESUS

The Birth of Jesus
  Matthew 1.18-2.15; Luke 2.1-20
Jesus Is Named and Presented
in the Temple
  Luke 2.21-40
The Young Jesus
  Luke 2.41-52
The Baptism of Jesus
  Matthew 3; Mark 1.1-11; Luke 3.21, 22
The Temptation of Jesus
  Matthew 4.1-11; Mark 1.12, 13;
  Luke 4.1-13
Jesus Calls His First Disciples
  Matthew 4.18-22; Mark 1.16-20;
  Luke 5.1-11
Jesus Chooses Twelve Apostles
  Matthew 10.1-4; Mark 3.13-19;
  Luke 6.12-16
The Transfiguration of Jesus
  Matthew 17.1-13; Mark 9.2-13

## JESUS' DEATH AND RESURRECTION

Jesus' Entry into Jerusalem
  Matthew 21.1-11; Mark 11.1-11;
  Luke 19.29-44; John 12.12-19
The Last Supper of Jesus
  Matthew 26.17-35; Mark 14.12-26;
  Luke 22.1-38
Jesus Prays in Gethsemane
  Matthew 26.36-46; Mark 14.32-42;
  Luke 22.39-46
Jesus' Trial and Crucifixion
  Matthew 26.47-27.66; Mark 14.43-15.47;
  Luke 22.47-23.56; John 18; 19
The Resurrection of Jesus
  Matthew 28.1-10; Mark 16;
  Luke 24.1-12; John 20
The Great Commission
  Matthew 28.16-20
The Ascension of Jesus
  Luke 24.50-53; Acts 1.1-12

## MIRACLES AND HEALINGS OF JESUS

Jesus Turns Water into Wine
  John 2.1-11
Jesus Feeds Many People
  Matthew 14.13-21; Mark 6.30-44;

Luke 9.10-17; John 6.1-15;
  Matthew 15.32-39; Mark 8.1-10
Jesus Calms a Storm
  Matthew 8.23-27; Mark 4.35-41;
  Luke 8.22-25
The Great Catch of Fish
  Luke 5.1-11
Jesus Walks on Water
  Matthew 14.22-33; Mark 6.45-52;
  John 6.16-21
Jesus Heals People with
Skin Diseases
  Matthew 8.1-4; Mark 1.40-45;
  Luke 5.12-16; Luke 17.11-19
Jesus Casts Out Demons
  Matthew 8.28-34; Mark 5.1-20;
  Luke 8.26-39; Matthew 12.22-37;
  Mark 3.20-30; Luke 11.14-23;
  Matthew 17.14-21; Mark 9.14-29;
  Luke 9.37-43; Mark 1.21-28;
  Luke 4.31-37
Jesus Heals the Blind
  Matthew 9.27-31; Matthew 20.29-34;
  Mark 10.46-52; Luke 18.35-43
Jesus Heals a Deaf Man
  Mark 7.31-37
Jesus Heals the Paralyzed and Crippled
  Matthew 12.9-14; Mark 3.1-6;
  Luke 6.6-11; John 5.1-8;
  Luke 14.1-6; Matthew 9.1-8;
  Mark 2.1-12; Luke 5.17-26
Jesus Heals Many Women
  Matthew 9.18-26; Mark 5.21-43;
  Luke 8.1-3; Luke 8.40-56;
  Luke 13.10-17; Matthew 15.21-28;
  Mark 7.24-30
Jesus Heals the Centurion's Servant
  Matthew 8.5-13; Luke 7.1-10
Jesus Heals Peter's Mother-in-law
  Matthew 8.14, 15; Mark 1.29-31;
  Luke 4.38, 39
Jesus Heals an Official's Son
  John 4.46-54
Jesus Revives an Official's Daughter
  Matthew 9.18,19,23-26;
  Mark 5.21-24,35-42; Luke 8.40-42,49-56
Jesus Raises the Dead
  Luke 7.11-17; John 11.1-44

366

## THE TEACHINGS AND PARABLES OF JESUS

The Sermon on the Mount
Matthew 5-7; Luke 6.20-49
The Beatitudes
Matthew 5.3-11; Luke 6.20-26
The Great Commandment
Matthew 22.37-39; Mark 12.29-31;
Luke 10.27
The Golden Rule
Matthew 7.12; Luke 6.31
The Grain of Mustard Seed
Matthew 13.31, 32; Mark 4.30-32;
Luke 13.18, 19
The Parable of the Sower
Matthew 13.1-23; Mark 4.1-20;
Luke 8.4-15
The Parable of the Growing Seed
Mark 4.26-29
Some Parables About the
Kingdom of Heaven
Matthew 13.24-52
The Parable of the Unforgiving Servant
Matthew 18.23-35
The Parable of the Workers
in the Vineyard
Matthew 20.1-16
The Parable of the Tenants
in the Vineyard
Matthew 21.33-46; Mark 12.1-11;
Luke 20.9-18
The Parable of the Wedding Feast
Matthew 22.1-14; Luke 14.15-24
The Parable of the Ten
Young Women (Virgins)
Matthew 25.1-13
The Parable of the Three
Servants and Their Coins
Matthew 25.14-30; Luke 19.11-27
The Parable of the Sheep and the Goats
Matthew 25.31-46

The Parable of the Good Samaritan
Luke 10.25-37
The Parable of the Shepherd
John 10.1-21
The Parable of the Rich Fool
Luke 12.16-21
The Parable of the Watchful Servants
Luke 12.35-48
The Parable of the Barren Fig Tree
Luke 13.6-9
The Parable of the Lost Sheep
Matthew 18.12-14; Luke 15.3-7
The Parable of the Lost Coin
Luke 15.8-10
The Parable of the Lost Son
Luke 15.11-32
The Parable of the Shrewd Manager
Luke 16.1-13
The Rich Man and Lazarus
Luke 16.19-31
The Parable of the Widow and the Judge
Luke 18.1-8
The Parable of the Pharisee and
the Tax Collector
Luke 18.9-14

## OTHER NEW TESTAMENT STORIES

The Birth of John the Baptist
Luke 1.57-66
John the Baptist Is Executed
Matthew 14.1-12; Mark 6.14-29
Peter Receives the Keys of the Kingdom
Matthew 16.13-20
The Holy Spirit Comes on Pentecost
Acts 2
Stephen, the First Martyr
Acts 6.5-15; 7.54-60
Philip Baptizes the Ethiopian Official
Acts 8.26-39
The Conversion of Paul
Acts 9.1-31
Peter and Cornelius
Acts 10
Peter in Prison
Acts 12.1-19
The Baptism of Lydia
Acts 16.11-15
Paul in Prison
Acts 16.16-40
The Riot at Ephesus
Acts 19.23-41
Paul's Voyage to Rome
Acts 27; 28

### What is a parable?

Parables are stories that use typical, everyday situations in order to teach important truths. Jesus used many parables to teach his followers about the Kingdom of God.

## NEW TESTAMENT PRAYERS

The Lord's Prayer
  Matthew 6.9-13
Jesus' Prayer in Gethsemane
  Matthew 26.36-44
Jesus' Prayer for His Disciples
  John 17
The Disciples' Prayer
  Acts 4.24-31
Paul's Prayer for Believers
  Ephesians 3.14-21

## SPECIAL BLESSINGS FROM THE NEW TESTAMENT

Invocations and Openings
  1 Corinthians 1.3; 1 Timothy 1.2;
  2 John 3; Revelation 1.4-6
Dismissals and Closings
  Romans 15.5,6,13; Romans 16.25-27;
  2 Corinthians 13.13; Ephesians 6.23,24;
  Philippians 4.7; Hebrews 13.20,21;
  Jude 24,25

## How to look up a New Testament reference.

Every verse in this New Testament is marked by its own *verse number*. To find any one of the passages listed in these reader's helps, you need to find the book, the chapter in the book, and the verse or verses within that chapter. The chapter number immediately follows the name of the book. This is followed by a period (.) which is followed by the number or range of numbers for the verses you seek. For example: 1 Corinthians 12.1-11 is the First Letter of Paul to the Corinthians, chapter twelve, verses one through eleven.

# Finding Help in the New Testament

## Help in Special Circumstances

**Being a friend**
Luke 10.25-37; John 15.11-17; Romans 16.1-2

**Being a leader**
1 Timothy 3.1-7; 2 Timothy 2.14-26; Titus 1.5-9

**Caring for the aged and widowed**
1 Timothy 5.3-8

**Celebrating the birth/adoption of a child**
Luke 18.15-17; John 16.16-22

**Celebrating a graduation**
Galatians 5.16-26; Philippians 4.4-9

**Celebrating a marriage**
Ephesians 5.21-33; Colossians 2.6-7

**Celebrating a wedding anniversary**
1 Corinthians 13

**Controlling your temper**
Galatians 5.16-26

**Controlling your tongue**
2 Thessalonians 2.16-17; James 3.1-12

**Discovering God's will**
Matthew 5.14-16; Luke 9.21-27; Romans 13.8-14; 2 Peter 1.3-9; 1 John 4.7-21

**Encountering a cult**
Matthew 7.15-20; 2 Peter 2; 1 John 4.1-6; Jude

**Encountering peer pressure**
Romans 12.1-2; Galatians 6.1-5; Ephesians 5.1-20

**Entering college**
Romans 8.1-17; 1 Corinthians 1.18-31

**Entering military service**
Ephesians 6.10-20; 2 Timothy 2.1-13

**Experiencing the death of a loved one**
John 11.25-27; John 14.1-7; Romans 8.31-39; Romans 14.7-9; 1 Thessalonians 4.13-18

**Experiencing illness**
Mark 1.29-34; Mark 6.53-56; James 5.14-16

**Experiencing suffering and persecution**
Matthew 5.3-12; John 15.18-16.4; Romans 8.18-30; 2 Corinthians 4.1-15; Hebrews 12.1-11; 1 Peter 4.12-19

**Facing a difficult decision**
Colossians 3.12-17

**Facing a divorce**
Matthew 19.1-9; Philippians 3.1-11

**Facing homelessness**
Luke 9.57-62; Revelation 21.1-4

**Facing imprisonment**
Matthew 25.31-46; Luke 4.16-21

**Facing life alone**
1 Corinthians 7.25-38; 1 Corinthians 12.1-31

**Facing a natural disaster**
Romans 8.31-39; 1 Peter 1.3-12

**Facing a trial or lawsuit**
Matthew 5.25-26; Luke 18.1-8

**Losing your job**
Luke 16.1-13; Philippians 4.10-13

**Losing your property and possessions**
Romans 8.18-39

**Managing your time**
Mark 13.32-37; Luke 21.34-36; 1 Timothy 4.11-16; Titus 3.8-14

**Moving into a new home**
John 14.1-7; Ephesians 3.14-21; Revelation 3.20,21

**Overcoming addiction**
2 Corinthians 5.16-21; Ephesians 4.22-24

**Overcoming a grudge**
Matthew 5.23-26; Luke 6.27-36; Ephesians 4.25-32

**Overcoming prejudice**
Matthew 7.1-5; Acts 10.34-36; Galatians 3.26-29; Ephesians 2.11-22; Colossians 3.5-11; James 2.1-13

**Overcoming pride**
Mark 9.33-37; Luke 14.7-11; Luke 18.9-14; Luke 22.24-27; Romans 12.14-16; 1 Corinthians 1.18-31; 2 Corinthians 12.1-10

**Overcoming procrastination**
Matthew 22.1-14; Matthew 25.1-13; 2 Corinthians 6.1-2

**Raising children**
Ephesians 6.4; Colossians 3.21

**Respecting civil authorities**
Mark 12.13-17; Romans 13.1-7; Titus 3.1-2; 1 Peter 2.13-17

**Respecting parents**
Ephesians 6.1-3; Colossians 3.20

**Retiring from your job**
Matthew 25.31-46; Romans 12.1-2; Philippians 3.12-21; 2 Peter 1.2

**Seeking forgiveness**
Matthew 6.14-15; Luke 15; Philemon; Hebrews 4.14-16; 1 John 1.5-10

**Seeking God's help**
Matthew 7.7-12

**Seeking salvation**
John 3.1-21; Romans 1.16-17; Romans 3.21-31; Romans 5.1-11; Romans 10.5-13; Ephesians 1.3-14; Ephesians 2.1-10

**Seeking strength**
Ephesians 6.10-20; 2 Thessalonians 2.16-17

**Seeking truth**
John 8.31-47; John 14.6-14; John 16.4b-15;
1 Timothy 2.1-7

**Sharing your gifts**
Luke 21.1-4; Acts 2.43-47; Acts 4.32-37;
Romans 12.9-13; 1 Corinthians 16.1-4;
2 Corinthians 8.1-15; 2 Corinthians 9.6-15

**Starting a new job**
Romans 12.3-11; 1 Thessalonians 5.12-18;
2 Thessalonians 3.6-13; 1 Peter 4.7-11

**Understanding your relationship with God**
John 15.1-17; Romans 5.1-11; Romans 8.1-17

**Understanding your relationship with others**
Matthew 18.15-17; Matthew 18.21-35;
Romans 14.13-23; Romans 15.1-16;
Galatians 6.1-10; Colossians 3.12-17;
1 John 4.7-12

**Worrying about the future**
1 Peter 1.3-5; Revelation 21.1-8

**Worrying about money**
Matthew 6.24-34; Luke 12.13-21;
1 Timothy 6.6-10

## Experiencing Troublesome Feelings

**Afraid?**
Mark 4.35-41; Hebrews 13.5-6; 1 John 4.13-18

**Afraid of death?**
John 6.35-40; Romans 8.18-39;
1 Corinthians 15.35-57; 2 Corinthians 5.1-10;
2 Timothy 1.8-10

**Angry?**
Matthew 5.21-24; Romans 12.17-21;
Ephesians 4.26-32; James 1.19-21

**Anxious? Worried?**
Matthew 6.24-34; Matthew 10.26-31;
1 Peter 1.3-5; 1 Peter 5.7

**Depressed?**
John 3.14-17; Ephesians 3.14-21

**Discouraged?**
Romans 15.13; 2 Corinthians 4.16-18;
Philippians 4.10-13; Colossians 1.9-14;
Hebrews 6.9-12

**Doubting your faith in God?**
Matthew 7.7-12; Luke 17.5-6; John 20.24-31;
Romans 4.13-25; Hebrews 11; 1 John 5.13-15

**Frustrated?**
Matthew 7.13-14

**Impatient?**
Hebrews 6.13-20; James 5.7-11

**Insecure? Lacking confidence?**
Philippians 4.10-20; 1 John 3.19-24

**Jealous?**
James 3.13-18

**Lonely?**
John 14.15-31a

**Overwhelmed? Experiencing stress?**
Matthew 11.25-30; John 4.1-30;
2 Corinthians 6.3-10; Revelation 22.17

**Rejected?**
Matthew 9.9-13; Luke 4.16-30; John 15.18-16.4;
Ephesians 1.3-14; 1 Peter 2.1-10

**Tempted?**
Luke 4.1-13; Hebrews 2.11-18;
Hebrews 4.14-16; James 1.12-18

**Tempted by sex?**
1 Corinthians 6.12-20; Galatians 5.16-26

**Tired? Weary?**
Matthew 11.25-30; 2 Thessalonians 3.16;
Hebrews 4.1-11

**Feeling useless? Inferior?**
Galatians 1.11-24; Ephesians 4.1-16;
1 Peter 2.4-10

**Vengeful?**
Matthew 5.38-42; Romans 12.17-21

# How to look up a New Testament reference.

Every verse in this New Testament is marked by its own *verse number*. To find any one of the passages listed in these reader's helps, you need to find the book, the chapter in the book, and the verse or verses within that chapter. The chapter number immediately follows the name of the book. This is followed by a period (.) which is followed by the number or range of numbers for the verses you seek. For example: 1 Corinthians 12.1-11 is the First Letter of Paul to the Corinthians, chapter twelve, verses one through eleven.

# What the New Testament Says about God's Forgiveness

**Every person is separated from God because of sin.**
Romans 3.9-20
Romans 5.12-21
Romans 7.14-25

**God has always sought to form a close relationship with people.**
Ephesians 1.3-14
1 Peter 1.1-10
1 John 3.1-10

**God has reached out to people in a personal way by sending Jesus Christ.**
Colossians 1.15-23
Romans 5.1-11
1 Peter 2.10-25
John 3.1-21
2 Timothy 1.3-10
Ephesians 2.1-10

**God's forgiveness through Jesus Christ is available to every person.**
1 John 1.5-10
Romans 10.5-13
Romans 8.31-39
Romans 3.21-26

**New life in Christ calls a person to live in a Christ-like way.**
Romans 6.1-14
Matthew 20.20-28
Ephesians 4.17-32
Galatians 5.16-26
1 John 4.7-21
Romans 12.1-21

Printed in the United States of America.

*other words for love*

W9-BPN-041

Lorraine Zago Rosenthal

# other words for love

EMBER

Text copyright © 2011 by Lorraine Zago Rosenthal
Cover photograph (top) copyright © 2011 by Melissa Breanne Jackson; cover photograph (bottom) copyright © 2011 by Hilary Elizabeth Upton

All rights reserved. Published in the United States by Ember, an imprint of Random House Children's Books, a division of Random House, Inc., New York. Originally published in hardcover in the United States by Delacorte Press, an imprint of Random House Children's Books, New York, in 2011.

Ember and the colophon are trademarks of Random House, Inc.

Visit us on the Web! www.randomhouse.com/teens

Educators and librarians, for a variety of teaching tools, visit us at www.randomhouse.com/teachers

The Library of Congress has cataloged the hardcover edition of this work as follows:
Rosenthal, Lorraine Zago.
Other words for love / by Lorraine Zago Rosenthal. — 1st ed.
p. cm.
Summary: In 1985 Brooklyn, New York, sixteen-year-old artist Ari learns about first love.
ISBN 978-0-385-73901-6 (hardcover) — ISBN 978-0-385-90765-1 (lib. bdg.)
ISBN 978-0-375-89692-7 (ebook)
[1. Coming of age—Fiction. 2. Family problems—Fiction. 3. Artists—Fiction. 4. Schools—Fiction. 5. Family life—New York (State)—New York—Fiction. 6. Brooklyn (New York, N.Y.)—Fiction.]
I. Title.
PZ7.R7194458 Oth 2011
[Fic]—dc22
2009053656

ISBN 978-0-385-73902-3 (tr. pbk.)

RL: 5.6

Printed in the United States of America

10 9 8 7 6 5 4 3 2 1

First Ember Edition 2012

Random House Children's Books supports the First Amendment and celebrates the right to read.

## acknowledgments

I would like to express my heartfelt appreciation to those closest to me for their unwavering support; my deepest gratitude to my agent, Elizabeth Evans, for her dedication and enthusiasm; and my sincere thanks to all the people at Delacorte Press—especially my editor, Stephanie Lane Elliott—who contributed their talents to this novel.

*other words for love*

# *one*

*In* 1985, just about everyone I knew was afraid of two things: a nuclear attack by the Russians and a gruesome death from the AIDS virus, which allegedly thrived on the mouthpieces of New York City public telephones.

My best friend, Summer, however, didn't worry about catching AIDS from a phone or anything else. She started kissing boys when we were twelve and wrote every one of their names in her diary, which had a purple velvet cover.

I didn't have a diary. I didn't need one because I had only kissed a boy once, in the Catskills during a family vacation between eighth and ninth grades. The Catskills boy was from Connecticut, and he turned on me after I kissed him. He claimed that I opened my mouth too wide and that I was *only a four on a scale of one to ten in the looks department.*

*Don't get any ideas,* he said. *You Brooklyn girls bore me. And I'm going home in two days, so we'll never see each other again.*

That was fine with me. I wanted to pretend that the kiss had never happened. It wasn't what I'd practiced on the back of my hand while imagining handsome faces from *General Hospital* and *Days of Our Lives*. None of those guys would have said I was only a four, and they definitely wouldn't have told me to watch where I was going after we bumped into each other at the breakfast buffet.

*What are you doing in there?* my mother asked later, while I was brushing my teeth in our motel bathroom and hoping there weren't any AIDS germs in my mouth. And I didn't tell Mom what had happened. She'd already warned me that bad things could hide in the most unlikely places.


Summer and I went to different high schools. I attended our local public school in Brooklyn, while she was a student at Hollister Prep, a fancy private school on the Upper East Side of Manhattan that charged tuition my parents couldn't afford.

Summer's parents *could* afford it, but that wasn't why she transferred there after only three months at my school. It was because some girls were spreading rumors about her, inventing filthy stories about how she supposedly serviced the entire wrestling team and went down on their coach in his office. *Summer Simon swallows*—that was what the girls wrote in bright red nail polish on a bathroom wall. Then they Scotch-taped Trojan *Ribbed for Her Pleasure* packets all over Summer's locker. That made her cry.

I peeled them off while she sobbed into her hands. *Forget it,* I whispered. *They're just jealous because all the guys like you.*

This was hard for me to say, because I was jealous myself. But Summer stopped crying and even smiled, and I was sure that I'd done something good. And she did lots of good things, too—like not ditching me after she started at Hollister and became a member of its popular crowd.

Now our sophomore year was over and Summer and I sat on folding chairs in my sister Evelyn's backyard in Queens. Toys were scattered across the grass, and Summer rolled a Nerf ball with her dainty foot.

"Eight whole weeks of vacation ahead of us," she said.

I nodded and looked at my nondainty foot. There was a callus on my heel and a scab on my ankle and I needed a pedicure, but Summer didn't. The sun bounced off her painted toenails and the long blond hair that was strategically highlighted around her pretty face. Her eyes were dark, she always wore flashy clothes, and she smelled of L'Air du Temps. She hadn't been without a boyfriend since junior high. Her latest conquest was a Columbia University sophomore she'd met last September who'd taken her virginity by Halloween. *He's nineteen, so it's illegal,* she'd told me in a giggly whisper the next day. *Nobody can ever know.*

I knew. And I was jealous. Since she'd started at Hollister,

3

everything had been so easy for her. She rarely studied, yet her name was a permanent fixture on the honor roll. She was good at math, she was a fashion expert, and she could recite the stats of every player on the Yankees. She lived as the only child in a palatial house in Park Slope. Even her name was perfect: Summer Simon, like a movie actress on a glitzy marquee.

I wondered if her parents had planned it that way, and I wished my parents had planned better. They should have known that guys would be more attracted to girls named Summer Simon than to girls named Ariadne Mitchell. I also wished that my mother was as interested in movies as she was in literature. It wasn't a smart idea to name me after some dusty old book by Chekhov.

But Mom was a reader. She had a master's degree in English and taught sixth-grade language arts at a public school. She thought my best friend was highly overrated. According to Mom, Summer was short, she was a shameless flirt, and she was totally manufactured—all dyed hair and makeup and fake nails. Mom said I had a much better figure than Summer because I was thinner and three inches taller, and *Jet-black hair with light blue eyes is very rare. You can thank your father for that.*

"Ari," Summer said. "Patrick is looking quite gorgeous today."

My attention shifted to Evelyn's husband, who was barbecuing hamburgers at the opposite end of the yard.

Patrick was thirty years old and six feet tall, and he had blond hair and brown eyes like Summer. He also had a killer

4

body. It was lean and muscular from lifting barbells in his basement and battling fires with the FDNY. I'd had a crush on him since we first met. He and Evelyn had a son named Kieran, whose fifth birthday we were celebrating, and now my sister was pregnant again.

"You're so boy-crazy," I answered, because what else could I say? Could I tell Summer that I knew Patrick was gorgeous and that whenever I slept at his house, I would press my ear against the guest bedroom wall to hear him and Evelyn having sex? I knew that made me a pervert.

"Take it easy, little sister," Patrick said when Mom and Summer and I were leaving, but he pronounced the last word "sistah" because he was from Boston. He also referred to the sprinkles on Kieran's birthday cake as *jimmies* and he complained that it was "wicked hot" today. He always called me little sistah, and I grabbed every chance to make fun of his accent.

"There's an *r* on the end of that word, Patrick Cagney," I told him.

"Don't be a wiseass," he said. "You criticize your father like that? He don't talk no better than me."

He *doesn't* talk *any* better than you, I thought, sure that Mom was cringing at Patrick's disgraceful grammar. But he was right. Dad did have a heavy Brooklyn accent, the accent that Mom had successfully discouraged in me but not in Evelyn. My sister's grammar was as bad as Patrick's, and she had the vocabulary of a drunken sailor, especially when she was angry.

She wasn't angry today, when we said goodbye at the front

5

door of her modest home, which was always messy and had wallpaper from 1972. Today she smiled and looked at me through her heavy-lidded green eyes. Bedroom eyes, that was what her high school friends used to call them. Evelyn had been as popular as Summer when she was our age. The boys in our neighborhood used to drool over her auburn hair, her delicate nose, and her pouty mouth.

"Come and spend the weekend soon," she said, hugging me tight. I felt her swollen stomach and noticed the thin layer of fat that had settled beneath her chin. Evelyn's face was still beautiful, but her first pregnancy had left a stubborn weight gain that she didn't try to lose.

I never criticized her figure out loud and neither did Mom, who wasn't in any position to criticize. Mom was thirty pounds overweight but she didn't care. She would never give up her favorite Hostess chocolate cupcakes or her homemade Sunday dinners with roasted chicken and potatoes drenched in gravy. *Food is one of life's simple pleasures,* she always said.

She lit a cigarette when she and Summer and I were in her old Honda, headed back toward Brooklyn. The windows were open because the air conditioner didn't work, and Mom's hair swirled around her head. It was shoulder-length, naturally auburn but now mixed with gray. In her wedding picture she looked like Evelyn, but her nose wasn't as small. And now her eyelids were a little too heavy.

"Are your parents at home, Summer?" Mom asked from the driver's seat next to me. I almost laughed. It was as if Mom thought we were eight instead of sixteen. But she believed that parents should be around a lot for their kids. That was why she'd become a teacher—so she could wait at the front door for me after school, so we could spend August afternoons together at Coney Island. She complained that Dad wasn't home enough, even though that wasn't his fault. He was a homicide detective in Manhattan, and the city was just so crime-infested.

"Yes, Mrs. Mitchell," Summer said, and I thought she sounded like one of Mom's students. Those kids were so intimidated by Mom, they practically wet their pants when her husky voice boomed across the classroom.

Mom stopped at the curb in front of Summer's house. All the houses on her block had double front doors, majestic bay windows, and elegantly angled rooftops. Her parents were outside, planting flowers in the tiny square of dirt that was their front lawn, and they both waved after we dropped Summer off and headed toward home.

Our house was in Flatbush, and it wasn't huge or imposing. It was similar to Evelyn's—all brick, two stories, three bedrooms, forty years old. But our house was much neater than hers, and there was a statue of Saint Anne on our lawn. She'd been abandoned by the previous owner, and I was sure she knew it. *She's the mother of the Blessed Virgin Mary,* Mom said. *So we can't evict her. That would be a terrible sin.* Saint Anne always looked like she was crying when it rained.

Evelyn thought we were nuts for keeping the statue. She also rolled her eyes and stuck a finger down her throat whenever Mom got religious. She said that Mom was a lapsed Catholic, a phony Cafeteria Catholic—one of those people who pick and choose the rules that suit them—and she wasn't wrong. We only went to church on Christmas and Easter, and we never abstained from meat on Fridays during Lent.

Once Mom even signed a pro-choice petition that a lady from NOW brought to our front door. *Women are entitled to their rights,* Mom had said after I gave her a funny look. *There are enough unwanted children in this world.*

Then I glanced at Saint Anne, standing there in a chipped blue gown with a gold shawl over her head and her baby daughter in her arms, and at that moment I thought she looked very sad.

"Is Summer seeing anyone?" Mom asked.

It was a few hours after we had come back from Evelyn's house and we sat on the living room sofa, enjoying the breeze that floated through a window screen. Illegal fireworks crackled outside, and I was polishing my toenails. There was barely enough light to see, but I didn't want to turn on a lamp because the darkness improved our plain furniture and hid the small charred hole in our La-Z-Boy. Mom had accidentally dropped a cigarette on the seat after she drank too much eggnog last Christmas Eve.

"Not right now. She broke up with the Columbia guy," I said, thinking about Summer's other ex-boyfriends. I asked her once if she missed any of them. She'd just shrugged and said, *I don't think much about guys from the past. I'm glad I knew them, but there's a reason they didn't make it into my future.* It surprised me that she could be so nonchalant, although I figured she was probably right.

"So she's actually without a boyfriend? That's shocking," Mom said, puffing on a Pall Mall. I wished she wouldn't smoke so much. I wished she wouldn't smoke at all. I didn't want her to get sick, or to end up as one of those people who have to lug an oxygen tank around. I used to beg her to quit, but she didn't even try. She was too addicted. Or too stubborn. Smoking was another one of her *simple pleasures*. So I'd given up on begging, but I silently worried. "She'll end up in trouble, if you know what I mean."

I knew, all right. Mom used to warn Evelyn about the same thing but it hadn't worked. Evelyn told our parents that she was "in trouble" during winter break of her senior year in high school. Then she took the GED, married Patrick before Easter, and gave birth to Kieran on a rainy June morning.

Later I sat in her old bedroom, which Mom had cleared out before we'd even finished eating Evelyn's leftover wedding cake. Now it was what Mom called my *studio,* the place where I sketched the faces of anyone who interested me. And I found them everywhere—in school, on the subway, at the supermarket. I only showed my drawings to Mom and my art teachers because nobody else understood. Mom noticed the details in an eye, the curve of a mouth. She believed that I had inherited her artistic gene, the one that drove her to write novels she never finished.

*I could've been a writer,* she sometimes said. *Or an editor at a publishing company in the city*. Then she'd look at me and smile, pretend it didn't matter, say that I was the best thing she ever created. And that I would have all the opportunities she never did.

I didn't expect an opportunity to arrive so soon. It happened after Mom and I came home from the barbecue and I went to sleep in my old canopy bed that was a hand-me-down from Evelyn. I woke to familiar noises downstairs—Dad's key in the front door, Mom's footsteps in the foyer, a midnight dinner frying on the stove.

They were talking as usual, but I didn't hear the normal words like *electric bill, plumber, that pain-in-the-ass neighbor blocked our driveway again.* Tonight it was something about a phone call and money, and Mom's voice was cheery but I wasn't sure why.

"Wait until the morning, Nancy," Dad said.

"But it's good news, Tom," Mom answered, and then she was in my room, telling me news that didn't sound good at all. "Uncle Eddie died," she said, and I saw Dad out in the hallway, Mom beside my bed, and Uncle Eddie in my mind. He was Dad's bachelor uncle who lived alone in a rent-controlled apartment.

"Oh," I said, remembering the many times I'd gone with Dad to check on Uncle Eddie. He was a kind old man who loved game shows and offered me chocolate from a Whitman's Sampler box. The thought of him watching *The Price Is Right* alone always made me sad. "That isn't good news, Mom."

My voice cracked. She pushed my long hair out of my face and glanced at Dad the way she did whenever my voice cracked. *Can you believe two tough cookies like us created such a delicate flower?* I once heard her say, and it was true, she and Dad were tough and I wasn't. But they had to be tough. Mom's parents had been alcoholics and not one of her four brothers had ever visited our house. Dad had been raised by a widowed mother who worked at a charity hospital to pay for the tiny apartment that she and Dad had shared, and he'd seen a lot of ugly things during his thirty years with the NYPD. *Kids are so spoiled these days,* he and Mom always said, and I didn't want them to say it about me. They thought that anyone who ate three meals every day and had two employed parents was spoiled.

"I know, Ariadne," Mom said, because she insisted on calling me by my full name. "But he did something nice for us. He left us his entire savings—a hundred thousand dollars. Now you can go to any college you want and we can send you to Hollister Prep in September."

I could go to any college I wanted and they were sending me to Hollister Prep in September. I wasn't sure how to tell Mom that I didn't want to go to Hollister. I knew I couldn't measure up to the girls there—girls like Summer who got sparkling report cards without opening a book and didn't leave the house if their shoes didn't match their purse. My current school wasn't great—my classmates seemed to think I was completely unremarkable—but it was nearby and at least the teachers liked me. So I hoped my parents would forget about Hollister.

I tried not to think about it when Mom and Dad were gone, when they were asleep in their bedroom down the hall and I couldn't possibly sleep. So I sat next to my window, studying the stars in the clear summer sky, shifting my thoughts to Uncle Eddie. I thought about him and his entire savings and the fact that he had nobody to leave it to except us.

# two

*There* were more people at Uncle Eddie's wake than I expected, so that was good. Other than me and my parents, and Patrick and Evelyn and Kieran, there were a few neighbors from Uncle Eddie's building and an attractive older lady who whispered to Dad that she and Uncle Eddie used to be *special friends*.

Summer was there too. She came with her mother, who had stringy brown hair and always looked tired. She probably *was* tired, because she owned and operated a business called Catering by Tina. She made the food herself and loaded it into a white van that she drove to people's homes in all five boroughs. Sometimes Summer and I helped with the cooking and went with Tina to the parties, where we stayed in the kitchen and arranged stuffed mushrooms on fancy silver trays.

Now Summer sat next to me in a stylishly appropriate dress. I glanced at my own dress, which I'd hastily chosen from a clearance rack at Loehmann's. It was baggy and dull, but I hadn't been thinking about style when I bought it. I'd been thinking about Uncle Eddie, about the fact that he would be buried alone, not next to a wife or children or anyone that mattered. I wanted him to know that someone cared, so I wrote a note telling him how much I appreciated the hundred thousand dollars. I also mentioned that because of him I could afford to go to college at the Parsons School of Design in Manhattan, which had been my dream since I was twelve.

The note was in an envelope that I clutched between my sweaty fingers. I wanted to give it to Uncle Eddie, who was lying inside that box at the front of the room, but I couldn't. The idea of being near a dead person made my knees shake.

"What's that?" Summer asked, nodding toward the envelope.

I folded it in my lap and glanced at Uncle Eddie. "He left my family some money. I know I can't really thank him, but I wanted to, so I wrote this letter. . . ." I turned back to Summer. She was sitting with her legs crossed at the ankles, her dark eyes fixed on my face. "I'm being stupid. It's not like he can read it."

She gave me a smile. "You're not being stupid. I think you're being nice."

I smiled back. "I still can't go up there, though."

Summer uncrossed her ankles. "Why not?"

"Because he's dead. It scares me."

She threw her hair behind her shoulders. "Don't be afraid of the dead, Ari. They can't hurt you. It's the *living* you should worry about."

She had a good point. Uncle Eddie couldn't do anything to me. But I stayed where I was, bending the envelope until it was wrinkled and damp.

Summer took it out of my clammy hands. She squeezed my shoulder and whispered in my ear. "Do you want me to do it? I'm not afraid."

That didn't surprise me. Summer wasn't afraid to do anything. "*I* should do it," I said. But I stayed where I was, wishing I wasn't so cowardly.

Summer stood up and extended her hand. I remembered all the times she'd done that before. She'd done it at her sweet sixteen, when I'd hidden in her bathroom because I didn't have the guts to mingle with the crowd of Hollister students in the living room. Summer coaxed me out and stuck with me the whole night, telling everybody, *This is my best friend, Ari.* That had made me think I might not be so unremarkable.

"Come on," Summer said, looking from me to Uncle Eddie. "We'll do it together."

* * *

I didn't go home with Mom and Dad after the wake. Instead I climbed into the back of Patrick's black Ford truck. Mom thought I had spent too much time in my room over the last few days and needed a change of scenery.

An hour later, I was helping Evelyn unload the dishwasher in her dingy kitchen. The outdated appliances were bile green and the wallpaper could make you dizzy if you stared at it for too long. It was covered with orange flowers, big leaves, and metallic swirls that weaved between the petals. Patrick had started to remove the wallpaper once, but he never found the time to finish. He was always working, either at the firehouse or doing odd jobs on his days off for extra money. Installing tiles, landscaping, anything to pay the mortgage.

"Look what I got for you," Evelyn said.

She stuck a Mrs. Fields bag in my face. It was filled with my favorite chocolate chip cookies, so I knew that Evelyn was in one of her good moods today. I liked her much better this way, when she was sweet and thoughtful the way she used to be, and not cranky and mean like she'd become over the past few years. *Dirty diapers and a husband with a dangerous job can make anyone grouchy,* Mom said. *I warned her.*

The worst was after Kieran was born. Evelyn broke out in a nasty case of eczema, and she cried every day and yelled at Patrick constantly. Mom had to call Summer's father for advice—he was a psychiatrist. He'd said he believed Evelyn had postpartum depression, and he recommended we send her to New York–Presbyterian Hospital in Manhattan. We did, and she had stayed for two months.

Her treatment hadn't been covered by Patrick's health insurance. My parents had cashed some savings bonds to pay for the whole thing, and they'd agreed when Evelyn's doctors recommended that she stop having children. But Evelyn didn't listen to anyone, especially Mom and Dad. She used to fight with them all the time. They fought about her failing grades, her trampy clothes, and the bag of marijuana that Mom once found in Evelyn's room. And there was always the issue of her revolving-door boyfriends and the fact that she'd gone alone to a clinic at the age of fifteen to get a prescription for birth control pills.

The biggest fight came when she was seventeen and announced that she was pregnant. Dad's mouth shrank into a thin white line and Mom yelled loud enough for our neighbors to hear. She said that Patrick was uneducated and ignorant and low class, she couldn't stand his South Boston accent, and he was lucky that she didn't hire someone to break his legs.

I had feared for his safety, worrying that some barbarous thugs would bind him and gag him and leave him bleeding somewhere in Bed-Stuy. But Mom chose not to solicit any criminal activity, and she changed her tune after Patrick and Evelyn left for their Florida honeymoon. Mom and Dad whispered in the car as we drove home from LaGuardia Airport, talking about how they'd done everything they could and they'd given Evelyn a nice wedding, and then Mom laughed and said, *She's Patrick's problem now.*

I shot Mom a stern look when she said that, because I didn't think it was right for a mother to refer to her daughter as a problem. And I wasn't shocked when Evelyn told us about the second baby. Being a mother seemed to make her feel like she wasn't just a girl who got married too young and worked part-time as a cashier at Pathmark. Now she was a playgroup organizer, a soccer coach, the woman who'd written a scathing letter to Hasbro after Kieran almost choked on a plastic game piece. Of course there were also the incessant comments from every direction about how handsome Kieran was, how he was blessed with Patrick's coloring and Evelyn's exquisite features.

She was striking, even with the extra weight. I sat across from her on the patio that night, admiring the way the fading sunshine accented the copper highlights in her long wavy hair. She was happy now, and she smiled with straight white teeth, let out throaty laughs that jiggled her cleavage.

I heard her laughing again after the sun was gone and I was alone in the guest bedroom, which would soon become a nursery. Patrick was laughing too, and then their voices lowered and changed into murmurs and moans and their headboard smacked the wall. I hadn't been expecting that sort of thing tonight because Evelyn was more than seven months pregnant, but I'd been wrong. And it was impossible not to listen. They were so loud and Patrick's noises made my heart race. He sounded like those professional tennis players who grunt whenever they hit the ball really hard.

Maybe it was the noise that gave me a headache. Either that or it was punishment for enjoying the sound of my brother-in-law having what my classmates jokingly called an *organism*, but I was in too much pain to decide. I was at the start of a migraine that blurred the vision in my left eye and made me see freaky things. Auras, that was what my doctor said they were called. They came around whenever I was stressed or upset or exposed to loud noises. *Don't bottle up your emotions,* the doctor said. *They'll manifest themselves physically and turn into headaches.*

I didn't follow his advice. And my migraines always started out the same way, with a web of fluorescent purple light that pulsated and grew until my medication kicked in. Tonight my medication wasn't here. I had been so preoccupied with Uncle Eddie that I'd forgotten to pack it in my overnight bag.

So I went across the hall to the only bathroom in the house, where I searched through a cabinet for Tylenol. But all I found was Patrick's Drakkar Noir and the bottle of ipecac that Evelyn had bought when Kieran was younger. She'd shown me where it was just in case he swallowed something dangerous while I was babysitting. She also made me go with her to a class where I learned to perform CPR and to diagnose broken bones.

I could see clearly through only one eye, and the pain in my head was so bad that I kneeled beside the toilet, ready to throw up. When I was down there, I spotted a book on the floor called *Name Your Baby.* I flipped through it and noticed that Evelyn had circled some names, but only girls' names. She'd refused a sonogram but was positive that she had a daughter on the way.

The names, the letters, Evelyn's scribbles in bright blue ink, made me feel worse, and I left the book on the tiles before I stood up. There was no reason to stay down there because nothing was happening, not even one lousy gag. I headed into the kitchen to search for Tylenol.

"What's wrong?" Patrick said.

I turned around. Patrick stood in the kitchen doorway, shirtless, his pajama pants resting low on his waist, a gold Celtic cross dangling from a chain around his neck.

"I'm trying to find some aspirin," I said.

He raked his hair back with his fingers but it was useless. Patrick's hair was very straight and it always fell over his forehead in a silky flaxen wave. "You got one of those headaches again?" he asked, and I nodded. Then he told me to sit down, he would find the aspirin, the bottle was hidden on a top shelf where Kieran couldn't get into it.

I didn't sit down. I stood on the linoleum watching Patrick rummage through the cabinets. I watched because he had a broad chest. A six-pack stomach. I hoped he wouldn't catch me staring at him and he didn't. He found a bottle of Tylenol and pointed to the table.

"I told you to sit down," he said, which was typical. Patrick was bossy, and words like *please* and *thanks* rarely came out of his mouth. Mom said it was because Patrick came from a family of eight kids with parents who were probably too frazzled to teach their children any manners. But I always followed his orders because I knew he meant well. So I took a seat and he sat opposite me, pushing two pills and a glass of water across the table. Then he reached over and pressed his palm against my forehead. "Are you sure it's only a headache? You ain't got no fever?"

*Fev-ah,* he said. No, Patrick, I thought, shaking my head. I don't have a fever. You could use a few lessons in Mom's class, but I won't tell you that. I can't hurt your feelings because you're so gorgeous and your hand feels nice on my face, hard and soft at the same time.

"So what brought this on? Are you still devastated about the corpse?" he asked, and I gave him a disapproving look that made him laugh. "Oh, come on, Ari. The man was almost ninety years old."

I shrugged, studying the ice in my glass. Then I told him what I'd been thinking, about how sad it was that Uncle Eddie had died in that gloomy apartment, that he didn't have a wife or children and his neighbors in the cemetery were strangers.

"I'm afraid of that," I said. "Dying alone."

He laughed again. "How do you come up with this morbid shit? You shouldn't worry about dying. You're a young kid."

But I do worry about it, I thought. I'm not Evelyn. Boys don't ring the doorbell for me and they don't call on the phone. I might never have a husband like you or a son like Kieran, and it's really confusing because I'm not even sure if I'd want to be like Evelyn. I wouldn't want to get in trouble and disappoint Mom so much that she'd laugh when I was gone.

"Come on," Patrick said, standing up. "You need some sleep."

I stayed where I was, watching the ice melt. I didn't want to sleep. I just wanted to sit there and think. Then he clamped his hand around my elbow and marched me to the guest bedroom. I wouldn't have let anyone except Patrick do that. I was sure he meant well.

Dad picked me up two days later. It was a humid morning and my legs stuck to the leather seats in his car.

"How was your weekend?" I asked, and repeated myself when he didn't answer. Some sports program was on the radio and he lowered the volume.

"I worked," he said, and turned it up again.

Dad's eyes were blue like mine and his hair used to be just as dark but now it was totally gray. He was tall and he didn't talk much. Not to me, anyway. He was a distant father, in Mom's opinion. But she said that he was also a good father because he kept a roof over our heads and food on the table. And he worked hard, all the time; he could have retired a decade ago but he didn't because retirement would drive him crazy. He wasn't interested in traveling or golf or anything except solving homicides, so he had to keep working. At least, that was what Mom told me. I never knew what Dad was thinking.

He sped back to work after I got out of the car in front of our house. Mom was inside, slicing bagels at the kitchen counter. She turned around and rested her hands on her hips.

"You look very thin, Ariadne. Didn't Evelyn feed you this weekend?"

I should have expected that; Mom always said critical things about Evelyn. *Didn't Evelyn feed you? Evelyn lets Kieran eat too much junk. Evelyn's house is a pigsty.* I wished she wouldn't. Evelyn might not have been perfect, but she wasn't so bad. Whenever she got cantankerous and snapped at me, I tried to remember the sweet things she did—like choosing me to be the maid of honor at her wedding and letting me tag along with her and her friends to the bowling alley, even though I was only eight at the time and nobody wanted me there.

"Of course she did," I said, but Mom looked skeptical. She toasted a bagel, slathered it with cream cheese, and watched while I ate it.

I went upstairs afterward, where I closed the door and opened the window in my studio. It was a sunny day, and our next-door neighbors—the annoying ones who constantly blocked our driveway—were having a party. Balloons bounced from their mailbox at the curb and guests were double-parking their cars, carrying cases of beer to the front porch. I watched for a while, and then I sat at my easel, sketching a tree across the street. The leaves, the bark, the rays of sunlight peeking through the branches. It wasn't the best thing to draw, not as interesting as faces, but my art teacher had said that I should practice drawing everything.

An hour passed before I heard Mom's voice. I saw her standing on our lawn, talking to the lady next door. Mom was calm at first, saying "I would appreciate it" and something about our driveway and when I looked at the driveway, I saw a Trans Am parked there with a dented Buick behind it. Our neighbor raised her voice and shouted something rude and so did Mom.

"Get those fucking cars off my property or I'll call the cops," Mom said. "My husband's on the force—I can get someone over here in five minutes."

Then I heard our front door slam and pots banging around in the kitchen. None of this was unusual, because Mom was feisty. That was the word Dad always used to describe her.

*I wouldn't have survived in my family otherwise,* I heard her tell him once, but I didn't know exactly what she meant. Mom had only mentioned her parents a few times in my presence, using a tone typically reserved for talking about something distasteful, like diarrhea or Evelyn's eczema. Her parents were both gone now, dead for years, although her brothers were still around. One of them had called our house a while back and Mom had hung up on him. She'd told Dad that her brother was a drunk looking for a handout and she didn't believe in handouts. She was proud that she'd done everything on her own. Even her degrees had been financed by loans that had taken twenty years to repay.

"Ariadne," Mom said, startling me. "Didn't you hear the phone?"

I hadn't heard. Now I looked away from my drawing and toward Mom, who was standing in the doorway, smiling and speaking in a gentle voice. She could flip the switch so easily, just like Evelyn. One minute Mom was screaming the F-word at somebody who cut her off in traffic, and the next minute she sounded as demure as a librarian.

I shook my head and she walked into the room, stopping behind me to examine my tree. "That's extraordinary," she said. "I'm glad you took your teacher's advice about drawing everything. He knows what it takes to make it as an artist."

"Or as a teacher," I said, and Mom rolled her eyes because she didn't want me to be a teacher. She wanted me to have an exciting career, better than what she had, even though that idea made me nervous.

But the thought of teaching didn't make me nervous. I imagined teaching art as fun and quiet and far from judgmental eyes. If I tried to be a real artist, people might say I had no talent, and that would ruin everything. There would be no point in drawing anymore, and life would be pointless without drawing. I'd have no reason to memorize people's faces on the subway.

"Summer called," Mom went on, adding that Tina was catering a party tonight and she could use my help with the cooking if I was interested, which I wasn't. I wanted to stay in my room and draw another tree, but Mom thought I had practiced enough for today.

She drove me to Summer's house, where she talked to Tina on the front steps and I went inside. Summer was sitting at the dining room table, cutting strips of dough with a pastry wheel. There was flour on her face, and she blew her bangs out of her eyes.

"How's your stud brother-in-law?" she asked.

Gorgeous as always, I thought. I love it when he walks around the house without a shirt. That weight lifting he does in the basement must really work, because his shoulders are huge. But of course I can't tell you that, Summer. He's married to my only sister and it's sinful for me to think these things.

24

"He's fine," I said.

Summer handed me a rolling pin and a bag of walnuts. I sat down and crushed the nuts, noticing that she wasn't wearing any makeup and thinking she looked much younger this way, more like she did before she blossomed and cast a spell over everyone. Back then—before puberty and highlights and operations to fix her lazy left eye and to straighten her nose—she used to just blend in. Except during the holidays, when some kids picked on her because she had a Christmas wreath on her door and a Hanukkah menorah in her window. *Make up your mind,* they used to say, and I told them they were ignorant. I said that Summer's mother was Episcopalian and her father was Jewish, and Summer was going to pick her religion someday but for now she was both.

"Ari," she said. "I'm sorry for drooling over Patrick, but I'm dying without a boyfriend."

"*You're* dying?" I said.

She knew what I meant—that I'd never had a boyfriend in my entire life. She reached over and squeezed my arm, leaving a smear of flour on my skin. "You'll get one. Then you'll see how nice it is to make love."

She smiled dreamily and I kept hearing those last two words even when she was quiet and cutting dough. She didn't say *screwing* or *banging,* and she called a guy's you-know-what a *magic wand* instead of the four-letter words that everybody tossed around at school. But Summer was mature and smart, and she'd read most of her father's medical books in his library down the hall.

She wanted to be a psychiatrist too, and she already acted

25

the part. She'd explained to me years ago that schizophrenics hear voices and that kidnapping victims can develop Stockholm syndrome, and she once had a talk with a boy in our seventh-grade class who had a crush on her. He used to call her house just to hear her answer the phone, he wrote sappy poems, and we actually found him collecting strands of her hair from her jacket in the coatroom. So Summer sat him down and explained that he wasn't in love with her, that he only thought he was in love because he was suffering from something else—a psychological word that I quickly forgot. Whatever it was, she said it was similar to lust but much worse because it could get you so stuck on somebody that you'd simply lose your mind.

He didn't bother her anymore after that. Summer considered him her first cured patient and started talking about UCLA, her father's alma mater. But I didn't want her to talk about any colleges that weren't in New York. Summer had been my best friend since first grade, and the possibility that she would go so far away was depressing.

"Ari," Tina said later on, when Summer and I were chopping raw steak into cubes. She gave me a piece of paper with a name and telephone number on it and ran her hand across her forehead. Her hair was limp and she looked exhausted as usual. "Please give that to your mother. She needs the name of someone to contact at Hollister."

"Thanks, Tina," I said, and I wasn't being disrespectful. Summer's parents didn't want me to address them as Mrs. Simon and Dr. Simon. They'd told me years ago to call them Tina and Jeff. Mom rolled her eyes when she found out about it and mumbled that Tina and Jeff were *progressive*.

I folded the paper and stuck it in my pocket. I felt Summer staring at me. I'd told her about our inheritance and the Parsons School of Design, but I had never mentioned Hollister Prep.

"Are you going to Hollister?" Summer asked.

She looked nervous. I guessed she was worried that I might accidentally mention embarrassing things to her Hollister friends, things like her eye surgery and her nose job. They must have believed that she was born perfect.

"My mother wants me to," I said. I was still secretly hoping that Mom would forget the whole thing and let me finish my last two years in Brooklyn. But I rarely got what I wanted.

A month later, my parents and I went to Queens for a Saturday-afternoon lunch. Patrick was on duty and I was sleeping over, because Evelyn's due date was getting close and he didn't want her to be alone.

I sat on the couch as Evelyn bent solicitously over Dad, offering him one of those mini hot dog things wrapped in a flaky biscuit. She was wearing a summery maternity dress with a neck that was too low and a hem that was too high. More weight had crept onto her recently and I could see the dimples above her knees.

"Evelyn," Mom said from her seat next to me. "Did Ariadne tell you that she's going to Hollister Prep in September?"

By this point, Mom and I had talked about Hollister Prep. Yesterday I'd admitted that I was afraid. I was afraid of new surroundings and new people, and I was sure I wouldn't make any friends because I hardly had any friends now, but Mom insisted that this was completely irrelevant. In her opinion, I was an interesting, intelligent, fabulous person, and if people didn't recognize that, then they could just go and screw themselves. Besides, it was only for two years, and I had to agree when she said that Hollister would help my college chances. So I was going.

"No," Evelyn said, lowering herself into a chair. Her stomach was gigantic and her feet were too swollen for shoes. "She didn't. So how are you paying for that?"

"Oh," Mom said. "Uncle Eddie left us some money. Didn't I mention it?"

Mom knew that she hadn't mentioned it. We all knew that she hadn't mentioned it. And I could almost hear what my sister was thinking: *Uncle Eddie left you some money, you're sending Ari to an expensive school, how much will that cost, and where's mine?*

That wasn't fair. Mom and Dad had given Evelyn lots of things, like a wedding and a two-month stay at New York–Presbyterian. But she could be very selfish sometimes.

"Well, that's nice," she said in the same bland voice she used lately whenever anything good happened to me, like when I entered a boroughwide art contest last year and won a second-place ribbon. I didn't know why she had to be that way, because I was always happy when good things happened to her. I'd been happy when she married Patrick, even though I'd wished he would marry me.

Evelyn changed the subject by bringing us upstairs to the guest bedroom. It was a nursery now, with walls painted a color called Valentine Rose.

"Sort of loud, isn't it?" Mom said.

Evelyn shrugged. "It's pink. Pink is nice for a girl."

"Yes," Mom laughed. "But you don't know if you're having a girl, sweetheart."

Evelyn's skin suddenly matched the walls and her expression was one I'd seen many times when she lived with us in Brooklyn. It was as if she was about to dissolve into tears or commit a fatal stabbing.

"Evelyn," Dad said. "Is lunch almost ready? I can't wait to eat your tuna casserole."

Tuna casserole was one of her specialties—along with meat loaf and sloppy joes.

Evelyn turned toward Dad. "It has potato chips on top," she said, giving him a faint smile. "Just the way you like it."

We had her tuna casserole for lunch, with her no-bake cheesecake for dessert, and after my parents went home, I washed dishes in the kitchen. Evelyn fell asleep on the couch, and Kieran asked if he could play in the backyard.

I nodded and changed into shorts and a bikini top. After that I sat on a folding chair while Kieran ran across the grass and dove on his Slip 'n Slide as if it was the most fantastic thing ever. It made me wonder who had come up with that brilliant idea—convincing kids that it was fun to skid across a slimy sheet of plastic on the hard ground.

The sun was fading when Evelyn joined us. She carried a bag of Doritos and dragged a chair next to mine.

"Do you know how much weight I've gained from this baby?" she asked, and I shook my head. "Well, I won't tell you because it's too embarrassing. I've turned into a big fat cow."

"Don't say that, Evelyn. You always look beautiful."

She snorted. "You're such a fucking liar, Ari. I mean . . . if you asked what I thought . . . I'd tell you that you've got a good body but your boobs are small and uneven."

What had happened to the sweet Evelyn? I knew that my breasts were small, but they were uneven, too? I looked down at my bikini top and she nodded toward my right breast.

"*That* one," she said. "It's a little smaller than the other side. I can't see it much in normal clothes, but it's obvious in a bathing suit. You should stuff your bra with tissues or whatever."

Later on, when Evelyn and Kieran were asleep, I stood at the bathroom mirror putting Kleenex in and pulling Kleenex out, and after an hour I decided that Evelyn was right. My right breast really was smaller than the left. This was especially upsetting because my list of flaws was long enough already.

There wasn't anything horribly wrong with me, like a receding chin or an oversized nose. My chin was strong and my nose was small and straight. I didn't even have any acne problems. But my face was kind of gaunt and pale, and one of my front teeth slightly overlapped the other. I had thick eyebrows that I had to tweeze relentlessly. Standing in front of a mirror, examining my reflection and criticizing myself, was something I spent a lot of time doing. My latest torture session, however, was cut short by Evelyn's voice outside the door. Her water had broken early and the contractions were starting.

\* \* \*

Sweet Evelyn emerged again on the way to the hospital. We'd had to wake up Kieran and leave him with one of Evelyn's neighbor friends. We also had to take a cab because I didn't drive yet and we couldn't reach Patrick. I'd called the firehouse and was informed that he was out. *Explosion in a high-rise,* the guy on the phone had said.

I left a message and lied to Evelyn. "It's just a grease fire in somebody's kitchen." She worried about Patrick enough; she didn't need to be worrying then, when she was in pain and clutching my hand.

I also called Mom and Dad, who met us at the hospital. Evelyn was being wheeled from the emergency room when she started talking about Lamaze, saying she needed Patrick for that, and Mom offered to take his place.

"No," Evelyn said. "Ari can come but nobody else."

This made me happy and sad at the same time. It was nice to be needed, to be part of Evelyn's inner circle—and I loved her for wanting me there—but I didn't enjoy leaving our mother out. Mom and Evelyn were very skilled at leaving each other out. *We have nothing in common,* Mom often said. *Evelyn has never finished a book in her entire life.*

Now Mom mumbled something that sounded like *Don't let me intrude,* but I wasn't sure. I was following behind Evelyn and a nurse, and we were getting too far away to hear.

We went to a room on the fifth floor that reeked of Lysol. I looked the other way while Evelyn undressed and slipped into a flimsy gown. Next there was a doctor and a needle that went into Evelyn's spine. That made me cringe and she got quiet. She drifted in and out of sleep while I watched television—a news reporter talking about the explosion in the high-rise—but Evelyn didn't notice. She was too busy with the doctor, who kept snapping on latex gloves, sticking his hands underneath her gown, and talking about centimeters.

I wished he wouldn't. It was all so stark and mechanical. How could soft moans behind a bedroom wall possibly result in needles and stirrups and K-Y Jelly? Even though I was still flattered to be a member of Evelyn's private club, I kept hoping that Patrick would show up before I had to help with that Lamaze business.

Luckily, he did. He dragged the scent of ashes with him and I read his jacket as he leaned over Evelyn's bed. CAGNEY. FDNY. ENGINE 258. He was kissing her cheek when he got yelled at by a nurse who ordered him to take a shower in an empty room next door and change into sanitary scrubs. I followed him to the hall and he laughed at me.

"Gross enough for you?" he asked as I studied the smears of dirt on his face. His hair dangled over his forehead and his firefighter clothes made him huge. The big black jacket with the horizontal yellow stripes, the matching pants, the thick boots. "I told your parents I'd send you back downstairs. And I'm warning you . . . Nancy seems pissed off."

So did Evelyn the next day, when my parents and I stopped by in the late afternoon. We'd stayed at the hospital until Evelyn gave birth, and we were so exhausted afterward that we slept until noon. Evelyn was exhausted too. Her labor had been long, she'd lost a lot of blood, and she was in a cranky mood.

"Here," she said, shoving the baby at a nurse. "I'm tired."

The baby wasn't a girl. He was a healthy boy with blond hair, a pink bedroom, and no name. Evelyn never even looked at the second half of the *Name Your Baby* book. Now she folded her arms across her chest, stared at *Days of Our Lives,* and didn't say goodbye when our parents left to get some coffee.

"Look, Evelyn," I said, lifting an elaborately wrapped box from Summer. There was a pair of baby pajamas inside, but they didn't make Evelyn feel better.

"This is for a girl," she said. "I didn't get a girl."

"It's yellow. Yellow is for a boy, too."

"Yellow is for faggots," she said, tossing the pajamas toward her night table.

They fell to the floor and I picked them up, thinking that she was being rude and ungrateful, because Summer had spent a lot of time wrapping that gift. I knew she was disappointed, that she'd wanted a daughter to dress in Easter bonnets, to sit side by side with at the beauty salon and share secrets. She probably wanted a do-over for all the fun things that didn't happen between her and Mom. But I was worried, too. She hadn't looked this miserable since Kieran was born.

# three

When Evelyn had been at New York–Presbyterian Hospital five years earlier, Mom had moved into her house. She'd taken care of Kieran while Patrick was at work, and she'd taught me how to hold a baby's head and how to change a diaper and the best type of formula to buy.

Now I took Mom's place, because she'd caught a stomach virus and Evelyn was still in the hospital. We weren't sure if it was because of all the blood she'd lost or if the doctors thought she was getting crazy again, and Evelyn wouldn't tell us. We only knew that there was a new baby in the family and Patrick couldn't miss work. He had two children and a thirty-year mortgage with a ten percent interest rate, after all. And his family couldn't help. They were in Boston and his mother had little kids at home. Patrick was the oldest; his youngest brother was in the third grade.

So the baby was my responsibility. His name was Shane, only because he couldn't leave the hospital until Evelyn came up with something to put on the birth certificate. She'd gotten the name from a soap opera and I wasn't sure she even liked it.

I held my nephew on a warm afternoon in his nursery, which wouldn't be pink for long. Patrick had already bought two gallons of blue paint because we couldn't let Evelyn come home to a reminder that she didn't get a girl.

Patrick joined me in the nursery that evening, freshly showered after a rough day at the firehouse. He settled into a rocking chair to feed Shane, while I stood there thinking that he was a good father. Not a distant one, either. Patrick changed diapers, and he knew to be careful of the soft spot on a baby's head. He also spent tons of time teaching Kieran how to throw a football and watching televised Red Sox games with him, which Dad didn't appreciate. He was horrified that his grandson was being raised to hate the Yankees and the Jets. It was blasphemy, in Dad's opinion. Brainwashing, too.

"You're doing a good job, little sistah," Patrick said. He also told me that I should take a break and go to the public pool with Kieran.

"I'll just stay for an hour," I said. "Then I'll make dinner."

Patrick rubbed Shane's cheek with his thumb. "I can't wait."

He loved my dinners. The night before, I'd made pork roast and broccoli with hollandaise sauce. The night before that it was stuffed peppers and zucchini in peppercorn vinaigrette. I took the recipes from a cookbook I'd found under the kitchen sink. Someone had given it to Evelyn as a Christmas gift and it was still wrapped in plastic.

Tonight we were having southwestern burgers and twice-baked potatoes, but Patrick didn't know that. I kept the menu a surprise. Then I changed into my bikini in the bathroom. I slipped a pair of denim cutoffs over it and stared at myself in the mirror, stuffing the right side of my top with tissues. But it didn't look realistic and I could just imagine the humiliation of Kleenex floating in the crowded pool if I decided to swim. Kieran banged on the door after a few minutes, and I pulled a T-shirt over my head to hide my deformity.

I kept the shirt on at the pool, where I sat on the edge and soaked my feet while Kieran played with his friends in the shallow end. I had only been here a few times before, but Evelyn was a fixture from Memorial Day to Labor Day. She and her friends spent each summer gossiping and chomping on the salty Goldfish crackers that were supposed to be for their children.

"Are you Evelyn Cagney's sister?" a voice asked.

I looked up and nodded. A vaguely familiar woman was standing there; I recognized the excessive eye makeup and the clear braces on her teeth. Angie, Lisa, Jennifer, what was her name again? It had to be one of these, because almost every woman who lived in Queens and was between the ages of twenty and forty was named Angie, Lisa, or Jennifer.

"So how is everything?" she said. "I heard that Evelyn's having problems."

And I heard that you took a crap on the table when you were squeezing out your fourth baby, I thought. Then I looked at the other end of the pool, where Kieran was splashing around with his friends, whose mothers were talking and glancing at me. They all knew about Evelyn's first meltdown and were probably dying for another one. The phone lines must have been sizzling with discussion of poor Evelyn Cagney and her pathetic relapse.

"No," I said. "That's not true. Evelyn's fine."

"But I heard she's still in the hospital."

"Only because she had some complications with the delivery," I said, which might have been the truth.

She nodded and changed the subject. "You know, I can't believe you're Evelyn's sister. You don't look anything alike."

Insult. For sure. Whether it was directed at me or Evelyn, I didn't know. She could have meant that my face wasn't as pretty as my sister's—that my top lip didn't have a Cupid's bow and there wasn't a natural arch in my eyebrows. Or she could have meant that Evelyn couldn't possibly fit into size-four shorts.

"Well," she said. "It was nice talking to you. I really have to go and pee."

*I really have to go and pee.* I hated when grown women said that. They all did, though. All my sister's so-called friends who were waiting for Kieran to leave so they could rip Evelyn to shreds. They were no different from those hyenas on PBS nature shows—standing in a circle, tearing a carcass apart. I could almost see fresh blood dripping from their chins. And I thought it was sad that some women were still as mean as they'd been in high school. This was their new clique, the housewives who just loved it when one of them couldn't measure up and got cut from the team.

Evelyn called from the hospital that night to say she was coming home in two days. I wanted everything to be perfect, so I stayed up late even though Patrick told me not to. He didn't want me to knock myself out, but I did anyway. I scrubbed the bathtub and cleaned out the hall closet. It was filled with cobwebs and shredded wrapping paper that had been there since Evelyn's first baby shower.

The next morning, Patrick refused to let me help him paint the nursery. "Just take it easy," he said. "You've been killing yourself."

I didn't take it easy. He painted and listened to the radio while I changed the contact paper inside the kitchen cabinets and rearranged the dishes. I was almost finished when Summer rang the doorbell. I answered it in my cutoffs and a shabby shirt. I was completely disheveled, but of course Summer wasn't. She'd taken the subway to Queens after an appointment at a ritzy hair salon in Manhattan and she looked fantastic.

"You look pretty," I made myself say as we walked into the kitchen.

She thanked me and stood on her tiptoes to peer into a cabinet. "It's so neat around here. I bet Evelyn will be happy when she gets back."

"I did a lot of work," I said. "I hope she'll like it."

"Well, she *ought* to. She doesn't know how lucky she is to have a sister like you."

I smiled. "You can watch TV if you want. I'll be finished with the cabinets soon."

She settled into the couch in the living room and turned on *General Hospital,* but she didn't watch it for long. Ten minutes later I found her standing in Shane's nursery, leaning against his crib, twisting a lock of newly highlighted hair around her finger.

She was talking to Patrick. Flirting with him, the way she did with every attractive man who crossed her path. She seemed to think she had to do this to find out if she really was beautiful, or if she was still that mousy girl with the lazy eye and the crooked nose.

I was used to her flirting, but not when it came to Patrick. She rarely saw him, and when she did, Evelyn was always around. Now Evelyn was in the hospital and Summer was wearing a short skirt. She kept sliding her foot out of her sandal and rubbing her heel against her calf. She reminded me of a hooker I'd once seen on Thirty-fourth Street in Manhattan.

Patrick was painting the closet door. Painting and talking but not flirting. Then he noticed that the knob was loose and he turned toward me. "Go get my toolbox," he said.

"'Go get my toolbox,'" Summer repeated. "Don't you know how to say *please*?"

He looked at her, his hair dripping over his forehead, his sleeves rolled to his shoulders. "This is my house. I don't say please to nobody here."

"Well," she said. "Somebody needs to teach you some manners, young man."

Unbelievable. Shameless. I saw her staring at Patrick's arms and it made me sick. She was so nervy to flirt with my sister's husband—in my sister's house—right in front of me and Evelyn's baby! At least I tried to hide my stares. But her comment made Patrick laugh, which annoyed me even more. I stood still until he reminded me about the toolbox, and I rushed to get it from the garage because I didn't want them to be alone for long.

"Can I touch your tools?" Summer asked after I came back and Patrick was rummaging through the box in search of a screwdriver. "I'll bet you've got some really big tools."

He nodded toward the door. "I'm busy, kid. Go play."

She smirked. "Will you play with me, Patrick? Or should I play with myself?"

The radio was still on. A screeching guitar, pounding drums, Eric Clapton. Patrick shook his head and went back to the doorknob, and Summer followed me to the living room. We sat on the couch and I gave her the cold shoulder.

"What's wrong?" she asked.

I spoke in a harsh whisper. "He's my sister's husband. Leave him alone."

She sank into the couch as if I'd hurt her feelings. "I didn't mean anything by it, Ari. It was nothing."

Later on, after Summer left and Patrick and I were cleaning up from dinner, I found out that he didn't think it was nothing. "Your friend is wicked bold for a high school girl," he said as I organized dirty glasses in the dishwasher.

She was *wicked bold.* He didn't approve of her. I loved that. "Do you think she's pretty?" I asked, staring down at the glasses, bracing myself for his answer.

"She's fake," he said. "Bleached hair and shit. And don't you get influenced."

I looked up. "What are you talking about?"

He dried his hands on a towel. He had big hands. *You know what they say about men with big hands,* Summer had told me repeatedly.

"She's not a nice girl. But you are. So stay that way."

"She's a nice girl," I said automatically, because I was so used to defending her. She always gave people the wrong idea. A girl in her neighborhood even called her a dumb blonde to her face. Summer and I laughed at that because we knew better. Tina and Jeff had her tested once and found out that she had a very high IQ.

Patrick raised an eyebrow. "You know what I mean, Ari."

I knew what he meant. I nodded and he left the towel hanging from the sink, all wrinkled and lopsided. I straightened it when he went into the living room to watch the Red Sox with Kieran, thinking that he loved my cooking and he said I was a nice girl, and if he wasn't my brother-in-law I would have kissed him. I was sure *he* wouldn't say that I opened my mouth too wide.

Later that night, I went to the basement with a basket of laundry. The basement was unfinished, with a concrete floor and two tiny windows. A washer and dryer stood against a wall and Patrick's barbells were lined up across the room. He was there now, on his back, bench-pressing God only knew how many pounds as I dropped stained bibs into the washing machine. I did everything slowly because I didn't want to go back upstairs. It was nicer here, with the smell of fabric softener and the sound of Patrick grunting and groaning.

I was filling a plastic cap with Tide when he finished. He stood up, took off his shirt, and used it to wipe his sweaty face. He threw it at me as he walked toward the stairs.

"Toss that in," he said.

"I'm not your maid," I answered, even though I didn't mind being his maid.

When he was gone, I looked at the shirt. It was navy blue with FDNY printed across the front in white letters, and it smelled of him—of beer and charcoal and cologne. The smell made me want to keep it, so I smuggled it into my overnight bag before tucking Kieran into bed. I adjusted his pillows and he mumbled something that I couldn't understand.

"What was that, Kieran?" I asked, sitting on his New England Patriots sheets. Brainwashed, I thought, hearing Dad's voice. Blasphemy.

"You're better than Mommy," he said with a sleepy smile, and I felt good for a second. He probably noticed that I was a more talented cook than Evelyn and that I never yelled at him the way she did. *You have no idea what you're talking about,* she'd said last year when I asked her not to raise her voice because it could hurt Kieran's self-esteem. *All you know is what you see on* Phil Donahue.

But the smug feeling quickly changed into guilt. "I'm not

better than your mommy," I said. "I'm just different. So don't say that to her because it would make her sad. Understand?"

He nodded and I was worried that he didn't understand. But he fell asleep before I could be sure.

The next morning, Kieran went with Patrick to pick up Evelyn at the hospital. I hung a new set of curtains on the kitchen window while dressed in my cutoffs and a sleeveless blouse that I knotted under my chest, and I didn't have time to change before everybody came back.

"You could've asked me," Evelyn said, about the curtains and the cabinets and everything else.

We were standing in the kitchen with Patrick and she didn't look good—there was a bumpy rash on her chin and her hair had frizzed in the humidity on the way home.

"Sorry," I said, disappointed that she wasn't grateful. "I was just trying to help."

She scratched her chin. "There's a difference between helping and taking over. This is *my* house, not yours."

"No kidding," I said.

"Ari," Patrick said in a warning tone that shut me up and annoyed me. I hated when he took Evelyn's side over mine, but of course he did—she was his wife, she'd just given birth to his baby. I assumed she was rightfully exhausted and grumpy, so I offered to take Kieran to the park.

When we came back, Patrick was gone. He was at a landscaping job in Manhasset with one of his firefighter friends. Kieran went to the backyard to play on his Slip 'n Slide, while

Evelyn stood by the stove boiling noodles for a tuna casserole.

"Need some help?" I asked, lingering in the doorway.

"What are you *wearing*?" she said.

I was still in my knotted-up shirt and my shorts, and she stared at my bare stomach and legs like I was a stripper on a pole. She seemed to forget about the skimpy things she used to wear when she could fit into skimpy things. But she made me so uncomfortable that I untied the shirt and let it fall over my hips.

"Nothing," I said. "Just . . ."

"What are you trying to do?" she asked, stirring noodles with a wooden spoon as steam rose into her face. "Get Patrick's attention?"

She turned away and laughed to herself, as if I was incapable of getting Patrick's attention. Or any man's attention. It made me so angry and embarrassed that I couldn't keep my mouth shut anymore.

"I don't want Patrick's attention," I lied.

Evelyn laughed again. She kept her back to me as she lifted the pot from the stove and dumped noodles into a strainer in the sink. "Yeah, sure. You used to climb on his lap whenever you got the chance."

Why did she have to bring that up? And it wasn't whenever I got the chance, it was just once, and I was only ten years old. Patrick had been dating Evelyn then, and he'd been sitting in our living room while she and Mom cooked dinner and I read a comic book on the floor.

He was on the couch watching TV, and I kept glancing

over my shoulder at his light hair and dark eyes. He didn't notice me, but I wanted him to. I had such a crush on him, even back then. So I jumped up on his knee with the comic book as if my only intention was to read him a particularly funny page, and Evelyn got aggravated after she came out of the kitchen. She told me to get lost, to leave Patrick alone, but he said he didn't mind, he had three younger sisters in Boston and they always sat on his lap. Then she charged into the kitchen and returned with Mom, who also told me to get lost. *Don't hang on him, Ariadne,* she'd said. *You're much too old for that.*

I didn't want to get into this now, so I set the table while Evelyn diced an onion that made my eyes water. She didn't say a word until I was finished, when I sat down with a magazine and she stuck the casserole into the oven.

"Mom is picking you up right after dinner . . . isn't she, Ari?"

She just couldn't wait. She acted like I was nothing but a pesky mosquito buzzing around her head. After a few seconds, she suggested that I go and watch TV. She was trying to cook for her family, if I didn't mind.

*Her family.* And what exactly was I? Who had taken care of her kids while she was gone? Was she ever planning to thank me? Oh, and by the way, Evelyn, those friends of yours at the pool aren't really your friends. I defended you to that dingbat with the braces on her teeth.

But I didn't want to tangle with Evelyn—she was too dangerous when she was like this—so I kept quiet in the living room until dinner, when Patrick came home. I sat across from

Kieran, who spit a mouthful of casserole into his napkin and griped that the noodles were too soggy.

Evelyn went to the refrigerator. "What do you want? I'll make a sandwich."

"No," Patrick said. He was sunburned and his eyes were bloodshot. "Kieran can eat what's given to him or he can go to bed hungry tonight."

She slammed a jar of mustard on the counter. "Just because you were raised that ignorant way doesn't mean I'm doing the same thing to my son."

A vein throbbed in Patrick's neck and I knew why. He was tired, his muscles were sore from mowing lawns, and things had been a lot more pleasant around here before Evelyn came back.

She gave Kieran his sandwich and it kept him quiet until dessert was served. It was another no-bake cheesecake, and according to the box, it was supposed to be *delicious* and *delightful*. Kieran didn't agree and he complained again.

"This is disgusting," he said, singing the last word. "Disgusting, disgusting, disgusting . . ."

Evelyn stared at him from her seat, and I wished Kieran would cut it out. The cake was fine; he was acting like a brat. Maybe I had spoiled him when she was away. Maybe if I'd raised my voice once in a while, he wouldn't be saying that same word over and over and Evelyn wouldn't have tears in her eyes.

Patrick must have been thinking the same thing. His voice was stern when he told Kieran to eat his dessert and stop being a pest, but Kieran didn't stop. He smashed his fork against the cake, turned it over, and left a mess on his plate.

"This is gross," he said. "How about a Twinkie?"

Patrick made a fist. "How about this?"

I knew Patrick would never touch him, but Kieran didn't, and he was stunned. Then he sat and sulked until he decided to hurt someone.

"What's on your face, Mommy?" he asked.

She lifted her hand to her chin. "It's eczema, Kieran. Just a rash."

"It's ugly," he said. "Ugly like you."

Evelyn's skin reddened and Patrick got furious. He ordered Kieran to his room, it didn't matter that another Red Sox game was on tonight, and was he planning to play on that Slip 'n Slide thing after dinner? Forget about it. It was going back into the garage until next summer.

Kieran slammed his bedroom door upstairs and the noise woke Shane. I heard him crying and Evelyn joined him. Tears spilled from her eyes, striping her cheeks with mascara. Patrick tried to talk to her but she wouldn't listen, so he followed her to the counter, where she turned her back, cried into her hands, and shoved him away.

"Go fuck your mother," she said.

Patrick just sighed because he knew what was going on. Her hormones were a mess and she couldn't be blamed for anything that came out of her mouth. Then he reached out to touch her but she wasn't done yet. She shoved him again, narrowing her eyes into an evil squint.

"That's what your mother likes, right? Pushing out eight

47

kids, getting knocked up at forty-four. Stupid Irish immigrant. Doesn't believe in birth control. She can't keep her scrawny legs shut."

Evelyn's hands were on her hips. Her body shook and this time she didn't shove Patrick away. He put his arms around her, ran his fingers through her hair, and I just sat there.

I wasn't angry with my sister anymore. Now she didn't seem mean and dangerous—she just seemed young and overwhelmed. I'm sorry, Evelyn, I thought, listening to her cry into Patrick's shirt. I'm sorry that you had a hard labor and you didn't get a girl. And I know I shouldn't feel the way I do about your husband, but I just can't help it.

# four

Right before school started, Summer stepped on a rusty nail in her front yard. The cut required seven stitches and a tetanus shot. She could get around on crutches but she didn't want to. She refused to be seen in public because she had a bandage on her foot and she couldn't fit into her Gucci shoes.

She was excused from school for a week, which was bad luck for me because Summer was the only person I knew at Hollister. Before her accident, she'd assured me that she would show me around and sit with me at lunch. Now I had to go to a new school all alone.

"It'll be okay," Summer said over the phone.

It was the night before the first day of school. I leaned against my kitchen counter, wrapping the phone cord around my wrist, watching it make white crinkles in my skin. "I don't think so, Summer. I don't even want to go."

"Of course you do. It's one of the best schools in the city, and it'll help get you into Parsons."

"What if I can't keep up with the work?" I asked, sighing and loosening the phone cord.

"Ari," she said calmly, the way she often did when I was nervous. "You'll do well, as usual. I know you'll be fine."

If Summer knew I'd be fine, I supposed I shouldn't worry so much. I relaxed a little, but the next morning I still wished she was around. On top of everything else I needed from her, I also wanted her fashion advice, because I couldn't count on Mom to validate my outfit. Mom said the teal shell looked fine under the black blazer and of course it was okay to wear white pants because it was still almost ninety degrees outside, but that didn't help because what Mom knew about fashion couldn't fill a thimble. And Hollister had a strict dress code. According to the student handbook, there were to be no sneakers and no jeans, not even a denim jacket. *Violators will be penalized,* I read. I didn't want to be penalized, especially not on the first day.

"Your ride is here," Mom said, and I saw a silver Mercedes parked outside our house. It belonged to Jeff Simon, who drove Summer to school every day because his office was just a few blocks from Hollister. Now he was my chauffeur too, even without Summer.

Jeff's car smelled of cigars. He was a tall fiftyish man with hair a mix of blond and gray and eyes the color of weak tea. He always spoke to me and Summer like we were his intellectual equals.

"How's Evelyn?" he asked as I sat beside him.

"She's okay," I said, although I wasn't really sure. Some days she seemed fine and other days my parents talked about spending some of Uncle Eddie's money to send her back to New York–Presbyterian Hospital.

Jeff nodded. "She's not symptomatic?"

*Symptomatic.* He had used that word five years earlier. *Is Evelyn symptomatic, is she displaying a flat affect?* I shrugged and he tuned the radio to a classical music station. Then we were on the bridge and I saw the skyline in the distance, below a smear of purple and orange across the early-morning sky.

"A new environment is always unsettling," Jeff said after we reached Hollister Prep and I was wringing my hands while watching a swarm of smartly dressed students file into the building. "Your mood will level out after you get used to it."

I was hoping Jeff was right when I reached homeroom, which was crowded, noisy, jammed with people who knew everyone but me. I sat in a chair against the wall, taking everybody in, sure that I wouldn't talk to anyone but that I'd definitely draw them later. The guy with his arm in a cast, a girl whose sunburned skin was peeling from her cheeks.

I leaned my head back and squeezed my eyes shut. I hadn't slept much the night before; the only thing that had helped was Patrick's shirt. I kept it hidden in my closet beneath a stack of winter scarves, where Mom wouldn't dust or snoop. I told myself that I hadn't stolen it—I had just borrowed it for a while, and nobody would notice because Patrick owned so many of those shirts. I needed it more than he did, anyway. I wore it in bed whenever I had a headache or trouble sleeping, and the smell of it relaxed me like a long hot bath.

"Damn," I heard somebody say, and I turned around to find a redhead searching through a handbag. She looked up and I saw hazel eyes, a small nose, lots of freckles, and no makeup. "Do you have any tampons?" she asked in a raspy voice. "Or some Stayfree? I'm a week early."

There were some Stayfree in my purse from last month, but now the teacher was here and she was taking attendance and I couldn't pull out a maxi pad in full view of the three guys sitting next to me. So I passed her my purse and said she could bring it to the bathroom, she would find what she needed in the left pocket.

She was Leigh Ellis. I found this out when she came back and the teacher called her name. Then the teacher said my full first name in a loud voice and I waited for stares, laughter, all the things I was used to, but nothing happened. There was just silence until I spoke up.

"It's Ari," I said.

"Why do you shorten it?" Leigh whispered in my ear, and I wondered if she had a sore throat. She sounded like she was on the verge of laryngitis.

I twisted around. She was leaning forward, resting her face on her hand. I noticed a widow's peak, a pointy chin, and tiny gold flecks in her irises.

"Why do you shorten your name? It's very pretty," she said, smiling with straight teeth, and I decided that I liked her. There was no way I couldn't. She was the first person besides Mom to say anything positive about my name in all my sixteen years. "It's the title of a book, you know. By Chekhov."

Now I liked her even better. Soon the bell rang and she was off, gliding solo down the hallway past rows of lockers. I walked past girls dressed in tailored pants, crisp blouses, antique earrings made of rubies and sapphires and pearls. Their eyelashes had only a little mascara; their lips, just a touch of gloss. There was nothing reminiscent of my school in Brooklyn—couples kissing against walls, big hair sprayed high and stiff with Aqua Net, Madonna wannabes. No fingerless gloves, no lace ribbon. Not one bustier.

I glanced down at my clothes as I walked into my next class. It was English literature, and I fit in. My light makeup, my straight hair—I was one of them, and that almost made me cry. I had never belonged at my other school, where I was ignored and dismissed as a dull, quiet girl who sat in the back of class and sketched faces in notebooks.

But I couldn't transform into one of those confident types that easily. So on my first day at Hollister Prep, I sat in the rear of each class. I ate my salami sandwich in a bathroom stall while everyone else socialized in the cafeteria. In art class I watched from five seats behind Leigh Ellis as her colored pencils moved across a sketch pad. She was drawing something abstract. It wasn't what the teacher had ordered us to do, but it was good, and more interesting than the bowl of fruit the rest of the class was copying.

I watched Leigh's freckled fingers clutch her pencils, her silver bracelet skim the paper, her thick red hair swish across her collar whenever she shifted her head. She caught me looking at her and I pretended that I wasn't, but I didn't have to pretend. She smiled, waved, pointed to herself and mouthed the word *homeroom,* as if there was any way she could be forgotten.

Jeff was a one-way chauffeur. He drove Summer to school and then she took the subway home, which I did that first day. It wasn't very crowded at four in the afternoon, but the station was warm and so was I. My skin was clammy underneath my blazer after I reached Brooklyn and walked up the steps into the sunshine and sticky air. There were people everywhere, going in and coming out of Asian food markets and Indian restaurants, speeding around on bicycles and honking horns at anyone who got in their way.

"Ariadne," I heard Mom say.

She was standing in front of me. Her hair frizzed as badly as Evelyn's in this weather, and there were dots of perspiration above her lip. She said something about waiting for me, she'd called my name three times, hadn't I heard her, and was I getting delirious from this hot weather?

I hadn't heard her. I'd been thinking that I'd chosen the right outfit that morning and my hair wasn't wrong, and nobody at Hollister had said a single thing that made me want to lock myself in my bedroom and spend the rest of my life there.

"So how was it?" Mom asked, holding her breath. She was probably hoping for something good but expecting something bad. She was more familiar with something bad, like when Summer was voted Prettiest Girl in junior high and I wasn't voted anything.

I heard Mom exhale as we were walking home and I finished telling her about Hollister. I mentioned how much I liked the fancy iron gates outside the school and the girl from my homeroom with artistic ability and knowledge of Chekhov.

Mom was happy. She smiled, put her arm around me, and gave me a squeeze as we stood at the curb and waited for a traffic light to change. She was wearing a tank top, but she shouldn't have been because her upper arms were heavy.

She and Evelyn had the same build. Now I imagined my sister at thirty, aged beyond her years, her beautiful face distorted by too many no-bake cheesecakes the way Mom's face was puffy from Hostess cupcakes. I saw Evelyn wearing a sleeveless housedress, flabby arms swaying as she washed dishes over her kitchen sink, but I didn't mention that. My first day at Hollister had gone well and Mom was taking me out for Chinese food to celebrate. I didn't need any gloomy thoughts banging around inside my head; they haunted me enough as it was. This time I refused to listen.


Leigh wasn't in homeroom the next morning. I worried that she'd never come back, that she'd moved away or transferred to a different school, which would be just my luck.

And I wished Summer hadn't stepped on that nail. I wished she'd come to school on crutches and sit with me in the cafeteria. Because if she did, I wouldn't have to eat lunch in the bathroom while thinking that Hollister wasn't so great after all. It seemed big and scary. Maybe I should have stayed in Brooklyn, where I'd spent my lunch breaks in the art room. The teacher had let me organize her supplies, and I wanted to be there, alone with brushes and paint, eating at a clean desk. Now I was eating on a dirty toilet. So I trudged through the rest of the day and barely noticed when a swish of red hair flew past at the beginning of art class.

"Hey," Leigh said, taking a seat behind me. She was in violation of the rules, dressed in jeans, Converse high-tops, and a maroon T-shirt with the words SUNY OSWEGO printed across the front. "Did I miss anything in homeroom?"

I shook my head, noticing a silver chain and matching arrowhead charm around her neck.

"Colossal waste of time," she said. "I never go."

I didn't know how she got away with breaking so many rules, but I couldn't have asked if I wanted to. The teacher started talking, telling us that this was a free drawing period and we could do whatever we wanted, as long as it wasn't potentially offensive.

"Censorship," Leigh muttered. "Nothing in art is offensive."

I agreed and she got inquisitive about where I was from and where I used to go to school. I answered her questions, adding that I was a friend of Summer Simon, and she gave me a blank stare.

"Never heard of her," Leigh said, and I was sure that she was just confused, because everyone knew Summer. Leigh sounded like she was still nursing a cold, so I decided that her head was congested and it was clogging her memory. I also decided not to mention her when I called Summer that night. The idea that someone was oblivious to Summer's existence would crush her, and I didn't want to be responsible for that.

# five

*I* packed my overnight bag on Sunday morning. Pajamas, underwear, my migraine pills just in case. I was going to spend the day with Evelyn because Patrick was on duty again.

This was Mom and Patrick's idea. But they pressured me to pretend that I had thought of it myself, because Evelyn would get suspicious otherwise. She needed my help, and they knew what was best for her.

They'd been talking about what was best for Evelyn since Shane was born. The two of them were constantly on the phone, which didn't seem ironic to anyone but me. Everybody else seemed to have forgotten that Mom once despised

Patrick and that she'd made a huge scene after Evelyn got in trouble. Mom had picked me up from school the day after she found out Evelyn was pregnant. She drove to Patrick's firehouse and screamed and swore at him on the sidewalk. I watched from her car as she called him a lowlife and a scumbag, and I shrank down in my seat when she asked him if he'd ever heard of a condom. *You should think with your brain,* she had said. *It's in your head, Patrick. Not in your pants.*

Now they were allies. A few times Dad mumbled something about how Mom shouldn't get involved, it wasn't right to meddle, but Mom didn't listen. She said that Evelyn had two children, her nasty attitude might drive Patrick away, and a divorce would be catastrophic because Evelyn had no education or job skills.

"You have nothing to worry about, Nancy," Dad told her as he drove us to Queens in Mom's car that afternoon. The windows were open because it was warm for the second week of September, and Mom's hair floated around her head in a frizzy swirl. "I think Patrick is very much in love with her."

I thought so too. He had to be in love to put up with everything she dished out.

Mom didn't seem convinced, because she made a disgusted face and breathed a stream of Pall Mall smoke through her nose like a bull. "Listen, Tom. I've never said anything about the weight she's put on. I could stand to drop a few myself. But between that and Evelyn's mood swings . . ." She shook her head, inhaled on her cigarette, and blew a gray cloud out the window. "My point is that she's giving Patrick plenty of reasons to screw around."

Dad glanced over at Mom, who was lifting her face to the

breeze and enjoying her cigarette. I thought he might argue with her, but he didn't. He never did. He just tuned the radio to the Yankee game. That was the only sound I heard until we rang Evelyn's doorbell.

It was one of her good days. She stood in the foyer, wearing a sundress that minimized what was wrong and exaggerated what was right. The skirt elongated her legs, the belt slimmed her waist. A beaded necklace got lost in her cleavage. Her hair had been blow-dried smooth, and it framed her refined features and the rare color of her eyes.

She made lunch for us. Chips and dip in the living room, stuffed shells covered with Ragu baked in the oven, Mrs. Fields cookies served with Neapolitan ice cream on paper plates.

"I know you like all three flavors, Dad," Evelyn said, running a scooper across the vanilla and the chocolate and the strawberry. She dropped a tricolored blob on his plate and sat down with Shane on her lap, and I wondered why Mom was so worried, because Evelyn seemed fine. She looked across the table at me and asked how school was going. "Any cute boys?" she said.

Mom was swallowing a spoonful of chocolate ice cream. "Boys are irrelevant," she answered before I could open my mouth. "Ariadne is at Hollister so she can get into a good college and make something of her life."

There was a clock over the sink and I heard it ticking. Mom went back to her ice cream and didn't notice how much Evelyn's face had changed—her jaw was stiff, her mouth tight. How could Mom be so clueless? College, making something of my life, everything Mom thought her firstborn daughter hadn't done. *Boys are irrelevant*—that had been Mom's favorite phrase when Evelyn was a teenager, and I knew what Mom was thinking: You didn't listen to me, Evelyn. And look at where that got you. You're an overweight twenty-three-year-old with a GED and two kids, sitting in an ugly kitchen that your husband can't afford to remodel.

"I love your dress, Evelyn," I blurted out, hoping a compliment would help, but it didn't. She smiled dully, mumbled something about changing Shane's diaper, and disappeared upstairs until it was time for Mom and Dad to leave.

"Don't be a sourpuss," Mom told her on the front steps. "Patrick will get sick of you."

Then she and Dad were gone. Evelyn slammed the door, went to the refrigerator, and plopped on the couch with a beer bottle.

"Fucking unbelievable," she said, prying off the cap. She took a swig and rested her feet on the coffee table. I just watched from the foyer. Sweet Evelyn had vanished as quickly as she'd appeared, and now I was afraid to go near my sister. "Don't listen to what our dear mother tells you about boys, Ari," she said, raising her middle finger to a photograph of Mom on the wall. It was a framed picture from Evelyn and Patrick's wedding, and everyone was smiling. "She'd keep you in a cage if she could. Make you do everything *her* way."

I stared at the picture. I remembered that it had been a sunny day. Mom had hemmed Evelyn's dress the night before, and she had invited Patrick's parents to sleep at our house because they couldn't afford a hotel. She'd driven Evelyn to ten different florists to find the prettiest bouquet, and she'd relinquished a strand of pearls Dad had given her, so that Evelyn would have something old.

"Mom means well," I said.

Evelyn laughed. "Are you aware that she wanted me to have an abortion when I was pregnant with Kieran?"

I was, but I shook my head anyway. I didn't want Evelyn to know that I heard the conversation almost six years ago through the wall that separated my room from hers. She and Mom were yelling and Evelyn was crying, and Mom said that an abortion would be the best way to solve this mess. Then Evelyn could finish high school and go to college—even if it was just Kingsborough Community College or Katharine Gibbs Secretarial School—anything would be better than having a baby before she turned eighteen.

"What a Catholic," Evelyn said. "Only goes to church on holidays and tells her daughter to kill a baby. She's a hypocrite, you know."

I didn't agree with that. Mom wanted what was best for Evelyn. I remembered her voice behind my lilac wallpaper, saying that Evelyn was throwing her future away, she was so young and so beautiful and Mom didn't want her to end up as a dependent housewife who had to ask her husband's permission every time she wanted to buy a new pair of socks.

"I don't think that's true, Evelyn," I started, but it was all I got to say.

"It is so," she said.

She turned on the television and finished her beer while

I went upstairs to the bathroom and swallowed two migraine pills. I was glad I hadn't forgotten them this time, because a fluorescent purple web was crawling into my left eye.

Later that night, I fell asleep in the living room because I had to. The guest bedroom didn't exist anymore. I woke up on the couch on Monday morning and heard Evelyn in the kitchen, asking Kieran what kind of cereal he wanted—Frosted Flakes, Apple Jacks, or Cap'n Crunch? Next there were Shane's babbling noises and Patrick slamming barbells against the basement floor, and soon Evelyn rushed past me with the kids, saying that Kieran was late for kindergarten and I should remind Patrick that he had to drive me to school. I didn't mind going to school, because I wouldn't have to eat lunch in the bathroom. Summer was coming back today.

The front door shut and I watched from the window as Evelyn sped away in her minivan. It was warm outside. A filmy haze covered the block, and everything was quiet except for the neighbor's Doberman barking and Patrick exercising downstairs. I went into the kitchen to eat breakfast and he came in a few minutes later, sweating, naked from the waist up.

"I gotta drive you to the city this morning, don't I?" he said, and I nodded as I tried not to stare at his chest. "I'd better hurry up and take a shower. What do they do at that place if you're late? Beat you with a ruler?"

I laughed. "I think they'd go to jail if they did *that*, Patrick."

"Not when I was in school. Those nuns used to smack the living shit out of me."

"There are no nuns at Hollister," I said, and he told me that nuns were sadistic and vicious and the reason why his kids were going to public school. Then he went upstairs. I heard the shower running and thought sadly about Patrick as a young boy in a stiff uniform, being terrorized by ferocious packs of ruler-wielding nuns.

Nobody could terrorize him now—he was too tall and strong. I admired his broad shoulders underneath his shirt as we climbed into his truck at the curb. He stuck a cassette into the tape deck, Bruce Springsteen singing about the Vietnam War or something like that, I wasn't really listening. Patrick was talking about Evelyn, saying that she seemed better lately, she was settling into a routine, and did she seem okay to me?

"I think she's fine," I said, because we both wanted it to be true.

Twenty minutes later, Patrick left me at Hollister and I had to fight my urge to clutch the back of his truck as he drove away. Even though Summer was here, I would have preferred to spend the day with Patrick, to hang out at the firehouse, maybe even sit in the fire engine as it raced around Queens, but of course that was just stupid.

"I'm back," I heard Summer say when I was spinning the combination on my locker.

We weren't in any classes together, not even homeroom, but at least I could eat lunch in the cafeteria like a normal person, which I did later that day.

Summer sat beside me, nibbling a Chipwich and talking

about some guys who'd installed new tile in her parents' bathroom. One of them was from Canada and was incredibly good-looking and flirty.

"He gave me his number," she said. "Not that I'll call. I'll just add it to my collection."

She meant her collection of phone numbers, which she kept in her bra drawer with the velvet diary. Her insistence on mentioning every single man who flirted with her was getting on my nerves. "That's nice," I said, glancing around the cafeteria.

I spotted Leigh Ellis a few tables away. She was sitting alone, skimming through a novel. She'd skipped homeroom again this morning and now she left the cafeteria early, waving at me on the way out. Summer was utterly shocked.

"You *know* her?" she asked.

"She's in my homeroom," I said.

Then Summer started talking. Gossiping, really. She told me that Leigh didn't have to go to class because one of her relatives had founded Hollister Prep and her uncle was some big-deal lawyer, and she was going to graduate from this school with good grades even if she lit the place on fire and danced nude in the ashes.

"She had a boyfriend," Summer whispered. "College guy. He died in a car crash upstate last winter. I heard she was driving . . . drunk, supposedly. She was out of school for three months after that but of course she didn't have to repeat the year. She seems to have recovered, because she's got a new boyfriend already . . . I've seen him pick her up in a Porsche. He's got a nasty scar on his mouth . . . I guess he must've been born with a cleft lip."

I nodded, dizzy from information overload. The bell rang and we walked out of the cafeteria and through the hall, where Summer pointed to a bronze plaque with words underneath a man's aristocratic profile. FREDERICK SMITH HOLLISTER, it read. FOUNDER OF HOLLISTER PREPARATORY ACADEMY, 1932.

"Leigh isn't directly related," Summer said. "I think the connection is through her uncle—the lawyer I told you about. It's his wife's father or something. I'm not sure because she doesn't talk to anyone." Summer waved to a group of guys who were walking past and then she spoke into my ear. "Listen, Ari . . . I'm glad you're here. But everybody at Hollister . . . they don't know about anything that happened in Brooklyn and I don't want them to know. Understand?"

I nodded. "It's our secret."

The next day I found out that Summer had been wrong when she said that Leigh didn't talk to anyone, because she talked to me in art class. We also talked during the cool, late-September mornings when she actually came to homeroom, throughout October while we drew the bright orange trees outside our art-class window, and into November, when all the leaves were gone and the sky filled with clouds and we sketched everything in black and gray.

It was on one of those afternoons that our teacher announced a project, a paper we had to write about a modern artist. He listed names on the blackboard and said that we could work in pairs, and Leigh and I both raised our hands when he pointed to *Picasso* scrawled in lime-green chalk.

"Do you want to come to my apartment tomorrow to

start working on it?" she asked from her seat behind me, and I turned around.

She was wearing her SUNY shirt and she was touching her silver bracelet. She looked optimistic, but I let her down. I paused for too long, thinking of everything Summer had told me. The car crash. The drunk driving. I liked Leigh but I wasn't sure if she was safe outside the iron gates of Hollister Prep.

She read my mind. Her face dimmed and I thought again about the gossip. It could all be a lie or a skewed version of the truth. Summer should have known better than to spread rumors. So I accepted the invitation.

# six

*Summer* slammed her locker door in a snit the next day. I'd just told her that we wouldn't be riding home together because I was going to Leigh's apartment, where we planned to extract Picasso information from books that we checked out of the Hollister library.

But that wasn't exactly what happened. Leigh and I were walking away from school beneath a dusky sky when she said something about Twenty-third Street. She thought she'd lost her bracelet but she hadn't—it had been found, she had to pick it up, and I didn't mind, did I? It would only take a few minutes and the bracelet meant a lot to her.

The wind bit at my cheeks as I shook my head. Then Leigh and I sat in a series of subway cars that took us to West Twenty-third Street, which was crowded with old row houses. They were narrow, four stories high, separated by just a sliver of an alley. We stopped at a building that had fire-escape ladders across the top three floors, and windows covered with plywood. I heard noise inside, rough voices and drills and hammers—construction workers, who I saw at the far end of the building after Leigh opened the door.

The place had a dank smell, mixed with sawdust that the drills were kicking up. I listened to men shout at each other about nails and bolts, and Leigh started walking up the staircase in front of us. It was slim, long, advancing into darkness. I followed her, hearing the steps creak beneath my feet.

"This is my cousin's place," Leigh said as she rapped a red door with a gold knocker. "He's planning to turn it into a dance club. His father thinks he's insane."

Her cousin opened the door and I saw his apartment— a renovated loft with exposed brick and a skylight and modern furniture, all black, leather, and glass. There was an adding machine on the coffee table, in the middle of stacks of receipts and cash.

"Ariadne Mitchell," Leigh said. "This is Delsin Ellis."

I guessed that Delsin Ellis was about twenty-four. He was stocky and average height, and he had dark hair, an aquiline nose, and eyes that were an unusual color. I couldn't tell if they were green or gray or both.

"Del," he said, extending his hand, and I took it.

"Ari," I replied, which made Leigh sigh.

"I can't believe either of you," she said. "Such distinctive

69

names and for some strange reason you shorten them." She looked at me. "My cousin was lucky enough to be given a name that reflects our Native American heritage."

I glanced at her necklace, at the arrowhead charm. Now it made sense.

" 'Native American heritage,' " Del repeated. "A hundred years ago, maybe. And mixed with German and Irish and everything else."

Leigh crossed her arms. "We have blood from the Shawnee tribe and you know that, Del." She looked at me again. "Del's father and my mother are brother and sister. They're from Georgia originally. The Shawnee used to be all over Georgia."

"Nobody gives a shit, Leigh," Del said, and waved us over to a bookcase. He took her bracelet from a shelf and she locked it around her wrist. It was an ID bracelet, the silver one she always wore. It wasn't meant for a girl, it was made for a man, with heavy links and the initials M. G.

"Take it to a jeweler and get it shortened so it doesn't fall off again. You might lose it in the street next time instead of in my car, and I don't want that to happen," Del said as I examined his face. I saw a ropy scar that began near the middle of his upper lip and weaved its way into his left nostril like a snake.

A scar on his mouth, a cleft lip—Summer was so wrong. Leigh hadn't already recovered from her dead boyfriend. The bracelet that meant so much to her was probably his. And she didn't have a new boyfriend. All she had was a cousin.

Leigh nodded and said that she and I should go, sounding raspy as usual. I'd recently figured out that there was never a cold or laryngitis, she was just naturally hoarse.

She kept talking after Del shut the door behind us and we

were heading down the staircase. Then we were on the side-walk and Leigh was talking about Del. I'd guessed his age correctly, and she was telling me other things—that his mother had died twelve years ago, that he had a younger brother, and that he was a college dropout.

"So many strings were pulled to get him into Northwestern," Leigh said. "He didn't exactly have the grades. Then he starts a fight with some engineering student over a parking space and gets himself expelled. . . . Del knocked out the guy's front teeth, if you can believe it. My uncle had to fork over a lot of money to make that one go away."

"Oh," I said, for lack of anything better.

The wind blew Leigh's hair across her face, long copper strands against freckled skin. "I shouldn't talk badly about him. Everybody else does," she said. "His name . . . it's Native American, and it means 'He is so.' My uncle always says 'He is so stubborn,' 'He is so angry,' 'He is so stupid.' This whole thing about starting a business . . . Del bought that dump with some of the trust-fund money he got from his mother. I hope it works, because nobody has any faith in him and he needs something meaningful in his life."

"Oh," I repeated, wondering why Leigh was telling me all this. But I was the only person she ever talked to at school, so I figured she was lonely and there was nobody else who would listen.


Leigh's apartment was in a modern building on East Seventy-eighth, with a doorman who ushered us through a glass door into a mirrored elevator that played Muzak as it

71

carried us to a small but well-decorated and bright apartment on the twentieth floor. It had fashionable furniture, windows covered with sheer turquoise drapes, and silver appliances in the kitchen.

We sat down at the kitchen table and pored over our library books, scribbling Picasso facts on loose-leaf. I was reading about one of his most famous paintings, *Les Demoiselles d'Avignon,* when I had to use the bathroom.

"Through the living room and down the hall on the right," Leigh said, pointing in that direction. She was too engrossed in Picasso to lift her head.

I walked through the living room, past a heather beige sofa, an oak coffee table the color of sand, and a Georgia O'Keeffe painting on the wall—an abstract flower, a blast of pink and orange and a light shade of turquoise that matched the curtains. Then I was in the hallway and a door at the end opened. I saw a tall, willowy young woman with spindly limbs, hair the same color as mine, and a beautiful face. She wore a short nightgown that was practically transparent.

"Hi," she said. "I'm Rachel."

"I'm Ari." I was closer now, so her face was clear. Her skin was olive-toned, smooth and flawless. Her nose was prominent but perfectly straight, her eyebrows were thin and arched, and her eyes were dark and shaped like almonds. Rachel was model-beautiful, as gorgeous as those women on the cover of *Vogue*. I couldn't imagine who she was, maybe Leigh's older sister, but they looked nothing alike.

"Do you need to use the girls' room?" she asked. "You go ahead . . . I'll wait."

I locked myself in the bathroom and took care of business quickly because I couldn't be rude and keep Rachel waiting. She slipped into the bathroom after I left. Leigh was still reading about Picasso in the kitchen when I walked in.

"We should go to MoMA," she said after I sat across from her. "To get a feel for his work. We can write about it better that way, don't you think?"

I nodded. Then I heard water running in the bathroom and Leigh heard it too. She said she didn't know that her mother was awake, and I couldn't imagine that the woman I'd just met could be anyone's mother, especially not someone as old as Leigh.

"Did you see her?" Leigh asked, and I nodded again. "She doesn't usually emerge from her slumber before five o'clock. You know . . . the fact that she's old enough to have a teenage daughter practically gives her the vapors. Not that she's really old enough to have a teenage daughter. She's only thirty-four."

I subtracted quickly—thirty-four, sixteen. Leigh was born when Rachel was eighteen. Evelyn had been three months short of eighteen when she gave birth to Kieran, but I wasn't inclined to blab my family secrets, so I didn't say anything.

Leigh told me that Rachel always slept during the day. I assumed she had some kind of night job, although I couldn't imagine what that was. She didn't seem the type to make change in a tollbooth or take care of sick people in a hospital.

"What does she do?" I asked, thinking that I was too nosy, but Leigh didn't mind.

"Hangs out at nightclubs, mostly. Studio Fifty-four was

her favorite when it was really popular. She's friends with one of the owners. He's sick now, though. AIDS." Leigh whispered the last word, like AIDS could be caught just by mentioning it. "My mother actually does have a job . . . she's a makeup artist on Broadway. It used to be *A Chorus Line* and now she's doing *Cats,* but only Tuesday through Thursday. She won't work on weekends—too busy with her social life. She's lucky that my uncle supports us or I don't know where we'd be. Living in a cardboard box on the corner, probably. Or in a trailer park in Georgia."

She said *Georgia* with a hokey Southern accent, and that was the last thing she said for a while. We went back to our books, to Picasso. We read about his rose period and his cubism period until I noticed that the apartment wasn't bright anymore.

"I'd better go," I said, glancing around for my coat. "It's late."

I'd forgotten that Leigh hung my coat in the hall closet. She brought it to me and I was closing the buttons when she said something about calling a car service to take me home.

"I'll be fine on the subway," I told her, thinking I only had a ten-dollar bill in my wallet and I was sure that wasn't enough to pay for a cab ride from Manhattan to Brooklyn.

"It's dark outside, Ari," Leigh said. "And dangerous. The subways are filled with people who've been kicked out of Bellevue too early. Don't you watch the news?" She picked up the phone and started dialing. "This is the service my uncle's firm uses and it's completely free . . . I won't take no for an answer."

I couldn't find a reason to argue. We rode the elevator downstairs, where we stood with the doorman until a glossy sedan arrived. I slid onto the backseat and watched Leigh wave goodbye through tinted windows. Then I listened to 1010 WINS while the driver sped through Manhattan, past skyscrapers and traffic lights in a swoosh of red and yellow and green.

Soon we were in Brooklyn and I saw different things—unassuming houses, Saint Anne on our lawn. The wind was so fierce that she and little Mary looked like they were huddling to stay warm.

Mom was in an apron on our steps. The front door was open behind her and I smelled our dinner from the sidewalk as the sedan drove off. I walked toward her, sure she was annoyed that I was late and that I hadn't bothered to call. Her expression was a combination of ticked off and puzzled, and she was looking down the street at the sedan, its scarlet brake lights glowing in the dark.

"What the hell is this?" she asked.

I assumed she was wondering why I'd been driven home by a chauffeur as if I was some kind of socialite, but I was thinking of other things. I was thinking of a dilapidated row house on West Twenty-third Street and a bright apartment on East Seventy-eighth, and Delsin Ellis with the Shawnee blood and the scar on his lip. I had no idea how to answer Mom's question because I couldn't explain any of it.

# seven

*Summer* didn't eat lunch with me the next day. She was supposed to—I went to the cafeteria carrying a paper bag that Mom had stuffed with ham on rye and a Hostess cupcake—but Summer immediately said something about her friend who lived in an apartment nearby. She whispered that every so often they'd sneak over there and order a pizza even though leaving campus during school hours was a blatant violation of Hollister rules.

"Do you want to come?" she asked, chomping on a square of Bubble Yum.

I looked over her shoulder at a group of girls who

belonged in a Bloomingdale's catalog. They were standing in the doorway with Louis Vuitton purses dangling from their wrists. And they were authentic Louis Vuitton—not the fake kind with the upside-down *L* and *V* that foreign guys sell in dark alleys.

I glanced back at Summer—at her indigo eye shadow, her lips that were wet from pearly peach gloss. She wore a tight angora skirt set with high-heeled boots that made her as tall as me, and a long strand of silver beads was looped around her neck three times.

"No," I said.

Her brow furrowed. "Why not?"

Your friends scare me, I thought. I don't know enough about designer shoes and dating rituals to fit in. But I couldn't admit all that, so I just shrugged.

"Ari," she said. "I really want you to come with us. I can't leave you by yourself."

"It's okay. I'll probably find Leigh around here some-place."

"Leigh?" Summer said. "She's a weirdo and a drunk driver."

"Summer," I said, and my voice held the scolding tone that usually comes from teachers and parents. "You shouldn't talk about people like that. Or spread rumors about them."

Her eyes widened as if I'd just shouted "Summer Simon swallows." "Yeah, I know," she said, and I ate my sandwich alone after she was gone because Leigh never showed up.

I didn't see her until last period, which made me wonder if she slept all afternoon like Rachel and just strolled in for art because it was the only class that didn't cause yawning fits.

"Want to go to MoMA after school?" she said.

She was wearing her Converses again, with the SUNY Oswego shirt underneath a blazer that didn't match. And I did want to go to MoMA, but Summer wasn't happy when I told her about it later that afternoon.

"We're supposed to ride home on the train together," she said, and she was right, so I compromised. I invited her to MoMA, where she and Leigh and I looked at Picasso and at melting clocks in the Dalí exhibit.

"This is idiotic," Summer said. She'd never been an art fan.

"I think it's amazing," Leigh answered, which Summer repeated in a sarcastic tone later when she and I were inside a subway car speeding toward Brooklyn.

"She's strange," Summer said, examining her fingers. She spotted a chip in her manicure, took a bottle of polish from her purse, and executed a skillful touch-up. "I'm sorry, but it's true. Haven't you noticed the way she dresses? I've seen her wearing that shirt three times in the past week. From what I hear, Oswego is where her dead boyfriend went to school. It's probably his shirt, and that's not psychologically healthy. She has to let go."

I shrugged as lights flickered inside the subway car. I thought about the shirt, wondering if it really had belonged to Leigh's boyfriend, if she never washed it because it smelled of him, if she wore it for the same reasons that I slept in Patrick's shirt. Then Summer mentioned Thanksgiving. She asked if we were eating at Evelyn's next week the way we usually did, and I shook my head.

"My mother is cooking this year" was all I said, because

she didn't need to know that Evelyn wasn't doing well lately, that Mom kept sneaking the telephone into our laundry room so that Dad wouldn't hear her conversations with Patrick, or that Evelyn didn't cook anymore, not even tuna casserole or no-bake cheesecakes. Patrick had told Mom that there was never anything in the house but Doritos and Dunkin' Donuts.

"We'll all have a nice day today," Mom said on Thanksgiving when she was bending into the stove and jabbing our turkey with a fork. "You'll help with the baby so Evelyn can relax. Everything will be just fine."

She nodded as if that would make it so. But she seemed disappointed during dinner, when Dad and Patrick argued about football and Evelyn did nothing but eat. She drowned her turkey in gravy and devoured three slices of pumpkin pie, and from the look on Mom's face, I knew she was worried that Evelyn's weight would be an excuse for Patrick to *screw around*.

Then a button popped off Evelyn's blouse and landed on Dad's plate. I wasn't surprised—she was bursting right out of her bra.

"Goddamn it," she said, snatching the button back. Her face turned splotchy like it had been during most of her first pregnancy, when she'd cried about the squiggly purple stretch marks that left scars on her skin.

"That happens to me all the time," I lied. "Things are made so cheaply these days."

Evelyn's jade eyes shot toward me. "Who the fuck asked *you?*"

I didn't think anyone had to ask me. I was just trying to be nice, but now I didn't know why I bothered. Forgive her, I thought. Her hormones are still out of whack and she has no idea what she's saying.

Mom tried to fix things. "Evelyn," she said. "Go find something else to wear in my closet. Take whatever you want."

Evelyn went upstairs. Dad took a walk to burn off some calories, Mom disappeared into the kitchen with the kids, and I heard the clang of dishes being washed while Patrick and I sat at the table.

"Well, that wasn't very nice," he said. "Go get me a ruler."

"For what?" I asked.

"So I can smack some sense into my wife."

I giggled. I loved him for being on my side. He was gone a few minutes later, off to work his shift at the firehouse, leaving Evelyn and the boys for Dad to drive back to Queens later on. I fed Shane his bottle on the couch while Kieran spread out on the carpet with a coloring book and a box of Crayolas.

"Mom," I heard Evelyn call from upstairs. "Can you come up here, please?"

Her tone was urgent, and I was worried that she couldn't find a single thing that fit. I was wiping formula off Shane's lips when Mom came out of the kitchen in her apron and slippers and headed up the stairs, and I'd just turned on the TV when she called my name.

I climbed the steps with Shane in my arms. The hall was

dark except for the light coming from my room, and my knees got wobbly when I saw Evelyn sitting on my bed with Patrick's T-shirt draped across her thighs.

Mom was in the doorway. Evelyn stood up and took Shane away from me. One of her curls smacked my right eye as she turned back to the bed. I felt sick. I had never expected that Evelyn would go rummaging through my closet.

"What's wrong?" I said, blinking the sting out of my eye, shocked at how calm I sounded. Nobody could possibly know that I was close to puking on Mom's terry-cloth slippers.

"Nothing," Mom said. "Evelyn found Patrick's shirt in your closet and she was wondering how it got there."

Evelyn rolled her eyes. "I *know* how it got there, Mom. Ari stole it from my house."

"Who gave you permission to snoop through my things?" I said.

"Why can't I snoop through your things?" Evelyn asked. "What are you hiding?"

"Evelyn," Mom said. "Patrick must've left that shirt here accidentally. Remember when he helped Dad paint the kitchen last spring? I know I did some laundry for him then, and it probably got mixed in with Ariadne's clothes."

"Yeah," I agreed, because this was such a reasonable, innocent explanation.

"Oh, please," Evelyn said, glaring at me. "You know he makes you cream your pants."

I despised that expression. It was so crude, so crass, the type of thing that Evelyn's low-achieving friends used to say while they smoked Marlboros on street corners instead of going to school. "You're disgusting," I said, clenching my fists so tightly that my nails dug semicircles into my palms.

"Girls, girls," Mom broke in before Evelyn could lunge at my jugular. She sat on the bed, stuffing Patrick's shirt into the front pocket of her *Kiss the Cook* apron. "Evelyn, you shouldn't talk to your sister that way. Patrick is your husband, and Ariadne would never do anything inappropriate. The idea is just ludicrous."

"Even if she did," Evelyn said, lifting her chin, "it wouldn't matter. Ari could strip naked in front of him and he wouldn't go for it. He isn't turned on by flat-chested teenagers, you know. Patrick only loves me."

The truth hurt. It hurt more than the worst migraine that ever festered inside my head. For a moment I hated Evelyn, sitting there all smug and haughty, the proud owner of Patrick's love. The worst part was that she was right. He did only love her, and he loved her so much that he overlooked the extra weight and the eczema, her roller-coaster moods and tuna casserole.

Then Shane started crying, which was good because it took the attention off me. But Evelyn got upset because his diaper was clean and he was fed, so there was no reason for him to be crying.

"I always get the criers," she said, pacing the floor while patting his back. "Kieran was exactly the same."

"They *all* cry," Mom told her.

"My friends' babies don't cry for nothing," Evelyn insisted, and she started crying for nothing too. She wiped her runny nose with her hand and I didn't hate her anymore. Don't listen to your friends, I thought. They're lying. Their babies cry too. Those horrible women want you to fail so they'll have something to gab about at the pool.

"I'll take him," I said. "Why don't you lie down on my bed for a while and relax?"

"Good idea," Mom chimed in. "Isn't that a good idea, Evelyn?"

Red lines marred the whites of Evelyn's eyes and she looked sorry for what she'd said before. She smiled; Mom and I closed the bedroom door and went to the living room with Shane. Dad took Evelyn and the kids back to Queens a few hours later, and I waved from the sidewalk as they drove away. It was cold outside, and crispy orange leaves spun in clusters on the cement. I turned back to the house, noticing Saint Anne watching me from the corner of her painted eye.

Inside, I hung my coat in the hall closet and felt Mom behind me. She gave my hair a sharp yank that made me lift my hand to my head, feeling for a bald spot.

"What was *that* for?" I asked.

She didn't answer. She smiled, holding up Patrick's shirt with her left hand. There was a laundry basket in her right. "I'll wash this and give it back to him."

Please don't, I thought. You don't know how much I need it. "Okay," I said, but my voice wasn't as steady as it had been in the bedroom, so I tossed my hair and cleared my throat to cover any sign of weakness.

"I figured you wouldn't mind," Mom went on, jamming the shirt into the basket along with gravy-stained dish towels and Dad's boxer shorts. "You've outgrown it, haven't you? You really should have by now."

At that moment I knew Mom hadn't forgotten the one time I sat on Patrick's lap. It was so humiliating that I wanted to disappear. And I thought about how Mom was a talented ringmaster, orchestrating everything in our circus of a family, trying to keep us all on the right track.

"Of course I have," I answered, wondering if I ever would.


Jeff's Mercedes was in front of my house on Monday morning. While Summer examined her face in a compact, I sat in the back and noticed that our neighbors had been busy over the weekend. All the Thanksgiving decorations were gone, replaced by wreaths and bows tied on mailboxes and lampposts.

"How is Evelyn doing?" Jeff said.

I shrugged. "Not great."

"Is she seeing anyone?" he asked, meaning a psychiatrist, and I shook my head.

When we reached Hollister, Summer went to her home-room and I went to mine. Leigh was actually there, dressed in an oversized SUNY Oswego sweatshirt. I wondered if it belonged to her boyfriend, but I couldn't ask.

"You're invited to a party," she said. "A week from this Saturday."

I turned around. Leigh's hair was pinned back. The arrow-head charm grazed her sweatshirt and her bracelet rested on her hand instead of her wrist because it was still too big. I thought she should hurry up and take it to a jeweler before it got lost forever.

"What party?" I asked.

She explained that her uncle was having his annual Christmas bash. It was at his apartment, a hundred people were invited, and he always let her bring a guest.

"Is your cousin going to be there?" I asked.

She knitted her brow. "You mean Del?"

Who else could I have meant? I nodded, thinking about his name. Del. Delsin Ellis. It was just as distinctive as Leigh had said.

"He'll be there," she said, then lifted her thumb to her mouth and chewed on her nail. She looked like there was something she wanted to tell me but wasn't sure she should. "He thinks you're pretty, you know."

I didn't know. I never would have thought that—compliments were hard to come by. Del's made me think about him all morning, through calculus and American history and even during lunch, while Summer babbled about an engagement party.

"Do you want to do it?" she said, but I was clueless. I wasn't listening. I was staring across the cafeteria at Leigh, who was flipping through *ARTnews*. I wanted her to look at me so I could wave her over to sit with us, but she probably wouldn't have, anyway. Summer hadn't exactly been charming when we'd been together at MoMA, and she was even less appealing now that she didn't have my undivided attention.

"You've got no idea what I'm talking about, do you?" she said, to which I meekly shook my head. Then she got huffy and spoke in a loud voice as if I was deaf or stupid. She told me that Tina was catering an engagement party next weekend and they could use my help if I was available.

I wasn't available. I'd been invited to a party at an apartment that was big enough to fit a hundred guests, with an older guy who allegedly thought I was pretty. I wanted to tell Summer, to brag the way she would, but I didn't. I lied. I told her I was spending the weekend in Queens, which was an acceptable excuse. I was sure she'd get huffy again if she heard the truth. It would devastate her to find out that I'd once again jilted my best friend for a girl who wore the same shirt three times in one week.

The next day Leigh gave me an invitation to her uncle's party. Even though the party was going to be at his home, the invitation had been mailed from his office. It was made of thick red paper, tucked inside a gold foil envelope with printing on the back: ELLIS & HUMMEL, P.A. EMPIRE STATE BUILDING. 350 FIFTH AVENUE. 98TH FLOOR. Leigh's uncle's name was Stanford Ellis.

I'd never been inside the Empire State Building and neither had my parents or Evelyn, because Mom said that real New Yorkers never did those touristy things. But I imagined that a man who owned a law firm on Fifth Avenue and whose Christmas-party invitation ended with the words *Black tie optional* expected his guests to wear something special.

"Can I get a new dress in the city?" I asked Mom the weekend before the party. It was Saturday morning, and she and Dad were sitting at our kitchen table reading the newspaper over a coffee cake. Mom was already smoking a cigarette, and she gave me a look like I had suggested a trip to Mars.

"In the city?" she said, as if the city wasn't only a few miles away. She looked at Dad and they let out a simultaneous laugh, went back to the newspaper, and left me standing on the tiles.

But I couldn't go to Stanford Ellis's party in some old clearance-rack rag from my closet. "The party is a semi formal, Mom. Black tie optional."

"Well," she said. "La-di-da."

Dad laughed and I almost cried. Didn't these people understand anything? Didn't they notice that I never went anywhere interesting or did anything exciting? I wanted to tell Mom that I had to look decent at the party because someone who might be attracted to me was going to be there, but I was smarter than that. *Boys are irrelevant,* she'd probably say.

We compromised. We went to a local Loehmann's, where she promised to buy me a dress that was practical and sensibly priced.

"This big-shot friend of yours," Mom said as we browsed the racks. "She might invite you to some other parties, so pick out something you love. I'm not buying a new dress every time, Ariadne. You're not Princess Diana."

I knew I wasn't Princess Diana. And Leigh wasn't a big shot. But I also knew Mom would make me leave the store empty-handed if I argued, so I didn't. An hour later we were back in the Honda, where I clutched a shopping bag, grateful for what was inside—a knee-length black velvet number that had been on sale for twenty percent off. A little black dress. Summer always said that every girl should have a little black dress.

I carefully packed it in a garment bag on the night of the party, and searched my dresser drawers for a pair of panty hose while Mom watched.

"Is your homework done?" she said.

"Yes," I answered, trying not to sound snotty even though she'd asked me that same question three times already.

"And Leigh's parents . . . they'll be at home?"

I was going to Leigh's apartment so we could get ready and take the car service to the party together, and I knew Rachel would be there, but the word *parents* threw me off. Leigh had never mentioned her father, and it would have been rude of me to ask. "Her mother will," I said.

"Her mother," Mom said. "What about her father?"

"I don't know, Mom. They're probably divorced. Just about everybody's parents are divorced."

She grunted. I didn't want to look at her, so I kept rummaging through the drawer. Then Mom gripped my arm and I had to look. Her eyes were puffy, and I wished she would dye her hair soon. She was so negligent about her hair.

"Be back by midnight, Ariadne. Not a minute later."

Midnight was fair. I agreed, and then I rode in the sedan that Leigh had ordered for me. The driver took me to Leigh's apartment, where Rachel opened the door. She was dressed in another nightgown, and her long hair cascaded over her shoulders.

"Can I tell you something?" she said a few minutes later. I was sitting beside her on the couch and Leigh was in a chair across from me, shaking her head.

"Oh, Mama," she said, which was weird. Everyone I

knew called their mother Mom or Mommy or Ma. The way Leigh said it reminded me of an old Elvis Presley interview I'd seen on television once. Mama and Daddy, that was how Elvis referred to his parents, and I guessed it made sense, because he was from the South too.

Rachel's accent was slight. I heard it after she ignored Leigh and spoke to me. "Ari," she said. "You have beautiful eyes. But honey, you're not tweezing those brows right. Let me fix them and I'll make you gorgeous."

Leigh seemed insulted. "Mama," she groaned. "What's wrong with you? Ari didn't ask for a makeover."

But I didn't mind. I couldn't pass up the opportunity for a professional makeup artist to make me gorgeous.

Rachel clicked her tongue. "*You're* the one who needs a makeover. I haven't seen you in lipstick for almost a year."

I'd never seen Leigh in lipstick either. Or mascara or anything else. Leigh's boyfriend had died almost a year ago, and I wondered if makeup didn't matter to her anymore.

"I'm fine," she said.

"You're not, but we'll discuss it later," Rachel said, and the next thing I knew, I was sitting on the edge of a bathtub and she was crouched in front of me with a look of intense concentration, as if she was performing microsurgery instead of plucking my eyebrows. When she was finished, she turned to Leigh. "See?" she said. "Wasn't I right?"

Leigh smiled and admitted that my arch was perfect. "You really opened up her eyes."

"Just keep her away from Del," Rachel said, then turned back to me. "He's a runaround like my father was. I swear he

*89*

wants that club so he can have a bar full of girls just a staircase below his bedroom."

I guessed Leigh wasn't kidding when she'd said that everybody talked badly about Del. She and Rachel left me alone to get dressed for the party, and I stared at myself in the mirror, thinking that I looked better. My eyebrows were artfully sculpted and they ended in tapered points at the outside corners of my eyes, which seemed bluer somehow. I stared for a while, zipped up my dress, and stepped into heels that made me much taller than Leigh.

She wore flat shoes. No makeup. Her dress was plain, the same color as a paper lunch bag and just as wrinkly. Rachel told her to find something else, she had a whole closet filled with more attractive things, but Leigh didn't listen and Rachel didn't argue. She was too busy working on her hair and her face and her dress, which was made of sequin-covered white satin that twinkled inside the sedan on our way to the party.

We weren't in the car for long. Stanford Ellis's apartment was only a few blocks away, in a tall building with a concierge and a granite floor in its lobby. We got into an elevator that played a symphony through invisible speakers; there was a leaf-shaped sconce on the wall made of frosted glass. Rachel pressed a button and we rode to the top floor, where the doors opened into what I thought was a shared hallway but was actually a private foyer.

We were standing on granite again. I felt heat from flames burning low in a fireplace and I smelled the greenery that covered a round table in the middle of the room. The walls around us were dark wood. We walked into a carpeted living room with floor-to-ceiling windows that boasted a breath-taking view of Manhattan.

I'd never seen the city from so high; I didn't think this place was really an apartment. It was a penthouse. It had a big kitchen and a formal dining room and a wide staircase of creamy pearl marble with an intricate iron railing. There were people sitting on the stairs wearing expensive suits and classy dresses, holding wineglasses and scotch glasses and cocktail napkins, probably because there was nowhere else to sit. The couches and chairs were filled with other people who were drinking and talking and laughing, and I noticed a man weaving his way through the crowd, spending just a moment with each person, like a bee pollinating flowers.

"That's Uncle Stan," Leigh said, pointing a freckled finger in his direction.

We were eating mini-quiches that we'd snagged from a gloved waiter's tray. We sipped Perrier and leaned against a wall and I watched Stanford Ellis, who wasn't what I expected. He wasn't as old as my parents and he wasn't as young as Rachel. I decided that he was in his forties and as handsome as any actor.

Leigh introduced him a few minutes later. He was Rachel's height and they had the same nose. His wheat blond hair was thick and his skin was tan. He didn't spend any more time with us than he did with his other guests, but he filled every second with smiles and charm.

"What's the matter with you, Leigh?" he said in a fading Southern accent, his dark eyes fixed on me. "Bringing such a pretty girl to the party. I'll have to lock up my sons."

He probably didn't mean it. But when he was gone, I

pretended he did and it got me all happy and excited and I kept sipping my Perrier, hoping Leigh wouldn't see that I was desperate for a compliment. She didn't seem to notice. She started talking about Del, who had just arrived and was working the crowd as expertly as his father.

We ran into him in the kitchen before dinner was served. The caterers were dropping sprigs of parsley on plates and Del was mixing his own drink.

He wasn't wearing a tie. The top of his shirt was open underneath his blazer and he smelled of cologne and tobacco. He smiled at me and Leigh with his scarred lip.

His eyes were greener than the last time I'd seen him. I hadn't realized until now how sharply his nose hooked downward at the tip, and I decided that he wasn't nearly as handsome as his father, but he made me much more excited.

"You ladies want a drink?" he asked.

I shook my head. I'd never had more than a Budweiser, and tonight wasn't the time to start experimenting. I needed to keep my wits about me so I wouldn't do anything stupid or embarrassing or both.

Leigh folded her arms. "We're underage. Not everybody breaks the law, Del," she said teasingly, and I remembered the engineering student with the missing teeth.

"Funny," he said.

She smiled, leaning against the counter. "Where's your brother?"

Del's drink was in his hand and he shook it to spin the rum inside. "Blake's upstairs. He's studying for finals like a good little boy."

Blake didn't join us for dinner, which was a buffet set up

in chafing dishes on the dining room table. Everyone loaded their plates and Leigh found an empty spot on a soft leather couch, where I settled down between her and Del and barely touched my food because I had to avoid getting spinach stuck in my teeth and dribbling marinara sauce down my chin. I couldn't humiliate myself, especially not with Del so close that his knee was touching mine.

His pants were smooth. He wore a gold bracelet and a diamond pinkie ring. He left twice to get more food and three times to refresh his drink, and I worried that I was boring and he wouldn't come back, but he always did.

"I'm opening my club on New Year's Eve," he told me. "You should come."

"I don't think I could get in," I said, because the minimum age for those clubs was twenty-one and I didn't have a fake ID. Del laughed and I felt a trickle of sweat roll down my back.

"That was cute," he said. "And don't worry. I won't let anyone keep you out."

I smiled and sat there talking to Leigh and Del until Rachel told us it was time to leave. Del walked with us to the foyer and Rachel looked at him after pressing the elevator button on the wall.

"Give me and your cousin a kiss goodbye, delinquent," she said.

He smirked and obeyed, then the elevator doors opened and he got close to me when Rachel's and Leigh's backs were turned. He whispered something in my ear, something that sounded like "Merry Christmas," and I felt the stubble on his chin as he kissed my cheek.

It was just a regular kiss. It was the same kiss he gave his aunt and cousin, the same nothing kiss that all the guests were giving to each other as they filed out of the party. But he clutched my shoulder and rested his hand on the small of my back, and it made me breathe faster because nobody had touched me that way since the Catskills boy.

"Leigh," Rachel said when we were in the car. "Did you see Blake tonight?"

Leigh shook her head. "Del told us he was studying."

"Hiding, more likely. Stan tells me he's still upset about that girl."

What girl? I wondered, but only for a moment. Rachel and Leigh were quiet now and I pressed my forehead against the window, watching lights whiz by while Del's kiss simmered on my skin.


When I walked into my house later that night, Dad was asleep and Mom was in the living room, smoking a Pall Mall and scribbling on a notepad.

"Are you working on a novel?" I asked.

"Aren't I always?" She ripped three pages from the pad, crumpled them in her hand, and told me to sit down. "I'll get a snack and you can tell me everything."

She went to the kitchen, came back with a plate of sandwiches, and handed me a warm glass. It was filled to the rim with milk and I didn't want it, but she wouldn't take no for an answer. Mom always forced milk on me and Evelyn to make our bones strong or whatever.

"I heated it up," she said. "It'll help you sleep tonight."

I was too excited to sleep. I kicked off my shoes and Mom and I sat cross-legged on the couch, where I told her about the fancy elevator and the penthouse. I mentioned Leigh's uncle but not her cousin, because Stanford Ellis was safe—I could talk about him the way I would any unattainable older man, like Don Johnson or Tom Selleck. But Del was twenty-four, like Patrick when he got Evelyn in trouble, so I kept him to myself.

# eight

*I* slept late the next morning. I would have slept even later if Dad wasn't so noisy when he climbed a ladder next to my window to line our roof with Christmas lights. I saw his feet on the rungs as I looked outside. I also saw a dusting of snow on Saint Anne's tranquil face. Mom was next to her, searching through a box marked *Extension Cords*.

There were more boxes in the living room. They gave off the scent of candles and the aerosol stuff that Mom always sprayed on our artificial tree to make it smell like real pine. The house reeked of Christmas and it boosted my mood, which was good already because I still felt Del on my cheek. I felt him while Mom and Dad were shouting at each other about whether they should use white or colored lights on our hedges, while I toasted a Pop-Tart, and even after the phone rang and I heard Patrick's voice.

"Evelyn has the flu," he said. "And I gotta go to work."

So we had to go to Queens, where I only got to see Patrick for a minute. He was waiting at the front door and he rushed past us without so much as a hello kiss because he was late for his shift.

This was the first depressing thing. There were many others, like the sound of Evelyn puking in the bathroom, the pile of dirty dishes in her kitchen sink, and the mountain of withered tissues that she hadn't bothered to clear from her coffee table. And even worse was the obnoxious blue Muppet that Kieran was watching on TV in the living room. I felt a headache starting and I didn't have my migraine pills, so I asked if he could watch something else, but he ignored me.

"Kieran," I said. "Please change the channel."

Dad was reading the newspaper in the kitchen, Mom was washing dishes, and Evelyn sneezed on the couch. She wiped her nose with a Kleenex but she didn't do a very good job, because when she looked at me, there was a sickening shimmer of snot above her lip.

"That's his favorite show," she said.

"It's giving me a migraine, Evelyn."

Her throat was filled with phlegm and she sounded like an old woman dying of pneumonia. "Oh, poor you. Go back to Brooklyn if your ears are so damn delicate."

She raised the volume on the TV and scratched her eczema, and I wanted to grab the tissues and use them to smother her. I wanted to tell her that she was nasty and rude and that I had come here to help even though I would rather be at home. I would rather be drawing or reading and not listening to some puppet sing a stupid song that was worse than nails drilling into my skull, but I didn't say that. I just went to the kitchen, where I complained to Mom.

"I know," she said. "But we have to be careful around her."

We had to be careful. I couldn't kill my sister. All I could do was set up a cot in the nursery and rest in the dark with Shane while Mom drove to the store to pick up some aspirin, Evelyn went to sleep in her bedroom, and Dad played with Kieran in the living room.

My blanket smelled of Patrick, which made me feel better. I stayed wrapped up in it until I heard a shrill noise and I went downstairs, where Kieran was rubbing his hair and crying.

"He hit his head on the table," Dad said in the airy tone adults use to convince children that they're not really in pain. But Kieran kept bawling and Dad put him on his lap on the couch while I watched from the bottom of the stairs.

That was what depressed me the most. More than the messy house and the puking and the snot. It depressed me because I only got that from Dad once, on a summer day when I was six years old. I accidentally slammed my finger in a drawer while Mom and Evelyn were at Pathmark. He came rushing into my bedroom, and after he checked that my finger was still attached, he scooped me up and told me in a soothing voice that everything was okay until I believed him.

That was the one and only time. There were other times

I wanted that kind of attention again, lots and lots of times, like when I came home from junior high with a tear-stained face because Summer had been voted Prettiest Girl. But Dad was working on his car in the garage and he just stared at me from ten feet away like I was ridiculous and said that Mom would be home soon.

At that moment I decided that I really was ridiculous, because I was twelve and my breasts were growing and my hips were curving, and I figured that breasts and hips were the things that made you a grown-up and grown-ups weren't supposed to cry to anyone. They weren't really supposed to cry at all, but if they did, they had to do it alone, locked in a bathroom or in the car when nobody else was there, and if anyone noticed their bloodshot eyes, they had to shake it off and be all stoic and say *Oh, I'm just fine.*

I believed this for a few years. I believed it and bravely accepted it until the first time I saw Evelyn cry to Patrick and he held her and stroked her hair, and I thought it was the most hopeful thing I'd ever seen.

Summer rushed to my front door on Monday morning, carrying a Bloomingdale's shopping bag. Her hair poked out of a fuzzy pink hat and there was a matching scarf around her neck with pom-poms that bounced against her black coat. She smiled, pulled a box out of the bag, and shoved the box at me as she stepped into my front hall.

"This is for Evelyn," she said. "For the baby, I mean. It's an outfit my mother and I bought at Bloomingdale's yesterday. . . . It's so precious that we just couldn't resist."

I considered telling Summer to bring the precious outfit back to Bloomingdale's for a refund because Evelyn was on Santa's bad list this year and she didn't deserve a baby gift. But I just thanked her and put the box under our Christmas tree.

"And here's something for *you*," Summer said as I turned around. She dug into the bag, took out a cedar box, and handed it to me. I saw EMPIRE STATE FINE ART SUPPLIES engraved in the wood. "My mother and I passed by there on our way to Bloomie's and I *had* to go in."

I opened the box. "Summer," I said with a gasp, running my finger across a row of pencils and charcoals, taking in their brand-new smell. "They're beautiful. But that store is expensive . . . you didn't have to spend so much money on me for Christmas."

"Oh, this isn't a *Christmas* present," she said. "It's just because you like to draw."

I closed the box and gave her a hug. We went outside and Jeff drove us to school, where Leigh didn't show up for homeroom or even art class. She must have gone to at least one of her classes, because I saw her in front of Hollister when Summer and I were leaving that afternoon.

She was walking across the street, heading toward a charcoal-colored Porsche with a young man leaning against it. He wore a long black coat and was smoking a cigarette, and it took me a second to figure out that he was Del.

Summer groaned. "There's the weirdo and her ugly boyfriend. Doesn't he look like an Indian? I heard somewhere that she's an Indian, so it makes sense. Maybe she's his squaw."

She laughed but I didn't. "Native American," I said, thinking that she sounded like a racist and wondering how someone who had the patience to psychologically counsel her own stalker could turn into a completely different person in matters relating to Leigh Ellis. It was such a change from this morning. "*Native American* is the proper term."

Summer seemed thoroughly insulted. "Whatever," she said, but she pronounced it "what-ev-er," breaking it into syllables as if the syllables were separate words.

"And she's only part Native American," I went on. "From way back."

We headed toward the subway, and for some reason Summer kept talking about Del.

"I think he looks like an Indian," she insisted. "His hair is so dark, and did you see his nose? And that hideous scar on his mouth? If Leigh marries him and has babies, they could get the same thing. I saw a picture in a medical book of a baby with a cleft lip—it was like a big wet gaping hole in the middle of the kid's face. I almost puked. That's a genetic birth defect, you know."

"My hair is dark," I said. "Lots of people have dark hair. And he has light skin and light eyes—and she's not going to marry him, Summer. He's her cousin."

She stopped walking. "How would *you* know anything about his eyes?"

Because I saw them when I was at his apartment, I thought. I also saw them at a penthouse party in the city on Saturday and I spent an hour last night mixing paint to match his shade. But I can't tell you that, Summer. I'll conjure up something believable and considerate to answer your question. You think I was in Queens instead of Manhattan on Saturday night and I wouldn't want to hurt your feelings, even though you're becoming so shallow it scares me.

A few days before Christmas vacation, when Summer sat with me during lunch period and she was all cheery because she'd reconciled with her Columbia guy, I caught Leigh's attention as she glanced up from *ARTnews*.

"Why did you have to do that?" Summer said after I waved across the cafeteria at Leigh, who closed her magazine and walked in our direction.

She settled down next to me; Summer was across from us. Leigh acted friendly and Summer sat stock-still in her chair like an absolute prig. Then Leigh started talking about Del and his club and the opening-night party on New Year's Eve.

"He told you about it, didn't he?" Leigh said, and I nodded and stiffened, feeling Summer's eyes sear holes in my face. "You can come, Summer . . . if you want to."

She did want to. I wasn't sure if it was because she liked the idea of being the private guest of a Manhattan nightclub owner—even one with a birth defect—or if it was just spite. And during the subway ride home that afternoon, she didn't ask where or how I had spoken to Del. She pretended that the entire issue was unimportant, which was even worse.

"I'll bring Casey," she said. "Leigh told me that I could bring a guest."

Casey was the Columbia guy. He was blond and good-looking and the mention of him reminded me that I didn't have a guest to bring, but I didn't feel bad. Normally I would have—I would have felt inadequate and unattractive and I would have spent hours pondering my uneven breasts—but this time I decided to be positive. I was going to see Del next week and he had kissed me and touched the curve in my back, and any guy who did such a thing to a girl had to have at least a smidgen of interest in her, didn't he?

But Mom couldn't know about that. I only told her that I wanted to go to a nightclub on New Year's Eve and that Leigh's cousin owned the place, and it was all perfectly safe because Leigh's mother would be there and I wouldn't have a single drink.

She puffed on a cigarette while I argued my case and then she demanded to meet *This Leigh Person,* as if I was five years old. But I agreed and Leigh stopped by on Christmas Eve so we could exchange gifts.

I gave her a sweater and she gave me an Eighty-eight-Shade Pro Eye Shadow Palette. It came in a glazed black case with a built-in mirror. She told me that Rachel had chosen this particular set because it was the appropriate match for my skin tone.

"Leigh is very nice," Mom said after she was gone. We were in the living room while Dad slept upstairs, and she handed me a plate of homemade butter cookies. "You can go to the club as long as you come home at a reasonable hour."

What a relief. I smiled and selected a cookie in the shape of a star.

The next day, Evelyn came to Brooklyn with Patrick and the boys. She'd lost seven pounds from the flu; her face was thinner, her eczema was almost gone, and she wore a royal blue dress with a Christmas present from Patrick—eighteen amethysts that formed a teardrop and hung from a gold chain around her neck. She whispered in my ear that they couldn't afford anything extra this year, but she'd been feeling so low lately that Patrick wanted to give her something special, so he just put it on their MasterCard.

I fawned over the necklace. I smiled after Mom whispered in a relieved voice that Patrick and Evelyn were getting along better. I snapped a Polaroid of them on the couch as Patrick's hand squeezed Evelyn's leg and Evelyn's head rested on Patrick's shoulder. And when they kissed under the mistletoe that hung from our kitchen doorway, I cheerfully agreed with Mom that they were a beautiful couple. Then I hid in the bathroom for a while. I was so jealous that I almost cried.

# nine

*It* was New Year's Eve and there was a party downstairs. Summer and I were in her bedroom, and she was frowning at my outfit.

"It's just too boring, Ari," she said, glancing at the imitation satin blouse that was my Christmas gift from Patrick and Evelyn. Then she reached into her closet and started tossing things on the bed until she found something supposedly appropriate—a black suede miniskirt and a bustier similar to the one she was wearing. "I hate to be so critical, but you usually want my advice and I'm only trying to help."

I knew that. But I couldn't wear a bustier. Hers was pink with jeweled lavender florets and underwire that hiked up her breasts; I couldn't imagine leaving the house in such a thing. "I can't, Summer. That top wouldn't look right on me."

"Well, maybe not. I know you're uneven up there. But it's barely noticeable."

She turned back to her closet and I felt the blood drain from my face, thinking that it couldn't possibly be *barely noticeable* because she had noticed it. And Evelyn had noticed it. And God only knew who else. Now I wanted to forget this whole thing, but Summer distracted me by latching a pearl choker around my neck.

"There. It's flashy but preppy. I know you love the preppy crap, Ari."

*Preppy crap.* That made me feel fabulous. I felt even better when she said my pants were too loose and my shoes were dull, but I took her advice because she did have a lot of fashion sense. So I ended up leaving her bedroom wearing my blouse, her choker, the suede skirt, and a pair of black pumps that she never wore because they were too big.

"You're going now?" Tina said.

Summer and I had just pushed through a crowd of guests on our way to the kitchen, where we found Tina staring through the window of her oven. The house smelled delicious and Tina looked exhausted.

"The car is outside," Summer said. "I won't stay out too late."

Tina pursed her lips and swung around to the counter. She peeled a sheet of wax paper from a tray of deviled eggs and shook her head. "I'm letting you off easy tonight, Summer.

But the next time I have a party at home or an event to cater, I expect your help."

"You don't have to work so hard," Summer said. "Dad makes plenty of money."

Tina was arranging eggs into a perfect circle on a plate. "Money has nothing to do with it. . . . I have a business and responsibilities. I have a reputation, you know."

They got into a tiff that lasted until Jeff and the scent of cigars joined us. He said that everyone was asking for Tina. Tina said she would be there in a minute and she didn't say anything else to Summer, so we left.

Once we were in the back of the sedan, Summer gave the chauffeur her boyfriend's address. I had to move to the front when Casey got into the car, but it was better that way, because as I checked my makeup in my compact, I saw the reflection of Casey and Summer kissing and groping. She only brushed his hands away after they reached her bustier.

"Wait until later," she said. "You're so pushy."

He was? She had never told me that. But I didn't think about it for long, because soon we were on West Twenty-third and there were so many cars and people in front of Del's building that the chauffeur had to drop us off way down the street. Summer was between me and Casey as we walked toward the club, and she kept saying "Isn't this exciting?" while the wind blew her hair into my face. It slapped my nose, but I didn't mind. Summer was right—this was *very* exciting. A strobe light flashed behind the windows in the two lower floors of Del's building, and we bypassed an endless line of people who gave us the stink eye while they waited behind a velvet rope.

The entrance wasn't the front door, which Leigh and I had used the last time we'd been here. It was on the side of the building. Summer and Casey and I waited there for Leigh so she could get us past the sinister-looking bouncer with the shaved head who was in charge of letting people in.

"What's the club called?" Summer asked.

"Cielo," Leigh said, suddenly behind me. "It means 'sky' in Spanish."

That was an appropriate name. Before Leigh had gotten here, I'd been staring at the pointed roof of the building, thinking that it nearly skimmed the moon, wondering if Del watched the stars through the skylight in his loft on clear nights.

Leigh spoke to the bouncer. He stepped aside and ushered us in, and the music was so loud I thought my eardrums might burst as I listened to Modern English—drums and a synthesizer and a male voice singing with a British accent. Lights pulsated in bursts of blue and yellow through smoke-filled air, and guys and girls were lifting their arms and grinding against each other on the dance floor. I thought I'd made a smart move by taking my migraine pills before I left home tonight. The lights and the noise would have given me a massive headache otherwise.

Summer, Casey, and I followed Leigh through the crowd until we reached a crescent-shaped bar surrounded by people sitting on stools covered in faux zebra skin. There were lit candles on the bar, a mirror behind it, and bottles of Stolichnaya and Johnnie Walker Black that were poured by three bartenders.

Leigh said something to one of them, I couldn't hear what, and the next thing I knew we were behind the bar, going through a door into a dark room that I guessed was an office because it had a desk and a phone, and then there was Del, standing in front of us in black pants and a silk shirt with the first three buttons undone.

Leigh made the introductions. Del shook hands with Casey and with Summer. He kissed Leigh and he kissed me and I felt his hand on the curve between my back and my rear end, which got me all shivery.

"No underage drinking, please," he said. "I'll lose my liquor license on my first night."

We nodded and Del said he had some things to do so he would see us later. Leigh and Summer and Casey and I went back to the club, where Casey found an empty barstool and stayed there because he wasn't a dancer.

The rest of us were. We carved out a space in the crowd, and we danced to the blare of Wham! and Duran Duran until our feet were sore and we had to take off our shoes and dangle them from our hands. Summer kept taking breaks to visit Casey, but Leigh and I were afraid to lose our spot, so we stayed right there.

I saw Del in the distance, working the crowd, and I also spotted Rachel, who looked beautiful in leather pants and a metallic halter top, dancing with various men. I caught her eye and she waved, jangling a jumble of bracelets on her wrist.

"Who's *that*?" Summer asked.

Her breath smelled of alcohol. I glanced across the club at Casey, who'd been sitting there all night with a glass in his hand, and I guessed that the glass had been refilled several times with something that wasn't Pepsi. He probably had a fake ID and was sharing his drinks with Summer. I was sure that neither one of them cared about Del and his liquor license.

"Leigh's mother," I said.

Her eyes grew big and round. "Really? Jesus."

We kept dancing and Summer kept crossing the room to be with Casey, and soon she started laughing too much and I knew she was drunk. Then she and Leigh and I got tired of dancing, so we stopped and found seats next to Casey at the end of the bar.

"Why did your cousin name this place Cielo?" Summer asked, yanking on her bustier, which had begun a downward slide.

Leigh was sipping a mock Pink Lady with an orange slice stuck on the rim. "His girlfriend is Spanish. She gave him the idea."

Summer nodded and touched up her lipstick, Leigh ate her orange slice, Casey ordered another drink, but for me the party was over. Del had a Spanish girlfriend and I was such an idiot.

"Hey," Summer said, reaching across me to tap Leigh on her sleeve. "Did Ari tell you I thought Del was your boyfriend?"

Leigh shook her head. What Summer said after that wasn't meant to be cruel—she was probably trying to be sympathetic and use her counseling skills when she said she was sorry that Leigh's boyfriend died, losing someone in such a tragic way must be horrible, blah blah blah. Summer's eyes were glassy and her face was flushed, and she didn't shut her mouth until Leigh opened hers.

"I think you've had enough to drink," she said, and Summer looked even more offended than she had when I'd told her that *Indian* wasn't the proper term. "You're not supposed to be drinking anyway. My cousin asked you politely, as I recall."

Leigh turned her head, gazing across the club. Summer was quiet at first. I knew she was formulating a good response, the way people do during the whole car ride home after they've been insulted at a party and they make a lengthy mental list of clever comebacks.

"*You're* one to talk," she said finally, as her bustier slid down and her cleavage bounced up. "At least I'm not planning to drive my boyfriend home tonight."

Leigh's face went pale and I thought I saw her lip quiver. "Fix your top," she said. "You don't want people to think you're a slut."

She shouldn't have said that. Leigh didn't know about the condoms on the locker or the nail polish on the bathroom wall. But Summer had never forgotten, and now her chest heaved up and down as she leaned across me again.

"Not that it's any of your business, Leigh . . . but I've only slept with one guy. And I haven't killed him."

I cringed. Leigh's eyes filled with tears. She jumped off the stool and shoved through the crowd toward Rachel while Summer muttered the word *bitch* and Casey put her coat over her shoulders.

"We'll get a cab," Summer said. "Right, Ari? Let's leave."

I watched her button her coat. I didn't want to leave. I

wanted to find Leigh and make sure she was okay. Summer was angry and flustered, and she seemed to think I was too. I just sat there until she stopped buttoning and looked at me.

"Right, Ari?" she said again. "Let's get out of here."

I touched the choker she'd given me. "I don't want to leave yet, Summer. I want to talk to Leigh before I go."

Her mouth fell open. "*Leigh?* Why would you talk to her after what she said to your friend?"

What about what you said to her? I thought. But I didn't say it; Summer was upset enough already. "She's my friend too. I can have two friends, can't I?"

Summer closed her mouth. She looked like I'd punched her. "You've never had two friends. *I've* always been your friend. You've always *needed* me to be your friend."

I didn't know what to say. There was a straw on the bar; I picked it up and started bending it in different directions. Now I knew why Summer had hated Leigh from the beginning—because it made her feel important to be my only friend. She was right when she said I had always needed her, and I supposed she wanted to be needed. I supposed everyone did.

"I never abandoned you," Summer went on, shouting over the music. "When I went to Hollister . . . and I made other friends . . . I never ditched you. I was always there for you."

I tossed the straw back onto the bar and looked at her. Her eyes were glistening. She was right again—she hadn't ditched me, even though most people would have. She had still invited me to her sweet sixteen and hadn't let me hide in the bathroom all night. She'd even stood next to Uncle

Eddie's coffin with me and put my thank-you note in his cold hand.

The strain between Summer and Leigh had worn me out. The music was deafening and I was tempted to jump in a cab and go home, but I couldn't do that to Leigh. "I know," I said tiredly, reaching over to squeeze Summer's shoulder through her coat. "I just want to stay for a while longer, that's all. It's New Year's Eve . . . and you know I never get to go any-place."

Summer tugged pink gloves onto her hands, looking at me disdainfully from the corners of her heavily made-up eyes. "Why aren't you on my side?"

"There aren't any sides," I said, thinking that having two friends was more complicated than I'd ever expected. "I don't want there to be."

She shook her head. "There are *always* sides, Ari. And I *hope* you're only staying because it's New Year's Eve."

I was sure we both knew that wasn't the reason, but we didn't talk about it anymore. Casey said goodbye, and he and Summer walked away, pushing past people as they headed to a bright red Exit sign. I looked over the crowd and saw Rachel and Leigh across the room. Rachel hugged Leigh and led her away, and I watched until I couldn't find them in the shimmery sea of people.

Then I watched Del. He was weaving in and out of the crowd, shaking men's hands and kissing women's cheeks, and every time he kissed a woman, he rested his hand on the small of her back. It was enough to make me wish I was back in Flatbush, eating Mom's leftover cookies and waiting for that stupid ball to drop over Times Square.

* * *

I wasn't sure how I ended up in the front hall, walking toward the staircase that led to Del's apartment. I had spent a long time alone at the bar, watching people dance and kiss and gaze longingly into each other's eyes while nobody gazed at me. Nobody except the sleazy overweight guy who kept offering to buy me an Alabama Slammer.

I didn't deserve that. I didn't deserve to be hit on by someone like him. I had shiny hair and well-groomed eyebrows and I was thin and above average height. I might not have been as sexy as Summer or as exotic as the image of Del's girlfriend that I'd spent the last hour concocting, but I was better than this fat creep with his three chins and his tacky pierced ear.

So I had bolted. I had given up on finding Leigh. I'd forced my way through the crowd until I saw a door that I hoped would lead to fresh air and a cab ride home. But of course I'd chosen the wrong door, and now I was in the front hall passing the staircase.

"It's all right, baby," I heard a voice say, and it was Rachel, huddling with Leigh on the lower steps. Leigh leaned her face against Rachel's neck and Rachel spoke in a comforting voice. They made me think of a widow and her child who'd been evicted by a greedy landlord. The two of them against the world.

It was a private moment, so I tried to sneak past. But when I heard my name, I turned around. Neither of them moved. They kept their arms around each other while Leigh apologized for ditching me.

"I'll call a car to take us home, Ari," she said, then turned back to Rachel. "You go inside, Mama. You were having fun before I ruined it."

Rachel held Leigh's face in her hands. "You didn't ruin anything, baby."

Leigh insisted. Rachel left and Leigh looked at me. "Let's go use Del's phone."

I didn't want to use Del's phone. I didn't want to see his loft with the exposed brick and the skylight with its amazing view of the stars. I wanted to forget about him, because how could I have expected that somebody like Del would be interested in me? The whole idea was preposterous. I just wanted the night to end.

I couldn't tell Leigh that, so I went. She had her own key, which she used to unlock the red door; then she picked up the telephone and I sat on a couch.

There were no partitions between the rooms. I stared at Del's bed on the far side of the loft. It was lacquered black with a mirrored headboard and rumpled sheets that dripped suggestively to the hardwood floor. There was a window next to it, and I saw gargoyles on the neighboring building. Or maybe they were dragons. I couldn't make them out from where I was, so I walked to the window and pressed my forehead to the glass, but I didn't see dragons or gargoyles. I saw spooky angel faces with apple cheeks and rosebud lips like Evelyn's.

I looked away, around the room, because Leigh's back was turned and she was still on the phone, and I had a chance to snoop. I slid open a bureau drawer, where I saw cigarettes and a pair of frilly panties that I was sure belonged to the Spanish girl. She probably had straight teeth and a cute accent and perfectly even breasts.

"Our ride will be here soon," Leigh called across the loft.

I closed the drawer. "Okay," I said, and felt Leigh's hand on my arm a minute later.

She sat on the bed and I sat with her. "Listen," she began, and I was uncomfortable. I couldn't stop imagining what had made the sheets so disheveled, and I wondered what it would feel like to lie down right here with Del next to me instead of Leigh. "You should know a few things," Leigh was saying.

Then she told me about her boyfriend. She said that he was a nineteen-year-old zoology major who had planned to become a veterinarian. She also said that whenever she had visited him in Oswego, he had let her drive his car for practice. She'd never so much as made an illegal turn until one Saturday last December. That night, they were driving back to his dorm after a movie when she skidded on an icy road. He hit his chest on the dashboard and was gone before the ambulance came.

"He had internal injuries," she said. "It was a freak accident. So people at school can tell all the stories they want . . . but that's the entire truth."

I believed her. The gossip was probably one of the reasons why Leigh rarely came to class. She probably walked around in her boyfriend's clothes because she felt him inside them. And I supposed there was no point in getting fixed up when the only guy you loved would never see your face again.

"Summer has no idea what she's talking about," Leigh said. "I didn't kill my boyfriend—it wasn't my fault—and

I never even slept with him. I made him wait because I was afraid of ending up pregnant. I was afraid he'd run off and disappear, because that's what happened to my mother. He was so understanding and patient but I made him wait anyway and it was the worst decision ever. Now I'll never get a second chance. And I'm not sure if I'll ever want anyone else. Most guys are jerks and phonies."

I rolled my eyes. "I know. They pay you compliments they don't even mean."

Leigh stared at me for a moment. "Are you referring to Del?"

I shrugged. I hadn't meant to give myself away, but the words just fell out of my mouth.

She leaned into the white ripples of the sheets. Then she told me that Del and his girlfriend had split up for a while and had gotten back together just a few days ago, and she shouldn't keep criticizing him but she was going to because I should hear the facts.

"He's a pig, Ari. You don't want him. Trust me."

"He's . . . ," I started to say, not sure if I'd heard her right.

"A pig," she said. "He's my cousin and I love him, but he really *is* a runaround. He cheats on his girlfriend constantly—he's always got a different chick up here." She patted the bed. "*Putas,* that's what Idalis calls them. They're just a bunch of skanky whores who get kicked out onto Twenty-third in the morning."

Who was Idalis? And I couldn't believe that every one of the girls Del brought up here was a *puta*. Some of them had to be regular girls who thought Del cared about them. That idea brought a disturbing image into my head. I pictured a pretty girl in high heels and smeared makeup stumbling on the sooty sidewalk after a night on these temptingly soft sheets. I saw her as a Christmas tree that got left on the curb with garbage cans and ratty old rugs like it had never been any better than the rest of the trash.

"Idalis?" I said.

She nodded. "His girlfriend. And he doesn't even protect himself. He caught an STD two years ago—I'm not sure which one—I heard my mother and Uncle Stan talking about it. It was cured with penicillin, but Del could end up with AIDS if he doesn't watch out. It's not just a gay disease, you know. A raging heterosexual like Del can get it too. I mean, when you sleep with one person, you're sleeping with everybody that person has been with and . . . it's like . . . endless."

"Yeah," I said, because I'd heard it all before in Sex Ed. But I wasn't sure if the rest was true. A part of me suspected that Leigh was sparing my feelings, like when a girl in junior high hadn't invited me to her birthday party and Mom had said, *You don't need that uppity little snob and her goddamned party. Who does she think she is, anyway? Her father spent two years in prison for tax evasion, from what I hear.*

But another part of me believed everything. And that part felt relieved, as if Leigh had snatched my hand away from a dog that was really cute but had razor-sharp teeth that could disfigure me for life.

# *ten*

When the holidays were over, I banished Del from my mind and focused on things that were supposed to be important, like grades and drawing and the practice SAT exams in a thick book Mom had picked up at Barnes & Noble.

At Hollister I ate lunch with Summer and without Leigh, who stuck to the opposite end of the cafeteria. But I talked to Leigh in homeroom and art class. I gave each one of my friends special attention to make up for New Year's Eve. I decided that Summer was oil and Leigh was water and they were both valuable in their own way, but they just couldn't mix.

I spent the first Saturday in January browsing at Bloomingdale's with Summer and the second at the Guggenheim with Leigh. The next day I accompanied Leigh to a Sunday-matinee performance of *Cats* at the Winter Garden Theater because Rachel got tickets for free. I warned Mom to keep my whereabouts a secret if Summer called while I was gone.

"Oh, Ariadne," she said with a laugh. "Is that really necessary?"

"Definitely, Mom," I told her. "Summer would be upset."

"Jealous, probably. She isn't used to sharing you."

That was a keen observation on Mom's part. I kept it in mind when January sixteenth came and Evelyn wanted to host a family dinner at her house for my seventeenth birthday. I invited Summer and not Leigh. Summer had been a fixture at my birthday dinners for years and Leigh knew nothing about them, so I wasn't snubbing anybody. At least, that was what I kept telling myself.

"I hope you like it," Summer said.

We were sitting on Evelyn's couch amid a field of tattered wrapping paper, and Summer's gift was my last. Mom and Dad had given me a garnet birthstone ring, and Patrick and Evelyn had bought me an imitation-angora sweater. Kieran's present was hilarious—a necklace he'd created in kindergarten, made of uncooked pasta. I wore the necklace because it made him happy. The rigatoni hung around my neck while I opened Summer's gift—a gold heart charm engraved with #1 FRIEND. She said I was her "best friend ever," which was really sweet. She had also brought cookies from Tina. They were arranged in a fancy container with a big bow and her new business card, which said CATERING BY TINA. TELL YOUR FRIENDS.

I filed the card in my wallet. Then we all sat around the kitchen table and ate the cookies and a cake that Evelyn had bought at Carvel. There were edible daisies on the outside and vanilla ice cream with those little chocolate crunchy thingies on the inside, and I thought that Summer wasn't the only one who was being sweet today.

Evelyn was in a good mood. She had lost more weight, she looked pretty, and she'd even served us dinner earlier—salad and garlic bread and lasagna. The lasagna was delicious, even though it was the kind that comes frozen in a box.

"Don't you want a cookie, Evelyn?" Summer asked.

Sabotage. That was exactly what sprang into my mind. Evelyn was on a diet—what was Summer trying to do, keep my sister chubby? Maybe Summer was hoping for a chance with Patrick, who sat across from me looking gorgeous, with his blond hair and those big hands that I was sure matched other big body parts.

"I can't," Evelyn said. "Weight Watchers, you know."

Summer nodded. "I can tell. You've lost a lot already."

That was nice. I was too suspicious. Summer excused herself to the bathroom, and Dad and Patrick went into the living room to watch the Rangers play the Bruins. Evelyn ate an apple, and I was proud of her—she was sticking to her diet. I wanted her to get thin enough to fit into her old high school clothes that were buried in our basement. There were tube tops and a Diane von Furstenberg knockoff dress and Jordache jeans that Mom couldn't stand. *They're so tight, I can see all your business,* Mom used to say. *You'll end up with a yeast infection worthy of the medical journals, Evelyn.*

She never got an infection. And those jeans were a decade

out of style now. But if Evelyn could fit into them, she might be inspired to get a new wardrobe that Mom and Dad could buy with some of Uncle Eddie's money. That might boost Evelyn's confidence enough for her to take some classes that would teach her to do more than ring up groceries at Pathmark.

"Evelyn," Mom said, finishing her second slice of cake. She grabbed a cigarette and I wanted to tell her to lay off those things, but I knew I'd be wasting my breath. "Did you know that your sister is on the honor roll again?"

I cringed. Why why why why why did she have to bring that up? Evelyn shook her head and Mom flicked her Bic and talked behind a billowy, menacing fog. She talked about my A in calculus and my A in English, and I thought she might have an *organism* when she brought up my art teacher.

"At the parent-teacher conference," Mom said, waving her hands around dramatically, holding her Pall Mall between two fingers, "he told me that Ari is loaded with talent and that she'll have no problem whatsoever getting into Parsons. No problem whatsoever."

*No. Problem. Whatsoever.* That was how she said it. And I was amazed that someone with a graduate degree could be so dense. Had she forgotten that we had to be careful around Evelyn and that talk of good grades and talent was the same as calling her a big fat stupid failure?

"That's nice," Evelyn said with a stiff grin, the way people do when they meet an ugly baby. *How cute. How adorable. That's the most hideous thing in existence but I'll just smile and tickle the unsightly creature because it's the polite thing to do.*

I wanted to change the subject, and I was struggling to

come up with one when Summer returned. She sat next to me, and Kieran started talking about his new racetrack set.

"Come and play with my cars, Aunt Ari," Kieran begged, tugging on my hand.

"Not now. I'm visiting with everyone," I said, but he didn't understand. He clung to me. He whined. He yanked at the rigatoni around my neck.

"Leave Aunt Ari alone, Kieran," Evelyn said. "I'll play with you later."

Then the worst thing happened. It was one of those *if only* moments—the kind of thing that makes you retrace your steps to pinpoint the exact second you could have averted the disaster. *If only I hadn't sat around in that wet bathing suit, I wouldn't have this kidney infection. If only I hadn't waxed the tiles, poor old Grandpa wouldn't have slipped and broken his neck. If only I had played with Kieran and his cars, he wouldn't have snapped at Evelyn like he was the spawn of Satan.*

"I don't want *you*," he said. "Aunt Ari is better than you."

Everyone was quiet. I heard Dad yelling at the television about a penalty, and Mom told Kieran to go and play in his bedroom. Her voice was low and husky and she wore the intimidating face she used with her students. It made Kieran skulk out of the room as she crushed her cigarette in an ashtray.

He was so moody. Maybe he got it from his mother, but that didn't matter right now. All that mattered was Evelyn. Last summer I had warned Kieran not to say I was *better* and I hadn't been sure he'd understood, so I had just let him fall asleep on those blasphemous New England Patriots sheets.

"He didn't mean that, Evelyn," Mom said. "Kids say the strangest things."

Evelyn's fingers shook as she cleared dishes from the table. Mom pointed at me and at Summer and nodded toward the living room.

Then Summer and I sat on the couch and watched the rest of the game with Dad and Patrick. Summer cheered and booed at the appropriate times, but it was just a blur to me. I had more important things on my mind, like the fact that Evelyn probably hated my guts and that an aura was floating around my left eye and my migraine pills were at home.

I sat in my studio the next Saturday afternoon, drawing hands with a pencil from the cedar box Summer had given me. I drew a man's hand and a woman's hand, intertwined. The man's was rugged, with veins that stretched from the wrist to the fingers like the pattern on a leaf, while the woman's was delicate and smooth as ivory.

"How beautiful," Mom said from the doorway.

She startled me. I'd been staring at my work, thinking that the hands were romantic. I imagined the feel of that strong hand against my palm, his fingers lacing into mine, fitting as perfectly as puzzle pieces.

That was probably because I'd seen Summer holding hands with Casey, who had picked her up from school every day last week in his BMW. He locked his hands into hers while she kissed him, and she waved to me from the window as they drove away.

It was sickening. But I couldn't let her know that I was

dying of envy, that I wished some handsome guy would whisk me away from school while my admiring classmates watched, and I couldn't complain about riding home alone on the subway. It was one thing for Summer to gripe about Leigh, but placing a boyfriend above everyone else was expected. It was the female code or whatever.

"I'm just practicing," I told Mom. "I'm terrible at extremities."

She lingered behind me. "On the contrary. You're very good."

I didn't think so. I flipped to a blank page in my sketch pad and Mom started talking about Queens. She said that Evelyn was desperate for a break from the kids, Patrick wanted to take her out tonight, and someone had to watch the boys.

"Oh," I said, sure that my birthday dinner had been forgiven and forgotten and Evelyn needed me. "What time are we leaving?"

"Well," Mom started, sitting down on a chair. She looked like she was about to tell me something important and was searching for the right words. She'd done the same thing years ago when she'd explained my *monthly visitor*. Now her eyes scanned the room as if the best words were written on the curtains or the walls. "Here's the thing . . ."

*Here's the thing.* That was the phrase Mom used to begin unpleasant conversations. It was what she'd said when Dad's mother died. Now it was the first sentence Mom chose when she told me that she and Patrick had decided it would be best if I didn't go to Queens for a while.

I knew Mom didn't mean Queens in general. She didn't

mean Shea Stadium or Flushing Meadows Park. She said Queens because she thought it sounded better than just coming right out and telling me that I wasn't welcome at Patrick and Evelyn's house.

"You mean they don't want me there?" I said. "Are you kidding? I've always tried so hard to help them."

"Of course you have," Mom said in that *You're not really in pain* tone. "But you know how Evelyn is. We want what's best for her . . . don't we, Ariadne?"

She spoke like I was too much of a delicate flower to handle this and she had to pretend everything was fine so I wouldn't start crying or get a migraine, and she was probably right. I almost did cry, and my head started to throb. We want what's best for her, I thought. I knew that *we* was Mom and Patrick. Of course he would sacrifice me for Evelyn. I might have been an excellent cook and a very nice girl, but Evelyn was his wife and the mother of his children. I was expendable.

# eleven

*Hollister* was stingy with its snow days. This I discovered two days later, after a Sunday-night blizzard that closed Mom's school the next morning but not mine.

Mom stood outside our house dropping rock salt on the front steps while I jammed my feet into a pair of boots in the foyer. I was zipping them up when Jeff's Mercedes arrived, and as I knotted a scarf around my neck, I saw him heading toward Mom.

What was he doing? Our storm door muffled their voices, and when I went outside, they clammed up and stared at me until I got the message and walked to the car, where Summer sat in the front seat.

She was wearing her fuzzy pink hat and she was happy, which was so obnoxious. She'd become one of those people who waltzed through life without so much as a split end, and I was still one of those people who changed diapers and babysat for free but still got treated like a rented mule.

"Studying?" Summer said, looking at the SAT book on my lap after I climbed into the back.

I nodded. "How about you? Did you get one of these books?"

"I don't need it," she said, tapping her forehead. "It's all up here."

That was obnoxious too. Of course she didn't need an SAT book, because she wasn't going to study. She never studied. I knew she planned to take the test without opening a book or enrolling in one of those tedious prep courses that met on Saturday mornings. Then the scores would arrive and hers would be stellar and she would go off to UCLA, where she'd fit in with blond surfer girls and glamorous Hollywood types and forget that I had ever existed.

Fine, Summer, I thought. Go to California. Leave me here like poor lonely Saint Anne on my lawn. Look at her, all covered in snow. She's getting so old and the paint on her face is cracking from the weather and I'm the only one who cares.

"He's giving your mother the names of a few psychiatrists in Queens," Summer said, pointing to Jeff and Mom. "She called him yesterday. I guess Evelyn is having problems again?"

I didn't know that Mom had called Jeff yesterday. She'd probably done it from the laundry room, where she whispered with Patrick about things she couldn't mention to me, especially since I'd been expelled from the inner sanctum.

"Yeah," I said. "She is."

Summer reached back and squeezed my hand. "You can't help what your nephew said, Ari. It wasn't your fault."

It wasn't? But she made me feel a little better until that afternoon, when she rushed to Casey's BMW with her hair flowing and they locked hands and kissed, and then I rode the subway to Brooklyn by myself.

The next day, I sketched in my notebook during homeroom until I felt a tap on my shoulder and heard a raspy voice in my ear.

"What's the matter with you?" Leigh asked. "You look sad."

I told her the truth. I told her about Evelyn and about Patrick, and she listened intently before inviting me to another party. This one was at the theater where we'd seen *Cats*.

"You need a night out, Ari. The party is a farewell for one of the cast members. My mother's planning it. It's supposed to be on Friday, but it might not happen because the caterer she hired just canceled. She's looking for another one."

I thought of Tina's *Tell Your Friends* card, pulled it out of my wallet, and gave it to Leigh. "I know you and Summer don't get along, but this is her mother's catering business, and she's very reliable."

Leigh shrugged. "We'd hire a mass murderer at this point."

A mass murderer would have been better. Because later

on, when it was nearly midnight and I was studying for the SAT at my kitchen table while Mom and Dad slept upstairs, the phone rang and it was Summer, who wasn't happy that Rachel had hired Tina for the farewell party.

"Are you retarded?" Summer asked.

Retarded. That was worse than calling Del an Indian. "Am I—" I began, thoroughly confused, but she cut me off.

"Retarded," she said. "I think you must be if you expect me to wait on Leigh Ellis like I'm some Puerto Rican maid."

She needed a few courses in respecting ethnicities and disabilities if she wanted to be a psychiatrist. And making her work as a maid wasn't what I'd meant to do at all.

"Summer—"

"Ari," she interrupted. "If a person is a true friend, she doesn't associate with people who'd disparage her best friend of many years by calling her names that are written on dirty bathroom walls and spoken aloud only by low-class individuals."

"Leigh isn't a low-class individual," I said as Mom and Dad walked into the kitchen with messy hair and the worried expressions they often wore after late-night phone calls. I suddenly got the feeling that Mom was right—Summer didn't want to share me. She preferred it when I sat at home on Friday nights while she was on dates and at parties.

Then I listened while Summer told me that she had plans with Casey on Friday and she wasn't going to the Winter Garden no matter how much Tina ranted and raved, and I should find my own way to school tomorrow.

"I told my father you're sick," she said. "I'm so mad right

now that I don't feel like riding to school with you for a few days. He thinks you're staying home for the rest of the week . . . and don't you dare tell him anything different or I'll never speak to you again."

I heard the dead hum of the dial tone. I hung up the phone while my parents stared at me, and I knew what they were thinking: Was that Patrick? Did something terrible happen and are we going to be visiting Evelyn at New York–Presbyterian Hospital soon?

They both relaxed after I explained that it was just Summer. Dad went upstairs and Mom sat across from me and asked me what Summer wanted; then she lit a cigarette and I told her everything.

"Well," Mom said. "I think I'll call Jeff and let him know that you're perfectly healthy."

"Do me a favor and stay out of it," I said, and the mention of Jeff got me thinking about psychiatrists in Queens and about Evelyn. I asked Mom what was going on and she sighed.

"Evelyn's seeing a shrink again. But you shouldn't worry about any of that."

"Of course I'm worried, Mom. I'm not welcome in my own sister's house."

She opened the window beside the table and tapped her ashes into the air, where they turned into fiery speckles before vanishing in the wind. "It's just for a while, Ariadne. Evelyn is in a delicate state right now and there's some jealousy going on . . . you know the crazy things she comes up with."

I felt guilty, thinking that not everything Evelyn came up

with was crazy and Mom knew it. But Evelyn had no reason to be jealous of me. She was the one with the refined features and the green eyes and the handsome husband who did things in their bedroom that made her moan and gasp.

"She shouldn't feel that way," I said. "I don't have anything Evelyn wants."

Mom shrugged. "Some people don't know what they want."

On Friday night, Leigh sent a car that took me to the Winter Garden Theater, and I decided to have fun even if it killed me. I forced myself to forgive Patrick for keeping me out of Queens. I was sure that the situation was only temporary. Evelyn's new psychiatrist would probably recommend an innovative medication, and soon she'd be buying me Mrs. Fields cookies by the dozens. So I was going to have a good time tonight. A fantastic, spectacular time with interesting theater people and Tina's deviled eggs.

This idea lasted approximately five minutes. Leigh met me at the front door and I followed her into the theater, where we walked beneath a gaudy gold ceiling past rows of empty chairs and through a big red curtain. Then I heard jazz music and voices and I saw Summer.

She was serving truffle canapés on a tray and she looked miserable. Her mouth was stiff and her feet dragged, and Rachel made everything worse. She ordered Summer around in a sharp, condescending tone, and I knew why. It was Summer's fault that Rachel's *baby* had cried on New Year's Eve, and this was payback.

"Summer," Rachel said, towering over her in a pair of silver stilettos and a matching dress. "Every party has a pooper, but I don't pay to have one at mine. Put on a happy face, sweetheart. And clean up that mess over there—stage right. My guests are getting tipsy and spilling their drinks."

Summer glanced around. "Right *what*?"

I heard someone laugh. Rachel did too, as if the entire world should be familiar with stage directions.

"*Stage* right," Rachel said, pointing a spindly finger. "Right, left . . . get it?"

Summer got it. She grabbed some napkins and crouched down on the floor, and I pitied her. Rachel acted like she was royalty and Summer was a peasant, and Tina only cared about her business—*I have a reputation, you know.* She expected Summer to be polite no matter what. I was glad I'd brought my medicine, because I had a headache. So I found a bathroom, stuck my mouth under the faucet, and swallowed two pills.

Leigh was standing by the door when I came out. "My bracelet's missing," she said.

I was sweaty. I wanted to go home because this whole mess was my fault, but I couldn't go anywhere. Leigh's ID bracelet was gone and she was panicking.

We looked everywhere—backstage, on the stage, in every row of the theater. We were searching the lobby when Rachel came in, wondering why we had ditched the party.

"I can't find my bracelet," Leigh said, and started to cry. I wished she'd brought that thing to a jeweler like Del had suggested.

"It's not here, baby," Rachel said after another search, and then she and Leigh and I went backstage, where everyone tried to help. Finally Tina told Leigh not to worry, she and Summer were going to clean up after the party and if the bracelet was here, they would find it.

Leigh's eyes shot toward Summer, who was standing *stage left* with a tray of Gorgonzola popovers in her hands, obviously eavesdropping on our conversation. Leigh's lip was quivering as she looked at Tina. "What if *she* finds it?" Leigh asked, nodding toward Summer.

Tina glanced over her shoulder and then back at Leigh. "You mean my daughter? She'll let you know if she finds it. Why wouldn't she?"

The story was too long to tell, and we wouldn't have shared all the sordid details with Tina anyway. Leigh shrugged and Rachel said that she and Leigh should go home, but Leigh shook her head.

"I'm always ruining your fun, Mama. You stay here. We'll go over to Uncle Stan's for a while. I just need to use the bathroom first."

She walked away and I dashed across the stage, where Summer was leaning over a table and refilling her tray.

"Summer," I said, lingering behind her. "You'll let Leigh know if you find her bracelet, won't you? I think it belonged to her boyfriend, and it means a lot to her."

She straightened up and put a hand on her hip. "Of course I will, Ari. What kind of person do you think I am?"

A few minutes later, the chauffeur was driving me and Leigh away from the Winter Garden while Leigh brushed tears from her face and I obsessed about Summer. I kept quiet as the chauffeur took us to the Upper East Side, where we found Leigh's uncle in the foyer of his luxurious penthouse. He was wearing a suit and he was all smiles, like last time. I addressed him as Mr. Ellis and he didn't correct me.

"Is Blake here?" Leigh asked.

"He's studying," Mr. Ellis said.

She made a sour face. "He needs to relax."

"He needs to stay on the dean's list, and he will. Blake knows I've had my share of disappointment—he won't give me more."

I was sure he meant Del. I thought of the fight with the engineering student and the college expulsion and the STD, whatever it was. I also thought of Evelyn, and I wondered if Blake and I had something in common. We were both trying to make up for things we hadn't even done.

"Where are you going at this hour, Uncle Stan?" Leigh asked, and he said something about work and a client. Then the elevator doors shut and she led me to the kitchen, where she sat at the table and sounded desperate. "That bracelet belonged to my boyfriend. If I don't get it back . . . I swear I'll kill myself."

"Stop it, Leigh," I heard someone say, and I turned to find a young man behind me. "Don't ever say that again."

"I can't help it, Blake," she said as tears dripped from her eyes.

He sat next to her. I was surprised that this was the studious Blake, because he didn't look studious. He wore jeans and a T-shirt over a body that was average height with muscles that rivaled Patrick's, he had a shock of deep brown hair that stood up from his head, and his eyes were a much brighter blue than mine.

"Are you all right?" he said after Leigh stopped crying, and I wanted him to say something else because his voice was so soft and smooth. Leigh nodded and excused herself to the bathroom, and we were alone. "Blake Ellis," he said, reaching his hand across the table, flashing a boyish grin worthy of a Colgate commercial. "Please pardon my family drama."

His two front teeth were slightly longer than the rest, and there was something cute about that. I was suddenly embarrassed by my own flawed teeth, but what did they matter? Blake was probably no better than Del, and I wouldn't have a chance with him even if my teeth didn't overlap. So I shook his hand and smiled back.

Mom didn't listen to me when I told her not to call Jeff about my perfect health. She did it on the sly, and the next thing I knew, it was Monday morning and Summer and I were sitting on the couch in my living room. Mom stood on the carpet with her arms folded while Jeff advised me and Summer to *work this thing out like adults*.

I wanted to work it out. Summer put on a big phony act. She pretended to understand that I had only wanted to help Tina when I gave her business card to Leigh, and she hugged me after the conversation ended, but it was the fakest thing ever. It was worse than an air kiss or those people who said "Let's do lunch."

Then she and I were at Hollister and I remembered

Leigh's bracelet as we passed the iron gates. I asked Summer if she had found it, and she looked at me with the disgust she usually reserved for chewed-up gum on the soles of her Gucci shoes.

"Did I find what, Ari?"

"Leigh's bracelet," I said.

"Oh, that." She took out her compact and examined her lip gloss as we walked through the entrance and past the plaque of Frederick Smith Hollister. "It wasn't in the theater. We checked everyplace. Leigh must've lost it somewhere else."

"Are you sure?" I said.

Summer snapped her compact shut and stopped walking. We were standing next to a row of lockers and a crowd of students maneuvered around us.

"Yes, I'm *sure*," she said, her dark eyes blazing. "What are you implying?"

She looked so offended that I felt guilty for bringing it up. Maybe she was right—I'd known her forever, she had her flaws, but she wasn't that kind of person. I shouldn't have accused her of stealing a dead boy's bracelet.

"Nothing," I said before heading to homeroom.


A few days later, I was sitting with Leigh in the cafeteria. Summer was eating pizza at her friend's apartment and I hadn't been invited.

"Are you really sure Summer doesn't have my bracelet?" Leigh asked.

"Positive," I said. "I know she can be sort of flaky

sometimes, but she doesn't mean it. She's a good person underneath. She wouldn't do something like that."

Leigh let out a heavy sigh. "So I guess it's gone and I just have to accept it." Then she started talking about California, and I almost choked on my sandwich.

"You're leaving?" I said, wondering if it was my destiny to be alone.

Leigh nodded and told me that her uncle owned a condominium in some city called Brentwood, and she and Rachel were moving there in June. Mr. Ellis also had a close friend whose aunt was the principal of a private school where Leigh would be accepted for her senior year, and another friend was a movie producer with connections who could get Rachel hired as a makeup artist at Warner Brothers.

"I need a new atmosphere," Leigh said as I noticed that she wasn't wearing anything printed with SUNY OSWEGO, which was a good thing. So I smiled and listened while she told me that she'd be going to UCLA because her family had donated money there and she would get in for sure.

UCLA. Of course. I imagined UCLA surrounded by palm trees and sidewalks with famous people's names carved into the cement. I saw it as a giant magnet with the power to drag my friends across the country. But I didn't say anything negative because Leigh seemed excited, and she changed the subject by asking about my college plans.

I mentioned Parsons and it sounded boring. But maybe *I* was boring because I wasn't interested in Brentwood or anyplace other than here. I didn't want to be far from my parents, and I couldn't move away from Patrick and Evelyn and the boys, even if they never wanted to see me again.

"Uncle Stan knows people at Parsons," Leigh said. "He can get you in. Do you want to work in art?"

"Sort of. I want to teach. But you're going to be a real artist, aren't you?"

"No," she said. "Art is mine."

That made sense. Her art was hers and my art was mine, and I wanted to keep it hidden in my studio like a newborn baby because nobody would ever love it the way I did. So I nodded and Leigh started talking about teaching on the college level, something about getting a master's and a PhD, and she suggested that I become an art professor.

"That's what Idalis is planning to do. And you're much smarter than she is, Ari."

I had no idea who she was talking about until she reminded me: Idalis, Twenty-third Street, the *putas* in Del's bed. According to Leigh, Idalis was finishing her master's in Spanish literature. She was going to start her PhD in the fall, and I could meet her and get some career advice if I went to Mr. Ellis's apartment for dinner on Saturday night.

"You *have* to come, Ari," Leigh said. "It won't be any fun without you. Del will be there, but who cares? You don't want him, anyway."

Not really. Maybe a little. But Del was a pig, so I started thinking about other things—things like very blue eyes, a Colgate smile, a smooth voice that gave me goose bumps. The possibility that Blake would be at the dinner too made me accept Leigh's invitation.

# twelve

*Idalis* Guzman was older than Del. I found out—over a four-course dinner served by two maids in Mr. Ellis's penthouse—that she was twenty-six, she was from Venezuela, and she wasn't serious about her boyfriend.

"I can't marry this guy," she said in perfect English with an accent that was even more appealing than I expected. "Then my name would be Idalis Ellis."

She had Rapunzel hair. It was honey brown and down to her waist, but not the kind that gets chopped off on those daytime talk shows where women neglect themselves and need a makeover. Hers was shiny and stylish. Her face wasn't the prettiest, but her skillfully applied makeup compensated for that. She wore classy clothes and expensive jewelry, and she carried herself like she was somebody special.

"If you want to teach," she said to me as we were eating our second course, which consisted of something I'd never seen before called sautéed leeks, "the university level is the way to go. Once you get tenure, you make good money and you have a flexible schedule, so you can work and still have time for a husband and kids. You can have it all, as they say."

I could have it all. I imagined myself as a professor: I would stand in a classroom and give lectures about Picasso to eager college freshmen. Then I would zip home to Brooklyn, where I would live in one of those elegant Park Slope houses, which I would be able to afford on my salary, and I'd be greeted at the door by my loving children, who would be as adorable as their father.

That idea got me excited and hopeful and it made me shift my gaze from Idalis to Blake. He sat opposite me, not eating his leeks, and his eyes reminded me of a marble that I had owned when I was nine years old. I'd had lots of others, but this one was my favorite, because it was transparent with a brilliant streak of sapphire blue that I would stare at and hold up to the sun. Then one day it disappeared. Mom took me to Woolworth's to find a match, but I didn't search very hard—I knew that something so beautiful only came around once.

"You don't need all that butter on your bread, Stan," Rachel said after the main course was served. "And slow down. You're eating too fast."

Mr. Ellis sat at the head of the table. He was digging into a slab of beef and he sounded annoyed. "I have to go out soon, Rachel. I'm meeting with a client."

Idalis laughed. "A client, sure. I think you've got a few lady friends stashed around Manhattan. And you should listen to your sister. You don't want another heart attack."

"That was three years ago," he said. "It won't happen again."

He still seemed annoyed and so did Blake, between dinner and dessert. I was in the bathroom upstairs when I heard his voice and Del's in the hallway. They were arguing, and I pressed my ear to the door.

"Tell your girlfriend to watch her mouth," Blake said.

Del laughed. "Why? You know she's right. Daddy keeps that apartment downtown for whoever he happens to be screwing at the moment. He can pretend he's faithful to Mama's memory all he wants, but that's just his usual hypocritical bullshit."

*Daddy and Mama.* That reminded me again of Elvis, even though Del and Blake both spoke like native New Yorkers. I listened while Blake said Del had no respect for their father and Del said their father led Blake around on a leash, and then Del started talking about some girl in Georgia.

"You've got nerve to criticize Idalis," Del said. "She's better than that little bleached-blond piece of trailer trash you banged for two years."

How scandalous. And interesting. The polite part of me wanted to turn on the faucet to drown out the conversation, but the nosy part was dying to hear what would happen next.

So I stayed where I was while Blake got angry and Del got angry.

"Don't talk about her," Blake said.

"Why?" Del asked. "She drops you with no explanation— she disappears without so much as a phone call—and you still defend her? It's pathetic, Blake. Get on with your life and stop moping about that chick. Be a fucking man, for Christ's sake."

And that was it. I heard footsteps on the stairs and I washed my hands and joined everybody in the dining room, where one maid was filling coffee cups and the other was lighting crème brûlée with a mini butane torch.

Blake didn't eat anything. Del devoured his dessert and swallowed two cups of coffee while I compared him to his brother. They were identical in height, and they both had dark hair and the exact same hands. Del was outgoing and a slick dresser, while Blake was quiet and wore casual clothes. His face wasn't quite as handsome as his father's, but it was much better than Del's. Blake's nose didn't hook down at the tip and there was no scar on his mouth. There was no way Summer could accuse him of having a birth defect.

"What's the matter?" Leigh asked Blake when she and Rachel and I were in the foyer with him, slipping into our coats. He shook his head and she patted his cheek, told him to cheer up, and suggested that they go skating at Rockefeller Center tomorrow.

"I love Rockefeller Center," I said, surprised at my boldness. I was fishing for an invitation, even though I shouldn't have because I had a chemistry test on Monday. Chemistry made my mind go numb. I had to work extra hard in that class to stay on the honor roll, so I'd been planning to study tomorrow, but Blake needed cheering up and this was a good excuse to see him again.

Leigh looked between me and Blake. "Oh," she said. "Do you want to come too, Ari?"

*More than anything.* I nodded, and Leigh told Blake we would meet him at noon. Then I was in the back of a sedan with Leigh and Rachel, and Rachel pointed at me.

"Blake would be perfect for this one," she said, and I was embarrassed to have been so transparent. But Rachel seemed to think the idea was her own.

Leigh glanced at me and back at Rachel. "Ari doesn't want your dating advice."

"Now, Leigh," Rachel said calmly, smoothing Leigh's hair. Leigh had a perturbed look on her face and her lips were puckered. "All three of you can be friends. I'm sure Ari wants to be friends with you *and* Blake."

That's right, I thought. I want to be friends with both of you. All three of us can be friends and I do want Rachel's dating advice, so shut up, Leigh.

Rachel turned toward me and started talking like a gossipy matchmaker. "Blake's a good boy, Ari. He doesn't prowl around the way Del does. And he's smart, too. He's a sophomore at NYU."

"He's nineteen, then?" I asked.

"Twenty," Leigh said, and I wondered if Blake hadn't started college right after high school, if he was one of those people who bummed around Europe for a year to find themselves. But she explained that he'd broken his leg when he was eight and was out of school for a while, and he'd had to repeat the third grade because he went to a school where the Ellis family hadn't donated any money. I was surprised that such a place existed.

"Del broke Blake's leg," Rachel said.

Leigh gave her a shove. "Don't say that, Mama."

"It's the truth, isn't it?" Rachel asked, then looked at me. "It was after their mother died. They got into a fight and Del pushed Blake down the stairs. That's the kind of temper he has."

Leigh told the driver to turn on the radio and we all got quiet. He dropped Leigh and Rachel off at their building, then drove me home, where Mom was waiting in the living room. There were sandwiches and warm milk on the coffee table and she wanted me to tell her everything. So we sat on the couch and I described the crème brûlée and the four courses, and asked if she'd ever eaten a leek.

"Once," she said. "At a swanky anniversary party."

Then I brought up my new plans. I talked about teaching college and becoming a career woman who could also have a husband and children and a house in Brooklyn with a flower garden and a hammock tied between two shady trees in the backyard, and I kept closing my eyes to see all of it. But when I opened them, Mom had a blank expression on her face, and that was so disappointing.

"Why would you want to live in Brooklyn?" she asked. "And being a college professor isn't what you think. Positions are hard to find, and nobody makes any money until they get tenure, which doesn't always happen." She stood up and brushed crumbs from her bathrobe. "Don't be in a rush to have children, either, Ariadne. Just look at Evelyn. She isn't exactly the portrait of fulfillment."

Mom went to bed and so did I, but I was too miserable to sleep. I switched between staring at the ceiling and through my window, wishing I could be what Mom wanted. I wished I could be like Summer, who wasn't afraid to go to UCLA or to put a note in a dead man's hand. She'd probably do all sorts of adventurous things that scared me, like move out of Brooklyn forever and travel solo around the globe. She'd probably become one of those independent women who didn't care about adorable children and flower gardens and hammocks.


There was an old pair of ice skates in our basement. I searched for them the next morning, remembering that they'd been a fourteenth-birthday gift from Mom and Dad to Evelyn, and Dad had said they were a goddamned waste because Evelyn had only worn them once.

They had to be here somewhere, lurking inside a cardboard box or buried in one of the plastic bins stacked against the wall. I was looking through a box marked EVELYN when I heard footsteps on the stairs.

"What are you doing?" Mom asked.

The skates weren't in the box. I saw a macramé purse, a container filled with seashells, and a pair of Jordache jeans that made me sad. But my mood was lousy anyway because Mom had crushed my dreams last night, and now I didn't want to look at her. I mumbled that I needed to find Evelyn's ice skates, and she started searching with me.

"Is it just going to be you and Leigh today?" she asked, pulling a hideous paisley dress from a box. "You didn't invite Summer?"

"Summer's always busy with her boyfriend," I said, watching as she held the dress against herself. It was a size eight, and I thought Mom should face reality and donate it to Goodwill. "You know that."

She must have read my mind. She tossed the dress onto an exercise bike that nobody ever used. "And all your home-work is done?"

"Yes," I said impatiently, and Mom put her hands on her hips. I wasn't looking in her direction—I was bent over, dig-ging through a box filled with musty old clothes—but I saw her from the corner of my eye and I wished she'd just go and eat something.

"Don't be so snippy, Ariadne. You want to get into Parsons, don't you?"

I straightened up. "Leigh told me her uncle has connec-tions there."

Mom found the skates. There wasn't a scratch on them, but they weren't exactly what I remembered. I thought they were white or tan, or something less ridiculous than silver with rainbow shoelaces and purple lightning bolts stitched into the leather.

She pushed them at me. "What do you mean, her uncle has connections?"

No wonder Evelyn only wore those skates once. They

couldn't have been stylish even in 1976, when teenagers walked around in bell bottoms with combs sticking out of their back pockets. So I jammed the skates into a box and turned to Mom. "Leigh's uncle knows people at Parsons. He can get me in. My grades probably don't even matter."

I might as well have told her that I was "in trouble." That was how horrified she looked. "We," she said, pronouncing the word in a virtuous tone, as if she was about to say *We Kennedys* or *We Vanderbilts,* "don't need anyone's connections. We stand on our own two feet in this family and you know that."

I did know that. I felt like a shallow sloth who wanted an escape from those brain-frying SAT practice tests, and that just wasn't who I was raised to be. So I nodded. I was about to go upstairs when Mom grabbed the skates and held them in the air.

"Forget something?" she asked, and I couldn't say that I wouldn't wear those ghastly things, because my parents had bought them with their hard-earned money and it didn't make sense to pay for rented skates at Rockefeller Center when these were practically brand-new.

They were snug, though. Painful, even. I forced them onto my feet an hour later as I sat on a bench at Rockefeller Center with Leigh. She had spotless white skates with matching laces, and she was too nice to say anything critical about mine.

When Blake showed up, he sat next to me. I slid my feet under the bench, hoping he wouldn't see my stupid lightning bolts.

I saw other things. I saw his outrageously blue eyes and the wind sweeping through his hair as he leaned over to tie his skates.

"Aren't you coming?" he asked.

"I have a headache," I lied. I told him and Leigh to go without me and they disappeared into a swarm of people gliding on the ice, listening to piano music from those Charlie Brown holiday specials.

I acted fast and unlaced my skates, stuck them in my knapsack, and put on my boots so I wouldn't be humiliated in front of Blake, although I wasn't sure why I cared. He was skating laps around the rink without ever stumbling or stopping to tie a wayward shoelace, and I felt like I had as much of a chance with him as I did with Del.

I watched anyway, as he zoomed by the United States flag and the Japanese flag and other flags I couldn't name, but I stopped watching when I heard a dull thump.

There was a boy on the ice just a few feet away from me. He was about ten years old, and he had fallen on his arm. Someone skated over his hat after it fell off.

"Are you all right?" I said, jumping off the bench. I stood over him, offering him my hand, and hoisted him up, which wasn't easy because he was a chubby kid. "Did you hurt your arm?"

"Yeah," he said, rubbing it with a gloved hand.

"Are you here by yourself?"

He nodded. "My mom went over to Saks. I promised I'd be careful, but now look at what I've done. My arm is probably broken." He was getting all worked up.

"Don't worry. I can check your arm," I said, remembering the class Evelyn had made me take a few years ago, the one where I learned about CPR and diagnosing broken bones. So I checked for swelling and bruising and asked if he'd heard a snap or a crack when he fell. He was shaking his head when Leigh and Blake came back. "You're fine," I said, zipping his jacket to his chin.

He sat with us until his mother appeared at the side of the rink, looking worried and carrying shopping bags. She thanked me before she and her son left, and Blake smiled after they were gone.

"You're good with kids," he said.

He was next to me on the bench again. His eyes were on my face and that made me edgy. I worried that my mascara had pooled into my tear ducts or that there was an unbecoming smear of lipstick across my overlapping teeth.

I shrugged. "My sister has two. I'm just used to them."

He raised his eyebrows. He seemed interested. I assumed he was just making conversation and that he'd go back to skating with Leigh, but he didn't.

"Don't you guys want to skate with me?" she asked, standing on the ice, her eyes darting between me and Blake. "Isn't your headache better yet, Ari?"

No, Leigh, I thought. My fake headache isn't better. And I really like you, but I like your cousin more. "Not yet," I said.

She chewed on her nail, looking disappointed. "Are you sure? Do you want to find a drugstore and get some aspirin? I can take off my skates and we can run across the street to—"

I cut her off. "No, I'll be fine."

She nodded and skated away with a sulky look on her face. Then I was alone with Blake, listening to the tinkle of piano keys and the flapping of flags in the wind.

"Is Leigh okay?" I asked.

He shrugged, watching her drag her feet at the other side of the rink. "She's been through a lot lately . . . and she's by herself too much. It's good she has you to hang out with. She needs a friend, especially someone who's got so much in common with her . . . I mean the art and everything," he said, and I suddenly felt bad that Leigh was skating alone. Then Blake changed the subject. "You mentioned your sister . . . how old is she?"

"Twenty-three. She has a five-year-old and a baby," I said without thinking. Twenty-three minus five—now he'd know that she was a teen mother. But Rachel was too, and he didn't seem to be subtracting. He was smiling and looking at the cloudy sky.

"Nice," he said wistfully. "It's good to have your kids when you're young."

Not *that* young, I thought. Then he said Leigh had mentioned that I had a brother-in-law who worked for the FDNY. Blake said that he'd always wanted to be a fireman, which was very ironic, in my opinion. People who lived on the Upper East Side didn't usually become firefighters.

"Firemen don't go to NYU," I told him.

"No," he said. "Lawyers do."

"So you want to be a lawyer like your father?"

He smiled, but it wasn't a happy smile. It was a wry smile

that lifted just one corner of his mouth. "Not exactly. My father wants me to be a lawyer like my father."

I got it. And I was right about the two of us having something in common. I realized, as we sat on the bench and talked while Leigh did laps and figure eights around the rink, that Blake had to compensate for Del the way I had to compensate for Evelyn. Mr. Ellis and Mom were cut from the same cloth. They wanted what was best for us, but they never asked what we wanted.

"My mother expects me to become an artist," I said after Blake told me that he was supposed to take over Ellis & Hummel someday. "As if *that's* a practical goal."

He smiled. This time he used both corners of his mouth. "Well, maybe it is. You should show me your work sometime."

I nodded at the same time the sun peeked out from behind a cloud. A ray struck Blake's right eye, and I decided that my lost marble finally had a match.

# thirteen

We were in the last days of March. The temperature was rising, and pea soup–colored grass burst through the melting snow, reminding me of prickly stubble on a bald man's head. The winter had eroded most of Saint Anne's nose. It was all so depressing that I never looked at our lawn anymore.

"What do you think?" Summer asked.

Dad was downstairs watching the Sunday-afternoon Knicks game. Mom was at Evelyn's house, helping to take care of Shane because he had the chicken pox. Or at least, that was what I thought she was doing. The flow of information had fizzled to a trickle since I'd been barred from Queens.

Now I looked at Summer, who had opened my curtain. I'd been keeping it closed lately to block out the gloom on the lawn. But she had the gall to open it so she could show off the red rose that had been tattooed on her ankle while she was in Key West with Casey for spring break.

"Pretty," I said, because it was. But I felt so blah and my voice came out that way.

"Our initials are on the petals," she said, pointing to an *S* and a *C* written in calligraphy. "Isn't it romantic?"

Casey was still in Florida. He was staying there for a few extra days, and I knew Summer was here because she was bored without him. The only contact we had lately was in Jeff's Mercedes every weekday morning, and romance wasn't a good topic for me right now. Weeks had passed since Rockefeller Center, and Blake had never asked to see my drawings or anything else.

"Sure," I made myself say.

"And the *C* will be easy to change when we break up."

I blinked. "Why would you get the tattoo if you're planning to break up?"

"Ari," she said in a sensible, psychiatrist-type voice. "The chances that Casey and I are going to live happily ever after are slim, don't you think? Besides, I'm not about to settle for the first guy who comes along. I need experience. And getting the rose was an experience too."

I studied the tattoo, imagining a sharp needle injecting the red ink and the black ink and the green ink beneath her skin. "It must've hurt," I said.

"So does sex the first time you do it, but I didn't let that stop me."

I sighed. This was such old news. "I know. You've told me fifty times already."

She sat on my bedspread. "Well, I'm just warning you in case you ever get a boyfriend."

I pulled the chair out from my desk and sat down, feeling limp and despondent and in the mood to denigrate myself. "Yeah . . . hopefully I'll get one before I turn all wrinkled and hunchbacked."

She gasped and covered her mouth. "I didn't mean it that way, Ari. That came out wrong. I always say things wrong. You know I meant *when*. *When* you get a boyfriend."

Whatever. I watched her zip her boots while my mind shifted back to her tattoo. It made me think of dirty needles and AIDS and people in hospital isolation units, wasting away with sores that blistered every inch of their bodies. I was about to ask if the tattoo parlor had taken the necessary precautions when she changed the subject.

"That Rachel Ellis is an even bigger bitch than her daughter. 'Stage left, stage right . . . ,' " she said, imitating Rachel by pointing her finger. "But my mother is all gushy about her because she got us a new account. A law firm or something."

"You mean Ellis and Hummel?"

She nodded. "We'll be handling their business meetings and stuff starting later this spring. I think it's in the Empire State Building."

Ninety-eighth floor, I thought. Then I got nervous because Summer might meet Blake, who probably wanted another bleached blonde to replace the one in Georgia, and I didn't stand a chance against Summer Simon. I wished she had never given me that *Tell Your Friends* card, because it had led to nothing but disaster.

I was glad when Summer went home, passing Mom on the front steps. Mom was carrying a grocery bag filled with marshmallow ducks, jelly beans, and eggs, which we dyed in the kitchen later on.

I dropped a yellow PAAS tablet into a cup filled with a combination of water and vinegar and watched it fizz. I'd already colored a dozen eggs and I was planning to do a dozen more. Mom and I always gave Kieran a huge Easter basket, and now we had to give one to Shane, too, even though he was less than a year old and mostly toothless.

"Is Shane better?" I asked, drawing a rabbit face on a fuchsia egg.

"Oh," Mom said. "He's fine."

I was drawing whiskers. I stopped because her voice sounded funny. It sounded like she was trying to keep something from me. "Well," I said, certain that my exile would be suspended on holidays. "I guess I'll find out next week."

"Ariadne," she said. "Here's the thing."

That was when I found out I wasn't going to Easter dinner in Queens. Mom acted like this was no big deal, it was a one-time occurrence. Evelyn had lost eleven pounds since my birthday, her psychiatrist was fantastic, and we wanted what was best for her, didn't we?

Mom was being a ringmaster again. I nodded and went back to drawing because I didn't want to talk about Evelyn anymore. What was the point, anyway? I'd just come off as spoiled and weak and a wimpy delicate flower if I complained that nobody ever put me first, not even Mom. I wasn't in the mood now for jelly beans or colored eggs, but I forced myself to organize them in Kieran's and Shane's Easter baskets. It wasn't their fault they had a very selfish mother.

On Monday I complained to Leigh about Easter. There was no other choice. I couldn't talk to Mom and I never talked to Dad, and Summer was too involved with herself to care. She rarely ate lunch at Hollister nowadays, Casey always picked her up from school, and she was constantly meeting with guidance counselors. She wanted to convince them to let her take extra classes next fall so she could graduate in January instead of in June, which just figured. Leigh would be gone soon and Summer probably would too, although it seemed as if she was far away already. *What do you care if I don't eat lunch in the cafeteria?* Summer had said last week. *You've got Leigh.*

"Well," Leigh said as we sat together in homeroom. I was surprised that she'd actually shown up, and I hadn't seen a SUNY Oswego shirt for weeks. Now she wore a dab of lipstick, a white eyelet blouse, and her chain with the arrow-head charm. It was a sunny morning, and she looked a lot more cheerful than I felt. "You'll just have to come to my place for Easter."

"I don't want to impose," I said.

She picked up her charm and pulled it back and forth across the chain. "Now you're being ridiculous. It's no imposition at all. We'll have plenty of food . . . my whole family will be there. I really want you to come—I'll even send a car to pick you up. Please come."

Her voice was tinged with desperation. Her face was close to mine, and there was a mix of hope and sadness in her eyes that made me nod, just so she wouldn't say please again. I also did it because I knew what it was like to be unpopular, because I knew how important it was to have at least one friend, and because I remembered that Leigh's *whole family* included Blake.

"Don't let this bother you, Ariadne," Mom said the next Sunday afternoon. We were standing on our front steps while Dad loaded the Easter baskets into his car.

"It doesn't bother me," I said, because I had to. My parents didn't think that missing one lousy Easter dinner was a big deal—they went through much worse when they were my age. *Kids are so spoiled these days.* Mom once said that her father had usually passed out drunk before the ham was served, and it was no secret that Dad's mother had spent every holiday emptying bedpans. So I pretended I didn't care.

Then a sedan arrived. It took me to the apartment on East Seventy-eighth, where I settled down at a cramped dining room table. Mr. Ellis sat at the head; Rachel was at the opposite end. Leigh sat next to me, and Blake and Del were across from us. I was surprised that I felt so comfortable eating Easter dinner with a family that wasn't mine.

"Pass that over here, sugar pie," Rachel said, gesturing to

a disposable aluminum tray beside Blake's elbow. Her accent was very Southern today, and so was the food. There were no maids or leeks or desserts set on fire. We had potato salad and pork chops and collard greens, and I ate the collard greens even though I'd never heard of them before. Rachel had cooked everything herself, and it wasn't exactly a penthouse party. It was the same kind of simple family gathering that was going on in Queens. There was another similarity too—I had to hide my Blake stares just like I hid my Patrick stares.

Blake ate more than he had at the penthouse. He dug into the potato salad and left four bare pork-chop bones on his plate. As we ate, he talked to me across the table. We talked about school and about grades, and at one point Mr. Ellis chimed in.

"A-plus on the Intro to Business Law midterm," he said proudly, patting Blake's shoulder in a way that was supposed to be affectionate, but he did it so forcefully that it probably hurt.

Rachel clapped her hands. "Congratulations, nephew. Now you get an extra piece of hummingbird cake." She turned to me. "You're not allergic to hummingbirds, are you, honey?"

Hummingbirds. Those were the little things with the thin beaks and the speedy wings. *Hummingbirds are of the* Trochilidae *family,* I remembered one of my science teachers saying. *They're the only birds that can fly backward.* I didn't remember her mentioning that hummingbirds were edible, but maybe it was a Southern thing. A delicacy or whatever.

"Aunt Rachel," Blake said. "Don't do that to her."

It was only a joke, thank God. Rachel went to the kitchen

and came back carrying a four-layer cake covered with cream-cheese frosting and chopped pecans. It tasted heavenly. Blake was cutting his second piece when Mr. Ellis rose from his chair.

"I have to get going," he said. "There's a trial next week and work on my desk."

Rachel twisted her mouth. "You push yourself too hard, Stan. You should get some of your associates to help you."

He smacked Blake's shoulder again. "This boy right here will be working for me over the summer. That'll be all the help I need."

Rachel offered to walk him to his car, adding that it was a beautiful day and we should all take a spin around the block to burn off dinner. Blake and Del shook their heads but Leigh sprang out of her chair and grabbed my hand.

"Come with us, Ari," she said.

I didn't want to. I wanted to stay here with her cousins, so I unlatched my hand from hers. "You go ahead, Leigh. Have a nice walk."

She stood there looking disappointed, like she had at Rockefeller Center. Her clinginess annoyed me a little, but I didn't want her to know, so I got up and went into the bathroom. When I came out, she and Rachel and Mr. Ellis were gone.

I went back to the dining room, where I sat at the table with Del and Blake. They made the room smell musky and masculine, from the things they drank or smoked or slapped on their skin, and I liked it, whatever it was.

"That was rude," Del said. He struck a match and lit a

cigarette. "Daddy leaving early, I mean. Who works on Easter?"

Blake ran a hand through his hair and it stood up straight. "You know he's busy."

"Yeah. Too busy to see my club. It's been open for three months and he hasn't shown up once. And neither have you." A long stream of smoke came out of Del's mouth. He pushed his chair back and it scraped the wall and that annoyed him. "This apartment is so fucking small. Why doesn't he get them a better one?"

"Del," Blake said. "There's a lady in the room. Watch your language."

That's okay, I thought. Nobody in my family watches their language, but thanks anyway, Blake. I'm flattered that you care. Del muttered an apology and Blake told him that Mr. Ellis paid Rachel and Leigh's rent and their bills, and wasn't that enough?

Del didn't seem to think it was, because he screwed up his face and started clearing the table. I watched him and tried to find the green in his eyes, but I only saw gray.

"You'd defend Daddy if he slit their throats," he said before disappearing into the kitchen. I heard water running and trays being crunched into the trash. Blake let out a heavy sigh.

"Sorry," he said. "Another family drama."

That's okay, I thought again. I'm familiar with family drama. Then I remembered the way Del had talked about Cielo and I felt sorry for him. "Your brother's club is nice . . . I was there for the opening-night party."

"I skipped that," he said, sliding his hand beneath the

neck of his shirt to rub his shoulder. I wondered if it was sore from when Mr. Ellis had pounded on it. I caught a glimpse of bare skin, and I also saw a silver chain. Then Blake turned slightly in his seat and I noticed something dark on the top of his back, near his shoulder. "So how old are you, Ari? Leigh's age, right?" He stopped rubbing and his shirt fell back into place before I could figure out what the mark was.

"Right," I said.

He smiled. "Then you're old enough to get into R-rated movies."

"Yeah," I said, wondering where he was going with this. "I'm old enough."

"You want to see one with me?" he asked. I couldn't believe it—Blake had just asked me on a date. Suddenly this was a very good Easter.


He called on Wednesday night. The phone rang when I was curled up on the couch with my calculus homework, and Mom answered it in the kitchen. Then she came into the living room with a puzzled expression on her face.

"It's for you," she said. "It's some boy."

She looked so surprised that a boy would deliberately dial my number, and that really irked me. Then she lingered in the kitchen while I talked to Blake. She opened and closed cabinets, pretending to search for cinnamon. She also rummaged through the refrigerator, checking the expiration dates on the milk and the sour cream and the butter, even though she knew good and well that they were all perfectly fresh.

She was even worse on Saturday night. I heard a car's engine at the curb and I flew down the stairs from my bedroom, calling "I won't be home too late," and I thought Mom would have the sense to stay inside, where a mother belongs, but she didn't. I was at the curb when I heard her husky voice behind me.

"Don't I get to meet your friend?" she said.

Go away go away go away, I thought. Blake is twenty years old and he drives this beautiful black Corvette convertible and you have no idea how much you're embarrassing me. Then Blake was on the sidewalk and he shook Mom's hand. Next he answered her probing questions with "Yes, ma'am" and "No, ma'am" and "I go to NYU, ma'am." She loved that *ma'am* business. She waved goodbye when I was in the car, and I watched her reflection in the rearview mirror as Blake drove away.

"I apologize," I said. "For her, I mean."

The Corvette had the scent of leather and plastic and other unknown substances that make a car smell new. It was a stick shift, and I marveled at how expertly Blake changed gears.

"Don't worry about it," he said. "I don't blame her. When I have a daughter, I plan to interrogate every guy who comes within a hundred yards. I'll probably get a polygraph machine and stick bamboo shoots underneath their fingernails."

I laughed. I wasn't embarrassed anymore. And I decided that Blake was different. He was better than the guys Evelyn had dated before Patrick, the ones who honked their car horns impatiently and rolled their eyes behind Mom's back and gave Dad weak handshakes. None of them ever said *ma'am.* I wondered if Blake's good manners were a sweet Southern thing, like Rachel's hummingbird cake.

He drove us to a movie theater in Manhattan, where he held every door for me, and the next thing I knew, we were eating dinner in a Little Italy restaurant with red-and-white-checkered tablecloths and a waiter who called me *Signorina.*

Blake seemed comfortable. So was I. The food was good and the atmosphere wasn't formal or fancy, which was fine with me. Our table was near the front door and I felt the cool April air, heard it rustling a tree outside, and saw Blake's Corvette parked across the street.

"You have a nice car," I said.

He shrugged. The waiter had just brought two bowls of chocolate gelato and Blake lifted his spoon. "My father gave it to me for Christmas. Total waste of money."

I wasn't sure how to answer, so I didn't. I lifted my own spoon and swirled it around the gelato, and Blake asked if I was seeing anybody else.

"No," I said. "I was dating someone for a while. It's over now."

It was a massive lie but I had to say it. I couldn't let Blake know the humiliating truth that this was my first real date. For some strange reason he didn't doubt me.

"Same here," he said.

I nodded and conjured up a vision of his bleached-blond girlfriend. I imagined her in a mobile home in Georgia, trying to make the place presentable by hanging up a wind chime and growing flowers in plastic containers out front. I saw Blake inside, having sex with her on a foldout couch while rain beat down on a metal roof, and I thought she was lucky even if she did live in a trailer.

"Who were you dating before?" I asked, as if I didn't know.

"A girl in Georgia," he said.

I acted all surprised. "Georgia," I echoed. "Do you go to Georgia much?"

"I used to. My grandmother lives down there. She has a little house far away from everything, underneath these big oak trees that were planted before the Civil War." He leaned his chair back and smiled at the ceiling. "I want a place like that someday."

I laughed. "But you live in a penthouse."

The check came. He tossed some cash on the table. "That's my father's taste," he said, popping a Life Saver into his mouth. "And Del's. I'd rather live in your neighborhood."

We were back in my neighborhood an hour later. It was dark now, and Blake parked the Corvette in front of my house as butterflies fluttered in my stomach. I remembered when Evelyn was a teenager and she would sit in parked cars on our street with her boyfriend of the month, while Mom paced the living room saying things like *She'll end up with trench mouth* and *I hope the neighbors don't see.*

I was looking out the window, checking for neighbors and hoping to give them something to see, when I felt Blake's hand on my chin. I looked at him, at his straight nose and his perfectly carved lips, feeling his finger move slowly back and forth on my skin. Don't ask me, I thought. Just do it.

He lifted my mouth to his and it was so much better than that stupid Catskills kiss. It was nice and gentle and he squeezed my shoulder and smoothed my hair, and he didn't get grabby with my off-limits-on-a-first-date areas or turn all critical when it was over.

"You want to sit over here?" he asked.

The only place to sit over there was on his lap. The invitation was so enticing and his voice was so soft that it made goose bumps pop all over me. I nodded and Blake smiled, hooking his arm around my waist, pulling me over the stick shift. Then I was on his thighs, and I loved it there, where I smelled aftershave and stayed wrapped up in his arms. He kissed me again, harder and deeper this time. I felt his tongue exploring my mouth and tasted a trace of his Wint-O-Green Life Saver. I wondered if he knew that they made tiny blue sparks if you crunched them in the dark.

"You're too pretty," he said when we were done.

I was? Those three words sent me floating over my lawn. The grass was growing in thick and green, and Saint Anne didn't seem lonely and old and chipped. Her dress was bright blue, her shawl was sparkly gold. She and little Mary looked like they were having a good day.

# fourteen

*Mom* was waiting on the couch. She made sandwiches and she heated milk, but I didn't want to tell her anything. The memory of tonight was as unblemished as new-fallen snow that I had to protect from careless footsteps. I just talked about the movie and the restaurant as Mom stared at me with her heavy-lidded eyes, waiting for something that never came.

"Don't you even want a sandwich?" she asked.

I shook my head. I heard her in the kitchen while I was brushing my teeth upstairs; she was tearing a sheet of aluminum foil to cover the sandwiches. I might have felt a lot guiltier if I wasn't so happy.

My happiness hindered my sleep. I stared at my bedroom ceiling later on, thinking about Blake, remembering the way he had touched me. He was careful and gentle, as if I was something fragile and important, like I was that soft spot on a baby's head.

He called on Sunday night. I wished there was a phone in my room. Evelyn used to have one, a powder-pink princess model that Mom and Dad bought after she whined and cried and nagged for weeks. Its cord had been woefully tangled and the dial had nearly fallen off from constant use, but she had still lugged it to Queens along with her Pet Rocks and Peter Frampton poster.

I'd never asked for a phone, and that was a mistake. If I had one, I could get some privacy from Mom and Dad, who were watching *60 Minutes* in the living room while I leaned against the kitchen counter, surprised at what came out of my mouth—girlish giggles and a flirty voice that made me wonder if I'd been possessed by Summer.

"What are you so cheery about?" Summer asked the next day as we strolled by Frederick Smith Hollister. You have a very handsome grandson, I thought, giving the plaque a puckish sideways glance.

"I went out with Leigh's cousin," I said.

Summer stopped walking. She made a noise like she'd just found a hair in her soup—*blech* and *ick* and *ugh* all rolled into one. "You mean that hideous Indian-looking guy with the messed-up lip?"

That was mean. She seemed to have forgotten that she hadn't always been flawless. Besides, Del wasn't hideous, and he couldn't do anything about his lip. I didn't want to talk about Blake anymore, but Summer said "Tell me tell me tell me" until I gave in.

"Leigh has another cousin you haven't met. He's Del's brother and he's adorable," I said.

She laughed. "Sounds like you've got quite a little crush brewing there, Ari."

I'd suffered through so many crushes. There was Patrick, and boys at school, but none of them had amounted to anything except a painful ache. They'd never resulted in what happened the next Saturday night—a handsome guy at my front door who willingly came inside and gave Dad a firm handshake and chatted politely with Mom before taking me to another movie and a dinner that he paid for with an American Express card.

Later that night, Blake and I sat in the Corvette, which he'd parked a block from my house, this time next to a vacant lot where another house used to be. The owners had torn it down with plans to build a bigger place because they'd won Lotto or risen in the ranks of the Mafia. Our neighbors were gossiping, but nobody was sure of the truth.

"Why did you park here?" I asked.

"Because," Blake said, "I can't go on kissing you in front of your house. That isn't nice, and I was brought up to be a gentleman. I want your parents to like me."

I like you, Blake, I thought when his mouth was on mine and his arms hugged my waist and our fingers laced together as perfectly as the ones on my sketch pad.

"Ari," Blake said, and I glanced at the clock on his dashboard, shocked at how late it suddenly was. "I should take you home now."

"Why?" I asked.

"Because it wouldn't be nice if I didn't," he said.

*Nice.* It wasn't nice to kiss in front of my house and it wasn't nice to kiss for too long. I wondered where all this niceness came from. It definitely didn't exist in Brooklyn guys or Connecticut boys who vacationed in the Catskills. I finally decided that it came from somewhere else—a faraway place where people ate collard greens and lived beneath pre–Civil War trees.


The next afternoon, a meteorologist on TV said the temperature was record-breaking. It was so warm that our obnoxious neighbors were sunbathing in their driveway and everybody else on the block was washing cars or mowing lawns.

I drew the lady next door as I watched her from the open window in my studio. She was spread out on a lounge chair, shiny from Coppertone, holding a foil collar beneath her double chin. Then I turned to a blank page in my sketch pad, but I wasn't motivated. I didn't even want to be here, with my pencils and my paper and my oil paints in their squashed tubes. I wanted to be outside soaking up the sunshine and the cut-grass smell, or on my driveway packing the car with Dad for a visit to Queens. But mostly I wanted Blake, who told me last night that he had an Intro to Business Law exam on Monday and planned to study for hours today.

"Ariadne," Mom said after I dragged myself to the kitchen. "What are you going to do while we're gone?"

I flopped into a chair, thinking that it was hot in here and why didn't this house have central air? All we had were noisy old window units that Dad hadn't taken out of the garage yet.

"Nothing," I said, watching as she put a tray of cupcakes in a cardboard box. They had homemade icing and multi-colored sprinkles, and I knew Patrick would enjoy them because he was a big fan of *jimmies*.

"You can study for the SAT," she suggested.

I rolled my eyes. Studying for the SAT and sketching in my studio seemed like death compared to keeping my eyes shut while Blake's tongue wandered inside my mouth.

Then my parents were gone. I watched television on the couch, listened to a group of kids play stickball on the street, and ignored my SAT book. Mom had left two cupcakes on a plate in the refrigerator, and as I bit into one, the phone rang. Blake was on the line.

"Leigh and my aunt Rachel convinced me to blow off studying today," he said. "We're driving out to the Hamptons. . . . I'm renting a car since we can't all fit in the Corvette. We'll pick you up in an hour if you want to come."

Of course I did. I wanted to go to the Hamptons more than anything in the world, even though I'd never been there before. So I ran upstairs and showered and shaved my legs.

Next I stood beside my dresser drawer and pulled out a bikini the color of a plum, which would have to be covered with a T-shirt because if Blake saw my uneven breasts, he might stop calling. The thought of that was too dismal for words.

He showed up right on time. Rachel jumped out of a black Toyota in a bikini top that wasn't covered by anything and a sheer sarong that was wrapped around her hips. A big pair of sunglasses—the same kind that Jackie O wore around Manhattan—rested on the bridge of her nose. She ushered me into the front seat next to Blake.

A couple of hours later, we arrived at a massive white house that resembled something out of *Miami Vice*. The walls inside were white, and there were endless windows and a balcony over the first floor. The furniture was modern, and Leigh showed me the indirect lighting in the five bedrooms and four bathrooms before whispering in my ear that the house belonged to her uncle.

"He has parties here during the summer," she said. "With his clients and stuff."

I nodded and followed her outside to the pool. It was four feet deep at one end and nine at the other, and was covered on the inside with sea green tiles except at the bottom, where black and yellow tiles formed the image of a scorpion.

I teetered at the edge of the pool to see a curvy tail, and then Leigh was next to me.

"I guess my mother was right about me and you and Blake. We can all be friends. We can do stuff like this for the next few months until I go to California," she said, glancing at the pool and the patio and the house. "I like to draw, but

I can't stand another spring alone in my apartment with my colored pencils."

I knew what she meant—I couldn't survive another spring locked in my studio, either.

"Sure, Leigh," I said. "We'll hang out together for the rest of the spring."

She smiled, crouched down, and moved her hand back and forth in the water to check the temperature. "Del and Idalis will be here soon. I'd like some ice cream before then."

So we went for a walk. Rachel sauntered down the road, waving at admiring male neighbors while Blake and Leigh and I trailed behind like baby chicks. We stopped at a quaint ice cream parlor near the beach that had a striped awning and smelled of roasted peanuts. Rachel ordered a cup of frozen yogurt, Leigh asked for vanilla ice cream in a waffle cone, and Blake and I both got a scoop of lemon sherbet. He paid for everything even though I took out my wallet. It didn't seem right that Blake should pay every single time we were together; it was 1986—the whole equality thing was supposed to have been settled years ago.

"Put that away, honey," Rachel said, jamming my wallet into my purse before Blake saw it. "A Southern man never lets a woman pay for anything. He wouldn't be a gentleman otherwise."

"But Blake isn't really a Southern man," I said.

She lifted a black eyebrow. "He was raised as one, and that's what matters."

\* \* \*

Del and Idalis were at the house when we got back. She floated around the pool on an inflatable raft with a piña colada in her hand, and she talked to Del in a mixture of Spanish and English while he sat at a table on the patio with his adding machine and a stack of receipts.

"Hey, *latoso*," she shouted. "You planning to sit there all day?"

He didn't answer and she yelled the question again. "I'm working, goddamn it," he said without looking up, and she got huffy and said a few things in Spanish that I didn't understand and something in English that I did.

"You can just lick me, then," she said, sticking out her tongue.

"Don't you wish," Del muttered over his receipts.

I laughed to myself. I knew they were talking about the thing that a lot of Catholic girls did instead of having sex because it was just bending the rules, not breaking them. It wouldn't give them a fatal disease or get them knocked up; they wouldn't become a disgrace to their rosary-carrying mothers. I didn't blame them, but it seemed to me that skirting the rules was a dirty trick and possibly more sinful than everything else.

Del wasn't dressed for the pool, he was dressed for work, and I got the impression that an afternoon in the Hamptons hadn't been his idea. Rachel became a mother hen and said things like "Oh, now, now" and "Mind your manners," and Leigh tried to help by dragging a volleyball net out of a shed and suggesting that we all play. Del ignored her and Rachel didn't want to wreck her nails, so the game turned into Leigh and Idalis against me and Blake.

"Are you keeping that shirt on?" Leigh asked. "I'm

wearing mine. I burn easily, in case you couldn't tell from my gazillion freckles."

"Same here," I said, grateful that she'd come up with an excuse before I had to. Then we sat at the edge of the pool while Blake installed the net and Idalis smashed a ball across the water in a way that told me she was one of those competitive girls I avoided in gym class.

"I have an idea," she said. "Ari can get on Blake's shoulders and Leigh can get on mine and we'll play that way. It's more challenging."

Leigh and Blake agreed, and I just nodded to go along. I waited while Blake finished setting up the net. His shirt was already off, and I saw that the silver chain I'd seen during Easter dinner had the same arrowhead charm that Leigh wore. The mysterious dark thing I'd seen was a tattoo on his left shoulder blade—a circle with a cross in the middle and three feathers dangling from the bottom.

"Hop on," he said a few minutes later.

He was crouching in four feet of water. I slid my calves over his shoulders, and I was glad I hadn't forgotten to shave my legs that morning. He gripped my ankles and I held on to his neck. His skin rubbed against my skin, and it was going to be hard to concentrate on this volleyball nonsense.

Leigh hit the ball with her fist and it came barreling toward my head. I ducked and Blake laughed, but Idalis didn't seem happy because she was probably expecting a real game. I stayed on Blake's shoulders while he retrieved the ball. That was the best part—just being close to him, clutching his strong shoulders with my bare thighs.

He gave me the ball and I tossed it back, but I had to do

that four times before it cleared the net. Idalis was frustrated and she switched positions with Leigh, which made me nervous. She was just about to hit the ball when Blake called a time-out because his father was standing on the patio.

"What are you doing here?" Rachel asked.

She was on a lounge chair. There was a blazer draped over Mr. Ellis's arm, and he loosened his tie. "I came to make sure the people I hired to clean this place were doing their job. I didn't know there was a party going on." He shaded his eyes and turned toward the pool. "Isn't there a test tomorrow, Blake? You should have your nose in a book instead of a girl on your shoulders."

"Come on, Daddy," Del said. "Let him have some fun for once."

"Nobody asked *you*," Mr. Ellis said sharply before directing a suave smile and a goodbye wave at the pool. I watched through a wall of windows as he went into the house, and then I heard a car start up and fade away in the distance.

"*Pendejo,*" Idalis called to Del. "Get some shorts on. Let's do boys against girls."

I wasn't sure what *pendejo* meant, but it couldn't have been a compliment because Del's face was darker than that scorpion in the pool. He kept punching numbers into his adding machine. Then Blake jokingly tossed the volleyball across the patio. It was wet and it landed on Del's receipts. Del grabbed the ball and shot it in Blake's direction, but it hit me right in the mouth.

Thick red droplets fell on Blake's chest. Next I was on the patio, surrounded by frantic people. I kept insisting that I was fine and I heard Del apologizing. Blake sneered at him.

"Fucking moron," he said.

He shouldn't have broken his *Watch your language around a lady* rule. It was just an accident; I could see that Del was sorry. Blake led me into the house, and I watched Del over my shoulder as Rachel wagged her finger and Leigh shook her head and Idalis screeched in Spanish.

I didn't hear her anymore after Blake took me to a bathroom and closed the door. It was completely white inside, with a granite countertop and towels emblazoned with the letter *E.* Blake ruined one of the towels by pressing it against my bloody lip.

He doted on me. He kept the towel on my mouth until the bleeding stopped, he soaked a cotton ball in iodine to clean what turned out to be just a minor cut, and he scoured the entire house for a Band-Aid. The one he found was the kiddy kind with a picture of Snoopy on it, but that was okay. Everything was okay because this was the best I'd ever felt.

Kindergarten. That was what was in my mind after Rachel and Leigh caught a ride home with Del and Idalis and I sat next to Blake as we sped down the parkway. The car windows were open, the sun was setting, and I thought that kindergarten was the last time the sun had looked so golden and the air had smelled so fresh. Little things had made me happy back then—little humdrum trivial nothing things, like polish on my toenails and strawberry shampoo and a crisp new dollar that I could spend on the Good Humor man. As I got older I'd noticed that nail polish chipped, and shampoo burned if it got in your eyes, and the Good Humor man's ice cream was no different from the stuff in the freezer case at Pathmark. The color slowly drained from everything and it was all just boring and pointless or both.

But tonight, when I got out of the car in front of my house, I could have sworn that Saint Anne was smiling. My neighborhood trees looked leafier than usual, the whole block smelled of a barbecue, Blake's face was more handsome than any I'd imagined while I was kissing my hand, and I felt like I was in kindergarten again.

It was getting dark and the air turned cool. Blake leaned against his car, draping his arms around my waist.

"Listen," he said. "Can we just say we're a steady thing?"

The lady next door was lugging her trash can to the curb. Crickets chirped and kids played stickball and I nodded. Then I saw Blake's Colgate smile. He held my face in his hands and kissed my forehead, and I was sure it meant something. A guy who didn't care about you just wanted to feel you up and feel you down, and Blake hadn't tried any of that. Only a guy who really cared would give a girl something as sweet and innocent as a forehead kiss on a dreamy April night.


My parents weren't home yet. I closed the front door after Blake was gone and walked around the house smiling and aimless, like I was giddy on champagne. I touched my Band-Aid, inventing a reason why it was there, because nobody needed to know about my amazing day in the Hamptons.

"You were fortunate, Ariadne," Mom said later that night, after I pretended that I'd tripped on a stair and bashed my mouth against the railing. I also pretended that the Snoopy Band-Aid had been in my dresser drawer for years and I didn't want it to go to waste. "You could've lost some teeth."

I was more fortunate than she knew—Del was good at making people lose their teeth. I held in a laugh and followed her to the kitchen, where we sat at the table and she handed me a Polaroid. It was a picture of Evelyn, but I thought it was an old one because her cheekbones were showing, and she was wearing a short skirt and there weren't any dimples above her knees. Her legs were thin and her hair wasn't frizzy, and she was leaning against Patrick with a seductive smile.

The Polaroid wasn't old. It had been taken just a few hours earlier. Mom told me that Evelyn had dropped twenty pounds since my birthday, her new medication was working, and I was invited to Queens next month for a Memorial Day barbecue. Then she lit a Pall Mall.

"Did you have a good time on your date last night?" she asked, to which I nodded and said that I really should do some SAT studying, but she wouldn't let me leave. She gripped my wrist and stared at me. "Look," she began, and stopped when Dad strolled in to raid the refrigerator. She kept quiet until he left with a sandwich to eat in front of the TV in the living room. "Blake seems very nice," she said. "But they all seem nice at first. You have to be careful."

Shut up, I thought. Please don't ruin this. "Careful?" I said.

She blew a smoke ring into the air. "You're sensitive. Men can be cruel. I don't want you getting upset or distracted from the important things."

*The important things.* I was sensitive. She wanted to lock me in my studio because a delicate flower is prone to wither. "We're going steady now," I said.

There was a flash of displeasure in her eyes that she smothered with a blink. "Steady," she said. "You know what *that* means, don't you?"

I thought so. I thought it meant that a guy actually liked me. "Sure, Mom. It means we're only seeing each other."

She laughed as if I was stupid. "It means he's looking for a regular screw and you could end up pregnant just like somebody else we know."

At that moment I wondered how other women spoke to their daughters. Did they refer to sex as a *screw*, and did they tell their future sons-in-law not to think with what was in their pants? This was one time I wished she could be more Catholic, that she could be one of those devout ladies who deluded themselves into thinking their daughters were going to save themselves for their wedding night. Those women would never initiate a conversation like this.

Why did she have to spoil everything? This was the first time a guy had shown the slightest interest and she had to go and get practical. I didn't want to hear about realistic things like ending up pregnant.

"We're not doing anything" was all I could say.

Mom scrunched her mouth into a skeptical smirk. "Not at the moment. But a twenty-year-old who looks like *that,*" she said, pointing toward the dishwasher as if Blake was standing there, "isn't exactly a virgin."

I made the same noise that Summer had when she

thought I was dating Del—the *blech* and *ick* and *ugh* combination. "Really, Mom," I said, amazed at how casually she used embarrassing words. But I couldn't argue because she wasn't wrong.

"Ariadne," she said. "I was young once too. I know what goes on. Now, if you want to go out with Blake, that's fine with me as long as you keep your grades up and you don't get serious. But remember, high school will be over before you know it and there are plenty of fish in the sea—you don't want to get stuck with the first one."

She was so sensible, so cynical, it was really depressing. I wanted to say that I'd love to get stuck with Blake, that I didn't care about the other fish in the sea, but there was no point. She'd just tell me that I was young and naive and that she knew best. Don't be so pessimistic, Mom, I thought. Things don't always turn out wrong.

"Besides," she went on, "you've taken Sex Ed—you know about AIDS. There's no way to tell who's got it. So you just make sure he keeps his jeans zipped and everything will be fine. He'll respect you more that way, anyhow."

AIDS, respect . . . she really knew how to complicate things. I just nodded and Mom smiled, reaching across the table to rub my cheek. She did it sort of the way Blake did—like I was something special.

# fifteen

*The* rest of April and half of May drifted along as innocently as the old Andy Hardy movies Dad watched on TV, starring Mickey Rooney as the boyfriend and Judy Garland as the girl-friend, holding hands in an all-American town with picket fences and cherry blossoms. Blake and I saw each other on Friday and Saturday nights but never during the week, because he had to stay on the dean's list and I couldn't fall off the honor roll. We went to the movies and to dinner, and the amount of time that Blake considered it *nice* to kiss kept growing.

Then it was the middle of May. Finals were coming and Hollister cut the school day in half on Wednesdays so we'd have time to study, although it seemed that I was the only one who actually did.

Leigh rarely showed her face at Hollister anymore—I figured she was busy getting ready for her move to California—but I saw her when she came to art class and when I went to Ellis family functions with Blake. Summer wasn't around much either, because she always sped off in Casey's BMW to activities that were more fun than studying.

It was on one of those Wednesdays that Blake parked his Corvette outside Hollister's iron gates. I didn't even see him at first. I was carrying a heavy stack of books and chatting with Summer; she stopped and gazed out at the street.

"Ooh," she said. "Who is *that*?"

I squinted from the sunshine and noticed she was looking at Blake like she wanted to tear off his clothes and slide underneath him. Or climb on top of him. Or let him get behind her, because she had told me she'd tried that position with Casey and it was *strangely exciting*.

"That's Blake," I told her, smiling and fighting the urge to skip.

"Oh my God you're kidding me," she said.

I shot her a hurt glance. *Oh my God you're kidding me.* She said it really fast, as if the six words were only one. "What's that supposed to mean?" I asked, even though I knew. She meant that Blake was filet mignon and I was Spam, and those two things couldn't possibly go together.

"Nothing," she said, squeezing my arm like she was sorry.

"That came out wrong. I just mean he's really cute. You're a lucky girl all of a sudden."

The sun was behind her head and it lit her hair into a golden halo. Her eye shadow sparkled, her lip gloss shimmered. She was gorgeous and it made me nervous. I didn't want her anywhere near Blake; I was sure she could take him away if she wanted to.

We walked toward the street, where Blake was leaning against his car in jeans and a Yankees T-shirt.

"This is my friend Summer Simon," I said, pretending I wasn't the most insecure person alive. "She's a big Yankees fan."

"Don Mattingly," she said. "*Love* him."

They started talking about other Yankees—Rickey Henderson and Mike Pagliarulo and whoever else. I couldn't join the conversation because I knew nothing about baseball.

"Pleasure meeting you," Blake said when Casey's car showed up.

Summer smiled. "You too. We'll have to do a double date sometime."

Don't count on it, I thought when Blake and I were in the Corvette. "What did you think of Summer?" I asked, trying to keep my voice free of envy, worry, and all the other pathetic emotions I loathed myself for feeling.

He stopped at a red light. "She seemed nice."

I nodded. He hit the gas and I looked out the window, at the Metropolitan Museum with its giant columns and sweeping steps.

"Do you think she's pretty?" I asked. I used a casual voice, like I didn't care about the answer.

"Yeah," he said. "She's very pretty."

I stared through the windshield. "I know. Everyone thinks so."

I kept thinking about Blake and Summer, how they might get to know each other better at Ellis & Hummel while Summer and Tina catered Mr. Ellis's business meetings and forget all about me. Then Blake reached over and turned my face toward his.

"You're much prettier," he said. "Than she is, I mean."

I almost said *You're full of crap,* but I didn't think he was. And I had never thought I'd find someone who would tell me that I was prettier than Summer Simon. So I didn't say anything—I just kept quiet and enjoyed it.

"Where are we going?" I asked a few minutes later as we were leaving Manhattan.

"You still haven't shown me your drawings," he said.

So we went to my house. My empty house. Mom was at school and Dad was at the precinct or collecting evidence or whatever it was he did to nab murderers. I opened a few windows on the first floor since Dad still hadn't installed those air-conditioning units, but Blake didn't seem to mind that the place was stuffy or that we didn't have our own elevator. He seemed comfortable. So I felt comfortable giving him a full tour of the living room and the dining room and the kitchen, where he saw Evelyn's Polaroid. Mom had taken more pictures that day—Kieran riding his tricycle, Shane in his crib—and they were stuck to the refrigerator with Mom's magnets that had corny sayings such as BLESS THIS NEST and SHOOT FOR THE STARS.

"Those are my nephews," I said.

"They're beautiful," Blake answered, and he mentioned again that it was a good thing to be a young parent.

"Evelyn was barely eighteen when she had Kieran," I said, because I'd known Blake long enough to stop keeping my sister's secrets. "That's way too young."

He nodded. "Twenty isn't, though. I'll be twenty-one in November and I'm wasting my life at NYU while I could be enjoying all of this." He waved his finger at the Polaroids.

"You're not wasting your life," I said.

He smiled at me. He smiled as if I made him feel good. He also cradled my face in his hands and asked again to see my drawings.

Then we climbed the stairs. I opened the windows in my studio as the floor creaked beneath our feet and an ambulance siren wailed in the distance. I felt nervous and twitchy and afraid that Blake might think I had no talent. Or he might tease or criticize, and that would just pulverize me into dust.

"I don't want to bore you with this stuff," I said, turning toward the door.

He caught my arm. "You're not boring me, Ari. Let me see."

I went slowly. Blake sat at my easel and I pulled things out of the closet—big sheets of paper and paint-splattered canvases. I showed him what had won me the second-place ribbon in the boroughwide art contest and even the hands on my sketch pad, because he was attentive and interested and that filled me with trust. He agreed with Mom that I could become a successful artist and I shook my head.

"You have to be extremely talented for that," I said, leaning against a wall.

He tilted backward in his chair. "And what do you think *you* are?"

I was flattered. Then we talked. I told him about my college plans and my career plans, and he said he just wanted to be a fireman with a comfortable little house and a bunch of unruly kids, and he hated the thought of working at Ellis & Hummel this summer. He'd rather quit college right now and take the FDNY entrance exam.

"So why don't you?" I asked.

"Because certain things are expected of me. And family is important," he said, which I completely understood. I nodded and we talked for a while longer, and then we were both startled by a deafening noise.

It was those stickball-playing kids. They had broken a window. Blake and I rushed down the hall and saw shattered glass covering my bedroom floor. I looked outside and saw three boys scatter in different directions. Two of them were in Mom's class and they were probably scared to death.

"They're in for it now," I said, picturing them cowering in corners when Mrs. Mitchell called their parents tonight. Then I crouched down and examined a long, jagged shard.

"Don't touch that," Blake said. "Where's your vacuum?"

I pointed to the hall closet. He used the vacuum to suck up the countless broken pieces, conscientiously checking the carpet for strays because he didn't want me to get a nasty surprise while I was barefoot.

He cared about me. I was sure of it. I thanked him and

he said he should leave because Mom might be home soon and if she found us alone together, she'd think it wasn't *nice*.

"She won't be back for another two hours," I said, draping my arms around his neck. I kissed him and he kissed me and the next thing I knew, I was lying on my neatly made bed and Blake was lying on me. I wrapped my legs around his waist. I heard sparrows chirping outside and nothing felt wrong, not even when he unbuttoned my blouse. He slid his hand inside and everything still seemed *nice* until his fingers moved to the clasp on my bra. I remembered my defective breasts and my talk with Mom, and I pushed him away.

"I can't," I said.

Our eyes were open now. His cheeks were flushed and he spoke in a patient voice. "Why?" he asked.

I held my shirt closed. "Because I'm kind of . . . uneven. Up here, I mean."

"No way. You're perfect."

I was not. But he made me feel a little better. "I still can't," I said, and I told him about Evelyn and about Mom. I also mentioned the shadowy virus that hid in unknown places and dragged people six feet underground. "I want you to respect me," I added, which was as true as everything else.

He nodded and sat up, and I sat next to him. "What about your other boyfriend?" he asked, and I had to stop myself from saying "What other boyfriend?" I just shook my head and he assumed things. "So it wasn't like that, then. Because most girls today . . ."

"Yeah," I said. "I know. Unfortunately I'm different from most girls."

I fiddled with an embroidered rose on the new bedspread that Mom had bought for me at JCPenney last week. I was waiting for him to leave, to go out and find a girl like Summer—a girl who had experience with various positions. But he just pushed a wisp of hair from my eyes and smiled.

"You're better than most girls. And all of this," he said, glancing at my bed, "it's okay if you love somebody. So I can wait until you feel that way."

*All of this.* He knew how to talk about sex a lot more delicately than Mom did. What he didn't know was that I loved him already.

There was a murder on Memorial Day. An entire family in Hell's Kitchen. The precinct called Dad at noon and he rushed off to work. Mom wasn't happy about it. We were in the middle of loading her Honda with a Budweiser-filled cooler and she got surly. She cursed and mumbled under her breath while we drove alone to Queens, as if those six people had some nerve to get stabbed to death on a holiday.

Blake was supposed to be here. The guest list for Patrick and Evelyn's party included their neighbors and Patrick's firefighter friends, and Blake had been invited too, but he had called last night and said he'd be a few hours late. Mr. Ellis was throwing his own party and Blake couldn't get out of it.

"That was a shitty thing to do," Mom said. "Bail out at the last minute."

She was in a rotten mood. But I wasn't the least bit upset about Blake. I couldn't criticize a guy who looked like *that* and was willing to wait for what he could easily get from any number of girls every day of the week.

I'd given in a little. I was sure that he cared about me and respected me, so it seemed okay to sneak him into my bedroom on Wednesday afternoons, where we talked and laughed and kissed on my bedspread, and I didn't push his hands away when they went inside my shirt. But that was as far as I would go, and Blake never did anything that made me say *I can't.*

"He didn't bail out, Mom," I said. "He's still coming. His father is having an important party in the Hamptons with clients and other lawyers from his firm. . . . Blake had to be there."

"Oh," she said in her *la-di-da* tone. "The Hamptons. How hoity-toity."

I dropped it. I was happy and I wasn't going to let her get me down. The week before, Mom had asked if the prescription for my migraine pills needed to be refilled and I had shown her the bottle, which was nowhere near empty because I hadn't seen an aura for quite a while. It made me wonder if feeling cheerful and pretty and cared-for all the time was a downright miracle cure.

"Hey there, little sistah," Patrick said as I stood on his front steps twenty minutes later.

He was so tall and tan, and I still felt something when he planted a peck on my cheek. But it was just a tiny tremor compared to the earthquake that came from Blake's kisses. I almost laughed, remembering how I used to eavesdrop through the bedroom wall and sleep in Patrick's shirt, and it was sort of like looking at an old toy and thinking: That doll sure is cute, but I'm way too grown up for it now.

"Hi," I said as Mom walked past us with the cooler. She opened the back door and went out to the yard, which was crowded with guests. I was heading in that direction when Patrick caught my elbow and spoke into my ear.

"You ain't mad at us, are you, Ari? I hated to keep you away."

I paused for a moment, studying the wave of hair that fell over his forehead. "Yeah," I admitted. "I was mad. Who wouldn't be?"

He smiled sympathetically, draped his arm around my shoulders, and led me to a quiet corner. "I don't blame you. But I have to put your sister first. Isn't that what you want?" he asked, and I nodded because it really was what I wanted. I couldn't stand it if Evelyn was married to some callous bum who put her last. "And you know I'm not big on saying thanks . . . but I appreciate what you've done for us, helping with the kids and everything. Please tell me you know that."

"Now I do, since you finally brought it up. But I'm not sure how much I can take . . . Patrick Cagney saying please and thanks all in one day . . . Somebody should call the *New York Times*."

"Wiseass." He laughed, leaning in close. "Evelyn's much better now, too—you'll see."

I saw her a minute later, standing at the kitchen counter, wrapping mini hot dogs in Pillsbury dough. She was thin and pretty and she was wearing a white sundress, white espadrilles, and a gold anklet with an engraved pacifier-shaped charm. MOMMY, it read.

"Is that something new?" I asked, lurking awkwardly in the doorway.

She looked away from a cookie sheet covered with pigs in blankets and down at her ankle. "Yeah . . . Patrick got it for me."

"It's beautiful," I said, noticing the care she'd taken with her eyeliner and her mascara, the polish on her nails. It was as if the old Evelyn had returned, and I was so happy to see her that I was willing to put everything behind us. "He really loves you," I added, and it didn't bother me to say it because now I had someone who might love me, too.

She wasn't angry anymore, I could tell. I wasn't either. She smiled, putting her arms around me. Her hair was blow-dried smooth and felt soft against my cheek. It almost made me cry, and I thought that Evelyn was also on the verge. We both sniffed and laughed when we stepped away from each other, and I knew that everything was better now.

"So," she said. "Where's this boyfriend of yours? I'm dying to see him."

She saw him later, when the sun cast an orangey gold hue over the house. Blake ate three hamburgers as if he hadn't had a morsel in the Hamptons. He fed Shane his bottle, played catch with Kieran, and settled into a chair beside mine.

"I saw your friend today," he told me.

"Summer?" I said.

He nodded. "Her mother catered the party. She handled a few meetings at the firm and now she'll be doing all my father's parties. Personally, I thought the food was way too salty."

I knew he hadn't eaten much at that party. And I felt nervous, panicky, the way I had the first time Blake and Summer

192

met. I imagined her flirting and laughing and talking about Don Mattingly, literally charming the pants off my boyfriend. But I remembered what he'd said in his car that day—that I was prettier—and I convinced myself that worrying was stupid.

"Do you want a beer?" I asked. It was a good subject-changer.

He shook his head. "I already had one. I don't drink much . . . I'd rather not turn into a lush like my brother."

"Del's a lush?" I asked. A pig, a lush, what was next?

"I guess it's a matter of opinion." He shrugged and threw one arm over the back of his chair. "This is exactly what I want," he said, taking in Evelyn and Patrick's modest house like it was the Taj Mahal. "Don't you?"

I loved that Blake knew what I wanted and didn't act as if it wasn't enough. "Yeah," I said. "But a nicer house. In Park Slope. With a hammock in the yard and a teaching job at a good college in the city."

He nodded. "My father has connections at schools in the city."

I sat there and tried to figure out why Mom was so anti-connections. I was starting to believe that connections were a good thing, because they could get you what you wanted without toil and drudgery and practice SAT exams. Then Blake stood up to get a soda and I watched him and Patrick on the patio.

They were getting along and I was thrilled. He and Patrick discussed football and baseball and the FDNY entrance exam, but I didn't get to hear everything because

Evelyn snatched me from my chair and coaxed me into the nursery, where she closed the door and clenched my hands.

"Holy shit," she said. "He's simply fetching."

I had never in my entire life heard Evelyn say the word *fetching*. I couldn't imagine where she'd found it other than in a half-read romance novel. But it was an accurate description, so I agreed and answered her questions about how Blake and I met, and then she asked his age.

"Twenty-one in November," I told her.

"Twenty-one," she said musingly. "So are you two doing it?"

She was worse than Mom. I shook my head as if I'd never even considered *doing it*.

"You're a liar, Ari. I know what's going on. Look at you, all glowing and crap."

I was glowing? I didn't know. And I hadn't expected that I'd want to talk to Evelyn about this, but I did. I couldn't talk to Mom and I didn't talk to Summer, and I wouldn't confide in Leigh—she was Blake's cousin, after all. And suddenly, standing in the middle of blue walls decorated with Red Sox pennants, I was grateful to have a big sister.

"I'm not lying," I said after telling Evelyn about my Wednesday afternoons. "We're really not doing anything."

"But you will," she said. "I'll give you my doctor's number. She works at a clinic in Brooklyn on Fridays. . . . They don't ask for insurance there, so you won't have to tell Mom . . . and you can get a prescription for the Pill. We don't want you getting knocked up, do we?" She laughed and then she scribbled on a piece of paper that she pressed into my palm.

"Evelyn," I said. "The Pill doesn't always work, does it? I mean—you—"

She interrupted me with a different sort of laugh. It was cunning and coarse and she lowered her voice. "They work if you take them every day. But I wanted to get out of Mom's house, so I skipped a pill here and there. I mean . . . Patrick always loved me, but he loved me more when I was carrying his baby. Guys are funny that way." She winked and put her hands on my shoulders. "Listen, Ari. There are all kinds of diseases out there, and I don't just mean AIDS. Make sure Blake doesn't have anything before you sleep with him. You should find out how many girls he's been with if you don't already know."

I only knew about the Georgia girl. But all I could think about now was how desperate Evelyn must have been to get out of Mom's house . . . and how Kieran was no accident.

# sixteen

*I* loved June. It was nothing but bright sunshine, fresh air, Wednesday afternoons on embroidered roses. I loved the music-box song that came from the Good Humor man's truck as he cruised my block after dinner each night, the smell of marshmallows roasting on our neighbors' barbecues, and the letter A written in encouraging red ink on my final exams.

"You're the most promising student I've seen in years," my art teacher said.

It was the last day of school. The classroom was empty. The windows were open and everybody milled around outside, talking and signing each other's yearbooks, and I listened to their voices until my teacher said something about a summer job. Then he handed me an index card printed with a Brooklyn address and the words CREATIVE COLORS.

"What kind of job is this?" I asked.

"It's a program for adults with mental disabilities," he said. "Down syndrome . . . brain injuries . . . that sort of thing. They do art therapy. A friend of mine owns the place and he needs some help, so I thought of you. Somebody with your talent should spread it around. You could do a lot of good there."

My talent. Did he really say that? The words repeated in my mind and I practically skipped to the subway station. Then I decided to stop by Creative Colors on my way home.

It was a few blocks from my house, on the first floor of a three-story Victorian with Doric columns and a wide porch. My teacher's friend's name was Julian; he was thirty-something, and he sported a brown goatee and wire-rimmed glasses. He said that I came highly recommended and he hired me right on the spot.

Mom wouldn't stop blabbing about my new job during dinner that night. "These people recognize talent when they see it," she said. "And you want to waste yourself on teaching." She held her hand out for my plate, overloaded it with macaroni salad, and turned to Dad. "This one just goes off and gets a job on her own. Remember when Evelyn was Ariadne's age? I begged her to find a summer job, but she wouldn't even fill out a Burger King application."

Mom was proud of me and that was great, but I didn't want compliments at my sister's expense. Evelyn had been so sweet lately—she always asked about Blake when we talked on the phone. And it had been considerate of her to hook me up with her doctor, even though it turned out I couldn't take birth control pills.

I'd found out a week ago. I had scheduled a secret appointment at the clinic, and I endured the humiliating exam with the flimsy gown and the latex gloves and the frigid instrument that could double as a shoehorn or a medieval torture device, and when it was over I felt like I'd crossed a finish line. I sat up from the examining table in that paper-thin gown, remembering a PBS program about these African boys who went through a ceremony and got their faces sliced with a razor and scarred for life because that was their rite of passage. So while the doctor sat on her stool and reviewed my medical history, I thought: This is my rite of passage. Now I'm no different from Summer or those other girls who see gynecologists regularly and swallow birth control pills faithfully, and I'm a member of the I've Got a Boyfriend Club.

Then I saw the doctor flipping through forms and scratching her head. She was a fleshy middle-aged woman who said she hadn't realized that I was a migraine sufferer and *The Pill isn't a good idea for you, Miss Mitchell. It'll only make your headaches worse.* Next she gave me a few pamphlets about pregnancy and STDs and birth control—as if I hadn't read the exact same things in Sex Ed at school—and said, *It's better if your boyfriend uses protection, anyway. You can never be sure of a man's sexual history, no matter what he tells you.*

So I'd worn that stupid gown for nothing. And Blake hadn't told me anything because I hadn't asked.

*  *  *

This was my first time at Delmonico's. I was sitting next to Blake on the Saturday after school ended, and I knew he wasn't comfortable. He was dressed in a suit—so was Mr. Ellis—and he kept tugging at his collar as if he couldn't breathe.

"Get used to it," Del said. "You'll be wearing a tie for the whole summer."

Rachel and Leigh and Idalis were there too. We all sat at a round table on leather chairs in a room that was dark even though the early-evening sun was blazing outside. There was a crimson carpet and a glitzy chandelier, and the waiter handed me a menu with prices that blew my mind.

I leafed through the menu as a basket of bread was being passed around the table. When it reached Leigh, she kept it beside her.

"Can I please have the bread, Leigh?" I asked, and even though she was sitting next to me, she didn't seem to hear. She was buttering a roll when I repeated my question.

"It's right *there*," she said without looking at me. "Get it yourself."

"Leigh," Blake said sharply. He was on my other side and he seemed as surprised by her nastiness as I was. "Don't talk to Ari like that."

"Blake," Rachel said from across the table, in the same chastising tone he'd used on Leigh. "Don't interfere. It's between the girls."

What was between the girls? I wondered as Blake reached

199

over Leigh's plate and snatched the bread away. He and I glanced at each other in confusion and shrugged it off. Then the waiter came back with a pad and pencil. Blake ordered a steak called the Classic and I ordered the same because I didn't know what else to do. Everybody was asking the waiter for things like *foie gras* and *au poivre,* which was baffling because Delmonico's wasn't even a French restaurant.

Mr. Ellis had a steak that cost more than fifty dollars. It was so rare that I had to look away after he cut into it. The meat was almost raw, and the sight of it turned my stomach.

"So will you miss us, Stan?" Rachel asked. "California is awfully far away, you know."

That was why we were here. Rachel and Leigh were leaving tonight on a flight to LAX out of JFK, and this was their farewell dinner.

"I won't miss paying your rent," Mr. Ellis said, and then he thanked me for recommending Catering by Tina. "Tina's food is excellent. And her daughter's a beautiful girl. She's your friend, isn't she?"

"Yes," I said, thinking that Mr. Ellis must like too-salty food, and that he'd called me a pretty girl the first time I met him but had never once said I was a beautiful girl. He never really spoke to me at all, other than hello and goodbye. I wouldn't have been surprised if he didn't know my last name.

"And what does her father do?" he asked.

"He's a psychiatrist," I said, which seemed to impress Mr. Ellis.

"I see. And what does your father do, Ari?"

"He's a cop. A homicide detective."

"How honorable," he said.

I wasn't sure he was still impressed. But I chose to take *honorable* as a compliment. I also tried to forget that beautiful is better than pretty and I focused on Blake, who was so handsome in his suit. But I could tell that he just wanted to tear it off.

After dinner we rode to the airport, in a limousine that Mr. Ellis arranged for us as if this was prom night. Del and Idalis had finished a bottle of wine by themselves during dinner and now they were loud and obnoxious. Blake was quiet, so I asked him what was wrong.

He whispered in my ear, "My mother died today."

He said it as if she had died this very day, this morning or this afternoon, instead of a long time ago. "You mean today is the anniversary?"

He nodded. "Thirteen years. We went to the cemetery this morning."

His voice was sad. I held his hand. Soon we were at JFK, where the chauffeur unloaded luggage from the trunk and everyone got out of the car. I wanted to give Leigh a goodbye hug even though she'd been so quiet in the limo and so touchy at the restaurant, but she was ignoring me.

"Leigh," I said, dashing ahead and catching her arm as she headed toward the airport's automatic doors. "Aren't you going to say goodbye? You have to give me your new phone number and your address so we can stay in touch."

She turned around. Her mouth was open. She looked like I'd just said something highly offensive. "Are you kidding?" she asked, and started walking.

"Leigh," I said again, following her. "What's wrong with you?"

She faced me. Then she grabbed my wrist and led me to an empty square of sidewalk, out of her family's earshot. I looked at the gold flecks in her eyes, the brown freckles on her skin. She was right—there were a gazillion of them.

"Why would you want my phone number?" she asked, perching her hands on her hips. "You won't use it. You didn't even call me when we lived across the bridge from each other. You said we'd hang out until I moved to California. Remember? In the Hamptons you said we'd hang out for the rest of the spring, but I ended up alone in my apartment as usual. I only see you at school or when you're with Blake and I just happen to be there. And he went to that Memorial Day party at your sister's house. But *I* didn't get an invitation. How come *I* didn't get an invitation?"

I was stunned. She was speaking quickly and raising her voice, and people walking by with suitcases and garment bags were staring. "W-well," I stammered. "I know we haven't seen each other much lately, but I thought you were busy getting ready to move."

She rolled her eyes and scoffed. "That's a weak excuse. As soon as you met Blake, you didn't care about me anymore. You used me to get to him . . . and it's not the first time this has happened. Lots of girls are interested in my cousins, and they don't care who they step on to get what they want. I didn't think you were like that . . . I thought you were different. I thought it would be okay to have you around them, that we could all be friends—but I was wrong. You dropped me and you didn't even notice."

I had a flashback to a four-course dinner and crème brûlée. I remembered standing in the penthouse, weaseling my way into an invitation to Rockefeller Center so I could see Blake again. I remembered Leigh telling Rachel not to give me dating advice when Rachel said Blake would be perfect for me. "I never meant to—" I started, but she raised her hand like she didn't want to hear any excuses. And maybe I was lying—maybe part of me really had meant to. I felt horrible, thinking about how friendly she'd been on my first day at Hollister, how I had let her ice skate alone, and I was shocked to realize that I was just like Summer. I'd put my boyfriend above everyone else and let Leigh sit at home on Friday nights. It was my fault that she'd spent the last few months alone in her apartment with nothing but colored pencils. It was even worse to think that this had happened to Leigh before, and that she considered me a girl who didn't care who she stepped on. I had never thought of myself as that sort of girl. "I'm so sorry," I said.

"Those are just words," Leigh said. "Do they make you feel better?"

Not at all. I wanted to make Leigh feel better, but I supposed it was too late now. "I guess you'll be back to visit soon?" I said meekly, hoping for another chance. "I mean . . . we can get together and maybe . . ."

"Yeah," she said, folding her arms. "I'll be back soon . . . to visit my *family*."

I got the message. I nodded, listening to car doors slamming and people saying "Have a safe trip." "Well . . . are you going to give me your new phone number? I promise I'll call you."

"Don't do me any favors." She spun around and stomped toward the terminal.

I knew I didn't deserve her phone number or her friendship. But I decided I would make it up to her somehow. I would ask Blake for Leigh's new address and send her a letter apologizing for everything. Maybe that would mean more than just saying I'm sorry.

I watched her walk toward Rachel, who was checking her suitcases curbside with a guy who had a Russian accent. I climbed into the limo with Blake, Del, and Idalis and just sat there thinking about Leigh.

"Can you give me Leigh's new address?" I asked Blake.

"Sure," he said. He reached into his pocket, took out his wallet, and started digging inside. The address was written on the back of an Ellis & Hummel business card that he pressed into my hand. "She didn't give it to you already?"

"I guess she forgot," I said, sticking the card in my purse, thinking it was nice of Leigh not to tell Blake that I was a person of questionable character. The fact that she hadn't made me feel even worse.

Blake nodded. "She was so snotty tonight. That's not like her. Maybe she's nervous about moving."

He hadn't noticed that I'd ditched her either. We'd been too busy with each other to give Leigh a second thought, even though we both knew how much she needed a friend. I just nodded at Blake and leaned my head against the window, watching Mr. Ellis as he tipped the guy who was taking Rachel's and Leigh's suitcases away.

The car door opened and Mr. Ellis slid onto the seat next

to Blake. "You have to give these people a good tip," Mr. Ellis said to nobody in particular. "Otherwise they'll put your bags on a plane to Moscow just to get even."

"Yeah," Del said. "Fucking commies."

He was drunk. But it was supposed to be a joke and I felt bad when Mr. Ellis didn't laugh. He turned his back on Del and spoke to Blake about starting at Ellis & Hummel on Monday, and I looked out the window because I got the feeling it was a private conversation.

Mr. Ellis stayed in the limo after the rest of us got out on the Upper East Side. He said something about work and a client and the car took him away. Then Blake and Del and Idalis and I were in the elevator and I tried not to watch as Idalis pushed Del into a corner and kissed him like they were alone.

They kept it up at the penthouse. I didn't think they would, because Del popped a movie into the VCR in the living room and we all sat together on the couch, but they started fooling around again during the opening credits. Blake had enough.

"Let's take a walk," he said, clutching my wrist.

Idalis disconnected her lips from Del's long enough to reach over and grab my arm. "Yeah," she said. "Why don't you take a walk upstairs to Blake's bedroom?"

*Upstairs to Blake's bedroom.* She said it long and slow, in a sultry voice that embarrassed and insulted me. I was sure I knew what she was thinking—that I was a sexless Debby Boone snoozefest and she was an erotic Madonna peep show. Blake pulled me up from the couch and Del rolled his eyes.

"Leave her alone, Idalis," Del said, and I adored him for it.

Then Blake and I were on the sidewalk. The sky had clouded over and I heard thunder in the distance. Blake was quiet as we walked to Central Park, where people started clearing from the grass after the sky lit up with an ominous spike of bluish white lightning.

Blake led me to a bench and we sat down. He pulled off his tie, took out his wallet, and showed me a yellowing picture of a young woman. She had big blue eyes and long blond hair that was parted straight down the middle, like a Wella Balsam ad from the seventies. Her skin was tan and her bone structure was regal, and she looked as if she was someone who never expected anything bad to happen to her.

"Is this your mother?" I asked.

He nodded and stared at the buildings in the distance before telling me that she had died while Del was playing Little League baseball. Blake and Del and Mr. Ellis had gone to the game and she'd stayed at home. Del had found her on the kitchen floor when they came back.

"Brain aneurysm," Blake said. "The doctor who did the autopsy said there was nothing anybody could've done. But Del thought it was his fault . . . he said we could've saved her if we'd been there. He never wanted to play baseball anymore after that. He was good at it too."

I wondered if anyone had ever told Del that it wasn't his fault. "I'm sorry," I said. "I bet she'd be proud if she could see you now."

He smiled. Thunder crashed, lightning ripped across the

sky, and we stayed on the bench with our arms around each other even though rain fell in heavy drops around us. I didn't mind getting soaked because it felt as if Blake needed me, and I wanted him to.

It was a Friday in late August when my boss, Julian, admitted that most of his employees quit after less than a week. The place was a downer for them because of the people who went there. They were called students, even though they were in their twenties and thirties, but they were really just being babysat until their parents came to pick them up at night, and they were easily entertained with crayons and finger paints.

One of them was named Adam. He was twenty-two and had cute dimples, and I was sure that he'd been a popular boy in high school until he got rammed in the head during a football game five years ago. Now he was mildly brain-damaged and he stuttered sometimes, and the highlight of his day seemed to be the pictures I sketched for him—pencil drawings of lakes and mountains. That was what he wanted because he used to hike and fish upstate, and I didn't mind drawing those things over and over if it made him happy.

"Do you have a boyfriend?" he asked.

"Yeah," I said, thinking that I'd answered the same question six times already, and if he hadn't gotten into that accident he could have chosen any girlfriend he wanted.

"You're pretty," he said. "You look like Snow White."

I almost cried. I convinced myself that helping Adam

with his painting would stimulate his mind and he might get better someday if I just kept trying.

Blake thought that this was a nice thing to do. He told me so that night, when I met him at work. It was six o'clock and we were standing beside a mahogany reception desk with the words ELLIS & HUMMEL printed across it in shiny gold letters.

"Leaving already?" we heard a voice say.

We both turned our heads and saw Mr. Ellis, who was holding a stack of papers in his hands and walking toward us.

"I left copies of the cases you wanted on your desk, Daddy," Blake said.

Mr. Ellis smiled and smacked Blake on the shoulder. A few minutes later, Blake and I were in the Corvette, where he said he wanted to stop at home to change before dinner. He went to his bedroom at the penthouse and I waited on the couch, admiring the skyline. As I was sitting there, I heard the elevator doors open. I looked toward the foyer and saw Del, who told me that he had come by to pick up an earring that Idalis lost the last time she'd been here.

"We broke up," he said, taking a seat next to me. "I was sick of her shit, anyway."

I wondered if that was true. I studied his eyes while he talked, thinking that they were much more green than gray tonight. "Oh, well," I said. "You're better off, I suppose."

He smiled. The scar on his lip curled. Then Blake was on the stairs and Del mentioned Ellis & Hummel. "Do you know what your boyfriend does at work?" he asked, and I shook my head. "He helps our father and his partners raid companies so decent people can lose their jobs."

I glanced over at Blake. He looked tired. "Cut it out, Del," he said.

Del didn't listen. "You know what else they do, Ari? They file frivolous medical-malpractice lawsuits. And they win. That's why health insurance costs so much and people dying of cancer go bankrupt."

"Enough already," Blake said, grabbing my arm. The next thing I knew, we were in the Corvette and Blake was saying he didn't want to stay in Manhattan. "Let's go to the Hamptons and order in. I've had enough of this city."

I didn't argue. He was quiet for the entire drive and when we ate a pizza at the kitchen table. Blake drank a beer and stared into space, and I knew what was wrong.

"You don't have to work there," I told him.

"I *do* have to work there, Ari. I can't let my father down."

I knew how he felt and I wanted to cheer him up. So I suggested that we sit on the lounge chairs by the pool because it was a nice night, but Blake wanted to swim instead.

"I don't have a bathing suit," I said, and he told me that Rachel had left one upstairs.

It was a hot pink bikini with a bottom that tied in a bow on the left hip. I found it in a dresser drawer along with T-shirts and sarongs, in one of those bedrooms with the in-direct lighting. Then I stood in front of a full-length mirror on the white carpet, examining my thin legs and my narrow waist and my chest. The bikini crowded my breasts together into a small semblance of cleavage, and I didn't think they were perfect, like Blake said, but they weren't all that horri-ble. So I decided to go to the pool wearing only the bikini and leave Rachel's shirts in the drawer.

I held my breath all the way down the stairs and across the patio, and I didn't exhale until Blake smiled at me. Then he picked me up and tossed me into the deep end.

"Jerk," I said, even though I didn't mean it. I rubbed chlorine out of my eyes as he dove into the pool, and everything was still blurry when he pulled me into a corner and I put my arms around his neck.

"You look much better in that bikini than Rachel does," he said.

His hair was slicked back. The lights beneath the water were reflected in his eyes, and I remembered lifting my favorite marble to the sun.

"I can't compete with Rachel. She's beautiful."

"*You're* beautiful," he said.

*Beautiful* sounded so much better than *pretty*. I smiled, fiddling with his arrowhead charm. "You and Leigh have the same necklace."

"My grandmother gave one to all of us . . . me and Leigh and Del. He never wears his, though."

"Have you spoken to Leigh lately?" I asked, thinking of the letter I had sent her at the end of June. I'd spent a half hour at Hallmark searching through *I'm Sorry* cards. The one I chose had a cartoon cat with forlorn-looking eyes and a daisy in its paw. I sat at my desk for a long time that night, writing *I didn't realize what I was doing* and *I hope you'll forgive me* and *Please give me a call so we can talk*. But Leigh had never called or written back, so I guessed she still hadn't forgiven me. I really couldn't blame her. Maybe she thought the card was stupid too. *I'm Sorry* cards were so sappy.

"Yeah," Blake said. "She called me the other day. Haven't you heard from her?"

"Not lately," I said casually. Then I looked at the tattoo on Blake's back and changed the subject. "What is this exactly?" I asked, tracing the circle and the cross and the three feathers with my index finger.

We treaded water while he explained. It was called a medicine wheel and it was a sacred Native American thing. It was also supposed to bring good luck. He'd gotten it from some old Shawnee man down in Georgia.

"Don't mention it to my father," Blake said. "He knows about the tattoo, but he wasn't happy when he found out, so I don't talk about it. He's been running from Georgia his whole life . . . he wants to forget that we have any Shawnee blood in us at all."

I wasn't surprised. I thought of Ellis & Hummel and the penthouse and Blake's mother with her aristocratic father. I imagined Mr. Ellis struggling through school and winning lawsuits so that he could afford to live on the Upper East Side and pretend he'd never eaten a collard green or a hummingbird cake.

"But he gave your brother a Native American name," I said.

"He didn't want to. That was his father's name and it was expected. So he did it." Blake leaned his head into the pool to soak his hair. He raked it back with his fingers and I watched water droplets collect on his cheeks. "Anyway . . . just don't mention the tattoo. Jessica has the same one—he didn't appreciate that very much, either."

I'd never heard of Jessica before, but I knew who she was when Blake apologized and said that it isn't nice for a guy to talk about an old girlfriend.

He was right. It wasn't nice. It made a queasy lump of envy rise from my stomach to my face. I saw blond hair and a trailer with flowerpots and Blake sleeping with Jessica for two whole years.

"What happened with her?" I asked, as if I had no clue.

"I don't know," he said. "She stopped returning my calls. I even went down there to see her, but she was just gone. No explanation."

That was a cruel thing to do and he didn't deserve it. "Oh," I said. "I'm sorry."

He shrugged as if he didn't care, but he was a bad actor. Then we kissed. The water in the pool was warm and so were Blake's lips and tongue as they touched mine. He untied my top and slid it off, and then his mouth was on my chest in a way that made me worry about the neighbors. But Mr. Ellis had a lot of property, so I doubted that anyone could see from two acres away.

"We have to stop now," Blake said suddenly. "Or I won't be able to stop."

I hated stopping. It was grating on my nerves. But I came to my senses when my top was back on and we were drying off on the patio. We rested on lounge chairs and Blake read the *New York Post* while I decided that he was smart to stop what we'd been doing in the pool. There were things to consider before I could have what he used to give to Jessica.

"Blake," I said.

He was reading the sports section: YANKEES CRUSH KANSAS CITY. "Yeah?"

"How many girls have you been with?"

There. I did it. I'd been wondering ever since Evelyn had brought it up on Memorial Day and I needed to know, because terrible things could dwell in the most unlikely places.

He rested the newspaper on his lap. "It isn't nice to talk about that."

"We have to. These days, people have to talk about it."

He nodded. Then he held up two fingers.

"Really?" I said. "Jessica and who else?"

"Somebody older. That was the first time." He rolled his eyes. "I barely knew her . . . I met her at a bar in the city that Del dragged me to when I was sixteen and it felt like she was going to the bathroom on me. That's how sex is if you don't care about each other—it's no good at all." He sat up and swung his legs over the side of the lounge chair. "Listen, Ari. I don't have AIDS or anything else. I'll get a blood test so you don't have to worry."

I wasn't worried anymore; he didn't need a blood test. I shook my head but he insisted that he'd see his doctor, and then he checked his watch and said that we should head back to the city.

I went upstairs. The bikini was dry now and I stood in front of the mirror again, studying my body. The door was open, and when I saw Blake's reflection pass by in the hall, I called his name. He joined me on the carpet and I waved my hand in front of my chest.

"Can you tell?" I asked. "I mean . . . that I'm uneven?"

He held his fist to my cheek. "You *aren't*. If you say that one more time, I'll make you sorry."

I laughed and we kissed again, even though Blake warned me that it was close to nine and we had a long drive ahead.

So what? Mom wanted me home at *a reasonable hour* and there was still plenty of time before the reasonable hours were gone. I distracted him from the clock by lying on the bed and crooking my finger. Then it was Wednesday afternoon all over again, this time on a white comforter stuffed with feathers that felt as soft as a field of cotton puffs.

"Ari," Blake said. He was lying on top of me and he still hadn't put a shirt on. His naked chest, the muscles in his stomach, and the trail of hair that began at his navel and disappeared inside his shorts got me all shivery, and I wasn't sure how much longer I could worry about being *nice*. "I love you."

I gasped. I wanted to say the same but he wouldn't give me a chance. He told me not to say it until I was ready and that I shouldn't say it unless I meant it, and I was about to ask him to shut up because I *was* ready and I *did* mean it. But I couldn't say a word because he kissed me again, and his hands were on that bow on my hip.

It was loose now, and I was nervous as his hands moved to my waistband. I felt it sliding south and I thought of Idalis floating in the pool and Del saying *Don't you wish*.

Blake was edging lower on the bed and I knew what he was about to do. It was the thing that people other than Idalis kept quiet or giggled about, the thing that was supposedly safe since it wouldn't get me pregnant, the thing that supposedly bypassed all the Catholic rules.

"Don't be scared, Ari," he said. "It won't hurt, I promise."

Then the bottom half of my bikini was lying on the carpet. Blake was between my legs and it definitely didn't hurt. I felt his lips and his tongue and his thick hair brushing against the soft inside of my thighs, and after a while there was a warm burst in the center of my body that flowed to my head and made noises come out of my mouth. They were like the sounds I heard through Evelyn and Patrick's bedroom wall, but I buried my face in my arm so that they wouldn't be as loud.

I kept my eyes shut against my arm, thinking that this was amazing and incredible, like devouring an entire box of chocolate all alone. It was sweet and delicious and I just couldn't help myself. But if anybody found out, I'd have to pretend that I could never ever ever do such a sinful thing.

# seventeen

One of the four bathrooms had a showerhead that looked like a mail slot in somebody's front door. It was a metal square with a rectangular opening and I almost expected a Con Edison bill to fall out.

Water flowed over me in a steady stream as I listened to Blake banging around in the bathroom next door. I'd rushed in here from the bedroom, saying I was saturated in chlorine and I needed some shampoo immediately, even though that was just a lame excuse.

I couldn't look at him. I couldn't speak. I was excited and elated and embarrassed all at once.

But I couldn't hide forever. I lingered in the shower until my hands wrinkled, then I wrapped a towel around myself and tiptoed down the hall. I ran into Blake, who was wet from the shower too. A towel was tied around his waist and his necklace skimmed his bare chest. He was so handsome, but I still couldn't look at him, even when he pressed his forehead against mine.

"You make such cute little noises," he said.

My cheeks flushed. I could have died. "I have to get dressed," I told him, but he caught my elbow as I walked away.

"Hey," he said gently. "What's wrong?"

He smelled of Irish Spring. I just stood there. "Nothing," I said.

He lifted my chin. "You think we did something bad?"

Yes. No. Maybe. "I don't know."

"Ari," he said with a laugh. "We didn't. And I wouldn't do it for just anybody. I don't get involved with someone unless I see a future."

*A future.* The idea that what happened tonight could lead to a Park Slope house and a hammock and kids with the bluest eyes made everything seem okay.

So I relaxed. I smiled. I danced alone around the bedroom while I changed into my clothes. Then we were in the car, where the top was down and my hair flowed in the breeze and everything felt perfect.


I thought I came home at a reasonable hour. It wasn't quite as reasonable as the time I usually came home, but it wasn't all that late. I didn't expect Mom to ambush me.

"Where were you?" she said.

I had just walked through the front door into the living room and I was startled at the sound of her deep voice in the pitch dark. I heard the click of a lamp and there she was, sitting on the couch with her arms folded and her legs crossed.

My eyes nervously searched the room. I saw the hole in the La-Z-Boy, a sealed pack of Pall Malls on the coffee table. "Where's Dad?" I asked.

"Where do you think? They pulled a body out of the East River tonight and he had to go to Manhattan." She reached for her cigarettes. "So where were you?"

I shrugged. I wondered if I was glowing and she'd figure everything out. "With Blake," I said.

She peeled plastic from the Pall Malls, slid out a cigarette, and tossed the pack onto the table. "I know that. Where exactly were you with Blake?"

"In the Hamptons," I said, and my voice sounded weak and small.

Mom flicked her lighter. "And what were you doing there all this time?"

"Nothing," I said.

She dragged on her cigarette and patted the couch. I sat beside her even though I just wanted to go upstairs and think about Blake.

"You're getting too serious," she said.

Here we go, I thought. Then I got defensive. "Why don't you like him?" I asked.

"I never said I didn't like him," Mom answered calmly. "He's very nice. He's respectful. I can see that he was brought up well. But you're my daughter and my concern is for you. You're too young to be serious about anyone."

Too young. Too serious. Too everything. "He thinks we have a future together," I said, and I thought I sounded mature and rational, but Mom didn't—she laughed as if I was an idiot.

"Ariadne, he has no idea what he wants. He's a young boy."

"He is not. He'll be twenty-one in November. You were only twenty-three when you married Dad."

"But that was 1957. It's a different world now . . . women have much more opportunity today. You," she said, pointing a finger at me, "have much more opportunity than I ever did. You don't know how lucky you are. And Blake better not be filling your head with all this *future* shit. It's just a ploy to get you in the sack." She leaned forward, staring into my eyes like they were two crystal balls. "He hasn't gotten you in the sack, has he?"

I wondered what she could see. Roses on a bedspread, a soft white comforter, a pool with a scorpion lurking at the bottom. "No," I said, and I didn't think it was a lie because *in the sack* meant going all the way, and Blake and I had only gone part of the way so far.

She settled into the couch and puffed on her cigarette. "Good. I'm glad to hear it. Because guys Blake's age are flighty—they'll tell you anything to get laid and then they move on to the next victim. There are some girls who can handle that—Evelyn, for example. She used to break up with one and find another without batting an eyelash. But you're not like Evelyn, and if this kid does anything to hurt you, I'll chop off his nuts and shove them down his throat." She snuffed out her cigarette in an ashtray. "And you tell him to bring you home earlier from now on. Understand?"

I understood. I understood that I would never tell her anything about Blake again and that my head hurt for the first time in months. "I'm going to bed now, Mom. I think I'm getting a migraine."

She wouldn't let me go to bed. She brought me to the kitchen, where she watched while I swallowed my medicine. Then she gave me a glass of warm milk and kissed my cheek.

"Good night," she said, and when she was gone, I wiped my cheek with a napkin and poured the milk down the sink.


Summer invited me to her house the next afternoon, which was surprising. I hadn't seen her once since school had ended, and she hadn't returned the four messages I'd left with Tina. But I missed her enough to forget all that and to ask Dad for a ride from Flatbush to Park Slope.

He dropped me off and waved to Tina before heading to work. I walked past her as she crouched on her little lawn, wearing a sun visor and plucking weeds.

"Hi, Ari," she said. "Long time no see. Go ahead inside— Summer's upstairs."

I slipped into the foyer and peeked into Jeff's library with its crowded bookshelves and Tiffany lamps. I heard Fleetwood Mac and I followed the sound to Summer's bedroom, where she was sitting in a chair with one foot perched on her desk. She was polishing her toenails and didn't see me.

I stood in the doorway and glanced around at her bedroom. It looked like it had been completely redecorated since the last time I'd been here. It was so fancy, so elegant. There was a paneled bed made of bleached wood set between two antique-looking night tables, a matching wardrobe chest, and taupe wallpaper speckled with shiny silver roses. The wallpaper matched the comforter on the bed, which had decorative pillows in the shape of circles and squares. Everything was perfect, like something from a fairy tale, and I wished I could sleep in a fairy tale instead of on Evelyn's rickety old canopy bed from when Lyndon Johnson was president.

"Your room is fantastic," I said, even though I had to force the words from my throat.

Summer looked up from her toes. She was wearing a short denim skirt with a pink halter top and indigo eye shadow, and she was as stunning as the room. But I remembered that I had Blake and he thought I was *much prettier,* which meant more to me than a fancy bedroom.

"Thanks," she said. "Sorry I haven't called lately. I've been busy."

I guessed she'd been busy with Casey, so I accepted the excuse. Female code and all. "No problem. I've been busy too."

She leaned back in her chair. "I broke up with Casey last week."

Surprised, I took a seat on her windowsill and watched as she pointed to the tattoo on her ankle. The *C* had been changed to an *S* so that now she was wearing her own initials.

"They did a good job," I said. "But I hope they used a clean needle."

"Of course they did, Ari. I got it done at a very reputable place on Bleecker Street a few days ago. I went there after a meeting that my mother and I catered at Ellis and Hummel," she said, and I tried not to react. I just nodded and crossed my legs as she flopped on her bed and hugged a pillow to her chest. "I think your boyfriend's father is gorgeous, by the way."

And my boyfriend's father thinks you're beautiful, I thought. But I didn't say it because she had a mischievous look on her face that didn't need encouragement.

"Forget it, Summer. He's old."

She rubbed one leg slowly across her comforter. "Not really. He's forty-seven."

"How would *you* know?" I asked.

"He told me. I talk to him all the time. . . . Stan's a friendly person."

She called him Stan. *I* didn't even call him Stan. He must have given her special permission, and I guessed he only did that for girls he considered beautiful. "Right," I said, and Summer flipped over onto her back and stared at her ceiling fan.

"Ari," she began. "Are you sleeping with Blake yet?"

I looked out the window; Tina was lugging a fertilizer bag down the stairs. "Why are you asking?"

She shrugged. "I was just wondering about . . . what he does and . . . what's normal for most guys. I mean . . . I dumped Casey because he was losing respect for me. He wanted a certain position all the time, not just once in a while, and I don't think that a guy really cares about you if he doesn't even look at your face while you're making love."

222

That image made me uncomfortable. "But you said that position was strangely exciting."

Summer shifted onto her stomach, resting her face on her fists. "Not every single time."

"Oh," I said.

"I'll bet Blake looks at your face. I've talked to him a few times at Stan's parties and I think he's a real gentleman. He always holds the door for me and he never even swears. He treats me with respect . . . like a man is supposed to treat a lady."

"That's how he is," I said proudly, and for the first time in my life, I knew that Summer envied me, that I had something she wanted. I felt victorious, but I tried not to act that way. She'd given herself to a guy who wouldn't even look at her face; she didn't need to get her feelings hurt again. "But the other stuff you asked about . . . I don't know. We haven't gotten that far."

"Jesus," she said. "After all these months? He really *is* a gentleman . . . Casey demanded sex after just a few dates."

I'd never known any of this—that Casey wasn't a gentleman, that he demanded things. Now I wasn't sure what to say, but it didn't matter because she changed the subject. She opened a dresser drawer, took out a letter from Hollister, and told me that she'd been approved to graduate early and was going to work full-time with Tina from January until college started next September. Then Tina called Summer from downstairs, asking for help with the twisted garden hose, and I was alone.

I walked around the room, examining Summer's pretty things: the carvings on her headboard, the old jewelry box with the spinning ballerina on her dresser. I glanced inside the drawer that she'd left open. I saw a lacy black bra, a purple velvet diary, and a silver bracelet engraved with the initials M.G.

Leigh's bracelet. The one she'd lost at the party at the Winter Garden. I couldn't believe it. I was furious. Leigh was desperate for that bracelet, and Summer had been holding it hostage all this time. I knew that Summer could be inconsiderate, but I'd never suspected that she was utterly heartless. I'd even defended her to Leigh. *She wouldn't do something like that.* I snatched the bracelet out of the drawer, holding it in my sweaty fist. My head was pounding and I was tired all of a sudden. A minute later Summer came back, smiling, completely unaware that she'd been found out.

"What's this?" I asked, dangling the bracelet in front of her.

"Oh, yeah," she said. "It turned up last week. I was going to tell you."

She wasn't going to tell me. And I was sure that she'd found it eons ago, the night of the Winter Garden party. Still, she stayed cool now, concocting a story—something about the bracelet getting tangled in a tablecloth that Tina hadn't used for ages.

"You're lying," I said. "You did this because you hate Leigh."

She slammed her drawer. "Why shouldn't I hate her? Remember what she said when we were at that club in the city? *You don't want people to think you're a slut.* I had enough of that crap in public school. And *you*," she said, pointing an acrylic nail at me. "You betrayed me, Ari. I always stuck by you, and I was always there for you when you needed me, but you weren't on my side against that weirdo and her bitch mother. It's unbelievable that they're related to Blake, because they're nothing like him."

I supposed she had a valid point about sticking by me and all, but I ignored that. I was so annoyed by the adoring look in her eyes when she spoke Blake's name that I couldn't be reasonable. "Stop talking about him," I said. "You don't know anything about him."

She folded her arms and let out a snarky laugh. "Neither do you."

"He's my *boyfriend,*" I said. "I *love* him."

Now she really laughed. "Oh, please. You don't love him. You barely know him. You haven't even slept with him. It's just a case of limerence, like that silly boy in seventh grade who kept a collection of my hair."

*Limerence.* That was the word I couldn't remember. The fact that she'd compare me to a poem-writing, hair-collecting seventh grader was just too much.

"Well," I said. "I wonder what Blake will say when I tell him what you did to his cousin. I know you have a high opinion of him, but I'm sure he won't think very much of you."

She chewed on her lip, staring at me for a second. Worry spread across her face but it quickly changed into disgust. "I don't know who you think you are," she said. "You've got this idea that you're something special because you landed a guy who's completely out of your league. But you won't have him forever, Ari. He'll figure it out."

She had hit a nerve, and it hurt. "Figure what out?" I asked as an aura crawled into my eye.

"That you're boring. That you're dull and boring and *average* in every possible way."

225

I was speechless. Maybe I should have shrugged it off. But I thought that it might be true, that I might be even less than average, and I fought back tears.

"You can't stand it that I finally have someone," I said after a moment, choking out the words as my throat closed up. "I never had a boyfriend, and I only had one friend, but you had everything . . . and that made you feel like you were better than me."

She tossed her hair. "I *am* better than you."

I couldn't talk anymore. My eyes were stinging and my face was burning. I rushed outside, past Tina, who was spraying shrubbery with her hose.

"Bye, Ari," she said, but I didn't say anything back.

I walked all the way home to Flatbush. I was exhausted by the time I opened my front door. I smelled potatoes roasting and Mom came out of the kitchen, drying her hands on a towel.

"You're home early," she said.

I thought I might faint. Mom looked distorted, like a reflection in a carnival mirror. "I'm done with Summer, Mom. And don't call Jeff about it."

She stared at me for a moment. "All right, Ariadne," she said finally.

The phone rang and it was Blake. He said he couldn't wait to see me at Evelyn and Patrick's Labor Day barbecue next week. After I hung up the phone, I sealed Leigh's bracelet in an envelope, wrote her Brentwood address on the front, tossed my #1 FRIEND charm and my cedar box filled with art supplies in the trash, and fell asleep on my embroidered roses.

# eighteen

On the Friday afternoon before Labor Day, I got dressed for my last day at Creative Colors while Dad showered for work and Mom shopped at Pathmark. I was on my hands and knees, trying to find a pair of matching shoes in my closet, when the phone rang. There was a pile of shoes around me and I didn't feel like answering the phone, but I ran to the kitchen anyway and picked up the receiver.

I heard a raspy voice, and it surprised me. "Hi, Ari," Leigh said as I leaned against the dishwasher, nervously wrapping the phone cord around my finger. "I'm only calling because I got the bracelet. It was in the mail yesterday."

That was the only reason she was calling. I supposed I shouldn't expect anything more. And I imagined that she was going to hide the bracelet in a chest or a drawer and never look at it again until she was ready. She might wait for years and years, until she was married and had children, and one day she'd take it out to show her teenage daughter and say something like, *This was from a boy I used to know. He was very special to me but that was so long ago.*

"Good," I said. The tip of my finger was turning red so I loosened the cord. "I'm glad."

"Who found it?" she asked.

"Summer." That was all I said. It was enough that Summer and I were done forever and that the #1 FRIEND charm had been taken away by a garbage truck. Even though I'd threatened otherwise, I had decided not to tell Blake about the bracelet. He might inform his father that Summer was a thief and a liar, and his father might fire Tina. For her sake, I didn't want that to happen. She worked so hard to uphold her reputation.

"I also got your note," Leigh said.

I remembered my *I'm Sorry* card with the dumb cat and the daisy. I expected her to say more, to say she'd forgiven me, but she didn't. And the flat, unfriendly voice she'd been using left me feeling very awkward. "Good," I said again. "So . . . do you like California?"

"It's okay so far. Some of my neighbors are our age, and they're much nicer than most people I knew in New York," she said, and I guessed I was one of those not-nice New Yorkers. Then she started talking about another neighbor, a guy our age from Vermont who'd moved the same week she had. "We're exploring Los Angeles together. He's a friend."

From the way she talked about him, I thought he might become more than a friend. She sounded happy all of a sudden and that made me happy, even though she was probably still mad at me and she cut our conversation short. I was glad that I'd gotten the bracelet back to her.

A few minutes later, I went outside into a sunny day. I walked to Creative Colors, past girls drawing hopscotch boards on cement. By the time I reached work, my muscles ached and I was tired even though I'd slept for nine hours the night before. I had no idea what was wrong with me. I wondered if I was seriously out of shape or if I was getting sick.

"Will you be back next year?" Adam asked.

It was the end of the day. We'd had a farewell-to-summer party—Dunkin' Donuts, and Kool-Aid in Dixie cups that I couldn't drink because my throat was sore. Adam was looking at me, his handsome face filled with hope, and he made me sad.

"Sure," I said, and my voice cracked.

He smiled. "What are you doing for Labor Day, Ari? Seeing your boyfriend?"

My boyfriend. He remembered. And he spoke without a stutter. It made me think that my work with Adam had actually done him good—that maybe all the painting had repaired his neurons or whatever was wrong inside his head. Maybe he was better off because of me. Believing that made me happy again.

*  *  *

Blake was on time for Evelyn and Patrick's Labor Day barbecue. He even brought an autographed Red Sox baseball for Kieran. When the sun began to set, I fell asleep on his shoulder as we cuddled together on a wicker patio sofa that Evelyn had ordered from Sears.

"Ari," he said, shaking me.

I opened my eyes. I wasn't sure how long I'd been asleep, and Blake looked worried. My hair stuck to the perspiration on my forehead and he pushed it away, asking why I hadn't eaten a thing all day.

"I'm not hungry," I said. "And my throat hurts."

"Then you should see a doctor."

"I don't want to. Tongue depressors make me gag."

"Baby," he said teasingly. "And speaking of doctors . . . I have something to show you."

He led me to the front of the house, where his car was parked at the curb. We climbed in and he took a piece of paper out of the glove compartment.

It was covered with words from Sex Ed—*chlamydia* and *gonorrhea* and *HIV*, plus a few others that my teacher had neglected to mention. They were listed on a chart and each one had a very good word next to it—*negative*.

"Did they stab you with a big needle?" I asked, scanning the chart, wondering which one of those filthy diseases Del had caught underneath his skylight. I despised needles and blood tests because I always ended up getting stuck at least five times. *Bad veins,* the nurses and phlebotomists always muttered while they turned my arm into swiss cheese.

"Needles don't bother me. And I'm not trying to pressure you with this, Ari. I just don't want you to worry about anything."

I smiled, folded the paper, and put it back in the glove compartment. "I'm not worried," I said, and he leaned over to kiss me but I covered my mouth. "Don't, Blake. You'll get sick."

"I don't care."

Later we went back to the sofa and watched Kieran and his friends skid on the Slip 'n Slide. I kept wondering about Del and I couldn't stop myself from whispering, "Which one of those diseases did your brother have?"

Blake's eyes widened. "Where did you get *that* from?"

I shrugged. "A little bird told me."

"Yeah . . . a little bird with red hair, I bet."

He didn't answer my question. I looked around the backyard at Patrick barbecuing hamburgers and Evelyn gossiping with her housewife friends until I couldn't stand it anymore and I asked again.

"Ari," Blake said. "It isn't nice to talk about that."

Nice, nice, *nice,* why did everything have to be so nice? "I won't tell anybody. I promise."

He sighed before whispering in my ear. "Syphilis," he said.

I gasped, remembering everything I'd learned in school about syphilis, like how it made people go blind. I couldn't think of anything worse than being blind. "That's a bad one, isn't it?"

"It's only bad if it doesn't get treated. Anyway . . . this isn't a polite topic of conversation, so let's drop it. My blabbermouth cousin never should've mentioned it to you. I talked to her last night, actually. She said you found her bracelet."

"Summer did," I said. "Summer and I aren't friends any-more, by the way."

"Really? I thought you two went way back."

An unexpected sadness rushed over me. We do go way back, I thought. But she's not the person I thought she was, and now you're my only friend. "These things happen," I said, then changed the subject because I didn't want to think about Summer. I just wanted to put my head on Blake's shoulder and pretend that this was my very own Sears sofa in my Park Slope backyard and that the giggly kids on the Slip 'n Slide belonged to us.

I felt strange the next morning. I was light-headed and warm, and even though my sore throat was gone and my empty stomach rumbled, I had no interest in Mom's blue-berry waffles or her fruit salad with the made-from-scratch whipped cream.

"Eat something, Ariadne," Mom said.

She was standing beside the kitchen table, wearing her *Kiss the Cook* apron and a smile. Dad sat across from me with his eyes on *Newsday* and his fork moving from his waffle to his mouth, and I told Mom I wasn't hungry but I shouldn't have. She looked disappointed and I didn't blame her—she had woken up at the crack of dawn to make this first-day-of-school, *It's the most important meal of the day* breakfast for me.

Then she got worried. "You're not sick, are you? You're very pale."

I was always very pale, but I was definitely sick. Still, I

didn't want to see a doctor who would poke me with needles and drain my blood into glass tubes.

"I'm just excited," I said. I had no idea where that had come from. It was as if my body had been inhabited by a clever spirit who knew the right thing to say.

"Of course you are," Mom said. "I'm excited too. I mean, it's your last year of high school and college will be here before you know it."

I didn't think about college that morning. I rode the subway alone, feeling really tired. And I thought about Blake, especially when I spotted Summer at the other end of the hall while I was walking to homeroom.

She was chatting with a group of girls and she looked blurry. She laughed and I wondered if she was laughing at me, if she was telling her friends about that weird Ari Mitchell, who was suffering from a serious case of limerence and believed she was in love with a guy she hadn't even slept with yet.

But I wanted to sleep with him. I thought about Blake all day, through homeroom and Calculus II, and while I read meticulously typed syllabi that were hot from the copy machine. I thought about him on the subway that took me back to Brooklyn and when the walk from the train station to my house seemed so long that I wasn't sure I'd make it.

Then I conked out on my bed. Dad was at work and Mom was at a faculty meeting that would keep her away for hours. When I woke up, the house was so quiet I could hear the freezer making ice cubes.

I stared at the ceiling, listening to ice fall into a plastic container. I didn't feel tired anymore—I felt beyond tired, sort of spacey and giddy. I got up, went to the bathroom, and looked in the mirror at a reflection that wasn't pale. My cheeks were ruddy and I probably had a fever, but I didn't feel sick. I looked reasonably pretty, and that made me decide to freshen up and go to Manhattan so I could surprise Blake at Ellis & Hummel.

I made my plans behind the shower curtain. I lathered my hair and watched water bead on a stomach that was disturbingly concave from lack of food. It didn't matter; I would eat later, someplace in the city with Blake, and afterward we would go to a nice hotel or to the penthouse if Mr. Ellis wasn't home. Then I would give Blake what he'd been so patient for, what I could do now because his tests were negative and he loved me and that made it okay.

I left the house an hour later. It was cloudy and a scorching wind blew through my hair, and Saint Anne seemed immersed in a radiant peace. I walked past her, rode the subway to Manhattan, and reached the Empire State Building at five o'clock, when swarms of people were flooding out of the lobby. The Catering by Tina van was parked on the street.

Tina didn't notice me because she was busy loading the van with chafing dishes. But Summer noticed. She looked through me as if I was nobody, as if she'd forgotten elementary school and junior high and my birthday dinners, and I pretended it didn't hurt. I turned away, rode the elevator to Ellis & Hummel, and filled my mind with Blake instead of Summer.

I asked for him at the front desk, where a gum-chewing

receptionist pointed toward a conference room with glass doors. I saw Blake inside, standing with Mr. Ellis and a few other men beside a long polished table. Mr. Ellis kept smacking Blake's shoulder and jokingly grabbing him in a choke-hold, as if Blake was a first-place trophy or a prize racehorse that he wanted to show off.

Blake saw me. He waved me over and broke away from his father; then we stood by the doors inside the conference room while Mr. Ellis filled the other men's glasses with liquor. I heard them talking, something about a "gentlemen's club," and the rest of the men laughed when Mr. Ellis said, "We're all gentlemen, aren't we?"

"What are you doing here?" Blake asked.

He was happy to see me. He smelled of aftershave. The darkness of his suit coaxed out the blue in his eyes, and just the sound of his voice gave me a warm shudder.

"I thought we could . . . ," I began, not sure how to fin-ish. *I thought we could spend some time together. I thought we could have a romantic dinner. I thought we could go to your apartment and have passionate sex until the sun rises in the morning.*

But I didn't say any of that because Mr. Ellis was suddenly beside us and so were the other men, and Mr. Ellis introduced me to them as "my boy's little girlfriend."

"This is Ari . . . ," he started, and looked at Blake for help.

"Mitchell, Daddy," Blake said. "Ari Mitchell."

I knew it. I knew he didn't remember my last name. And being called Blake's little girlfriend didn't exactly boost my self-esteem. A little girlfriend, a little crush—why did everybody have to take something that seemed so big and squash it into a tiny speck of nothing?

"Of course," Mr. Ellis said, summoning his charming smile. "Forgive me, Ari. I'm getting close to fifty and the memory's the first thing to go."

Everybody laughed. Mr. Ellis put his son in another chokehold, rubbed his knuckles against Blake's scalp, and told him not to take too long. He and the other men would be waiting in the lobby.

I was so disappointed. "Where are you going?"

Blake seemed uncomfortable, and not just from his suit. "Dinner at Delmonico's. And some bar later on."

I folded my arms. "What kind of bar?" I asked, imagining a place where cheap, desperate girls in G-strings would grind on his lap for a twenty-dollar bill.

"It's just business, Ari. I'm not interested in those places. My father always takes his clients there. I have to go. You understand, right?"

I didn't want to understand. But I nodded and he hugged me. He said that I felt really warm, I should see a doctor, and I couldn't ride the subway back home all alone. He told the receptionist to call the car service and then we took the elevator to the lobby, where I left him with Mr. Ellis and got into a car that whisked me away from all my beautiful plans.

I fell asleep in homeroom the next day. My teacher tapped my shoulder and I lifted my head to find the entire class staring at me. Then I went to the school nurse and she asked if I was on drugs, which was hilarious. I'd never even smoked a cigarette or been drunk, and I wouldn't have any idea where to find drugs, unless Evelyn had left a stash of marijuana in the basement with her Jordache jeans.

The nurse called Mom, who took me to my doctor's office, where a phlebotomist tied a rubber tube above my elbow. I looked away as his needle pricked my arm seven times to find a vein. When I looked back, he had filled so many vials with blood I was surprised to still be alive.

I only felt semi-alive. I was exhausted and my muscles ached, and the doctor said he couldn't be sure until the tests came back but he was almost certain that I had mono-nucleosis.

"You know where you got this," Mom said.

We were in her Honda, heading toward Flatbush. "Where?" I asked.

"*Where?* From Blake, where else?"

I should have known she'd say that. I had felt her eyes on me when the doctor was talking, explaining that mono was common in teenagers because *adolescents are typically involved in intimate behavior.*

"Blake isn't sick," I said. "I didn't get it from him."

"He doesn't have to be sick, Ariadne. Didn't you hear the doctor? He said that some people carry the virus but never show symptoms. It's called the kissing disease. Didn't you hear the doctor?"

How many times was she going to ask me that? I was fed up with the sound of her voice, but I still had to listen to it when I was in bed later and she called my school from the phone in the kitchen. She told the principal that I had mono and I had to stay home for eight weeks, and that she was very concerned because I was planning to attend the Parsons School of Design next year, so I couldn't veer off track.

I didn't want to veer off track. Blake and I had a future together that couldn't be delayed. So I was glad when Mom came to my room and said that everything had been worked out. She was driving to Manhattan tomorrow to pick up my books. My teachers were going to write down my assignments every week and fax them to Mom at her school, and I could go back to Hollister in November as if nothing had ever happened.

She left me alone after that. I rested in bed, listening to the end-of-summer sounds outside—the Good Humor truck making its final rounds, people setting off firecrackers left over from the Fourth of July. I was inhaling the smell of a neighbor's barbecue when I decided that this mono thing might not be so terrible. My best friend was history, Leigh was in California, and I didn't have anyone to sit with in the cafeteria anymore. Now I wouldn't have to spend the next two months eating lunch in a bathroom stall.


I did have mono. The doctor called a few days later to confirm his diagnosis. But Blake didn't have it. I insisted he get another blood test to prove Mom wrong.

He came to my house the next week while she was at school and Dad was at work. He surprised me, driving to Brooklyn after his last class on a Thursday afternoon.

I let Blake in, and he followed me upstairs and settled into bed with me. I was on my side, his arm was around my shoulders, and I wanted to fall asleep with him. But Mom would be home in a few hours, so that just couldn't happen.

"I should teach you to drive," he said.

"You have to be eighteen to get a license in New York," I answered.

"You'll be eighteen in four months, Ari. You can get a permit now. I can give you driving lessons."

I didn't want driving lessons. Driving lessons were dangerous. I could skid on an icy road and Blake could hit his chest on the dashboard. I shrugged and he turned my face toward his, trying to kiss me. I pulled away and jammed my lips into my pillow. "You can't, Blake. I'm diseased."

He laughed. "You are not."

"I am too. I don't want you to get sick—you'll miss school. Your father would be mad."

"Let him be mad, then," Blake said. "So what?"

*So what?* I smiled into my pillow, thinking I'd been right a few weeks ago when I decided it was okay for me and Blake to sleep together. If he was willing to risk catching mono and missing school and letting his father down, then he meant it when he said he loved me.

But I still didn't want him to get sick—I couldn't be responsible for him feeling as tired and achy as I felt. "You can't kiss me, Blake," I said when he tried again, even though I was dying to kiss him. "I have germs in my mouth."

He laughed, moved my hair, and kissed my bare neck.

He ran his tongue from the base of my skull to the tip of my spine. It sent waves of electricity through me. "You don't have any germs right here, do you?"

"No," I said. But even if I did have germs, I couldn't have told him to stop.

He came back the next Thursday, and he brought gifts— books and magazines, so I wouldn't go stir crazy. He came to visit me every Thursday, and each time he brought presents, like boxes of dark chocolate from a fancy candy store in the city.

We'd stay in bed for hours. He'd put his arms around me and kiss the back of my neck, and sometimes I wondered if he'd try to do more than that. My parents weren't home and I wouldn't have objected, even though I was sick and contagious. I knew that most guys would see an empty house and a willing girl as an easy opportunity, but Blake didn't. And that made me love him even more.

"How are you feeling?" he asked one day. I was on my side in bed; he snuggled up next to me and draped his arm across my shoulders.

"Not good," I said, hearing early-October rain tap my window. "My whole body's sore . . . especially my back. It feels better if I lie on my stomach."

"Then lie on your stomach."

I shifted on the bed and pressed my face into my pillow, listening to the rain. It was getting heavier now and sounded like rocks hitting the roof. I also heard Blake moving, and then he was straddling me, massaging my back through my shirt, gently kneading his fingers into my skin and my aching muscles. His thighs felt warm and strong as they squeezed my hips. I thought I might melt into the sheets.

"Is that better?" he whispered into my ear as his cheek skimmed mine.

"Much better," I mumbled. I was falling asleep.

Blake touched my face and spoke in a louder voice that snapped me out of my trance. "You're really warm," he said, reaching over to my night table. He picked up a bottle of Tylenol and shook it. "This is empty, Ari. Do you have any more?"

I blinked and turned around. His eyebrows knitted together like he was worried.

"I don't know," I said, stretching and yawning, flattered that he was worried.

He went across the hall to the bathroom and I heard him riffling through the medicine cabinet. When he came back, he grabbed his leather jacket, which he'd chucked across my bed earlier.

"Where are you going?" I asked, sitting up halfway.

Now he was next to my desk, picking up his wallet. "To the drugstore to buy Tylenol. You need to get rid of that fever."

I looked outside. I saw water spilling down the window, and a tree across the street. Its leaves were deep orange and bright yellow, and they were sagging beneath the steady rain.

"You can't go out, Blake. It's pouring." I didn't want him to go anywhere, not even just down the street. I wanted him to get under the covers with me and massage my back again. So I sat up all the way and moved to the end of the

241

bed, kneeling on the mattress. "Stay here," I said, feeling cold all of a sudden. I glanced at the mirror above my dresser; I saw pasty skin and dark circles around my eyes. I was so gory-looking lately. "My mother can pick up the Tylenol when she gets home from work."

He shook his head. "She shouldn't have to go out again in this weather."

That was a considerate observation. He was more considerate of Mom than I was. Then my teeth started to chatter. Mono was crazy—broiling one minute, freezing the next.

"I hate it when you leave," I admitted.

A smile spread across his lips. It was a lazy, sensual smile. "You hate it when I leave?" he said, like he wanted to hear it again. I nodded, and then he gathered up my bedspread and wrapped it around me as I looked into his eyes and absorbed his smell—leather and aftershave and toothpaste.

He gently pushed me back down to the pillows and kissed my entire face. He kissed me everywhere—my forehead, my cheeks, my mouth, my jaw, my chin, the space between my eyes. I was flattered again. I had thought I was too hideous and clammy to be kissed.

"Get some rest," he said afterward. "I'll be back soon."

I couldn't argue with him anymore, because I needed the Tylenol. The chills were the worst. So I put my head on my pillow and listened to his footsteps on the stairs, his car pulling away from the curb, and the rain beating against my house. It was so nice to be taken care of, especially by him.

\* \* \*

Mom wasn't impressed by Blake's presents. She saw me eating the chocolate and accused me of deliberately slowing my recovery. She wanted me to drink milk and eat meat so I'd regain my strength. She was particularly skeptical of my favorite gift—a pure white teddy bear covered with velvety soft fur. She shoved the bear aside one night when I was filling out an application for Parsons and she was dusting my dresser.

"Blake gives you cheap gifts," she said. "Especially for a rich boy."

I scoffed. "That bear isn't cheap, Mom. It's from FAO Schwarz. Besides, I thought you weren't impressed by money."

Touché. I got her good on that one. She rolled her eyes and changed the subject, telling me for the tenth time to request applications from a few other schools.

"You'll get into Parsons," she said. "But it's smart to have some backups just in case."

I nodded and returned to my application, but I had no intention of requesting anything from other schools. I knew I didn't need backups because I had something better: connections.

It seemed to take forever for me to recover from mono. The truth was, I wasn't sure I *wanted* to recover, because it was nice to do my schoolwork at home and to lie in bed with Blake's arms around me every Thursday. It was Halloween when my doctor said that I was healed, that I should rest for another week and then get back into my normal routine.

Mom was happy, but I wasn't. I tried to think of pleasant things, like Blake's twenty-first birthday party, which was scheduled for the following Friday at the Waldorf Astoria. Mr. Ellis had invited two hundred people and the party was black tie optional. I was excited, but Mom was worried because the party was the night before the SAT.

"You'd better come home early, Ariadne. And don't even think about asking me to buy another dress. You have a perfectly good dress in your closet that you've only worn once."

I didn't ask for another dress. I wasn't going to have it on for long, anyway. I had decided that I was going to give Blake a very special birthday gift, something I'd been saving for what felt like forever.

"Can we get a room here tonight?" I asked.

The party had just started. Blake and I stood inside a reception hall at the Waldorf among lots of men in suits and women in dresses. Blake was sipping a Heineken and his forehead crinkled.

"Why?" he said.

I whispered into his ear, "Because I love you."

He got it. He smiled. I wanted to kiss him but I couldn't because Mr. Ellis came by. He took Blake away and led him around the room, smacking his shoulder and tousling his hair, introducing him to people as "my boy Blake" while I sat alone.

I watched them move through the crowd. After a few minutes I saw two familiar faces. I should have expected that

Tina and Summer would be here—it seemed as if Mr. Ellis's guest list included every single person he and Blake knew, and everybody but Rachel and Leigh had accepted.

"Having fun?" Del said, sitting down next to me.

He was in a suit, wearing his pinkie ring, and he smelled of tobacco and cologne. We started talking and he got me feeling the way I had at the Christmas party last year—excited and nervous. I had to stop feeling like that and I had to stop trying to figure out what color his eyes were, because Blake was my boyfriend, Del wasn't nearly as handsome, and I was going to be his sister-in-law someday.

But Del was seated at table three for dinner, like me. I walked with him to a room with ornate chandeliers and flower arrangements. He sat on my left and Blake sat on my right. Other people joined us—women escorted by men who Blake told me were his father's partners at the firm—and then Mr. Ellis was there, and suddenly the two seats next to him were filled with Tina and Summer.

"Hi, Ari," Tina said, waving across the table, her stringy hair brushing the collar of her plain gray dress. I wondered what Summer had told her, what story she'd crafted to explain why I never called anymore. "Look, Summer," Tina said, smiling and pointing at me the way parents point when they take their kids to the zoo. *Look, there's a giraffe, there's a bear, there's an average boring girl.* "It's Ari. Did you see Ari?"

"I saw her," Summer said, unrolling the silverware in her napkin. She mumbled a greeting across the table that I returned, only because we were in public and I had to be civil.

"Why is *she* at this table?" I whispered to Blake.

He shrugged. "My father handled the seating arrangements. You don't mind, do you?"

I shook my head. I pretended not to mind. I ate my salad even though it was made with a kind of lettuce that was more suited to rabbits than humans.

"Who's that floozy?" Del whispered into my ear.

"She's not a floozy," I whispered back. "She's an ex-friend of mine. She and her mother cater your father's parties. You've met her before, actually—at your club on New Year's Eve."

"Oh, yeah. I forgot." He picked up his drink and finished it off. It was his third, but he asked the waiter for another. "My father loves introducing Blake to chicks like her. There are two kinds of women, he always says. The nice ones you marry and the cheap ones you screw. He thinks that guys need a lot of cheap girls before they end up with a nice girl."

I felt my stomach drop as I realized that Mr. Ellis was more like Mom than I'd ever imagined. *Guys need a lot of cheap girls before they end up with a nice girl. There are plenty of fish in the sea. You don't want to get stuck with the first one.*

I wished Del hadn't opened his mouth. Now I was concerned about Mr. Ellis, who was smiling at Summer like she was the most adorable thing in the room. I thought back to the day before I'd found out about the mono, when Blake had *had* to go to a strip club with his father. How long had Mr. Ellis been introducing *cheap girls* to Blake? And what did he think about his father's philosophy?

I tried not to think about it during dinner. I tried to enjoy the melon wrapped in prosciutto, the grilled pork tenderloin with the caramelized apples, and the butternut squash. Blake held my hand beneath the table and when the meal was finished, he slow-danced with me to a Spandau Ballet song. My heartbeat quickened when a cake with HAPPY 21ST BIRTHDAY written on it arrived, because the party was winding down and soon we'd be alone.

"Here's something for you, son," Mr. Ellis said while I was eating my cake. He crouched between me and Blake and handed him a wrapped box that Blake opened. There was a gold watch inside. Blake thanked him and Mr. Ellis slapped his cheek. "Just keep making me proud," he said.

Blake lied to him when the party was over. He said that he was going out with some friends and he wouldn't be home until late, and then he brought me to a room with a queen-size bed, beige curtains, and a matching carpet covered with rows of brown squares.

"My gift isn't as nice as this," I said, stroking his watch.

He left it on a night table. "Your gift is much nicer than this."

I smiled and started thinking about practical things. "I can't take the Pill because I have migraines," I said, because I couldn't think of a better way to mention the practical things.

"Since when do you get migraines?" he asked.

"Since always. I haven't had one for a while. But I'm still considered a migraine sufferer," I said, which he found funny for some reason. He laughed and I kept babbling. "So do you have—you know—"

"Protection?" he said with another laugh.

I nodded and he told me that he'd been carrying protection in his wallet for months. Then we went to the bed, where he slipped off his tie, unbuttoned his shirt, and dropped them on the floor. I was still in my dress but not for long. Soon it was next to Blake's shirt, resting on those neatly lined-up squares. I reached over and turned off the lamp. The only light in the room came from behind the curtains, from the building across the street. I heard car horns honking, voices traveling up twelve floors, and my own breath.

There was enough light to see Blake. He leaned over me and I trembled at the muscles in his arms, the pearly glimmer of his smile. His pants joined the rest of his clothes on the floor and he guided my fingers below the path of hair on his stomach, where he felt long and warm inside my palm, hard but soft, like Patrick's hands. Then his mouth was all over me and noises came out of my mouth, little panting sounds like the ones I'd made in the Hamptons, but they didn't embarrass me this time. Nothing did. Nothing seemed dirty or sinful or wrong, even though I was about to break a major Catholic rule. I kept my eyes closed until I heard paper ripping and a snapping noise.

"Don't be scared," Blake said.

I felt his weight on me and I was definitely scared. "Wait," I said. "You didn't make a promise like you did in the Hamptons."

I saw a sympathetic smile in the hazy light. "I can't promise that."

He kissed my forehead before pressing his groin into mine, and I heard talking in my head—my voice saying that Summer's tattoo *must've hurt* and her voice saying *So does sex the first time you do it, but I didn't let that stop me.*

Summer was right. But I wasn't going to let it stop me

either, and the painful part passed quickly and turned into something fantastic. Blake gripped my hands and held them flat on the bed, his chest rubbing mine as he moved with slow thrusts, while I absorbed every part of him and he took every last inch of me.

"Are you okay?" he whispered.

I nodded, feeling a fiery jolt in the middle of my body that rose to my head. I guessed that Blake was feeling the same thing, because he made those tennis-player-hitting-the-ball noises and tilted his head back. Then I knew that I was much better than okay, and I couldn't imagine feeling any other way.

# nineteen

*I* hadn't planned to fall asleep. I'd known I wasn't going to get home early like Mom wanted—I assumed I might sneak in at one or two and still have time to get some rest before the SAT—but I'd never expected to wake up at the Waldorf with my head on Blake's stomach. I looked at his rising and falling chest, his slightly parted lips, and the sheet that started at his waist and ended at his feet. The sight of him made me ignore Mom and the SAT.

I kept looking until Blake opened his eyes. He smiled and pushed my hair out of my face, and I thought that Mom had been wrong when she said *They'll tell you anything to get laid and then they just move on to the next victim.* I knew he wasn't going anywhere.

Then I glanced at the digital clock on the night table. It was after seven and the SAT was at nine. I panicked, gathered the sheet around my body, and slid to the edge of the bed.

"What's the matter?" Blake asked.

"I'm supposed to take the SAT this morning. I'll be late."

"You won't be late," he said. "I'll drive you straight there."

"But I have to go home and change . . . I can't show up like *this*," I said, reaching down to the carpet to pick up my dress. "I need to take a shower and wash off my makeup, and eat something. . . . I can't screw up the SAT. I have to get into Parsons."

He laughed, grabbed my arm, and pulled me toward him. "Don't worry so much, Ari. The SAT is no big deal. My father will get you into any school you want. You know that."

I still wanted to do well on the test. A low score would disappoint me and devastate Mom. I could already hear all the critical, cutting things she'd say if I blew it.

But it was hard to tear myself away from Blake. I stayed in bed with him for a while longer, wrapped in his arms while he kissed the back of my neck and made me feel like I had nothing to worry about anymore, like I wasn't a four out of ten in the looks department and I wouldn't die alone and I didn't have to fight and struggle for everything the way Mom did.

\* \* \*

It was eight-thirty when Blake dropped me off at my house. He wanted to come in with me, to second my story that we'd gone dancing at Del's club and lost track of time, to convince Mom that we hadn't done anything that wasn't *nice*. But I wouldn't let him because I was afraid of the humiliating things Mom might say, things like *You should think with your brain. It's in your head, Blake. Not in your pants.*

I ran to the front steps as Blake drove away, and Mom opened the door when my key touched the lock.

"What the hell is going on here?" she yelled in my face.

I was in the foyer as she slammed the door with a deafening bang that made me flinch. I stood there in my wrinkled dress, feeling like Evelyn in high school, strolling in after one of her late nights with God-knows-who doing God-knows-what.

"We went dancing after the party," I said. "I lost track of time."

"Dancing," Mom said. "Where? On the backseat of Blake's car?"

"Corvettes don't have backseats, Mom."

I regretted that sentence as soon as it came out of my mouth. It sounded snotty. Mom stared at me like I was someone else, like I was a big disappointment, worse than Evelyn. But what Blake and I had done wasn't wrong, and I couldn't let her tell me that it was, so I kept on lying. I swore that nothing happened and that I was sorry for staying out late without calling and it would never happen again. Then I felt really guilty because she believed me.

"Wash your face and brush your hair," she called after me

as I raced up the stairs toward my room. But there wasn't any time for that. I tore off my dress, threw on jeans and a sweatshirt, and rushed outside into a cold day. Mom had already started the car.

I took the SAT at my old school instead of Hollister because Brooklyn residents were allowed to take the test in their own borough. Summer did the same thing. She sat one row away from me and six seats ahead, looking well rested in a white turtleneck and designer jeans while I looked positively mangy. She turned around and glanced at me once, obviously aghast at my messy hair and the black mascara smeared under my eyes. Then she went back to pretending I didn't exist.

For a moment I wished I could talk to her, that I could tell her what had happened last night. Last night was the kind of thing that a girl wants to share with people like sisters and best friends. But Evelyn and Patrick had driven to Boston with the kids this weekend for a Cagney family reunion, I wouldn't have discussed it with Leigh even if we *had* patched things up, because it wouldn't be *nice* to discuss sex-related things about her cousin, and of course I couldn't talk to Summer anymore. So I focused on the test, on the verbal section, the endless analogies.

I was exhausted and my head was killing me. The words on the page blurred together—*medicine: illness:: law: anarchy; extort: obtain:: plagiarize: borrow; tenet: theologian*— What exactly was a tenet? I'd seen that word when I was taking practice tests, but now I couldn't remember much of anything.

We took a break before the math part and I watched the back of Summer's head while I invented my own analogy: *real* is to *fake* as *love* is to *limerence,* and you had a lot of nerve to tell me that I have a *little crush* on Blake, Summer. I love him and he loves me and now you can't say that I barely know him and that I haven't even slept with him because none of that is true anymore.

I wanted to sleep. I wanted to eat. I wanted to think about Blake and last night. But after the break, I just sat and held my forehead in my hands, reading about *Susie,* who had to *visit towns B and C in any order.* There were lines on a diagram, and I was supposed to figure out how many routes she could take, *starting from A and returning to A, going through both B and C, not traveling any road twice.*

I couldn't possibly have cared less about Susie or her routes.

Summer, on the other hand, looked like she knew exactly how Susie could go through B and C without traveling any road twice. I stared at her while she breezed through the questions, twirling her hair as she filled in the answers with a pencil. She was done before anyone else, so she closed the exam book, leaned back in her chair, and examined her perfectly manicured nails.

I wanted to grab her pencil and plunge it through her heart. This wasn't fair. She never even studied. But she'd probably had the sense to go to bed early last night and to eat a healthy breakfast this morning. My stomach was growling and time was running out, and I knew I was bombing the SAT even though I'd aced so many practice tests, while Summer hadn't taken a single one.

When it was over, I found Mom waiting outside. "I hope you did well," she said nervously as she drove us back home. "Do you think you did well?"

I stared through the windshield, mustering up the strength to lie. "I think I did okay."

Mom's head snapped toward me. "*Okay?* What does *that* mean?"

"Nothing," I said, feeling queasy.

We stopped at a red light and I listened to her wedding ring tap the steering wheel.

"Well," she said, "if you didn't score as high as you should have, you can take it again."

I guessed that made her feel better. I just nodded and kept quiet. My headache was getting worse and my mind was racing with thoughts of last night. I was worried about the test, but I remembered what Blake had said this morning. I told myself that the SAT didn't matter because Mr. Ellis was going to get me into any school I wanted.

Mr. Ellis wasn't at home the next weekend when Blake brought me to the penthouse and took me upstairs to his room. I'd never been in there before and it was surprisingly small, with an old shag rug and lots of textbooks scattered across a desk.

His bed was pushed against a wall and his wool blankets scratched my skin while we made love for the second time. We went there every chance we could find, through Thanksgiving decorations coming down and Christmas lights going up. Mr. Ellis was never home. Sometimes we had sex and sometimes Blake repeated what he did in the Hamptons, and I didn't hide my face in my arm anymore. Then there were other times when all we did was stay in bed for hours with our arms around each other, and it was as nice as everything else.

"I've been thinking," he said.

It was two days before Christmas and one of those nights when we just kissed and talked while we were wrapped up in woolly blankets. There was snow on the ground outside and the temperature was brutally low, and I loved being in his hide-away of a bedroom, where we were safe from the entire world.

He told me that he didn't want to go to law school. Spending the summer at Ellis & Hummel had been proof that he couldn't stand wearing suits and that legal work bored him to tears. But he couldn't come up with a way to break the news to his father, so he was going to finish college, take the firefighter exam, and tell Mr. Ellis when the time was right.

"You have to do what you want," I said. "I've figured that out lately."

He smiled, pulling off his clothes and mine. I felt his lips on my skin and his breath on my neck.

"Blake," I said afterward. "Everything we talked about—the house and the kids and the future—you don't mind waiting for a few years, right? I mean . . . until I'm done with college and grad school? Because I want those things . . . but I won't be ready for a while."

"I'd rather have it now. But for you . . . I'll wait." Then he said that he had an early Christmas present for me and he put on a pair of shorts, walked across the room to his desk, and returned to bed holding out a tight fist. He uncurled his fingers to show me a big square ruby attached to a gold chain. "This belonged to my mother," he said. "I want you to have it."

His mother. I realized that he loved me even more than I'd thought, because he wouldn't give such a precious gift to just anyone.

Blake fastened the chain around my neck and got under the blankets with me, where we quickly passed out. I wasn't sure how long we'd been asleep when I heard a cough—and opened my eyes to find Mr. Ellis standing in the doorway, wearing a suit and an unhappy face.

It was so humiliating. My bra had been flung wantonly onto the carpet and Blake was cuddled up behind me, his arm draped over my bare shoulders. I nudged his ribs to wake him, and Mr. Ellis said that he wanted to see Blake downstairs.

I got dressed in a flash after they were gone. I heard voices: a thick New York accent and a light Georgia twang. I couldn't understand a word, so I tiptoed into the hallway to eavesdrop, but I still couldn't hear anything except footsteps. I dashed into the bathroom, closed the door, and stayed inside until Blake knocked.

"It's okay," he said. We were in the hallway now and he saw that my face was flushed. "I'll take you home, all right?"

"I'll take her home," Mr. Ellis interrupted from the bottom of the stairs. "I have some errands to do anyway. Is that okay with you, Blake?"

I wanted him to say that it wasn't okay. I stared at him, hoping he could read my mind, but he didn't seem to have the strength. The next thing I knew, I was sitting next to Mr. Ellis in a Porsche like Del's, struggling to act dignified, pretending that he hadn't just caught me naked in bed with his son.

The radio was on, 1010 WINS. *You give us twenty-two minutes, we'll give you the world.* The leather seats were heated, and a medallion swung from the rearview mirror. FORDHAM LAW, it read. CLASS OF 1964. I absentmindedly touched the ruby on my neck with one hand and nervously twisted my hair with the other.

Mr. Ellis saw my necklace. Our eyes met for a second but he didn't say anything. I tucked it beneath my shirt, thinking that my gift belonged to his poor dead wife and he probably didn't want me to have it.

He didn't act that way, though. He flipped the charm switch and engaged me in polite conversation about the weather. Next he started talking about how he'd spent years toiling at some sweatshop firm in Midtown to repay his student loans and to get enough experience to open his own place. It was all for his kids, he said. Too bad Blake was the only one who appreciated it.

"My son told me about your college plans," he said when we were close to Flatbush. "I can help you with that. I know quite a few people at Parsons."

I hoped he'd be able to tell them my last name. "Thank you, Mr. Ellis."

He ran a hand through his hair. "Is there anything else you want, Ari? I mean . . . is there anything I can do for you?"

We were a block from my house and he parked next to that lot where Blake and I used to sit in the Corvette and kiss. It was still vacant; the latest rumors were that the owners had either squandered all their Lotto money or gone to jail for killing some Mafia kingpin.

I was confused. Why had he stopped the car and what was he talking about? I shook my head and he asked if I was sure, because there were many things he could do, like finance my college education and buy me any kind of car I wanted.

"I don't need anything, Mr. Ellis," I said.

He turned in his seat and I got a clear view of his face. He was so handsome, better-looking than either of his sons, but I felt afraid of him suddenly, of what was behind that suave smile and those deep brown eyes. They were so dark that I couldn't find the pupils.

"You know something, Ari," he began. "Blake's been acting very strangely these days. His grades are dropping and he's preoccupied . . . and last week I found an application for a firefighter exam in his room. You don't know anything about that, do you?"

I wanted to run home. Instead I shook my head and listened to him talk about how Blake had acted this way once before, when he was dating a girl in Georgia, and he had even considered quitting school and moving down there to marry her and work at some dead-end blue-collar job, and could I believe that?

I could believe it. I felt sick. I remembered the night at the penthouse when Del and Blake had talked about Jessica. Del had said that Blake was with her for two years and she lived in a trailer and she'd dumped him without so much as a phone call. She probably didn't have a cent and hadn't been able to resist when Mr. Ellis asked if there was anything he could do. He'd probably done a lot to get rid of her so that she wouldn't spoil the plans he had for his prize racehorse.

But I wasn't Jessica. I didn't need anything except Blake. Mr. Ellis kept asking what I wanted, saying that he'd buy absolutely anything for me and my family.

"My family and I have everything we need," I said.

He stared at me for a second, as if his eyes could melt my will. When that didn't work, he turned away, started the car, and drove me home. He didn't say another word until we were across the street from my house. Dad was on a ladder, twisting bulbs on a string of lights that lined the roof, trying to identify the one that had caused the rest of them to die.

"Is that your father?" Mr. Ellis asked. "The detective?"

I nodded and reached for the door, but he stopped me.

"Ari," he said. "I'm sure you wouldn't want him to know what you've been up to. I mean . . . spending time alone in a young man's bedroom doing things that could cause a lot of trouble. You wouldn't want your parents to know about that, would you? I'm sure they have a high opinion of you—you wouldn't want anything to spoil it."

He'd switched from bribery to blackmail, and my face flushed again because he was staring right through me like he could see everything that Blake and I had done in his bedroom. I sprang out of the car, raced past Dad, and ran upstairs, where it took me hours to fall asleep.


Blake called the next morning as if nothing had happened. Of course, he didn't know what had happened. Mr. Ellis wasn't going to mention our conversation, and I didn't rat him out. I couldn't shatter Blake's illusions by informing him of the cold hard truth that his father was a snake.

Blake invited me back to the penthouse for Christmas Eve, and Rachel was standing in the foyer when I walked in. She looked as beautiful as ever, holding a glass of cider in her hand and saying goodnight to a man who was putting on his coat. She wore a black knit dress with a slit up the thigh, and I felt nervous when she glanced in my direction. I wondered if she thought I was as bad as Summer for hurting Leigh, and I worried that she'd tower over me in her high-heeled suede boots, pointing a skinny finger.

I dashed by her. I had almost made it to the living room when I felt someone touch my arm.

"Ari . . . aren't you going to say hello to me, honey?" Rachel said in her faint Southern accent, and I turned around. I played it cool, pretending I hadn't even seen her.

"Hi," I said, clenching my fists and waiting for something awful to happen.

"Leigh is here," Rachel said, nodding toward the living room.

I thought she was about to say that I was a selfish, scheming user and that I didn't deserve a friend like Leigh. But she just put an arm around me and bent her head toward mine.

"I think you two should patch things up," she whispered. "You didn't know what you were doing. A girl can lose her head when she has feelings for a guy. I've been there, God knows. And like I've said before . . . all three of you can be friends. Isn't that right?"

I let out a relieved sigh, nodded, and veered around wine-drinking guests in the living room until I found Leigh. She was standing by the floor-to-ceiling windows, holding a red mug and staring at Manhattan. I tapped her shoulder and she turned around.

"Ari," she said with a serious face that looked prettier than I'd ever seen it. Her hair was pulled back, and Rachel must have done her makeup. It was all the right colors—apricot-hued lipstick, sparkly gold eye shadow. She wore a green velvet dress with a silver belt cinched around her waist.

I was nervous. I tugged on one of my fingers, trying to crack the knuckle. "Merry Christmas," I said, looking at the miniature marshmallows floating in her hot cocoa.

She leaned against the window. "Merry Christmas," she said coldly.

That disappointed me, but I decided to give my apology a try. "Leigh," I began. "You didn't deserve what I did to you. I know that saying sorry doesn't mean much, but it's all I can do. I'd really like to be friends again."

The city lights blinked behind her as she sipped from her mug. I thought she was ignoring me, that Rachel was wrong, that it was hopeless. So I turned away, but then she grabbed my elbow.

"Okay, Ari. I accept your apology. But don't ever treat me like that again."

"Promise," I said, sticking out my hand to seal the deal. She hugged me instead.

I saw Mr. Ellis later on. What a phony. He was all smiles and charm and "Merry Christmas, Ari. So glad you could come."

I smiled back, deciding that I'd be just as fake as he was and that I wouldn't let him or anyone else take Blake away. I wouldn't accept bribes and I wouldn't be blackmailed, even if he'd been clever enough to place hidden cameras all over the Hamptons house and the apartment. I wondered if he had X-rated evidence that he planned to show my parents if I didn't disappear, like videotape of me topless in the pool or of Blake's head between my thighs or of the two of us going at it on those scratchy blankets.

That was paranoia, I told myself. Or maybe it was a story-line from *Days of Our Lives*. But after last night, I wouldn't have put anything past Stanford Ellis. He could call Mom and Dad to expose me as a liar and their second letdown of a daughter, and even though I prayed that wouldn't happen, I told myself it didn't matter—because it was okay if you loved somebody.

"Want to see what I got for Christmas?" Blake asked.

We were sitting on the couch with Del and Rachel and Leigh. Leigh had told me that the guy from her building was her boyfriend now, and her face lit up every time she mentioned him, which made me think the California move had been a good idea.

"Blake got a stereo system from our father," Del said. He'd been drinking and he was slumped on the couch with a cigarette in his hand. "And you know what I got, Ari? I got turned down on a loan for my club. Now I have to go to the bank and get raped on a fucking ten-percent interest rate."

"Watch your mouth," Blake said. "And don't expect Daddy to bail you out every time you get in trouble. It's not his fault that your business isn't doing well. He warned you not to open that place."

"He'd bail *you* out," Del said. "He'd do anything for you."

Blake didn't answer. He must have known it was true. Then he took my hand and led me upstairs, where he showed me an expensive stereo system and looked disappointed when I wasn't enthusiastic.

"What's the matter?" he said.

"Nothing," I answered, stepping closer to kiss him. I asked if he would come to my house for Christmas tomorrow but he said he couldn't, one of his father's partners had invited them for dinner and he couldn't get out of it. "Oh, come on," I whined. "Can't you blow it off for me?"

And he did. He showed up at my house the next afternoon with gifts for the kids and a Lindy's cheesecake for dessert. I had a gift for Blake. I gave him a bottle of his favorite aftershave. It wasn't special and precious like what he'd given me, but he seemed to appreciate my Christmas present as much as I treasured his.

"It's huge," Evelyn said after dinner when she and I were washing dishes, Mom was playing with the boys, and Dad and Patrick and Blake were watching TV in the living room. Evelyn was looking at the ruby that hung over my shirt and she whispered into my ear, "Is *he* huge too?"

I nodded and held my finger to my lips when she let out a raunchy laugh. I had told her everything about me and Blake—about the Waldorf and the time we spent in his bedroom—and she'd promised to keep it a secret from Mom.

An hour later, we ate Mom's butter cookies around the dining room table and Blake blended in like he was a member of the family. It made me think that Blake would learn to stand up to Mr. Ellis the way I was learning to stand up for myself. If he'd turn down Christmas with his father to spend it with me and my family, then he was definitely making progress.

"I love my gift," I said, twirling the ruby between my fingers.

Everyone had moved to the living room and Blake and I sat together on the couch, where he took off his NYU sweat-shirt and gave it to me because I was cold. It smelled of him and it was going to keep me warm in bed tonight. I was glad I didn't have to hide it under the scarves in my closet.

# twenty

*Mr.* Ellis had his second heart attack at his partner's Christmas dinner. Leigh called my house to tell Blake, and he and I rushed to St. Vincent's Hospital in Manhattan.

Leigh and Del and Rachel were waiting for us in the emergency room. Rachel's cheeks were striped with tears, and when Blake saw her as we ran through the automatic doors, the frightened look on his face made me regret the moment in the car when I'd wished that this Christmas would be his father's last.

The hospital allowed two people at a time into Mr. Ellis's

room. *Just family,* a nurse said. The only reason I wanted to go in was to be with Blake, who I saw through a window in the door. He was sitting in a chair next to the bed and Rachel was sitting next to him, rubbing his back. I wished I could rub his back. He looked so sad. His eyes were on Mr. Ellis, who had a tube in his arm and another up his nose and a ghostly pallor covering his skin.

I stood in the hallway as Rachel came out and Del went in and Del came out and Leigh went in. The only constant was Blake, who finally left the room when a doctor wanted to speak to everybody. Then I listened to the doctor tell us that Mr. Ellis had gotten to the hospital in time, that he had to stay at St. Vincent's for a few days, but he'd be all right if he watched his diet and stopped working so hard and avoided stress.

Rachel breathed a sigh of relief. She put her arm around Leigh and they went back to the room, and then I was alone with Blake and Del. Del looked at his watch.

"This poor girl has been standing here for hours," he said to Blake. "I'll take her home."

I thought that was very considerate but Blake didn't. His face turned stormy and his voice was peevish when he told Del that nobody had asked him to take me home. Ten minutes later, Blake and I were back in the Corvette. I didn't say a word as we drove from Manhattan to Brooklyn because Blake didn't seem interested in talking.

"I should've been there" was the first thing he said.

We were parked in front of my house and he didn't look at me. His eyes were fixed on the windshield, through which

I saw piles of snow on the sidewalk and intoxicated people leaving Christmas parties.

"Your father will be fine, Blake. The doctor said so. You couldn't have done anything if you'd been there."

"But I would've been there, Ari."

He never said he blamed me. He didn't have to. I didn't get a good-night kiss, and that said it all.

Blake didn't want to welcome 1987 together. He called a few days after Christmas and said his father was home from the hospital and it wouldn't be right to leave him alone on New Year's Eve. He also said that Rachel was helping out, but she and Leigh were itching to go to Times Square and Del was working at his club, so the only one left to play nurse was him.

"You understand, don't you?" he asked, and I pretended I did. I told myself that it didn't matter, that Mr. Ellis would recover soon and Blake and I could pick up where we had left off on those scratchy blankets.

Then I went with Mom and Dad to spend New Year's Eve in Queens, where my positive thinking evaporated. I sat on the couch in a funk while Kieran raced his Matchbox cars in the basement with Evelyn, and Dad and Patrick played poker in the dining room. Mom plopped down next to me. She tore open a pack of Pall Malls, turned on the television, and watched *It's a Wonderful Life* as I stared into space and caressed my necklace.

"This isn't a cheap gift," I said.

Mom grabbed the remote control and lowered the volume. "What was that?"

"I said this isn't a cheap gift. You accused Blake of giving me cheap gifts and this is an expensive gift."

"Of course it is," Mom said. She put her arm around me, pried my hand from the necklace, and squeezed my fingers in hers. "It's a lovely gift. And I'm sure that Blake would've spent tonight with you if his father wasn't sick. But he has his life to lead and you have yours. Believe me, this time next year you'll be in college and you'll look back on tonight and laugh."

For a minute there I had thought she understood. I'd thought she was going to tell me that everything would be fine with Blake and that I had nothing to worry about . . . but instead she dismissed him as somebody I'd barely remember in twelve months.

And why did she have to bring up college? I was sure that I hadn't exactly aced the SAT, and I hadn't applied anywhere other than Parsons. If Mr. Ellis could get me in, he could probably keep me out. Our conversation in his car had made it crystal clear that he wouldn't give me something for nothing. Now I understood why Mom was so anti-connections.


Leigh called on New Year's Day and invited me to the penthouse, which was strange. It wasn't her penthouse, and Blake should have done the inviting. I asked where he was and what he was doing, and there was a pause before she answered.

"He went to some deli on the other side of town to buy chicken noodle soup," she said. "Uncle Stan is very picky about his chicken noodle soup."

Her tone was sarcastic, and I imagined Blake shivering in the cold outside Katz's or the Carnegie Deli and trying not to spill a container of scalding hot soup as he rushed home. This made me even angrier at Mr. Ellis than I already was, but my mood wasn't too terrible, because I assumed that Blake had told Leigh to call and everything was fine.

So I fixed my hair and makeup and rode to Manhattan in a car that Leigh sent to Brooklyn. It left me at Blake's building, where I took an elevator to the top floor. My heart sank when I reached the penthouse and he wasn't there.

"He'll be back soon," Leigh said. "He had to pick up some deposition transcripts . . . Uncle Stan won't stop working no matter what the doctors say."

She told me that Mr. Ellis was resting upstairs and Rachel was asleep in the guest bedroom because she'd been out clubbing until six that morning. She led me to the living room, where Del was sitting on the couch smoking a cigarette and watching a football game. Leigh sat down next to him, so I sat next to her and stared at the television, thinking that the penthouse didn't feel the same. It seemed empty and boring and grim without Blake.

He came home an hour later and I rushed to the foyer. There was a stack of spiral-bound documents in his hands and a dusting of snow on his coat, which I brushed off.

"Look," I said, raising my index finger to show him a snowflake. "They say no two are alike. Isn't it amazing?"

He didn't say anything, just smiled a half smile, as if it

wasn't amazing and he pitied me for thinking it was. "I guess Leigh invited you," he said, and this gave me a chill because I'd convinced myself that he wanted me there.

"Of course I did," Leigh said from behind me. "I figured you forgot to do it yourself. A guy wants to spend New Year's Day with his girlfriend unless he's made a resolution to become a total bastard."

So Blake hadn't wanted me there. And Leigh had definitely forgiven me—she was looking out for me even though I'd pushed her aside. We sat back down on the couch, where Del and Leigh paid attention to the game and Blake didn't pay attention to me.

"Let's go upstairs," I said into his ear, because I was sure he was in a bad mood from being an errand boy all morning and I could cheer him up.

"Upstairs?" he said. "But my whole family's here. It wouldn't look nice."

Nice, nice, nice, I didn't *care* about nice. And I doubted that anyone would notice. Rachel was still asleep and Mr. Ellis's bedroom door was shut, and Leigh and Del were arguing about whether a penalty on the Jets was deserved. So I pouted and whined until Blake brought me to his room, where he acted like his old self again. He kissed me and I kissed him back, then he was on top of me on the bed and I started to undo his belt because I craved him so much that I couldn't stand it anymore.

"Don't," he said.

"It's okay," I whispered. "We'll be quiet. Nobody will know."

He shook his head, sat up, and rubbed his temples as if he

had one of my migraines. I sat next to him and asked if something was wrong, because he'd been acting so funny lately.

"Here's the thing," he said. "I think we should cool things off for a while."

He wasn't looking at me. He was touching his knee, scratching a bleach stain on his jeans as if scratching would do any good. What he said felt like a thousand bee stings all over my body. Then he said something about falling off the dean's list last semester and about law school, and when I reminded him that he didn't want to go to law school, he reminded me that his father needed him and he couldn't let him down, especially now that he was sick and stress could make him sicker.

I wished that Mr. Ellis *would* get sicker. I wished that he'd have another heart attack and not make it to St. Vincent's in time, and I didn't care if that was a sinful thing to wish because he was ruining everything.

"I'm sorry," Blake said, looking at me with a tired face. "I didn't want to tell you until after the holidays. It's just that I'm not sure what I'm going to end up doing, so it's better for me to be alone for a while to figure things out. And I can't keep lying to my father."

"I lie," I said. "I lie to my mother all the time. I've told her so many lies about us that I can't even remember them anymore. And you shouldn't be so eager to please your father— he's not as perfect as you think."

There was a flash of anger in his eyes and he broke his *Watch your language around a lady* rule again. "What the hell is that supposed to mean?"

It means that he threatened me, I thought. It means that

he tried to bribe me and he did the same thing to Jessica. She didn't disappear on her own, you know. Stanford Ellis made that happen so he could have you all to himself. But I didn't say anything because I could barely talk. Blake had never raised his voice to me before, and his tone brought tears and an aura to my eyes.

"Nothing," I answered, and my voice cracked.

He noticed and it softened him. He reached out and ran his knuckles across my cheek, and I gripped his wrist to keep his hand where it was. "Don't be upset," he said. "I don't want to hurt you, Ari. We'll just see what happens, okay?"

I nodded, trying not to cry, wanting him to put his arms around me so I could bury my face in his chest, but he didn't. He led me downstairs, where Leigh and Del were getting into their coats. They said that Leigh wanted to go back to her hotel and Del had work to do at the club, and a car was waiting for them outside.

"Take Ari with you," Blake said. "She needs to go home."

Now it was much harder to keep myself from crying, but I managed somehow. I stepped into the elevator with Leigh and Del while Blake stood in the foyer with his face as blank as a soldier's. He didn't kiss me goodbye. Then the doors slammed shut and he was gone.

Downstairs in the lobby, the doorman ushered us into a miserable day. The snow had turned to rain, and our driver must have had the flu because he kept sniffing and coughing. His cough was so deep I felt it in my chest.

"Are you all right?" Leigh asked in her raspy voice. She was sitting between me and Del, and I guessed she was asking because I hadn't said a single word in the last fifteen minutes. She didn't know it was because I was afraid I'd break into a fit of sobs if I dared to open my mouth. So I nodded and she kept looking at me, studying my face with her hazel eyes, and she said that Blake had been acting weird since Christmas. "He's all mixed up in his head, Ari," she said quietly, so Del couldn't hear. "He'll get over it."

I nodded again, hoping she was right. The sedan parked at her hotel, and as she got out she said that she and Rachel would be back in New York next month. Del told the driver that the next stop was West Twenty-third and we were off again, riding over slick streets, past mountains of filthy gray snow that I wished would melt because they were depressingly ugly.

"I'm not contagious, you know," Del said.

At first I thought he was referring to the syphilis. But of course he wasn't. He'd been cured, and he didn't even know that I knew about it. He just meant that I was sticking to the opposite side of the car. I was still afraid to talk, so I forced a smile and slid a few inches toward him on the seat. He asked if it would bother me if he had a cigarette. I shook my head and he rolled down the window to blow smoke into the rain. We were both quiet and I kept glancing at his hands because they came from the exact same mold as Blake's.

When we reached Cielo, Del tossed his cigarette into the gutter. Then he leaned across the seat to put his hand on the curve in my back and to kiss my cheek, wishing me a happy new year. A raw gust of wind blew into my face as he opened the car door and I had a sinking feeling this wasn't going to be a happy year.

# twenty-one

*January* was awful. I went back to Hollister, where I had nobody to talk to or to sit with during lunch. Just about every day I tossed Mom's homemade sandwiches and her Hostess cupcakes in the trash because the sight of food was sickening. I knew this was a disgraceful thing to do, especially since people were starving in Ethiopia, but I couldn't help it.

I kept thinking of the Ethiopians, sitting in the merciless African sun with flies crawling into their eyes and up their nostrils. It wasn't fair that they had to suffer so much, but of course nothing was fair. I guessed that compared to them, my problems weren't important. People without food didn't lose sleep over a boyfriend who had stopped calling.

Blake's silence drove me to start making deals in my head, deals like *He'll call if I wear his mother's necklace every day* and *If I get an A on the Calculus II exam, he'll send me a birthday card that says he can't live without me.* But nothing worked, and the mailman brought only my dreaded SAT scores on the morning I turned eighteen.

Mom tore the envelope open before I could get near it. She was in the foyer when I was coming down the stairs, and she stood on an area rug in her slippers and apron, shock on her face. I wanted to tiptoe backward and pretend I hadn't seen her, but she caught my eye before I could move. Her expression changed to anger—her eyes narrowing and her mouth tightening—and I knew I was about to get chewed out.

"Very *nice*, Ariadne," she said, shoving the score report at me. I looked at it and my results were so low, so pathetic, I almost cried. "I can't believe that a girl as smart as *you*," Mom went on in her husky voice, "could do *so* badly on a test *this* important that you spent *months* studying for. This is your *future* we're talking about."

I had known she'd say cutting things. I turned around and started up the stairs to escape, but she followed me.

"That's what happens," she said, "when you make stupid decisions . . . when you run around Manhattan right before a test and dance at a club all night with a damn *boy*."

I wasn't dancing, I thought. I was sleeping with that *damn boy*, and he doesn't seem to want me anymore. I sniffed, holding back tears, and headed to my room. Mom trailed behind me the whole way.

"What do you have to say?" she asked when we reached my door. "Don't you have anything to say?"

I turned to face her. A tear slipped out of my eye and I wiped it away. "What do you want, Mom? I'm sorry. I know I've ruined everything."

Another tear rolled down my cheek and I dried it with my sleeve. I guessed she remembered that I was sensitive, because her face softened and so did her voice. She stopped talking like a teacher.

"Okay," she said. "It's okay. It's your birthday . . . I shouldn't yell at you."

I didn't care about my birthday. I just wanted to go back to bed.

But Mom kept talking. "I guess it isn't *that* bad," she said, like she was trying to convince herself. "You can just retake the test, that's all. You'll study some more and get a good night's sleep . . . and I'll make sure you have a decent breakfast. You'll do much better next time. Right, Ariadne?"

The thought of taking that horrid test again made me want to hurl myself down the steps. But Mom looked hopeful and she was trying to be encouraging, so I couldn't tell her the truth.

"Right, Mom," I said, walking into my room. I closed the door behind me, leaving her alone in the hall.


That night, Patrick and Evelyn drove to Brooklyn with the boys. Mom didn't mention the SAT again. She pretended that everything was fine. She cooked dinner and ordered a cake from the bakery, and Kieran gave me a picture frame made of bottle caps. Everyone kept telling me how pretty I looked and there were big phony smiles on their faces, the same kind people use when they're trying to cheer up somebody with a terminal illness.

They meant well, so I went along with the act. I forced cake down my throat and played a board game with Kieran. He'd brought the game in a schoolbag filled with other stuff, like Play-Doh and an Etch A Sketch. Then he pulled out the autographed Red Sox baseball that Blake had given him, and my head started to pound. I excused myself and pretended I was going upstairs to take my migraine pills, when I was actually planning to lie facedown on my bed until tomorrow.

Patrick came out of the bathroom as I hit the top step. His hair swept across his forehead and he looked handsome, but not as good as Blake.

"Are you okay?" he asked, and I nodded unconvincingly. Then he got back into the *Let's cheer up Ari* routine by reminding me that I was eighteen now and could get my driver's license, which made me feel worse.

"Blake offered to teach me how to drive," I said. My voice broke on the last word, and that wasn't lost on Patrick.

"I'll teach you how to drive," he said.

He was such a good guy. But I couldn't think about driving. All I wanted to do was vegetate in my room, which I did for an hour before Mom and Evelyn crept in and surrounded me on the bed.

It seemed as if they were a team suddenly, a more unlikely match than the Nancy Mitchell–Patrick Cagney pairing. It got me wondering if they had secret conversations about what was best for me. And I didn't bother to lift my face from my pillow when Mom made pleasant suggestions. She said that the three of us should go shopping next weekend, maybe in the city, and it would be a "girls' day out."

I thought I must be really bad off if Mom was proposing a shopping trip to Manhattan. It didn't sound like fun to me—nothing did anymore—so I just mumbled an excuse into my pillow. Then Mom mentioned Blake.

"Is that what's been bothering you lately?" she asked. "Is it all because Blake dropped you?"

Now I looked at her. "He didn't drop me. We're just taking a break for a while."

That was what I'd been telling myself. In my mind, the proof was that he hadn't asked for his mother's necklace back. I brought this up as evidence, but I didn't convince anyone.

"Ari," Evelyn said. She grabbed an elastic band from my night table and used it to knot her hair into a bun. "You have to snap out of this. Don't let that jerk upset you."

"He's not a jerk," I insisted. "I thought you liked him. You said he was good-looking. *Fetching,* you said."

She rested her hand on my shoulder. "Any guy who doesn't treat my sister right is a jerk. And you know what? Guys are no different from buses. If one drives past, you just wait for the next and hop right on. So if Blake wants to be a prick, then he can rot in hell as far as I'm concerned. You don't need him."

I knew she was trying to make me feel better, but it didn't work. Mom had been right—Evelyn wouldn't bat an eyelash over this. And Mom had been right about me, too. I wasn't like my sister and I didn't want to hop on another bus.

* * *

I never expected I'd lose interest in drawing, but that was exactly what happened. Not once since New Year's Day had I even thought of walking into my studio.

I'd be lucky if I earned a C⁺ in art this semester. I'd be lucky if I earned a C⁺ in any of my classes because I had stopped striving for good grades. What did they matter, anyway? Everybody knew that the second half of senior year made no difference. The college-acceptance letters were practically in the mail.

I even took the SAT again like Mom wanted. I went to bed early the night before, I ate her blueberry waffles for breakfast, and I forced myself to try, only because she'd go nuts if I didn't. But my mind was foggy so I couldn't remember definitions and formulas, and there were more of those impossible logic questions that made me choose answer C over and over again. *When in doubt, choose C*—that was what everybody at school always said—but it was bad advice. When my scores came back, they were only slightly higher than last time.

I was starting to wonder if Mom and my teachers were wrong about me. Maybe I wasn't so bright, maybe I wasn't a good student, and maybe I'd somehow managed to fake it throughout my entire academic career. The look on Mom's face when she saw my results made me think she was wondering the same thing.

College-acceptance letters were supposed to arrive by the end of February, and I hoped for a miracle. I hoped that Mr. Ellis had put in a good word for me at Parsons. Or maybe he'd put in a bad word for me, or maybe he hadn't said anything and I'd get in on my twelve years of good grades alone. Or maybe I wouldn't get in and I'd have nobody to blame but myself.

I put the whole sickening mess out of my mind on a cold Tuesday afternoon toward the middle of February, while I sat in the library at Hollister and pretended to study. I couldn't study for real; basic addition and subtraction had become impossible and there was no point in trying to remember historical facts and all that meaningless drivel. Information just poured in and flowed out of my brain like it was a strainer.

I couldn't go home, either. Home was where Mom tiptoed around me as if I was a soufflé in danger of falling. She was trying so hard to make me feel better, it was exhausting to watch.

Unfortunately, the library closed at four on Tuesdays. A librarian wearing sensible shoes reminded me of that in an unfriendly way when I was still there at four-fifteen. So I gathered my books and went outside. I stood by the iron gates, trying to come up with a destination. I couldn't go back to Brooklyn and I didn't want to go to Queens—but Blake's penthouse wasn't far away. Maybe I could take a stroll past his building. Maybe he'd be on his way home from NYU and we'd cross paths on the sidewalk, and he'd tell me that he missed me and that we should go upstairs and make love in his bedroom like we used to.

This idea seemed ingenious until I actually got to the Upper East Side and saw Tina's van parked at the curb. Summer had graduated early, according to her plan, and I assumed that she was working with her mother. She was probably at the penthouse flirting with Blake—and with Mr. Ellis, if he was feeling better.

Summer was welcome at the penthouse and I wasn't. Even if she was just an employee, the thought of her up there made me want to scream or cry or both, yet I couldn't do either. I just stared at the building and the van until I heard a car door slam and felt a tap on my shoulder. I smelled cigarettes and I turned to find Del behind me.

"What are you doing here?" he asked. "Did you and Blake get back together?"

So he really had dropped me. We weren't just cooling things off for a while and I was a fool. "No," I said, and the word came out so faintly that Del got the picture and seemed sorry for opening his mouth. "I have to go," I told him. "I have to go home."

"How are you getting there?" he asked.

"I don't know," I said, because I didn't. My mind was so sluggish lately.

A scarf hung from my shoulders and he wrapped it gently around my neck. "You have to think of these things, Ari. It's freezing out here."

He offered to drive me home. I got in the Porsche, where Del tried to make conversation as we headed to Brooklyn. All he got in return were one-word answers because I didn't have the strength for anything more.

"You should know something," he said when we were a few blocks from my house. "Blake is seeing that friend of yours. The blond chick."

I wanted to die. I stared through the windshield while Del went on, telling me that Mr. Ellis thought Blake needed more experience and Summer was just the kind of girl to give it to him.

Then we were in front of my house and Del turned to me. I stared at the scar on his lip while he spoke. "Maybe I shouldn't have told you," he said, most likely because my chin was shaking. "But you don't care, do you? I mean, a girl like you . . . you've probably got another boyfriend already."

I shook my head. He changed the subject to Leigh and Rachel, who were flying into JFK this weekend. He said that they were all going to Cielo for Valentine's Day, so I should stop by. And Blake might be there too, but I would come anyway, wouldn't I?

I nodded after he passed me a little red square. It was a piece of paper printed with the name of his club and VALENTINE'S DAY SPECIAL. HALF-PRICE DRINKS FOR ALL LADIES. FRIDAY, FEBRUARY 14.

He smiled, leaned toward me, touched my back, and kissed my cheek. For a while there I had thought that Del's kisses meant nothing, but now I wasn't so sure.


When Summer was voted Prettiest Girl in junior high, I had thought it was the worst thing that could happen. But I was only twelve, and was clueless about all the bad things that could happen. That was just a scratch compared to the stab wound I'd been nursing ever since Del told me about her and Blake.

I couldn't stop thinking about the two of them together. I saw them in the Corvette and in the penthouse and in the Hamptons, all day long and in my dreams. I imagined Summer sneaking Blake into her fairy-tale room and I figured he liked it better there than on my crummy JCPenney bedspread. I especially thought about them on Valentine's Day, while I sat by my bedroom mirror with wet hair and my Eighty-eight-shade Pro Eye Shadow Palette.

A few days earlier, I had made a decision. I wasn't going to look like a Hollister student anymore, with simple hair and preppy pearls, because simple and preppy hadn't gotten me anywhere. Simple preppy girls wasted their youth and got dumped by their boyfriends, while flashy sexy girls lived it up in Manhattan, where they dished out *experience*. I decided that I was going to be someone else—someone glamorous and sophisticated, someone who wasn't dull and boring and average, someone who wasn't afraid of doing sinful things.

I outlined my eyes in black and smeared them with gray, then chose a lipstick the color of a ripe cherry. My clothes were waiting on the bed—a satiny bustier I'd picked up at one of those trendy stores where women who wear five-inch heels tend to shop. I also bought snug leather pants, stiletto pumps, and dangly earrings that grazed my shoulders.

My hair hung straight and dark around my face. I couldn't let it stay that way—it was nothing but *preppy crap*— so I grabbed a pair of scissors and cut a long bang that brushed my left eye. I threw some hot rollers into the rest and sprayed everything with Aqua Net after I took them out, and when I was in my bustier and my leather pants and my

284

heels and my ruby necklace, I barely recognized myself. I looked like what I was—a girl whose parents were at a second cousin's third wedding in Yonkers, tricked into believing that their daughter was spending the night with her calculus books.

So what if I lied? Being good didn't get me anywhere. I'd spent my entire life being good, studying and babysitting and trying not to hurt anyone's feelings. I was through with being nice.

I didn't exactly have a plan for that night. All I knew was that Blake might be there and that Del would definitely be there, and I wasn't sure which one of them I wanted to see.

At first I only saw Leigh, who was wearing a tweed cap and matching coat and waiting for me in the cold. There was a bouncer beside her who handed me five of the half-price drink coupons.

"Are you in disguise?" she asked, looking me up and down.

"No," I said. "I'm new and improved."

Her forehead wrinkled. "Why? You were fine the way you were before."

"Not quite," I said, and started walking toward the door.

The club was just the way I remembered it—smoky air and flashing lights, music so loud that I had to read Leigh's lips. She pulled off her hat and nodded at the coupons in my hand. "Those will be wasted on us . . . you can give them to my mother if you want to."

"I don't want to," I said, because I wanted to try drinking and forget everything.

Leigh clutched my arm and spoke into my ear. "Ari," she said. "I don't like the way Blake's treated you, and I hope this *new and improved* stuff isn't for him. You're better than that."

This was the last thing I wanted to hear. Leigh was being practical, like Mom, and I wasn't in a practical mood. So I ignored her and walked toward the bar. It was a cinch to get the first drink, and the second and the third, because the bartender was so busy staring at my chest that he didn't bother to ask for ID. It was probably too dark to notice that I wasn't exactly even.

I felt like I was levitating. The floor blinked in yellow and red and blue while Rachel and Leigh and I danced, but after a while I ran out of steam and Rachel got all motherly.

"How much did you have to drink, honey?" she asked.

I shrugged. I had ordered a beer and a wine cooler and two White Russians that I downed quickly because they tasted as harmless as chocolate milk. Rachel shook her head and wagged her finger and told me to get a big glass of water. So I sat on faux zebra skin at the bar, guzzling Evian and watching bartenders juggle bottles.

I was there for a half hour before I saw Blake, who was at the other end of the bar. He was dressed differently than usual, similar to Del, in a dark blazer and a shirt with the top few buttons undone, and he was talking with two girls. Neither of them was Summer, but they were so much prettier than me. Then I looked around at all the pretty girls in the club. There were tons of them, swarming like a million ants on a discarded piece of candy. I couldn't even count them all. Why would Blake want me when he could choose any of them?

It was so depressing. I sat on the stool watching him, even though he didn't notice. He walked away a few minutes later and I stalked him through the club. He disappeared into the men's room and I waited outside, thinking this was my chance and I had to take it.

He didn't recognize me when he came out. He walked by and didn't turn his head until I called his name. "Ari?" he said, like I was wearing a Halloween costume.

He looked down at me and I smiled up at him. "Hi," I said as my heart pounded.

"What's all this?" he asked, motioning to my clothes and my stiletto heels.

"I don't know," I said, flirtatiously lifting a bare shoulder. "Don't you like it?"

He shrugged. "I don't know."

I wanted to talk to him. I wasn't sure what I was going to say. But it was too loud to hear myself think, so I nodded toward the men's room. It was empty and we locked ourselves in a stall.

I pressed my back against the partition that separated our stall from the next. Blake stood opposite me, leaning into the wall.

"You've been drinking, haven't you?" he asked. "I can smell it on you."

I shrugged and tried to be flirty again. "Maybe a little."

"You don't drink," he said, moving his eyes from my heels to my hair. "This isn't you."

"Good. I don't want to be me." I looked down at the tiles beneath my feet. They were ceramic, the high-quality kind.

I was sure that Del had spent a lot of money on this bathroom, but nobody respected it. They just scribbled on the walls and left empty toilet-paper rolls on the floor. "Anyway, I thought you'd like my outfit. It's the kind of thing Summer wears. You two are close friends now, from what I've heard."

He sighed. "We aren't. I don't care about Summer."

"Then why did you sleep with her?" I asked. "I thought you were a gentleman. I thought you didn't sleep with girls you didn't care about. You told me it wasn't any good that way."

"I don't want to talk about it. She was a mistake," he said, and that wasn't the denial I craved. So I just stood there in a stony silence until he opened his mouth again. "I miss you, Ari. I think about you constantly."

"Liar," I said. "You don't care about me anymore."

"I care about you too much. That's the whole problem."

That wasn't a problem. That couldn't be a problem. A rush of hope flooded through me and I forgave him for everything as I threw myself across the stall and into his arms, where he kissed me and I kissed him back.

I heard the bathroom door creak, men's voices over the faucet running. They were talking about money in hushed tones: I was probably eavesdropping on a drug deal, but it didn't matter. It didn't matter that Blake and I were in a filthy bathroom, kissing beside a toilet. The only important thing was that we were kissing.

It was comforting and familiar—his smell, his taste, his tongue on my skin. His hand went down my bustier and I hooked one leg around his waist and then he said, "We can't. I don't have anything with me."

I knew he was talking about protection and I started to think crazy things, desperate things, like Evelyn saying that Patrick had loved her more when she was carrying his baby, and I thought that Blake might love me again if I was carrying his. *Guys are funny that way.* So I stayed where I was and I moved my hand downward to feel him through his pants.

"Stop it," he said. "We can't."

I dropped to my knees and unbuckled his belt. "Can we do this?"

I didn't even sound like me. I sounded like some other girl who was used to wearing trashy clothes and tempting men by getting on her knees. Blake gripped my arms and pushed me away.

"Don't, Ari."

"Why? I want to."

"Stop it," he said again, sharply this time. He yanked me to my feet, adjusted my bustier because it was falling off. I tried to kiss him but he wouldn't let me, and that didn't make sense because he missed me and he thought about me constantly. So I kept trying until he held my wrists to make me stop. "Look at where we are, Ari. This isn't you. You're a nice girl."

"I don't want to be a nice girl," I said, sliding my hand to his groin.

He stepped back. "Don't talk like that."

Nothing I did was right. "How do you want me to talk? I'll do whatever you want."

Blake took off his jacket and put it over my shoulders. "I want you to go home," he said. "And keep this on. You shouldn't be walking around in that getup. People will get the wrong idea."

I started to cry. Softly at first, and then harder, until I could barely see through my tears and I lost it. I screeched at Blake that I couldn't think straight anymore and that I didn't care about school or life and I would never love anybody but him and I just wanted to die.

"Don't say that," he said. "I'm not worth it."

But I thought he was worth it. So I said it again and again and then his palm cracked against my cheek. It was the kind of slap that people use to wake someone from a fainting spell or a fit of hysterics.

"I'm sorry," he said. "Just calm down. Please. I can't stand seeing you this way."

He couldn't stand seeing me this way? It was his fault that I *was* this way. My cheek was stinging and I felt angry suddenly. I sniffed, wiped my nose, and struggled to compose myself.

"Summer stole your cousin's bracelet, you know." I had stopped crying and now I stood there with my chest heaving and my hands on my hips. "She kept it hidden for months even though she knew how much it meant to Leigh. And if you're wondering why Jessica ran off, ask your father. He's the one who made her dump you. He bribed her. He probably tried to blackmail her too—that's what he pulled on me, but I didn't fall for it."

I was so proud of myself for saying that, but I didn't feel proud when I noticed how Blake was looking at me. It was like he didn't believe me, like I was nothing but a pathetic liar. It made me angrier and I ripped off his mother's necklace, threw it at his feet, and stormed from the bathroom into the smoky air.

Five minutes later I was alone, crying into my hands on the steps that led to Del's apartment. I wished I hadn't come here. I wished I hadn't thrown the necklace at Blake. I wished I'd never been born.

My head was killing me and the noise from the club made it worse. The thought of taking my migraine pills before I left home tonight hadn't even crossed my mind. I heard the jingle of keys and I turned toward the banister, hoping that whoever was coming would just keep going. Then there were feet in front of me and I heard a deep voice.

"What's the matter?"

I looked up and saw Del. "Nothing. I've got a headache. I have to go."

He crouched down and touched my arm. I glanced at his hand and it was the same as Blake's except for the pinkie ring, and that made me cry again.

"You're not crying about my brother, are you?" he asked. "He's just a stupid kid."

"He is not," I said.

Del sat next to me, watching tears pour down my face. Then he massaged my aching temples with his fingertips. It surprised me and it felt really nice. It felt even better when he put both arms around me and I leaned my head against his strong shoulder and his silky shirt that smelled of cigarettes.

"It's okay," he said. "Don't cry. Blake doesn't deserve you."

My mascara was melting onto my cheeks and I couldn't stop bawling, but Del didn't make me feel ridiculous. He held me the way Patrick held Evelyn, the way I wanted, and I hoped he wouldn't let go because there was nothing else keeping me together.

The next thing I knew, we were walking up the steps and into his apartment, where I saw his skylight and the waning moon. Del tossed his keys onto a table and we sat on his messy sheets. I was sniffling and shaking and he dried my face with his hands, which felt almost as good as Blake's kisses on my neck.

"You like me, don't you?" he asked. "You've always liked me."

I nodded, thinking that his eyes were very green tonight.

"I've always liked you too," he said as he traced my jaw with his finger.

That weakened me. I missed being touched, especially by someone who might not stop me from touching him back. I heard myself breathing, felt my heart pounding again. Del wasn't Blake but he was as close as I could get, and I was thinking more crazy things.

"Really?" I said.

He nodded and I blinked because there were still tears in my eyes. The dark room looked dim and blurry, yet I saw his face getting closer to mine. He paused when our mouths were almost touching, as if waiting for me to back away, but I didn't. I let him kiss me and I felt his scar. It was like a thick piece of twine against my lip. Soon he was lying on me and Blake's jacket was on the floor and the top of my bustier was down at my ribs. I kept my eyes shut and I didn't stop him from doing anything, even when he slid off my pants and tossed them away.

They landed on the hardwood with a thump and that woke me up. The music downstairs seemed louder, my vision was clear, and Del's eyes had somehow changed to gray. Then I heard his belt buckle open and I was scared.

Del didn't tell me not to be scared. He didn't kiss my forehead. "Del," I started, but my voice was so faint that he didn't hear me and it was too late. I'd already let this go too far—we'd gone all the way. And it didn't feel good anymore. It felt wrong. It felt like nothing. Now Del looked ugly—the gash on his lip, the downturn of his nose.

I was about to push him away but I didn't need to. Everything had happened so fast, he was done already. He slumped against me, then rolled off and stared through the skylight as he tried to catch his breath. I looked around the room, at the bachelor-pad furniture and the mirror on the headboard. It all seemed tawdry and disgusting and what was I doing here? I should have stayed at home and studied calculus. I never should have said that I didn't want to be a nice girl. Nothing felt worse than not being a nice girl.

I was getting queasy. I had a migraine, and what I'd just done made me want to jump out the window, to fly through the glass toward those creepy angels on the building across the alley. I wanted to pretend that this hadn't happened. I wanted to erase it like my miserable first kiss.

I pulled up my bustier, slid into my pants, but didn't pick up Blake's jacket. "Don't you ever tell your brother about this," I said, standing over Del. "Don't you ever tell anybody."

He looked up at me from the bed, and I actually felt sorry for him because my voice was cold and he seemed hurt. Then I remembered Leigh and Idalis and the parade of *putas* that came in and out of here. I remembered Evelyn getting in trouble and STD pamphlets and Leigh saying *Del could end up with AIDS if he doesn't watch out.*

"Did you use anything?" I asked. It sounded so crass but I had to know.

He was getting dressed. He zipped his pants and buttoned his shirt. "No," he said. "I figured you were on the Pill or whatever."

I rushed down the stairs, thinking he had filled me with something toxic that could destroy my life or end it with a gruesome death. I'd been so careful before, I was always so careful, but this one moment might ruin me forever.

Del was behind me, calling my name down the stairs. I ignored him and ran through the front door into the frigid night, stumbling in my tacky shoes. I glanced around for a cab but instead I saw Blake and Rachel and Leigh at the curb.

They were probably waiting for one of those glossy sedans to take them home. I didn't want them to see me but they glanced in my direction at the sound of Del's voice. He was here now, asking what was wrong like he had no idea. Blake looked at him and looked at me with my messed-up hair and my mascara-stained face, and then he charged toward Del.

"What did you do to her?" he demanded.

"Nothing," Del said. "Mind your own business."

Blake's face was red and he yelled and swore. He shoved his brother, who stumbled backward on the sidewalk. Then Del straightened up and punched Blake square in the face. Blood gushed from Blake's nose and Del shouted at him.

"You had that coming," he said. "You only dumped her

because of Daddy. You didn't have the guts to choose her over him."

It was so quiet. Leigh and Rachel were staring at me from the curb. Blake didn't answer, and I guessed he was surprised that Del wasn't as dumb as everybody thought.

# twenty-two

*I* dove into a cab, escaping the commotion, and watched Rachel through the window as she searched her coat pockets and then held a handkerchief to Blake's face. A big part of me wanted to jump out of the car and help him, but the rest of me thought Del was right. Blake did have that coming.

When I got home, Saint Anne pierced me with her reproachful gaze. My parents weren't back yet, the house and the front yard were dark, and I squinted across the lawn. Don't look at me like that, I thought. Not everyone can be as perfect as your daughter.

I hurried past Saint Anne, locked myself in the house, and dry-heaved over the toilet. Mom and Dad came back and soon Mom was banging on the bathroom door. She wanted to know if I was sick. The stomach flu was going around, she said.

The knocking was like a hammer crushing my skull. She had no idea how sick I was—that I was just a sick excuse for a human being. I was sick for getting into bed with Del and I was sick for practically begging to go down on Blake in a public restroom, and now I might get morning sickness or syphilis or an incurable virus that could put me in a box that Mom and Dad would buy with Uncle Eddie's money. *At least poor Ariadne got to use that money for something,* I imagined Mom saying.

The thought made me vomit. Mom knocked on the door as a half-digested dinner mixed with wine and beer and Kahlúa spewed from my mouth. I gripped the toilet, wishing she'd go away. She kept telling me to unlock the door, but I couldn't. I couldn't let her see me until I got rid of my outfit.

She finally gave up and I stripped off my clothes, burying my underwear in the trash can beneath crumpled tissues and frayed dental floss. Then I stepped into the shower, where I scrubbed every bit of myself in scalding hot water that I hoped would sterilize me. I wanted everything to disappear— the makeup, the Aqua Net, the smell of cigarettes in my hair.

I let my mouth fill with water and I spit into the drain, over and over, trying to purge the millions of microscopic germs that Del had probably left.

*  *  *

An hour later, I walked down the hall toward my bedroom wearing a bathrobe and clutching my clothes in a ball. I remembered rumors I'd heard about foiling a pregnancy with things like soda or vinegar and I considered trying both, but I quickly changed my mind. Those were ignorant myths; someone who had taken Sex Ed should know better.

"Ariadne," Mom said. "Are you all right? You were in there for so long."

She came out of nowhere with a pungent tuna sandwich and I stifled a gag.

"I'm fine," I said. "Just leave me the hell alone for once."

She looked stunned. I couldn't have cared less. I walked away, shut my door, and collapsed into bed, where I watched numbers change on my clock and stared at the teddy bear on my dresser.

Blake. I thought of him and of the past year. I thought about when colors had been outrageously bright and the air had smelled incredibly good and when I had forgotten how it felt to be sad. Now I remembered, and I thought Blake was no better than some street-thug heroin dealer. He had gotten me hooked on him and then he'd cut off my supply. I'd heard that addicts would do anything, would degrade themselves in every way to get another fix, and now I understood how that could happen, because it was happening to me.

I wished that tonight had been just a bad dream. I wished that Blake had some backbone. I wished he'd chosen me over his father, but he hadn't, and now all I had left was a stuffed animal and an NYU sweatshirt. The sweatshirt was tucked inside my night table, and I took it out and wrapped it around myself. It was the only thing that could get me to sleep.

Leigh called at noon. Mom came in and shook my shoulder to wake me up.

"I don't want to talk to her," I said, because last night wouldn't have happened if it wasn't for Leigh. It was her fault that I had met Blake and Del. Of course, I could have been a good friend instead of chasing after her cousins. And I was going back on my word too. On Christmas Eve I'd told her that I would never treat her badly again. Maybe now I was getting what I deserved, but I couldn't tolerate any more blame. It was too heavy for me to carry alone.

Mom just assumed I was too sick to talk on the phone. She walked away and I heard her telling Leigh that I had the flu or whatever was going around. I went along because it was convenient—sick people get to stay in bed all day, and I wanted to stay in bed all day. A minute later, Mom hung up the phone and yelled from the kitchen that Leigh said she'd call me the next time she was in New York. I didn't care if she ever called me again.

I went back to sleep, and stayed in bed for most of the day and most of the next week, faking the flu so I could skip school. I didn't change out of the NYU sweatshirt and I didn't shower and I only left the house once. I went to the library, where I hid between bookshelves and shuddered as I skimmed the pages of a medical dictionary and worried that Del's STD wasn't really cured.

*Untreated syphilis can cause damage in the brain, spinal cord, heart, and other organs,* I read. *Signs and symptoms of late-stage syphilis include paralysis, numbness, gradual blindness, and dementia. This damage may be serious enough to cause death.*

Blindness scared me more than everything else, including death. I imagined seeing absolutely nothing and depending on Mom to dress me and brush my hair and she wouldn't do any of it right. I'd get old and my hair would turn gray and she'd hardly ever dye it, and I'd probably end up doddering around Brooklyn with dark glasses, banging the sidewalk with a cane like some shriveled old witch who would frighten the neighborhood kids.

Then I decided I needed a pregnancy test and a blood test immediately, even if I had to get poked fifty times to find a vein.

"Do you have a faculty meeting tomorrow?" I asked Mom that night.

She nodded from her seat on the couch, where she was smoking a Pall Mall and trying to write a novel based on some idea that had come to her while she was scrubbing the kitchen sink. She smiled down at her notebook. She'd bought a spiral-bound one with a perky pink cover, like a student with high hopes for a new school year. "It would be nice if this novel works out. But I probably won't finish."

"Probably not," I said, because I knew the odds were against anything working out. Mom's smile dimmed, but it was the truth, so I didn't feel bad.

She put the notebook aside. "Are you going to take a shower someday? Your hair is greasy. I don't know why you cut those bangs . . . they're always in your eyes. And you've been wearing that sweatshirt forever."

Mom was right about the sweatshirt. I was turning into Leigh. But it was much easier for her, because M.G. hadn't left her on purpose.

"So what?" I asked. "Nobody cares how I look."

"I care," Mom said.

That seemed irrelevant. So I didn't change my clothes or do anything about my hair the next day. I had an appointment at the clinic at three. When I got there, I gave my name to a woman with coffee-colored skin and cornrows. She flipped through a book and asked if I was sure I hadn't made the appointment somewhere else.

"No," I said. "I called here."

She figured out that I had called there, but when I'd asked for a Friday appointment, she had thought I meant next Friday. So I was turned out into the street for another week of paranoia.

That night I sat at the kitchen table with Mom and Dad. My plate was filled with mushy mashed potatoes swimming in thick brown gravy and meat loaf covered in a crispy ketchup glaze that reminded me of dried blood. Mom didn't seem to think I had enough food, so she shoveled three spoonfuls of fried onions onto my plate and filled a glass with milk.

"Eat up," she said. "You're so thin, Ariadne. You really have to gain some weight back. You need your strength for school."

I kept my eyes on my food, made tracks in the potatoes with a fork, and wondered if starvation could cause a miscarriage. A miscarriage would be better than the stirrups and the instruments and whatever else doctors used to fix a big mistake.

"I'm not going back to school," I said.

"Of course you are. You're not sick anymore."

That was what *she* thought. I ignored her and hid a piece of meat loaf under my napkin when nobody was looking. Dad wasn't looking because he was busy reading the newspaper. Mom accused him of having bad manners. She said that dinnertime was when people were supposed to talk to each other.

He paused for a moment, searching for something to talk about. "I ran into someone today," he said.

"Who?" Mom asked.

"Summer Simon. I had to see a potential witness in the Empire State Building and Summer was walking out when I was walking in."

Dinnertime conversation was so overrated. The mention of that name and the Empire State Building made me nauseous, so I headed to my room. I was on the staircase when I felt Mom's hand on my elbow.

"Get off," I snapped.

"What's the matter with you?" she said in her stern teacher voice. "Why are you acting like this?"

I didn't tell her. She'd warned me and I couldn't stomach an "I told you so."

Later, when Mom and Dad were watching TV downstairs, I took a bubble bath because I was nervous and restless and I couldn't come up with anything else to do. TV didn't interest me and schoolwork didn't interest me and drawing

302

was stupid. It was nothing but a useless hobby, I couldn't do anything with it, I would never become an artist, and the idea of teaching had suddenly lost its luster.

I tried not to think about anything when I was in the bathtub, covered with suds up to my neck. I closed my eyes, listening to water swishing and the canned sitcom laughs coming from downstairs. Then there was a knock at the door and Mom walked in even though I didn't give her permission.

"What are you doing?" I said. "I'm naked in here."

"Oh, please. I can't see anything." She sat on the toilet-seat lid and her tone was much nicer than the one she'd used on the staircase. "What's wrong, Ariadne? You've been acting so strangely."

Just go away, I thought, closing my eyes again. "Nothing is wrong, Mom. I'm fine."

She didn't believe me. I listened to her say that I was sulky and irritable and that I never drew anymore. Then she mentioned Summer and I wanted to slide down the drain and into the sewer with the rest of the filth. That was where somebody who would get on her back for her boyfriend's brother belonged, anyway.

"What exactly happened between the two of you?" she asked.

"Nothing," I said again.

She was quiet for a moment and I heard her slipper tapping the tiles. "Did it have something to do with Blake?"

My eyes sprang open. "Of course not. It had nothing to do with him. Absolutely nothing."

I should have stopped at *Of course not*. I had protested too much and she didn't believe a word.

"You know what?" she said. "I should call that boy and tell him what I think about the shitty way he's treated you."

"Don't you dare," I said, but she didn't pay any attention.

"Who does that little prick think he is? Just because his father is some big-shot lawyer and he lives on the fucking Upper East Side doesn't mean he can get away with upsetting my daughter. Look at what he's done to you, for God's sake—you haven't been yourself for weeks, and you're getting worse. I really ought to go into the city and tell him off in person."

"Don't you dare!" I said, shouting this time, and I sounded as psychotic as I had in the men's room at Cielo. "Don't you dare call him or go anywhere near him. If you say one word to Blake . . . I swear I'll kill myself."

I was definitely turning into Leigh. Mom stared at me. She stared at me as if she could see everything I'd tried so hard to hide.

"What's going on?" she said. "What happened? Something must have happened to make you act like this."

"Nothing happened," I said through my teeth. "Just go away."

She stayed where she was. "Ariadne, was your relationship with Blake more serious than you let on? I can't imagine you'd be this distraught if all the two of you did was hold hands. I mean . . . did he . . . did you let him . . ."

Did he? Did I let him? That sounded awful. Obscene. Sleazy and vile and foul. She kept asking, my head was pounding, and I didn't care anymore if she knew.

"Yes, Mom," I said, sarcastic and loud. "He did. I let him. I let him do anything he wanted whenever he wanted and you were right—he lied and he dumped me and I hope you're happy now."

*I hope you're happy now.* I said it four times in increasing volume and shrillness while she begged me to calm down. Then I grabbed a towel, wrapped it around myself as I sprang from the tub, and ran down the hall, leaving soggy footprints on the carpet. I slammed my bedroom door so hard that it shook the walls and my bear tumbled from the dresser. I left it on the floor while I listened to Mom and Dad out in the hallway. Mom said I was hysterical and she didn't know what to do, and Dad said I'd yelled loud enough for the whole neighborhood to hear and he had never expected something like that from someone like me.

Later that night, I heard my parents whispering and Mom talking on the phone to Evelyn, who'd surely broken her promise not to tell Mom anything. I guessed that Evelyn had to tell her everything now, since I was losing my mind and all. At that moment I thought that things couldn't get worse, but they did the next day when our mailman delivered a tellingly thin envelope from the Parsons School of Design. I got rejected and had to admit to Mom that I hadn't applied anywhere else.

I knew she wanted to yell and scream and tell me how disappointed she was and how idiotic I'd been to rely on connections, but she didn't say anything. I guessed she thought a delicate flower whose petals were barely hanging on couldn't withstand a harsh wind. Then she brought up Hollister, saying I could stay at home for another week and I should spend a few days in Queens because a change of scenery might do me good.

I didn't think so. Queens was just as miserable as Brooklyn, and I couldn't stop thinking that all my studying and drawing had come to absolutely nothing, that it was all just a colossal waste of life. And I was turning out even worse than Evelyn, because at least she was married. Marriage was a respectable place to hide from her failures, a place where she could organize playgroups and be admired for her beautiful children. I had nowhere to go and nothing to do, and that made me want to swallow my entire bottle of migraine pills, which I considered the next morning while I stood in the bathroom and scrutinized the label. ACETAMINOPHEN, it read. BUTALBITAL.

Butalbital sounded nice and lethal. But I didn't have the nerve to do it, and the fact that I was a coward on top of everything else made me hate myself. I decided that I might try again later and I took two pills like I was supposed to, and then I sat in Mom's Honda as she drove me to Queens in silence. I wondered if this was how my sister had felt when she left home with her pregnant stomach and her princess phone.

Soon we were at Evelyn's house, and she rushed down the front steps with her auburn curls flowing behind her. She hugged me on the stairs as Mom drove away, and I held on a little longer than usual. It was a relief to be with someone who knew what it was like to be the object of Mom's disappointment.

Evelyn set up the cot in Shane's room and arranged two dozen Mrs. Fields cookies on a paper plate after lunch. She and Patrick and the boys and I were sitting around the kitchen table when she pushed the plate toward me.

"No thanks," I said.

"You love these, Ari. I got them especially for you."

"No thanks," I said again, and I felt awful because I kept letting everybody down.

She sighed, turning her attention to Shane in his high chair, and tickled him. She laughed when he did and she kept saying "I love you I love you I love you."

I watched them. They made me remember my imaginary Park Slope house and my imaginary husband and my imaginary kids, and knowing that all of it would never be anything but imaginary brought tears to my eyes.

Patrick noticed. "Come on," he said. "Get up. I'm giving you a driving lesson."

I didn't want a driving lesson but I had no choice. He pulled my chair from the table while I was still sitting in it, took me by the arm, and told me to put on my coat. I followed him out to his truck even though I just wanted to sleep until the new millennium.

I sat in the driver's seat and it felt uncomfortable and confusing there. "I don't even have my learner's permit," I said. "It's against the law to drive without a learner's permit."

Patrick snorted. "Who gives a shit? We won't get pulled over. Now stick the damn key in the ignition and let's go."

"I can't," I said, and saw tears dropping onto my jeans. I didn't want to cry, so I fought it by sniffing and wiping my nose, but nothing worked.

He handed me a tissue from his glove compartment. "You know something, Ari?" he said. "Most guys are assholes."

I guessed we were talking about Blake. I wondered if Mom and Evelyn had told him everything. I couldn't even imagine what Patrick would think of me if he ever found out about what happened with Del. And I wouldn't blame him if he was disappointed, because I hadn't taken his advice about staying a nice girl.

"*You're* not," I said.

He smiled, put on his sunglasses, and told me again to start the car. Then I had my first driving lesson, and I couldn't have asked for a better teacher. We went back to the house an hour later, where I sat on the couch and nobody asked me to do anything, not even help with the boys or set the table for dinner.

We all went upstairs early that night, and Patrick made love to Evelyn at nine o'clock. I heard them when I was on the cot in Shane's room. But I didn't want to listen. And I didn't feel jealous. I bent a pillow around my ears to block out the noise and all I felt was lonely.

I stayed in Queens for another four nights. Patrick took me home on a windy Friday morning. He was driving away when I noticed a silver Mercedes parked at the curb, and it gave me the urge to clutch the back of Patrick's truck and spend the day in his fire engine.

But he was already halfway down the street. I was too tired to run, so I just sat on the front steps with my chin in my hand until the door opened and I smelled cigars. Then I looked up at Jeff Simon and wondered if he was about to handcuff me and haul me kicking and screaming to New York–Presbyterian, where I'd fit in with the rest of the loonies. *Are you Evelyn Cagney's sister?* people wearing straitjackets would ask. *You sure don't look like her, but you're obviously just as nutty as she used to be. Seems like you both inherited the wacko gene.*

"How are you feeling?" he asked.

I turned my eyes to a brown leaf that somersaulted across our dead lawn, thinking that Jeff had a lot of nerve to inquire about my well-being when it was partially his daughter's fault that I wasn't doing well at all.

"I'm not one of your patients, Dr. Simon . . . even if my mother wants me to be."

I called him Dr. Simon to sound rude and distant. It worked. He stared at me for a moment, scratched his head, and sighed.

"Don't be difficult," he said. "Tell me how you're feeling."

I gave up. "Not good," I said, and he suggested that I "talk to someone," which was a lousy suggestion. I didn't want to talk and I didn't want a prescription for the kind of pills that Evelyn took. But I said I would think about it so he'd leave me alone.

"I told Nancy that postponing college until next year is the best thing for you," he said. "It's my professional opinion that you need a break, Ari. Don't you agree?"

I agreed. I nodded. "Thank you," I said.

Jeff got into his car and drove away; then I went inside, where I found Mom sitting on the couch with a cigarette.

"How are you feeling, Ariadne?" she asked in a delicate

way. She acted like I'd explode into bits and pieces if she wasn't careful.

"Fine," I said blandly, and headed for the stairs.

"If you need your medication," she called after me, "I've got it."

I turned around and she was smiling as if she could trick me, as if neither one of us had the slightest inkling that too much butalbital could be fatal or that she'd stolen my pills while I was in Queens. It was probably something else Jeff had advised.

# twenty-three

*I* hated March. March was when I worried about my *monthly visitor* because it hadn't shown up. It still hadn't come by my Friday-afternoon appointment at the clinic.

A young nurse kept saying "Sorry, I'm new at this" as she used my left arm as a pincushion. I wanted to tell her that it wasn't her fault and that I had bad veins, but I was too tired to bother. She hit the right spot on the sixth try and handed me a plastic cup.

"Pee in this," she said, and I thought she could have been more professional. A nurse should use better terminology than Evelyn's brainless friends. "The restroom is down the hall. Bring your sample back here when you're finished."

I walked past a waiting room, jammed with knocked-up teenagers, toward a bathroom the size of a broom closet. It had one of those dreary old-person safety rails on the wall, and I was so nervous about blindness and blisters and my late period that I couldn't fill the cup. I thought of things like waterfalls and rainy days, and that worked until someone banged on the door.

"Just a minute," I said, and I felt rushed and sweaty and the minute turned into much longer. Then I finally had my sample and I wondered how I was supposed to get it back down the hall without anyone noticing, but I didn't have much time to think because the banging started again. So I put the lid on the cup and stuck it in my purse and prayed that it wouldn't spill.

"It's about time," a girl said when I came out. She was my age and visibly pregnant under a T-shirt printed with the words TOUCH MY BELLY AND LOSE A HAND. There was a baby in her arms and she looked like she wanted to strangle me. "You kept me waiting for fifteen minutes. Nobody around here ever hogs the bathroom for fifteen minutes."

I didn't answer. I just walked away because I didn't know the rules and I didn't belong here with tough-faced girls who were probably headed toward a life of food stamps and black eyes from worthless men.

"When should I call for the results?" I asked the nurse after I gave her my sample.

"We can't do it over the phone," she said. "You'll have to speak with the doctor in person."

"Why?" I said, but I knew. It was because the clinic didn't want to be responsible for what people might do while they were alone if their test results came back positive. They might get crazy ideas in their heads, ideas like swallowing a bottle of migraine pills.

"It's our policy. You can make an appointment at the front desk."

I went to the desk, where I found that I couldn't catch a break. Nothing was easy, not even scheduling my appointment. The receptionist flipped through her book and told me to come back in three weeks, which might as well have been three years.

I was helpless to do anything about it, so I just nodded. Then I trudged through the waiting room, where phrases like "my baby's daddy" and "my overdue child support" were being tossed around. They stuck with me even after I was outside in the dusky afternoon, listening to the morbid sound of church bells that reminded me of a funeral. I ignored them and kept going, feeling numb and trying to figure out how I'd gotten here.

On a Monday morning I noticed that the snow on our lawn was melting and the grass was growing in sparse clusters around Saint Anne's feet. Early spring was hideous. I couldn't stand the sight of it, so I decided to keep my bedroom curtains permanently shut. Then I gathered my books as Mom smiled at me from my doorway and used her delicate voice.

"Would you like a ride today, Ariadne?" she said.

She'd been asking that question every day since I'd gone

back to Hollister, and I shook my head like I always did. I didn't think it would be fair to make her drive to Manhattan— I was enough trouble already.

I left the house and stared straight ahead. I didn't want to see her standing at the living room window, clutching the curtain and watching me walk down the street. She was as worried about my future as she used to be about Evelyn's, and that made me want to cry.

So I didn't look back. I kept going even though my walk to the train station seemed to have expanded several miles and the ride to Manhattan was endless and claustrophobic. The subway car was warm and I spotted a *Safe Sex* pamphlet on an empty seat, and knowing that I had to wait another ten days for my test results made me panic. Everything felt small and cramped and I had to get out at a station that wasn't mine just to catch my breath.

That made me late for school. A pimply hall monitor stopped me at the front door; I considered wrestling him to the ground and threatening to snap his neck because he was shorter than I was and only a sophomore. But he'd probably accuse me of assault, and that might give Mom a legitimate reason to commit me to New York–Presbyterian, so I just let him fill out his stupid tardy slip, which led me to the principal.

I'd never even seen this woman before. I'd never been on academic probation and had never violated the dress code, so there had been no reason to see her.

"I hope you have a good explanation for being late," she said.

She was much younger than I expected, and she was using

Mom's teacher voice, which annoyed me. I belonged in the principal's office as much as I belonged at the clinic. Why was everything so upside-down? A few wrong turns had changed me into something I had never wanted to be. I felt like waving my second-place ribbon and my old report cards in her face and saying "See? This is who I really am."

"The subway stalled," I said, and the words fell right off my tongue because I was used to being a liar. "I was stuck in the tunnel for an hour."

She eyed me skeptically and dismissed me as if I was a total write-off. This put me in a crabbier mood and I couldn't pay attention in my classes because I was fed up with everything. It got worse later, when I was in the bathroom and heard some girls gushing about the senior prom and what kind of flowers they wanted in their corsages. They also talked about going away to college in the fall, to New England and to Midwest campuses with old stone buildings and football games where they planned to sit on bleachers while they were wrapped in blankets made of wool.

I didn't want to be reminded of wool blankets. I didn't want to hear about the prom and corsages and everything else that was passing me by. Those were once-in-a-lifetime things, things as special and fleeting as Halley's comet. And if you missed them, you could never get them back.

I rode home on the subway later that day, feeling irritable and disgusted and thinking about Blake. I was usually sad when he crept into my mind, but now I was angry about what he'd done and what I'd done and the big disaster it had all turned out to be. Then I shifted my anger to Mr. Ellis, because this mess was his fault. I wouldn't have had any problems if it wasn't for him. If he'd kept out of Blake's business, I would have been as happy and carefree as those girls in the bathroom whose biggest concern was whether they got lilies or roses.

The three weeks were finally over. Now I sat in the doctor's office at the clinic, sweating and biting my nails even though I never bit my nails. Then the doctor came in and I watched as she sat at her desk and skimmed through a folder filled with charts and notes. The suspense was killing me. I was about to leap across the desk and look at that folder myself.

"You're not pregnant," she said.

I didn't believe her. "But I'm late. My period is weeks late."

"Stress interferes with your system . . . it can make you skip a month." Her eyes rose over her bifocals. "You also tested negative for HIV and everything else."

"Negative?" I said with a smile that felt weird because I hadn't used it for so long.

"That's right. But you should come back in three months for another blood test, because HIV and some other STDs don't show up immediately."

"Oh," I said as my smile disappeared.

She looked at her folder. "I wouldn't be overly concerned, Miss Mitchell. From what I see here, you've only had two sexual partners . . . and one of them used protection every time. So AIDS, while not impossible, is unlikely."

*Unlikely* sounded good. *Two sexual partners* didn't. The thought of Del made me wring my hands, and the doctor got suspicious.

"The second man," she said. "The relationship was consensual, wasn't it?"

I sort of wished I could say that it wasn't, that Del had forced me by holding a switchblade against my throat, but he hadn't. His only weapon had been a shoulder for me to cry on.

I nodded at the doctor, who started offering me diaphragms and sponges, and I almost laughed because she seemed to think I needed those things. She didn't know that I couldn't let anybody touch me except Blake, and he was never going to touch me again.

"No thanks," I said, and left the clinic, breathing a huge sigh of relief.

March was almost over, the snow was gone, and daffodils were popping through the dirt around a tree that I passed on my way home. They were pretty and hopeful, and the church bells ringing a mile away didn't remind me of a funeral. This was the closest to normal I had felt since Christmas.

At home, I sat on my bed, opened my calculus book and tried hard to remember the method of integration by parts, because failing out of high school would be almost as bad as everything else that had happened recently. I didn't want to end up working at Pathmark or getting locked in a padded room at New York–Presbyterian, so I had to try to heal on my own.

The rusty wheels in my brain were slowly turning when I glanced away from the book and saw my teddy bear. It was facedown on the carpet, exactly where it had fallen after I'd slammed my door in February. I picked it up and brushed dust from its ears. I felt angry with Blake again, and I thought that I should move it, maybe hide it in one of those boxes in the basement, but I couldn't. It reminded me of things like soft kisses on the back of my neck and the idea that somebody loved me once. So I put it on my dresser because that was where I still thought it should be.

In June I decided to skip my graduation ceremony. Dressing up in a dopey gown and marching down an aisle past gawking strangers would be overwhelming; I didn't need to go through all that to get my diploma. Hollister could just send it in the mail. This was another letdown for Mom, even though she didn't say so.

"You still want a party, don't you?" she asked.

I didn't. But she'd been so considerate and patient over the past few months that I couldn't deprive her of everything. "A small one," I said. "Just family."

That was good enough for her. So on a sunny day at the end of the month, she cooked a big dinner and bought a chocolate cake with words written in pink icing: CONGRATU-LATIONS, ARIADNE, CLASS OF 1987.

I stood by the open refrigerator and stared at the cake. Mom was getting dressed upstairs, Dad was buying beer at Pathmark, and I felt awful. I didn't deserve a party. I hadn't gotten into college and I'd been moping for months, and Mom must have been out of her mind with worry because she still kept my migraine pills locked up. Then she was in the kitchen, wearing a cheerful flower-print dress and pearl earrings, and I thought I might cry but I didn't. I was completely cried out.

"I'm sorry," I said, my eyes on the cake.

"For what?" she asked.

I shrugged. "For everything."

"Ariadne," she said. "It's fixable. You can reapply to Parsons. You aren't in trouble and you didn't catch anything. Isn't that right?"

She sounded a little worried. "Right," I said, even though I was only positive about the pregnant part.

"So everything is fine. You've been going through a bad time, that's all. It's just a bump in the road. Someday it won't matter."

I couldn't imagine that day. "Then I'm sorry for not being what you wanted."

She took me by the shoulders and spoke in a serious voice. "You're *exactly* what I wanted," she said, her eyes firmly set on mine, and I was so surprised. Mom didn't think I was a disappointment . . . and I wasn't completely cried out after all.

"I think I'm getting a headache," I said, grabbing a tissue to dry my eyes.

She left the kitchen and came back carrying my migraine pills. "Here," she said, sticking the bottle in my hand. "You can keep these now, can't you?"

"Yeah," I answered. "I can. You don't have to worry anymore, Mom."

"I'll always worry," she said, and I knew she was talking about normal things, like worrying about me getting mugged on the subway. The possibility of her daughter overdosing on butalbital wasn't something she had to worry about anymore.

A few days later, I got a call from Julian at Creative Colors. He said he'd love to have me back this summer and so would Adam, who never stopped asking if he would see me again.

The idea of working was tiring, but I couldn't let Adam go on wondering if he was ever going to see me again. So I promised Julian I would be there next week, and that I'd work until September.

I hung up the phone and told Mom I was going for a walk, even though that wasn't true. I was actually heading to the clinic for another blood test to make sure I hadn't caught anything from Del.

The nurse at the clinic was getting better at finding veins—she only stabbed me twice. I went back a week later and the doctor showed me a chart—a list of diseases and the word *negative* typed beside every one. It was relief, but the chart was like the one Blake had shown me last year. The thought of him made me sink into my chair.

"What's wrong?" the doctor asked as we sat in her office. "It's good news."

I stared at diplomas on the wall behind her. "I know. I'm just thinking about someone."

She leaned forward at her desk. "Who are you thinking about?"

I moved my eyes to a credenza across the room. It was

covered with framed pictures of what looked like children and grandchildren. "My ex-boyfriend," I said, turning back to her. Saying it made me sink even lower.

"Well," she said. "You've been through a difficult situation . . . waiting to find out whether you were pregnant, worrying about lab results. Have you confided in anyone?"

I shook my head. "I can't do that. I don't want anybody to know."

The doctor nodded and reached into her desk. Then she handed me a business card with the name of the clinic's psychiatrist, and she said that I should make an appointment, but I didn't want to. I couldn't lie on a couch or sit in a chair and talk about Blake for hours. In my opinion, it was better not to talk about him at all.

Adam wanted me to draw all the same old things, but I didn't mind. My pictures made him smile a big smile that broke out two deep dimples, which made me happy and sad at the same time. I was happy that I could give him a little joy, and sad because he was even better-looking than last year. He was growing into a handsome man with a brain that would never keep up.

"You're a good artist, Snow White," he said at the beginning of July.

I smiled weakly. "I'm not an artist, Adam."

"Sure you are," he said, lifting one of my drawings by its edge as proof.

Maybe his brain wasn't all that damaged. Maybe he knew

more than I did. And his was the first face that had interested me in a very long time. So that night, I went into my studio and sat down at my easel. My pencils were dusty and my paper was discolored from being left alone by the window for so long, but it didn't matter. I still knew how to draw. Maybe I actually was an artist, because before I knew it, Adam's face was staring back at me from my sketch pad.

"Oh," Mom gasped from the doorway. "You're drawing again."

I couldn't match her excitement. I still didn't have the strength. I just nodded and she backed off, saying she had some silverware to polish, and I heard her walking away.

"Mom," I said.

She poked her head into the room. "Yes, Ariadne?"

"Don't polish the silverware. Work on your novel."

She rolled her eyes. "For what? I'll never finish. I'm not a real writer."

"Sure you are," I said, the same way Adam said it to me, and just as sincerely. If I could be interested in drawing again, then anything was possible.

We went to Queens a few days later for the Fourth of July. Dad drove Mom's Honda and I sat in the back, my hair blowing into knots because all the windows were open.

"You really should get the air conditioner fixed," I called toward the front seat.

"We will," Mom said. "We'll fix it when you start driving."

What was she talking about? I had only driven once, in

February, when Patrick gave me my first lesson. Then Mom said that Patrick had offered to give me more lessons and to take me to the DMV to get my license, and soon she was going to buy a new car and I could have this one and wouldn't I like that?

"Yeah," I said. "I won't have to walk everywhere."

"And it'll come in handy later on . . . when you start college."

Dad's head snapped toward Mom. "Nancy," he said in a chastising tone, as if I was hobbling on crutches and she was pressuring me to run.

That shut her up. I looked at Dad's gray hair, saw his fingers on the steering wheel, the wedding ring he never took off. My hand was at my side and it moved toward him, toward his shoulder, which I wanted to squeeze. But I didn't because we didn't touch each other much, and if we did, it wasn't in a mushy way. I just held the back of his seat instead, hoping he could feel me through the leather.

At Patrick and Evelyn's house, we joined a backyard crammed with off-duty firefighters, Queens housewives, and kids who played catch on the grass. Patrick spent the day slaving over his barbecue, so I didn't talk to him until the crowd thinned out. The sun had just started to set when he plopped down next to me on the Sears sofa and I felt something hit my ankle. Then Kieran chased a ball as it rolled across the patio, grabbed it, and held it up to my face.

"Remember this?" he asked. I did—it was the Red Sox baseball from Blake. "Your boyfriend gave it to me. Where is he?"

Kieran was too young for tact. I squirmed in my seat and Patrick rescued me.

"Don't ask nosy questions," he said. "And put that damn thing away before I make sure you never see it again."

Kieran was used to his father's tough talk. He skipped into the house and I felt a headache brewing. I rubbed my temples and Patrick stood up, reached into his pocket, and tossed his key ring onto my lap.

"I don't feel like driving right now," I said.

"Did I ask how you feel? You'll be nineteen in six months and you still don't have your license. That's wicked lame."

*Wicked lame.* I laughed a little and I swallowed two Tylenol in the bathroom before Patrick and I hit the road in his truck, where I had my second driving lesson. There were more lessons after that, through the rest of July and into August, and one day toward the end of summer he said I was ready for the DMV.

I wasn't sure how ready I was, but I gave it a shot and ended up with a New York State driver's license. I passed the test on my first try, and it gave me a familiar feeling, the feeling of pride I used to get from the letter A written on exams at school. I hadn't felt that way for months, and I hadn't realized how much I missed it.

The next time I felt like that was during my last day at Creative Colors. Adam was upset because I was leaving, so I gave him his portrait and it cheered him up. Julian looked at my drawing over Adam's shoulder and I felt very small, worrying that Julian might be one of those critical people who had haunted my imagination for years. But I was wrong.

"This is really good, Ari," he told me.

"It is?" I said.

He chuckled and gave me an invitation to his wedding, which was going to be in October on one of those rented yachts that sailed around New York Harbor.

Later that night, I was drawing in my studio when I decided to take the SAT again. Maybe I could do well enough to get into Parsons this time. But if not, there were other schools in Manhattan, and now I had the sense to fill out more than one application.

My decision made Mom very happy. After I told her, she made a squealing noise and spent hours scribbling in her perky pink notebook. And that made *me* very happy.

The next morning I cornered Dad while he was eating breakfast and Mom was taking a shower. I reminded him that Mom was working on her novel and that she'd finished six chapters already, and she couldn't possibly write the whole thing with a ballpoint pen.

"Let's buy her a typewriter," I said. "An electric one. You can leave work early today and we can go shopping together."

What was I thinking? Dad never left work early. But he agreed that the typewriter was a good idea and took some money out of his wallet, and I bought a Smith Corona that afternoon. Mom was thrilled and I acted like it was Dad's idea. Then she kissed him and typed until midnight.

Mom gave me her car the night before Labor Day, after she and Dad went to a dealership in the Bronx to pick up a brand-new Honda. It was a color called Desert Mist. Dad had finagled a good price because the salesman was his partner's wife's ex-husband or something.

The next day we took it to Patrick and Evelyn's house, where Evelyn told me and Mom that she'd signed up for a secretarial course at Queensborough Community College.

"It's only for a semester," she said. "To learn office skills and all that crap. I may try to get a job when Shane starts nursery school. Patrick thinks it's a good idea."

So did I. And so did Mom, who looked as if Evelyn had been granted a full scholarship to Yale. "That's fantastic, Evelyn," I said.

"But here's the thing," she began, and that worried me even though there was no need to worry. She just said that her classes were on Mondays and Wednesdays and she needed a babysitter and I wouldn't mind taking care of the kids, would I?

"Well, I have nothing else to do," I said with an unexpected laugh, and it didn't sound so tragic.

# twenty-four

*It* was mid-September, the time of year when fall edges up on summer and the air smells of lighter fluid because everyone wants to use their barbecues before they can't anymore. Dad was busy figuring out who raped and murdered a girl in Battery Park, Mom was intimidating a brand-new pack of sixth graders, and Evelyn was learning how to type.

I was proud of Evelyn. Early on Mondays and Wednesdays I drove the Honda to Queens, where I found her waiting at the front door clutching textbooks to her chest. Then she sped off in her minivan, and I drove Kieran to second grade and spent the rest of the day taking care of Shane and studying for the SAT.

On one of those Wednesday mornings I filled out my second Parsons application, and my first for three other colleges in the city. Later I strapped Shane into his car seat and stopped at the post office to mail the four envelopes before I picked up Kieran at school.

That night, I drove home to Brooklyn and found the house empty. Dad was working, Mom was at a faculty meeting, and the red light on our answering machine was blinking. I pressed it and heard the raspy voice of a girl saying I should give her a call at the Waldorf. Room 163.

It was a warm night but I felt a nervous chill. I didn't want to think about the Waldorf or Leigh or anyone connected to her. I was afraid that if I did, it would pull me into the deep dark hole that had been so hard to escape.

"I could go for some ice cream," Mom said after dinner.

She and I were sitting at the kitchen table. She licked her lips and suggested a Carvel Flying Saucer or a pint of Jamoca Almond Fudge from Baskin Robbins, but I didn't want ice cream and I came up with excuses because I couldn't tell Mom the truth. I couldn't tell her that Leigh's voice had rattled my shaky foundation and now I couldn't stop thinking that it was much easier to recover from mono than from Blake Ellis.

"Come on," Mom said. "Food is one of life's simple pleasures."

Maybe she was right. Maybe something as simple as Jamoca Almond Fudge would help. So I smiled and stood up from the table. Then the phone rang and it was Evelyn, who wanted Mom to know that Kieran had won the second-grade spelling bee and that Evelyn had earned a B⁺ on a typing test, and I didn't want Mom to have to cut the conversation short.

"I'll run over to Baskin Robbins," I whispered. "I'll be back soon."

She nodded and I went outside. The warm air had been chased away by a cool breeze that rustled the trees, and there was a bunch of grade-school girls with braids and ponytails riding their bicycles in circles on the street. Our neighbor was standing on her driveway, talking to another woman with curlers in her hair who kept shading her eyes from the sun. They both waved as I drove past and headed to Baskin Robbins, where I bought a gallon instead of a pint.

I left my windows open as I drove home, enjoying the crisp air and the sound of kids laughing on street corners. I was almost there when a bicycle cut in front of me. I slammed on my brakes and heard my tires screech, and then nobody was laughing.


I'd never been in a hospital before. Of course I'd been *to* a hospital, but I'd never been *in* a hospital, where I was the patient and doctors asked me questions like *What's your full name?* and *Who's the president of the United States? Ariadne Mitchell* and *Ronald Reagan*—that was how I answered—and everybody seemed impressed even though the questions were so silly. For a minute I wondered if I'd finally gone nuts and I was in New York–Presbyterian, but it didn't seem that way because I wasn't tied up in a straitjacket. This was just a normal room with a television and a bed and a powerful smell of

Lysol. I was in the bed, there were sheets pulled to my waist, and I was hooked up to a machine that measured my heart rate and never stopped beeping. I was also wearing a gown that I didn't remember putting on.

"Where are my clothes?" I asked Mom, who was standing next to me.

"They took them off," she said. "You were unconscious."

The fact that some random strangers had removed my clothes was more disturbing than finding out I'd been unconscious. I tried to remember which bra I'd worn today. I hoped that it was decent, that it didn't have ripped elastic or holes, but I couldn't remember anything and my head was killing me. Mom kept talking, saying I hit the brakes so hard to avoid the girl on her bike that I had slammed my forehead against the steering wheel.

"Is she okay?" I asked.

"She's fine," Mom said. "A moron, but fine. Who the hell rides a bike in the middle of the damn street?"

Then I found out that I wasn't exactly fine, that I had a big bump and a purplish gray bruise growing and darkening across my forehead, and that I might have a concussion, but the doctor wasn't sure so I had to stay in the hospital overnight for observation.

I didn't think I had a concussion and neither did a matronly nurse who checked on me after Mom left. And I was starting to feel better. My head didn't hurt all that much by the time the ten o'clock news started, and I was settling into my pillows to watch a story about that dead girl in Battery Park when I heard the door open.

I thought it would be the nurse. But when I turned my head, I saw long red hair and eyes with gold flecks.

"Wow, you got banged up good," Leigh said.

I was nervous again. The feeling lingered while I listened to her talk. She said she hadn't been sure I'd gotten her message, so she'd stopped by my house but nobody was home, and my next-door neighbor had told her I'd been in a car accident and she could find me at Kings County Hospital. I wished my neighbor had kept her mouth shut, because now Leigh was sitting on the empty bed beside mine. She was smiling and telling me about UCLA, and I couldn't smile or answer. Her arrowhead charm swung from her neck and it brought back memories that kept me very quiet.

I felt guilty, too. I hadn't contacted her after Valentine's Day. I blamed her for having introduced me to Blake and Del when she was completely blameless, and yet here she was, acting like I didn't deserve the Worst Friend of All Time award. But maybe she was taking pity on me because she knew what it was like to lose someone you love.

"Uncle Stan had a triple-bypass operation," she said. "He's not doing so well."

Good, I thought. I haven't been doing so well either because of him. "Oh," I said, and nothing else, even though Leigh seemed to be waiting for something else, something considerate or encouraging. But I just couldn't give it to her.

She twirled her hair around a finger. "I'm glad you're okay. Accidents like this can turn into something much worse, as I know all too well."

She meant M.G. I wanted to ask if she still thought about

him, if she still missed him, and how long it took to be completely over someone, but I couldn't do that either. "I'm glad I'm okay too," I told her instead.

She nodded. "Listen, Ari . . . Blake is out in the car."

My heart skipped a beat. I wondered if it registered on that machine. "Why?" I asked.

"I told him you were in an accident and he wanted to see if you were all right." She touched her charm, and I couldn't take my eyes off it. "I'm not sure if that's all . . . but he wants to see you. Do you want to see him?"

Why couldn't she ask me one of those easy questions like *Who's the president of the United States?* That had been a cinch to answer. This one was so confusing. Part of me wanted to see Blake more than anyone in the world, and the other part didn't want to see him ever again because he had betrayed me and I had betrayed him and he would never betray his father, especially if his father was sick. So there wasn't any point.

"No," I said. That word wasn't easy to say, but I thought it was the best word.

"Are you sure?" Leigh asked.

"No," I said again.

She stood up from the bed. "I understand. Well . . . I'm sure you're tired. I'll get out of here and let you relax. Take care of yourself, okay?"

She headed for the door and I reached out and clutched her hand to stop her. I held it in mine for a moment, regretting that I'd never been the friend she deserved. She seemed to understand that, too.

"Take care, Leigh," I said.

She smiled. "Get better, Ari."

Leigh left without promising to call me the next time she was in New York. I think we both knew that I had to make a clean break from the Ellis family if I was ever going to forget about them.

A few minutes later, the nurse came in and asked me how I was feeling. When I tried to talk, my voice broke and a tear rolled down my cheek.

"What's wrong?" she said.

I wiped my face. "Someone came to see me but I decided not to see him."

She nodded. "We have mental health counselors here. Do you think you'd like to talk to someone?"

I wasn't even sure why I was talking to her. I didn't talk about Blake with anyone, although I was starting to think that keeping everything to myself wasn't such a bright idea. *Don't bottle up your emotions*—that was what the doctor who diagnosed my migraines had advised a long time ago. I really should have listened.

"Not tonight," I said. "But I'll be ready soon."

I didn't have a concussion and I didn't talk to a counselor at the hospital. Instead I made an appointment with a psychiatrist at the clinic. I went there the next Friday afternoon with a bruise on my forehead and spoke with a forty-something woman named Dr. Pavelka. She wore cat's-eye glasses and lipstick the color of Pepto-Bismol. She had a soothing Slavic accent and a comfortable couch in an office with plants on the windowsill. I liked her immediately. I liked her enough to tell her things I'd never told anyone else, such as how I had kept my curtains closed to block out the sight of Saint Anne's face and spring grass poking through slushy snow.

She bit the tip of her pencil as she sat in an oversized chair. "Since when do you feel this way?" she asked.

"Since . . . ," I said, searching the stucco ceiling for an answer. Then I looked back at her, at the strawberry blond hair that was piled on top of her head and secured with two chopsticks. "Since after kindergarten. I felt really good in kindergarten."

"I see. And this statue—this saint—you think it talks to you?"

"Oh, no," I said quickly, wondering if she thought I was schizophrenic and I heard voices coming from plaster. "No, it just . . ."

I stopped because I didn't know which words to choose. I needed some that wouldn't make me sound certifiably insane. Dr. Pavelka kept biting her pencil, and I waited for men in white uniforms to swoop in and take me away.

"Is hard to explain," she said. "It may take a while to figure out. Right?"

"Right," I said, thrilled that she didn't think I was a blathering lunatic.

She stuck the pencil behind her ear and crossed her legs. "Your migraines, Ari . . . there's no physical cause? Your physician said that they're brought on by stress?"

I relaxed into the cushions on her couch. "Stress," I

agreed. "Loud noises, being upset . . . and keeping everything to myself."

Dr. Pavelka uncrossed her legs. "Come back next Friday," she said. "I get feeling you should've come here long time ago. We have lots to talk about, no?"

I went back the next Friday. She didn't admit me to a psych ward or give me medication. All we did was talk, and we did have lots to talk about. We discussed Blake and my parents and Evelyn, and Dr. Pavelka wasn't shocked about anything. She acted as if feeling depressed was no different from having mono. And she wasn't the least bit disgusted when I told her about Del and that I used to have a crush on my own brother-in-law.

"Isn't that strange?" I asked. "I mean . . . the way I felt about Patrick?"

"Is normal," she said.

She made me feel normal. I saw her the next Friday afternoon, and the one after that, and soon the leaves on the trees outside her office window turned from green to brown.

"I still think about Blake," I told her on a crisp day in October.

"How much?" she asked. "On scale of one to ten."

I shrugged. "Maybe a six."

"Of course," she said. "He was first boyfriend. First love. Not easy to forget so quick. But you have to remember, Ari . . . you have future ahead. Yesterday is gone."

She stood up because our session was over. I stayed where I was, thinking that yesterday was gone and I couldn't get it back and that was really sad. But then I thought that going

335

back to yesterday might feel like visiting elementary school, where the desks were small and you couldn't believe that you had ever fit in them, and you knew you didn't belong there anymore.

I walked home afterward, my mind on Julian's wedding and the fact that I had nothing to wear. That night, while Mom tapped away at her typewriter in the kitchen, I stood in my bedroom riffling through my clothes and trying to find something appropriate for a wedding cruise around Manhattan. I came across a black dress, the one I'd worn to Mr. Ellis's Christmas party, the one that had ended up on the floor after Blake's twenty-first birthday. I took it out, touched it and stared at it, and then Mom was beside me.

"I'll buy you a new dress," she said, gently detaching it from my hands. "Something that's in fashion."

That dress was still in fashion. A little black dress is always in fashion. But Mom didn't know any better, so I didn't correct her. Besides, I thought she might actually have a point. That dress was very yesterday.

We went to Loehmann's the next morning and bought a purple skirt set that matched the bruise that still wasn't completely gone from my forehead. It was small now, just a few speckles above my left eyebrow, but Julian noticed. He saw it after the ceremony, when he was officially married and I was standing alone, leaning on the yacht's railing and staring over the water at the skyline.

"Did you get mugged or what?" he said.

I laughed and told him about the accident. It was a beautiful autumn night with a clear sky and a cool breeze, and Julian wanted to know what I'd been up to since the summer.

I said that I hadn't really been up to anything except planning to start college next year, and he asked where I wanted to go.

"Parsons, I hope. I have to retake the SAT next month. I really blew it last time."

He laughed. "The SAT seems important now, but it won't matter later on, especially for somebody with your talent. You know, I showed that portrait you drew of Adam to a friend of mine—a guy who owns an advertising agency in the city—and he was impressed. He said he might have a part-time opening next spring if you're interested."

"An opening," I said, imagining myself answering phones or stuffing envelopes. "What kind of opening?"

"For an artist, Ari," he said, like I was a total ditz. "Are you interested?"

There was a time when I would have said I wasn't interested, when being an artist seemed big and scary, like something that would dissolve me into thin air. But now I didn't say I wasn't interested, because a lot of big and scary things had come my way lately and I was still here.

"What do you think?" Evelyn asked.

It was New Year's Eve and I stood behind her as she examined herself in her full-length bedroom mirror. She'd just slipped into a beaded party dress with an Empire waist, and she nervously checked her reflection from different angles. She studied the embroidery on her skirt, the showgirl-type shoes on her feet. We'd bought everything together at one of those hole-in-the-wall shops where they sold vintage clothes at affordable prices, and I knew she was going to out-shine everyone at the party she and Patrick were attending tonight. It was at a catering hall on Long Island, hosted by a neighbor who'd recently inherited some money and wanted to welcome 1988 in style.

"I think it's beautiful," I said. "And stop fidgeting."

She smiled. "Will you be okay with the kids? They just can't shake these colds."

I adjusted her hair around her face and smiled back. The boys had been sick since Christmas, coughing and sneezing and fighting low-grade fevers, but I didn't want Evelyn to worry. She and Patrick deserved a carefree night filled with shrimp cocktail and champagne.

"We'll be fine," I said, handing her the silver clutch purse that a saleslady had told us was made in 1928. "Just have a good time."

She gripped the purse with one hand and unclumped her mascara in the mirror with the other. "Call Mom if you have any problems," she said, and I nodded even though I had no intention of calling Mom. She and Dad were throwing their own New Year's Eve party at home, with brandy-spiked eggnog and throngs of NYPD and their spouses, and they deserved a good time too.

I pushed her toward the living room, where Patrick sat on the couch with Kieran by his side and Shane on his lap. He rubbed Shane's back and held a tissue for Kieran to blow his nose. He was dressed in a sleek black suit and a silky blue tie.

"You clean up nice," I told him.

He tugged at his collar. "I'm suffocating in this thing."

That comment reminded me of someone else who would have preferred a T-shirt and jeans to a fancy suit. It made me remember that I didn't have anyone to kiss at midnight.

I took the kids away from Patrick to distract myself. Dr. Pavelka had told me to distract myself whenever I felt the slightest hint of depression. *Don't dwell,* she said. Then Shane held my neck and coughed into my sweatshirt while Kieran used my sleeve to dry his nose, and the three of us stood in the front hall watching Patrick and Evelyn slip into their coats.

Patrick opened the door and held it for Evelyn. There was a Christmas wreath on the door and I heard its bells jingle. I also felt the cold air and Evelyn's soft cheek on mine when she leaned over to say good night.

"Thanks for taking care of the boys," she said.

It was something she said a lot more than she used to. "Enjoy the party," I answered.

When they were gone, I supervised Kieran playing with his new train set after Shane went to bed. Kieran finally fell asleep on the couch, and I moved him to his room with the Jets sheets that Dad had given him for Christmas. I laughed to myself as I closed the door, thinking that Patrick was going to burn them to a crisp when Evelyn wasn't around.

Then I plopped onto the couch with the remote control, but not for long. I heard Shane coughing in his room, so I raced upstairs and gave him a dose of medicine.

"Feel better?" I asked, pushing damp hair away from his warm forehead.

"I want to watch TV," he said.

So we sat together on the couch, and I was flipping through the *Daily News* when the doorbell rang. I scooped up Shane, walked toward the front hall, and opened the door. I heard bells and saw a petite girl with straight blond hair cut into a chin-length bob. She wore a cream-colored coat and matching gloves, and she smelled of L'Air du Temps.

"Hi, Ari," Summer said. "Happy New Year."

She looked so different. Her clothes weren't flashy. She'd lost six inches of hair. There was no shimmery lip gloss or indigo eye shadow. Her makeup was subdued except for the matte red lipstick on her mouth, and she was prettier than ever. She reminded me of photographs I'd seen of women in the 1920s, the ones who carried the sort of purse that Evelyn had brought to the party tonight.

"Hi" fell out of my mouth, in a weak voice that I could barely hear. I hadn't seen Summer since last year, and I had never expected to see her again.

"I stopped by your parents' house," she said. "Your mother told me you were here. She was having a party."

"I know," I said, my voice louder. I wished Mom hadn't disclosed my location, but I couldn't be angry with her. Even though Mom suspected various things, I had never told anyone but Dr. Pavelka about what had happened between me and Summer. It would sound too ugly outside her office.

Summer shifted her eyes from me to Shane. "Oh, you've gotten so big," she said. She reached out to stroke his cheek but I jerked him away.

"Leave him alone," I said.

Her smile disappeared and her arm fell limply to her side

as if she knew she deserved that. It made me feel sorry for her, even though sorry was the last thing I wanted to feel. Is this a new look, Summer? I thought. Are you new and improved? I tried that once and it didn't work.

"Well," she said, her breath hitting the air and changing into steam. "Can I come in, Ari? I mean . . . I want to talk to you."

I thought of slamming the door. I thought of kicking her down the stairs. But a nagging little part of me remembered Uncle Eddie's wake and a sweet-sixteen party and a box of art supplies, and the rest of me was curious, so I let her in.

She glanced around the living room—at the blinking Christmas tree, the messy pile of torn-open gifts on the floor. The place hadn't changed at all since the last time she'd been here, and I wondered if she was going to turn up her big-shot UCLA nose at everything, but she didn't. She just yanked off her gloves and sat on the couch.

I sat across from her in the new plaid La-Z-Boy that was Patrick's Christmas gift to himself. He said he planned to enjoy a lot of Red Sox games in it next season. Shane started rolling a toy fire engine on the kitchen floor while I stared blankly at Summer.

"I thought you'd be in California," I said, folding my arms across my chest.

She unbuttoned her coat. "I'm visiting my parents for the holidays."

Which holiday? I thought. Hanukkah or Christmas? Did you choose a religion yet, Summer? Make up your mind. "Oh," I said.

She seemed nervous and I wasn't going to do anything to put her at ease. I just watched as she leaned forward and selected a Hershey's Kiss from a bowl on the coffee table.

"Ari," she said, peeling silver foil. "Do you ever see Blake anymore?"

*Blake.* It seemed to echo against every wall in the house. I never said his name outside of Dr. Pavelka's office, and it was unsettling to hear it now, especially from Summer.

"No," I said, clutching Patrick's chair, terrified of the question I was about to ask. "Do you?"

"Me?" she said with wide eyes and chocolate melting in her palm. "No. I haven't seen him in a long time, and I don't want to. My mother doesn't even work for Ellis and Hummel anymore—she picked up a bigger account last spring, so she doesn't have time for them. She's expanded her business—she's got a few people working for her now."

"Oh," I said again, releasing my grip on the chair. "That's . . . good for your mother."

Summer nodded, abandoning her chocolate on the table. "Ari," she said. "I was wrong about everything. I thought Blake was a nice guy, but he wasn't. He wasn't a nice guy at all."

"Blake was a nice guy," I said, the same way and for the same reason that I'd protested when Patrick had said that Summer wasn't a *nice girl* and when Del had called Summer a *floozy*. "He just wasn't a strong guy."

"Yeah," she agreed. "You're right. His father really bossed him around. Honestly, I think Stan liked me more than Blake did. Anyway, Blake had the wrong idea about me. The whole thing was a huge mistake."

Where had I heard that before? And lots of people had the wrong idea about Summer. It gave me a satisfied feeling to know that both she and Blake regretted what they did, but I also pitied her again. I knew that Mr. Ellis had used her, that Blake had used her, that she'd been searching for a guy who would look her in the eyes when they made love, and I doubted that Blake had, even if he'd been right on top of her.

"Yes," I said. "It was a mistake."

She nodded once more, stood up, and brushed foil fragments from her coat. "Ari," she said. "I'm not better than you. And I don't think you're average."

I guessed this was her idea of an apology. I accepted a tiny fraction of it and gave her a half smile. Then she quickly changed the subject as if my silence equaled forgiveness. She started talking about her new boyfriend and she pulled a wallet from her purse.

"This is him," she said as I looked inside the wallet at a picture of an attractive young man. He stood beneath a palm tree with his arm around Summer. The picture was as perfect as the ones that always came with wallets—the photos of happy couples. I guessed that her new look was for him, for California, for starting over. "He's a little older . . . he graduated from UCLA five years ago and now he's working on his MBA. I think it's good to go out with older guys—they're more mature and they treat you better."

I could tell that the guy in the picture treated Summer better than Casey had, better than Blake had, better than any of those names in her diary, and I was surprisingly glad. I also got the feeling she wasn't seeking *experience* anymore.

"That's great, Summer," I said. "Really."

She smiled and we walked to the front hall, where I opened the door and smelled burning wood in the air.

"Goodbye," she said.

She walked down the stairs and I listened to her heels tap the sidewalk as she headed up the block. Shane ran out of the kitchen, I picked him up, and the two of us watched Summer's bright coat disappear into the darkness.

"Bye-bye," Shane said, waving a tiny hand.

Bye-bye, I thought, almost sure that I'd never see her again. But if I did—if we ran into each other someday—I knew we would smile and say polite things like *How are you?* and *Give my regards to your parents,* and we would secretly remember that we used to mean something to each other. And even if that never happened, if we never spoke again, I was grateful that we'd have tonight.

# twenty-five

*Parsons* accepted me. In February, the mailman brought a thick envelope and then I had to take a portfolio of my work to the city and interview at the school, and soon they sent another letter that I tore open while Mom peered over my shoulder. *Dear Ariadne,* I read. *Welcome to the Parsons School of Design, Class of 1992.*

She was ecstatic and so was I, and we were both just as happy when I met with Julian's friend in May. He offered me a part-time job at his agency in Midtown, where I worked as an entry-level illustrator under senior artists and art directors, and none of them ever said I didn't have any talent. Sometimes people at the office would show me their work and ask, "What do you think of this, Ari?" and the idea that someone cared what I thought made me feel even more important than being given a ruby necklace for Christmas. The whole thing made Mom change her mind about the value of connections, just as long as there weren't any strings attached.

So I kept working through my freshman year of college, and soon it was the summer again. I spent three days each week in the city and two at Creative Colors, and I found out that Adam still liked drawings of lakes and mountains.

"Do you have that same boyfriend?" he asked one Friday afternoon in August.

I was filling in a lake with a cobalt pencil and I shook my head.

"Oh," he said. "That's okay. You'll find another one when you're ready."

I laughed because he was right.

The next day, my parents and I went to a citywide firefighters' picnic at a park in Manhattan with Evelyn and Patrick and the boys. It was warm and sunny, and we sat on folding chairs around a table covered with food. I was drinking a glass of lemonade when Kieran came running across the grass, panting and saying he had to tell me something.

"I saw your old boyfriend, Aunt Ari."

"Shhh," Evelyn said, grabbing his arm and shoving him into a chair. Mom shushed him too and Patrick kept his eyes on his hamburger. I knew they meant well, as usual, but they didn't have to protect me anymore. I didn't want anything from Blake. I just needed to see him one last time so that I would never need to see him again.

"Where?" I asked.

"It was probably just someone who looked like him," Mom said, lighting a Pall Mall. "Eat your lunch, Ariadne."

"Where?" I said again, staring at Kieran.

"He's over at the track," Dad said.

We all looked at him. He was sitting at the head of the table and he glanced down at his plate as if he hadn't just done the nicest thing ever.

I got out of my chair and dared to put my arms around him. "Thank you, Dad," I said, and he actually hugged me back. It wasn't for long—just a few seconds—but it was something.

I walked away, across the park, where I saw Blake. He was running laps on the track, dressed in black shorts and a gray T-shirt. I stood at the edge of the asphalt and called his name as he passed.

He stopped running. He turned around and walked toward me, and I saw his handsome face. Time had matured his features; he looked more like a man than a boy.

"Ari," he said with a smile I didn't expect. I wasn't sure he would want to see me, especially since I'd refused to see him at Kings County Hospital. But I hadn't been ready then. Now I was. "How are you?"

"Fine," I answered, nervous and not sure what to say next.

His eyes moved around my face. "You look good."

"I do?" I said, and he laughed as if I hadn't changed at all, but he was wrong. Then he asked if I was at Parsons and I said

I was. I also told him about my job, and nothing surprised him.

"I always knew you could be an artist," he said.

I smiled because that was true. He had always believed in me. "What are you doing these days?" I asked, hoping he'd tell me he was planning to become a fireman and was running laps so he could ace the physical portion of the FDNY entrance exam.

He shrugged one shoulder and tugged at the bottom of his shirt. It was damp and clinging to his chest. "I'm in law school now."

My heart sank, even though I wasn't shocked. "But you wanted to be a firefighter."

He paused for a moment, looking down at a rock on the track. He kicked it toward the grass before looking at me again. "You remember that?"

Of course I remembered. How could he think I wouldn't? But so much time had passed—I *was* starting to forget things, things like what kind of chocolate he'd given me when I was sick with mono. "It was so important to you," I said.

He nodded slowly and rubbed the back of his neck. "Yeah . . . I still think about it sometimes. But things took a different turn."

"They sure did," I said, struggling to keep sarcasm out of my voice. I wasn't sure I'd succeeded. "Well . . . I guess your father is happy you're in law school."

He ran a hand through his hair. It stood up straight just like it used to. "My father died a while back, Ari. He never followed the doctor's advice . . . he still ate whatever he wanted and he worked himself into the ground, even after he had surgery. Aunt Rachel's taken it really hard, but she'll be okay eventually. Time heals all wounds, as they say."

He was right. And I didn't feel the same as I had when Leigh told me that Mr. Ellis wasn't doing well. I didn't feel hatred anymore. I wanted to say something to make Blake feel better, but I couldn't think of what that would be.

"I'm sorry" was all that came to mind.

Blake shrugged as if he wasn't sad, but I knew better. He was still a bad actor. Then he moved closer, touching my hand as it hung at my side. "Me too," he said.

I knew he wasn't talking about Mr. Ellis. I knew this was the day Mom had told me about, the day when everything that had happened didn't matter anymore. I looked into Blake's eyes, remembering my lost marble and thinking that even though it was gone forever, there could be another match out there. There might be another guy who would kiss my forehead, a guy who was just as sweet but was strong enough to choose me over everybody else.

I nodded. He squeezed my fingers in his, stepped back, and changed the subject.

"Del sold his club and moved to California. He opened another place in Los Angeles. You know Del and I never got along . . . but he's doing well and I'm happy for him."

"That's great," I said, and I could tell that Blake had no idea what had happened in the loft on Valentine's Day. Del kept it a secret, like I'd asked—he wasn't such a pig after all. "But you're alone in New York now, aren't you?" I asked, thinking that his closest relatives were either dead or in California.

"I'm going to school in LA," he said, yanking his shirt

again. UNIVERSITY OF SOUTHERN CALIFORNIA was printed across the fabric in red letters. I hadn't even noticed.

"Oh," I said, surprised. "Do you like California? I mean—is law school okay?"

He sighed. "It's what I expected. So is California. But Aunt Rachel wanted me nearby. . . . I think I should be around my family for now. And my father always planned for me to become a lawyer."

I glanced at my sandals and back at him. "Your father is gone, Blake."

He stared at me for a second. "So you don't think I should do what he wanted?"

"I think you should do what *you* want. He isn't here."

There was a wounded look on Blake's face. He shook it off quickly and spoke in a determined voice. "I know he isn't—and that makes following his plans even more important. His partners are running Ellis and Hummel. I've kept an apartment here in the city, and I come back every month or so to check in at the office. I'll start working there permanently after I graduate. Eventually I'll be in charge of everything."

I remembered New Year's Day at the penthouse when he'd broken up with me. I remembered him standing by the elevator as I left, looking brave and dutiful, like a soldier. He looked the same way now, and I realized he hadn't changed much. It made me sad for him.

"Ari," he said. "Are you seeing anybody?"

"No," I answered, shaking my head. "Are you?"

He shrugged. "Since we broke up, there hasn't been anybody important."

I felt a little smug. I thought he should have realized

sooner that important people don't show up very often, and you should hold on to them when they do. Maybe I was smarter than he was all along, because that was something I'd always known.

From the way Blake was looking at me, I got the feeling he'd finally figured it out. Maybe that was one thing about him that *had* changed. But it had taken him too long.

I remembered the things we used to talk about, the things we'd planned, everything that had taken me so long to leave behind. But now I wanted other things, new things, like the career that people at work kept telling me I was sure to have. I'd probably want the house and the kids and the husband one day, but not yet. There were so many things I wanted to do between now and then. I also knew that Park Slope wasn't the only place to plant a flower garden. There were even better places out there somewhere.

Blake stared at me and I sensed what he was getting at—there wasn't *anybody important,* he was going to be in New York *permanently* after law school. As I stood there looking at him, Summer popped into my mind. I heard her saying *I don't think much about guys from the past. I'm glad I knew them, but there's a reason they didn't make it into my future.* Back then I had thought she was probably right. Now I was sure.

I took a deep, quivering breath. "Well," I said. "I hope you find somebody important. I hope you get everything you want, Blake."

He looked like I'd let him down. I didn't want to hurt him, and it wasn't easy to say what I said, but I knew it was right.

Blake sighed, gave me a faint smile, and wrapped his hand around my elbow. "Thanks," he said, holding me tightly. He still smelled like aftershave and toothpaste. "I hope you do too."

"Thank you," I said, and my voice cracked. "Goodbye."

He let me go. "Good luck, Ari."

He started running down the track and I turned away. I walked across the grass toward my family, feeling the warm August air against my face and the sunshine on my hair. I really meant it when I told Blake that I hoped he'd get everything he wanted. I hoped I would too.


That night, I cleaned my room while Mom typed in the kitchen. I sorted through wrinkled test papers from Hollister, and threw junk into garbage bags and everything else into boxes for Goodwill. I cleared off my dresser and got rid of dusty magazines and dried-up nail-polish bottles, and then the only thing left was my teddy bear. I picked it up and stroked its face and the smooth brown beads that were its vacant eyes.

"Ariadne," Mom said.

She startled me. I hid the bear behind my back and she didn't see it because she was too excited. She said she had just finished her novel.

"Oh, Mom," I said. "Congratulations."

"It still needs work. But it's done," she said, taking a seat on my bed.

"Your next goal," I said, "will be to quit smoking."

She gave me a half-annoyed, half-amused look. "Maybe," she said, so I didn't push it. At least she didn't say no. *Maybe* was progress. Then she looked down at the embroidered roses on my bedspread and rubbed one with her fingertip. "Ari-adne," she said again, her eyes on the rose. "When you used to see that doctor . . ."

"Dr. Pavelka, you mean? I still see her, Mom . . . just not as much. Every third Friday."

"Right," Mom said. "When you see Dr. Pavelka . . . when you talk to her . . . does she ever say that . . . that when you went through that bad time . . . that it was because of me? Because of something I did? I mean . . . I always meant well." She glanced up. "You know that, don't you?"

Mom's face was tired. Her eyes were swollen from late nights bent over the Smith Corona. She couldn't know that Dr. Pavelka and I had spent countless hours talking about her, and about Dad, and about Evelyn and everything else, and that I had always known Mom meant well. I didn't blame anyone for that bad time—not even Blake.

"I know, Mom."

That made her happy. She stopped touching the rose and looked around the room. "Well," she said, standing up. "It seems like you're moving things along in here. I'll leave you alone to finish . . . I really need to get some sleep."

When she was gone, I went to the basement, found an empty box, and sealed the teddy bear and the NYU sweatshirt inside with heavy-duty tape. I started thinking about Leigh's ID bracelet and I imagined that one day, maybe years and years from now, I might open the box and say the same thing to my daughter that Leigh might say to hers: *This was from a boy I used to know. He was very special to me, but that was so long ago.*

And later on, when my room was clean and all the important things had been packed away, I carried two trash bags to the curb and saw Saint Anne on my way back inside. Her shawl glistened from the glow of the streetlight; her dress was a bright shade of blue. She didn't look lonely, and I could have sworn she was smiling.

*Lorraine Zago Rosenthal* was born and raised in New York City. She earned a bachelor's degree in psychology and a master's degree in education from the University of South Florida. She also earned a master's degree in English, with a concentration in American and British literature, from Northern Kentucky University. In addition to writing fiction, Lorraine enjoys reading, watching movies, and spending time with her husband. *Other Words for Love* is her first novel.